Lecture Notes in Computer Science 12919

More information about this subseries at http://www.springer.com/series/7410

Debin Gao · Qi Li · Xiaohong Guan ·
Xiaofeng Liao (Eds.)

Information and Communications Security

23rd International Conference, ICICS 2021
Chongqing, China, November 19–21, 2021
Proceedings, Part II

Springer

Editors
Debin Gao
Singapore Management University
Singapore, Singapore

Qi Li
Tsinghua University
Beijing, China

Xiaohong Guan
Xi'an Jiaotong University
Xi'an, China

Xiaofeng Liao
Chongqing University
Chongqing, China

ISSN 0302-9743 ISSN 1611-3349 (electronic)
Lecture Notes in Computer Science
ISBN 978-3-030-88051-4 ISBN 978-3-030-88052-1 (eBook)
https://doi.org/10.1007/978-3-030-88052-1

LNCS Sublibrary: SL4 – Security and Cryptology

This Springer imprint is published by the registered company Springer Nature Switzerland AG
The registered company address is: Gewerbestrasse 11, 6330 Cham, Switzerland

Preface

This volume contains papers that were selected for presentation and publication at the 23rd International Conference on Information and Communications Security (ICICS 2021), which was jointly organized by Chongqing University, Xi'an Jiaotong University, and Peking University in China during November 19–21, 2021. ICICS is one of the mainstream security conferences with the longest history. It started in 1997 and aims at bringing together leading researchers and practitioners from both academia and industry to discuss and exchange their experiences, lessons learned, and insights related to computer and communication security.

This year's Program Committee (PC) consisted of 141 members with diverse backgrounds and broad research interests. A total of 202 valid paper submissions were received. The review process was double blind, and the papers were evaluated on the basis of their significance, novelty, and technical quality. Most papers were reviewed by four or more PC members. The PC meeting was held online with intensive discussion over more than two weeks. Finally, 49 papers were selected for presentation at the conference giving an acceptance rate of 24%.

A "Best Paper Selection Committee" with five PC members of diverse backgrounds from around the world was formed, which selected the two best papers after a lengthy discussion. The paper "Rethinking Adversarial Examples Exploiting Frequency-Based Analysis" authored by Sicong Han, Chenhao Lin, Chao Shen, and Qian Wang received the Best Paper Award, while the paper "CyberRel: Joint Entity and Relation Extraction for Cybersecurity Concepts" authored by Yongyan Guo, Zhengyu Liu, Cheng Huang, Jiayong Liu, Wangyuan Jing, Ziwang Wang, and Yanghao Wang received the Best Student Paper Award. Both awards were generously sponsored by Springer.

ICICS 2021 was honored to offer two outstanding keynote talks: "Engineering Trustworthy Data-Centric Software: Intelligent Software Engineering and Beyond" by Tao Xie and "Securing Smart Cars – Opportunities and Challenges" by Long Lu. Our deepest gratitude to Tao and Long for sharing their insights during the conference.

For the success of ICICS 2021, we would like to first thank the authors of all submissions and the PC members for their great effort in selecting the papers. We also thank all the external reviewers for assisting the reviewing process. For the conference organization, we would like to thank the ICICS Steering Committee, the general chairs, Xiaohong Guan and Xiaofeng Liao, the publicity chairs, Qingni Shen, Qiang Tang, and Yang Zhang, and the publication chair, Dongmei Liu. Special thanks to Tao Xiang for the local arrangements. Finally, we thank everyone else, speakers, session chairs, and volunteer helpers for their contributions to the program of ICICS 2021.

Last but not least, we wish to extend a huge thank you to healthcare frontliners and our colleagues in the research of vaccine and immunization in fighting COVID-19. ICICS 2021 could not have become one of the first mainstream security conferences returning to an in-person setting without their enormous contribution.

November 2021

Debin Gao
Qi Li

Organization

Steering Committee

Robert Deng	Singapore Management University, Singapore
Dieter Gollmann	Hamburg University of Technology, Germany
Javier Lopez	University of Malaga, Spain
Qingni Shen	Peking University, China
Zhen Xu	Institute of Information Engineering, CAS, China
Jianying Zhou	Singapore University of Technology and Design, Singapore

General Chairs

Xiaohong Guan	Xi'an Jiaotong University, China
Xiaofeng Liao	Chongqing University, China

Program Committee Chairs

Debin Gao	Singapore Management University, Singapore
Qi Li	Tsinghua University, China

Program Committee

Chuadhry M. Ahmed	University of Strathclyde, UK
Cristina Alcaraz	University of Malaga, Spain
Man Ho Au	The University of Hong Kong, Hong Kong, China
Zhongjie Ba	Zhejiang University, China
Joonsang Baek	University of Wollongong, Australia
Guangdong Bai	The University of Queensland, Australia
Jia-Ju Bai	Tsinghua University, China
Diogo Barradas	Universidade de Lisboa, Portugal
Yinzhi Cao	Johns Hopkins University, USA
Guangke Chen	ShanghaiTech University, China
Rongmao Chen	National University of Defense Technology, China
Songqing Chen	George Mason University, USA
Ting Chen	University of Electronic Science and Technology of China, China
Xiaofeng Chen	Xidian University, China
Xun Chen	Samsung Research America, USA
Yaohui Chen	Facebook, USA
Sherman S. M. Chow	The Chinese University of Hong Kong, Hong Kong, China

Mauro Conti	University of Padua, Italy
Wenrui Diao	Shandong University, China
Jintai Ding	Tsinghua University, China
Xuhua Ding	Singapore Management University, Singapore
Josep Domingo-Ferrer	Universitat Rovira i Virgili, Spain
Ruian Duan	Palo Alto Networks Inc, USA
Xinwen Fu	University of Massachusetts Lowell, USA
Zhangjie Fu	Nanjing University of Information Science and Technology, China
Jose Maria de Fuentes	Universidad Carlos III de Madrid, Spain
Fei Gao	Beijing University of Posts and Telecommunications, China
Xing Gao	University of Delaware, USA
Joaquin Garcia-Alfaro	Institut Polytechnique de Paris, France
Dieter Gollmann	Hamburg University of Technology, Germany
Stefanos Gritzalis	University of Piraeus, Greece
Le Guan	University of Georgia, USA
Fuchun Guo	University of Wollongong, Australia
Shuai Hao	Old Dominion University, USA
Jiaqi Hong	Singapore Management University, Singapore
Hongxin Hu	University at Buffalo, SUNY, USA
Pengfei Hu	Shandong University, China
Jun Huang	Massachusetts Institute of Technology, USA
Xinyi Huang	Fujian Normal University, China
Shouling Ji	Zhejiang University, China
Jinyuan Jia	Duke University, USA
Chenglu Jin	CWI Amsterdam, The Netherlands
Georgios Kambourakis	University of the Aegean, Greece
Sokratis Katsikas	Norwegian University of Science and Technology, Norway
Dongseong Kim	The University of Queensland, Australia
Doowon Kim	University of Tennessee, Knoxville, USA
Hyoungshick Kim	Sungkyunkwan University, South Korea
Shujun Li	University of Kent, UK
Wenjuan Li	The Hong Kong Polytechnic University, Hong Kong, China
Feng Lin	Zhejiang University, China
Jingqiang Lin	University of Science and Technology of China, China
Yan Lin	Singapore Management University, Singapore
Jian Liu	Zhejiang University, China
Tongping Liu	University of Massachusetts Amherst, USA
Xiangyu Liu	Alibaba Inc., China
Zhuotao Liu	Tsinghua University, China
Giovanni Livraga	University of Milan, Italy
Javier Lopez	UMA, Spain
Jian Lou	Emory University, USA

Kangjie Lu	University of Minnesota, USA
Bo Luo	The University of Kansas, USA
Xiapu Luo	The Hong Kong Polytechnic University, Hong Kong, China
Haoyu Ma	Xidian University, China
Christian Mainka	Ruhr University Bochum, Germany
Daisuke Mashima	Advanced Digital Sciences Center, Singapore
Jake Massimo	Amazon Web Services, USA
Weizhi Meng	Technical Universtiy of Denmark, Denmark
Jiang Ming	UTA, USA
Chris Mitchell	Royal Holloway, University of London, UK
Yuhong Nan	Purdue University, USA
Jianbing Ni	Queen's University, Canada
Jianting Ning	Singapore Management University, Singapore
Liang Niu	New York University, USA
Satoshi Obana	Hosei University, Japan
Rolf Oppliger	eSECURITY Technologies, Switzerland
Roberto Di Pietro	Hamad Bin Khalifa University, Qatar
Joachim Posegga	University of Passau, Germany
Giovanni Russello	The University of Auckland, New Zealand
Nitesh Saxena	Texas A&M University, USA
Shawn Shan	University of Chicago, USA
Vishal Sharma	Queen's University Belfast, UK
Qingni Shen	Peking University, China
Wenbo Shen	Zhejiang University, China
Purui Su	CAS, China
Hung-Min Sun	National Tsing Hua University, Taiwan, China
Kun Sun	George Mason University, USA
Willy Susilo	University of Wollongong, Australia
Qiang Tang	Luxembourg Institute of Science and Technology, Luxemburg
Yuzhe Tang	Syracuse University, USA
Luca Viganò	King's College London, UK
Binghui Wang	Duke University, USA
Cong Wang	City University of Hong Kong, Hong Kong, China
Ding Wang	Nankai University, China
Gang Wang	University of Illinois at Urbana-Champaign, USA
Haining Wang	Virginia Tech, USA
Haoyu Wang	Beijing University of Posts and Telecommunications, China
Lei Wang	Shanghai Jiao Tong University, China
Lingyu Wang	Concordia University, Canada
Shuai Wang	The Hong Kong University of Science and Technology, Hong Kong, China
Ting Wang	East China Normal University, China

Xiuhua Wang	Huazhong University of Science and Technology, China
Zhe Wang	ICT, China
Jinpeng Wei	University of North Carolina at Charlotte, USA
Weiping Wen	Peking University, China
Daoyuan Wu	The Chinese University of Hong Kong, Hong Kong, China
Zhe Xia	Wuhan University of Technology, China
Xiaofei Xie	Nanyang Technological University, Singapore
Dongpeng Xu	University of New Hampshire, USA
Jia Xu	NUS-Singtel Cyber Security R&D Lab, Singapore
Jun Xu	Stevens Institute of Technology, USA
Minhui Xue	The University of Adelaide, Australia
Toshihiro Yamauchi	Okayama University, Japan
Feng Yan	University of Nevada, Reno, USA
Qiben Yan	Michigan State University, USA
Guomin Yang	University of Wollongong, Australia
Zheng Yang	Southwest University, China
Roland Yap	National University of Singapore, Singapore
Xun Yi	RMIT University, Australia
Qilei Yin	Tsinghua University, China
Meng Yu	Roosevelt University, USA
Yu Yu	Shanghai Jiao Tong University, China
Xingliang Yuan	Monash University, Australia
Chuan Yue	Colorado School of Mines, USA
Tsz Hon Yuen	The University of Hong Kong, Hong Kong, China
Chao Zhang	Tsinghua University, China
Fan Zhang	Zhejiang University, China
Fengwei Zhang	SUSTech, China
Jialong Zhang	ByteDance, China
Jiang Zhang	State Key Laboratory of Cryptology, China
Kehuan Zhang	The Chinese University of Hong Kong, Hong Kong, China
Yang Zhang	CISPA Helmholtz Center for Information Security, Germany
Yinqian Zhang	Southern University of Science and Technology, China
Lei Zhao	Computer School of Wuhan University, China
Qingchuan Zhao	Ohio State University, USA
Tianwei Zhang	Nanyang Technological University, Singapore
Yuan Zhang	Fudan University, China
Yongjun Zhao	Nanyang Technological University, Singapore
Yunlei Zhao	Fudan University, China
Yajin Zhou	Zhejiang University, China
Yongbin Zhou	Chinese Academy of Sciences, China
Shuofei Zhu	Pennsylvania State University, USA

Additional Reviewers

Isaac Agudo
Md Rabbi Alam
Cristina Alcaraz
Ahsan Ali
Saed Alsayigh
Enkeleda Bardhi
Christof Beierle
Christian Berger
Alessandro Brighente
Cailing Cai
Giovanni Calore
Xinle Cao
Kwan Yin Chan
Jinrong Chen
Long Chen
Min Chen
Tianyang Chen
Tommy Chin
Murilo Coutinho
Andrei Cozma
Handong Cui
Vasiliki Diamantopoulou
Qiying Dong
Minxin Du
Orr Dunkelman
Alexandros Fakis
Pengbin Feng
Ankit Gangwal
Yiwen Gao
Nicholas Genise
Junqing Gong
Qingyuan Gong
Kamil D. Gur
Yonglin Hao
Ke He
Xu He
Jiaqi Hong
Xinyue Hu
Yupu Hu
Mengdie Huang
Huiwen Jia
Xiangkun Jia
Ziming Jiang
Georgios Karopoulos
Maria Karyda
Andrei Kelarev
Minjune Kim
Felix Klement
Vasileios Kouliaridis
Gulshan Kumar
Jianchang Lai
Qiqi Lai
Chhagan Lal
Gregor Leander
Bo Li
Huizhong Li
Shaofeng Li
Wanpeng Li
Yannan Li
Zheng Li
Ziyuan Liang
Kyungchan Lim
Chaoge Liu
Gang Liu
Songsong Liu
Xiaoning Liu
Xueqiao Liu
Yichen Liu
Yiyong Liu
Yuejun Liu
Yunpeng Liu
Zengrui Liu
Eleonora Losiouk
Xin Lou
Junwei Luo
Lan Luo
Xiaolong Ma
Zhou Ma
Ahmed Tanvir Mahdad
Fei Meng
Vladislav Mladenov
William H. Y. Mui
Lucien K. L. Ng
Shimin Pan
Dimitris Papamartzivanos
Bryan Pearson

Henrich C. Pöhls
Hunter Price
Xianrui Qin
Yue Qin
Tingting Rao
Pengcheng Ren
Yujie Ren
Ruben Rios
Shalini Saini
Md Sajidul Islam Sajid
Stewart Santanoe
Shiqi Shen
Siyu Shen
Menghan Sun
Shuo Sun
Azadeh Tabiban
Fei Tang
Jiaxun Steven Tang
Utku Tefek
Guangwei Tian
Guohua Tian
Zhihua Tian
Yosuke Todo
Zisis Tsiatsikas
Payton Walker
Hongbing Wang
Jiafan Wang
Jianfeng Wang
Kailong Wang
Lihchung Wang
Lu Wang
Shu Wang
Ti Wang
Ting Wang
Wenhao Wang
Xinda Wang
Xinying Wang
Yunling Wang
Rui Wen
Mingli Wu
Yi Xie
Guorui Xu
Jing Xu
Shengmin Xu
Bolin Yang
Fan Yang
Hanmei Yang
Shishuai Yang
Wenjie Yang
Xu Yang
Zhichao Yang
Amirhesam Yazdi
Quanqi Ye
Jun Yi
Xiao Yi
Qilei Yin
Pinghai Yuan
Syed Zawad
Zhe Zhao
Zhiyu Zhao
Ziming Zhao
Chennan Zhang
Yuexin Zhang
Yubo Zheng
Ce Zhou
Jin Zhou
Rahman Ziaur
Max Zinkus
Yang Zou
Yunkai Zou

Sponsors

Gold Sponsor

Silver Sponsors

TRUSTED®
COMPUTING
GROUP

Keynotes

Engineering Trustworthy Data-Centric Software: Intelligent Software Engineering and Beyond

Tao Xie

Peking University

Abstract. As an example of exploiting the synergy between AI and software engineering, the field of intelligent software engineering has emerged with various advances in recent years. Such field broadly addresses issues on intelligent [software engineering] and [intelligence software] engineering. The former, intelligent [software engineering], focuses on instilling intelligence in approaches developed to address various software engineering tasks to accomplish high effectiveness and efficiency. The latter, [intelligence software] engineering, focuses on addressing various software engineering tasks for intelligence software, e.g., AI software. However, engineering trustworthy data-centric software (which AI software components are part of) requires research contributions from compiler, programming languages, formal verification, security, and software engineering besides systems and hardware. This talk will discuss recent research and future directions in the field of intelligent software engineering along with the broad scope of engineering trustworthy data-centric software.

Securing Smart Cars – Opportunities and Challenges

Long Lu

NIO

Abstract. As cars become more intelligent and connected, the security of on-car systems, software, and data has caught heavy attention from academia, industry, and regulators. This talk will discuss the key technical aspects of smart car security, including low-level system security, secure and robust autonomous driving, V2X security, data security, etc., highlighting the research and technical opportunities and challenges.

Contents – Part II

Security Analysis

Post-quantum Cryptography

Applied Cryptography

Contents – Part I

Machine Learning Security

Exposing DeepFakes via Localizing the Manipulated Artifacts

Wenxin Li[1], Qi Wang[1], Run Wang[1,2], Lei Zhao[1,2(✉)], and Lina Wang[1,2]

[1] School of Cyber Science and Engineering, Wuhan University, Wuhan, China
leizhao@whu.edu.cn

[2] Key Laboratory of Aerospace Information Security and Trusted Computing, Ministry of Education, Wuhan, China

Abstract. In recent years, *DeepFake* has become a public concern due to the abuse of advanced generative adversarial networks (GANs). Researchers have proposed various approaches to fight against DeepFakes by identifying whether an image or video is synthesized by GANs. Due to the imperfect design of GANs, the introduced artifacts serve as a promising clue for detection, which is captured by many proposed methods. However, these methods failed in presenting the artifacts in an interpretable manner. In this paper, we propose a novel approach by focusing on the artifact regions with dual attention (channel attention and spatial attention) to localize the observable and invisible artifacts for assisting *DeepFake* detection. Specifically, our proposed approach is agnostic to the specific backbone, which could be easily plugged into any DNN models to improve their performance. Experimental results show that our proposed dual attention could be deployed in any DNN based classifiers to improve their performance in detecting various DeepFakes. The detection accuracy on six current open-source *DeepFake* datasets is improved by 3.50%, 2.56%, 1.64%, 1.36%, and 0.89% in average on MesoNet, Meso-Inception, VGG-19, Xception, and EfficientNet, respectively. Besides, experimental results also show that our attention mechanism can serve as an asset for pixel-wise manipulation localization.

Keywords: DeepFake forensics · Localization · Dual attention

1 Introduction

Artificial Intelligence (AI) is developing rapidly at present. Among types of AI techniques, Generative Adversarial Networks (GANs) (e.g., ProGAN [12], StyleGAN [13] and FaceSwap-GAN [14]) have been widely used in multimedia synthesis and show great power. However, these advanced techniques can also be abused to generate so-called *DeepFake* videos or images. For example, multiple applications, such as *FaceApp* [2], *FaceSwap* [3], or *DeepFaceLab* [1] can generate faked videos where one's face can be swapped with someone else's. With these tools, users can generate *DeepFake* videos without any expert knowledge.

D. Gao et al. (Eds.): ICICS 2021, LNCS 12919, pp. 3–20, 2021.
https://doi.org/10.1007/978-3-030-88052-1_1

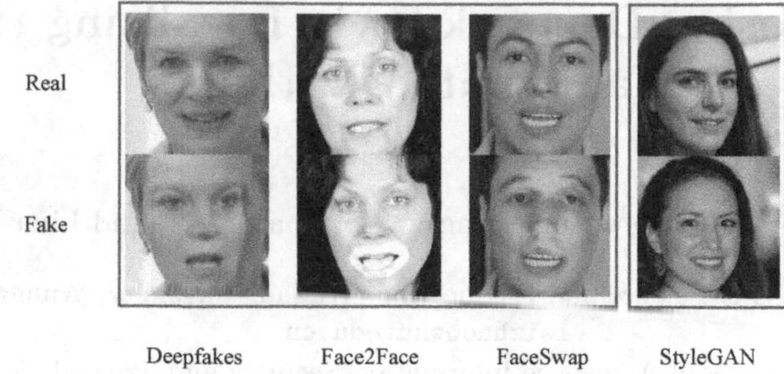

Fig. 1. Artifacts in DeepFake images.

The widespread of such *DeepFake* videos on the Internet seriously endangers the legitimate rights and interests of individuals and may result in a much worse impact if such videos are used for political and commercial purposes. Consequently, *DeepFake* brings a new yet significant threat to Cyber Security.

To fight against DeepFakes, previous studies have proposed multiple detection techniques. Based on the observation that synthesized images will inevitably introduce various artifacts due to the imperfect design of GANs, capturing artifacts is a promising approach for detection. Early techniques define features related to observable artifacts and then leverage these features for detection [5,14,27]. However, artifacts may not always be obvious because advanced GANs can often remove or reduce observable artifacts, which brings a challenge to early techniques. For example, we can observe from Fig. 1 that images synthesized with *Deepfakes* [20] have obvious blending boundaries, images created by *Face2Face* [20] show observable artifacts in the mouth region, and images created by *FaceSwap* [20] have unnatural light around the eyes and nose. By contrast, it is difficult to identify artifacts for images synthesized with *StyleGAN* [13].

To address the challenge caused by invisible artifacts, researchers proposed to design deep neural networks (DNNs) to learn the artifacts automatically [4,9,16]. A series of detection studies improve the generalization capability of DNNs using data augmentation [10] or detecting the blending boundary [24].

Despite the advances in *DeepFake* detection techniques, the interpretability of *DeepFake* has not been well investigated. For digital forensics, it is also critical to interpret how a detected DeepFake is manipulated by localizing the manipulated region. To achieve this purpose, a recent study [8] proposed an attention-mechanism-based technique for detecting and localizing artifacts in DeepFakes. This technique trains a neural network to focus on the ground truth mask regions and then leverage the attention map for localization. The main limitation of this technique is that it requires amounts of paired real/fake samples because it utilizes supervised learning that relies on ground truth manipulation masks for training. However, constructing the ground truth is challenging due to the scarce of paired samples. What's more, the resolution of the attention map is limited to a coarse-grained block level because it is designed to mask the high-dimensional features.

In this paper, we propose a novel approach for *DeepFake* detection and manipulated artifacts localization. The core of our approach is a dual-attention (channel attention and spatial attention) model to identify artifact regions. Compared with the previous technique [8] that leveraged supervised learning, our approach only relies on the labels and does not require the pair of synthesized images and the source images as the ground truth. To be more specific, we leverage neural networks to extract features and learn the connection between features and labels. Furthermore, dual attention enables the neural networks to adaptively refine critical features related to artifacts. Thus our attention is generated without the guidance of ground truth manipulation masks.

In detail, we leverage channel attention to figure out the channels related to the most critical features where artifacts may exist, and then leverage spatial attention to learn the distribution of features in the feature map. As channel attention and spatial attention are complementary, it is promising to combine such dual attention for better detection. Furthermore, the attention mechanism focuses on artifact regions. Thus, we can leverage the attention map to localize the manipulated pixels, and each pixel in the attention map corresponds to the pixel in the original image. In conclusion, our dual attention mechanism can focus on artifact regions that assist detection, as well as providing clues to locate the manipulated pixels with artifacts at a fine-grained pixel level.

To demonstrate the effectiveness of our approach, we construct experiments on five backbone models of different architectures and six datasets containing a diversity of *DeepFake* synthetic techniques. Experimental results show that our attention can be deployed to different models, improving the accuracy by 3.50% on MesoNet, 2.56% on Meso-Inception, 1.64% on VGG-19, 1.36% on Xception, and 0.89% on EfficientNet in average. Take MesoNet as an example, the model with dual attention reaches an accuracy of more than 92% on most datasets and an AUC of more than 0.92 on all datasets, outperforming the corresponding model without attention, with single attention, or with an extra convolution layer. Meanwhile, our approach performs fine-grained manipulation localization, and the PBCA of our attention maps reaches more than 0.7 while the IINC is less than 0.7 on all datasets, which outperforms the previous technique [8].

In summary, we make the following contributions:

- We propose to leverage the dual attention mechanism to detect artifacts that existed in the synthesized images. The attention mechanism focuses on channels and spatial distributions of critical features where artifacts may exist. And our approach can capture both observable and invisible artifacts.
- Beyond detection, our attention mechanism can further help to locate the manipulated pixels in an unsupervised manner. We learn the attention from the labels, instead of the ground truth manipulation masks, and leverage the attention map for localization.
- The dual attention mechanism proposed in our approach is scalable to convolutional neural networks of different architectures. Evaluation results show

that our attention mechanism improves the performance on different backbone models including MesoNet, Meso-Inception, VGG-19, Xception, and EfficientNet.

2 Related Work

2.1 DeepFake Creation

GANs have made great progress in image synthesis. Recently, a variety of GANs like ProGAN [12], StyleGAN [13], and FaceSwap-GAN [14] have been widely used for *DeepFake* generation. According to the tampered regions, there are two types of fake images synthesized with GANs: entire face synthesis and partial manipulation. As for the entire fake face synthesis, the whole facial image is synthesized with GANs. And partial manipulation includes expression swap, identity swap, and facial attributes editing. Specifically, expression swap transfers the facial expression from the source image to the target image, while identity swap replaces the whole target face with the source, and facial attributes editing modifies the facial attributes such as eyes or mouth. However, artifacts are inevitably introduced for both entire face synthesis and partial manipulation due to the imperfect design of GANs. Some artifacts are observable to humans while others are not, which could be captured by carefully designed models, and both of them provide critical clues for *DeepFake* detection.

2.2 DeepFake Detection

Existing *DeepFake* detection techniques can be roughly divided into two categories. One is detecting manually defined features with observable artifacts. Yang et al. [27] built the head pose vector using facial landmarks to capture the inconsistency between facial landmarks and head position, and trained an SVM classifier for detection. Agarwal et al. [5] designed an individual-specific monitor to capture the biological signals and trained an SVM classifier to detect them. But these techniques are rarely used at present, because existing artifacts may be removed with the development of GANs, and it cannot adapt to the changes. The other is based on DNNs by learning the artifacts automatically. Afchar et al. [4] built a convolutional neural network called MesoNet for *DeepFake* detection. They also added the Inception module and designed Meso-Inception to enable the model to extract additional features. Meanwhile, classical convolutional neural networks were also applied for *DeepFake* detection, such as VGGNet [21], InceptionNet [9], and Xception [20], etc. Among them, EfficientNet [22] has been proved to achieve the state-of-the-art performance in *DeepFake* detection. Besides, Wang et al. [25] improved the detection approaches by training a classifier based on ResNet and generalized it to unseen architectures using pre-/post-processing and data augmentation. Li et al. [15] trained their model to detect the blending boundary. Due to the strong self-learning ability of neural networks, deep learning is still the mainstream for *DeepFake* detection. However, there are still limitations because they provide no clues about the existence and location of artifacts in the fake images.

2.3 Attention Mechanism

Attention mechanism was widely adopted in NLP at first. Bahdanau et al. [6] applied the attention mechanism to solve the long-term dependence on contextual semantics problems in machine translation. Google's machine translation team also adopted the attention structure for the machine translation task [23]. Later, research about attention mechanism in the field of computer vision has been raised to simulate the way human views images. It can be divided into soft attention and hard attention. Soft attention is differentiable, which is trained by gradient descent and back propagation algorithm, while hard attention usually requires the prediction of the areas to be focused and applies reinforcement learning. On the whole, the soft attention mechanism has better performance in computer vision and is easier to be implemented in an end-to-end neural network. Woo et al. [26] proposed Convolutional Block Attention Module (CBAM), which is an effective soft attention module for feed-forward convolutional neural networks. Inspired by the excellent performance of the CBAM module, we apply the similar soft attention mechanism to help the neural networks capture observable and invisible artifacts in the synthesized images.

3 Our Approach

3.1 Insight

We observe that the images synthesized with GANs, including entire face synthesis and partial manipulation, will inevitably introduce various artifacts due to the imperfection of GANs. Some artifacts are observable while others are not, and both of them serve as a clue for *DeepFake* detection. However, a key challenge is that existing detection techniques cannot locate the pixels where artifacts exist even if they correctly detect fake images. In other words, they provide no evidence about the existence and location of artifacts, thus fail to present the artifacts in an interpretable manner.

To address this challenge, we propose a novel approach for *DeepFake* detection and manipulated artifacts localization by focusing on the artifact regions with dual attention. Specifically, we leverage channel and spatial attention to figure out the channels and spatial distributions of the most critical features related to the artifacts. Thus, our attention mechanism helps the neural networks automatically capture and focus on the artifacts of different GANs as well as locating the manipulated pixels. On the whole, our detection approach has three main advantages. The first is that the detection performance of different DeepFakes can be further improved since the attention mechanism helps neural networks concentrate on the specific artifacts to better cope with the changes and differences of GANs. The second is locating manipulated regions at pixel-level through unsupervised learning. The attention is obtained according to the labels instead of the ground truth manipulation masks so that we don't need to collect paired real/fake samples. Thirdly, our attention has a good generalization capability, which is agnostic to the specific backbone and can be easily plugged into any convolutional neural network to improve their performance significantly.

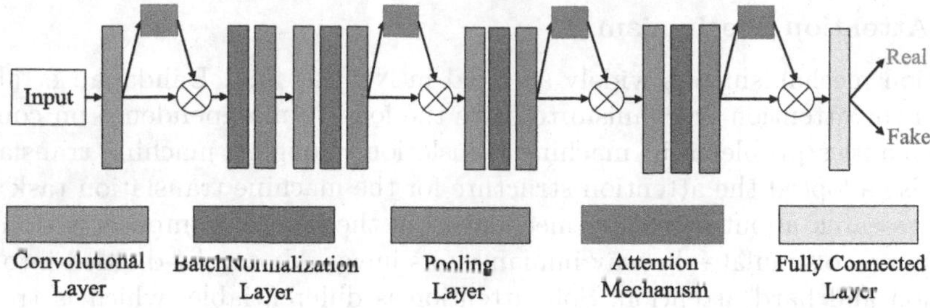

Fig. 2. The framework of our model. It consists of four basic blocks, each block contains a convolution layer, a batch normalization layer, and a pooling layer, and then connect to a fully connected layer. Attention is added to the extracted feature map of convolution layer for block one and pooling layers for the rest.

3.2 Framework

Here, to better illustrate the basic idea of our proposed approach, we choose MesoNet as the backbone model case and add our attention mechanism to the extracted feature maps. First, we focus on the artifacts of the *DeepFake* image rather than the whole image like prior studies. So we choose a shallow CNN that pays more attention to local features where artifacts exist. Additionally, we expect the network to pay more attention to the channels and regions concerning about the main artifacts in *DeepFake* images, so we add the attention mechanism to build our CNN model. Our attention mechanism can also be applied to arbitrary convolutional neural networks and more explanation refers to Sect. 4.

The framework is shown in Fig. 2. It consists of four basic blocks, each block includes a convolution layer, a batch normalization layer, a pooling layer, and further with a connection to a fully connected layer. For each basic block, the convolution layer extracts the latent semantic features of the image, and the feature maps are passed to the pooling layer for feature selection. The batch normalization layer is added in the middle to enhance the fitting ability of the model. For the first block, we calculate the attention and add it to the convolution layer, since the first convolution layer extracts the most detailed features that provide fine-grained localization. And for the rest blocks, attention is added to the pooling layers which have already filtered out excess information and we hope that our attention can mask the high-dimensional features to assist detection.

3.3 Dual Attention for Detection and Localization

The attention mechanism is used to simulate the way human views images. Humans usually only focus on important areas of images, and the attention mechanism enables important features in the feature maps to be further concerned and expressed, while other less important features are inhibited. We add two modules of attention mechanism: channel attention and spatial attention [26].

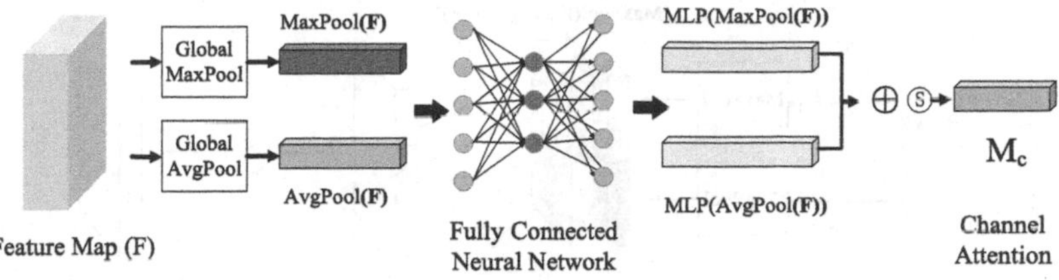

Fig. 3. The process of calculating channel attention.

Channel attention helps the model focus on important channels where artifacts may exist, and spatial attention focuses on the location distribution of artifacts in the feature map.

Channel Attention. For a convolutional neural network, different channels represent different features in the extracted feature map. Some channels represent important features for *DeepFake* detection such as eyes or mouth, while others are unnecessary like the background. Therefore, we add channel attention to help the neural network focus on channels concerned about the most important features where artifacts may exist. Suppose the output feature map of a convolution layer in CNN is $F \in R^{C*H*W}$, where C represents the channels of the feature map, H and W are height and width. Then we add channel attention M_c to the feature map. The new feature map with channel attention added can be represented as $F' = M_c(F) \bigotimes F$, where $M_c \in R^{C*1*1}$, and $\bigotimes$ means element-wise multiplication.

The specific implementation process of calculating channel attention M_c is shown in Fig. 3. First, the input feature map is compressed using global max pooling and global average pooling. We use them at the same time, because average pooling has a global receptive field and captures overall characteristics, while max pooling focuses on unique features in the feature map. The combination of them helps to fully express channel attention. Then these vectors are fed into a fully connected neural network with shared dense layers. The network is used to explicitly model the correlation between channels, and the importance of each channel is expressed through nonlinear transformation. To reduce the parameters of the network, the hidden layer parameters are compressed, which also filters out some unimportant information. After obtaining these one-dimensional vectors representing the correlation and importance between channels, we calculate the sum of these two vectors and get the final channel attention M_c. This process can be expressed with Formula 1:

$$M_c(F) = \sigma(MLP(GAP(F)) + MLP(GMP(F))) \tag{1}$$

In formula (1), $M_c(F)$ is a one-dimensional matrix representing channel attention of the feature map. σ represents the activation function *Sigmoid*. *GAP(F)* means global average pooling and *GMP(F)* means global max pooling.

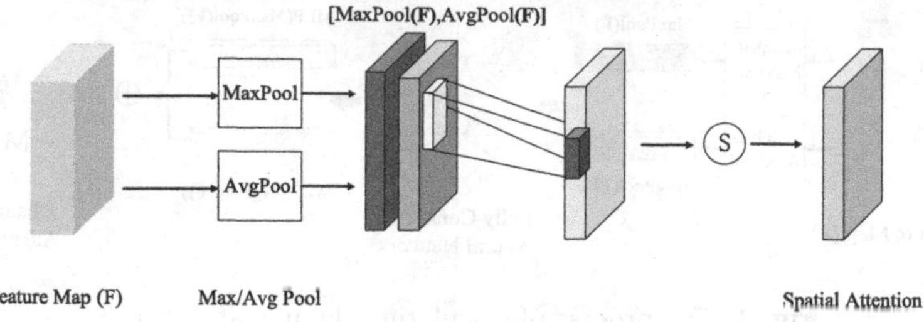

Fig. 4. The process of calculating spatial attention.

Spatial Attention. Different from channel attention, the spatial attention mechanism mainly focuses on the location information of the feature map, because the important features concentrate in a certain region and the location is uncertain. The idea is similar to the channel attention mechanism. A neural network can pay more attention to the areas with important features concerning artifacts by assigning different weights to different areas in the feature map. Suppose M_s represents spatial attention of the feature map, then we have $M_s(F) \in R^{H*W}$, wherc F is the input feature map, H and W represent height and width.

Figure 4 shows the specific implementation process of calculating M_s. First, max pooling and average pooling are used on the channel dimensions of the feature map. Similarly, max pooling focuses on the location of unique features, while average pooling focuses on the overall information of target features. And an effective feature descriptor of the feature map is formed by these two pooling operations. Then the convolution operation is performed on the feature descriptors to encode and model the locations that need to be emphasized or suppressed in the feature map. After that, we get the spatial attention $M_s \in R^{H*W}$. This process can be expressed with Formula 2:

$$M_s(F) = \sigma(f([F^S_{avg}, F^S_{max}])) \tag{2}$$

In formula (2), $M_s(F)$ is a two-dimensional matrix representing spatial attention of the feature map. σ represents the activation function *Sigmoid* and f represents convolution operation. F^S_{avg} is the descriptor of the average pooling on the feature map and F^S_{max} is the descriptor of the max pooling.

Dual Attention. The channel attention mechanism and spatial attention mechanism of the feature map are complementary. Channel attention focuses on information about the feature and its importance, while spatial attention focuses on the distribution of features in the feature map. Therefore, it is effective to combine them for better detection. It can not only help the neural network to pay more attention to key features, but also improve the ability to take control of the key feature distribution in space. Furthermore, the regions that our attention mechanism focuses on provide clues for localization.

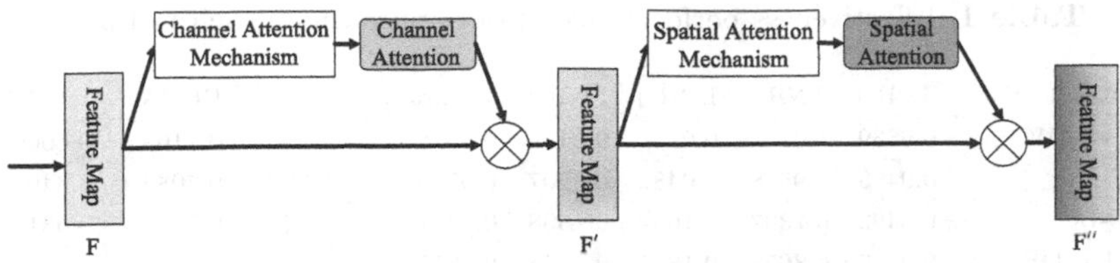

Fig. 5. The process of combining channel attention with spatial attention. For the input feature map, channel attention is calculated at first, because it will not interfere with the calculation and addition of spatial attention. Spatial attention is calculated later and added to the feature map that channel attention has been added to.

By combining channel attention with spatial attention and perform a linear transformation on the input feature maps, attention can be added to channel and space at the same time. The process of combining channel attention with spatial attention is shown in Fig. 5. For the input feature map, channel attention is calculated at first, because it will not interfere with the calculation and addition of spatial attention. After getting the feature map $F^{'}$ with channel attention added, spatial attention of $F^{'}$ is calculated. Then we add spatial attention to $F^{'}$ and get feature map $F^{''}$ with both attention added.

4 Experiment

4.1 Experimental Setup

Datasets. In this paper, we select six available open-source datasets for evaluation, namely Deepfake-Timit (DT) [14], UADFV [27], FaceForenscics (FF) [19], Celeb-DF (v2) [17], DeeperForensics (DeeperF) [11], and StyleGAN [13], including both images and videos. These datasets cover a wide range of GANs for *DeepFake* generation and their quality is relatively high. Among them, Deepfake-Timit uses FaceSwap-GAN for training, and the corresponding real videos come from VidTIMIT. UADFV is consist of both real and fake videos generated with *FakeApp*. FaceForenscics contains real YouTube videos and fake videos generated with *FaceSwap*. They are divided into three categories by the compression rate: Raw, HQ (High Quality), and LQ (Low Quality). Celeb-DF (V2) is also based on public YouTube videos, using an improved *DeepFake* synthesis technique, and has better visual quality. DeeperForensics is a video dataset generated by a newly proposed end-to-end face-swapping framework. These videos are first split into several frames, then the facial area of each frame is extracted to produce training and test images. We divide each dataset into disjoint training and test sets on a scale of approximately 9 to 1 except Celeb-DF (v2) according to its official documents. More details of the datasets are shown in Appendix A.

Implementation Details. We choose MesoNet [4], Meso-Inception [4], VGG-19 [21], Xception [7] and EfficientNet-B0 [22] as backbone to evaluate the

Table 1. Effectiveness performance of our approach on each test set.

Datasets	TPR ↑	TNR ↑	FPR ↓	FNR ↓	Accuracy ↑	AUC ↑	PBCA ↑	IINC ↓
FF-RAW	0.9839	1.0	0.0	0.0164	0.9918	0.9997	0.7168	0.6006
FF-HQ	0.9493	0.9518	0.0482	0.0507	0.9505	0.9925	0.7082	0.6404
FF-LQ	0.8492	0.7307	0.1693	0.1508	0.8401	0.9217	0.7113	0.6319
Celeb-DF (v2)	0.9469	0.8658	0.1811	0.0378	0.8975	0.9673	–	–
UADFV	0.9528	0.9960	0.0042	0.0451	0.9744	0.9792	0.8404	0.6869
DT-HQ	1.0	1.0	0.0	0.0	1.0	1.0	–	–
DT-LQ	1.0	1.0	0.0	0.0	1.0	1.0	–	–
DeeperF	0.9875	0.9815	0.0184	0.0126	0.9845	0.9982	0.7094	0.6211
StyleGAN	0.9060	0.9385	0.0636	0.0910	0.9223	0.9748	–	–

effectiveness of our added attention in improving the detection performance. Specifically, we add channel and spatial attention to every block in MesoNet as described in Sect. 3.2 (referred to as **our approach** in the following sections). And we insert our attention module after both block 1 and 4 in Meso-Inception, between block 1 and 2 of Xception, and at the last block for VGG-19 and EfficientNet. For VGG-19, we also add batch normalization layer after each block to avoid over-fitting. The performance when our attention is added to different places of the backbone models is analyzed in Sect. 4.3. We used Adam optimizer with $\beta_1 = 0.9$, $\beta_2 = 0.999$, and a fixed learning rate of 0.001. In the module of channel attention mechanism, the compression ratio in the shared fully connected layer is set to 8. And in the module of spatial attention mechanism, the kernel size used for modeling spatial attention is set to 7 * 7.

4.2 Detection Effectiveness

In evaluation, we adopt six different metrics, namely TPR (recall, true positive rate), TNR (true negative rate), FPR (false positive rate), FNR (false negative rate), accuracy, and AUC (area under curve). The detection effectiveness of our approach on each test set is shown in Table 1. Its detection accuracy in all datasets except FaceForensics LQ and Celeb-DF (v2) reaches over 92%, and the average FPR and FNR of all datasets are 0.0539 and 0.0449. The AUC of our approach on all datasets can reach more than 0.92, indicating the good detection performance for a variety of GANs. On the whole, results show that our model performs well in various datasets and achieves good performance in these evaluation metrics. AUC and accuracy are relatively low in the FaceForensics LQ dataset possibly because the high compression rate causes serious image distortion and it is even hard for humans to distinguish, which also causes a high FNR.

Baselines. To evaluate the performance of our approach comprehensively, we manually reproduce the existing facial forgery detection techniques to train them on the same training sets as our model and test on the corresponding

Table 2. Comparison of detection accuracy with baseline techniques on each dataset. The improvement relative to the corresponding baseline has been highlighted.

Approach	FF-RAW	FF-HQ	FF-LQ	Celeb-DF (v2)	UADFV	DT-HQ	DT-LQ	DeeperF	StyleGAN
Head pose	0.5253	0.5301	0.4822	–	0.9444	0.7099	0.7326	0.4400	–
VA-MLP	0.7439	0.7105	0.6688	0.6908	0.7170	0.8205	0.8707	0.7384	0.5833
VA-logistic	0.7730	0.7398	0.6426	0.6661	0.6604	0.8405	0.9138	0.7783	0.6401
FWA	0.8357	0.7680	0.5544	0.5969	0.7215	0.7520	0.9986	0.4028	0.4923
MesoNet	0.9616	0.9017	0.8048	0.8470	0.9439	1.0	1.0	0.9750	0.8818
MesoNet+Att.	**0.9918**	**0.9505**	**0.8401**	**0.8975**	**0.9744**	1.0	1.0	**0.9845**	**0.9223**
Meso-Inception	0.9877	0.9170	0.8411	0.8616	0.8869	1.0	1.0	0.9892	0.9153
Meso-Inception+Att.	**0.9918**	**0.9316**	**0.8694**	**0.9019**	**0.9661**	1.0	1.0	**0.9908**	**0.9267**
VGG-19	0.9918	0.9371	0.8647	0.9284	0.8734	1.0	1.0	0.9882	0.9798
VGG-19+Att.	0.9918	**0.9566**	**0.8713**	**0.9477**	**0.9331**	1.0	1.0	**0.9932**	**0.9848**
Xception	0.9915	0.9624	0.8502	0.9611	0.9606	1.0	1.0	0.9972	0.9892
Xception+Att.	**0.9918**	**0.9668**	**0.9022**	**0.9717**	**0.9801**	1.0	1.0	**0.9988**	**0.9962**
EfficientNet	0.9918	0.9719	0.8706	0.9683	0.9812	1.0	1.0	0.9968	0.9965
EfficientNet+Att.	0.9918	**0.9859**	**0.9048**	**0.9756**	**0.9845**	1.0	1.0	**0.9982**	**0.9985**

test sets for comparison. Table 2 reports the detection accuracy. According to the results, detection approaches based on manually defined features, including Head Pose [27], VA-MLP [18], VA-Logistic [18], and FWA [16], are only effective on some limited datasets. As for other learning-based approaches, including MesoNet [4], MesoNet-Inception [4], VGG-19 [21], Xception [20], and EfficientNet [22], accuracy is relatively high on all datasets, even for the simplest network like MesoNet. However, our approach still has an improvement compared with the corresponding backbone models. Specifically, the accuracy is improved by 3.50%, 2.56%, 1.64%, 1.36%, and 0.89% in average on MesoNet, Meso-Inception, VGG-19, Xception, and EfficientNet, respectively. Accuracy reaches 100% on Deepfake-Timit, suggesting that it is simple for learning-based approaches to detect, thus is not taken into account here and in the following sections. Results show that our attention mechanism has the capability to improve the detection performance for different *DeepFake* generation techniques and backbone models, and is especially effective for shallow networks such as MesoNet and Meso-Inception.

Cross-dataset Evaluation. We also evaluate the generalization capability of our approach, which is trained on FaceForensics RAW dataset and tested on other datasets. As shown in Table 3, generally, the detection accuracy of our approach is slightly lower than the backbone model when they are tested on datasets other than FF-RAW. The possible reason is that our attention mechanism focuses mainly on the artifacts of specific method, thus the trained model is less effective in dealing with unknown GANs.

However, we argue that as long as our attention mechanism has seen the images synthesized with the new GANs, even in the case of multiple mixed generation methods, it can also pay attention to the respective artifacts of different methods. To confirm this, we mix training images in FF-RAW, Celeb-DF (v2),

Table 3. Detection accuracy in the cases of cross-dataset and mixed training set.

Approach	Train	Test				
		FF-RAW	Celeb-DF (v2)	UADFV	DeeperF	StyleGAN
MesoNet	FF-RAW	0.9616	**0.6155**	0.4990	**0.4980**	**0.5002**
MesoNet+Att.	FF-RAW	**0.9918**	0.5897	**0.5165**	0.4810	0.4980
MesoNet	mixed	0.8562	0.7482	0.9175	**0.9740**	0.8383
MesoNet+Att.	mixed	**0.9597**	**0.8109**	**0.9330**	0.9645	**0.8658**

Table 4. Comparison of accuracy when added with single attention, dual attention, and a normal convolution layer.

Approach	FF-RAW	FF-HQ	FF-LQ	Celeb-DF (v2)	UADFV	DeeperF	StyleGAN	Parameters
MesoNet	0.9616	0.9017	0.8048	0.8470	0.9439	0.9750	0.8818	28073
MesoNet+Att-c	0.9906	0.8816	0.8059	0.8205	0.9321	0.9812	0.9062	28287
MesoNet+Att-s	0.9912	0.9189	0.7909	0.8641	0.9589	0.9832	0.9190	28465
MesoNet+Att.	**0.9918**	**0.9505**	**0.8401**	**0.8975**	**0.9744**	0.9845	**0.9223**	28679
MesoNet+Conv.	0.9836	0.9101	0.7972	0.8892	0.9404	**0.9848**	0.9137	29681

UADFV, DeeperForensics, and StyleGAN to create a mixed training set. Then we train MesoNet as well as our approach on this dataset, and they are tested on the original test sets. Results in Table 3 show that detection accuracy of our approach substantially outperforms the backbone model, especially in FF-RAW and Celeb-DF (v2), indicating the capability for our attention mechanism to focus on artifacts of different GANs.

4.3 Ablation Study

Effectiveness of Dual Attention. To evaluate the effectiveness of dual attention, we compare our approach with several cases, including: (i) MesoNet, (ii) MesoNet+Att-c: MesoNet with only channel attention added to the corresponding places of each block, (iii) MesoNet+Att-s: MesoNet with only spatial attention added, (iv) MesoNet+Att.: MesoNet with dual attention added, (v) MesoNet+Conv.: an extra convolution layer is added to the first block of MesoNet to match the number of parameters with our approach. The detection accuracy and the number of trainable parameters are shown in Table 4. In general, the best results are obtained by using dual attention mechanism, while single attention mechanism improves detection accuracy slightly in some datasets and decreases in others. By adding a convolution layer, the accuracy is improved in most datasets. The average improvement is 1.47%, less than 3.50% when added with dual attention, even though it has more trainable parameters. This suggests the effectiveness of dual attention and shows that the improvement in accuracy does not entirely come from the increase in the number of parameters.

Table 5. Comparison of accuracy when our attention is added to different places of backbone models.

Approach	Position	FF-RAW	FF-HQ	FF-LQ	Celeb-DF (v2)	UADF.V	DeeperF	StyleGAN	Improve(avg)
MesoNet	–	0.9616	0.9017	0.8048	0.8470	0.9439	0.9750	0.8818	–
	block1	0.9902	0.9366	0.8332	**0.8973**	**0.9671**	**0.9882**	**0.9203**	3.10%
	block2	0.9771	0.9384	0.8464	0.8913	0.9661	0.9872	0.9035	2.78%
	block3	**0.9912**	0.9294	0.8376	0.8756	0.9589	0.9820	0.9042	2.33%
	block4	0.9903	**0.9472**	**0.8596**	0.8770	0.9610	0.9882	0.9123	**3.14%**
Meso-Inception	–	0.9877	0.9170	0.8411	0.8616	0.8869	0.9892	0.9153	–
	block1	**0.9921**	0.9458	**0.8728**	0.8794	0.9293	**0.9930**	**0.9395**	**2.19%**
	block2	0.9918	0.9399	0.8568	0.8890	0.9311	0.9900	0.9255	1.79%
	block3	0.9918	0.9183	0.8662	0.8773	0.9066	0.9858	0.9093	0.81%
	block4	0.9918	**0.9534**	0.8348	**0.8936**	**0.9567**	0.9910	0.9187	2.02%
VGG-19	–	0.9918	0.9371	0.8647	0.9284	0.8734	0.9882	0.9798	-
	block1	0.9918	0.9530	0.8199	0.9465	0.9003	0.9918	**0.9930**	0.47%
	block2	0.9918	0.9274	0.8600	0.9348	0.8938	0.9910	0.9685	0.06%
	block3	0.9915	0.9427	0.8508	0.9141	0.9217	0.9895	0.9832	0.43%
	block4	0.9918	0.9453	0.8458	0.9373	0.9049	0.9840	0.9758	0.31%
	block5	0.9918	**0.9566**	**0.8713**	**0.9477**	**0.9331**	**0.9932**	0.9848	**1.64%**
Xception	–	0.9915	0.9624	0.8502	0.9611	0.9606	0.9972	0.9892	–
	block1	0.9918	0.9668	**0.9022**	**0.9717**	**0.9801**	**0.9988**	**0.9962**	**1.36%**
	block4	0.9918	0.9627	0.8650	0.9692	0.9681	0.9982	0.9962	0.56%
	block12	0.9918	0.9652	0.8584	0.9674	0.9795	0.9985	0.9762	0.35%
	block13	0.9918	**0.9718**	0.8863	0.9652	0.9634	0.9975	0.9918	0.79%
EfficientNet	–	0.9918	0.9719	0.8706	0.9683	0.9812	0.9968	0.9965	–
	stem	0.9918	0.9747	0.8715	0.9720	0.9819	0.9975	0.9960	0.12%
	middle	0.9918	0.9775	0.8742	0.9685	0.9842	0.9978	0.9965	0.19%
	top	0.9918	**0.9859**	**0.9048**	**0.9756**	**0.9845**	**0.9982**	**0.9985**	**0.89%**

Ablation Study on the Depth of Attention Module. We further investigate the effects of our attention mechanism when added to different depths of different backbone models. For MesoNet, Meso-Inception, and VGG-19, we add the attention module to the end of each block respectively. Since Xception and EfficientNet are much deeper, we select only four typical blocks of Xception, representing the beginning of entry flow (block1), middle flow (block4), exit flow (block12), and the ending of exit flow (block13), and three positions of EfficientNet that are before the first block (stem), between block3 and 4 (middle), and after the last block (top). Attention is added to these places respectively. Then we train and test each model with different placements of attention on each dataset. Results in Table 5 shows that accuracy of models with attention added is relatively higher than the original ones regardless of the placements, indicating that the attention mechanism can indeed improve the detection performance of different backbone models. Generally, it is more effective when attention is added to the beginning and exit flow, especially for deeper neural networks such as Xception. Moreover, since the feature extraction capability is relatively weak for shallow networks, attention can be added in multiple locations to enhance the detection effectiveness. For example, the accuracy is improved by 3.50% with attention added to all blocks of MesoNet (refer to Table 2), better than adding to any single block.

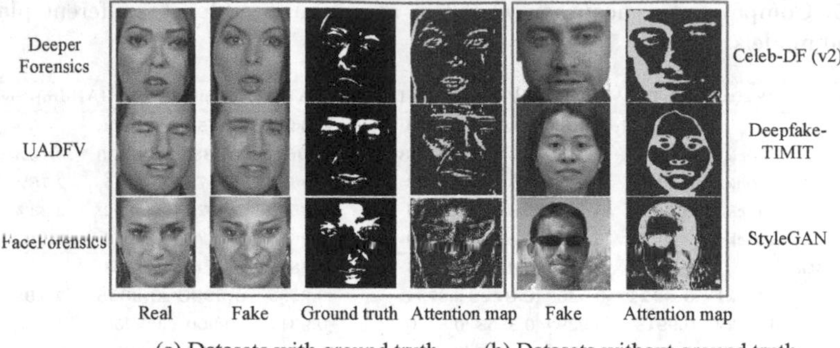

(a) Datasets with ground truth. (b) Datasets without ground truth.

Fig. 6. Visual effects of localization. For DeeperForensics, UADFV and FaceForensics, the attention maps are visually consistent with the ground truth. As for Celeb-DF (v2), Deepfake-TIMIT, and StyleGAN, attention is concentrated on facial areas.

Table 6. Comparison with FFD.

Approach	Accuracy ↑	PBCA ↑	IINC ↓
Xception	0.9729	–	–
FFD	0.9752	0.8289	0.6574
MesoNet	0.9664	–	–
Our approach	**0.9753**	**0.8315**	**0.6454**

4.4 Manipulation Localization

Our attention mechanism can focus on manipulated pixels of the synthesized images, hence we utilize the spatial attention from the first convolution layer for localization. Each pixel in the attention map corresponds to the pixel in the original image. To quantify the localization effectiveness, we need to compare our attention map with the ground truth, thus we only evaluate *DeepFake* images in datasets where ground truth can be obtained. We choose PBCA (Pixel-wise Binary Classification Accuracy) and IINC (Inverse Intersection Non-Containment) [8] as the evaluation metrics. Higher PBCA and lower IINC means better performance. As shown in Table 1, we have a considerable PBCA of more than 70% and IINC less than 70% on all datasets. And the visual effects of our attention maps are shown in Fig. 6. For datasets with ground truth, our attention maps are visually consistent with the ground truth maps. As for datasets without ground truth, attention is concentrated on facial areas, indicating that artifacts mainly exist in facial areas for generated videos and images. More visualization results can be found in Appendix B.

We also compare our localization effectiveness with previous work by Dang et al. [8] (referred to as FFD). The detection accuracy, PBCA, and IINC on *faceapp*, a dataset provided in Dang's work, are reported in Table 6, and the comparison of visual effects is shown in Fig. 7. Overall, the detection accuracy,

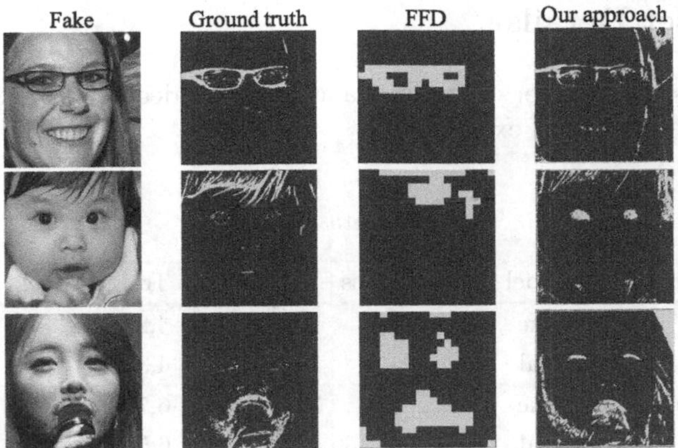

Fig. 7. Comparison of visual effects with FFD. By comparing the attention maps produced by both techniques with the ground truth, we can observe that our approach is obviously more fine-grained and precise.

PBCA, and IINC of our approach are slightly better than FFD. And though our approach is similar to FFD in terms of these metrics, the attention maps of our approach are obviously more fine-grained and precise.

5 Conclusion

In this paper, we propose a novel *DeepFake* detection approach by focusing on the observable and invisible artifact regions with dual attention. We add channel attention and spatial attention to help the neural networks to better focus on essential features and their spatial distribution in the images where artifacts mainly exist. Our proposed approach can automatically learn artifacts for different GANs, which not only helps for better detection performance but also provides a clear clue for localization. We evaluate our approach with five backbone models of different architectures and six datasets covering a diversity of GANs. Experimental results show that the detection accuracy is improved by 3.50%, 2.56%, 1.64%, 1.36%, and 0.89% in average on MesoNet, Meso-Inception, VGG-19, Xception, and EfficientNet respectively, and our attention mechanism can perform pixel-wise manipulation localization.

Acknowledgement. This work was supported in part by National Natural Science Foundation of China under Grant U1836112 and 61876134, the Fundamental Research Funds for the Central Universities No. 2042021kf1030.

A Dataset Details

Table 7 details the number of training and testing videos and images of the six DeepFake datasets in our experiments.

Table 7. Datasets details.

Datasets	Label	Train videos	Test videos	Train images	Test images
UADFV	Fake	39	10	4,237	1,483
	Real	39	10	4,343	1,487
Deepfake-Timit HQ	Fake	288	32	6,728	703
	Real	507	52	6,591	676
Deepfake-Timit LQ	Fake	288	32	6,730	705
	Real	507	52	6,591	676
FaceForenscics RAW	Fake	135	15	1,2736	1,618
	Real	135	15	12,721	1,559
FaceForenscics HQ	Fake	135	15	12,736	1,618
	Real	135	15	12,720	1,576
FaceForenscics LQ	Fake	135	15	12,712	1,618
	Real	135	15	12,699	1,553
Celeb-DF (V2)	Fake	5,299	340	26,429	1,695
	Real	712	178	10,579	2,646
DeeperForensics	Fake	900	100	1,8000	2,000
	Real	900	100	18,000	2,000
StyleGAN	Fake	–	–	18,000	2,000
	Real	–	–	18,000	2,000

B Visualization

Figure 8 presents the visualization results of our attention maps. For datasets with ground truth, including DeeperForensics, UADFV, and FaceForensics, we pair the fake images with the real ones to calculate the manipulated pixels. And then we calculate the manipulated pixels from our spatial attention mechanism for localization. Experimental result shown that our attention maps are visually consistent with the ground truth. As for datasets without ground truth, we also calculate the attention maps obtained from the spatial attention mechanism to understand the artifact regions of these images. Results show that attention is concentrated on facial areas for Celeb-DF (v2), Deepfake-TIMIT, and StyleGAN, which are the main artifact regions.

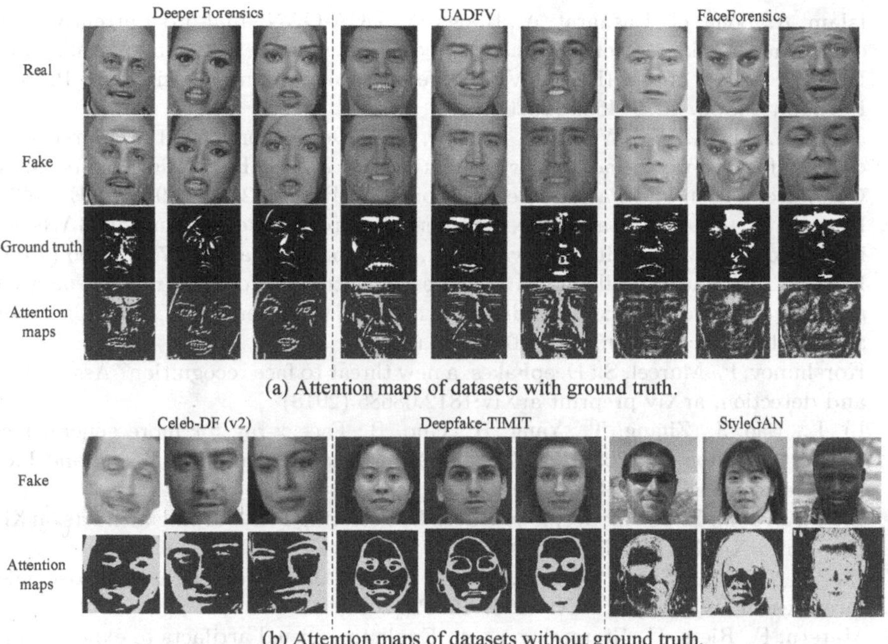

Fig. 8. Visualization results of localizing the manipulated artifacts.

References

1. Deepfacelab. https://github.com/iperov/DeepFaceLab. Accessed 20 Apr 2021
2. Faceapp. https://faceappdownload.org/. Accessed 11 Apr 2021
3. Faceswap github. https://github.com/deepfakes/faceswap. Accessed 20 Apr 2021
4. Afchar, D., Nozick, V., Yamagishi, J., Echizen, I.: MesoNet: a compact facial video forgery detection network. In: 2018 IEEE International Workshop on Information Forensics and Security (WIFS), pp. 1–7. IEEE (2018)
5. Agarwal, S., Farid, H., Gu, Y., He, M., Nagano, K., Li, H.: Protecting world leaders against deep fakes. In: CVPR Workshops, pp. 38–45 (2019)
6. Bahdanau, D., Cho, K., Bengio, Y.: Neural machine translation by jointly learning to align and translate. arXiv preprint arXiv:1409.0473 (2014)
7. Chollet, F.: Xception: deep learning with depthwise separable convolutions. In: Proceedings of the IEEE Conference on Computer Vision and Pattern Recognition, pp. 1251–1258 (2017)
8. Dang, H., Liu, F., Stehouwer, J., Liu, X., Jain, A.K.: On the detection of digital face manipulation. In: 2020 IEEE/CVF Conference on Computer Vision and Pattern Recognition (CVPR) (2020)
9. Güera, D., Delp, E.J.: Deepfake video detection using recurrent neural networks. In: 2018 15th IEEE International Conference on Advanced Video and Signal Based Surveillance (AVSS), pp. 1–6. IEEE (2018)

10. Islam, A., Long, C., Basharat, A., Hoogs, A.: DOA-GAN: dual-order attentive generative adversarial network for image copy-move forgery detection and localization. In: Proceedings of the IEEE/CVF Conference on Computer Vision and Pattern Recognition, pp. 4676–4685 (2020)
11. Jiang, L., Li, R., Wu, W., Qian, C., Loy, C.C.: DeeperForensics-1.0: a large-scale dataset for real-world face forgery detection. In: 2020 IEEE/CVF Conference on Computer Vision and Pattern Recognition (CVPR), pp. 2886–2895. IEEE (2020)
12. Karras, T., Aila, T., Laine, S., Lehtinen, J.: Progressive growing of GANs for improved quality, stability, and variation. arXiv preprint arXiv:1710.10196 (2017)
13. Karras, T., Laine, S., Aila, T.: A style-based generator architecture for generative adversarial networks. In: Proceedings of the IEEE Conference on Computer Vision and Pattern Recognition, pp. 4401–4410 (2019)
14. Korshunov, P., Marcel, S.: DeepFakes: a new threat to face recognition? Assessment and detection. arXiv preprint arXiv:1812.08685 (2018)
15. Li, L., Bao, J., Zhang, T., Yang, H., Guo, B.: Face x-ray for more general face forgery detection. In: 2020 IEEE/CVF Conference on Computer Vision and Pattern Recognition (CVPR) (2020)
16. Li, Y., Lyu, S.: Exposing deepfake videos by detecting face warping artifacts. arXiv preprint arXiv:1811.00656 (2018)
17. Li, Y., Yang, X., Sun, P., Qi, H., Lyu, S.: Celeb-DF: a new dataset for deepfake forensics. arXiv preprint arXiv:1909.12962 (2019)
18. Matern, F., Riess, C., Stamminger, M.: Exploiting visual artifacts to expose deepfakes and face manipulations. In: 2019 IEEE Winter Applications of Computer Vision Workshops (WACVW), pp. 83–92. IEEE (2019)
19. Rössler, A., Cozzolino, D., Verdoliva, L., Riess, C., Thies, J., Nießner, M.: FaceForensics: a large-scale video dataset for forgery detection in human faces. arXiv preprint arXiv:1803.09179 (2018)
20. Rossler, A., Cozzolino, D., Verdoliva, L., Riess, C., Thies, J., Nießner, M.: FaceForensics++: learning to detect manipulated facial images. In: Proceedings of the IEEE International Conference on Computer Vision, pp. 1–11 (2019)
21. Simonyan, K., Zisserman, A.: Very deep convolutional networks for large-scale image recognition. arXiv preprint arXiv:1409.1556 (2014)
22. Tan, M., Le, Q.: EfficientNet: rethinking model scaling for convolutional neural networks. In: International Conference on Machine Learning, pp. 6105–6114. PMLR (2019)
23. Vaswani, A., et al.: Attention is all you need. In: Advances in Neural Information Processing Systems, pp. 5998–6008 (2017)
24. Wang, S.Y., Wang, O., Owens, A., Zhang, R., Efros, A.A.: Detecting photoshopped faces by scripting photoshop. In: Proceedings of the IEEE International Conference on Computer Vision, pp. 10072–10081 (2019)
25. Wang, S.Y., Wang, O., Zhang, R., Owens, A., Efros, A.A.: CNN-generated images are surprisingly easy to spot... for now. arXiv preprint arXiv:1912.11035 (2019)
26. Woo, S., Park, J., Lee, J.-Y., Kweon, I.S.: CBAM: convolutional block attention module. In: Ferrari, V., Hebert, M., Sminchisescu, C., Weiss, Y. (eds.) ECCV 2018. LNCS, vol. 11211, pp. 3–19. Springer, Cham (2018). https://doi.org/10.1007/978-3-030-01234-2_1
27. Yang, X., Li, Y., Lyu, S.: Exposing deep fakes using inconsistent head poses. In: ICASSP 2019–2019 IEEE International Conference on Acoustics, Speech and Signal Processing (ICASSP), pp. 8261–8265. IEEE (2019)

Improved Differential-ML Distinguisher: Machine Learning Based Generic Extension for Differential Analysis

Gao Wang[1] and Gaoli Wang[1,2(✉)]

[1] Shanghai Key Laboratory of Trustworthy Computing, East China Normal University, Shanghai 200062, China
glwang@sei.ecnu.edu.cn

[2] State Key Laboratory of Cryptology, P.O. Box 5159, Beijing 100878, China

Abstract. At CRYPTO 2019, Gohr first proposes a deep learning based differential analysis on round-reduced Speck32/64. Then Yadav *et al.* present a framework to construct the differential-ML (machine learning) distinguisher by combining the traditional differential distinguisher and the machine learning based differential distinguisher, which breaks the limit of the ML differential distinguisher on the number of attack rounds. However, the results obtained based on this method are not necessarily better than the results gained by traditional analysis. In this paper, we offer three novel greedy strategies (M_1, M_2 and M_3) to solve this problem. The strategy M_1 provides better differential-ML distinguishers by considering all combinations of classical differential distinguishers and ML differential distinguishers. And the strategy M_2 uses the best ML differential distinguishers to splice classical differential distinguishers forward, while the strategy M_3 adopts the best classical differential distinguishers to splice ML differential distinguishers. As proof of works, we apply our methods to round-reduced Speck32/64, Speck48/72 and Speck64/96 and get some improved cryptanalysis results. For the construction of differential-ML distinguishers, we can reach 11-round Speck32/64, 14-round Speck48/72 and 18-round Speck64/96 with 2^{27}, 2^{45}, 2^{62} data respectively.

Keywords: Differential analysis · Machine learning · Lightweight ciphers · Speck

1 Introduction

As an important branch of symmetric cryptography, block ciphers play an irreplaceable role in the field of information security. Differential cryptanalysis proposed by Bihma and Shamir [6] is one of the most effective analysis methods in block cipher analysis, and it is also one of the indispensable indicators to measure the security of a block cipher.

D. Gao et al. (Eds.): ICICS 2021, LNCS 12919, pp. 21–38, 2021.
https://doi.org/10.1007/978-3-030-88052-1_2

In 1994, Matsui [19] proposes a branch-and-bound algorithm to search for the best differential characteristic for DES [7]. But for large block sizes, it is difficult to find useful differential trials with the branch-and-bound based method. Then some automated search tools are applied to solve this problem, such as Mixed Integer Linear Programming (MILP) [26,34], Constraint Programming (CP) [14,24] and Boolean satisfiability problem or satisfiability modulo theories (SAT/SMT) [18,23]. In recent years, cryptanalysts have begun to explore how to use the machine learning technique for differential analysis.

At CRYPTO 2019, Gohr [15] first presents the real and random differences approach to develop neural distinguishers for differential analysis based on the all-in-one differential cryptanalysis [1]. And he also proposes an effective key search policy by adopting a variant of Bayesian optimization. With the help of this policy, he can use 2^{38} encryptions to achieve a 11-round key recovery attack on Speck32/64 compared with 2^{46} in [12]. In addition, he presents a greedy algorithm to derive good input differences without human knowledge. This algorithm allows the neural network to find a good difference rapidly with the help of transfer learning [27] and few-shot learning [29] techniques. But the real and random differences approach only works for Markov ciphers.

Inspired by Gohr's work, Baksi *et al.* [2] propose a new strategy to build ML differential distinguishers for the non-Markov cipher or the cipher with large block sizes by simulating the all-in-one differentials [1]. They choose t ($t \geq 2$) input differences and consider all the output differences of these input differences. To prove the effectiveness of their approach, they train several ML differential distinguishers to reduce the search complexity reported by the designers for round-reduced Gimli-Hash [5] and Gimli-Cipher [5]. To choose a preferable machine learning model for the ML differential distinguisher, they try several different neural network types and their variants (the neural network with different width and depth) with manual way, including multi-layer perceptron (MLP), Convolutional Neural Network (CNN), and Long Short-Term Memory Network (LSTM). And they suggest employing the MLP network (with 2 hidden layers and 1024 neurons in each hidden layer) as the machine learning model for ML differential distinguishers.

Then Jain *et al.* [17] produce a simpler network to distinguish the 3/4/5/6-round Present [9], which can provide better result in less time compared with the MLP network Baksi recommended. Instead of randomly selected input differences in [2], they also adopt the best 14-round differential characteristic in [28] to improve the ability of the ML differential distinguishers.

Bellini *et al.* [4] compare the performance of conventional distinguishers and neural network based distinguishers. They use two different network architectures to build neural distinguishers for round-reduced TEA [30] and RAIDEN [21]. The result indicates that neural network based distinguishers outperformed classical distinguishers and the former can get the results with bits of the computation.

Due to the limitation of computer computing power, the ML differential distinguishers can only attack a few rounds. To solve this problem, Yadav *et al.* [32] propose a strategy to combine the conventional differential distinguisher and ML differential distinguisher. They adopt the 2-round output difference of the best 9-round differential trail to build the 6-round differential-ML distinguisher with 2^{21} data compared with 2^{26} in [8] for Speck32/64.

However, the Yadav's approach has some improvements to make, which is because the distinguishers constructed by Yadav's method are not necessarily better than the traditional approach. For example, although Yadav can use 2^{21} data to build a 6-round distinguisher for Speck32/64, the best 6-round differential probability is 2^{-13} obtained by the classical method in [13]. We further explore how to solve this problem in this paper.

Table 1. Summary of the data complexity against Speck

Cipher	Speck32		Speck48		Speck64	
r	[13]	This paper	[13]	This paper	[13]	This paper
1	2^0	2^0	2^0	2^0	2^0	2^0
2	2^1	2^0	2^1	2^0	2^1	2^0
3	2^3	2^0	2^3	2^0	2^3	2^0
4	2^5	2^2	2^6	2^0	2^6	2^0
5	2^9	2^4	2^{10}	2^2	2^{10}	2^1
6	2^{13}	2^6	2^{14}	2^6	2^{15}	2^4
7	2^{18}	2^7	2^{19}	2^9	2^{21}	2^7
8	2^{24}	2^{12}	2^{26}	2^{11}	2^{29}	2^{10}
9	2^{30}	2^{17}	2^{33}	2^{15}	2^{34}	2^{15}
10	2^{34}	2^{22}	2^{40}	2^{21}	2^{38}	2^{23}
11		2^{27}	2^{45}	2^{29}	2^{42}	2^{28}
12		2^{33}	2^{49}	2^{38}	2^{46}	2^{34}
13				2^{43}	2^{50}	2^{40}
14				2^{45}	2^{56}	2^{43}
15				2^{52}	2^{62}	2^{46}
16					2^{70}	2^{51}
17						2^{55}
18						2^{62}

1.1 Our Contributions

In this work, we present three novel greedy strategies to develop the differential-ML distinguishers, which can improve the performance of distinguishers in [32] and tackle the limitations of machine learning techniques in cryptanalysis.

We first experimentally show that the differences with low hamming weights are more appropriate to develop ML differential distinguishers. Inspired by this and the idea of greedy strategy, three greedy strategies (M_1, M_2 and M_3) are proposed to improve the framework in [32]. A brief introduction is as follows, for more information please refer to Sect. 4.

(a) *Greedy strategy based on considering all possible combinations (M_1).* This strategy allows us to get better R-round differential-ML distinguisher by picking the best one from multiple R-round distinguishers instead of constructing only one distinguisher in [32].

(b) *Greedy strategy based on the ML differential distinguisher (M_2).* This strategy first ensures that the following ML differential distinguisher is the best, and then extends it forward to get the differential-ML distinguisher.

(c) *Greedy strategy based on the classical differential distinguisher (M_3).* In contrast to the strategy M_2, this strategy develops the differential-ML distinguisher by combining the best classical distinguisher and the ML differential distinguisher.

To prove the effectiveness of our three optimization strategies, we apply them to round-reduced Speck32/64, Speck48/72 and Speck64/96. For each variant of Speck, we achieve better results than the best-known ones in [13], as summarized in Table 1. We reach 11-round Speck32/64, 14-round Speck48/72 and 18-round Speck64/96 with 2^{27}, 2^{45}, 2^{62} data, while the authors can only get 9-round Speck32/64, 11-round Speck48/72 and 15-round Speck64/96 with 2^{30}, 2^{45}, 2^{62} data in [13].

1.2 Organization

Section 2 provides a brief description of the block cipher Speck and some preliminary knowledge used in this paper, including MILP aided differential analysis, ML differential distinguisher and basic differential-ML distinguisher. Section 3 shows that the ML differential distinguisher can get better accuracy when the input differences with low hamming weights. In Sect. 4, the three improved methods with greedy strategy are introduced in detail. We apply the improved approaches to round-reduced Speck32/64, Speck48/72 and Speck64/96 in Sect. 5. Section 6 concludes this paper. Section 7 gives the project and fund support of this work.

2 Preliminaries

2.1 Brief Description of Speck

Speck [3] is a lightweight block cipher with Feistel structure proposed by the US National Security Agency (NSA, USA) in June 2013. There are several versions of Speck and their parameters are specified in Table 2. Its round function is composed of ARX components, which include left and right circular shifts ($\lll$ or $\ggg$), bitwise XOR ($\oplus$) and addition modulo 2^n ($\boxplus$).

Round function Assuming (x_i, y_i) and (x_{i+1}, y_{i+1}) are the input and output of the i-th round and the round key of the i-round is k_i, while α and β represent the parameters of circular shifts. Their relationship is as follows:

$$\begin{cases} x_{i+1} = (x_i \ggg \alpha) \boxplus y_i \oplus k_i \\ y_{i+1} = x_{i+1} \oplus (y_i \lll \beta) \end{cases}$$

which is shown more clearly in Fig. 1.

Table 2. Speck parameters

Block size-$2n$	Key size-mn	Rounds-T	α	β
32	64	22	7	2
48	72	22	8	3
48	96	23	8	3
64	96	26	8	3
64	128	27	8	3
96	96	28	8	3
96	144	29	8	3
128	128	32	8	3
128	192	33	8	3
128	256	34	8	3

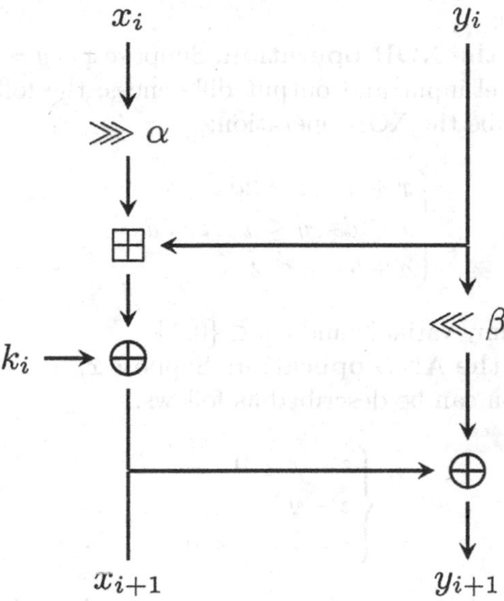

Fig. 1. Round function of Speck.

Key schedules Suppose $K = (l_{m-2}, ..., l_0, k_0)$ represents the key of Speck$2n$, where $l_i, k_0 \in GF(2)^n, m \in \{2, 3, 4\}$. The round key k_i and sequences l_i are defined by

$$\begin{cases} l_{i+m-1} = (k_i + S^{-\alpha} l_i) \oplus i \\ k_{i+1} = S^{\beta} k_i \oplus l_{i+m-1} \end{cases}$$

where S^j and S^{-j} stand for left and right circular shifts j bits.

2.2 MILP Aided Differential Analysis

Mixed Integer Linear Programming (MILP) uses a series of linear inequalities or equalities to define the propagation rules of the cipher. In the beginning, the MILP is used to search the minimum number of active S-boxes for word-oriented ciphers [20]. Then Sun *et al.* [26] extend the MILP technique to search for the differential characteristics. Afterward, it is also extended and adapted to ARX based cipher [13] and other analysis methods such as integral cryptanalysis [31], zero-correlation linear analysis [11] and impossible differential analysis [22]. Here we only focus on MILP aided differential analysis.

When we need to perform differential analysis on a cipher, we only need to model the different components of the cipher, such as XOR, AND, S-box, Modular Addition, and son on. Then we can get the optimal differential probability and differential characteristic with the help of the optimized solver such as CPLEX [10] and Gurobi [16]. The study of MILP modeling techniques alone is not the focus of this paper, we briefly introduce two basic operations (XOR and AND) as follows:

Constraints on the XOR operation. Suppose $x \oplus y = z$, where $x,\ y,\ z \in \{0,1\}$ are the bit-level input and output differences, the following inequalities are adopted to describe the XOR operation:

$$\begin{cases} x + y + z \geq 2d_{\oplus} \\ x \leq d_{\oplus}, y \leq d_{\oplus}, z \leq d_{\oplus} \\ a + b + c \leq 2 \end{cases}$$

where $d_{\oplus}$ is the dummy variable and $d_{\oplus} \in \{0,1\}$.

Constraints on the AND operation. Suppose $x,\ y,\ z \in \{0,1\}$ and $x \wedge y = z$, the AND operation can be described as follows:

$$\begin{cases} z - x \geq 0 \\ z - y \geq 0 \\ z - x - y \leq 0 \end{cases}$$

Regarding the modeling of other operations (such as Objective Function, S-box, Modular addition, etc.), we recommend referring to [13,25,26,33,34].

2.3 ML Differential Distinguisher

The real and random differences method proposed by Gohr [15] can be adopted to develop the ML differential distinguisher.

We divide the construction of a ML distinguisher into two phases: offline and online. In the offline (training) phase, the N training samples are first generated based on the given difference and cipher. Each training sample is composed of ciphertext pair $(C, C^{'})$ and label Y. Half of the data comes from the selected difference with label $Y = 1$ and the other half belongs to random input differences with label $Y = 0$. Then the training samples are used to train the distinguisher.

If the accuracy of distinguisher $a > 0.5$, it means that a working ML distinguisher is obtained successfully. Otherwise, no suitable distinguisher is available.

In the online (testing) phase, the goal is to identify whether *Oracle* is *Random* or *Cipher*. The attacker can find a threshold τ and a cutoff C_τ on the number of predictions with probability greater than τ. τ is a fixed threshold $(0.5 < \tau \leq 0.8)$, depending on the verification accuracy of the distinguisher. The first step is to generate C_τ samples from the same source (*Random* or *Cipher*). Then the test accuracy $a^{'}$ can be calculated by substituting the data into the model obtained in the training phase. Finally, we can judge whether *Oracle* is *Random* or *Cipher* based on the test accuracy $a^{'}$ and threshold τ.

2.4 Basic Differential-ML Distinguisher

Yadav *et al.* [32] present a framework to combine the classical differential distinguisher and the ML differential distinguisher. We divide their attacks into three phases:

1) *Deriving the input difference.* They first intercept an r-round differential trial with probability P_r from the $r^{'}$-round $(r^{'} > r)$ differential characteristic given in the previous study. And then they take the r-round output difference ΔX_r as the input difference of the ML differential distinguisher instead of the plaintext difference ΔX_0.
2) *Developing the ML differential distinguisher.* Then they adopt the ΔX_r and the real and random differences method introduced in Sect. 2.3 to train and evaluate a s-round ML distinguisher. To evaluate the s-round ML distinguisher as precisely as possible, they conduct 5 experiments and adopt 100 samples (half of the samples belong to the r-round output difference and the other half belongs to the randomly selected difference) to get 96% or higher accuracy for each experiment.
3) *Evaluating the differential-ML distinguisher.* In the end, they can obtain an R-round $(R = r+s)$ differential-ML distinguisher by combining the r-round classical differential distinguisher and the s-round ML differential distinguisher. In theory, C_τ/P_r data is enough to get 96% or higher accuracy for the R-round differential-ML distinguisher, but in fact, more data is needed. We define the data complexity of the R-round differential-ML distinguisher as C_R $(C_R \geq C_\tau/P_r)$.

3 The Relationship Between Input Difference and ML Differential Distinguisher

The choice of input difference affects the accuracy of the ML differential distinguishers and the number of rounds that the distinguishers can attack. The all-in-one approach [1] considers all the output differences with one input difference. It is well known in classical differential cryptanalysis that the differences with low hamming weights diffuse relatively slowly, so we use experiments to explore whether this theory can be applied to ML-based analysis methods.

To observe the relationship between the accuracy of ML differential distinguishers and the hamming weights of the input differences, the best way is to exhaust all the input differences with different hamming weights. But it requires an enormous amount of calculation, so we randomly choose W differences for every different hamming weights to simplify the calculation. For a lightweight block cipher with block length BL, the number of differences we need to compare is $BL \times W$.

If we retrained the model every time we have to evaluate a new input difference, it would take a long time because the differences we need to examine are too many. So we adopt few-shot learning and transfer learning techniques to speed up this work. We first train a Gohr's ML model as the first model with N training samples generated by a randomly chosen difference. Then when we need to evaluate a given input difference, the first step is to bring the data of $N^{'}$ training samples X obtained by the given input difference into the first model. Then we take the output of the penultimate layer $Y^{'}$ and the label of training samples Y as the input to the second model to get its accuracy. The linear model Ridge Regression with $\alpha = 0.01$ is sufficient as the second model for identification, which is faster than nonlinear models. Algorithm 1 summarizes the general pseudo-code for calculating maximum, minimum, average accuracies of the input differences with different hamming weights.

We apply Algorithm 1 to 4-round Speck32/64, Speck48/72 and Speck64/96 with $N = 10^6$, $N^{'} = 10^4$ and $W = 100$, the results are presented in Fig. 2. We can intuitively observe that the ML differential distinguisher can get better accuracy when the input differences with low hamming weights.

4 Improved Differential-ML Distinguisher with Greedy Strategy

In this section, we present three greedy strategies to optimize the construction of the differential-ML distinguisher. For convenience, we call these three strategies M_1, M_2 and M_3 respectively.

4.1 Greedy Strategy Based on Considering All Possible Combinations (M_1)

Unlike Yadav's work, we adequately consider all $(r + s)$-round differential-ML distinguishers instead of just one, which can enhance the analysis results. For example, Yadav only combines a 2-round classical differential distinguisher and a 4-round ML distinguisher to construct a 6-round differential-ML distinguisher for Speck32/64, while we consider all the cases where the 6-round differential-ML distinguisher can be constructed, such as 1-round classical differential distinguisher and 5-round ML differential distinguisher, 2-round classical differential distinguisher and 4-round ML distinguisher, 3-round classical differential distinguisher and 3-round ML distinguisher, and so on.

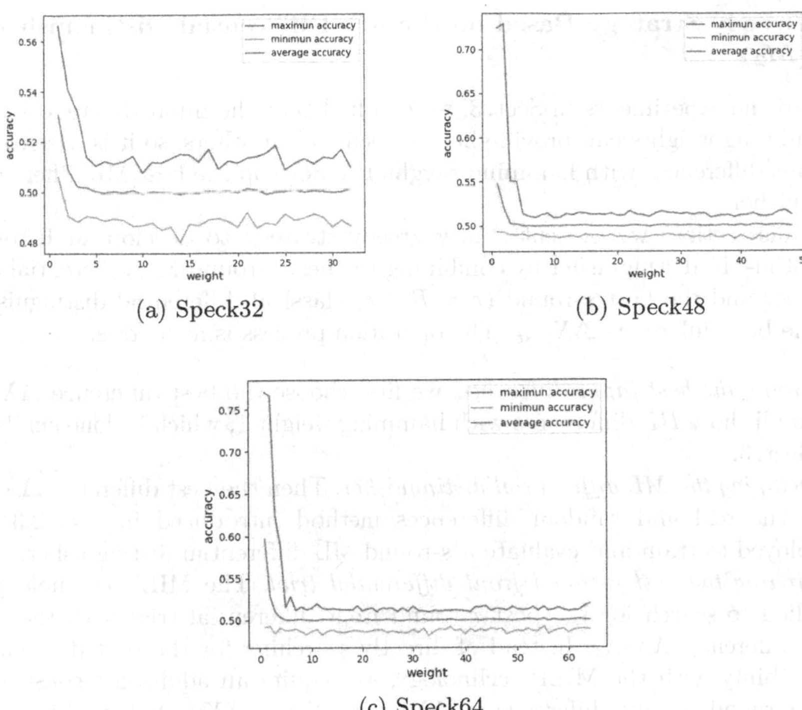

(a) Speck32 (b) Speck48

(c) Speck64

Fig. 2. Accuracy of 4-round ML differential distinguishers with different hamming weights

Algorithm 1. Calculate maximum, minimum, average accuracies of the input differences with different hamming weights

```
Randomly generate an input difference ΔX
X, Y ← GetData(ΔX, s, N), s is the number of rounds
Net = Train(X, Y)
MaxResults, MinResults, AvgResults ← ∅
for all i ← 0, BL do
    Result = []
    for all k ← 0, W do
        Randomly generate ΔX with hamming weight i
        X, Y ← GetData(ΔX, s, N')
        Y' = Net[−2].predict(X)
        (Net[−2] denotes the output of the penultimate layer of the Net)
        accuracy = RidgeRegression(Y', Y)
        Result.insert(accuracy)
    end for
    Insert Max(result), Min(result), Avg(result)
    into MaxResults, MinResults, AvgResults
end for
return MaxResults, MinResults, AvgResults
```

4.2 Greedy Strategy Based on the ML Differential Distinguisher (M_2)

Through the experiments in Sect. 3, we can find that the input differences with low hamming weights can provide better results than others, so it is wise to use the input differences with hamming weight 1 to develop the best ML differential distinguisher.

In this section, we present a new greedy strategy to develop an R-round differential-ML distinguisher by combining the best s-round ML differential distinguisher and the best r-round ($r = R - s$) classical differential distinguisher with the best difference ΔX_{best}. The operation process is as follows:

1) *Deriving the best input difference.* we first choose the best difference ΔX_{best} from all those BL differences with hamming weight 1, which is done similarly to Sect. 3.
2) *Developing the ML differential distinguisher.* Then the best difference ΔX_{best} and the real and random differences method introduced in Sect. 2.3 are employed to train and evaluate a s-round ML differential distinguisher.
3) *Searching the best r-round front differential trial.* The MILP technology is applied to search for the best r-round front differential trial with the output difference ΔX_{best}. Instead of directly searching for the best differential probability with the MILP technology, we require an additional constraint: the r-round output difference is ΔX_{best} ($\Delta X_r = \Delta X_{best}$). By adding this constraint we can find the best differential probability and differential trial for extending r rounds forward.
4) *Evaluating the differential-ML distinguisher.* Finally, the $(r + s)$-round differential-ML distinguisher, which is composed of the s-round ML differential distinguisher and the r-round classic differential distinguisher, has the same evaluation method as Sect. 2.4.

4.3 Greedy Strategy Based on the Classical Differential Distinguisher (M_3)

To make the differential probability of the classical differential distinguisher as small as possible, we can take the output difference of the best r-round differential trial as the input difference of the ML differential distinguisher.

There may be multiple differential trials with the best differential probability, but we only consider those whose r-round output difference has the minimum hamming weight based on the finding in Sect. 3. For all those differential trials that satisfy the above condition, we choose the best one according to the performance of ML differential distinguishers constructed by their r-round output differences. Finally, we can get a differential-ML distinguisher by combining the classical differential distinguisher and ML differential distinguisher. The specific steps are as follows:

1) *Obtaining the maximum r-round differential probability* (P_r). This work can be easily completed with the MILP technology introduced in Sect. 2.2.
2) *Acquiring all r-round differential trials with the minimum hamming weights* (W_r). There are three differences between this task and searching for the maximum r-round differential probability. The first is that the objective function becomes the sum of the r-round output difference ($\sum_{i=0}^{BL} \Delta X_{r\_i}$), which can minimize the hamming weights of the r-round output differences. The second is that we need an additional condition: the differential probability of the r-round differential trial is P_r, which can be expressed as $\sum_{i=0}^{r} Pr_i = P_r$ (Pr_i is the differential probability of i-th round). The last is that the newly obtained result cannot be in the previous results, which can be defined as follows:

$$\begin{cases} \#\ ResultsSet\ is\ a\ set\ of\ results\ initialized\ to\ \varnothing \\ \#\ i\ is\ the\ subscript\ of\ a\ nonzero\ position \\ for\ \Delta X_r\ in\ ResultsSet: \\ \qquad \sum \Delta X_{r\_i} \leq W_r - 1 \end{cases}$$

The search can be stopped when the new minimum hamming weight is greater than the one we get initially.
3) *Developing the ML differential distinguisher.* All the r-round output differences are used to train and evaluate the s-round ML differential distinguishers based on the real and random differences method in Sect. 2.3.
4) *Evaluating the differential-ML distinguisher.* The evaluation method of the differential-ML distinguishers obtained by combining the ML differential distinguishers and the classical differential distinguishers is same as that in Sect. 2.4.

5 Applications

In this section, we apply our three greedy strategies (M_1, M_2 *and* M_3) to round-reduced Speck32/64, Speck48/72 and Speck96/96. All the ML differential distinguishers are built based on Gohr's network structure in [15], except for the following two differences: the depth of the residual block is set to 1 and the epoch of the model is set to 50 to avoid overfitting. For more information about Gohr's network structure, we refer to [15].

The experiment is performed on a single PC (Intel(R) Xeon(R) CPU E5-2620 v4, 2.10 GHz, NVIDIA GeForce GTX 1080 Ti GPU, 32.00 GB RAM, Windows). The construction of ML differential distinguishers are done by GPU, and the MILP models are solved with the powerful mathematical optimization solver Gurobi [16] on the CPU.

First of all, we adopt the strategy M_1 in Sect. 4.1 and the best differential trials in Table 4 to build the differential-ML distinguishers. For Speck32/64, we first adopt r-round output difference ΔX_r ($0 \leq r \leq 9$) of the best 9-round differential trial to develop and evaluate the s-round ML differential distinguishers. Then the r-round classical differential trial and s-round ML distinguisher are combined into a R-round ($R = r + s$) differential distinguisher for Speck32/64. For Speck48/72 and Speck64/96, the similar method is carried out.

Afterwards, the strategy M_2 in Sect. 4.2 is applied to do this work. The best input differences ΔX_{best} and their corresponding ML differential distinguishers are shown in Table 5. For the s-round ML differential distinguisher, we can get the $(r + s)$-round differential-ML distinguisher by combining the r-round differential trial forward.

Subsequently, the strategy M_3 in Sect. 4.3 is employed to derive the differential-ML distinguishers. The relevant information of the first 6 rounds is shown in Table 6. When the round number is greater than 6, it takes too much time to search for all the output differences with minimum hamming weight and the best r-round differential probability, so we directly use a differential trial with the best r-round differential probability to experiment.

Finally, we can pick the best R-round differential-ML distinguisher based on the data complexity of all R-round distinguishers constructed by these three greedy strategies. The results are listed in Table 3. In [13], the authors could provide the best 9,11,15-round differential distinguisher for Speck32/64, Speck48/72 and Speck64/96 with 2^{30}, 2^{45}, 2^{62} data respectively, while we can use 2^{27}, 2^{45}, 2^{62} data to achieve 11,14,18-round differential distinguisher for the three variants of Speck respectively.

Table 3. The best results for Speck

R	r	s	ΔX_0	ΔX_r	$log_2 C_R$	$Strategy$
1	0	1	0x00400000	0x00400000	0	M_2
2	0	2	0x00400000	0x00400000	0	M_2
3	0	3	0x00400000	0x00400000	0	M_2
4	0	4	0x00400000	0x00400000	2	M_2
5	1	4	0x00408000	0x00000002	4	M_3
6	2	4	0x00102000	0x80008002	6	M_3
7	3	4	0x28000010	0x81008102	7	M_3
8	4	4	0x02110a04	0x81008102	12	M_1
9	6	3	0x02110a04	0x850a9520	17	M_3
10	7	3	0x0a204205	0x850a9520	22	M_3
11	7	4	0x0a204205	0x850a9520	27	M_3
12	8	4	0x14881008	0x850a9520	33	M_3

(*continued*)

Table 3. (*continued*)

R	r	s	ΔX_0	ΔX_r	$log_2 C_R$	*Strategy*
1	0	1	0x000080000000	0x000080000000	0	M_2
2	0	2	0x000080000000	0x000080000000	0	M_2
3	0	3	0x000080000000	0x000080000000	0	M_2
4	0	4	0x000080000000	0x000080000000	0	M_2
5	1	4	0x009000000010	0x000080000000	2	M_2
6	1	5	0x000080800000	0x000000000004	6	M_3
7	3	4	0x009000000010	0x808000808004	9	M_3
8	4	4	0x001202020002	0x808004808020	11	M_3
9	5	4	0x820200001202	0x8000848400a0	15	M_3
10	6	4	0x020082120200	0x80a00085a420	21	M_3
11	7	4	0x400052504200	0x0080a02085a4	29	M_3
12	9	3	0x08080242084a	0x80842484a905	38	M_3
13	9	4	0x001202020002	0x200100200000	43	M_1
14	10	4	0x001202020002	0x202001202000	45	M_1
15	11	4	0x001202020002	0x210020200021	52	M_1
1	0	1	0x0000008000000000	0x0000008000000000	0	M_2
2	0	2	0x0000008000000000	0x0000008000000000	0	M_2
3	0	3	0x0000008000000000	0x0000008000000000	0	M_2
4	0	4	0x0000008000000000	0x0000008000000000	0	M_2
5	1	4	0x0000008080000000	0x0000000000000004	1	M_3
6	1	5	0x0000008080000000	0x0000000000000004	4	M_3
7	2	5	0x0000008080000000	0x0000000400000024	7	M_3
8	4	4	0x0000120202000002	0x8080000480800020	10	M_3
9	5	4	0x0082020000001202	0x8000800484008020	15	M_3
10	6	4	0x4010420000400240	0x8400802080008124	23	M_3
11	7	4	0x4000409210420040	0x8080a0808481a4a0	28	M_3
12	8	4	0x0082020000001202	0x2020000001206008	34	M_3
13	9	4	0x2400008000040080	0x02080800124a0800	40	M_3
14	11	3	0x0000900000000010	0x0000080800004808	43	M_3
15	11	4	0x0000900000000010	0x0000080800004808	46	M_3
16	11	5	0x0000900000000010	0x0000080800004808	51	M_3
17	13	4	0x0082020000001202	0x0800480008020840	55	M_3
18	14	4	0x0409240020040104	0x8000800484008020	62	M_1

6 Conclusions

In this paper, we propose three new greedy strategies (M_1, M_2 and M_3) to derive the differential-ML distinguisher for differential cryptanalysis, which improves

Yadav's work in [32] and enlarges the application of machine learning techniques in cryptanalysis.

We first experimentally show that the differences with low hamming weights are more suitable for building ML differential distinguishers, which is the basis of the strategies M_1 and M_2. Then we propose three greedy strategies to enhance the analysis method in [32]. The first strategy (M_1) considers all combinations of classical differential distinguishers and ML differential distinguishers. The second strategy (M_2) employs the best ML differential distinguishers to splice classical traditional distinguishers in front, while the third strategy (M_3) adopts the best classical traditional distinguishers to splice ML differential distinguishers. Finally, the improved approaches are applied to round-reduced Speck32/64, Speck48/72 and Speck64/96 and provide better results than the best-known ones. Of course, this method is also applicable to other block ciphers, here the block cipher Speck is only used as an application example.

Moreover, how to balance the ML differential distinguisher and the traditional differential distinguisher in a better way is still an interesting topic, we leave this research as our future work.

Acknowledgment. This work is supported by the National Natural Science Foundation of China (No. 62072181), the National Cryptography Development Fund (No. MMJJ20180201), the International Science and Technology Cooperation Projects (No. 61961146004).

A The Best Differential Trails for Speck

Table 4. The best differential trails for Speck

Rounds	Speck32		Speck48		Speck64	
i	ΔX_i	$\log_2 Pr_i$	ΔX_i	$\log_2 Pr_i$	ΔX_i	$\log_2 Pr_i$
0	0x02110a04		0x001202020002		0x0409240020040104	
1	0x28000010	−4	0x000010100000	−3	0x2000082020200001	−6
2	0x00400000	−2	0x000000800000	−1	0x0000000901000000	−4
3	0x80008000	0	0x800000800004	−0	0x0800000000000000	−2
4	0x81008102	−1	0x808004808020	−2	0x0008000000080000	−1
5	0x8004840e	−3	0x8400a08001a4	−4	0x0008080000480800	−2
6	0x85329508	−8	0x608da4608080	−9	0x0048000802084008	−4
7	0x50020420	−7	0x042003002400	−11	0x06080808164a0848	−7
8	0x00801000	−3	0x012020000020	−5	0xf240004040104200	−13
9	0x10015001	−2	0x200100200000	−3	0x0082020000001202	−8
10			0x202001202000	−3	0x0000900000000010	−4
11			0x210020200021	−4	0x0000008000000000	−2
12					0x8000000080000000	0
13					0x8080000080800004	−1
14					0x8000800484008020	−3
15					0x808080a0a08481a4	−5
$\log_2 P_r$	−30		−45		−62	

B The Partial Results for Sect. 5

Table 5. The partial results of the strategy M_2 for Speck

Cipher	ΔX_{best}	s	a	τ	$\log_2 C_s$
Speck32/64	0x00400000	3	1.0	0.8	0
		4	0.994	0.8	2
		5	0.927	0.75	6
		6	0.786	0.6	7
		7	0.614	0.55	13
Speck48/72	0x000080000000	3	1.0	0.8	0
		4	0.998	0.8	0
		5	0.949	0.7	4
		6	0.726	0.6	8
Speck64/96	0x0000008000000000	3	1.0	0.8	0
		4	1.0	0.8	0
		5	0.989	0.7	4
		6	0.857	0.65	5
		7	0.632	0.55	10

Table 6. The partial results of the strategy M_3 for Speck

Cipher	r	$-\log_2 P_r$	W_r	ΔX_r
Speck32/64	1	0	1	0x00000002
	2	1	3	0x0002000a, 0x80008002
	3	3	5	0x8000840a, 0x81008102
	4	5	5	0x8000840a
	5	9	5	0x8000840a
	6	13	10	0x850a9520
Speck48/72	1	0	1	0x000000000004
	2	1	3	0x000004000024, 0x800000800004
	3	3	5	0x808000808004
	4	6	6	0x808004808020
	5	10	7	0x8000848400a0
	6	14	10	0x080a02085a4, 0x80a00085a420
Speck64/96	1	0	1	0x0000000000000004
	2	1	3	0x0000000400000024, 0x8000000080000004
	3	3	5	0x8080000080800004
	4	6	6	0x8080000480800020
	5	10	7	0x80008004840080020
	6	15	9	0x8400802080008124

References

1. Albrecht, M.R., Leander, G.: An all-in-one approach to differential cryptanalysis for small block ciphers. In: Knudsen, L.R., Wu, H. (eds.) SAC 2012. LNCS, vol. 7707, pp. 1–15. Springer, Heidelberg (2013). https://doi.org/10.1007/978-3-642-35999-6_1
2. Baksi, A., Breier, J., Dong, X., Yi, C.: Machine learning assisted differential distinguishers for lightweight ciphers. IACR **2020**, 571 (2020). https://eprint.iacr.org/2020/571
3. Beaulieu, R., Shors, D., Smith, J., Treatman-Clark, S., Weeks, B., Wingers, L.: The SIMON and SPECK lightweight block ciphers. In: Proceedings of the 52nd Annual Design Automation Conference, pp. 175:1–175:6. ACM (2015). https://doi.org/10.1145/2744769.2747946
4. Bellini, E., Rossi, M.: Performance comparison between deep learning-based and conventional cryptographic distinguishers. IACR **2020**, 953 (2020). https://eprint.iacr.org/2020/953
5. Bernstein, D.J., et al.: GIMLI: a cross-platform permutation. In: Fischer, W., Homma, N. (eds.) CHES 2017. LNCS, vol. 10529, pp. 299–320. Springer, Cham (2017). https://doi.org/10.1007/978-3-319-66787-4_15
6. Biham, E., Shamir, A.: Differential cryptanalysis of des-like cryptosystems. J. Cryptol. **4**(1), 3–72 (1991). https://doi.org/10.1007/BF00630563
7. Biryukov, A., Cannière, C.D.: Data encryption standard (DES). In: van Tilborg, H.C.A., Jajodia, S. (eds.) Encyclopedia of Cryptography and Security, pp. 295–301. Springer, Heidelberg (2011). https://doi.org/10.1007/978-1-4419-5906-5_568
8. Biryukov, A., Roy, A., Velichkov, V.: Differential analysis of block ciphers SIMON and SPECK. In: Cid, C., Rechberger, C. (eds.) FSE 2014. LNCS, vol. 8540, pp. 546–570. Springer, Heidelberg (2015). https://doi.org/10.1007/978-3-662-46706-0_28
9. Bogdanov, A., et al.: PRESENT: an ultra-lightweight block cipher. In: Paillier, P., Verbauwhede, I. (eds.) CHES 2007. LNCS, vol. 4727, pp. 450–466. Springer, Heidelberg (2007). https://doi.org/10.1007/978-3-540-74735-2_31
10. CPLEX: Cplex optimizer (1988). https://www.ibm.com/analytics/cplex-optimizer
11. Cui, T., Jia, K., Fu, K., Chen, S., Wang, M.: New automatic search tool for impossible differentials and zero-correlation linear approximations. IACR **2016**, 689 (2016). http://eprint.iacr.org/2016/689
12. Dinur, I.: Improved differential cryptanalysis of round-reduced speck. In: Joux, A., Youssef, A. (eds.) SAC 2014. LNCS, vol. 8781, pp. 147–164. Springer, Cham (2014). https://doi.org/10.1007/978-3-319-13051-4_9
13. Fu, K., Wang, M., Guo, Y., Sun, S., Hu, L.: MILP-based automatic search algorithms for differential and linear trails for speck. In: Peyrin, T. (ed.) FSE 2016. LNCS, vol. 9783, pp. 268–288. Springer, Heidelberg (2016). https://doi.org/10.1007/978-3-662-52993-5_14
14. Gerault, D., Minier, M., Solnon, C.: Constraint programming models for chosen key differential cryptanalysis. In: Rueher, M. (ed.) CP 2016. LNCS, vol. 9892, pp. 584–601. Springer, Cham (2016). https://doi.org/10.1007/978-3-319-44953-1_37
15. Gohr, A.: Improving attacks on round-reduced speck32/64 using deep learning. In: Boldyreva, A., Micciancio, D. (eds.) CRYPTO 2019. LNCS, vol. 11693, pp. 150–179. Springer, Cham (2019). https://doi.org/10.1007/978-3-030-26951-7_6
16. Gurobi: Gurobi optimizer (2008). http://www.gurobi.com

17. Jain, A., Kohli, V., Mishra, G.: Deep learning based differential distinguisher for lightweight cipher PRESENT. IACR **2020**, 846 (2020). https://eprint.iacr.org/2020/846
18. Liu, Y., Witte, G.D., Ranea, A., Ashur, T.: Rotational-XOR cryptanalysis of reduced-round SPECK. IACR Trans. Symmetric Cryptol. **2017**(3), 24–36 (2017). https://doi.org/10.13154/tosc.v2017.i3.24-36
19. Matsui, M.: On correlation between the order of S-boxes and the strength of DES. In: De Santis, A. (ed.) EUROCRYPT 1994. LNCS, vol. 950, pp. 366–375. Springer, Heidelberg (1995). https://doi.org/10.1007/BFb0053451
20. Mouha, N., Wang, Q., Gu, D., Preneel, B.: Differential and linear cryptanalysis using mixed-integer linear programming. In: Wu, C.-K., Yung, M., Lin, D. (eds.) Inscrypt 2011. LNCS, vol. 7537, pp. 57–76. Springer, Heidelberg (2012). https://doi.org/10.1007/978-3-642-34704-7_5
21. Polimón, J., Hernández-Castro, J.C., Estévez-Tapiador, J.M., Ribagorda, A.: Automated design of a lightweight block cipher with genetic programming. Int. J. Knowl. Based Intell. Eng. Syst. **12**(1), 3–14 (2008)
22. Sasaki, Y., Todo, Y.: New impossible differential search tool from design and cryptanalysis aspects - revealing structural properties of several ciphers. In: Coron, J., Nielsen, J.B. (eds.) EUROCRYPT 2017 (2017)
23. Sun, L., Wang, W., Wang, M.: Automatic search of bit-based division property for ARX ciphers and word-based division property. In: Takagi, T., Peyrin, T. (eds.) ASIACRYPT 2017. LNCS, vol. 10624, pp. 128–157. Springer, Cham (2017). https://doi.org/10.1007/978-3-319-70694-8_5
24. Sun, S., et al.: Analysis of aes, skinny, and others with constraint programming. IACR Trans. Symmetric Cryptol. **2017(**1), 281–306 (2017). https://doi.org/10.13154/tosc.v2017.i1.281-306
25. Sun, S., et al.: Towards finding the best characteristics of some bit-oriented block ciphers and automatic enumeration of (related-key) differential and linear characteristics with predefined properties (2015)
26. Sun, S., Hu, L., Wang, P., Qiao, K., Ma, X., Song, L.: Automatic security evaluation and (related-key) differential characteristic search: application to SIMON, PRESENT, LBlock, DES(L) and other bit-oriented block ciphers. In: Sarkar, P., Iwata, T. (eds.) ASIACRYPT 2014. LNCS, vol. 8873, pp. 158–178. Springer, Heidelberg (2014). https://doi.org/10.1007/978-3-662-45611-8_9
27. Tan, C., Sun, F., Kong, T., Zhang, W., Yang, C., Liu, C.: A survey on deep transfer learning. In: Kůrková, V., Manolopoulos, Y., Hammer, B., Iliadis, L., Maglogiannis, I. (eds.) ICANN 2018. LNCS, vol. 11141, pp. 270–279. Springer, Cham (2018). https://doi.org/10.1007/978-3-030-01424-7_27
28. Wang, M.: Differential Cryptanalysis of reduced-round PRESENT. In: Vaudenay, S. (ed.) AFRICACRYPT 2008. LNCS, vol. 5023, pp. 40–49. Springer, Heidelberg (2008). https://doi.org/10.1007/978-3-540-68164-9_4
29. Wang, Y., Yao, Q., Kwok, J.T., Ni, L.M.: Generalizing from a few examples: a survey on few-shot learning. ACM Comput. Surv. **53**(3), 63:1–63:34 (2020). https://doi.org/10.1145/3386252
30. Wheeler, D.J., Needham, R.M.: TEA, a tiny encryption algorithm. In: Preneel, B. (ed.) FSE 1994. LNCS, vol. 1008, pp. 363–366. Springer, Heidelberg (1995). https://doi.org/10.1007/3-540-60590-8_29
31. Xiang, Z., Zhang, W., Bao, Z., Lin, D.: Applying MILP method to searching integral distinguishers based on division property for 6 lightweight block ciphers. In: Cheon, J.H., Takagi, T. (eds.) ASIACRYPT 2016. LNCS, vol. 10031, pp. 648–678. Springer, Heidelberg (2016). https://doi.org/10.1007/978-3-662-53887-6_24

32. Yadav, T., Kumar, M.: Differential-ML distinguisher: machine learning based generic extension for differential cryptanalysis. IACR **2020**, 913 (2020). https://eprint.iacr.org/2020/913
33. Zhang, Y., Sun, S., Cai, J., Hu, L.: Speeding up MILP aided differential characteristic search with Matsui's strategy. In: Chen, L., Manulis, M., Schneider, S. (eds.) ISC 2018. LNCS, vol. 11060, pp. 101–115. Springer, Cham (2018). https://doi.org/10.1007/978-3-319-99136-8_6
34. Zhou, C., Zhang, W., Ding, T., Xiang, Z.: Improving the MILP-based security evaluation algorithm against differential/linear cryptanalysis using A divide-and conquer approach. IACR Trans. Symmetric Cryptol. **2019**(4), 438–469 (2019). https://doi.org/10.13154/tosc.v2019.i4.438-469

Black-Box Buster: A Robust Zero-Shot Transfer-Based Adversarial Attack Method

Yuxuan Zhang[1,2], Zhaoyang Wang[1,2], Boyang Zhang[1], Yu Wen[1(✉)], and Dan Meng[1]

[1] Institute of Information Engineering, Chinese Academy of Sciences, Beijing, China
{zhangyuxuan,wangzhaoyang,zhangboyang,wenyu,mengdan}@iie.ac.cn

[2] School of Cyber Security, University of Chinese Academy of Sciences, Beijing, China

Abstract. Recent black-box adversarial attacks can take advantage of transferable adversarial examples generated by a similar substitute model to successfully fool the target model. However, these substitute models are either pre-trained models or trained with the target model's training examples, which is hard to obtain because of the security and privacy of training data. In this paper, we proposed a zero-shot adversarial black-box attack method that can generate high-quality training examples for the substitute models, which are balanced among the classification labels and close to the distribution of the real training examples of the target models. The experiments demonstrate the effectiveness of our method that significantly improves the non-target black-box attack success rate around 20%–30% of the adversarial examples generated by the substitute models.

Keywords: Adversarial attack · Substitute model · Zero data

1 Introduction

Deep neural networks (DNNs) have been widely applied in various domains (e.g., object detection, face recognition, autonomous vehicles), and have achieved state-of-the-art performance. However, DNNs are vulnerable to adversarial examples, i.e., small perturbations on the images can mislead DNNs to produce an incorrect output with high confidence [21]. Many studies have shown that the vulnerability caused by adversarial attack is inevitable appeared in almost all the classifiers, whose data are distributed in a high-dimensional space [1].

According to the attacker's knowledge of the target model, two types of attacks can be performed: white-box and black-box. In a white-box attack, the attacker has full access to the model's parameters and architectures. However, this attack scenario is probably the least frequent in real-world applications due to privacy and security. In the black-box setting, an adversary can only obtain the outputs of the target model, making it more difficult to carry out such attacks.

D. Gao et al. (Eds.): ICICS 2021, LNCS 12919, pp. 39–54, 2021.
https://doi.org/10.1007/978-3-030-88052-1_3

Despite this, but the attacker can still mislead the classifiers with the transferability of adversarial examples. Szegedy et al. [21] demonstrated that adversarial examples generated by one model can also fool another model. Therefore, in the black-box attack, the target model can be attacked by the adversarial examples generated on the substitute model.

Substitute models need to be trained by target models' training data, which is hard to acquire because of the security and privacy. For example, some online machine learning service platforms (e.g., Microsoft Azure) protect their models and intellectual property, and their operators do not disclose their training datasets. Therefore, attackers can only obtain the predictions. Papernot et al. [19] assumed that attackers had partial access to the training dataset of the target model and then proposed the synthetic data generation technology on the Jacobian matrix. These data samples better capture the characteristics of the target model. Besides, some other works [5,18] assumed that the auxiliary dataset with a similar data distribution can be used as the training dataset of the substitute model. Correia-Silva et al. [5] used random unlabeled data to steal the target model. Orekondy et al. [18] had shown that constructing a dataset with other large datasets related to the target model task can as well achieve a considerable attack effect. Specifically, they provide a combination strategy for selecting task-related data and irrelevant data by active learning.

However, it is difficult for attackers to achieve the above data in multiple fields. For example, in MRI cancer diagnosis, MRI imaging datasets of the same parts are needed. However, to protect the privacy of patients, it is impossible for attackers to partially access the training data or find a suitable auxiliary dataset.

Hence, how to train a substitute model without the dataset of the target model is worth exploring. Generative adversarial networks (GANs) [9] have been widely applied for generating samples. To learn a portable substitute network without original data, we exploit GAN to generate training samples with the available output information of the given target network.

We explore three questions related to the transfer-based adversarial attack without the training data:

1) How to ensure that each generated sample is more realistic and closer to the target model training dataset?
2) How to ensure that generated samples are sufficient and each category is balanced?
3) How does the number of sample categories affects the transfer-based adversarial black-box attacks?

For the first question, we optimize a generator G based on the output probability of the target model, where max output probability's index is considered as a predicted label. By constraining the distance between output probability and the pseudo ground-truth label, the generated images are more compatible with the target network's training datasets.

For the second question, it is mainly to deal with the mode collapse of GANs. Previous work [23] trains multiple GANs for different categories, which is time consuming and clumsy. Instead, we utilize information entropy. Specifically, when it maximizes, the categories are evenly distributed.

For the third question, we conduct an ablation study. We test the same target model (ResNet-34) and substitute model (ResNet-18) on the datasets (e.g., CIFAR-10, CIFAR-100) with the same task but a different number of categories.

We rigorously evaluate our proposed method by attacking three target models: MediumNet, VGG16, ResNet34 respectively on three datasets: MNIST, CIFAR10, CIFAR100. The performances (transferable attack success rate) show the improvements over baseline: above DaST-P around 20%–30%. In addition, to highlight the superiority of this study, we reproduce two other types of dataset generation methods: Synthetic datasets (JBDA), Auxiliary datasets (Knockoff). We utilize these algorithms to implement transferable attacks on the same model. The result demonstrates that our method improved by 40%–60% than the two methods on the accuracy of the substitute model. In summary, we experimentally show that in terms of both the accuracy of the substitute model and the success rate of the transferable attack, our method has strong advantages.

The main contributions of this study are summarized as follows:

- We propose a novel zero-shot adversarial black-box attack method that can generate high-quality training examples for the substitute models, which are balanced among the classification labels and close to the distribution of the real training examples of the target models.
- To evaluate the transferability, we utilize four attack methods to generate adversarial examples, which include FGSM, BIM, projected gradient descent (PGD), C&W.
- Comparing to substitute training methods using synthetic datasets and auxiliary datasets, our method shows the superiority in terms of both the accuracy of the substitute model and the transferable attack success rate.

The rest of our paper is organized as follows: in Sect. 2, we sum up the related works. Section 3 introduces the threat model: attack ability and attack goal. The proposed method is described in Sect. 4. We detail the experiment setup, results, and performance evaluation in Sect. 5. Conclusions are drawn in Sect. 6.

2 Related Work

In this section, we introduce the background knowledge of adversarial examples and adversarial attacks, including white-box attack and black-box attack. Besides, we cover the main substitute training methods with same datasets, synthetic datasets, auxiliary datasets and without datasets.

2.1 Adversarial Examples and Adversarial Attacks

Adversarial Examples are input examples deliberately designed with some imperceptible perturbations, which cause the target model to give an erroneous output with high confidence. Based on the knowledge of target model information, adversarial attacks are generally divided into two categories: white-box and black-box. In the white-box setting [2,10,17], an adversary has full access to the structure, parameters and training dataset of target model. Recently, researchers have proposed several effective white-box attacking methods to craft adversarial examples like FGSM [10], BIM [14], PGD [17], and CW [2]. In practice, it is not always possible to access model information. Most of the online machine learning application platforms are not open source and reluctant to share their data due to privacy. There are more restrictions in black-box attack as only the outputs of the target model can be obtained, whereas, it better represents real-world attack scenario.

In black-box attacks, query-based attacks [3,4,22] utilize inputs query feedback to guide the attack method to generate adversarial examples. Chen et al. [4] proposed a zeroth order-based attack (ZOO) to convert a black box to a white box by estimating the gradients. The probability differences caused by positive and negative perturbations are used to estimate the first gradient and second gradient, then Adam or Newton's method is applied to update sample X. Towards query-based attacks, defenders implement a limit to the number of times a single sample can be queried. And in real life, online machine learning platforms typically limit the number of queries allowed within a certain period time. For example, the Cloud Vision API from Google currently allows 1,800 requests per minute to prevent adversaries from making large-scale attacks.

Transferability of adversarial examples was first validated by Szegedy et al. [21] that adversarial examples generated by one model are also very likely misclassified by another model. Transfer-based attacks take advantage of this feature and generate adversarial examples by using a standard white-box attack method on a pre-trained source model to fool the target model [6,12,16,19]. Different from query-based attacks, training datasets are necessary.

2.2 Substitute Training

Same Datasets. Some existing works [8,10,12] supposed the attackers can obtain the training data of the target models, they focus on improving the transferability of adversarial examples across different models under the assumption. Attackers firstly trained a substitute model on the same training datasets, and then generate adversarial examples in a white-box manner.

Synthetic Datasets. Papernot et al. [19] assume that an attacker can access a subset of training dataset D_{sub}. For example, if the target model is used to classify handwritten numbers, the attacker collects 10 images for each number from 0 to 9, and the distribution of this set does not have to be consistent with the training set distribution of the target model. Nevertheless, the adversary does not have enough nature samples to train a model, so they generate synthetic samples x' by using Jacobian Based Dataset Augmentation (JBDA) which are labeled using the predictions of target model $y' = T(x')$. The substitute model S is trained by synthetic datasets: $D_{syn} = \{x', y'\}$, and D_{sub}. However, in most cases, this method is not realistic, a subset of the training dataset is also unavailable.

Auxiliary Datasets. Some works [5,18] use common datasets which have similar distributions to the original datasets as auxiliary datasets D_{aux} to train substitute models. Orekondy et al. [18] demonstrated model stealing can be performed without access to seed samples, they used large datasets (e.g. ImageNet1K) as auxiliary datasets to query the target model to construct a labeled dataset by the predictions of the target model. This labeled dataset is used to train the substitute model. Correia-Silva et al. [5] use random unlabeled data to steal the target model. Unfortunately, sometimes it is hard to find an auxiliary dataset, and data in some areas is not public.

Without Datasets. Unlike above, substitute training can also be performed without training data. It's the hardest setting as adversaries can't access any prior knowledge of the model (training dataset, detailed architecture information, model parameters, model hyperparameters, etc.) and do not have any auxiliary datasets associated with the task domain. A recent work by Mingyi et al. [23] generate a substitute training dataset by GAN. Their optimization goal is to minimize output differences between the target model and the substitute model. Unfortunately, this technique only seems to be effective for small models trained on simple datasets. Our goal is to develop an attack method that can train a highly accurate substitute model only using black-box target model probabilities.

3 Problem Statement

3.1 Adversarial Ability

We assume a black-box target model $\mathbf{T}(\mathbf{x})$ outputs probability as prediction, where $\mathbf{x}$ denotes sample from the input space of the target model $\mathbf{T}$. We can access the output probabilities $P_T(\cdot \mid x)$ associated with each class. Although the model's training dataset, model parameters, model hyperparameters, etc. cannot be acquired in the black-box setting, we argue that output probability can serve as a strong proxy for an adversarial transferable attack.

3.2 Adversarial Goal

Given an original image $\mathbf{x}$ with the ground-truth label $\mathbf{y}$, a non-target adversarial attack can be formulated when an adversarial example x' satisfies the following limits:

$$T(x') \neq y \qquad \|x - x'\|_F \leq \rho \tag{1}$$

This formula defines the region of imperceptible changes, it is a small hypersphere centered around the original image $\mathbf{x}$ with radius ρ. The symbol $\|\cdot\|_F$ denotes the $\mathbf{F}$ norm, a distance measurement function between the clean input $\mathbf{x}$ and the perturbed input x', $F \in \{0, 2, \infty\}$, i.e. the magnitude of the perturbation. Here, L_2 norm is considered as a distance metric.

4 Methods

In this section, we describe an optimization framework for performing a transferable adversarial attack. We firstly introduce a training method to train a substitute model S, capable of imitating a target model T. Then, we use the adversarial examples crafted from the substitute model in a white-box manner to fool the target model as a transfer-based attack (see Fig. 1).

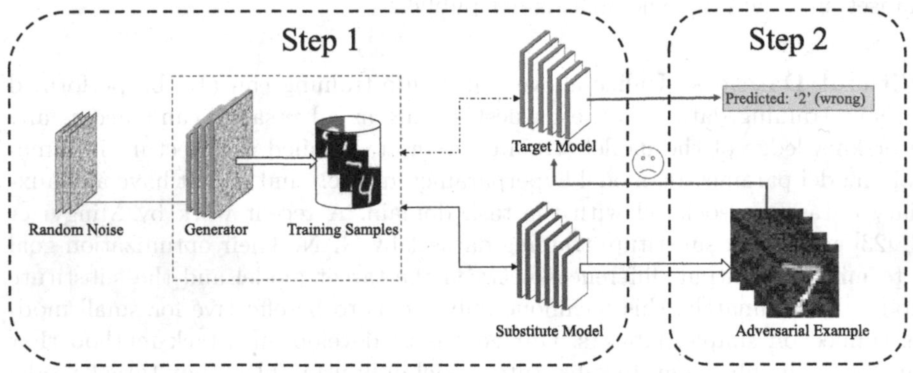

Fig. 1. The proposed framework for zero-shot transfer-based adversarial attack

4.1 Substitute Training

As mentioned above, we introduce the substitute model's training method without prior knowledge. Substitute training aims to build a model S that is functionally equivalent to the target model T, which means they have a similar decision boundary. Our algorithm is divided into two steps. The first step is that the generator produces the training dataset. Specifically, the input (image)-output (prediction) pair $(X, T(X))$ is used to train substitute model S. The second one is that the substitute model is employed to estimate parameters. These two steps are executed interactively to obtain an imitator of the target model.

Step1: Firstly, we randomly initialize a latent noise vector $Z = \{z_1, z_2, \dots, z_n\}$, and then use a generator G to map Z to the desired data $X = \{x_1, x_2, \dots, x_n\}$, i.e. $G : z \rightarrow x$. Secondly, the generated images are fed into the target model T and we get the output probabilities $Y = \{y_i = T(x_i) \mid y_i^j \in (0, 1), \sum_{j=1}^{k} y_i^j = 1\}$, where k is the number of categories, and y_i^j means the probability of belonging to j_{th} category.

In the image classification task, the classifiers use the cross-entropy loss function in the training stage to supervise the network to output the same results as the real labels. In the multi-classification task, the network output should be close to a one-hot vector, with the probability of '1' for only one category and '0' for the others. If the images generated by G have the same distribution as the training dataset, their predictions should also be similar. Hence, the loss function should encourage the predictions of generated images close to one-hot vector, leading generator G to generate images similar to the target model training dataset. Then we optimize G as follows that the generated training data can be more similar to the real dataset:

$$L_G = \sum_{i=1}^{n} CE(T(x_i), l_i) \tag{2}$$

where y_i denotes the output probabilities of T, l_i indicates the i_{th} image's pseudo-ground-truth label, $l_i = \arg\max y_i$ means the index of max output probability. CE donates the cross-entropy loss function. While the training dataset X is the real image, the output Y should be sparse, that is, there should be one particular category with a very high probability. Constraining the distance with pseudo ground-truth ensuring that the generated images are compatible with the target model's training dataset, rather than any other real scenario.

In addition, to make the generated samples covering all categories in our method, we take the information entropy into account. Assuming that there are K categories of images, and the probability vector of each category is $P = \{p_1, p_2, \ldots, p_k\}$. Information entropy, i.e., the amount of information P owns:

$$H(P) = -\sum_{i=1}^{k} p_i log(p_i) \tag{3}$$

Information entropy measures the degree of chaos. When $H(P)$ reaches the maximum value, any $p_i = 1/k$. For output probabilities $Y = \{y_1, y_2, \ldots, y_n\}$, generated frequency of every category of images is $F = \frac{1}{n}\sum_{i=1}^{n} y_i$, ideally, every value in vector F is equal to $1/k$. Under this situation, generator G can generate images of each category in roughly the same probability.

The uniformity of category distribution is proportional to the value of H, define $L_H = -H(F)$, which shows minimize L_H can result in generated images evenly distributed in each category. We sum up the original objective function L_G and regularization term L_H and minimize the new objective function:

$$L_G = \alpha \sum_{i=1}^{n} CE(T(x_i), l_i) + \beta L_H \tag{4}$$

However, the backpropagation of the above equation needs the gradient information of the target model T, violating the rules of black-box attacks. We need to generate training samples without the gradient information of T.

Algorithm 1. Substitute Training

Input: Targeted model T, number of epoch N, hyperparameter α, β
Output: Substitute model S

Randomly initialize latent noise vector $Z = \{z_1, z_2, \dots z_n\}$
Generate training samples $X \leftarrow G(z)$
while $t \leq N$ **do**
    $T \leftarrow X_t$
    Generate training samples.
    min $L_G = \alpha \sum_{i=1}^{n} CE(S(x_i), l_i) + \beta L_H$
    Train the substitute model S:
    min $\sum_{i=1}^{n} \|T(x_i), S(x_i)\|_F$
end while

In the process of constant imitation, target model T and substitute model S get closer and closer, the equation can be approximated as the following formula.

$$L_G = \alpha \sum_{i=1}^{n} CE(S(x_i), l_i) + \beta L_H \tag{5}$$

where α and β denote the hyperparameter to adjust the value of regularization. In the experiment, we set α as 1.

Step2: Train the substitute model by the input (image)-output (prediction) pair $(X, T(X))$, minimizing the distance between target model T and substitute model S:

$$\sum_{i=1}^{n} \|T(x_i), S(x_i)\|_F \tag{6}$$

where $\|\cdot\|_F$ denotes the F norm, $F \in \{0, 2, \infty\}$, here, L_2 norm is considered as a distance metric. Our method is shown in Algorithm 1.

Similar to the current substitute attack algorithms, the substitute model S trained by our algorithm is used to generate adversarial examples to attack target model T.

4.2 Adversarial Transferable Attack

FGSM [10] is an attack framework based on first-order projected gradient descent. FGSM finds adversarial examples by maximizing the loss function to increase the diversity between the predicted value and the real category label:

$$x^* = x + \epsilon \cdot sign(\nabla_x J(x, y))$$

where $J(x, y)$ is the loss function used in the neural network model and ∇_x finds the gradient of loss about x. The symbol $sign(\cdot)$ is used to obtain the direction of gradient descent and ϵ is the perturbation strength set by manual.

BIM and PGD are iterative FGSM and the difference between the two methods is that PGD increases the number of iterations and adds a layer of randomization. C&W is an adversarial example generation algorithm based on optimization, Carlini and Wagner crafted some perturbations with minimizing $L_p$norm, which is generally considered to be one of the most powerful white box attack algorithms.

By taking advantage of the transferability of the adversarial examples, we generate adversarial examples in the way of a white box on the substitute model to deceive the target model. We utilize four attack methods which include FGSM, BIM, PGD, and C&W following DaST [23]. For testing, we use AdverTorch library [7] to generate adversarial examples.

5 Experiment

5.1 Experimental Setup

Datasets and Architecture. We use MNIST [15] and CIFAR-10 [13] to evaluate our proposed method. For generator architecture, we design a generative model with 3 convolutional layers. After the convolutional layers, it's equipped with a BatchNorm layer and LeakyReLU to make a nonlinear transformation. In the experiment, we use an Adam optimizer with an initial learning rate of 0.2 to train the generator.

We are not ignorant when designing substitute model architectures, at least we know input data type, whether the input is image data, text data, or voice data. Next, we understand the function of the model, whether it is a classification task or a detection task. In our experiments, the basic architecture for image classification is a CNN due to its properties of translational invariance and locality. Besides, layers' number, size, and type have little effect on the results [19].

In the experiments, we choose a medium network, VGG16 [20] as our target model, and large network, ResNet50 respectively as our substitute model. In sensitivity analysis, we choose ResNet34 [11] as the target model, and ResNet18 as the substitute model.

Criterion for Learning Accuracy. For evaluating the performance of our method, we set the DaST [23] as the baseline. The success rate of black-box transferable attack is largely dependent on the transferable property of adversarial examples. To this end, the key to implement an effective attack is to train a substitute model that is as similar to the target model as possible. A typical criterion is to compare the accuracy (**AC**) of the trained substitute model to the pre-trained target model on the same dataset.

Criterion for Transferability. As for the adversarial transferable attack, we focus on the model assigning the perturbed input to one category different from the label of the original input. It is meaningless to verify the transferability of an adversarial example between two models which cannot classify the original image correctly. Therefore, in our experiment, we only generate adversarial examples on the images, which are correctly classified by the target model. The transferability of the attack is measured by calculating the success rate of adversarial examples spoofing the target model. A higher success rate means better non-targeted transferability. The success rate is calculated by m/n, where n and m respectively are the total number of adversarial examples and the number of which can fool the target model.

5.2 Experiments on MNIST

In this subsection, we employ the proposed method to train a substitute model for adversarial attacks on the MNIST dataset and evaluate the performance in terms of attack success rate in DaST-P, Knockoff, JBDA, and our method.

Following DaST-P [23], we set the medium network (four convolutional layers) as the target model on MNIST and the large model (five convolutional layers) as the substitute model. To demonstrate our superiority, we reproduce two existing methods of generating substitute models from auxiliary datasets [18] and synthetic datasets [19] respectively. We also utilize the two substitute models to generated adversarial examples to attack the target model on the same test set (1,000 images in MNIST). Configuration of existing attacks are as follows:

1. KnockoffNets: We use FashionMNIST as an auxiliary dataset on the medium network. In this case, we query the target model with the training samples of FashionMNIST, then use the dataset constructed from these queries to train the substitute model for 20 epochs using an SGD optimizer with a learning rate of 0.01. The paper proposes two strategies on how to sample images to query: random and adaptive. We use the random strategy in the paper since adaptive resulted in marginal increases in an open-world setup.
2. JBDA: We pick 100 seed samples from MNIST as the initial data and then use Jacobian Based Dataset Augmentation (JBDA) to enlarge the training dataset. Data augmentation step is set as 6, and the synthetic datasets formed at the query limit 8,000 to the black-box target model. Other hyperparameters are default set as Papernot [19].

Table 1. AC of four methods on MNIST and CIFAR10

Datasets	Substitute training			
	DaST-P	Knockoff	JBDA	Ours
MNIST	97.82	11.70	83.70	**98.10**
CIFAR10	25.15	36.50	17.50	**79.87**

Our experiments show that the performance of the substitute model on MNIST converges after about 20 epochs (Fig. 2). The substitute model accuracy (%) of DaST-P, Knockoff, JBDA, and ours on MNIST is shown inTable 1 on the first line. The substitute model trained by our method achieved 98.10% accuracy on the test set, higher than the other three methods, especially Knockoff. Moreover, it's reflected that substitute training using auxiliary datasets is greatly influenced by the choice of the dataset on the side.

Table 2. Attack success rate (%) of four methods on MNIST

Attack	Substitute training			
	DaST-P	Knockoff	JBDA	Ours
FGSM	69.76(5.41)	64.99(5.37)	68.98(5.42)	**90.64(5.71)**
BIM	96.36(4.81)	69.24(5.21)	76.06(5.52)	**96.78(5.44)**
PGD	53.99(3.99)	47.36(3.92)	51.87(4.09)	**85.19(4.09)**
C&W	27.35(2.74)	13.38(1.26)	13.51(2.12)	**44.40(2.19)**

The attack success rates (%) of DaST-P, Knockoff, JBDA, and ours on MNIST are shown in Table 2 and () denotes the average Lp perturbation distance per image. As can be seen from this table, our method's success rates are higher than the baseline method (20.88%, 0.4%, 31.2%, 17.05% higher than DaST-P on FGSM, BIM, PGD and C&W respectively). Besides, the substitute model generated by our method outperform the models trained by the auxiliary datasets and synthetic datasets. Even on CW, our method achieved more than 30% accuracy.

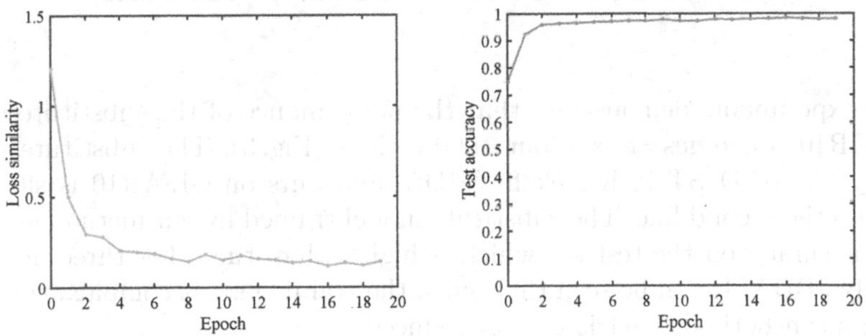

Fig. 2. Substitute model loss and accuracy on MNIST during the attack

5.3 Experiments on CIFAR10

To further evaluate the effectiveness of our method, we conduct experiments on the CIFAR10 dataset following DaST and compare attack success rates in DaST-P, Knockoff, JBDA, and our method.

Following DaST-P [23], we set the VGG16 as the target model on CIFAR10 and ResNet50 as the substitute model. To demonstrate our superiority, we reproduce two existing methods of generating substitute models from auxiliary datasets and synthetic datasets respectively. Configuration of existing attacks are as follows:

1. KnockoffNets: We use CIFAR100 as an auxiliary dataset on the VGG16. In this case, we query the target model with the training samples of CIFAR100 and then use the dataset constructed from these queries to train the substitute model for 100 epochs using an SGD optimizer with a learning rate of 0.01. We also use the random strategy in the section.
2. JBDA: We pick 100 seed samples from CIFAR100 as the initial data and then use Jacobian Based Dataset Augmentation (JBDA) to enlarge the training dataset. Data augmentation step is set as 2 and the synthetic datasets formed at the query limit 20,000 to black-box target model. Other hyperparameters are default set as Papernot [19].

Table 3. Attack success rate (%) of four methods on CIFAR-10

Attack	Substitute training			
	DaST-P	Knockoff	JBDA	Ours
FGSM	39.63(1.54)	12.99(1.53)	10.11(1.53)	**62.35(1.53)**
BIM	59.71(1.18)	7.27(1.00)	6.31(1.03)	**64.78(1.15)**
PGD	29.10(1.10)	7.46(1.05)	7.12(1.06)	**53.01(1.09)**
C&W	13.52(0.74)	2.77(0.66)	2.25(0.73)	**15.54(0.45)**

Our experiments demonstrate that the performance of the substitute model on CIFAR10 converges after about 1000 epochs (Fig. 3). The substitute model accuracy (%) of DaST-P, Knockoff, JBDA, and ours on CIFAR10 is shown in Table 1 on the second line. The substitute model trained by our method achieved 79.87% accuracy on the test set which is higher than the other three methods, especially JBDA. It can be seen that when the training set is complex, the effect of using a synthetic dataset is greatly reduced.

The attack success rates (%) of DaST-P, Knockoff, JBDA, and ours on CIFAR10 are shown in Table 3 and () denotes the average Lp perturbation distance per image. As can be seen from this table, our method's success rates are higher than the baseline method (22.72%, 5.07%, 23.91%, 2.02% higher than DaST-P on FGSM, BIM, PGD, and C&W respectively). Besides, the substitute model generated by our method outperforms the models trained by the auxiliary datasets and synthetic datasets, almost over 50% in accuracy except CW.

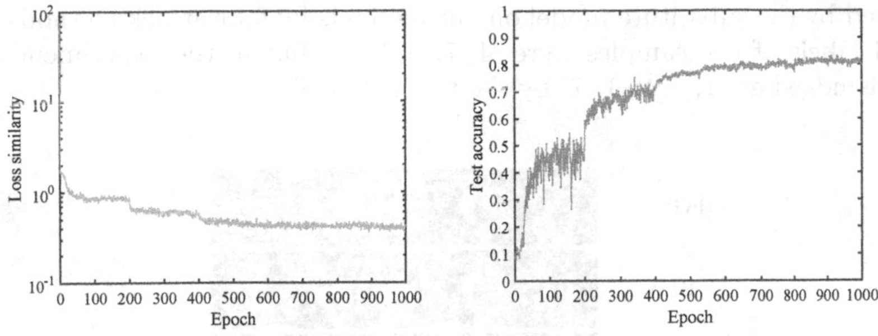

Fig. 3. Substitute model loss and accuracy on CIFAR10 during the attack

5.4 Sensitivity Analysis

In the above sections, we have verified the effectiveness of our proposed method for transfer-based adversarial attacks without training data. We further conduct the sensitivity analysis experiments for an explicit understanding and analysis.

The sensitivity experiment is conducted on the architecture ResNet34 and ResNet18. We use CIFAR10 and CIFAR100 as datasets for comparison. Table 4 depicts the results of the impact of datasets scale on the effect of transfer-based adversarial attacks. And () denotes the average Lp perturbation distance per image. For the experimental results, we observe that the attack success rates with different data sizes have a big gap, compared with using the same architecture. It is obvious that the attack effect is more effective when the data volume is small. CIFAR10 is 37.36%, 32.01%, 31.94%, 4.58% higher than CIFAR100 on FGSM, BIM, PGD, and C&W respectively on attack success rate. We suspect that the reason for this phenomenon might be that models developed from larger volumes of the dataset are more complex and harder to learn.

Table 4. Attack success rate (%) of the methods on CIFAR-10 and CIFAR-100

Attack	Datasets	
	CIFAR-10	CIFAR-100
FGSM	**83.39(1.65)**	46.03(1.62)
BIM	**98.00(2.15)**	65.99(2.46)
PGD	**84.55(1.91)**	52.61(1.87)
C&W	**6.68(0.52)**	2.10(0.31)

5.5 Visualization Results

After investigating the effectiveness of the proposed method, we further conduct visualization on the MNIST dataset. Figure 4 illustrates the adversarial examples generated by the substitute model on our methods by four attack methods. The original labels of the samples were '4, 7, 3, 9, 5', but in the experiment, they were misjudged as '1, 5, 9, 1, 7' by the target model.

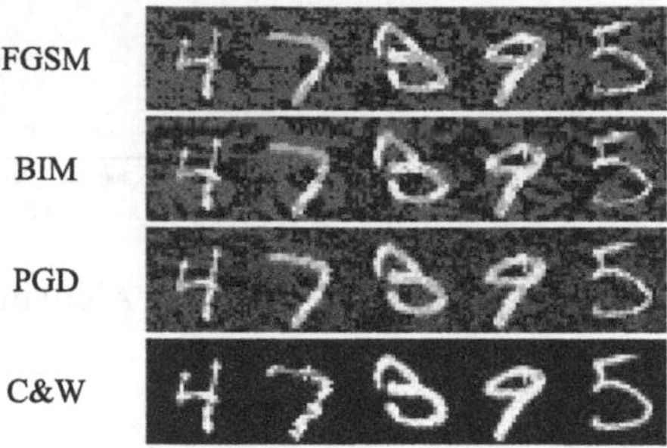

Fig. 4. Visualization of the adversarial examples on MNIST

Similar to the above, we conduct visualization on the CIFAR10 dataset. Figure 5 illustrates the adversarial examples generated by the substitute model on our methods by the four attack methods. The original labels of the samples were 'truck, deer, automobile, frog, bird', but in the experiment, they were misjudged as 'deer, ship (frog/airplane), cat (airplane), dog, cat' by the target model.

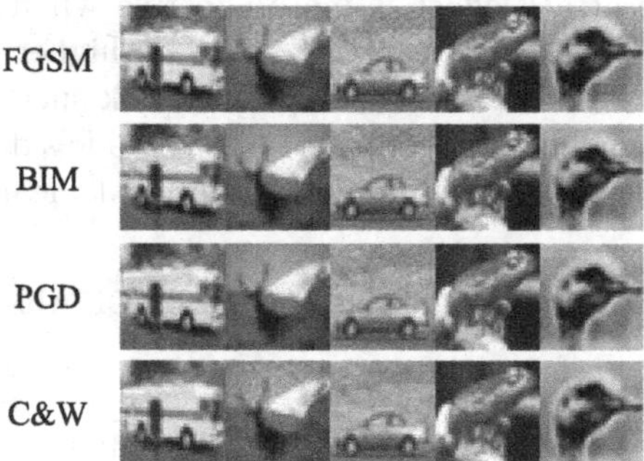

Fig. 5. Visualization of the adversarial examples on CIFAR10

6 Conclusion

In this paper, we propose a new zero-shot substitute training method that can perform an effective transferable adversarial attack. Our method directly obtains a fine substitute model without the original training dataset, and the adversarial examples generated by this substitute model can fool the target model with very high probability. The experiments show the effectiveness and excellence of our method.

We evaluated the approach on three common datasets (MNIST, CIFAR-10, and CIFAR-100), using popular classifiers (e.g., ResNet, VGG). The experimental results show that our method can achieve a very high success rate under the real-world black box setup.

Acknowledgment. This work is supported by the Strategic Priority Research Program of Chinese Academy of Sciences, Grant No. XDC02010300.

References

1. Athalye, A., Carlini, N., Wagner, D.: Obfuscated gradients give a false sense of security: circumventing defenses to adversarial examples. In: Proceedings of the 35th International Conference on Machine Learning, pp. 274–283 (2018)
2. Carlini, N., Wagner, D.: Towards evaluating the robustness of neural networks. In: 2017 IEEE Symposium on Security and Privacy (SP), pp. 39–57 (2017)
3. Chen, J., Jordan, M.I., Wainwright, M.J.: HopSkipJumpAttack: a query-efficient decision-based attack. In: 2020 IEEE Symposium on Security and Privacy (SP), pp. 1277–1294 (2020)
4. Chen, P.Y., Zhang, H., Sharma, Y., Yi, J., Hsieh, C.J.: ZOO: zeroth order optimization based black-box attacks to deep neural networks without training substitute models. In: Proceedings of the 10th ACM Workshop on Artificial Intelligence and Security, pp. 15–26 (2017)
5. Correia-Silva, J.R., Berriel, R.F., Badue, C., de Souza, A.F., Oliveira-Santos, T.: Copycat CNN: stealing knowledge by persuading confession with random non-labeled data. In: 2018 International Joint Conference on Neural Networks (IJCNN), pp. 1–8 (2018)
6. Demontis, A., et al.: Why do adversarial attacks transfer? Explaining transferability of evasion and poisoning attacks. In: 28th USENIX Security Symposium (USENIX Security 19), pp. 321–338 (2019)
7. Ding, G.W., Wang, L., Jin, X.: Advertorch v0.1: an adversarial robustness toolbox based on Pytorch. CoRR (2019)
8. Dong, Y., Liao, F., Pang, T., Su, H., Zhu, J., Hu, X., Li, J.: Boosting adversarial attacks with momentum. In: 2018 IEEE/CVF Conference on Computer Vision and Pattern Recognition, pp. 9185–9193 (2018)
9. Goodfellow, I., et al.: Generative adversarial networks. In: Advances in Neural Information Processing Systems 3 (2014)
10. Goodfellow, I.J., Shlens, J., Szegedy, C.: Explaining and harnessing adversarial examples. In: 3rd International Conference on Learning Representations ICLR (2015)
11. He, K., Zhang, X., Ren, S., Sun, J.: Deep residual learning for image recognition. In: 2016 IEEE Conference on Computer Vision and Pattern Recognition (CVPR), pp. 770–778 (2016)
12. Huang, Q., Katsman, I., Gu, Z., He, H., Belongie, S., Lim, S.N.: Enhancing adversarial example transferability with an intermediate level attack. In: 2019 IEEE/CVF International Conference on Computer Vision (ICCV), pp. 4732–4741 (2019)

13. Krizhevsky, A., Hinton, G.: Learning multiple layers of features from tiny images. Computer Science Department, University of Toronto, Technical Report 1 (2009)
14. Kurakin, A., Goodfellow, I.J., Bengio, S.: Adversarial examples in the physical world. In: 5th International Conference on Learning Representations ICLR, Workshop Track Proceedings (2017)
15. Lecun, Y., Bottou, L., Bengio, Y., Haffner, P.: Gradient-based learning applied to document recognition. Proc. IEEE **86**(11), 2278–2324 (1998)
16. Liu, Y., Chen, X., Liu, C., Song, D.: Delving into transferable adversarial examples and black-box attacks. In: 5th International Conference on Learning Representations ICLR (2017)
17. Madry, A., Makelov, A., Schmidt, L., Tsipras, D., Vladu, A.: Towards deep learning models resistant to adversarial attacks. In: 6th International Conference on Learning Representations ICLR (2018)
18. Orekondy, T., Schiele, B., Fritz, M.: Knockoff nets: stealing functionality of black-box models. In: Proceedings of the IEEE/CVF Conference on Computer Vision and Pattern Recognition (CVPR), pp. 4954–4963 (2019)
19. Papernot, N., McDaniel, P., Goodfellow, I., Jha, S., Celik, Z.B., Swami, A.: Practical black-box attacks against machine learning. In: Proceedings of the 2017 ACM on Asia Conference on Computer and Communications Security, pp. 506–519 (2017)
20. Simonyan, K., Zisserman, A.: Very deep convolutional networks for large-scale image recognition. In: 3rd International Conference on Learning Representations ICLR (2015)
21. Szegedy, C., et al.: Intriguing properties of neural networks. In: 2nd International Conference on Learning Representations ICLR (2014)
22. Tu, C., et al.: AutoZOOM: autoencoder-based zeroth order optimization method for attacking black-box neural networks. In: The Thirty-Third AAAI Conference on Artificial Intelligence, pp. 742–749 (2019)
23. Zhou, M., Wu, J., Liu, Y., Liu, S., Zhu, C.: DaST: data-free substitute training for adversarial attacks. In: 2020 IEEE/CVF Conference on Computer Vision and Pattern Recognition (CVPR), pp. 231–240 (2020)

A Lightweight Metric Defence Strategy for Graph Neural Networks Against Poisoning Attacks

Yang Xiao[1], Jie Li[2(✉)], and Wengui Su[3]

[1] State Key Laboratory of Integrated Services Networks, School of Cyber Engineering, Xidian University, Xi'an, Shanxi, China
yxiao@xidian.edu.cn

[2] State Key Laboratory of Integrated Services Networks, School of Telecommunications, Xidian University, Xi'an, Shanxi, China

[3] Guangxi Key Laboratory of Manufacturing System and Advanced Manufacturing Technology, School of Mechanical Engineering, Guangxi University, Nanning, China
wgsu@gxu.edu.cn

Abstract. Graph neural networks (GNN) are a specialized type of deep neural networks on graph structured data by aggregating the learned representations of node neighborhood, which has been widely applied in a variety of domains. However, recent studies demonstrate that using unnoticeable, artificially-crafted perturbations on graph structure can drastically damage the performance of GNNs. Hence, developing robust algorithms to defend poisoning attacks is of great significance. A natural idea to defend them is to delete perturbed edges from a poisoned graph and several efforts have been taken. However, current works either adopt specific threshold as a criteria to filter out poisoned effect for particular graphs or design quite complicated framework with higher time consumption, which can't well be scablable in practice. Thus in this work, we first investigate the distinction of perturbed edges and normal edges behaved on metric space, then design a defense strategy, called MD-GNN based on Jaccard similarity. Its core principle is to discern the perturbed edges via deleting those edges with lower metric values. Besides, to preserve the valuable information of graph structure and avoid the appearance of the single node during deleting process, MD-GNN deploy the minimum connectivity principle as the terminated condition. Extensive experiments on three real-world datasets show that MD-GNN can effectively preserve state-of-the-art performance of GNNs in the face of poisoning attacks with less time consumption.

Keywords: Graph neural networks · Defence · Metric space · Similarity computation

1 Introduction

Graph neural networks (GNNs), which expand traditional deep neural networks to graphs, pave a new way to effectively learn representations for graphs [9],

D. Gao et al. (Eds.): ICICS 2021, LNCS 12919, pp. 55–72, 2021.
https://doi.org/10.1007/978-3-030-88052-1_4

and have gained significant success in numerous areas such as social networks [22], traffic networks [1], chemistry [4] and finance [19], etc. The key to such huge success of GNNs is the neural message passing framework where neural messages are propagated along the edges of graphs and typically optimized for performance on a downstream task.

Despite their fabulous performance in various tasks, recent studies have shown that GNNs are susceptible to poisoning attacks, i.e., deliberately designed small perturbations on graph structures or node features [27,28]. To be specific, attackers rewire the graph topology via changing a few edges or inject artificially designed perturbations on node features to contaminate the neighborhoods of nodes, which brings errors/noises to node representation during learning and degrades the performance of GNNs significantly. The lack of robustness and resistance against the perturbation effect become a crucial issue of GNNs in many applications, including those where perturbations interfere the judgement of detecting systems [20], damage public trust [12] and even influence human health [8]. Therefore, it is urgent to escalate the robustness of GNNs in the presence of poisoning attacks. Recent studies of poisoning attacks on GNNs suggest that adding perturbed edge is more effective than deleting edges or adding noises to node features [17]. This is because node features are usually high-dimensional, requiring larger expense to attack. Deleting edges only result in the loss of some information during message aggregation while adding edges is easy to infect information aggregation. Hence in this work, we mainly focus on defense against the poisoned attack that a graph is poisoned with injected perturbed edges.

To protect GNNs from the injected perturbed edges, an intuitive idea is to delete these poisoned edges or reduce negative impacts. Several efforts have been made in this direction [10,21,25,26]. Wu et al. [21] use Jaccard similarity to prune perturbed graph with the assumption that connected nodes have higher similarity. Jin et al. [10] explore graph properties of sparsity, low rank and feature smoothness to design robust graph neural networks. GNNGuard [25] learns how to best assign higher weights to edges connecting similar nodes while deleting edges between unrelated nodes via neighbor importance estimation and layer-wise graph memory. However, there exist two key challengings in the above methodologies: 1) Methodologies targeted on deleting poisoned edges generally set a specific threshold as a criteria to purify the poisoned graph. However, the defaulted threshold tightly depends on particular graphs, which is hard to apply in other different graphs directly. 2) To better distinguish the poisoned effect, some schemes consider too much graph properties and design complicated defense framework, which extremely increases time consumption and thus decrease its practicability.

Based on the discussion above, we design a lightweight metric defense strategy for GNNs called MD-GNN, which is just based on *metric similarity* (here we choose Jaccard similarity). In our work, we first characterize the property of poisoned edges from the metric similarity based on our empirical analysis on three real-word datasets. Second, we design a criteria based on minimum connectivity of nodes to delete the poisoned edges, which not only immeasurably reserves the graph structure information to learn an accurate representation, but also break up the dependency on the specificity of graph. Concretely, given a node in a poisoned graph, MD-GNN[1] first computes the metric value of edges connecting with its neighbourhood and form a candidate edge set, then deletes those edges with lower value until this node attains minimum connectivity. Finally, the new purified graph will be regarded as the input of any GNN models. The main contributions of our work are listed as follows:

- We explore a new characteristic between clean graph and poisoned graph from the perspective of metric similarity, which is more effective to recognize the difference of poisoned edges and normal edges. We are motivated to investigate whether and how metric similarity can facilitate an active defense technique against poisoning attacks induced by a wider range of metric alterations on GNN.
- We propose MD-GNN, a general lightweight metric defense framework which not only substantially improves the robustness of GNNs against various poisoning attacks, but also reduces the time consumption of representation learning.
- Extensive experiments on three datasets validate that MD-GNN can efficiently defend poisoning attacks and outperforms the state-of-the-art defense methods in node classification task.

The rest of this work is organized as follows. We first review some related works about poisoned attack and defense in Sect. 2, then introduce some preliminaries and formulate the problem in Sect. 3. Next, we give the details of MD-GNN in Sect. 4 and report the experimental results in Sect. 5. Finally, we conclude our work in Sect. 6.

2 Related Works

In this section, we briefly describe related work on adversarial attacks and defense for graph structured data. Recently, extensive studies have proved that deep neural networks (DNNs) are vulnerable to adversarial attacks [2,16]. As the extension of DNNs to graphs, graph neural networks (GNNs) have been demonstrated to inherit this vulnerability [9,24,25,27]. Different from image data, the graph structured data is discrete and the nodes are dependent on each other, thus making the defense on graph data far more challenging. Generally, there are two major categories of adversarial attacks, namely evasion attack and poisoning attack. Evasion attack focuses on generating fake samples for a trained model. Dai et al. [5] proposed an evasion attack based on reinforcement learning. Conversely, poisoning attack mainly changes training data, which can impair the performance of GNNs extremely. For example, Zügner et al. [27] propose *nettack* which misleads GNNs to make wrong prediction on any targeted node by modifying its neighbor connections. They further develop *mettack* [28] which

[1] Our source code is released to https://github.com/lizi-learner/MD-GNN.

reduces the overall performance of GNNs via meta learning. Compared with evasion attack, poisoning attack methods are usually more powerful and can lead to an extremely low performance because of its contamination of training data. In addition, it is almost impossible to clean up a graph which is already poisoned. Therefore in this work, we focus on defending the poisoning attack of graph data.

In order to protect GNN models from poisoning attacks, some initial attempts have been made. Zhu et al. [26] proposed RGCN by adopting Gaussian distributions as the hidden representations of nodes to absorb the effects of poisoned changes and further escalate the robustness of GCN. Wu et al. [21] propose a defense methodology via removing the edges from perturbed graphs that connects the nodes with low feature similarity score. Entezari et al. [7] propose GCNSVD which deploys a low-rank approximation of adjacency matrix that drops noisy information through an SVD decomposition. Zhang et al. [25] proposed GNNGuard to detect and quantify the relationship between the graph structure and node features, and exploit it to mitigate negative effects of the poisoning attack. Jin et al. [10] propose a jointly learning method ProGNN which simultaneously learn a structural graph and a robust GNN model from the poisoned graph. Tang et al. [17] proposed PA-GNN, which relies on a penalized aggregation mechanism that directly restrict the negative impact of perturbed edges by assigning them lower attention coefficients. However, the aforementioned works consume too much time in discerning the poisoned effects, which can not appropriately be applied in practice.

Different from the previous works, we aim to design a scalable defense approach with high efficiency for GNNs via inducing metric distance to explore the poisoned effects, which not only guarantees the robustness, but also consumes less computation time.

3 Preliminaries

In this section, we summarize the notations used in this work and introduce our motivation in detail.

3.1 Problem Definition

We use $\mathcal{G} = (\mathcal{V}, \mathcal{E}, \mathcal{F})$ to denote a graph, where $\mathcal{V} = \{v_1, v_2, ..., v_n\}$ is the set of n nodes, $\mathcal{E} \subseteq \mathcal{V} \times \mathcal{V}$ represents the set of edges, and $\mathcal{F} = \{f_1, f_2, ..., f_n\}$ indicates node features, where $f_j \in \mathbb{R}^K$ is the k-dimensional node feature for node $v_j \in \mathcal{V}$. Let $\mathcal{A} \in \mathbb{R}^{N \times N}$ denote an adjacency matrix whose element $\mathcal{A}_{ij} \in \{0, 1\}$ indicates the existence of edge e_{ij} connecting v_i and v_j. We use $\mathcal{N}(v_i)$ ($\mathcal{N}(v_i) = \{v_{i_1}, v_{i_2}, ..., v_{i_k}\}$) to denote the neighbourhood of node v_i. In addition, each node has its unique label that help GNN models to accomplish precise classification. Let $\mathcal{C} = \{c_1, c_2, ..., c_l\}$ denotes the set of labels, we use $\widehat{y}_i$ to represent the prediction derived from a GNN model for v_i. To dramatically decrease the performance of GNN, attackers usually fake few edges to

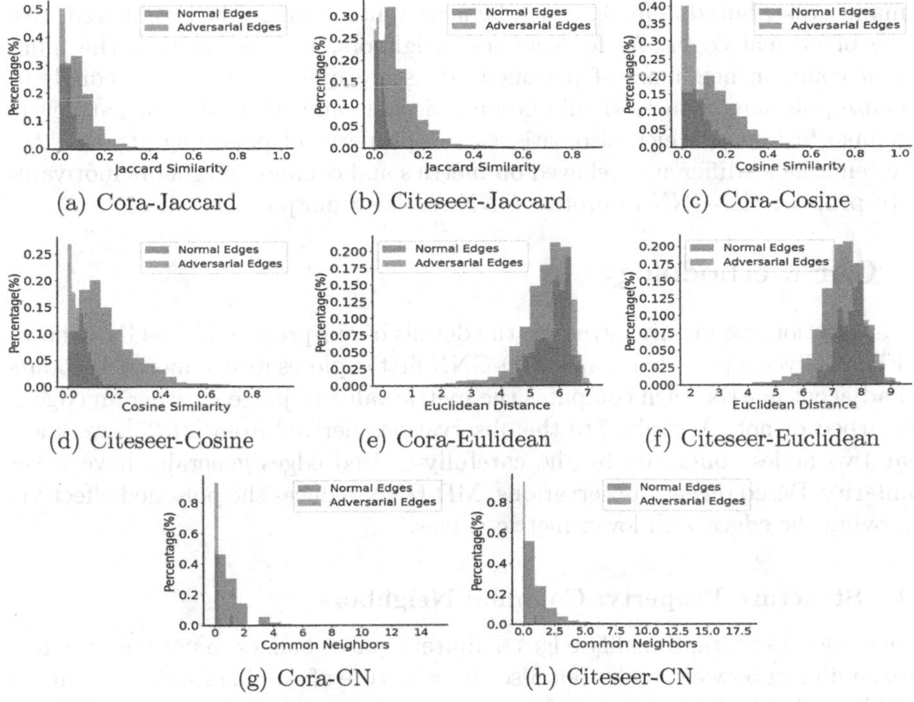

(a) Cora-Jaccard (b) Citeseer-Jaccard (c) Cora-Cosine (d) Citeseer-Cosine (e) Cora-Eulidean (f) Citeseer-Euclidean (g) Cora-CN (h) Citeseer-CN

Fig. 1. Metric analysis

change the structure of $\mathcal{A}$, which results in the poisoned version of $\mathcal{G}$, namely $\mathcal{G}' = \{\mathcal{V}, \mathcal{E}', \mathcal{F}\}$.

With aforementioned notations, the problem we aim to solve in this work is formally stated as follows:

Given a poisoned graph $\mathcal{G}' = \{\mathcal{V}, \mathcal{E}', \mathcal{F}\}$ with the adjacent matrix $\mathcal{A}$ perturbed by artificially faking edges and feature $\mathcal{F}$ unchangeable, a robust GNN model is needed to accomplish the correct node classification for candidate nodes with unknown labels under poisoned settings.

3.2 Why Using Metric Methods in Defense

In this section, we mainly discuss our motivation of applying metric in defending against poisoned samples in graph shown in Fig. 1, where the perturbation rate of metattack [28] is set as 25%. Because of page limitation, we mainly display the analysis on Cora and Citeseer datasets under metattack setting. Here we adopt three common metrics, i.e., Cosine similarity, Jaccard similarity, Euclidean distance, and node common neighbours (CN) to distinguish the difference between normal edges and poisoned edges.

As shown in Fig. 1, we find that the Cosine similarity and Jaccard similarity of poisoned edges are mainly distributed in [0, 0.2] and their Eudildean distance is mainly distributed in [6, 9], which behaves quite distinguished compared with those of normal edges. As for common neighbors, we observe that the number of common neighbors of poisoned edges are quite rare (mainly equals 0) because poisoning attacks should be unnoticeable and slight and thus attackers just fake few ones, which also satisfies the property of poisoning attacks [27]. The remarkable difference behaved on metrics and common neighbors motivates us to propose MD-GNN to protect GNN models from poisoned effect.

4 Our Methodology

In this section, we mainly introduce the details of our proposed MD-GNN shown in Fig. 2. Given a poisoned graph, MD-GNN first explores its common neighbours via adjacent matrix, then computes the metric value to judge whether an edge is perturbed or not. According to the observations derived from [21,25], we know that two nodes connected by the carefully-crafted edges generally have lower similarity. Based on such observations, MD-GNN reduces the poisoned effect via removing the edges with lower metric values.

4.1 Structure Property: Common Neighbors

Poisoning attacks that modify edges definitely make changes to not only the feature similarity between nodes but also the structure of graph, especially common neighbors. From the viewpoint of network topology, common neighbors (CN) is considered as the simplest method to define similarity based on semi-structural information of the graph [6]. The more common neighbors two nodes have, the more similarity they own. In our work, the computation of CN is defined as:

$$CN(i,j) = A_i A_j^T \tag{1}$$

where A_i means the ith column of adjacent matrix $\mathcal{A}$.

4.2 Feature Property: Metric Methods

According to the characteristic of poisoning attacks, attackers generally tend to attack the nodes with different labels and features [25]. Thus, the similarity of features has potential to serve as a guidance to clean the perturbed edges from the poisoned graph. In this work, we mainly adopt Jaccard similarity to differentiate the poisoned edges from the normal edges according to Sect. 3.2. Here we adopt Jaccard similarity because the features of many datasets are bag-of-word. For the graphs with other types of features, such as numeric features, cosine similarity may be available. The details of Jaccard similarity are elaborated as follows.

Let f_i and f_j be the feature vector of node v_i and v_j, where the element of the feature vector is binary, i.e., users like or do not like an item, we utilize Jaccard similarity to measure their similarity, which is defined as follows:

$$Jaccard(i,j) = \frac{L_{11}}{L_{01} + L_{10} + L_{11}} \tag{2}$$

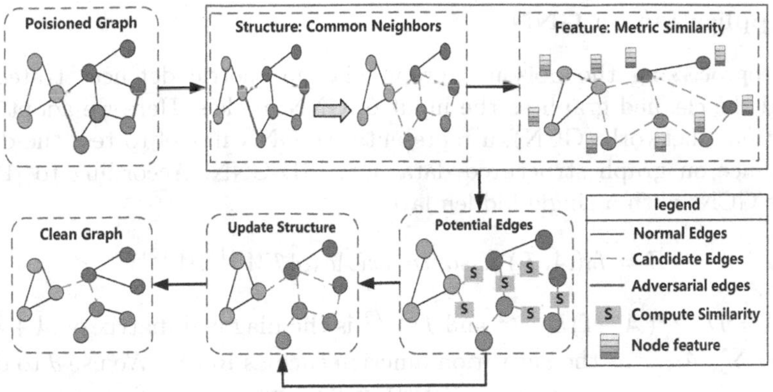

Fig. 2. Illustration of metric defense strategy

where L_{11} is the number of features where both node v_i and v_j have a value of 1. L_{01} is the feature number where the value of the feature is 0 in v_i but 1 in v_j. Similarly, L_{10} is the total number of features which have a value of 1 in v_i but 0 in v_j.

4.3 Clean Perturbed Edges

In our work, all the edges that connect nodes with low metric value (e.g., Jaccard similarity) are selected as candidates to remove, which means that some normal edges with lower metric score may be also deleted. Thus, how to define a proper threshold to balance the number of removed clean edges and perturbed edges becomes quite important. However, it is intractable to determine a perfect threshold for each graph. Moreover, we observe two findings: 1) simply removing edges will cause single nodes which only have their own features without connection and can not participate in the message aggregation process during training, which will decrease the performance of GNN models. 2) The number of CN between two nodes connected by the poisoned edges is mainly 0 based on our metric analysis shown in Fig. 1(g)–(h). Thus for any node, we first collect its edges connected with other nodes and form a set, then computing the metric value for each edge. Next, we remove the edges with lower metric from this set. To against the appearance of single nodes, we set the terminated condition as holding the minimum connectivity [14] of each node.

Our metric defense strategy is pre-processing based. We perform a pre-processing on a given graph before training. In our work, all the edges that connect nodes with low similarity score are selected as candidates to remove. Although some normal edges with lower similarity may be deleted, we find that removing these clean edges does little harm to the performance of GNN models. On the contrary, the removal of these edges may even reduce the time consumption of training and improve the accuracy of GNN models.

4.4 Application on GNN

After preprocessing the poisoned graph via our metric defence strategy, we regarded the cleaned graph as the input of GNN models. Here we adopt graph convolutional network (GCN), a representative GNN model to test the defense performance on graph structured data, i.e., MD-GNN. According to [11], we consider GCNs with a single hidden layer:

$$Z = f_\theta(\mathcal{A}, \mathcal{F}) = softmax(\widehat{\mathcal{A}}\sigma(\widehat{\mathcal{A}}\mathcal{F}W^{(1)})W^{(2)}) \tag{3}$$

where $\widehat{\mathcal{A}} = \widetilde{D}^{-1/2}(\mathcal{A}+\mathbf{I})\widetilde{D}^{-1/2}$ and $\widetilde{D}^{-1/2}$ is the diagonal matrix of $\mathcal{A}+\mathbf{I}$ with $\widetilde{D}_{ii} = 1+\sum_j \mathcal{A}_{ij}$. σ is the activation function such as ReLU. We use θ to denote the set of all parameters, i.e., $\theta = \{W^{(1)}, W^{(2)}\}$. The optimal parameters θ are then learned in a semi-supervised fashion by minimizing cross-entropy loss on the output of the labeled samples, which is formulated as

$$\min_\theta \mathcal{L}_{GCN}(\theta, \mathcal{A}, \mathcal{F}, \mathcal{C}) = \sum_{v_i \in \mathcal{V}_L} (l(f_\theta(\mathcal{A}, \mathcal{F}), c_i) \tag{4}$$

where $\mathcal{V}_L$ is the set of nodes with known labels. we adopt Adam optimizer with the learningrate of 0.01 to minimize the loss function and update the model parameters. Overall, the time complexity of MD-GNN is $\mathcal{O}(n)$.

5 Experiments

In this section, we mainly estimate the effectiveness of MD-GNN against various graph poisoning attacks. To be specific, our comparisons aim to answer the following questions:

- **RQ1**: How does MD-GNN perform compared to the state-of-the-art defense approaches under various poisoning attacks (See Sect. 5.2)?
- **RQ2**: What is the scalability of MD-GNN transplanted into other GNN models? (See Sect. 5.3)
- **RQ3**: What about other metrics applied in defense strategy? (See Sect. 5.4)
- **RQ4**: What is the effect of our threshold strategy? (See Sect. 5.5)
- **RQ5**: Does the MD-GNN work as expected? (See Appendix A.1)
- **RQ6**: How do the parameters deployed in our work affect the defense performance (See Appendix A.2)?

5.1 Experimental Settings

Datasets. We validate our proposed methodology on the three publicly available datasets, i.e., Cora, Cora_ml, Citeseer. Following [7,27], we select the largest connected components and normalize all feature vectors in the experiments. The statistics of preprocessed datasets are shown in Table 1.

Table 1. The Statistics of preprocessed datasets

Datasets	Cora	Cora_ml	Citeseer
EDGES	10138	15962	7385
NODES	2485	2810	2120
Classes	7	7	6
Features	1433	2879	3703

Compared Schemes and Attacks. To evaluate our methodology, we compare it with the following state-of-the-art GNN models and defense approaches.

- **GCN** [11] and **GAT** [18]: These two GNN models are baselines, which have been widely used for comparison.
- **HGCN** [3]: HGCN is another variant of GCN by mapping the embedding features into a continuous hyperbolic space.
- **RGCN** [26]: RGCN adopts Gaussian distributions as the hidden representations of nodes in each convolutional layers, which absorbs the negative effects caused by adversarial perturbations.
- **GCNJaccard** [21]: GCNJaccard preprocesses the attacked graph by deleting the edges between nodes with low feature similarity computed by Jaccard distance [15]. This approach only works on the nodes with features.
- **GCNSVD** [7]: This method originally aims to solve high-rank attacks (e.g., *nettack*), which vaccinate GCN with the low-rank approximation of the perturbed graph. However, it is also straightforward to extend it to non-targeted and random attacks.
- **ProGNN** [10]: ProGNN is a general defense framework which jointly learns a structural graph and a robust graph neural network model from the perturbed graph via exploring the properties of graph.
- **GNNGuard** [25]: GNNGuard is a general scalable graph defense framework, which learns how to best assign higer weights to edges connecting similar nodes while pruning edges between unrelated nodes.

We compare all the approaches under the following four graph attacks implemented by PyTorch DeepRobust [13] package[2]:

- **Random Attack** [10]: We randomly inject artificial edge on graphs, which can be regarded as adding random noise on clean graphs.
- **Nettack** [27]: This attack is a representative targeted attack which aims to attack several specific nodes via changing the number of their neighborhoods.
- **Metattack** [28]: Metattack is a non-targeted global attack, which generates poisoning attacks based on meta-learning.

Implementation. For each dataset, we randomly split 10% of nodes for training, 10% of nodes for validation and the rest 80% of nodes for testing. For each experiment, we record the average performance of 10 runs. For tuning

[2] https://deeprobust.readthedocs.io/en/latest/.

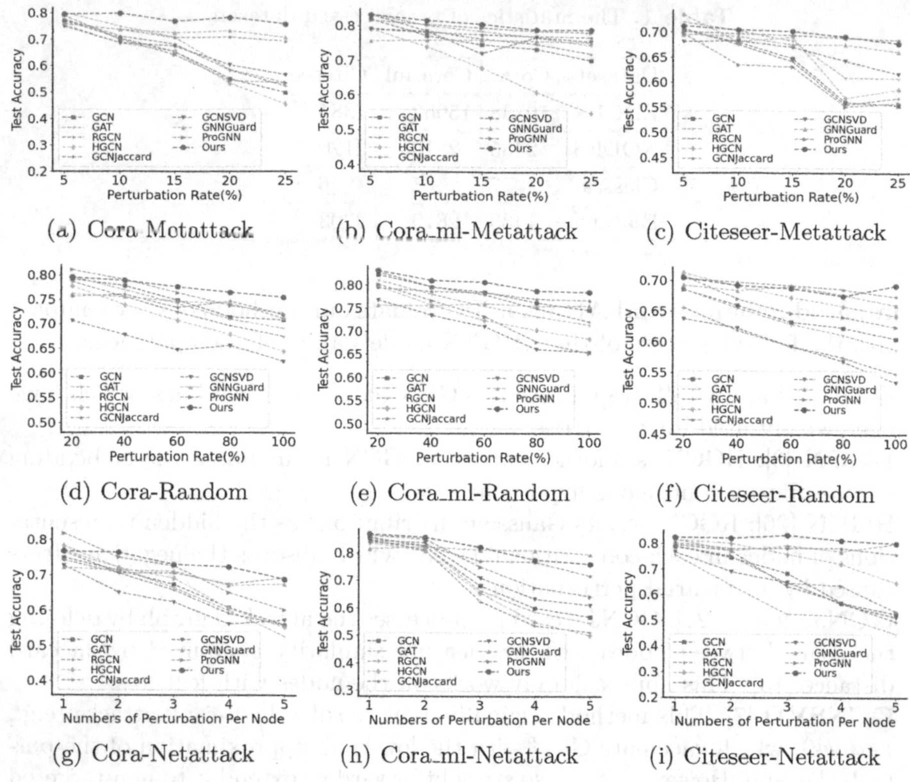

(a) Cora-Metattack (b) Cora_ml-Metattack (c) Citeseer-Metattack

(d) Cora-Random (e) Cora_ml-Random (f) Citeseer-Random

(g) Cora-Netattack (h) Cora_ml-Netattack (i) Citeseer-Netattack

Fig. 3. Node classification performance (accuracy±std) under various attacks

the hyper-parameters, we pick out the approaches that perform best on datasets based on classification accuracy. All the approaches are trained until convergence, i.e., if the performance does not improve after 40 epochs. All the approaches are trained for a maximum of 400 epochs. For GCN, GAT, HGCN, ProGNN and GNNGuard, we adopt the same parameters setting defaulted in the original works. For RGCN, the latent embedding dimension is set as 16. For GCNJaccard, the threshold of Jaccard distance for filtering edges is randomly selected from {0.02, 0.04, 0.06, 0.08, 0.1}. For GCNSVD, the reduced rank is randomly selected from {5, 10, 15, 50, 100, 200}. All the experiments are implemented via Pytorch 1.5.0, on a 4-core Windows 10 professional machine with a Intel(R) Xeon(R) CPU E3-1230(v5) and NVIDIA Quadro P400 GPU.

5.2 Defense Performance Analysis

In this section, we mainly analyze the overall performance of compared schemes under poisoning attacks, i.e., *metattack*, *random attack* and *nettack*, from the perspectives of both classification accuracy and time consumption. As shown in Fig. 3 and Table 2, the perturbation rates of *metattack* and *random attack* are varied from 5% to 25% with a step of 5%, and from 20% to 100% with a step

Table 2. Time Consumption (seconds) under metattack, random attack and nettack

Metattack										
Dataset	PTB(%)	GCN	GAT	RGCN	HGCN	GCNJaccard	GCNSVD	GNNGuard	ProGNN	MD-GNN
Cora	5	6.11	14.24	21.00	**3.75**	5.33	8.15	49.23	2319.06	4.13
	10	6.36	14.91	21.86	**3.86**	5.22	8.28	52.43	2315.65	4.24
	15	6.66	14.70	21.97	**3.81**	5.51	8.33	52.12	2323.29	4.58
	20	6.48	14.98	22.29	**3.90**	5.54	8.42	52.63	2315.74	4.36
	25	6.55	15.15	20.94	**3.84**	6.07	7.96	52.42	2318.18	4.59
Cora_ml	5	7.76	21.10	30.04	**3.91**	9.05	11.32	82.04	3252.38	7.98
	10	7.84	21.40	29.73	**3.66**	9.33	11.41	81.86	3248.09	8.51
	15	7.81	21.82	29.14	**3.63**	10.22	12.16	81.45	3243.71	8.40
	20	7.88	22.16	29.00	**3.69**	9.99	12.17	81.97	3248.55	8.73
	25	7.84	22.63	28.99	**3.68**	10.01	11.77	81.68	3246.00	8.92
Citeseer	5	5.35	15.71	23.38	**3.50**	4.79	6.46	60.92	1491.79	4.34
	10	5.31	15.85	23.20	**3.45**	4.87	6.40	61.08	1495.60	4.49
	15	5.31	16.08	23.73	**3.46**	4.91	6.26	60.49	1585.72	4.53
	20	5.39	16.19	24.25	**3.47**	5.11	6.28	60.77	1680.87	4.61
	25	5.30	16.38	24.33	**3.19**	5.08	6.23	61.04	1564.78	4.73
Random attack										
Dataset	PTB(%)	GCN	GAT	RGCN	HGCN	GCNJaccard	GCNSVD	GNNGuard	ProGNN	MD-GNN
Cora	20	6.34	15.06	18.50	**3.87**	6.43	8.18	50.85	2318.80	4.32
	40	6.15	16.17	18.17	**3.86**	6.10	8.05	51.19	2326.55	4.74
	60	6.37	17.17	18.43	**4.05**	6.92	8.79	52.96	2323.81	4.98
	80	6.25	18.18	18.49	**4.15**	6.88	7.95	52.48	2326.09	5.63
	100	6.78	19.22	19.28	**4.03**	7.50	8.16	50.30	2336.90	5.93
Cora_ml	20	7.89	22.21	29.10	**3.69**	9.52	11.59	81.67	3250.06	8.58
	40	8.00	23.92	29.30	**3.74**	10.31	12.18	81.17	3255.03	9.23
	60	8.40	25.26	29.00	**3.77**	10.36	11.37	81.70	3261.08	10.10
	80	8.27	26.97	29.08	**3.98**	11.75	11.34	81.46	3268.76	10.38
	100	8.49	28.57	28.93	**4.17**	11.68	12.54	81.33	3268.45	10.85
Citeseer	20	5.37	16.17	24.22	**3.55**	4.98	6.61	60.78	1621.65	4.82
	40	5.34	17.01	23.89	**3.68**	5.42	6.61	61.46	1736.70	5.08
	60	5.40	17.71	23.30	**3.48**	5.64	6.24	61.16	1744.29	5.48
	80	5.49	18.43	23.48	**3.60**	5.60	6.16	61.47	1669.52	5.36
	100	5.46	19.32	23.49	**3.54**	5.97	6.18	61.50	1618.80	5.74
Nettack										
Dataset	PTB-E	GCN	GAT	RGCN	HGCN	GCNJaccard	GCNSVD	GNNGuard	ProGNN	MD-GNN
Cora	1	6.29	14.21	18.19	**3.81**	5.83	8.35	52.27	2309.82	4.08
	2	6.12	14.37	18.25	**3.87**	5.44	8.07	52.26	2316.35	4.03
	3	5.98	14.30	18.11	**3.89**	5.57	8.04	51.98	2316.85	4.23
	4	6.04	14.33	18.19	**3.90**	5.18	8.40	51.59	2310.77	4.11
	5	6.19	14.33	18.17	**3.75**	5.71	8.22	52.52	2317.46	4.05
Cora_ml	1	7.92	20.81	29.01	**3.57**	9.49	12.45	82.61	3241.12	7.83
	2	7.81	20.95	29.04	**3.61**	9.44	11.46	80.82	3242.64	7.76
	3	7.85	21.63	28.96	**3.66**	9.66	11.85	82.45	3243.58	8.04
	4	7.83	22.02	29.10	**3.65**	9.96	12.06	80.88	3244.59	8.12
	5	7.73	21.97	28.98	**3.64**	9.82	12.07	80.69	3256.04	8.17
Citeseer	1	5.30	15.54	23.21	**3.47**	4.88	6.28	60.89	1512.52	4.51
	2	5.30	15.70	23.19	**3.39**	4.74	6.28	60.53	1492.02	4.35
	3	5.33	15.71	23.54	**3.55**	4.94	6.42	60.78	1495.86	4.38
	4	5.43	15.84	23.86	**3.62**	4.65	6.34	61.01	1501.70	4.36
	5	5.27	16.30	24.27	**3.56**	4.95	6.32	61.04	1502.83	4.38

of 20%, respectively. As for *nettack*, following [10,26], we vary the number of perturbations made on each targeted node from 1 to 5 edge with a step size of 1, and the nodes in test set with degree larger than 10 are set as target nodes. For classification accuracy, all the experiments are conducted 10 times and we report the average accuracy with stand derivation. For time consumption, we record the total time of 200 epochs. All the best performance on node classification and time consumption are highlighted in bold. Several observations are derived as follows:

- As a whole, our proposed MD-GNN outperforms other state-of-the-art approaches under most various poisoning settings. Under metattack setting, MD-GNN easily defeats GCN, RGCN, GCNJaccard, GNNGuard and ProGNN in classification accuracy. As for random attack, MD-GNN behaves better robustness compared with three GNN model (i.e., GCN, GAT and HGCN). In comparison with other defence schemes, MD-GNN also attains highest classification accuracy in most cases. Although ProGNN and GNN-Guard strike higher accuracy on few nettack settings operated on Cora and Cora_ml datasets, they cost too much time to accomplish it.
- From Table 2, we find that the time consumption of HGCN is fewer than other approaches whereas it behaves worse in classification accuracy shown in Fig. 3. Although MD-GNN spends more time in classification compared with HGCN and GCN on Cora_ml, it can attain higher accuracy. Another finding is that ProGNN and GNNGuard produce more time consumption in node classification, which means that they will spend more time in learning features and decreasing poisoning effect.

To conclude, our proposed MD-GNN not only achieves remarkable classification accuracy, but also consumes less time in comparison with other approaches.

5.3 Scalability Analysis

In this section, we mainly discuss the scalablity of MD-GNN. To be fair, we transplant our metric defense strategy into other GNN models (i.e., GCN, GAT and HGCN) and defense approaches, where we select RGCN as the baseline owe to its higher classification accuracy and less time consumption according to Table 2. Because of page limitation, here we test the experiments on Cora and Citeseer datasets under metattack and nettack settings. Specifically, given a poisoned graph dataset, MD-GNN first clean it via removing the perturbed edges according to metric difference and a cleaned graph is generated. Then we take it as the input of other models. Note that we adopt the same parameter settings mentioned in the Sect. 5.1.

To better illustrate the comparison, we classify four candidate approaches into two groups, i.e., GCN and GAT belong to the 1st group, (named as "dataset-Attack-1"), RGCN and HGCN belongs to the 2nd group (named as "dataset-Attack-2"). The new reconstructed GNN model is named by "MD-name" shown in Fig. 4. Obviously, the classification accuracy of MD-GCN/GAT/RGCN/HGCN on test datasets has gained remarkable improvement compared with the original models, which further demonstrates the scalability and efficiency of our metric defense strategy.

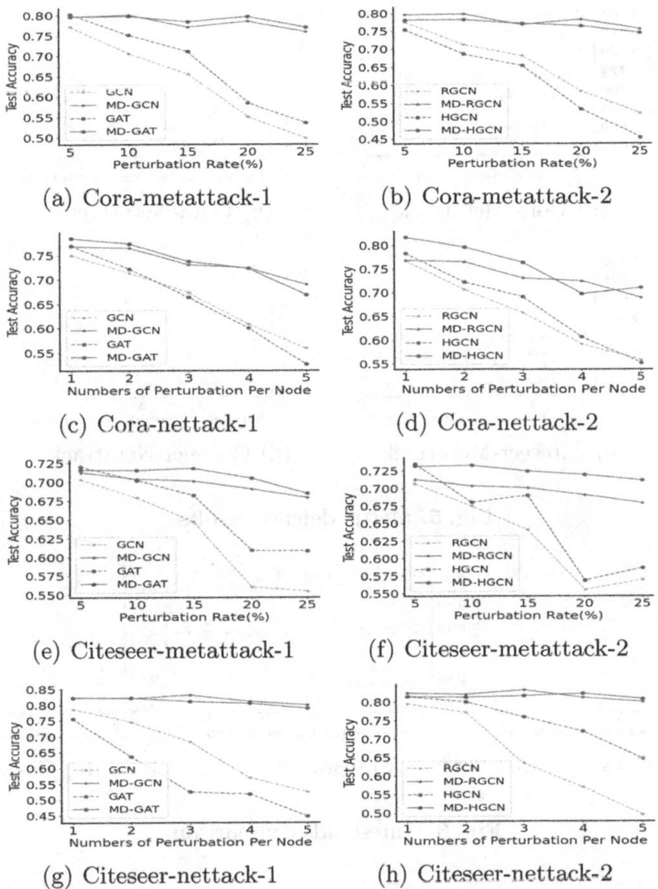

(a) Cora-metattack-1 (b) Cora-metattack-2

(c) Cora-nettack-1 (d) Cora-nettack-2

(e) Citeseer-metattack-1 (f) Citeseer-metattack-2

(g) Citeseer-nettack-1 (h) Citeseer-nettack-2

Fig. 4. Scalability results

5.4 Metric Discussion

In this section, we further explore the performance of various metric methodologies on defense strategy. Specifically, We deploy other three common metric methods, i.e., Cosine similarity, Euclidean distance and Manhattan distance into MD-GNN (Note that our MD-GNN adopts Jaccard similarity). As shown in Fig. 5, we find that applying Euclidean distance and Manhattan distance can not well reduce the poisoned effect because their test accuracy decreases dramatically. Besides, although Cosine similarity behaves much better than Euclidean distance and Manhattan distance in test accuracy, its defense performance can't catch up with Jaccard distance. Thus, Jaccard distance exhibits better defense performance compared with other common metric methodologies.

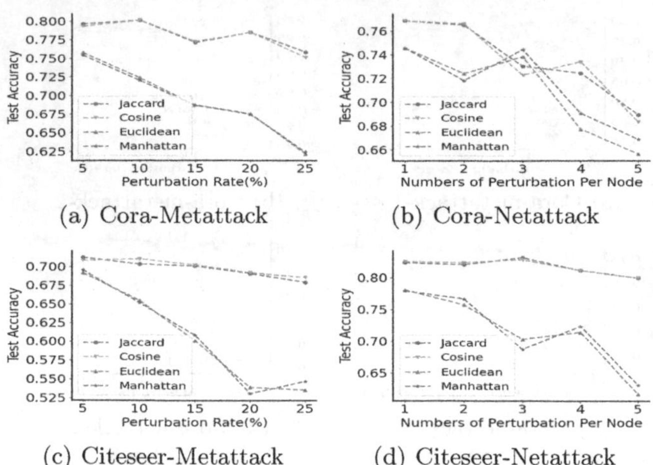

(a) Cora-Metattack (b) Cora-Netattack

(c) Citeseer-Metattack (d) Citeseer-Netattack

Fig. 5. Metric defense results

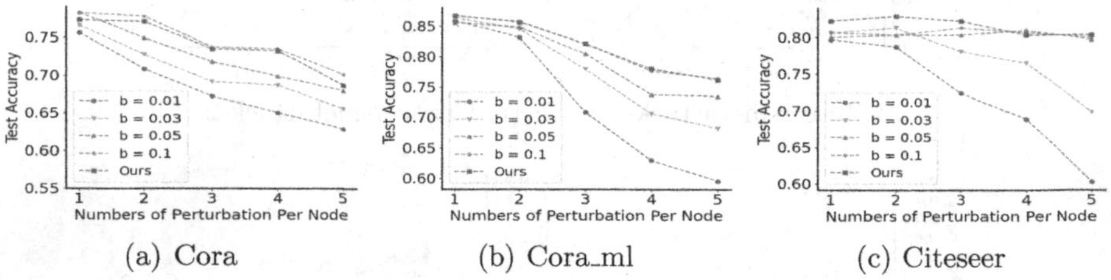

(a) Cora (b) Cora_ml (c) Citeseer

Fig. 6. Thresholds comparison

5.5 Threshold Discussion

In this section, we mainly discuss the performance induced by threshold b. We execute the comparison under nettack settings, where we set b from $\{0.01, 0.03, 0.05, 0.1\}$. As shown in Fig. 6, we find that our threshold strategy, i.e., minimum connectivity, outperforms other numerical threshold settings in reducing the poisoned effects. For numerical threshold, we also find that the higher value leads to the better defense performance against poisoning attacks.

6 Conclusion

Graph neural networks can be easily fooled by poisoning attacks. Hence in this work, we investigate the distinguished properties of perturbed edges and normal edges behaved on metric space, and propose MD-GNN based on Jaccard similarity. The proposed MD-GNN can accurately discern the poisoned effect according to metric value, and simultaneously save the information of graph topology as much as possible. Compared with current state-of-the-art approaches, MD-GNN not only reduces the poisoned effect in a less time period, but also can be scalable to other GNN model to promote their accuracy in node classification tasks.

Acknowledgements. This work is supported by the National Key Research and Development Program of China under Grant 2020YFB1807500, the Fundamental Research Funds for the Central Universities under Grant XJS211513, the Key Research and Development Programs of Shaanxi (No. 2021ZDLGY06-03, No. 2019ZDLGY13-07, No. 2019ZDLGY13-04), and Research on information collaboration technologies of supply chain based on block chain 17-259-05S007.

A Appendix

A.1 Visualization

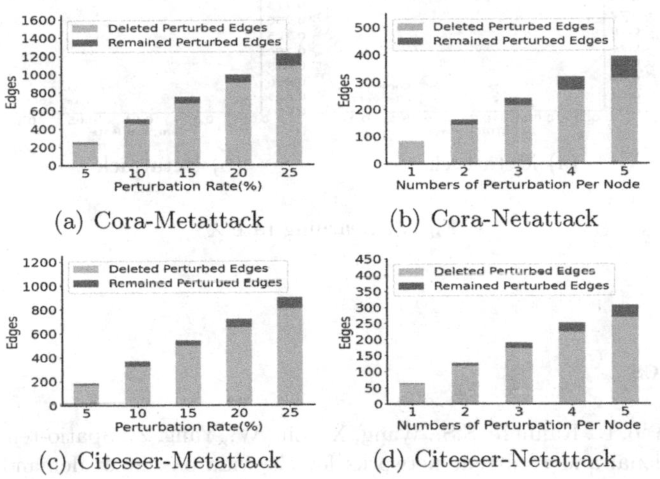

(a) Cora-Metattack (b) Cora-Netattack

(c) Citeseer-Metattack (d) Citeseer-Netattack

Fig. 7. Visualizations

In this section, we mainly display the visualization of new graph cleaned by MD-GNN shown in Fig. 7. Here we only show the results on Cora and Citeseer datasets under metattack and nettack settings for page limitation. As shown in Fig. 7, the total perturbed edges include the deleted perturbed edges (colored by cyan) and the remained perturbed edges (colored by orange). We find that most perturbed edges in a poisoned graph has been cleaned via executing MD-GNN only once, which validates that MD-GNN can extremely decrease the poisoned effect in node classification task.

A.2 Parameter Settings

In this section, we mainly study learning rate λ on the defense performance of MD-GNN. Here we use control variable method to accomplish the experiments on parameters, which keeps one parameter changeable while others are held unchangeable during experiments [23]. All the experiment settings about parameters are defaulted as that in Sect. 5.2. For evaluating λ, we fixed perturbation rate of metattack as 25% and perturbation edges of nettack as 5. The results of parameters are shown in Fig. 8. From the above figure, we find that with the increase in λ, the test accuracy of defending metattack become continuously increased on Citeseer dataset, while become decreased on Cora dataset when λ is larger than 0.01. As for nettack shown in Fig. 8(b), the tendency of test accuracy become fluctuated with the increase of λ.

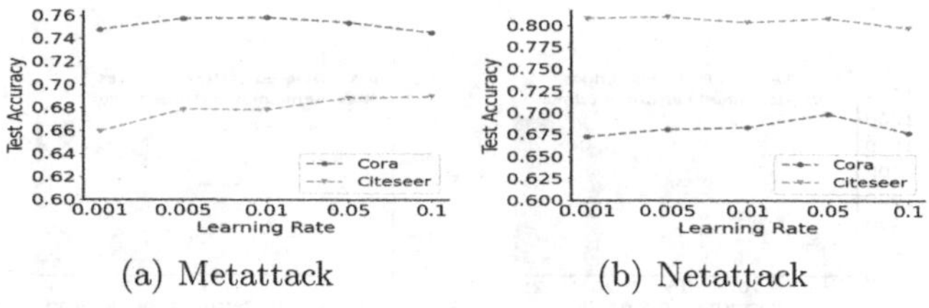

(a) Metattack (b) Netattack

Fig. 8. Learning rate λ

References

1. Bai, L., Yao, L., Kanhere, S.S., Wang, X., Liu, W., Yang, Z.: Spatio-temporal graph convolutional and recurrent networks for citywide passenger demand prediction. In: Proceedings of the 28th ACM International Conference on Information and Knowledge Management, pp. 2293–2296 (2019)
2. Cao, Y., Chen, X., Yao, L., Wang, X., Zhang, W.E.: Adversarial attacks and detection on reinforcement learning-based interactive recommender systems. In: Proceedings of the 43rd International ACM SIGIR Conference on Research and Development in Information Retrieval, pp. 1669–1672 (2020)
3. Chami, I., Ying, Z., Ré, C., Leskovec, J.: Hyperbolic graph convolutional neural networks. In: Advances in Neural Information Processing Systems, pp. 4868–4879 (2019)
4. Coley, C.W., et al.: A graph-convolutional neural network model for the prediction of chemical reactivity. Chem. Sci. **10**(2), 370–377 (2019)
5. Dai, H., et al.: Adversarial attack on graph structured data. In: Dy, J.G., Krause, A. (eds.) Proceedings of the 35th International Conference on Machine Learning, ICML 2018, Stockholmsmässan, Stockholm, Sweden, 10–15 July 2018. Proceedings of Machine Learning Research, vol. 80, pp. 1123–1132. PMLR (2018). http://proceedings.mlr.press/v80/dai18b.html

6. Dehmamy, N., Barabási, A.L., Yu, R.: Understanding the representation power of graph neural networks in learning graph topology. arXiv preprint arXiv:1907.05008 (2019)
7. Entezari, N., Al-Sayouri, S.A., Darvishzadeh, A., Papalexakis, E.E.: All you need is low (rank) defending against adversarial attacks on graphs. In: Proceedings of the 13th International Conference on Web Search and Data Mining, pp. 169–177 (2020)
8. Finlayson, S.G., Bowers, J.D., Ito, J., Zittrain, J.L., Beam, A.L., Kohane, I.S.: Adversarial attacks on medical machine learning. Science **363**(6433), 1287–1289 (2019)
9. Jin, W., Li, Y., Xu, H., Wang, Y., Tang, J.: Adversarial attacks and defenses on graphs: a review and empirical study. arXiv preprint arXiv:2003.00653 (2020)
10. Jin, W., Ma, Y., Liu, X., Tang, X., Wang, S., Tang, J.: Graph structure learning for robust graph neural networks. In: Proceedings of the 26th ACM SIGKDD International Conference on Knowledge Discovery & Data Mining, pp. 66–74 (2020)
11. Kipf, T.N., Welling, M.: Semi-supervised classification with graph convolutional networks. In: 5th International Conference on Learning Representations, ICLR 2017, Toulon, France, 24–26 April 2017, Conference Track Proceedings. OpenReview.net (2017)
12. Kreps, S., Kriner, D.: Model uncertainty, political contestation, and public trust in science: evidence from the covid-19 pandemic. Sci. Adv. **6**(43), eabd4563 (2020)
13. Li, Y., Jin, W., Xu, H., Tang, J.: Deeprobust: a pytorch library for adversarial attacks and defenses. arXiv preprint arXiv:2005.06149 (2020)
14. Pavlikov, K.: Improved formulations for minimum connectivity network interdiction problems. Comput. Oper. Res. **97**, 48–57 (2018)
15. Real, R., Vargas, J.M.: The probabilistic basis of Jaccard's index of similarity. Syst. Biol. **45**(3), 380–385 (1996)
16. Sun, L., Dou, Y., Yang, C., Wang, J., Yu, P.S., Li, B.: Adversarial attack and defense on graph data: a survey. arXiv preprint arXiv:1812.10528 (2018)
17. Tang, X., Li, Y., Sun, Y., Yao, H., Mitra, P., Wang, S.: Transferring robustness for graph neural network against poisoning attacks. In: Proceedings of the 13th International Conference on Web Search and Data Mining, pp. 600–608 (2020)
18. Velickovic, P., Cucurull, G., Casanova, A., Romero, A., Liò, P., Bengio, Y.: Graph attention networks. In: 6th International Conference on Learning Representations, ICLR 2018, Vancouver, BC, Canada, 30 April–3 May 2018, Conference Track Proceedings. OpenReview.net (2018)
19. Wang, D., et al.: A semi-supervised graph attentive network for financial fraud detection. In: 2019 IEEE International Conference on Data Mining (ICDM), pp. 598–607. IEEE (2019)
20. Waniek, M., Michalak, T.P., Wooldridge, M.J., Rahwan, T.: Hiding individuals and communities in a social network. Nat. Hum. Behav. **2**(2), 139–147 (2018)
21. Wu, H., Wang, C., Tyshetskiy, Y., Docherty, A., Lu, K., Zhu, L.: Adversarial examples for graph data: deep insights into attack and defense. In: Proceedings of the 28th International Joint Conference on Artificial Intelligence, pp. 4816–4823. AAAI Press (2019)
22. Xiao, Y., Pei, Q., Xiao, T., Yao, L., Liu, H.: MutualRec: joint friend and item recommendations with mutualistic attentional graph neural networks. J. Netw. Comput. Appl. **177**, 102954 (2021)
23. Xiao, Y., Pei, Q., Yao, L., Wang, X.: Recrisk: An enhanced recommendation model with multi-facet risk control. Expert Syst. Appl. **158**, 113561 (2020)

24. Xu, H., Li, Y., Jin, W., Tang, J.: Adversarial attacks and defenses: frontiers, advances and practice. In: Proceedings of the 26th ACM SIGKDD International Conference on Knowledge Discovery & Data Mining, pp. 3541–3542 (2020)
25. Zhang, X., Zitnik, M.: Gnnguard: Defending graph neural networks against adversarial attacks. In: Advances in Neural Information Processing Systems 33: Annual Conference on Neural Information Processing Systems 2020, NeurIPS 2020, 6–12 December 2020, virtual (2020)
26. Zhu, D., Zhang, Z., Cui, P., Zhu, W.: Robust graph convolutional networks against adversarial attacks. In: Proceedings of the 25th ACM SIGKDD International Conference on Knowledge Discovery & Data Mining, pp. 1399–1407 (2019)
27. Zügner, D., Akbarnejad, A., Günnemann, S.: Adversarial attacks on neural networks for graph data. In: Proceedings of the 24th ACM SIGKDD International Conference on Knowledge Discovery & Data Mining, pp. 2847–2856 (2018)
28. Zügner, D., Günnemann, S.: Adversarial attacks on graph neural networks via meta learning. In: 7th International Conference on Learning Representations, ICLR 2019, New Orleans, LA, USA, 6–9 May 2019. OpenReview.net (2019)

Rethinking Adversarial Examples Exploiting Frequency-Based Analysis

Sicong Han[1], Chenhao Lin[1(✉)], Chao Shen[1(✉)], and Qian Wang[2]

[1] Xi'an Jiaotong University, Xi'an, China
siconghan@stu.xjtu.edu.cn, linchenhao@xjtu.edu.cn,
chaoshen@mail.xjtu.edu.cn
[2] Wuhan University, Wuhan, China
qianwang@whu.edu.cn

Abstract. Deep neural networks (DNNs) have been recently found vulnerable to adversarial examples. Several previous works attempt to relate the low-frequency or high-frequency parts of adversarial inputs with the robustness of models. However, these studies lack comprehensive experiments and thorough analyses and even yield contradictory results. This work comprehensively explores the connection between the robustness of models and properties of adversarial perturbations in the frequency domain using six classic attack methods and three representative datasets. We visualize the distribution of successful adversarial perturbations using Discrete Fourier Transform and test the effectiveness of different frequency bands of perturbations on reducing the accuracy of classifiers through a proposed quantitative analysis. Experimental results show that the characteristics of successful adversarial perturbations in the frequency domain can vary from dataset to dataset, while their intensities are greater in the effective frequency bands. We analyze the obtained phenomena by combining principles of attacks and properties of datasets and offer a complete view of adversarial examples from the frequency domain perspective, which helps to explain the contradictory parts of previous works and provides insights for future research.

Keywords: Adversarial examples · Model robustness · Frequency analysis

1 Introduction

With the widespread deployment of deep learning systems in various fields, the robustness of deep learning models has become of paramount importance. Deep learning models are highly vulnerable to adversarial examples [19], which may lead to serious security breaches and irreparable financial loss as they have been integrated into various safety-critical systems, e.g., self-driving cars.

Adversarial examples, in the context of the image classification, look similar to the original images while they have the ability to fool the model into producing incorrect outputs with high confidence [5]. Numerous adversarial attack

D. Gao et al. (Eds.): ICICS 2021, LNCS 12919, pp. 73–89, 2021.
https://doi.org/10.1007/978-3-030-88052-1_5

methods [1,13] and defense methods [10,25] have been proposed to improve the effectiveness of attacks and enhance models' robustness, respectively. Meanwhile, the studies on understanding the intrinsic nature of adversarial examples have attracted increasing attention with various theories, including Linearity hypothesis [5], boundary tilting [20] and curvature of decision boundaries [12].

Recently, some studies attempt to understand the adversarial examples from the perspective of the frequency domain. It is argued in [21] that the generalization of convolutional neural networks (CNNs) can be related to how they process the high-frequency information of images. Besides, the performance of the attacks can be promoted by finding adversarial perturbations in specific frequency bands [4,6,16]. However, a small number of attacks and a single dataset are usually adopted in previous works, resulting in weak generalization and some contradictory parts among proposed theories.

To address the limitations of existing works, we comprehensively analyze and evaluate the adversarial examples in the frequency domain. Two categories of six attack methods in total and three commonly used datasets are adopted in this paper. We first visualize the distribution of frequency components of successful adversarial perturbations, then we decompose them into signals of two frequencies to explore which one plays a leading role in reducing the accuracy of the model. We further propose an evaluation method to quantitatively compare the differences between the distribution of successful perturbations and unsuccessful ones within the effective frequency bands to figure out what leads to the different effects of both perturbations. The bridge between the robustness of models and the properties of adversarial perturbations in the frequency domain on different datasets is built in this paper. Based on the observations and analyses, we draw several important findings and provide insights for future research:

- Unlike previous works [22,23], in which they claim that successful adversarial perturbations for naturally trained models concentrate more on the high-frequency domain, our results suggest that the distribution of successful adversarial perturbations can vary from dataset to dataset, so as the effectiveness of different frequency bands of successful perturbations on misleading models. As a result, it is not accurate to solely relate high-frequency components of images with the target features of adversarial attacks. Besides, filtering the fixed frequency bands of information of images cannot provide universal defense.
- Previous studies [4,6] illustrate that constraining adversarial directions in different frequency bands on ImageNet can obtain progress in improving the effectiveness of attacks. However, the principles behind those results are not provided systematically. Our findings and analyses show that both low- and high-frequency components of successful adversarial perturbations on ImageNet have a noticeable effect on reducing the model's accuracy. Therefore, performing adversarial attacks in specific frequency bands can be a reasonable way to promote the performance of attacks on this dataset, explaining the rationality of previous works.

- Furthermore, we find the effective frequency bands for various attacks under changeable constraints, within which the successful adversarial perturbations can reduce the accuracy of the model rapidly. Through the proposed quantitative comparison between the intensities of the distribution of both successful and unsuccessful perturbations, we conclude that within the effective frequency bands, the distribution of successful perturbations has larger intensity upon most occasions, thus misleading the model.
- We associate the characteristics of successful adversarial examples in the frequency domain with the space occupied by the objects that belong to the ground truth classes, which is a noticeable difference among the three datasets. By exploiting the rules we found, it is possible to establish the defensive measure from the perspective of the frequency domain by adopting the properties of the datasets or usage scenarios as the prior information, but providing high-performance universal defense is still a challenge.

2 Related Work

Various viewpoints have been introduced to understand the adversarial examples and explore how they mislead the DNNs. Szegedy *et al.* [19] argued that those adversarial examples were rarely observed in the test set due to the extremely low probability, while they were actually dense and thus could be found in every test case. Goodfellow *et al.* [5] illustrated that the infinitesimal changes to the input of a simple linear model could accumulate to one large change to the output due to the sufficient dimensionality. Moosavi-Dezfooli *et al.* [11] associated the robustness of DNNs to the curvature of decision boundaries.

The counter-intuitive phenomenon brought by adversarial examples arouses the discussion about the gap in the visual information processing between humans and machines. Intuitively, human visual sensitivity for the different frequency components of the images can be various. As a result, analyzing adversarial examples from the frequency perspective provides a possible way to explore the robustness of DNNs [22]. Wang *et al.* [21] found that the CNN could make correct predictions using only high-frequency counterparts of images, which were not perceivable to humans. They attempted to exploit the high-frequency components of images to explain the trade-off between the accuracy and the robustness of CNNs. Yin *et al.* [23] demonstrated that adversarial perturbations generated towards a naturally trained model concentrated on the high-frequency domain, while after adversarial training, those perturbations became more low-frequency.

In addition to exploring the distribution of target features of adversarial attacks, several works focused on improving the strength of adversarial examples by finding perturbations in different frequency bands. Guo *et al.* [6] illustrated that adversarial directions might occur in high density in the low-frequency subspace of images. Therefore, finding adversarial perturbations in the low-frequency domain could result in improving the query efficiency of attacks. Besides, low-frequency perturbations were showed to be highly effective against defended models [16]. On the other hand, performing universal attacks on middle and high frequency bands could balance the fooling rates and perceptiveness [4].

In the literature related to analyzing adversarial examples in the frequency domain, proposed views align well with the local empirical observations. However, these views can be contradictory to each other. Finding adversarial perturbations in low-frequency [6] and high-frequency bands [4], as mentioned above, are examples that are not consistent well with each other. Besides, a single dataset and a small number of attack methods with limited norms of constraints are used in previous works, which results in weak consistency of existing illustrations. Therefore, a comprehensive analysis of adversarial examples in the frequency domain on multiple datasets and diverse attack methods with changeable constraints are urgently required to address the limitations of existing works.

3 Methodology

We first define the basic notations used in this paper. $\mathcal{F} : x \in \mathbb{R}^{d\times d} \rightarrow z \in \mathbb{R}^k$ is defined as a neural network which takes x as an input and outputs logits z, where k is the number of classes. We denote the ℓ_p norm as $\|\cdot\|_p$, and $p \in \{2, \infty\}$ is considered in this paper. The image x that can be correctly classified as its ground truth label y will be attacked to generate corresponding adversarial example x^{adv}. Let $v = f(x)$ denote the Discrete Fourier Transform (DFT) of x and $f(\cdot)^{-1}$ represent the inverse DFT (IDFT), where $v \in \mathbb{C}^{d\times d}$ and $v(i,j)$ represents the value of v at position (i,j). Low-frequency components are shifted to the center when we visualize the frequency spectra of adversarial perturbations.

3.1 Adversarial Attack Methods

We adopt untargeted white- and black-box attacks in this paper, due to targeted attacks may make biases on obtained perturbations when targets are specified. The principles of six used attacks are illustrated as follows:

FGSM Attack. Fast Gradient Sign Method (FGSM) [5] focuses on efficiently generating adversarial examples. By using the gradients of the loss function $\mathcal{L}(x,y;\mathcal{F})$, pixels of the original example are modified to increase the loss in a single step. Formally, FGSM Attack can be expressed as:

$$x^{adv} = \text{clip}\{x + \epsilon \cdot sign(\nabla_x \mathcal{L}(x,y;\mathcal{F}))\}, \tag{1}$$

where ϵ is the constraint that ensures the ℓ_∞ perturbation is small enough to be undetectable, and the clip function forces x^{adv} to be a legitimate image.

BIM Attack. Basic Iterative Method (BIM) [8] is an iterative variant of FGSM, which follows the update rule:

$$x_0^{adv} = x,\ x_{n+1}^{adv} = \text{project}\{x_n^{adv} + \alpha \cdot sign(\nabla_x \mathcal{L}(x_n^{adv}, y; \mathcal{F}))\}, \tag{2}$$

where α is the step size, the number of iterations n is set to be $\min(\epsilon+4, 1.25\epsilon)$, and the project function keeps x_{n+1}^{adv} residing in both ℓ_∞ ϵ-neighbourhood of the original image x and the image value range.

PGD Attack. Compared with BIM, Projected Gradient Descent (PGD) [10] has more iterations and performs random starts as the initialization to improve the diversity. It is a strong first-order adversary that can be expressed as:

$$x_0^{adv} = \text{clip}(x + \mathcal{S}),\ x_{n+1}^{adv} = \text{project}\{x_n^{adv} + \alpha \cdot sign(\nabla_x \mathcal{L}(x_n^{adv}, y; \mathcal{F}))\}, \tag{3}$$

where $\mathcal{S} \in \mathbb{R}^{d \times d}$ is the random vector which is chosen from the uniform distribution of $[-\epsilon, \epsilon]$, the clip function makes x_0^{adv} stay in the image value range, and the project function keeps the generated adversarial example within in both ℓ_∞ ϵ-neighbourhood of the original image and the image value range.

DeepFool Attack. The aim of DeepFool Attack [13] is to compute a minimal ℓ_2 perturbation for the target image. This method starts from the original image and calculates the vector, leading the image to step over the decision boundary of the approximated polyhedron iteratively.

CW Attack. The untargeted version of Carlini & Wagner (CW) Attack [2] uses a new loss function to maximize the distance between the ground truth class y and the most-likely class outside of y, which can be expressed as:

$$\mathcal{L}_{CW}(x, y; \mathcal{F}) = \max(\mathcal{F}(x)_{(y)} - \max_{i \neq y} \mathcal{F}(x)_{(i)}, -\kappa), \tag{4}$$

where $\mathcal{F}(x)_{(t)}$ represents the output logit of class t and κ encourages the solver to find the adversarial example that decreases the original class's prediction probability with high confidence. The ℓ_2 perturbation δ is optimized as follows:

$$x^{adv} = x + \arg\min_\delta \{c \cdot \mathcal{L}_{CW}(x + \delta, y; \mathcal{F}) + \|\delta\|_2^2\}, \tag{5}$$

where c is a constant found by the binary search and an Adam optimizer can be used to effectively solve this optimization problem.

Boundary Attack. Boundary Attack [1] starts with the image that is already adversarial, which can be achieved by sampling each pixel of the initial image from a uniform distribution. Furthermore, a random walk is performed to keep the adversarial image in the adversarial region and decrease the distance towards the clean image simultaneously. In this way, the minimal ℓ_2 perturbation is found.

3.2 Frequency-Based Analysis Methods

Distribution of Adversarial Perturbations. Inspired by [23], we visualize the distribution of successful adversarial perturbations in the frequency domain to understand adversarial examples by adopting

$$v_{dis}^{sec} = \sum \frac{|f(x_{sec}^{adv} - x)|}{\|x_{sec}^{adv} - x\|} \Big/ num_{sec}, \tag{6}$$

where num_{sec} is the number of adversarial examples than can mislead the target model successfully. For the 3-channel input image, DFT and the norm calculation will be performed in each channel separately.

Normalization is used to visualize the distribution of adversarial perturbations produced by different attack methods under various constraints. Since different attack algorithms result in different successful adversarial examples on the same dataset for the target model, the norms and numbers of perturbations are considered in Eq. (6) to avoid the biases among the obtained distribution brought by the differences in quantities and contents of different successful adversarial perturbations.

Effectiveness of Different Frequency Bands of Adversarial Perturbations. To explore how different frequency bands of successful adversarial perturbations influence the prediction results of models, we adopt

$$v_l = Mask_{low}^r(f(x_{sec}^{adv} - x)), \tag{7}$$

$$v_h = Mask_{high}^r(f(x_{sec}^{adv} - x)), \tag{8}$$

to preserve low-frequency components v_l and high-frequency components v_h of the transformed perturbation respectively.

To be specific, $Mask_{low}^r$ and $Mask_{high}^r$ can be seen as the low-pass filter and high-pass filter respectively to preserve the corresponding parts of the transformed perturbations. Let (c_n, c_m) denote the centroid, and $Mask^r$ operation is formally defined as:

$$\begin{aligned} Mask_{low}^r(v(i,j)) &= \begin{cases} v(i,j), & \text{if} d((i,j),(c_n,c_m)) \le r \\ 0, & \text{otherwise} \end{cases}, \\ Mask_{high}^r(v(i,j)) &= \begin{cases} 0, & \text{if} d((i,j),(c_n,c_m)) \le r \\ v(i,j), & \text{otherwise} \end{cases}, \end{aligned} \tag{9}$$

where $d(\cdot)$ quantifies the distance between two positions, which is set as Euclidean distance, and r is the predefined radius. Furthermore, successful adversarial examples are reconstructed by performing IDFT on certain frequency bands of perturbations and adding them to original images. Inputting those reconstructed images to the model can help with figuring out which frequency band of perturbations mainly results in reducing the accuracy. The process mentioned above can be expressed as:

$$\mathcal{F}(x + f^{-1}(Mask^r(f(x_{sec}^{adv} - x)))). \tag{10}$$

It should be noted that the DFT, mask operation and IDFT of 3-channel adversarial perturbations is performed in each channel respectively, and then three 1-channel filtered perturbations are connected to be added to the original images.

Quantitative Analysis on Intensity. After verifying which frequency band of perturbations makes main contributions to the false predictions of the network, i.e. low-frequency band or high-frequency band, we attempt to figure out the differences between the distribution of successful and unsuccessful adversarial perturbations generated by various attacks within their concrete effective frequency bands on three datasets.

At first, we illustrate the concept of the effective frequency band. As mentioned before, the clean images are added to the low- or high-frequency parts of perturbations preserved by the predefined radius r to form the reconstructed images. The area specified by the pair of radii (r_h, r_l) that leads to the accuracy of the network against the reconstructed images drop rapidly from a high value acc_{r_h} (e.g., 90%) to a relatively low value acc_{r_l} (e.g., 50%) is referred as the effective frequency band. It should be noted that when the low-frequency band of information has the main effect on reducing the accuracy, $r_l > r_h$, while $r_l < r_h$ when high-frequency components mainly lead to the decrease of the accuracy.

The distribution of successful perturbations v_{dis}^{sec} and the distribution of unsuccessful ones v_{dis}^{unsec} are obtained using the same way described in Eq. (6) respectively. Then the values reside within the effective frequency band (r_h, r_l) are preserved discretely in k areas. When the low-frequency components play a leading role in reducing the accuracy, the preservation can be expressed as:

$$\begin{aligned} v_{dis}^{sec,k} &= Mask_{low}^{r_l-k+1}(v_{dis}^{sec}) - Mask_{low}^{r_l-k}(v_{dis}^{sec}), \\ v_{dis}^{unsec,k} &= Mask_{low}^{r_l-k+1}(v_{dis}^{unsec}) - Mask_{low}^{r_l-k}(v_{dis}^{unsec}), \end{aligned} \tag{11}$$

where $k = 1, 2, \cdots, r_l - r_h$. If high-frequency components of perturbations mainly result in the false predictions, the preservation can be expressed as:

$$\begin{aligned} v_{dis}^{sec,k} &= Mask_{high}^{r_l+k-1}(v_{dis}^{sec}) - Mask_{high}^{r_l+k}(v_{dis}^{sec}), \\ v_{dis}^{unsec,k} &= Mask_{high}^{r_l+k-1}(v_{dis}^{unsec}) - Mask_{high}^{r_l+k}(v_{dis}^{unsec}), \end{aligned} \tag{12}$$

where $k = 1, 2, \cdots, r_h - r_l$.

We propose an evaluation method to compare the intensities of the distribution of both successful and unsuccessful adversarial perturbations within the effective frequency band. We first calculate the proportion of the pixels of the successful perturbation distribution that have higher values in every discrete area, and then allocate coefficients to these items according to the resulting decrease of the accuracy. The evaluation method is formally defined as:

$$score = \sum_{k=1}^{|r_h - r_l|} \frac{p_k}{q_k} \times \frac{\Delta acc_k}{acc_{r_h} - acc_{r_l}}, \tag{13}$$

where p_k is the number of positions where $v_{dis}^{sec,k}(i,j) > v_{dis}^{unsec,k}(i,j)$ in the k-th area, q_k is the number of pixels in the k-th area, and Δacc_k is the decrease of accuracy brought by the k-th area of perturbations. A higher score indicates successful perturbations within effective frequency band have higher intensities.

4 Results and Analyses

4.1 Experimental Setup

Datasets. The MNIST database [9] contains a training set of 60000 examples and a test set of 10000 examples, which are all 28 × 28 grey-scale images with handwritten digits of numbers 0–9. There are 50000 training images and 10000 test images on CIFAR-10 [7], which are all 32 × 32 RGB images in 10 classes. ILSVRC2012 [15] is a large dataset which chooses RGB images in 1000 classes from ImageNet [3] dataset. A small subset of the validation set on ILSVRC2012 will be used in this paper, which is briefly referred to as ImageNet, and each image is resized to 299 × 299 × 3 to be input to the network.

Models. For the MNIST classification task, we use two convolutional layers followed by a fully connected hidden layer. Each convolutional layer is followed by a 2×2 max-pooling layer. WideResNet [24] is adopted for the CIFAR-10 classification task. The architectures, selected hyper-parameters and training approaches of both models are identical to [10]. We achieve 99.22% accuracy on MNIST, and 93.81% accuracy on CIFAR-10. For the complex dataset ImageNet, we use the pretrained Inception-v3 network [18] provided by Keras and it achieves 77.9 % top-1 accuracy and 93.7% top-5 accuracy.

Attacks. Six mainstream attack methods, which can be divided into two categories, are applied in this paper. The first one attempts to increase the loss to mislead the model, *i.e.* FGSM, BIM, and PGD attacks. Perturbations generated by this strategy are constrained in ℓ_∞-norm. The second one pursues minimal perturbations, *i.e.* DeepFool, CW and Boundary attacks, which are ℓ_2-norm and are calculated by using Foolbox [14]. Pixel values of images on MNIST and CIFAR-10 are resized to $[0, 1]$, while the ones on ImageNet are resized to $[-1, 1]$ according to the request of using the pre-trained model. Specific constraints chosen for different attack methods and the numbers of used images on each dataset are shown in Table 1.

Table 1. Constraints and numbers of used images of attacks on each dataset.

Dataset	Attack method	Constraint	Number of images
MNIST	FGSM, BIM, PGD	0.1, 0.2, 0.3	10000
	DeepFool, CW, Boundary	2	10000
CIFAR-10	FGSM, BIM, PGD	2/255, 4/255, 8/255	10000
	DeepFool, CW, Boundary	0.5	1000
ImageNet	FGSM, BIM, PGD	2/255, 4/255, 8/255	1000
	DeepFool, CW, Boundary	3	500

4.2 Analysis on MNIST

Distribution of Adversarial Perturbations. As illustrated in Fig. 1(a) and (b), we visualize the distribution of adversarial perturbations generated by various attacks under different constraints on MNIST in the frequency domain, where the red represents higher intensity, while the blue means lower intensity. It can be seen that adversarial perturbations generated by FGSM, BIM, and PGD attacks all concentrate on the low-frequency domain. With the increase of ℓ_∞-constraints, BIM, and PGD attacks concentrate more on a low-frequency domain, which is implied by the extension of the deep red area in the centers of the frequency spectra in Fig. 1(a). Nevertheless, the distribution of perturbations generated by the FGSM attack changes very little, which may be because FGSM is a one-step attack and the positions of attacked pixels hardly change.

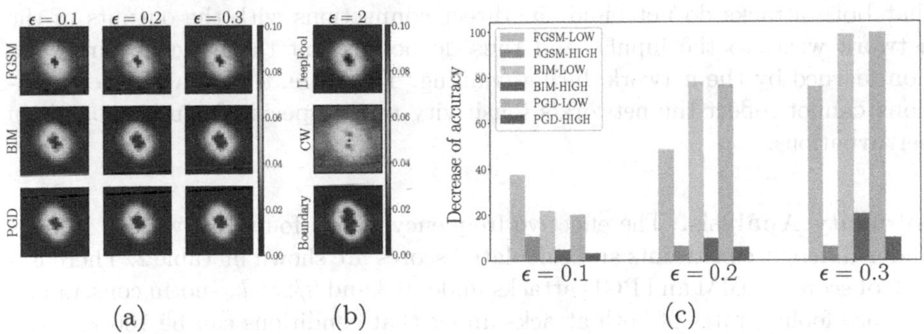

Fig. 1. The distribution of successful adversarial perturbations generated by FGSM, BIM, and PGD attacks on MNIST is depicted in the leftmost image and the distribution of the ones generated by DeepFool, CW and Boundary attacks is shown in the middle. The rightmost image shows the decrease of accuracy brought by two frequency bands of perturbations produced by FGSM, BIM, and PGD attacks on MNIST.

When it comes to DeepFool, CW, and Boundary attacks, we do not change the constraints because they belong to the strategy that finds the minimal perturbations. The ℓ_2-constraint is set to guarantee the imperceptibility. It is shown in Fig. 1(b) that all the perturbations are low-frequency as well. Compared with the other two attacks, the CW attack generates relatively more high-frequency perturbations, because it tends to find the perturbations that modify the outlines of digits instead of the images' backgrounds.

Decrease of Accuracy. Low frequency and high frequency are two relative concepts, and it is hard to specify a constant radius to separate images on each dataset. As a result, we change the radius from zero to the maximum value to separate the low- and high-frequency components of perturbations, and add the filtered perturbations to the original images to obtain the decrease of accuracy brought by those perturbations. Then we choose a proper radius according to the size of the image to show experimental results. On MNIST, results obtained when $r = 8$ are depicted in Fig. 1(c). It is shown that low-frequency components mainly contribute to the decrease of accuracy while high-frequency components have a subtle influence on launching successful attacks on MNIST, which is consistent with distribution of adversarial perturbations shown in Fig. 1. The degree of decrease of accuracy is proportional to the intensity of the attack.

The decrease of accuracy results from low- and high-frequency components of DeepFool perturbations are 37.31% and 7.77% respectively. We can know that low-frequency components still play a leading role in reducing the accuracy. An exciting phenomenon emerges when we separate perturbations produced by CW and Boundary attacks: neither low-frequency components nor high-frequency components reduce the accuracy. In other words, adversarial perturbations of both attacks are out of operation after the separation in the frequency domain. This phenomenon also exists on the rest two datasets. It may be attributed to that both attacks do not build the direct connections with the outputs of the network w.r.t. to the inputs, and thus do not exploit the frequency information learned by the network during training. Therefore, the obtained perturbations cannot reflect the network's sensitivity to the specific frequency bands of perturbations.

Intensity Analysis. The effective frequency bands found for various attacks under different constraints and calculated scores are shown in Table 2. There is a lack of scores of BIM and PGD attacks under 0.3 and 8/255 l_∞-norm constraints, because fooling rates of both attacks under that conditions can be 100%.

On MNIST, acc_{r_h} is set to be 95%, and acc_{r_l} is set to be 65%. Table 2 illustrates that the pixels of successful perturbation distribution have higher intensities within effective frequency bands, which can be seen as a reason that those perturbations are equipped with the ability to mislead the model. While for PGD attack constrained in 0.1 l_∞-norm constraint, the score is less than 0.5, and it may be attributed to the area divided by the r_l does not strictly belong to low-frequency area. Unsuccessful perturbations can attack the area other than the low-frequency area harder, i.e., the image's background.

Table 2. The effective frequency bands and results of intensity comparison on three datasets.

Dataset	MNIST				CIFAR-10				ImageNet			
Attack	Constraint	r_h	r_l	Score	Constraint	r_h	r_l	Score	Constraint	r_h	r_l	Score
FGSM	0.1	3	7	0.69	2/255	19	15	0.72	2/255	13	31	0.48
	0.2	4	7	0.72	4/255	19	15	0.72	4/255	11	25	0.61
	0.3	3	6	0.54	8/255	20	16	0.80	8/255	9	21	0.60
BIM	0.1	5	10	0.50	2/255	18	15	0.70	2/255	18	40	0.41
	0.2	4	6	0.77	4/255	19	16	0.56	4/255	17	35	0.48
PGD	0.1	5	10	0.36	2/255	18	15	0.65	2/255	19	41	0.45
	0.2	4	6	0.52	4/255	19	16	0.53	4/255	19	38	0.49
DeepFool	2	4	7	0.54	0.5	20	16	0.89	3	48	105	0.57

4.3 Analysis on CIFAR-10

Distribution of Adversarial Perturbations. The properties of the distribution of successful adversarial perturbations on CIFAR-10 are pretty different from those on MNIST. As shown in Fig. 2(a), adversarial perturbations generated by FGSM, BIM, and PGD attacks mainly concentrate on high-frequency domains. Compared with the distribution of perturbations produced by FGSM, which still hardly changes when the predefined constraints enlarge, target features attacked by BIM and PGD attacks gradually concentrate on the low-frequency domain, leading to both center and margin of the frequency spectra being high-value. This may be attributed to that both attacks find perturbations iteratively, leading to the reduction of differences between adjacent pixels, and the generated perturbations contain more low-frequency information. Besides, the intensity of the central area of perturbation distribution produced by the

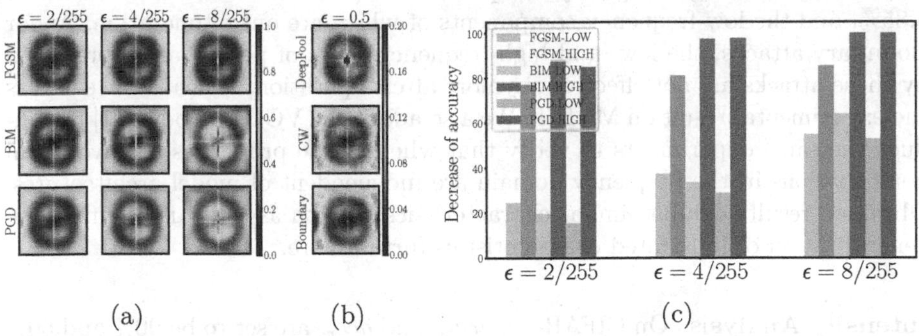

Fig. 2. The distribution of successful adversarial perturbations generated by FGSM, BIM, and PGD attacks on CIFAR-10 is depicted in the leftmost image and the distribution of the ones generated by DeepFool, CW and Boundary attacks is shown in the middle. The rightmost image shows the decrease of accuracy brought by two frequency bands of perturbations produced by FGSM, BIM, and PGD attacks on CIFAR-10.

PGD is lower than the one produced by the BIM, which results from the noises introduced by random initialization at the beginning of the PGD attack.

Adversarial perturbations generated by DeepFool, CW, and Boundary attacks also exhibit high-frequency characteristics, which are shown in Fig. 2(b). Compared with CW and Boundary attacks which mainly focus on attacking high-frequency components, the DeepFool attack generates perturbations on extremely low-frequency domains. The ℓ_2-norm of distortions caused by DeepFool attacks are at least 3 times bigger than that caused by CW and Boundary, which leaves that its perturbations contain more low-frequency information.

Decrease of Accuracy. Here we show the results when $r = 10$ is used to filter the low- and high-frequency components of adversarial perturbations on CIFAR-10. It can be seen from Fig. 2(c) that high-frequency parts of adversarial perturbations have a superior effect on misleading the model. With the increase of ℓ_∞-constraints of FGSM, BIM, and PGD attacks, the gap of effectiveness on deceiving the model between low- and high-frequency components generated by each attack is narrowed. When $\epsilon = 8/255$, both frequency bands of perturbations of each attack can reduce the accuracy by more that 50%.

Low- and high-frequency components of perturbations generated by the DeepFool attack reduce the accuracy by 18.47% and 80.33%, respectively. While it can be seen from Fig. 2(b) that the central spectrum of perturbations generated by DeepFool has an extremely high value, the effectiveness of the most low-frequency components is minimal, which may because models are hardly sensitive to the additive perturbations in lowest frequencies [23]. The experimental results also imply this phenomenon that the accuracy remains above 99% until radius $r > 3$ in most cases when the model is attacked by low-frequency parts of adversarial perturbations added to the original images. The decrease of accuracy brought by high-frequency components of perturbations of CW attack is 5.85%, and the low-frequency components of which are out of operation. As for Boundary attacks, the low- and high-frequency parts of perturbation produced by these attacks are not effective anymore after separation, which is the same as the experimental result on MNIST. We also adopt the VGG16 model [17] to conduct the same experiments to verify that whether the properties of adversarial perturbations in the frequency domain are independent of model architectures. Obtained results exhibit similar characteristics in both aspects and confirm the generalization of illustrated characteristics furthermore.

Intensity Analysis. On CIFAR-10, acc_{r_h} and acc_{r_l} are set to be 90% and 50% respectively. Evaluation results in Table 2 show that unsuccessful perturbation distribution exhibits extremely lower intensity compared with the successful perturbation distribution in some cases. Successful perturbation distribution gets a score of over 0.5 in every situation, which is assumed by us to be an explanation for the failure of unsuccessful perturbations on cheating the model.

4.4 Analysis on ImageNet

Distribution of Adversarial Perturbations. Figure 3(a) shows that the distribution of successful adversarial perturbations generated by FGSM, BIM, and PGD attacks mainly concentrates on low-frequency domains, similar to that on MNIST. However, compared with the BIM attack that constantly attacks low-frequency components, the PGD attack gradually increases the intensity of the attack on high-frequency components. In our experiments, besides more iteration steps, PGD attack introduces the random initialization at the beginning of the attack. To figure out which one is the main factor that leads to the difference mentioned above, we force both attacks to have the same numbers of iterations under changeable constraints and obtain similar results, which implies that the random initialization can be the reason for changing the distribution of adversarial perturbations generated by the PGD attack.

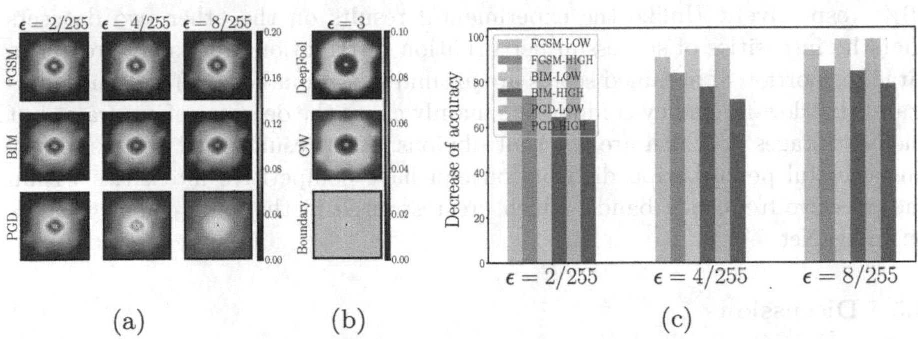

Fig. 3. The distribution of successful adversarial perturbations generated by FGSM, BIM, and PGD attacks on ImageNet is depicted in the leftmost image and the distribution of the ones generated by DeepFool, CW and Boundary attacks is shown in the middle. The rightmost image shows the decrease of accuracy brought by two frequency bands of perturbations produced by FGSM, BIM, and PGD attacks on ImageNet.

It is shown in Fig. 3(b) that DeepFool and CW attacks exhibit the property of taking the low-frequency components as the target features. In contrast, the adversarial perturbations produced by Boundary attack are uniformly distributed across the frequencies. After comparing the attacked and clean images, we find that the Boundary attack modifies attacked pixels in each image to a similar extent. However, the CW and DeepFool attacks mainly target at attacking concrete objects of each image.

Decrease of Accuracy. Because the image's resolution is large, we do not change the radius continuously but choose several radii values to record the decrease of accuracy instead. The experimental results obtained when $r = 80$ are depicted in Fig. 3(c). Low-frequency components are the main factors that reduce the accuracy of the model, while high-frequency components have an obvious effect on misleading the model as well, which may be attributed to that the accuracy of model on original images is not high enough, leaving the model vulnerable to both frequencies of perturbations. The results explain the fact that both of the works [4,6] promote the performance of attacks while finding the adversarial examples in different frequency bands. With the increase of constraints, the gap between the effectiveness of low- and high-frequency components is narrowed, which is similar to the trend exhibiting on CIFAR-10.

Low-frequency components of perturbations produced by DeepFool reduce the accuracy of the model by 36.50%. However, the high-frequency components of perturbations result in a 13.87% decrease of accuracy, which is consistent with the distribution of perturbations shown in Fig. 3(b). As to CW and Boundary attacks, the perturbations are still out of operation after the separation.

Intensity Analysis. On ImageNet, acc_{r_h} and acc_{r_l} are set to be 90% and 50%, respectively. Unlike the experimental results on the other two datasets that the intensities of successful perturbation distribution are visibly greater, a large proportion of obtained scores are around 0.5. From Fig. 2(c) we can understand that low-frequency components mainly cause the decrease of accuracy, but the advantages of which are not that obvious. As a result, both successful and unsuccessful perturbation distribution can have competitive intensities within the effective frequency bands, which are restricted in the low-frequency bands on ImageNet.

4.5 Discussion

For the successful adversarial perturbations produced by the attack strategy that increases the loss to mislead the model, with the improvement of the constraints of attacks, the distribution of perturbations generated by FGSM has no apparent changes. Adversarial perturbations generated by BIM and PGD attacks gradually concentrate on the low-frequency domain during this procedure, while the random initialization introduced by PGD attack may change this trend as the proportion of the background in the image enlarges. For the successful adversarial perturbations generated by the attack strategy that pursues the minimal perturbations, because of the vast differences among the principles of attacks, they do not have unified laws on three datasets while maintaining the same concentration area with the ones generated by the first attack strategy.

We find that the high-frequency components of successful adversarial perturbations have a minimal effect on MNIST. While on CIFAR-10, high-frequency components play a leading role in fooling models. Both low- and high-frequency components of successful perturbations on ImageNet can obviously affect models, and low-frequency ones have superior performance. Although the characteristics of successful adversarial perturbations vary from dataset to dataset, the evaluation results illustrate that they have larger attack intensities within different effective frequency bands compared with the unsuccessful ones in most situations, which can be seen as the factor that misleads the model successfully.

Since the distribution of successful adversarial perturbations varies from dataset to dataset, we assume that it can be associated with how much space the object occupies in the images. Attacking the objects in the images makes pixel values of corresponding parts of perturbations change dramatically due to the complex outlines and texture of objects, which means high-frequency information will remain in the perturbations. The backgrounds in the images are relatively smooth, and attacks tend to change backgrounds to a small extent to remain imperceptible, which leaves low-frequency information.

Figure 4 illustrates three pairs of clean images and successfully attacked images and visualizes the DFT of their perturbations. It is shown that, the number is placed in the center of the image on MNIST and takes up less than a quarter of space of the image. Consequently, there is more low-frequency information in the perturbation. On CIFAR-10, the object takes up almost all the space in the image, resulting in much high-frequency information in the perturbation. While on ImageNet, most of successfully attacked images have more information of backgrounds rather than objects, thus leaving perturbations concentrating on the low-frequency domain. Such visualized analyses also validate our hypothesis.

Fig. 4. The DFT of perturbations on MNIST, CIFAR-10 and ImageNet. In each 3 × 1-image part, the first one is the clean image, the second one is the adversarial image, and the last one is the DFT of corresponding adversarial perturbation.

Consequently, taking the properties of datasets or some specific usage scenarios where the sizes of objects are relatively constant may enhance the robustness of deep learning models from the perspective of the frequency domain. However, the universal defense that achieves high accuracy on both adversarial and clean images remains challenging.

5 Conclusion and Further Work

In this paper, six classic attack methods and three commonly used datasets are adopted to comprehensively analyze and evaluate the adversarial examples in the frequency domain. We explore the effectiveness of different frequency bands of perturbations through a quantitative analysis. Our significant findings successfully explain the contradictory parts of previous works. Evaluation results show that compared with the distribution of unsuccessful adversarial perturbations, the distribution of successful ones exhibits higher intensity within the effective frequency bands, providing an explanation for launching attacks successfully.

Besides addressing the limitations of existing theories, we obtain a better understanding of adversarial examples from the frequency domain perspective and provide an idea on enhancing the robustness of models by considering the frequency properties of datasets in advance. Further work is required to conduct analyses on adversarially trained models from the frequency domain perspective and build efficient and effective defense by exploiting the frequency properties.

Acknowledgement. This research is supported by the National Key Research and Development Program of China (2020AAA0107702), the National Natural Science Foundation of China (62006181, 61822309, 61703301, 61822309, 61773310, U20A20177, U1736205) and the Shaanxi Province Key Industry Innovation Program (2021ZD LGY01-02).

References

1. Brendel, W., Rauber, J., Bethge, M.: Decision-based adversarial attacks: reliable attacks against black-box machine learning models. arXiv preprint arXiv:1712.04248 (2017)
2. Carlini, N., Wagner, D.: Towards evaluating the robustness of neural networks. arXiv preprint arXiv:1608.04644 (2016)
3. Deng, J., Dong, W., Socher, R., et al.: ImageNet: a large-scale hierarchical image database. In: 2009 IEEE conference on CVPR, pp. 248–255. IEEE (2009). https://doi.org/10.1109/CVPR.2009.5206848
4. Deng, Y., Karam, L.J.: Frequency-tuned universal adversarial attacks. arXiv preprint arXiv:2003.05549 (2020)
5. Goodfellow, I.J., Shlens, J., Szegedy, C.: Explaining and harnessing adversarial examples. arXiv preprint arXiv:1412.6572 (2014)
6. Guo, C., Frank, J.S., Weinberger, K.Q.: Low frequency adversarial perturbation. arXiv preprint arXiv:1809.08758 (2018)
7. Krizhevsky, A., Hinton, G., et al.: Learning multiple layers of features from tiny images (2009)
8. Kurakin, A., Goodfellow, I., Bengio, S.: Adversarial examples in the physical world. arXiv preprint arXiv:1607.02533 (2016)
9. LeCun, Y.: The MNIST database of handwritten digits (1998)
10. Madry, A., Makelov, A., Schmidt, L., et al.: Towards deep learning models resistant to adversarial attacks. arXiv preprint arXiv:1706.06083 (2017)
11. Moosavi-Dezfooli, S.M., Fawzi, A., Fawzi, O., et al.: Analysis of universal adversarial perturbations. arXiv preprint arXiv:1705.09554 (2019)
12. Moosavi-Dezfooli, S.M., Fawzi, A., Fawzi, O., et al.: Universal adversarial perturbations. arXiv preprint arXiv:1610.08401 (2016)
13. Moosavi-Dezfooli, S.M., Fawzi, A., Frossard, P.: DeepFool: a simple and accurate method to fool deep neural networks. arXiv preprint arXiv:1511.04599 (2015)
14. Rauber, J., Zimmermann, R., Bethge, M., et al.: Foolbox native: fast adversarial attacks to benchmark the robustness of machine learning models in PyTorch, TensorFlow, and JAX. J. Open Source Softw. **5**(53), 2607 (2020). https://doi.org/10.21105/joss.02607 https://doi.org/10.21105/joss.02607
15. Russakovsky, O., Deng, J., Su, H., et al.: ImageNet large scale visual recognition challenge. arXiv preprint arXiv:1409.0575 (2014)

16. Sharma, Y., Ding, G.W., Brubaker, M.: On the effectiveness of low frequency perturbations. arXiv preprint arXiv:1903.00073 (2019)
17. Simonyan, K., Zisserman, A.: Very deep convolutional networks for large-scale image recognition. arXiv preprint arXiv:1409.1556 (2014)
18. Szegedy, C., Vanhoucke, V., Ioffe, S., et al.: Rethinking the inception architecture for computer vision. arXiv preprint arXiv:1512.00567 (2015)
19. Szegedy, C., Zaremba, W., Sutskever, I., et al.: Intriguing properties of neural networks. arXiv preprint arXiv:1312.6199 (2013)
20. Tanay, T., Griffin, L.: A boundary tilting persepective on the phenomenon of adversarial examples. arXiv preprint arXiv:1608.07690 (2016)
21. Wang, H., Wu, X., Huang, Z., Xing, E.P.: High frequency component helps explain the generalization of convolutional neural networks. arXiv preprint arXiv:1905.13545 (2019)
22. Wang, Z., Yang, Y., Shrivastava, A., et al.: Towards frequency-based explanation for robust CNN. arXiv preprint arXiv:2005.03141 (2020)
23. Yin, D., Lopes, R.G., Shlens, J., et al.: A Fourier perspective on model robustness in computer vision. arXiv preprint arXiv:1906.08988 (2019)
24. Zagoruyko, S., Komodakis, N.: Wide residual networks. arXiv preprint arXiv:1605.07146 (2016)
25. Zhang, H., Yu, Y., Jiao, J., et al.: Theoretically principled trade-off between robustness and accuracy. arXiv preprint arXiv:1901.08573 (2019)

Multimedia Security

Compressive Sensing Image Steganography via Directional Lifting Wavelet Transform

Zan Chen[1], Chaocheng Ma[1], Yuanjing Feng[1(✉)], and Xingsong Hou[2]

[1] College of Information Engineering, Zhejiang University of Technology, Hangzhou, China
fyjing@zjut.edu.cn

[2] Department of Information and Communications Engineering, Xi'an Jiaotong University, Xi'an, China

Abstract. This paper proposes a deep-based compressive sensing (CS) image steganography scheme that inserts the plain image into the directional lifting wavelet transform (DLWT) domain of the carrier image. For the data hiding processing, we exploit two logistic maps to create the measurement matrix and simulated noise respectively, which are used to randomly under-sample and diffuse the plain image to obtain the secret image. Then, we employ singular value decomposition (SVD) to embed the secret image into the DLWT domain of the carrier image, which generates the meaningful stego image. For the data extraction, we introduce the deep-based CS reconstruction algorithm to enhance the quality of the reconstructed image. Experimental results show that the proposed approach maintains security while achieving a high quality of the stego image and the reconstructed image.

Keywords: Image steganography · DLWT · Compressive sensing

1 Introduction

Image steganography performs an essential role in the data security field [1]. It refers to hiding sensitive plain images into carrier images such that the existence of the sensitive data is hard to sense. One of the main pursuits of image steganography is to embed more sensitive information with less damage to the quality of the carrier image at the encoder side and extract the secret image as accurately as possible at the decoder side [2]. Broadly, the image steganography methods can be classified into two categories, namely the spatial domain approaches and transform domain approaches [3].

Spatial domain approaches directly modify the intensity value of the carrier image to hide information. For instance, the authors in [4] designed a least significant bit (LSB) replacement method to embed the plain image bits. The authors in [5] exploited the brightness, edges, and texture masking for data hiding, which can avoid abrupt changes in edge areas of the carrier image. The authors in [6]

D. Gao et al. (Eds.): ICICS 2021, LNCS 12919, pp. 93–109, 2021.
https://doi.org/10.1007/978-3-030-88052-1_6

added chaotic mapping with pseudo-random keys to improve the security of the image. However, for the above approaches, too much hiding information would affect the perceptual characteristics of the carrier image to a certain extent [3]. Besides, spatial domain steganography approaches are more sensitive to noise or attacks [7].

Transform domain approaches can remedy these problems by embedding the information into the high-frequency subband of the carrier image. It can improve the perceptual characteristics of the carrier image [8]. Meanwhile, the plain image hiding in the transform domain is robust to noise and attacks [3]. However, the hiding capacity of the transform domain steganography heavily relies on the sparse representation ability of the adopted transform domain. Most existing schemes still utilize traditional transform methods, such as discrete cosine transform (DCT) [9], and discrete wavelet transform (DWT) [8].

Existing transform domain steganography approaches have two faults. First, they do not exploit directional information of image texture, which limits the hiding capacity of the carrier image. Second, they directly hide the plain image without considering the encrypting and compressing process, which limits the security of the hidden sensitive information. To solve the above problems, we propose a compressive sensing (CS) image steganography scheme based on directional lifting wavelet transform (DLWT). First, we randomly under-sample and diffuse the plain image by a measurement matrix and simulated noise, which are generated from two logistic maps. Then, we employ singular value decomposition (SVD) to embed the secret image into the DLWT domain of the carrier image, which generates the meaningful stego image. For the data extracting process, we further introduce a deep-based CS reconstruction algorithm to enhance the quality of the reconstructed plain image. Our scheme improves the visual quality of the reconstruction while ensuring security.

The rest of this paper is organized as follows. In Sect. 2, we introduce the background of the transform domain and compressive sensing for image steganography. Section 3 presents the proposed image steganography scheme including steganography based on DLWT-SVD, encryption based on chaotic system, and reconstruction based on Deep-based CS. Section 4 evaluates the experiential results of visual quality analysis and encryption performance analysis. Section 5 offers conclusions.

2 Background

2.1 Steganography in the Transform Domain

Steganography in the transform domain has developed rapidly due to its advantages of efficiency and robustness. In [8], the authors proposed an image steganography technology based on single-level DWT, which can resist various image attacks. The authors in [7] proposed a steganography method based on integer wavelet transform (IWT) with SVD to increases the robustness of protecting stego images from geometrical and image processing attacks. In [10], the authors proposed an efficient DWT steganography scheme of using diamond encoding to enhance security and reduce the distortion added to the stego image. The authors in [9] proposed a steganography technology to embed two bits of the compressed form of the secret message by utilizing the difference between the DCT coefficients. However, all these methods only exploit the traditional sparse transformation without considering the optimal direction of texture or edge. Thus, we introduce DLWT into the image steganography to enhance the capacity of the carrier image to hide information.

2.2 Compressive Sensing for Steganography

Compressive sensing (CS) is a technique for reconstructing a sparse or compressible signal from under-sampling measurements, i.e.

$$y = \Phi x, \tag{1}$$

where x is the original signal, y is the CS measurement, and Φ refers to the measurement matrix [11,12]. By utilizing compressive sensing, image compression and encryption can be achieved simultaneously [13,14]. For the properties of privacy-preserving, easy-implement, and robustness to noise, many researchers have exploited CS in steganography schemes. For example, in [15], the authors proposed a CS steganography scheme by using the characteristic of dimensional reduction and random projection. The authors in [16] proposed a CS image steganography scheme based on the combination of framelet and SVD to improve the imperceptibility of the carrier image. The authors in [17] proposed an efficient and robust CS image coding and transmission scheme, which can reconstruct the original image accurately while still supporting error resilience. The authors in [18] proposed a visually safe CS image steganography scheme, in which a plain image is transformed into wavelet coefficients and confused by a zigzag path. However, all these schemes utilize traditional hand-crafted CS reconstruction algorithms such as BCS-SPL [19] and NLR-CS [20], limiting the qualities of the reconstructed plain images.

3 Proposed Image Steganography Scheme

Figure 1 shows an overview of the proposed image steganography scheme. For the data hiding processing, we use the logistic map with initial values $\{k_1^0, k_2^0\}$ to obtain the measurement matrix Φ for under-sampling and simulated noise η for diffusion, which are used to generate the secret image S from the original plain image x_p. Then, we apply DLWT-SVD on the carrier image x_c to embed the secret image S and obtain the stego image x_s. For the data extraction, we apply the inverse processing of the data hiding to obtain the secret image $\tilde{S}$. Then, we adopt a deep-based CS algorithm to reconstruct the final original image x_r from the secrete image $\tilde{S}$. In the following subsections, we detail DLWT-SVD, encryption, and deep-based CS reconstruction algorithm used in the proposed image steganography scheme.

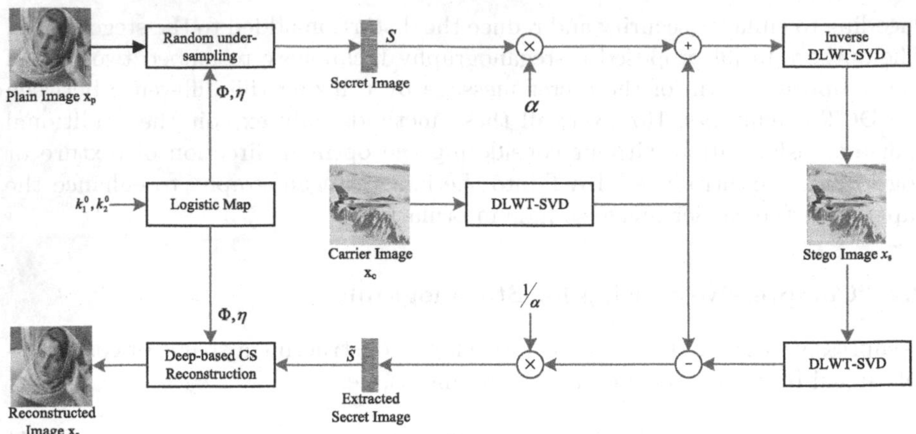

Fig. 1. Overview of proposed image steganography scheme.

3.1 Steganography Based on DLWT-SVD

Note that the conventional DWT does not exploit the geometrical structure of images efficiently, which leads to the limited capability of sparse representation. Thus, we apply DLWT on the steganography scheme to reduce the energy of the high-subband coefficients (LH, HL, HH) of the carrier image and achieves more energy clustering in the low-frequency coefficient (LL). We can generate the above three high-pass subbands LH, HL, and HH and a low-pass subband LL by applying the one-level decomposition of DLWT on the carrier image. Figure 2 shows the quadtree segmentation and optimal direction of DLWT for Barbara. As observed from the figure, DLWT technology can effectively segment the image and predict the image pixels along the best direction of local areas.

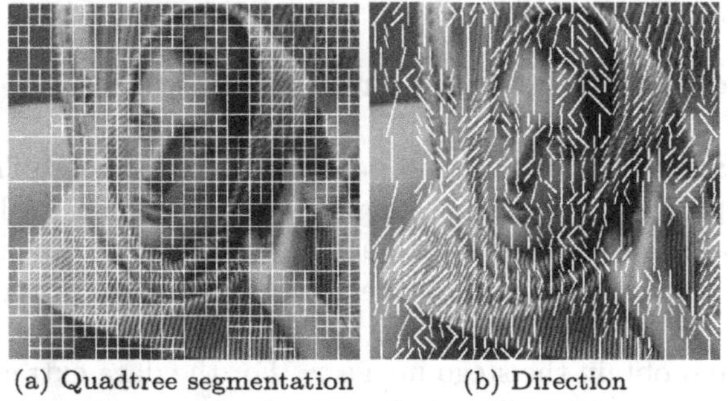

(a) Quadtree segmentation (b) Direction

Fig. 2. Quadtree segmentation and optimal direction of DLWT for Barbara.

For data hiding processing, we first apply DLWT (denoted as F) on the carrier image x_c to generate the transformation coefficients C_{LL}, C_{LH}, C_{HL}, C_{HH},

$$[C_{LL}, C_{LH}, C_{HL}, C_{HH}] = \mathrm{F}(x_c). \tag{2}$$

Then, we decompose the C_{HH} by SVD, which can be represented as

$$C_{HH} = U \cdot \Sigma \cdot V^T, \tag{3}$$

where Σ is a diagonal matrix, and U and V^T are two unitary matrices.

Instead of directly hiding the original plain image, we compress and encrypt the plain image first, and embed the secret image into the carrier image. The details of the encryption based on the chaotic system are presented in the next subsection.

To insert the secret image S into the carrier image x_c, we modify Σ by the following equation

$$\Sigma_M = \Sigma + \alpha \cdot S, \tag{4}$$

where α is a gain factor to adjust the intensity of the secret image S. We further update Eq. 3 by replacing Σ with Σ_M and keeping U and V^T unchanged, which can generate a new high-subband $\tilde{C}_{HH}$, i.e.

$$\tilde{C}_{HH} = U \cdot \Sigma_M \cdot V^T = U \cdot (\Sigma + \alpha \cdot S) \cdot V^T. \tag{5}$$

Next, we apply the inverse DLWT (F^{-1}) to generate the stego image x_s,

$$x_s = \mathrm{int}(\mathrm{F}^{-1}(C_{LL}, C_{LH}, C_{HL}, \tilde{C}_{HH})), \tag{6}$$

where int is the integer operation necessary for image storage and transmission. For the data extraction process, we can obtain the secret image $\tilde{S}$ from the stego image x_s by reversing the above DLWT-SVD at the decoding side. Note that $\tilde{S}$ is slightly different from the S for the integer operation of image pixel values. By utilizing the deep-based CS reconstruction algorithm described below, we can recover the plain image x_r from the extracted secret image $\tilde{S}$.

3.2 Encryption Based on Chaotic System

To achieve both compression and encryption, we utilize a random under-sampling to generate the secret image S as follows

$$S = \mathrm{int}(\Phi x_p + \eta), \tag{7}$$

where $\Phi \in R^{m \times n}$ $(m << n)$ is the measurement matrix for sampling and η is the simulated noise for diffusion. Both of them are generated by the logistic map with initial values, i.e. secret keys $\{k_1^0, k_2^0\}$. In this way, the encoder and decoder side can synchronize the noisy CS measurement only by transferring the secret keys $\{k_1^0, k_2^0\}$. Specifically, we generate the chaotic sequence using the logistic map formulated as follows

$$\begin{cases} k_1^{i+1} = (a-1)k_1^i - a(k_1^i)^2, \\ k_2^{i+1} = (b-2)k_2^i - b(k_2^i)^2, \end{cases} \tag{8}$$

in which we set the ranges of the secret keys as $k_1^0 \in (0, 0.5)$, $k_2^0 \in (0, 0.5)$. From Eq. 8, we obtain two pseudo-random sequences $\{k_1^i\}$ and $\{k_2^i\}$, which can further generate the measurement matrix and simulated noise. For measurement matrix Φ, we can obtain the value of Φ at position (i, j) by the following equation

$$\Phi(i,j) = \begin{cases} 0, \, k_1^{(i-1)n+j+c} \leq 0.5 \\ 1, \, k_1^{(i-1)n+j+c} > 0.5 \end{cases}, \tag{9}$$

where $c = 1500$. By discarding the former 1500 values, we can obtain a more random measurement matrix. For the value of simulated noise at position i, we can obtain as follow

$$\eta(i) = 255 * (k_2^{i+c} - 0.5). \tag{10}$$

Finally, we can obtain the noise-like secret image S by Eq. 7, which can maintain the security and achieve the compression of the stego image simultaneously.

3.3 Reconstruction Based on Deep-Based CS

We need to reconstruct the plain image from the extracted secret image. Thus, the adopted CS reconstruction algorithm is crucial for the quality of the final reconstructed image. Since Φ is rank deficient, there exists more than one solution to satisfy Eq. 7. Thus, we solve this ill-posed inverse problem by introducing some deep-based prior as follows

$$x_{\mathrm{r}} = \arg\min_{x_{\mathrm{r}}} ||\tilde{S} - \Phi x_{\mathrm{r}}||, \;\; s.t. \; x_{\mathrm{r}} \in C, \tag{11}$$

where C is the natural image set, and $\tilde{S}$ is the secret image extracted from the stego image x_{s}. We utilize a deep learning network to describe the natural image set C and solve the optimal matter of Eq. 11 by a proximal gradient descent algorithm

$$x_{\mathrm{r}}^k = P(x_{\mathrm{r}}^{k-1} - \tilde{v}^{k-1}), \tag{12}$$

$$\tilde{v}^{k+1} = \Phi^{\mathrm{T}}(\Phi x_{\mathrm{r}}^k - \tilde{S}) + \frac{1}{m}\tilde{v}^k \,\mathrm{div}P(x_{\mathrm{r}}^{k-1} - \tilde{v}^{k-1}), \tag{13}$$

where k is the iteration step, and $P(\cdot)$ is a proximal operator that can project the image into the set C. And we utilize a pre-trained end-to-end denoising convolutional network same as [21] to emulate the $P(\cdot)$. Besides, we estimate the expected value of $\mathrm{div}(\cdot)$ same as [22]

$$\mathrm{div}P(p) = \frac{\eta}{\epsilon}(P(p + \epsilon\eta) - P(p)), \tag{14}$$

where $\epsilon = \frac{||\tilde{p}^k||_\infty}{m}$ and $\eta \sim N(0, I)$. We set the initial guesses of x_r^0 and $\tilde{v}^0$ both to be zeros. Finally, we can obtain the reconstructed plain image x_{r} by iterating Eqs. 13 and 12, which can highly improve the overall performance of the CS steganography scheme [23].

Fig. 3. The first two rows illustrate eight plain images, i.e. Barbara, Boats, Cameraman, Foreman, House, Lena, Monarch and Parrots. The last row illustrates four carrier images, i.e. Sailboats, Bridge, Peppers and Jet.

4 Experimental Results

In our experiences, we test eight plain images of size 256 × 256 and four carrier images of size 256 × 256 as shown in Fig. 3. We performed all training and testing on a PC with an Intel i5 CPU and an Nvidia RTX 2070 GPU. The designed networks are trained with PyTorch over 60 epochs. And we use the same dataset and parameters as in [24] for training. To verify the effectiveness of our steganography scheme, We analyze the metrics of visual quality and encryption performance respectively.

4.1 Visual Quality Analysis

In this section, we conduct several simulations to study the performance improvement from DLWT-SVD, deep-based CS reconstruction algorithm, and CS sampling rates, respectively. For convenience, we denote $\mathrm{PSNR_{ste}}$ as the PSNR results between stego images x_s and carrier images x_c, and $\mathrm{PSNR_{rec}}$ as the PSNR results between reconstructed images x_r and plain images x_p. By adjusting the gain factor α in Eq. 4, we can realize to generate stego images and reconstructed plain images with different $\mathrm{PSNR_{ste}}$ and $\mathrm{PSNR_{rec}}$. The visual quality can reflect undetectability and reconstructed image quality can indicate the amount of original information obtained. There exists a trade-off between the quality of the stego image and the reconstructed image. We provide the $\mathrm{PSNR_{rec}}$-$\mathrm{PSNR_{ste}}$ curve (R-S curve) to reflect the steganography efficiency.

Effect of DLWT. We evaluate the effect of DLWT-SVD for steganography by replacing the adopted transformation in Eq. 2 from DLWT to DWT and remaining other settings unchanged. Figure 4 (a) shows the R-S curves of DLWT-SVD

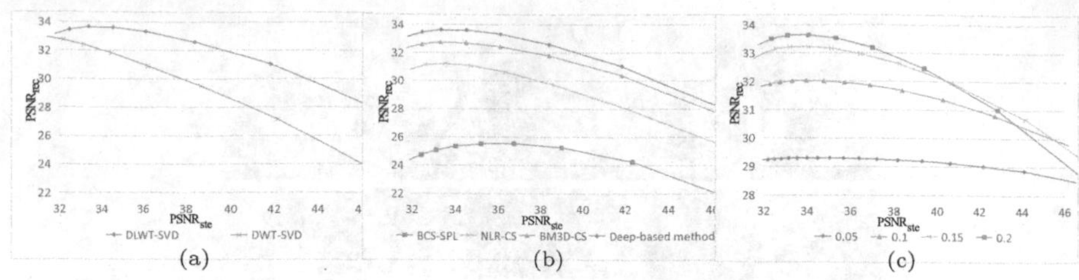

Fig. 4. Average PSNR (dB) comparison: (a) DLWT-SVD and DWT-SVD; (b) different CS reconstruction algorithms; (c) different sampling rates.

and DWT-SVD, where the X-axis and Y-axis represent the average PSNR_{ste} of four carrier images and average PSNR_{rec} of four eight plain, respectively. From Fig. 4, we can see that the curve of DLWT-SVD is above that of DWT-SVD, bringing about 2 dB improvement at PSNR_{ste} of 36 dB. And DLWT-SVD brings more PSNR_{rec} improvement as PSNR_{ste} increases.

Effect of the Deep-Based CS Reconstruction. To test the improvement of the adopted deep-based CS algorithm for image steganography, we further apply some traditional hand-crafted CS algorithms to reconstruct the plain image from the secret image. Especially, we test BM3D-CS [25], NLR-CS [20], and BCS-SPL [19], in which BM3D-CS achieves state-of-the-art performance before the popularity of deep learning technology. Figure 4 (b) shows the R-S curves when using different CS reconstruction algorithms, where the sampling rate is fixed at 0.25. We can see that the deep-based method can deeply improve the R-S curve, bring about 1.0 dB improvement over the image steganography using BM3D-CS. These hand-crafted methods are computationally costly and frequently include difficult-to-determine hand-selected parameters. Deep learning regularisation learns realistic image priors from a large amount of training data, resulting in improved performance.

Effect of Sampling Rate. The sampling rate (SR) defined as $\frac{m}{n}$ is one of the important settings to affect the R-S curve, as it determines the size of the secret image embedded into the carrier image. Figure 4 (c) illustrates the R-S curves of the proposed image steganography at different sampling rates. We can see that R-S curve at a high sampling rate changes dramatically with PSNR_{ste}, while the curve at a low sampling rate is relatively stable.

Qualitative Evaluation. Also, we compare the qualitative results of reconstructed plain images using DLWT-SVD and DWT-SVD. Figure 5 shows the reconstructed image (Parrots) with different quality of the stego image (Jet), in which the first, second and last row represent reconstructed plain images for DLWT-SVD, reconstructed plain images for DWT-SVD, and the corresponding

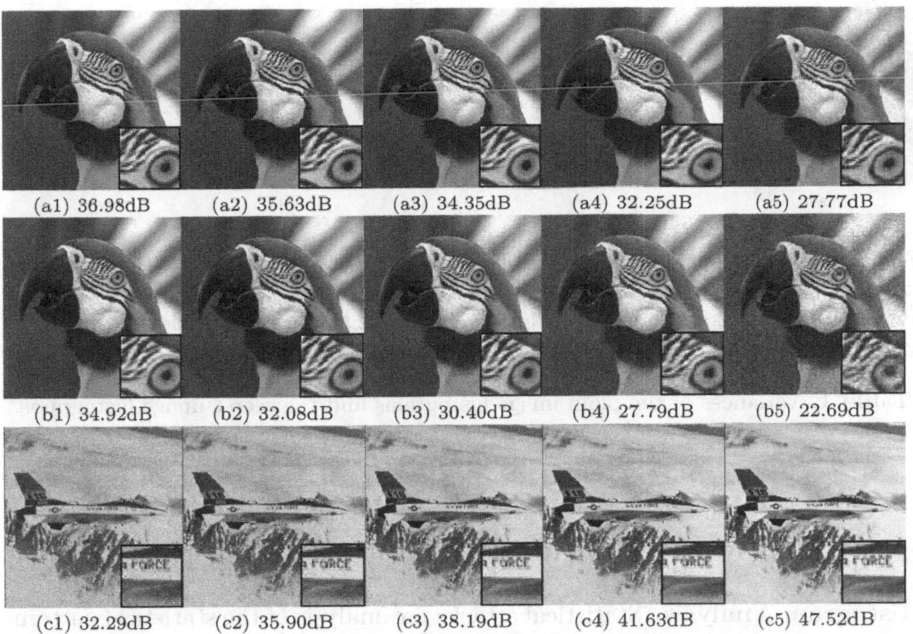

Fig. 5. Different visualization of the reconstructed plain images and stego images by adjusting α in Eq. 4. (a1)–(a5) are reconstructed plain images hided by DLWT-SVD; (b1)–(b5) are reconstructed images hided by DWT-SVD; (c1)–(c5) are the corresponding stego images.

stego images, respectively. We can see that our scheme using DLWT-SVD preserves the textures of the plain image well, whereas the scheme using DWT-SVD produces some noise artifacts.

4.2 Encryption Performance Analysis

In this section, we verify the security of the secret image by providing the analysis on the secret key, histogram, correlation of adjacent pixels, information entropy, noise attack, and randomness.

Secret Key Analysis. Brute force attacks crack a system by trying possible keys. Key sensitivity can reflect the security performance of the secret image, and high key sensitivity means that the scheme has strong resistance to brute force attacks. The secret keys in our scheme contain two initial values of the logistic map used to generate the random measurement matrix and the simulated noise.

Besides, we show the effect of key sensitivity on the reconstructed image in Fig. 6. As can be seen from the figure, when the key is changed slightly at the decoding side, the reconstructed image will present useless information similar to noise. Therefore, only a completely correct key can obtain the desired information of the original image.

Fig. 6. Key sensitivity analysis: (a) plain image; (b) secret image at 0.25 bpp when stego image is Jet; (c) reconstructed image with a correct key; (d-e) reconstructed image with wrong keys, in which only one element of the secret keys deviates $\epsilon = 2^{-52}$ from the correct keys.

Table 1. Variances of the plain image histograms and the secret image histograms.

Images	Barbara	Boats	Cameraman	Foreman	House	Lena	Monarch	Parrots
Plain image	29761	102311	110973	137339	300755	40483	40207	71508
Secret image	81.5781	66.3750	74.7969	71.6406	74.3984	67.4453	74.8047	76.1484

Histogram Analysis. Statistical attacks use analysis of the statistical patterns of secret images and plain images to break the system. Histogram reflects the distribution of image pixel values, thus attackers cannot find useful information from a uniform histogram of the secret image. Figure 7 illustrates the histograms of the three test plain images, corresponding secret images, carrier images, and stego images. From which we can see that the histograms of the secret images are uniform distribution, and the histograms of the carrier images and stego images are similar. Besides, the variance can well represent the uniformity of the image histogram with the following formula:

$$var(H) = \frac{1}{2l}\sum_{i=1}^{l}\sum_{j=1}^{l}(h_i - h_j)^2, \tag{15}$$

where h_i denotes the number of pixels with a gray value equal to i, $l = 255$ is the greyness level, and H is the vector of the image histogram. Table 1 shows the variance of the histograms, which quantificationally indicates that the secret

Table 2. Correlation coefficients of the plain image and secret image.

Image		Horizontal	Vertical	Diagonal
Plain image		0.9688	0.9528	0.9306
Secret image	0.10	−0.0168	0.0102	−0.0061
	0.15	0.0027	0.0065	0.0062
	0.20	−0.0086	−0.0026	−0.0085
	0.25	0.0006	0.0060	0.0020

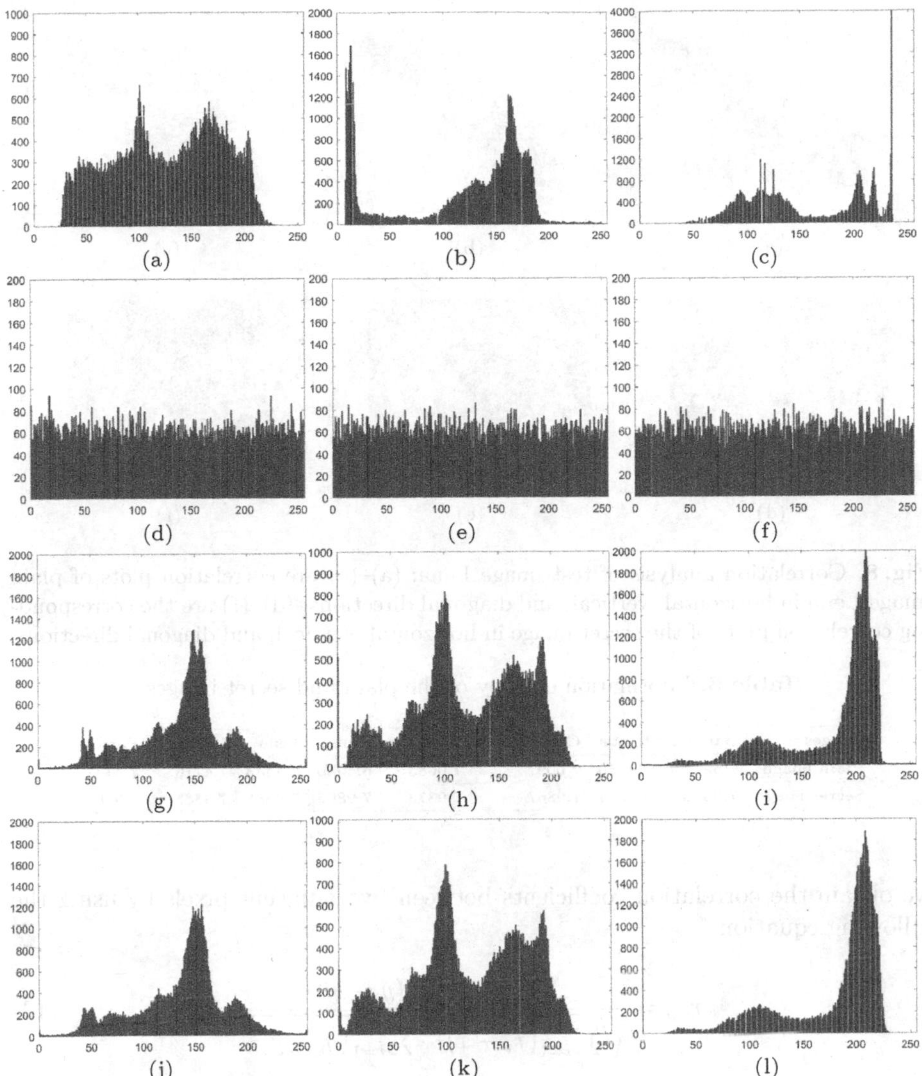

Fig. 7. Histogram analysis: (a)–(c) are the histograms of the test plain images Barbara, Cameraman and Foreman; (d)–(f) are the histograms of the secret images; (g)–(i) are the histograms of the carrier images Sailboats, Peppers and Jet; (j)–(l) are the histograms of the stego images.

images of our scheme have desirable uniformity. Therefore, our scheme can resist statistical attacks effectively.

Correlation of Adjacent Pixels. To measure the degree of similarity between adjacent pixels in the horizontal, vertical, and diagonal directions respectively,

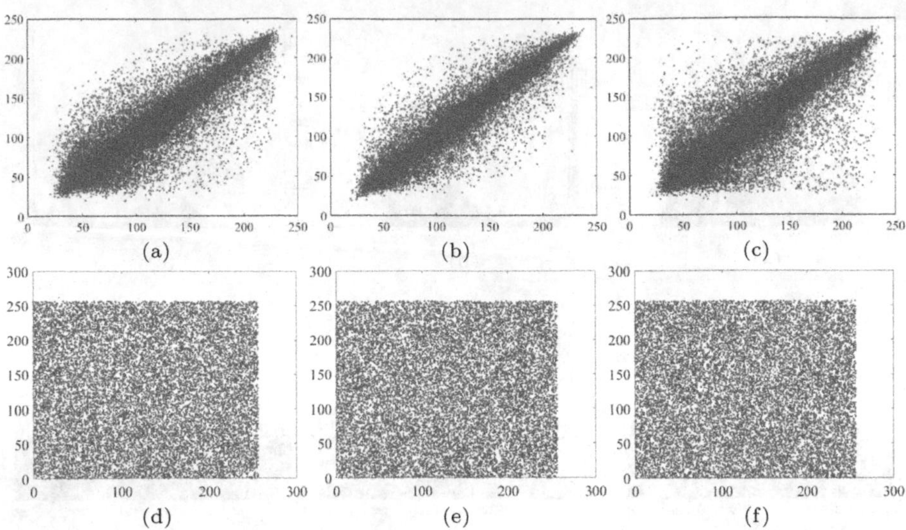

Fig. 8. Correlation analysis of test image Lena: (a)–(c) are correlation plots of plain image Lena in horizontal, vertical, and diagonal directions; (d)–(f) are the corresponding correlation plots of the secret image in horizontal, vertical, and diagonal directions.

Table 3. Information entropy of the plain and secret images.

Images	Barbara	Boats	Cameraman	Foreman	House	Lena	Monarch	Parrots
Plain image	7.5252	7.1456	7.0097	7.0083	6.4930	7.4443	7.4716	7.4141
Secret image	7.9852	7.9884	7.9867	7.9873	7.9866	7.9881	7.9865	7.9863

we obtain the correlation coefficients between two adjacent pixels by using the following equation

$$r_{xy} = \frac{\sum_{i=1}^{N}(x_i - \bar{x})(y_i - \bar{y})}{\sqrt{\sum_{i=1}^{N}(x_i - \bar{x})^2 \cdot \sum_{i=1}^{N}(y_i - \bar{y})^2}}, \tag{16}$$

where $\bar{x} = \frac{1}{N}\sum_{i=1}^{N} x_i$ and $\bar{y} = \frac{1}{N}\sum_{i=1}^{N} y_i$. Table 2 shows the correlation coefficients of the plain image and the secret image. From the table, we can obtain that the plain image has a high correlation in the horizontal, vertical, and diagonal directions, while the correlation coefficient of the secret image is close to 0. Figure 8 reflects the resistance of the secret image to statistical attacks by comparing the correlation coefficients of Lena's plain image with the secret image.

Information Entropy. Entropy attacks can crack a system through a trivial linear combination of the "stale" packets collected or intercepted. Information

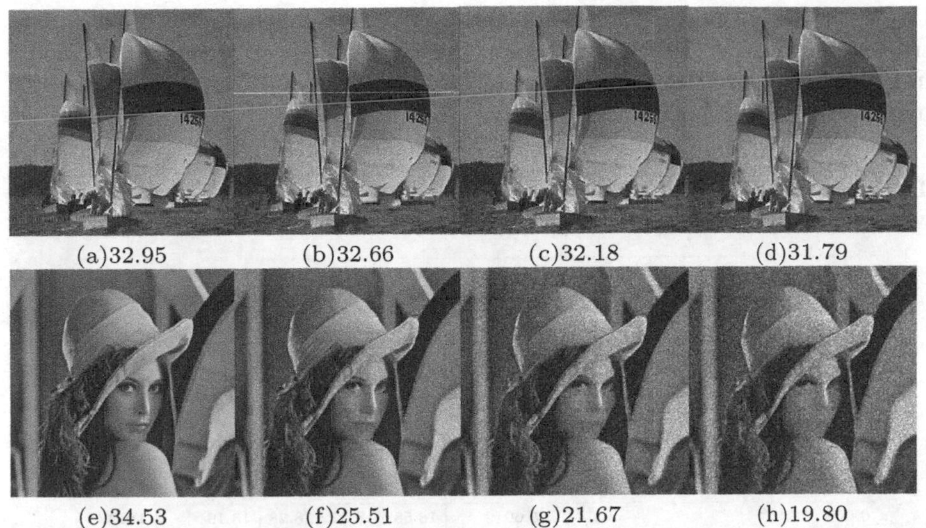

Fig. 9. Noise attack: (a) stego image Sailboats; (b–d) stego image Sailboats with Gaussian noise of intensities 0.0001%, 0.0003%, 0.0005%; (e) reconstructed image Lena without noise; (f–h) reconstructed image of (b–d).

entropy is to measure the randomness of an image, formulated as follows:

$$H(x) = -\sum_{i=1}^{n} p(x_i) \log_2 p(x_i), \tag{17}$$

where n is the total number of pixels, and $p(x_i)$ is the probability of x_i. The information entropy of different plain and secret images are shown in Table 3, from which one can see that each information entropy of plain images is relatively small, while the entropy values of secret images are close to 8. The results show that the secret images of our scheme can resist the entropy attack.

Noise Attack. Decoding errors are likely to result from an additive white Gaussian noise assault on the stego image. Considering the stego image may be contaminated by noise during transmission, we add Gaussian noise of different intensities, i.e. 0.0001%, 0.0003%, and 0.0005% to the stego image Sailboats for testing. Figure 9 depicts the reconstructed Lena with $\mathrm{PSNR_{rec}}$ are 34.53 dB, 25.51 dB, 21.67 dB, and 19.80 dB, respectively. The results demonstrate that our steganography scheme can resist noise attacks to some extent.

In addition, we compare our method with other steganography methods, including LSB [6], LSB-PVD [26], DWT [8], DCT [27], IWT [28], IWT-SVD [29]. LSB is a method of embedding the secret data directly into the least significant bit of the carrier image, and LSB-PVD uses LSB substitution to embed the secret data bits into the upper left corner pixel of every 2 × 2 pixel block [3].

DWT, DCT, IWT, and IWT-SVD are methods for embedding secret data into transform domains. Table 4 lists the average PSNR results of the reconstructed image with different Gaussian noise intensities, from which we can see that our method achieves higher PSNR results.

Table 4. PSNR (dB) of the reconstructed image for image steganography methods with different Gaussian noise intensities.

Gaussian noise intensity (‰)	Methods						
	LSB	LSB-PVD	DWT	DCT	IWT	IWT-SVD	Proposed
0.001	17.72	5.60	25.93	26.03	24.31	24.24	**26.24**
0.002	12.09	5.57	23.67	23.68	22.65	22.57	**24.04**
0.003	8.98	5.65	22.27	22.25	21.51	21.42	**22.66**
0.004	7.29	5.64	21.21	21.18	20.61	20.53	**21.62**
0.005	6.37	5.65	20.38	20.33	19.89	19.81	**20.80**
0.006	5.87	5.68	19.68	19.63	19.27	19.19	**20.11**
0.007	5.57	5.65	19.11	19.04	18.75	18.67	**19.53**
0.008	5.44	5.60	18.58	18.52	18.28	18.19	**19.02**
0.009	5.39	5.48	18.12	18.06	17.85	17.78	**18.57**

Randomness Analysis. We test the randomness on the secret images by NIST SP800-22 [30]. Table 5 shows the secret results of the NIST SP800-22 test suite of Cameraman and House. We can see that p-values of 17 metrics all larger than the significance level $\alpha = 0.01$ suggested by NIST, which means that our scheme has a randomness to resist attacks.

Table 5. Secret results of NIST SP800-22 test suite of Cameraman and House.

Statistical test	p-value of Cameraman	p-value of House	Result
Frequency	0.474706	0.295157	SUCCESS
Block frequency (m = 20, 000)	0.921740	0.664308	SUCCESS
Runs	0.089741	0.308369	SUCCESS
Longest runs of ones	0.367556	0.829401	SUCCESS
Rank	0.928664	0.165484	SUCCESS
Spectral DFT	0.599481	0.853537	SUCCESS
Non-overlapping templates (m = 9)	0.520506	0.504029	SUCCESS
Overlapping templates (m = 9)	0.295484	0.984835	SUCCESS
Maurers universal	0.744794	0.759849	SUCCESS
Linear complexity (m = 500)	0.088364	0.088314	SUCCESS
Serial p-value1 (m = 16)	0.719065	0.362367	SUCCESS
Serial p-value2 (m = 16)	0.612280	0.388961	SUCCESS
Approximate entropy (m = 10)	0.266238	0.351563	SUCCESS
Cumulative sums (Forward)	0.830463	0.472380	SUCCESS
Cumulative sums (Reverse)	0.268736	0.212095	SUCCESS
Random excursions (x = −1)	0.422975	0.472099	SUCCESS
Random excursions variant (x = −1)	0.154259	0.624297	SUCCESS

5 Conclusion

This paper proposes an efficient image steganography scheme based on DLWT-SVD and the deep-based CS reconstruction algorithm. We first use the measurement matrix and simulated noise to randomly under-sample and diffuse the plain image to obtain the secret image. Then, we apply DLWT-SVD to embed the secret image into the DLWT domain of the carrier image, which generates the meaningful stego image. For data extracting, we utilize a deep-based CS reconstruction algorithm to recover the original plain image from the secret image. The experimental results indicate that the proposed scheme has the outstanding ability to hide security information in the carrier image while achieving the high quality of the reconstructed plain image.

Acknowledgments. This research was sponsored in part by the National Natural Science Foundation of China (Grant Nos. 62002327, 61976190), and Natural Science Foundation of Zhejiang Province (Grant No. LQ21F020017)

References

1. Hussain, M., Wahab, A.W.A., Idris, Y.I.B., Ho, A.T., Jung, K.H.: Image steganography in spatial domain: a survey. Signal Process.: Image Commun. **65**, 46–66 (2018). https://doi.org/10.1016/j.image.2018.03.012
2. Kadhim, I.J., Premaratne, P., Vial, P.J.: Improved image steganography based on super-pixel and coefficient-plane-selection. Signal Process. **171**, 107481 (2020). https://doi.org/10.1016/j.sigpro.2020.107481
3. Kadhim, I.J., Premaratne, P., Vial, P.J., Halloran, B.: Comprehensive survey of image steganography: techniques, evaluations, and trends in future research. Neurocomputing **335**, 299–326 (2019). https://doi.org/10.1016/j.neucom.2018.06.075
4. Chan, C.K., Cheng, L.: Hiding data in images by simple LSB substitution. Pattern Recogn. **37**(3), 469–474 (2004). https://doi.org/10.1016/j.patcog.2003.08.007
5. Yang, H., Xingming, S., Sun, G.: A high-capacity image data hiding scheme using adaptive LSB substitution. Radioengineering **18**(4), 509–516 (2009)
6. Rajendran, S., Doraipandian, M.: Chaotic map based random image steganography using LSB technique. Int. J. Netw. Secur. **19**(4), 593–598 (2017). https://doi.org/10.6633/IJNS.201707.19(4).12
7. Singh, S., Singh, R., Siddiqui, T.J.: Singular value decomposition based image steganography using integer wavelet transform. In: Advances in Signal Processing and Intelligent Recognition Systems. AISC, vol. 425, pp. 593–601. Springer, Cham (2016). https://doi.org/10.1007/978-3-319-28658-7_50
8. Kumar, V., Kumar, D.: A modified DWT-based image steganography technique. Multimedia Tools Appl. **77**(11), 13279–13308 (2017). https://doi.org/10.1007/s11042-017-4947-8. Kindly note that the References [8] and [27] seems to be same. So we have delete the duplicate reference and renumbered accordingly. Please check and and correct if necessary
9. Attaby, A.A., Ahmed, M.F.M., Alsammak, A.K.: Data hiding inside JPEG images with high resistance to steganalysis using a novel technique: DCT-M3. Ain Shams Eng. J. **9**(4), 1965–1974 (2018). https://doi.org/10.1016/j.asej.2017.02.003

10. Atawneh, S., Almomani, A., Al Bazar, H., Sumari, P., Gupta, B.: Secure and imperceptible digital image steganographic algorithm based on diamond encoding in DWT domain. Multimedia Tools Appl. **76**(18), 18451–18472 (2016). https://doi.org/10.1007/s11042-016-3930-0
11. Chai, X., Wu, H., Gan, Z., Zhang, Y., Chen, Y., Nixon, K.W.: An efficient visually meaningful image compression and encryption scheme based on compressive sensing and dynamic LSB embedding. Opt. Lasers Eng. **124**, 105837 (2020). https://doi.org/10.1016/j.optlaseng.2019.105837
12. Chen, Z., Hou, X., Shao, L., Wang, S.: Revising regularisation with linear approximation term for compressive sensing improvement. Electron. Lett. **55**(7), 384–386 (2019). https://doi.org/10.1049/el.2018.8019
13. Chen, Z., Hou, X., Gong, C., Qian, X.: Compressive sensing reconstruction for compressible signal based on projection replacement. Multimedia Tools Appl. **75**(5), 2565–2578 (2015). https://doi.org/10.1007/s11042-015-2578-5
14. Zhang, B., Xiao, D., Xiang, Y.: Robust coding of encrypted images via 2D compressed sensing. IEEE Trans. Multimedia **23**, 2656–2671 (2020). https://doi.org/10.1109/TMM.2020.3014489
15. Pan, J.-S., Li, W., Yang, C.-S., Yan, L.-J.: Image steganography based on subsampling and compressive sensing. Multimedia Tools Appl. **74**(21), 9191–9205 (2014). https://doi.org/10.1007/s11042-014-2076-1
16. Xiao, M., He, Z.: High capacity image steganography method based on framelet and compressive sensing. In: MIPPR 2015: Multispectral Image Acquisition, Processing, and Analysis, vol. 9811, p. 98110Y (2015). https://doi.org/10.1117/12.2205279
17. Chen, Z., Hou, X., Qian, X., Gong, C.: Efficient and robust image coding and transmission based on scrambled block compressive sensing. IEEE Trans. Multimedia **20**(7), 1610–1621 (2017). https://doi.org/10.1109/TMM.2017.2774004
18. Chai, X., Gan, Z., Chen, Y., Zhang, Y.: A visually secure image encryption scheme based on compressive sensing. Signal Process. **134**, 35–51 (2017). https://doi.org/10.1016/j.sigpro.2016.11.016
19. Mun, S., Fowler, J.E.: Block compressed sensing of images using directional transforms. In: 16th IEEE International Conference on Image Processing, pp. 3021–3024 (2009). https://doi.org/10.1109/ICIP.2009.5414429
20. Dong, W., Shi, G., Li, X., Ma, Y., Huang, F.: Compressive sensing via nonlocal low-rank regularization. IEEE Trans. Image Process. **23**(8), 3618–3632 (2014). https://doi.org/10.1109/TIP.2014.2329449
21. Zhang, K., Zuo, W., Chen, Y., Meng, D., Zhang, L.: Beyond a gaussian denoiser: residual learning of deep CNN for image denoising. IEEE Trans. Image Process. **26**(7), 3142–3155 (2017). https://doi.org/10.1109/TIP.2017.2662206
22. Metzler, C., Mousavi, A., Baraniuk, R.: Learned D-AMP: principled neural network based compressive image recovery. In: Advances in Neural Information Processing Systems, pp. 1772–1783 (2017)
23. Chen, Z., Hou, X., Shao, L., Gong, C., Qian, X., Huang, Y., et al.: Compressive sensing multi-layer residual coefficients for image coding. IEEE Trans. Circuits Syst. Video Technol. **30**(4), 1109–1120 (2020). https://doi.org/10.1109/TCSVT.2019.2898908
24. Chen, Z., Guo, W., Feng, Y., Li, Y., Zhao, C., Ren, Y., et al.: Deep-learned regularization and proximal operator for image compressive sensing. IEEE Trans. Image Process. **30**, 7112–7126 (2021). https://doi.org/10.1109/TIP.2021.3088611

25. Metzler, C.A., Maleki, A., Baraniuk, R.G.: From denoising to compressed sensing. IEEE Trans. Inf. Theory **62**(9), 5117–5144 (2016). https://doi.org/10.1109/TIT.2016.2556683
26. Swain, G.: A steganographic method combining LSB substitution and PVD in a block. Procedia Comput. Sci. **85**, 39–44 (2016). https://doi.org/10.1016/j.procs.2016.05.174
27. Saidi, M., Hermassi, H., Rhouma, R., Belghith, S.: A new adaptive image steganography scheme based on DCT and chaotic map. Multimedia Tools Appl. **76**(11), 13493–13510 (2016). https://doi.org/10.1007/s11042-016-3722-6
28. Wang, H., Xiao, D., Li, M., Xiang, Y., Li, X.: A visually secure image encryption scheme based on parallel compressive sensing. Signal Process. **155**, 218–232 (2019). https://doi.org/10.1016/j.sigpro.2018.10.001
29. Zhu, L., et al.: A robust meaningful image encryption scheme based on block compressive sensing and svd embedding. Signal Process. **175**, 107629 (2020). https://doi.org/10.1016/j.sigpro.2020.107629
30. Bassham, L.E., Rukhin, A.L., Soto, J., et al.: A statistical test suite for random and pseudorandom number generators for cryptographic applications. National Institute of Standards & Technology (2010)

Remote Recovery of Sound from Speckle Pattern Video Based on Convolutional LSTM

Dali Zhu[1,2], Long Yang[1,2], and Hualin Zeng[1,2](✉)

[1] Institute of Information Engineering, Chinese Academy of Sciences, Beijing, China
{zhudali,yanglong,zenghualin}@iie.ac.cn

[2] School of Cyber Security, University of Chinese Academy of Sciences, Beijing, China

Abstract. In the field of security surveillance, remotely acquire the sound signal of the target is an attractive research topic. The research has broad application prospects, such as counter-terrorism, rescue, medical monitoring, and so on. To obtain clear and accurate sound signal of the target, we propose a method based on convolutional LSTM network to recover the sound. The principle of our method consists of two steps. First, we record the speckle images of target remotely. Then we utilize the convolutional LSTM network to extract the subtle movement from speckle images. The results demonstrate that our network is superior to convolutional neural network in the accuracy and efficiency of processing temporal-spatial speckle image data. The influence of different sampling rates on sound extraction is revealed through appropriate experimental settings. In addition, we also reveal the principle that our network has stronger generalization ability than convolutional neural network. Benefit from the powerful generalization ability of the network, our method could perform accurate and robust sound extraction to unseen objects. The excellent performance of our method proves that it is a significant development in the field of remote sound acquisition.

Keywords: Laser speckle images · Speckle movement · Convolutional LSTM · Convolutional neural network · Contactless sound acquisition · Remote sound recovery

1 Introduction

Remotely acquiring sound of the target is a meaningful and challenging research in the field of public security. In recent years, researchers have proposed various methods [4,5,8,18,25] to monitor the target speech remotely, many of which are based on the principle of laser detection. Laser detection is one of the fastest developing technologies recently because of the development of imaging system and laser technology. The main idea of laser detection is to illuminate an object

D. Gao et al. (Eds.): ICICS 2021, LNCS 12919, pp. 110–124, 2021.
https://doi.org/10.1007/978-3-030-88052-1_7

with a laser beam and collect the laser information reflected by the object. When the object is excited by the subtle vibration caused by sound, the laser information we collect contains the vibration characteristics about the sound. With subsequent analysis, we can recover the sound from the collected laser information. Compared with traditional detection methods, laser detection can achieve non-invasive and covert detection, meanwhile, the operation is easy and can be carried out in hundreds of meters away.

At present, there are mainly two methods to realize laser detection: one is Laser Doppler Vibrometer (LDV) [5,8,18] based on photodetector, and the other is speckle image measurement based on image acquisition system. LDV is a non-contact optical technology with high spatial and temporal resolution, and its results are real-time and less dependent on atmospheric conditions. The main disadvantages of LDV are that it is not reference-free, and it can not fulfill the full field detection. To overcome the limitations of LDV, authors of [25] advanced a method based on speckle image measurement. They proved that, with proper optical settings, the speckle image moves in the two-dimensional plane when the object vibrates in space. Tracking the movements of speckle images can recover the motion of the object. It is a full-field and non-contact detection technology without a reference laser. The quality of recovered sound is determined by two factors: the quality of speckle images and the performance of the recovery algorithm. The quality of speckle images is determined by the optical system and imaging sensors, which has been greatly improved by [25]. However, the common recovery algorithms are inefficient, low precision, and vulnerable to noise in speckle images, such as digital image correlation [4,17,19,24], optical flow method [7], convolutional neural networks based method [26], and so on.

To overcome the deficiencies of the above recovery algorithms, we introduce recurrent neural networks (RNN) into the application of sound extraction. In this paper, we propose a deep neural network (model) based on convolutional LSTM [20] to analyze and extract the movement from speckle images and recover the sound that caused the movement. Convolutional neural network (CNN) can extract static features of images well, but it can not capture temporal information from sequence data as RNN. Speckle images are spatiotemporal data, so CNN is not the best choice to extract sound from them. ConvLSTM combines the basic architecture of RNN and CNN, which enables it to extract static spatial features and capture temporal information simultaneously. In the following sections, we will illustrate the powerful performance of our model for sound extraction.

This paper makes two main contributions:

- We introduce ConvLSTM into speckle image processing for the first time and verified its superiority over CNN in the practical application of sound recovery.
- We implement a sound acquisition method based on deep learning technology. The method overcomes many shortcomings of previous methods, and achieves accurate speech extraction with high efficiency and strong robustness.

The Rest of this Paper is Organized as Follows. In Sect. 2, we summarize related works of sound recovery. In Sect. 3, we describe the theory of the speckle image and build our model. Section 4 is about data processing and experiment details. In Sect. 5, we evaluate the performance of our model and discuss the experimental results. Finally, conclusions and further discussions.

2 Related Work

We exploit the ConvLSTM architecture to extract subtle movements from speckle images and recover the sound of the target. This paper connects related works in deep learning, optical technology, and signal processing and uses all these connections to extend traditional methods.

2.1 Optical Methods

Sound derives from mechanical vibration. Objects in the path of sound propagation will be forced to vibrate according to the characteristic of sound. Although the subtle motion of object caused by sound is so small that hard to be measured directly, it can be detected by some elaborate systems. Due to imaging technologies promoted and high-speed cameras available, [25] proposed a novel method to recover sound from secondary speckle patterns. They monitor tiny vibrations by continuously recording the speckle images through the high-speed camera. The sound is recovered by extracting shifts between speckle patterns. Their method has low requirements for the imaging system and optical devices, and its working range can reach several hundred meters. But the extraction algorithm is digital image correlation (DIC) [4,19,24], which is inefficient and resource-consuming with the output of low quality.

Recently, the authors of [2] studied the audio signal recovery algorithms from speckle pattern. Their work allows non-contact vibration measurements with inexpensive devices. The methods they used are efficient except the MIT method [6]. One imperfection of their experiments is that the sampling rate (maximum 886.05 Hz) they used is relatively low compared with the frequency of voice (up 2000 Hz). The other imperfection of their work is that the results lack high accuracy.

[26] proposed a novel convolutional neural network instead of DIC to extract displacement from speckle images. In their experiments, they proved that CNN is superior to DIC in accuracy and reliability, and revealed the potential of CNN in the real-time system. However, CNN inherently lacks the ability to predict and analyze spatiotemporal data, which is necessary to better understand sound and video data.

2.2 Deep Learning Technology

RNN architecture is of great significance to solve many problems involved with temporal sequences in deep learning. One interesting idea in RNN is that it can connect current problems with previous information, for example, using the content of previous frames in a movie to help understand the later content of the movie. This property of RNN makes it especially suitable for spatiotemporal data because the contents of spatiotemporal data are related in time.

As a variant of RNN, Long Short Term Memory (LSTM) [11,13,14,23] is intended to alleviate the long-range dependence problem of RNN. It has been successfully used to perform a variety of sequence learning tasks, such as action recognition [22], video caption [16], speech recognition [3], and so on. The major drawback of LSTM in handling spatiotemporal data (e.g. image, video) is that it can not encode the spatial information of images, because it does not contain convolutional module, which has been proved to be essential for feature extraction from images. Researchers [20] replaced part of the original modules with convolutional modules in LSTM, thus introduced convolutional LSTM (ConvLSTM) to realize the connection of CNN and LSTM in a more concise way. They proved the excellent performance of ConvLSTM than FC-LSTM [9] in precipitation nowcasting.

In order to make full use of spatiotemporal data and exploit the spatial information of speckle images, we will leverage ConvLSTM to extract motion from speckle patterns and finally recover sound signals.

3 Background

In this section, we first introduce the theory of extracting sound from speckle images. Then we present the basics of ConvLSTM network structure, describe the architecture of CNN model and our model.

3.1 Speckle Pattern

The object located in the range of a sound source will produce same vibration as the sound source under the influence of sound. Therefore, by tracking the motion trajectory of the object, we can recover the sound signal. When illuminating an object with a laser, speckle pattern will be observed on the rough surface of the object. The distribution of speckle is determined by the surface roughness and does not change with the distance between the laser and the object. As described in [21,26], the motion of speckle pattern is very sensitive to the movement of the object. The speckle pattern will produce detectable displacement even the object is moved negligibly.

Researchers [25] have proved that under appropriate imaging conditions, the speckle pattern will move with the movement of the object, while the speckle pattern remains unchanged. The relative shift β of speckle pattern is proportional to the change of the spatial position of speckle pattern due to the object vibration. From [15,25], the conversion of object movement to the relative shift β of speckle pattern is as follows, refer to Fig. 1,

$$\beta = \frac{4\pi \tan \alpha}{\lambda} \approx \frac{4\pi\alpha}{\lambda} \quad (1)$$

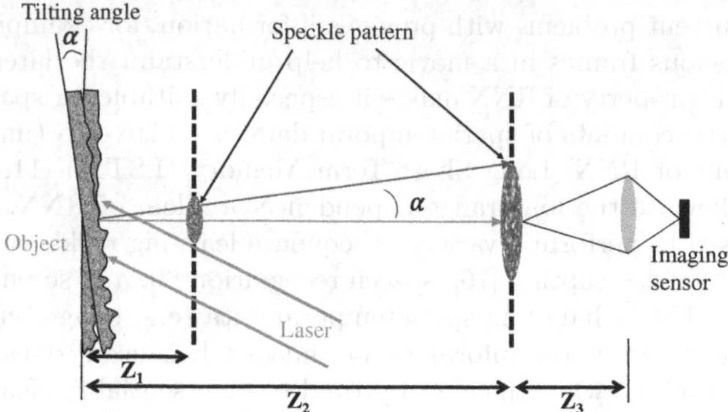

Fig. 1. Theory description. The conversion of object vibration to the displacement of the speckle pattern. In the near field (at position Z_1), the speckle pattern is varied randomly. In the far field (at position Z_2), there is almost no change in speckle pattern, only shift.

where α is the tilting angle of the object, and λ is the wavelength of laser. Since object vibration caused by sound is very small, we can assume that the change in the tilting angle α is small enough, then we obtain a linear proportion between the relative shift and the tilting angle.

Refer to Fig. 2, let I_1 and I_2 be the images captured by high-speed camera at two time consecutively. I_2 could be the shifted speckle image of I_1,

$$I_2 = I_1(x + \Delta x, y + \Delta y), \tag{2}$$

where (x, y) are the image coordinates, and $\Delta x, \Delta y$ are the relative displacements of image I_2 with respect to I_1 in X-axis and Y-axis respectively. By temporal tracking the motion of captured speckle images, β can be recovered, and then the audio signal can be recovered.

3.2 ConvLSTM

An example architecture of ConvLSTM is described in [20]. In this paper, we follow the formulation of ConvLSTM as in [20], the key equations are shown in Eq. (3) below:

$$\begin{aligned}
i_t &= \sigma\left(W_{xi} * \mathcal{X}_t + W_{hi} * \mathcal{H}_{t-1} + W_{ci} \circ \mathcal{C}_{t-1} + b_i\right) \\
f_t &= \sigma\left(W_{xf} * \mathcal{X}_t + W_{hf} * \mathcal{H}_{t-1} + W_{cf} \circ \mathcal{C}_{t-1} + b_f\right) \\
o_t &= \sigma(W_{xo} * \mathcal{X}_t + W_{ho} * \mathcal{H}_{t-1} + W_{co} \circ \mathcal{C}_t + b_o) \\
\mathcal{C}_t &= f_t \circ \mathcal{C}_{t-1} + i_t \circ \tanh(W_{xc} * \mathcal{X}_t + W_{hc} * \mathcal{H}_{t-1} + b_c) \\
\mathcal{H}_t &= o_t \circ \tanh(\mathcal{C}_t)
\end{aligned} \tag{3}$$

where '$*$' denotes the convolution operator, and '$\circ$' denotes the Hadamard product.

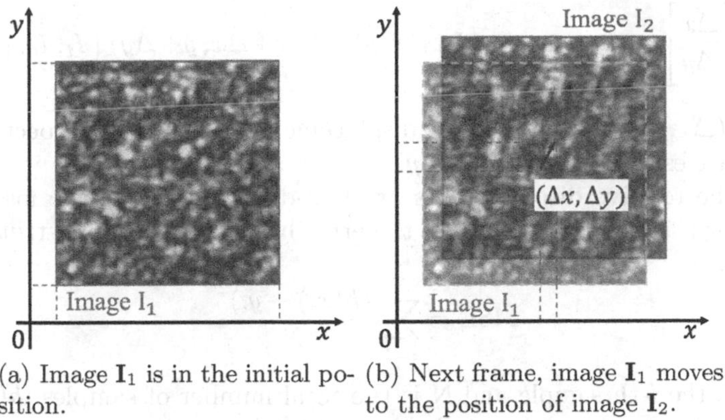

(a) Image $\mathbf{I}_1$ is in the initial position.

(b) Next frame, image $\mathbf{I}_1$ moves to the position of image $\mathbf{I}_2$.

Fig. 2. The motion of speckle images. The displacements from image $\mathbf{I}_1$ to image $\mathbf{I}_2$ are Δx and Δy in X-axis and Y-axis respectively. Note that the speckle images are grayscale images, we colored them here for illustration. Best viewed in color.

ConvLSTM uses a convolution operation in the state-to-state and input-to-state transitions to encode spatial information. The cell output $\mathcal{C}_t$ is updated with the input $\mathcal{X}_t$ and the last step hidden state $\mathcal{H}_{t-1}$, as well as the cell output $\mathcal{C}_{t-1}$. The hidden state $\mathcal{H}_t$ is updated with the cell output $\mathcal{C}_t$. The gates i_t, f_t control the update of $\mathcal{C}_t$ and o_t controls the update of $\mathcal{H}_t$. For every step, the cell takes as input $\mathcal{X}_t$ and output the features encoded through convolutional transitions and "memories" stored in the hidden state. By comparing the encoded features and "memories", it can infer the relative displacement information of speckle pattern with time.

Network Architecture. The network architecture in our experiment is shown in Fig. 3. To keep consistent with the settings of the CNN model in [26], the input of our model is two cropped speckle images with size 32×32. Then we stacked two convolutional layers to extract basic features from the input speckle pattern. The first convolutional layer has 128 kernels with kernel size 7×7 and strides 2. The second convolutional layer has 256 kernels with kernel size 5×5 and strides 2. After the convolutional layer, three ConvLSTM layers are used to capture the spatial and temporal features from the convolutional layer output. The first ConvLSTM layer has 256 kernels with kernel size 5×5 and strides 2. And the later two ConvLSTM layers have the same 128 kernels with kernel size 3×3 and strides 1. There is a normalization layer [1] between every two ConvLSTM layers to reduce the internal covariate shift of layer inputs and achieve a training speed-up. After the ConvLSTM layers are two fully connected (FC) layers with units 2048 and 1024 respectively, which are used to infer the relative displacement. The output layer has two units to produce the relative displacements of speckle images in the X-axis and Y-axis. Feed the network with speckle images sequence, the convolutional and ConvLSTM layers extract the spatial and temporal information of the input sequence and encode the extracted features into hidden state tensors, then the fully-connected layers exploit the hidden state to produce the estimation,

$$\begin{bmatrix} \hat{\Delta x} \\ \hat{\Delta y} \end{bmatrix} = \arg\max_{\Delta x, \Delta y} p\left[I_{t+1}(x,y) = I_t(x+\Delta x, y+\Delta y) \mid I_t, I_{t+1}\right] \tag{4}$$

where the $(\Delta x, \Delta y)$ are the relative displacements of I_{t+1} with respect to I_t, and $(\hat{\Delta x}, \hat{\Delta y})$ are estimations of $(\Delta x, \Delta y)$.

Since the relative displacements are non-discrete, we use the loss of mean square error (MSE, (5)) to measure the error between the ground-truth and the estimation.

$$\mathrm{MSE} = \sum_{i=1}^{N} \frac{(h(x_i) - y_i)^2}{N} \tag{5}$$

where x_i is the i-th sample and N is the total number of samples. $h(x_i)$ is the estimation of input x_i, and y_i is the ground-truth.

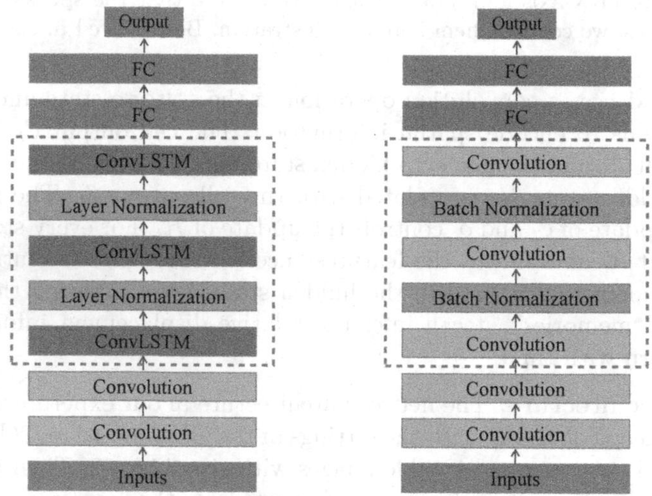

(a) The architecture of our ConvLSTM model.

(b) The architecture of CNN model for comparative experiments.

Fig. 3. The architecture of models. To ensure the fairness of the comparative experiments, we adopted the CNN model in [26] with the same convolution layer added after the fourth convolution layer to expand the model.

3.3 CNN Model for Comparative Experiments

The CNN architecture in [26] is used for comparative experiments with our model. We add a convolution layer after the fourth convolutional layer for a reasonable comparison. The CNN model shown in Fig. 3(b) has the same number of kernels in each corresponding layer as our model, i.e., the number of kernels in the first five layers in the CNN model are 128, 256, 256, 128 and 128, and the units in the following two FC layers are 2048 and 1024 respectively. The batch normalization [12] acts the same role as layer normalization in our model. In the Sect. 5, we will compare the performance of the CNN model and our model.

4 Experiment Setup

In this section, we first introduce the details of data collection, including experimental setups, objects and the methods used in the data preprocessing. Then we describe the training details such as weights initialization method and optimizer settings. The last part is the metrics that will be used in later evaluation.

4.1 Data Collection

The data we used to evaluate the model is speckle image sequence. Like the optical settings in [25], we used a laser beam of wavelength 532 nm to illuminate the object from 2 m away, and a speaker was used to excite the object. A high-speed camera that can record up to 5000 frames per second (FPS) was placed near the laser source to capture the speckle images. Inspired by the experiments in [6], we collected speckle images of several objects, such as cartons, tissue paper, plant leaves, because these targets are accessible and unobtrusive in daily life. We recorded the speckle images with different frame rates for every object to evaluate the relationship between the quality of recovered sound and the frame rate. After we finished data collection, the relative displacement of every image with respect to a reference image was computed by using a correlation algorithm [21]. In the end, we have a dataset (see details in Table 1) contains speckle images of three objects captured at the different frame rates and the relative displacements of the speckle images.

Table 1. Data collection

Sampling frequency (FPS)	The number of speckle images		
	Carton	Tissue paper	Plant leaves
1000	15366	16030	10582
1500	14622	15712	18890
2000	15235	15440	19155
2500	17346	18139	16352
3000	19934	18232	25730
Total	82503	83553	90709

Data Preprocess: In order to improve the stability of calculation and accelerate the convergence of model in the training process, we scaled all images to mean zero by subtracting the mean value of the training set from each pixel. We also applied data augmentation to reduce overfitting. As illustrated in [26], the image patch of size 32 × 32 is qualified for representing the whole speckle image. With randomly crop the whole speckle image (256 × 256) at size 32 × 32 in one of four fixed locations, we extended the training set four times larger than that without the augmentation. The crop method is fulfilled by randomly selecting one of the four fixed pixels as the center of the cropped image patch. Note that we cropped a single patch from every image in the validation set and testing set.

4.2 Training Details

The model is implemented by Tensorflow, which is a dataflow graph based machine learning framework. The activations σ of gates i_t, f_t, o_t are relu. In cooperation with the relu activation, we initialized kernels with the initialization method introduced in [10]. Mini-batch stochastic gradient descent is used to optimize the model with batch size 64. Learning rate exponential decay is applied to increase the stability of training process with an initial learning rate of 0.01 and a decay rate of 0.95 for every epoch.

4.3 Evaluation Metrics

In addition to the MSE metric, we also use mean absolute error (MAE) to quantify the estimation error with respect to the ground truth. If each signal has N scalar observations, then the mean absolute error is defined as:

$$\mathrm{MAE} = \frac{1}{N}\sum_{i=1}^{N}|h(x_i) - y_i| \tag{6}$$

where $h(x_i)$ is the estimation of input x_i, and y_i is the ground-truth.

5 Results

We have conducted various experiments to validate the performance of the model in sound extraction. In this section, we first investigate the accuracy and efficiency of our model on test data. Then we show the influence of sampling rate on the speech extraction results. Last, we investigate the generalization ability of our model on unseen data.

5.1 Overall Evaluation

For the overall evaluation of the model, we divided all data into training data (80%), validation data (10%) and test data (10%). We trained the model over the training data as described before. The training process ends when the epoch number reaches 100 or the validation error is no longer reduced. Figure 4 is the results of the well-trained model on test data. Waveforms of the estimation

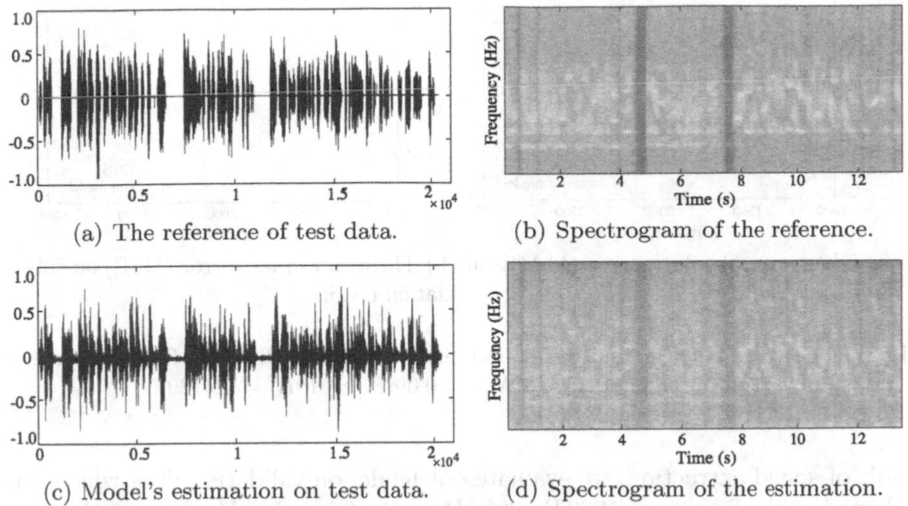

(a) The reference of test data. (b) Spectrogram of the reference.

(c) Model's estimation on test data. (d) Spectrogram of the estimation.

Fig. 4. The reference and the model's estimation of test data. The errors between estimation and the reference: MAE = 0.105, MSE = 0.026.

and the reference are very similar, and their spectrograms are also very similar. The signal in Fig. 4(c) is the model output that has no post-processing except centralization (i.e. align the mean value to zero). The MSE of the output is 0.026, which is a relatively small error. As a result, the recovered voice is clear and of high quality.

In addition to the above overall accuracy evaluation, we also conduct comparative experiments to demonstrate the high accuracy of our model. The comparative model is the CNN model shown in Fig. 3(b). Refer to Fig. 5 (see more details in 5.2), the results show that our model is better than CNN in the accuracy of the estimation. At different sampling frequencies, our model outperforms CNN with a large margin in the MAE and MSE metrics. On average, the MAE of our model is 28.4% less than that of CNN, and the MSE of our model is 37.1% less than that of CNN.

We also test the efficiency of our model by running 100 epochs on a dataset of 44,416 samples, and the result indicates that our model slightly faster than CNN. The reasoning speed of our model is 1.34 ms (milliseconds) per sample. By contrast, CNN takes 1.42 ms to process a sample.

5.2 Influence of Sampling Rates

As a general application of signal sampling, the higher the sampling rate, the more accurate the recovered signal. In this experiment, higher sampling rate means that more speckle images are recorded at the same time, which means more expensive imaging equipment is needed and more compute resources are consumed. To illustrate the influence of different sampling rates on the final

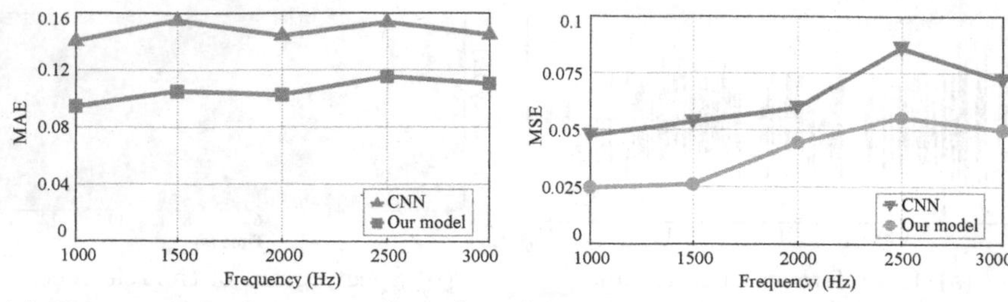

(a) The mean absolute error (MAE) on validation data.

(b) The mean square error (MSE) on validation data.

Fig. 5. The error between the result and the reference at different frequencies. The standard deviation of our model: $\sigma(\text{MAE}) = 0.0078$, $\sigma(\text{MSE}) = 0.0139$.

result of sound extraction, we evaluate our model on validation data which was collected at the frequency 1000 Hz 3000 Hz with strides 500 Hz. We use the metrics of MAE and MSE to measure the errors of our model as well as the CNN. Figure 5 is the result of our experiment.

The higher sampling rate also leads to the smaller displacement between two continuous speckle images. That means it becomes more difficult to extract the smaller movements from speckle images. As a consequence, refer to Fig. 5, while the sampling rate increases 1000 Hz 3000 Hz, MAE increases slightly and MSE increases significantly for both our model and CNN, which indicates that our model and CNN are relatively insensitive to extremely small motion in speckle images.

Contrary to the evaluation metrics, the auditory characteristics of recovered sounds improve with the increase of the sampling rate, which is a reasonable result, because the higher the sampling rate is, the more details are recorded in the speckle images. We provide an intuitive comparison of the results at different sampling rates in Fig. 6. We select 2000 data points from each of the three results extracted from speckle images with different sampling rates. Through intuitive evaluation, we can infer that the higher the sampling rate is, the more subtle the result is.

5.3 Generalization Performance

We show the generalization performance of our model on different objects that are unseen to the model before validation. Due to the small number of objects in the dataset, we choose the leave-one-out method to investigate the generalization ability. To be specific, we remove all data corresponding to an object from the training set during the training process, and then we validate the generalization ability of the well-trained model on the data we removed. In this way, we could reveal the generalization ability of our model on unseen data.

The test results of generalization ability are shown in Fig. 7, which demonstrates that our model is superior to CNN in dealing with the subtle nuances

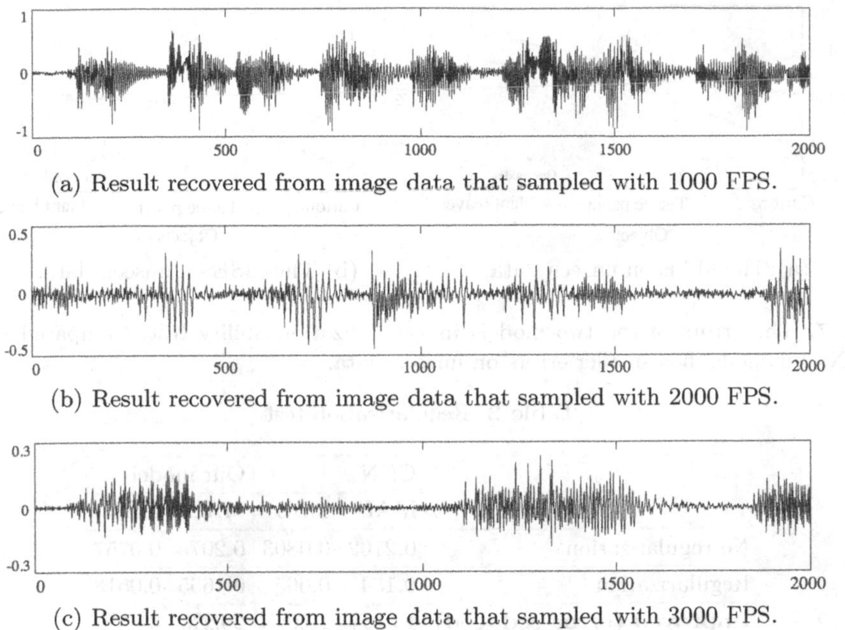

(a) Result recovered from image data that sampled with 1000 FPS.

(b) Result recovered from image data that sampled with 2000 FPS.

(c) Result recovered from image data that sampled with 3000 FPS.

Fig. 6. The intuitive comparison of results at different sampling rates. All three signals contain 2000 data points.

between speckle patterns. Due to the different materials of the three objects, their vibration characteristics are also different, which further leads to slightly different speckle patterns. It can be seen that our model and CNN have the strongest generalization ability for cartons and the weakest generalization ability for plant leaves. Accordingly, in the practical sound extraction, cartons may be a better choice target than plant leaves.

Since the ConvLSTM module have the potential to capture the spatial-temporal relationship from temporal data, we may infer that the better generalization ability of our model comes from regularization settings and the ConvLSTM architecture. In order to confirm the inference, we conducted a regularization test to evaluate the generalization performance of the model with and without regularization settings. Table 2 shows the errors of model on unseen data. In contrast, without regularization settings, the MAE and MSE of our model are reduced by 20% and 31% respectively, while that of CNN are reduced by 15% and 19% respectively on unseen data. Therefore, the ConvLSTM architecture contributes to the generalization performance of the model, which makes our model has stronger generalization ability than CNN and more suitable for processing unknown temporal data than CNN.

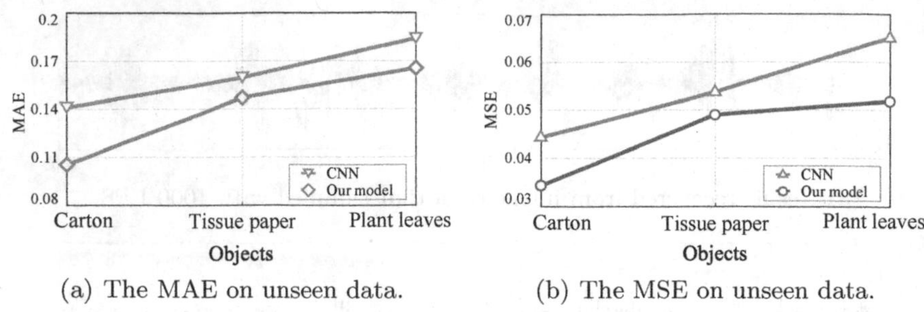

(a) The MAE on unseen data. (b) The MSE on unseen data.

Fig. 7. The errors of the two models in generalization ability test. Compared with CNN, our model has smaller errors on unseen data.

Table 2. Regularization test

	CNN		Our model	
	MAE	MSE	MAE	MSE
No regularization	0.2162	0.0803	0.2075	0.0757
Regularization	0.184	0.065	0.1655	0.0518
Improved (error reduced)	14.9%	19.0%	20.2%	31.5%

6 Conclusion

We present an effective and efficient method based on ConvLSTM to extract sound from speckle images, prove its excellent performance by various experiments. Compared with CNN, our model has advantages in accuracy, efficiency, and generalization ability. Through experiments, we illustrate the influence of sampling rate on sound extraction and demonstrate that the experimental results are consistent with the sampling theorem. In the generalization ability test, our model outperforms CNN with a large margin on different objects. As a conclusion, the ConvLSTM is better than CNN in extracting subtle motions from speckle images, and our method is a significant progress in speech signal extraction. Despite the good results of experiments, there are still some challenges with our approach. One obvious problem is that speckle images are sensitive to noise and disturbance, so improving the noise tolerance of our model is of great significance for future research. In practice, the sampling rate of speckle images is up to 2000 FPS, but now our model can only process 750 images per second. Therefore, accelerating the inference speed of our model is one of the other research directions, we should try to realize the practical sound recovery system.

References

1. Ba, J.L., Kiros, J.R., Hinton, G.E.: Layer normalization (2016). http://arxiv.org/org/abs/1607.06450v1

2. Barcellona, C., et al.: Remote recovery of audio signals from videos of optical speckle patterns: a comparative study of signal recovery algorithms. Opt. Express **28**(6), 8716–8723 (2020). https://doi.org/10.1364/OE.386406
3. Billa, J.: Dropout approaches for LSTM based speech recognition systems. In: 2018 IEEE International Conference on Acoustics, Speech and Signal Processing (ICASSP), pp. 5879–5883 (2018). https://doi.org/10.1109/ICASSP.2018.8462544
4. Blaber, J., Adair, B., Antoniou, A.: Ncorr: open-source 2D digital image correlation matlab software. Experiment. Mech. **55**, 1105–1122 (2015)
5. Castellini, P., Martarelli, M., Tomasini, E.: Laser doppler vibrometry: development of advanced solutions answering to technology's needs. Mech. Syst. Signal Process. **20**(6), 1265–1285 (2006). https://doi.org/10.1016/j.ymssp.2005.11.015
6. Davis, A., Rubinstein, M., Wadhwa, N., Mysore, G.J., Durand, F., Freeman, W.T.: The visual microphone: passive recovery of sound from video. ACM Trans. Graph. **33**(4) (2014)
7. Diamond, D.H., Heyns, P.S., Oberholster, A.J.: Accuracy evaluation of sub-pixel structural vibration measurements through optical flow analysis of a video sequence. Measurement **95**, 166–172 (2017)
8. Garg, P., et al.: Measuring transverse displacements using unmanned aerial systems laser doppler vibrometer (UAS-LDV): development and field validation. Sensors **20**(21) (2020). https://doi.org/10.3390/s20216051
9. Graves, A.: Generating sequences with recurrent neural networks. ArXiv abs/1308.0850 (2013)
10. He, K., Zhang, X., Ren, S., Sun, J.: Delving deep into rectifiers: surpassing human-level performance on imagenet classification. In: Proceedings of the IEEE International Conference on Computer Vision (ICCV), December 2015
11. Hochreiter, S., Schmidhuber, J.: Long short-term memory. Neural Comput. **9**(8), 1735–1780 (1997). https://doi.org/10.1162/neco.1997.9.8.1735
12. Ioffe, S., Szegedy, C.: Batch normalization: accelerating deep network training by reducing internal covariate shift (2015)
13. Kritsis, K., Kaliakatsos-Papakostas, M., Katsouros, V., Pikrakis, A.: Deep convolutional and lstm neural network architectures on leap motion hand tracking data sequences. In: 2019 27th European Signal Processing Conference (EUSIPCO), pp. 1–5 (2019). 10.23919/EUSIPCO.2019.8902973
14. Mutegeki, R., Han, D.S.: A cnn-lstm approach to human activity recognition. In: 2020 International Conference on Artificial Intelligence in Information and Communication (ICAIIC), pp. 362–366 (2020). https://doi.org/10.1109/ICAIIC48513.2020.9065078
15. Ozana, N., et al.: Demonstration of a remote optical measurement configuration that correlates with breathing, heart rate, pulse pressure, blood coagulation, and blood oxygenation. Proc. IEEE **103**(2), 248–262 (2015). https://doi.org/10.1109/JPROC.2014.2385793
16. Pasunuru, R., Bansal, M.: Multi-task video captioning with video and entailment generation. In: Proceedings of the 55th Annual Meeting of the Association for Computational Linguistics (Volume 1: Long Papers), pp. 1273–1283 (Jul 2017)
17. Peters, W.H., Ranson, W.F.: Digital imaging techniques in experimental stress analysis. Optical Eng. **21**(3), 427–431 (1982). https://doi.org/10.1117/12.7972925
18. Rothberg, S., et al.: An international review of laser doppler vibrometry: making light work of vibration measurement. Optics Lasers Eng. **99**, 11–22 (2017). https://doi.org/10.1016/j.optlaseng.2016.10.023

19. Shao, X., Zhong, F., Huang, W., Dai, X., Chen, Z., He, X.: Digital image correlation with improved efficiency by pixel selection. Appl. Opt. **59**(11), 3389–3398 (2020). https://doi.org/10.1364/AO.387678
20. Shi, X., Chen, Z., Wang, H., Yeung, D.Y., Wong, W.k., Woo, W.C.: Convolutional LSTM network: a machine learning approach for precipitation nowcasting. In: Proceedings of the 28th International Conference on Neural Information Processing Systems - Volume 1, p. 802–810. NIPS 2015 (2015)
21. Smith, B.M., O'Toole, M., Gupta, M.: Tracking multiple objects outside the line of sight using speckle imaging. In: 2018 IEEE/CVF Conference on Computer Vision and Pattern Recognition, pp. 6258–6266 (2018). https://doi.org/10.1109/CVPR.2018.00655
22. Srivastava, N., Mansimov, E., Salakhutdinov, R.: Unsupervised learning of video representations using LSTMs. In: Proceedings of the 32nd International Conference on International Conference on Machine Learning - vol. 37, pp. 843–852. ICML 2015 (2015)
23. Xu, Z., Li, S., Deng, W.: Learning temporal features using lstm-cnn architecture for face anti-spoofing. In: 2015 3rd IAPR Asian Conference on Pattern Recognition (ACPR). pp. 141–145 (2015). https://doi.org/10.1109/ACPR.2015.7486482
24. Yang, D., Su, Z., Zhang, S., Zhang, D.: Real-time matching strategy for rotary objects using digital image correlation. Appl. Opt. **59**(22), 6648–6657 (2020). https://doi.org/10.1364/AO.397655
25. Zalevsky, Z., et al.: Simultaneous remote extraction of multiple speech sources and heart beats from secondary speckles pattern. Opt. Express **17**(24), 21566–21580 (2009). https://doi.org/10.1364/OE.17.021566
26. Zhu, D., Yang, L., Li, Z., Zeng, H.: Remote speech extraction from speckle image by convolutional neural network. In: 2020 IEEE Symposium on Computers and Communications (ISCC), pp. 1–6 (2020). https://doi.org/10.1109/ISCC50000.2020.9219652

Secure Image Coding Based on Compressive Sensing with Optimized Rate-Distortion

Di Xiao(✉) and Shuwen Lan

Chongqing University, Chongqing, China

Abstract. Secure image coding schemes have attracted much attention in the information field. However, most of the secure image transmission schemes suffer from poor rate-distortion (R-D) performance. In this paper, the property of the measurement matrix and the correlation among the compressive sensing (CS) measurements are utilized to develop a secure image data transmission scheme with optimized rate-distortion. At the encoder side, block CS is applied to capture an image with the DCT matrix. Next, the measurements need to be divided into three parts and then quantized with different bit-depths, where the residual coefficients are quantized with fewer bits. Lastly, all bits will be scrambled into an image and then it will be diffused with the forward-reverse diffusion. At the decoder side, the image will be reconstructed with the corresponding decryption and decoding algorithm. Compared with the adopted benchmarks and some existing works, the proposed scheme can reach a higher level of R-D performance. Moreover, the simulation analyses prove that the proposed cryptoscheme has a good performance in terms of security.

Keywords: Compressive sensing · Security · Secure image coding · Rate-distortion performance

1 Introduction

With the rapid development of smart city, Internet of Things (IoT) has attracted considerable attention owing to its various kinds of applications. IoT plays an important role in several monitoring domains [1], such as intelligent tracking, in-home fall detection and object identification. Consequently, IoT monitoring applications produce the exponential growth of surveillance images or videos. The enormous surveillance data should be transmitted to data centers for intelligent data analysis. Therefore, it is critical to design an image transmission scheme that can protect data privacy and reduce the data volume simultaneously.

As a sub-Nyquist sampling technology, compressive sensing (CS) [2,3] can sample and compress an image in a single step. CS has been gradually utilized to design image cryptoschemes [4–14] because the CS-based image cryptoscheme can achieve data protection and reduction simultaneously. Zhou et al.

D. Gao et al. (Eds.): ICICS 2021, LNCS 12919, pp. 125–141, 2021.
https://doi.org/10.1007/978-3-030-88052-1_8

[4] proposed an encryption scheme, where image encryption is achieved by scrambling the CS measurements of two adjacent blocks. Subsequently, Zhou et al. [5] proposed a two-dimensional (2D) encryption scheme, where measurements are encrypted by the nonlinear fractional Mellin transform. Then in [6], Zhou et al. employed the measurement matrix constructed of chaotic sequences to perform CS and then scramble the measurements. Li et al. [7] designed a chaotic-based cryptoscheme in the spatial domain, where the chaotic sequences are exploited to construct measurement matrix and implement the forward-reverse diffusion to the quantized measurements. Hu et al. [8] constructed multiple measurement matrixes cooperated with the counter mode operation and then CS is applied to each column of an image with each measurement matrix parallelly. Finally, the diffusion process in a cross manner is used to evenly spread the energy of measurements. Luo et al. [9] proposed a chaotic-based image encryption scheme in the Haar wavelet domain. Diffusion is directly applied to the quantized LL component. CS is performed to HL component with a higher sampling ratio than LH and HH components. Finally, the permutation is employed to scramble the quantized measurements and the diffused LL component. Zhu et al. [10] divided the DCT coefficients into three parts and employed CS to each part with different sampling ratios. Finally, they used the diffusion and permutation to obtain the encrypted images. In recent years, the rate-distortion (R-D) performance of the CS-based image cryptoschemes has been improved, but the R-D performance can be further improved by designing the encoder delicately.

Some CS-based image coding works improve the R-D performance of image transmission works by elaborately designing the encoder. Wang et al. [15] proposed a uniform quantization scheme by exploiting the measurements correlation to discard the most significant bits of several measurements. Chen et al. [16] proposed a non-uniform quantization scheme, which can recover images well by imposing the low-rank constraint. Later in [17], Chen et al. proposed a novel image coding scheme by quantizing multilayer residual coefficients with the same bit-depth uniformly. Moreover, this work can perform well by exploiting the deep learning-based DAMP-CS algorithm. However, these works do not consider information security.

In CS coding scheme, the quality of the reconstructed image is determined by the sampling ratio and the quantizer step. We can exploit the property of the measurement matrix and the correlation among the CS measurements to obtain better R-D performance. By using the DCT measurement matrix, we can obtain measurements with uneven energy. By allocating more quantization steps to high energy measurements, we can obtain better rate-distortion performance than allocating the same quantization steps. After dividing measurements into three parts, the predicted measurements of the last part can be obtained by using the correlation among the CS measurements, so the quantization step of the last part can be further reduced. The main contributions of this paper are given as follows:

Firstly, we propose a secure image coding scheme which can achieve better R-D performance by allocating different bit-depths to different parts. After demonstrating the feasibility of the scheme, we further graphically represent the better R-D performance of the proposed scheme by adopting two benchmarks.

Secondly, we fit the encryption algorithm for encrypting the values which are expressed in different length bits. This algorithm first applies bit-wise permutation to the different length values and then performs forward-reverse diffusion to the reshaped image.

Thirdly, we show that the proposed secure image coding scheme can achieve good image encryption performance by simulations.

Table 1 lists the commonly used symbols in this paper. This paper is organized as follows: Sect. 2 gives the basic knowledge of compressive sensing and Logistic-Tent map. Section 3 contains the overview of the proposed scheme and the algorithms of the encoder and decoder are detailed. Section 4 shows the performance of the proposed image coding scheme in terms of reconstruction and security. Finally, our conclusion is presented in Sect. 5.

Table 1. From left to right: (a) symbols of the frequently used variables and functions in this paper. (b) Denotations of these symbols. (c) some remarks of the symbols

Variable or Function	Meanings	Remarks
$\mathbf{X} \in \mathbb{R}^{N \times N}$	Plaintext Image	Sparse in $\boldsymbol{\Psi}$
$\boldsymbol{\Phi} \in \mathbb{R}^{M \times N}$	Measurement Matrix	
$\boldsymbol{\Psi} \in \mathbb{R}^{N \times N}$	Sparsifying Basis	Discrete wavelet transform
$\mathbf{Y} \in \mathbb{R}^{M \times N}$	Measurements	$\mathbf{Y} = \text{BCS}(\mathbf{X})$
$\mathbf{Y}_1 \in \mathbb{R}^{1 \times N}$	The first part of the measurements	$\mathbf{Y}_1 = \mathbf{Y}(1,:)$
$\mathbf{Y}_2 \in \mathbb{R}^{m \times N}$	The second part of the measurements	$\mathbf{Y}_2 = \mathbf{Y}(2:m+1,:)$
$\mathbf{Y}_3 \in \mathbb{R}^{(M-m-1) \times N}$	The third part of the measurements	$\mathbf{Y}_3 = \mathbf{Y}(m+2:M,:)$
$\tilde{\mathbf{e}}_3 \in \mathbb{R}^{(M-m-1) \times N}$	Residual coefficient	
$\mathbf{C} \in \mathbb{R}^{\frac{N}{2} \times N}$	Ciphertext Image	Every pixel is in [0,255]
B_j	The bit-depth of the jth part	$j = 1, 2, 3$
$\tilde{\mathbf{I}}_j$	The quantized values of the jth part	$j = 1, 2, 3$
$\mathbf{K}_j$	$gen\_Logistic\_Tent(z_j, r_j, d_j, [M, N])$	
$\text{Q}_{B_j}(\cdot)$	Quantization with B_j bits	Uniform quantization
$\text{Q}_{B_j}^{-1}(\cdot)$	Dequantization	
$\text{BCS}(\cdot)$	Measure with BCS	
$\text{BCS}^{-1}(\cdot)$	Reconstruct with BCS-SPL	
$\text{P}(\cdot)$	Permutation	
$\text{P}^{-1}(\cdot)$	Reverse Permutation	
$\text{D}(\cdot)$	Forward-Reverse Diffusion	
$\text{D}^{-1}(\cdot)$	Reverse-Forward Diffusion	
gen_Logistic_Tent($\cdot$)	Sequence Generation by iterating Logistic_Tent map	

2 Background

2.1 Compressive Sensing Theory

Compressive sensing (CS) can sample and compress in a single step. It can reduce the dimension of a signal by multiplying underdetermined sensing matrix. When CS is applied to two-dimensional images, block-wise compressive sensing (BCS) is a popular sensing method.

In BCS, an $N \times N$ image $\mathbf{X}$ is divided into $\sqrt{N} \times \sqrt{N}$ non-overlapping blocks. Then CS is applied to every vector which is vectorized from a block in parallel. Finally, we get measurements $\mathbf{Y} \in \mathbb{R}^{M \times N}$. To guarantee the successful reconstruction of the signal from the measurements, it is vital to ensure that the signal $\mathbf{X}$ is either exactly K-sparse or approximately sparse in the transform domain.

BCS with smooth projected Landweber (BCS-SPL) [18] is the reconstruction algorithm. When the measurement matrix $\mathbf{\Phi}$ satisfies the restricted isometry property (RIP) [3], BCS-SPL can output the correct reconstruction image $\mathbf{X}$ with the inputs of measurements $\mathbf{Y}$ and the corresponding measurement matrix $\mathbf{\Phi}$. If the sampling ratio is bigger, the quality of the reconstruction image is higher.

2.2 Logistic-Tent Map

Due to the properties of ergodicity, unpredictability and high sensitivity to related parameters, chaos has become a popular approach to design cryptoschemes. Refer to [8] by combining Logistic map and Skew Tent map, Logistic-Tent map can outperform Logistic map and Skew Tent map in distribution, key space size and statistical property.

Logistic-Tent map can be represented by

$$z^{k+1} = \begin{cases} (rz^k(1-z^k) + \frac{((4-r)z^k)}{2}) - \lfloor (rz^k(1-z^k) + \frac{((4-r)z^k)}{2}) \rfloor, & z^k < 0.5 \\ (rz^k(1-z^k) + \frac{(4-r)(1-z^k)}{2}) - \lfloor (rz^k(1-z^k) + \frac{(4-r)(1-z^k)}{2}) \rfloor, & z^k \geq 0.5 \end{cases} \tag{1}$$

where $k = 0, 1, 2, ..., (MNd)$, the control parameter $r \in (0, 4]$, the initial state value $z^0 \in (0, 1)$ and the sampling distance $d \in [1, 10]$. The output of the function gen_Logistic_Tent($z^0, r, d, [M, N]$) is $\{z^{n_0 + i \times d}\}_{i=0}^{MN-1}$, where the first n_0 values are discarded. In this paper, Logistic-Tent map is employed to generate the index vector for permutation and the key streams for diffusion.

3 The Proposed Image Coding Scheme

3.1 The Overview of the Proposed Image Coding Scheme

The architecture of the proposed image secure coding scheme is shown in Fig. 1.

The secure image coding scheme is mainly aimed at protecting private images so that the attacker can not infer the content of private images. For protecting privacy images, the secure image coding scheme should have the ability to resist the brute force attack, the statistical attack and the differential attack [7,12].

To overcome the poor R-D performance of the CS-based secure image coding scheme, we design the encoder elaborately. Inspired by the fact that the R-D performance is dominated by the quantization step and sampling ratio, we can allocate the sampling ratio and the quantization step properly to obtain a better R-D performance. Although suitably increasing the sampling ratio and reducing the quantization step can improve the R-D performance, we can employ the property of the measurement matrix and the correlation among the CS measurements to further improve the R-D performance.

In this paper, the one-dimensional DCT matrix is treated as the measurement matrix. Because of the energy compaction property of DCT, the energy of measurements is distributed unevenly. Most of the energy focuses on the upper part of measurements so that most of the information concentrates on the same part. In uniform quantization, the quantization distortion is inversely proportional to the quantization step, so the part with more information needs to be quantized with a longer quantization step in order to reduce the distortion. To reduce the transmitted data volume further, the correlation among the CS measurements is also exploited. By utilizing the correlation among the CS measurements, we can use the measurements of the first two parts to obtain the predicted measurements of the third part. The residual coefficient between the predicted measurements and the third part of measurements can be quantized with a shorter quantization step. Therefore, by suitably allocating quantization steps for three parts, the proposed scheme can achieve better R-D performance.

The encoder is responsible for compression, quantization, and encryption. After applying BCS to an image $\mathbf{X}$, the obtained measurements $\mathbf{Y}$ is divided into three parts. Only the last part $\mathbf{Y_3}$ is replaced by the residual coefficient $\tilde{\mathbf{e}}_\mathbf{3}$ between the measurements $\mathbf{Y}_3$ and the predicted measurements $\tilde{\mathbf{Y}}_\mathbf{3}$. Then each part is quantized with different bit-depths. Next, permutation is adopted to scramble the bits of each quantized measurement, and then the encrypted result is shaped into an image. Finally, the image is diffused into the ciphertext image $\mathbf{C}$ to enhance the security of the cryptoscheme.

The decoder can reconstruct the image by the corresponding decryption, dequantization, and decompression. After receiving the ciphertext image $\mathbf{C}$, the decoder performs the reverse-diffusion and reverse-permutation to obtain $\tilde{\mathbf{I}}$. Then, dequantization is applied to acquire the measurements $\tilde{\mathbf{Y}}_\mathbf{1}$ and $\tilde{\mathbf{Y}}_\mathbf{2}$ and the residual coefficient $\tilde{\tilde{\mathbf{e}}}_\mathbf{3}$. Finally, after recovering the last part of the measurements $\tilde{\tilde{\mathbf{Y}}}_\mathbf{3}$ from the residual coefficient $\tilde{\tilde{\mathbf{e}}}_\mathbf{3}$, the measurements $\hat{\mathbf{Y}}$ is used to reconstruct the plaintext image $\hat{\mathbf{X}}$.

3.2 The Image Coding with the Elaborate Encoder

The $N \times N$ image is converted to $M \times N$ measurements $\mathbf{Y}$ by using BCS. The measurements are divided into three parts. The first part of the measurements,

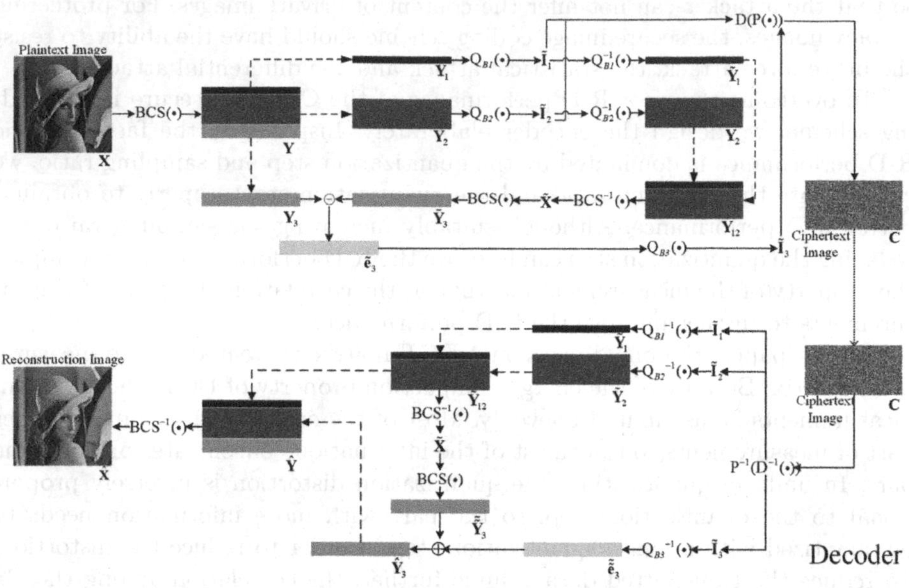

Fig. 1. The framework of the proposed image coding scheme. The dotted line means combination or partitioning.

$\mathbf{Y}_1$, only includes the first row of $\mathbf{Y}$. The second part of the measurements, $\mathbf{Y}_2$, contains the m rows of the measurements $\mathbf{Y}$. The third part of the measurements, $\mathbf{Y}_3$, involves the last $(M - m - 1)$ rows of $\mathbf{Y}$. Before quantizing each part, only the last part of the measurements needs to be processed. With the first two parts of the measurements, we can get the residual coefficient $\tilde{\mathbf{e}}_3$ between the third part measurements $\mathbf{Y}_3$ and the corresponding predicted measurements $\tilde{\mathbf{Y}}_3$.

Algorithm 1: Framework of the Encoder Side

Data: $\mathbf{X}$, M, m
Result: $\mathbf{C}$

$\mathbf{Y} \leftarrow \mathrm{BCS}(\mathbf{X})$;
$\mathbf{Y_1} \leftarrow \mathbf{Y}(1,:)$; $\mathbf{Y_2} \leftarrow \mathbf{Y}(2:m+1,:)$; $\mathbf{Y_3} \leftarrow \mathbf{Y}(m+2:M,:)$;
$\tilde{\mathbf{I}}_\mathbf{1} \leftarrow \mathrm{Q}_{\mathrm{B}_1}(\mathbf{Y_1})$; $\tilde{\mathbf{I}}_\mathbf{2} \leftarrow \mathrm{Q}_{\mathrm{B}_2}(\mathbf{Y_2})$;
$\tilde{\mathbf{Y}}_\mathbf{12} \leftarrow [\mathrm{Q}^{-1}_{\mathrm{B}_1}(\tilde{\mathbf{I}}_\mathbf{1}); \mathrm{Q}^{-1}_{\mathrm{B}_2}(\tilde{\mathbf{I}}_\mathbf{2})]$;
$\tilde{\mathbf{Y}}_\mathbf{3} \leftarrow \mathrm{BCS}(\mathrm{BCS}^{-1}(\tilde{\mathbf{Y}}_\mathbf{12}))$;
$\tilde{\mathbf{e}}_\mathbf{3} \leftarrow \mathbf{Y_3} - \tilde{\mathbf{Y}}_\mathbf{3}$;
$\tilde{\mathbf{I}}_\mathbf{3} \leftarrow \mathrm{Q}_{\mathrm{B}_3}(\tilde{\mathbf{e}}_\mathbf{3})$;
$\tilde{\mathbf{I}} \leftarrow [\tilde{\mathbf{I}}_\mathbf{1}(:); \tilde{\mathbf{I}}_\mathbf{2}(:); \tilde{\mathbf{I}}_\mathbf{3}(:)]$;
$\mathbf{C} \leftarrow \mathrm{D}(\mathrm{P}(\tilde{\mathbf{I}}))$;

The detailed process to obtain the residual coefficient $\tilde{\mathbf{e}}_3$ is given as follows. The first two parts are quantized firstly and then dequantized to obtain the new measurements $\tilde{\mathbf{Y}}_{12}$ which lose some information. After applying BCS-SPL to $\tilde{\mathbf{Y}}_{12}$, the predicted reconstruction image $\tilde{\mathbf{X}}$ can be obtained. The predicted third part measurements $\tilde{\mathbf{Y}}_3$ can be acquired by executing BCS($\tilde{\mathbf{X}}$). The residual coefficient $\tilde{e}_3$ is obtained by subtracting the predicted measurements $\tilde{\mathbf{Y}}_3$ from the measurements $\mathbf{Y}_3$.

Next, the first two parts of the measurements, $\mathbf{Y}_1$ and $\mathbf{Y}_2$, and the residual coefficient $\tilde{\mathbf{e}}_3$ are quantized into $\tilde{\mathbf{I}}_1$, $\tilde{\mathbf{I}}_2$ and $\tilde{\mathbf{I}}_3$. Then, the quantization values $\tilde{\mathbf{I}}_1$, $\tilde{\mathbf{I}}_2$ and $\tilde{\mathbf{I}}_3$ is shaped as the binary vector $\tilde{\mathbf{I}}$ which contains $M \times N \times 4$ bits. Finally, we apply the encryption to the binary vector $\tilde{\mathbf{I}}$ for protecting the image information. The whole encoding procedure is described in Algorithm 1.

The encryption can be described as $\mathbf{C} = \mathrm{D}(\mathrm{P}(\tilde{\mathbf{I}}))$, which is composed of permutation and forward-reverse diffusion. Permutation scrambles the bits of $\tilde{\mathbf{I}}$ according to the index vector by sorting the Logistic-Tent sequence. Forward-reverse diffusion focuses on altering the pixels of the permuting results with the Logistic-Tent key streams. The detailed procedure of the encryption is presented in Algorithm 2.

Algorithm 2: The Encryption for the Binary Vector $\tilde{\mathbf{I}}$

Data: $\tilde{\mathbf{I}}$, N, z_1, z_2, z_3, r_1, r_2, r_3, d_1, d_2, d_3
`//` z_1, z_2, z_3, r_1, r_2, r_3 `are the secret keys`
Result: $\mathbf{C}$

$\mathbf{K_1} \leftarrow \text{gen\_Logistic\_Tent}(z_1, r_1, d_1, [1, N \times N \times 4])$; $[\sim, \tilde{\mathbf{K}}_1] \leftarrow \text{sort}(\mathbf{K_1})$;
$\mathbf{K_2} \leftarrow \text{gen\_Logistic\_Tent}(z_2, r_2, d_2, [1, N \times N/2])$;
$\tilde{\mathbf{K}}_2 = \text{mod}([\text{round}(\mathbf{K_2} \times 10^{16})], 256)$;
$\mathbf{K_3} \leftarrow \text{gen\_Logistic\_Tent}(z_3, r_3, d_3, [1, N \times N/2])$;
$\tilde{\mathbf{K}}_3 = \text{mod}([\text{round}(\mathbf{K_3} \times 10^{16})], 256)$;
$\mathbf{T} \leftarrow \tilde{\mathbf{I}}(\tilde{\mathbf{K}}_1)$;
for $i \leftarrow 1$ **to** $N \times N/2$ **do**
  $\tilde{\mathbf{T}}(1, i) \leftarrow \text{bin2dec}(\mathbf{T}(8 \times (i-1) + 1, 8 \times i))$
end
$\mathbf{B}(1, 1) \leftarrow \tilde{\mathbf{K}}_2(1, 1) \oplus \tilde{\mathbf{T}}(1, 1)$;
for $i \leftarrow 2$ **to** $N \times N/2$ **do**
  $\mathbf{B}(1, i) \leftarrow \mathbf{B}(1, i-1) \oplus \tilde{\mathbf{K}}_2(1, i) \oplus \tilde{\mathbf{T}}(1, i)$;
end
$\mathbf{C}(1, N \times N/2) \leftarrow \tilde{\mathbf{K}}_3(1, N \times N/2) \oplus \mathbf{B}(1, N \times N/2)$;
for $i \leftarrow N \times N/2 - 1$ **to** 1 **do**
  $\mathbf{C}(1, i) \leftarrow \mathbf{C}(1, i+1) \oplus \tilde{\mathbf{K}}_3(1, i) \oplus \mathbf{B}(1, i)$;
end
$\mathbf{C} \leftarrow \text{reshape}(\mathbf{C}, [N/2, N])$;

3.3 The Decryption and Decoding of Received Image

The reconstruction procedure is similar to that of the encoding process but in reverse order. The images can be reconstructed successfully only when the decoder applies decryption and decoding to the received image correctly. After receiving the encrypted image at the decoder side, the encrypted image needs to be decrypted at first. The decryption can be described as $\mathrm{P}^{-1}(\mathrm{D}^{-1}(\mathbf{C}))$, which is consisted of reverse-forward diffusion and permutation. The detailed steps of the decryption are described in Algorithm 3.

Algorithm 3: The Decryption for the Ciphertext Image **C**

Data: $\mathbf{C}$, N, z_1, z_2, z_3, r_1, r_2, r_3, d_1, d_2, d_3
`//` z_1, z_2, z_3, r_1, r_2, r_3 `are the secret keys`
Result: $\tilde{\mathbf{I}}$

$\mathbf{K_1} \leftarrow$ gen_Logistic_Tent$(z_1, r_1, d_1, [1, N \times N \times 4])$; $[\sim, \tilde{\mathbf{K}}_\mathbf{1}] \leftarrow$ sort$(\mathbf{K_1})$;
$\mathbf{K_2} \leftarrow$ gen_Logistic_Tent$(z_2, r_2, d_2, [1, N \times N/2])$;
$\tilde{\mathbf{K}}_\mathbf{2} = \mathrm{mod}([\mathrm{round}(\mathbf{K_2} \times 10^{16})], 256)$;
$\mathbf{K_3} \leftarrow$ gen_Logistic_Tent$(z_3, r_3, d_3, [1, N \times N/2])$;
$\tilde{\mathbf{K}}_\mathbf{3} = \mathrm{mod}([\mathrm{round}(\mathbf{K_3} \times 10^{16})], 256)$;
$\mathbf{C} \leftarrow \mathbf{C}(:)$;
$\mathbf{B}(1, N \times N/2) \leftarrow \tilde{\mathbf{K}}_\mathbf{3}(1, N \times N/2) \oplus \mathbf{C}(1, N \times N/2)$;
for $i \leftarrow N \times N/2 - 1$ **to** 1 **do**
  $\mathbf{B}(1, i) \leftarrow \mathbf{C}(1, i+1) \oplus \tilde{\mathbf{K}}_\mathbf{3}(1, i) \oplus \mathbf{C}(1, i)$;
end
$\tilde{\mathbf{T}}(1,1) \leftarrow \tilde{\mathbf{K}}_\mathbf{2}(1,1) \oplus \tilde{\mathbf{B}}(1,1)$;
for $i \leftarrow 2$ **to** $N \times N/2$ **do**
  $\tilde{\mathbf{T}}(1, i) \leftarrow \mathbf{B}(1, i-1) \oplus \tilde{\mathbf{K}}_\mathbf{2}(1, i) \oplus \tilde{\mathbf{B}}(1, i)$;
end
$\mathbf{T} \leftarrow$ dec2bin$(\tilde{\mathbf{T}}, 8)$;
$\tilde{\mathbf{I}}(\tilde{\mathbf{K}}_\mathbf{1}) \leftarrow \mathbf{T}$;

After decryption, the dequantization is directly applied to the recovered bits. With the auxiliary dequantization parameters, we can recover the measurements $\tilde{\mathbf{Y}}_1$, $\tilde{\mathbf{Y}}_\mathbf{2}$ and the residual coefficient $\tilde{\tilde{\mathbf{e}}}_\mathbf{3}$. The base image is obtained by applying BCS-SPL to the measurements $\tilde{\mathbf{Y}}_\mathbf{1}$ and $\tilde{\mathbf{Y}}_\mathbf{2}$ and then the predicted measurements $\tilde{\mathbf{Y}}_\mathbf{3}$ is gotten by using BCS with the base image. The predicted measurements $\tilde{\mathbf{Y}}_\mathbf{3}$ plus the residual coefficient $\tilde{\tilde{\mathbf{e}}}_\mathbf{3}$ is the measurements $\hat{\mathbf{Y}}_\mathbf{3}$. Finally, we can obtain the refined image with the measurements $\tilde{\mathbf{Y}}_1$, $\tilde{\mathbf{Y}}_\mathbf{2}$ and $\hat{\mathbf{Y}}_\mathbf{3}$. Algorithm 4 details the procedures of the decoding algorithm.

4 Experimental Results

In this section, we show the R-D performance and the security analyses of the proposed scheme. The standard gray images "Barbara", "Boat", "Cameraman", "Foreman", "House", "Lena", "Monarch", "Parrots" are used as plaintext images. Without loss of generality, the discrete wavelet transform (DWT) is the sparsifying basis. The DCT matrix is the measurement matrix. The size of all the images is 256×256. The sampling distance d_1, d_2, d_3 are 4, 2 and 7, respectively. The secret keys are randomly selected under the limitation of $r \in (0, 4]$ and $z \in (0, 1)$ as $z_1 = 0.52$, $z_2 = 0.21$, $z_3 = 0.68$, $r_1 = 1.37$, $r_2 = 2.56$, $r_3 = 3.26$. In the subsection of feasibility and security analyses, we use $M = 141$, $m = 36$, $B_1 = 8$, $B_2 = 8$ and $B_3 = 7$. (In fact, since there are a lot of variable combinations of these parameters, we select the best combination for Lena.)

4.1 Feasibility

In the case of using the correct key, a secure and efficient image coding scheme has the ability to successfully reconstruct the image. The peak signal-to-noise ratio (PSNR) is usually utilized as the indicator to estimate the quality of the reconstruction image, and it is given by

$$PSNR = 10 \lg \frac{H \times L \times 255^2}{\sum_{i=1}^{H} \sum_{j=1}^{L} [\hat{\mathbf{X}}(i,j) - \mathbf{X}(i,j)]^2} \tag{2}$$

where H and W are the height and width of the image respectively. With the correct keys, we can reconstruct the encoding images successfully as Fig. 2. Furthermore, the space complexity is $\mathcal{O}(N^2)$ and the time complexity is $\mathcal{O}(N^2)$.

4.2 The R-D Performance of the Proposed Scheme

If an image coding scheme can achieve better R-D performance, the higher quality images can be reconstructed with the same bit rate.

Formulating the parameter setting to an optimization problem turns out to be an extremely difficult problem. The CS reconstruction performance depends

Algorithm 4: Framework of the Decoder Side

Data: $\mathbf{C}, N, M, m$
Result: $\hat{\mathbf{X}}$

$\tilde{\mathbf{I}} \leftarrow \mathrm{P}^{-1}(\mathrm{D}^{-1}(\mathbf{C}))$;
$\tilde{\mathbf{I}}_1 \leftarrow \tilde{\mathbf{I}}(1 : N)$;
$\tilde{\mathbf{I}}_2 \leftarrow \tilde{\mathbf{I}}(N+1 : (m+1) * N)$; $\tilde{\mathbf{I}}_2 \leftarrow \mathrm{reshape}(\tilde{\mathbf{I}}_2, [m, N])$;
$\tilde{\mathbf{I}}_3 \leftarrow \tilde{\mathbf{I}}((m+1) * N + 1 : end)$; $\tilde{\mathbf{I}}_3 \leftarrow \mathrm{reshape}(\tilde{\mathbf{I}}_3, [M - m - 1, N])$;
$\tilde{\mathbf{Y}}_1 \leftarrow \mathrm{Q}^{-1}_{\mathrm{B}_1}(\tilde{\mathbf{I}}_1)$; $\tilde{\mathbf{Y}}_2 \leftarrow \mathrm{Q}^{-1}_{\mathrm{B}_2}(\tilde{\mathbf{I}}_2)$; $\tilde{\tilde{\mathbf{e}}}_3 \leftarrow \mathrm{Q}^{-1}_{\mathrm{B}_3}(\tilde{\mathbf{I}}_3)$;
$\tilde{\mathbf{Y}}_{12} \leftarrow [\tilde{\mathbf{Y}}_1; \tilde{\mathbf{Y}}_2]$;
$\tilde{\tilde{\mathbf{Y}}}_3 \leftarrow \mathrm{BCS}(\mathrm{BCS}^{-1}(\tilde{\mathbf{Y}}_{12}))$;
$\hat{\mathbf{Y}}_3 \leftarrow \tilde{\tilde{\mathbf{Y}}}_3 + \tilde{\tilde{\mathbf{e}}}_3$;
$\hat{\mathbf{X}} \leftarrow \mathrm{BCS}^{-1}([\tilde{\mathbf{Y}}_{12}; \hat{\mathbf{Y}}_3])$;

(a) 35.2715dB (b) 39.2441dB (c) 31.7627dB (d) 38.0588dB

(e) 35.9261dB (f) 36.8792dB (g) 32.8040dB (h) 33.3540dB

Fig. 2. The reconstructed images with the correct keys.

on the sampling ratio R and the quantization step sizes. However, there is no exact closed-form expression for the CS reconstruction performance. Although several upper bounds for the mean square reconstruction error are given in [19], using any of these upper bounds as a substitute to the actual mean square error is not practical. Therefore, we use exhaustive search to find the parameter set under the condition of $B_1 + B_2 \cdot m + B_3 \cdot (M - m - 1) = 128 \times 8$. In this paper, we restrict the $M \in [128, 148]$, $m \in [1, 127]$, $B_1 \in [8, 12]$, $B_2 \in [4, 8]$, $B_3 \in [8, 12]$ to obtain the parameter set Ω.

Evaluating the R-D performance of the proposed image coding scheme is a problem in our scheme. In this subsection, we adopt two benchmarks:

The first benchmark is the PSNR value P_1 of the reconstructed image in the case of no dividing, a quantization step of 8 and the same size of the encrypted image. In other words, the PSNR value P_1 is the reconstruction quality of the special ciphertext image $\mathbf{C}_1$. The steps to obtain $\mathbf{C}_1$ are as follows: we apply BCS to Lena with a 0.5 sampling ratio to get the measurements. Then, the measurements are uniformly quantized with 8 quantization steps. Finally, the quantized measurement is encrypted with the same encryption algorithm to get $\mathbf{C}_1$.

The second benchmark is the PSNR value P_2 of the reconstructed image in the case of no dividing, no quantization and the 0.5 sampling ratio. In other words, the PSNR value P_2 is the reconstruction quality of the special ciphertext image $\mathbf{C}_2$. The algorithm to obtain $\mathbf{C}_2$ is similar to the steps to obtain $\mathbf{C}_1$. The different part is only we would not quantize the measurements in this algorithm.

From Fig. 3, a large proportion of the black points are over the green line and the red line. In other words, under the condition that the ciphertext image size is the same, the reconstruction quality of the proposed scheme is better than that of the quantization steps of 8, even better than that of the unquantized

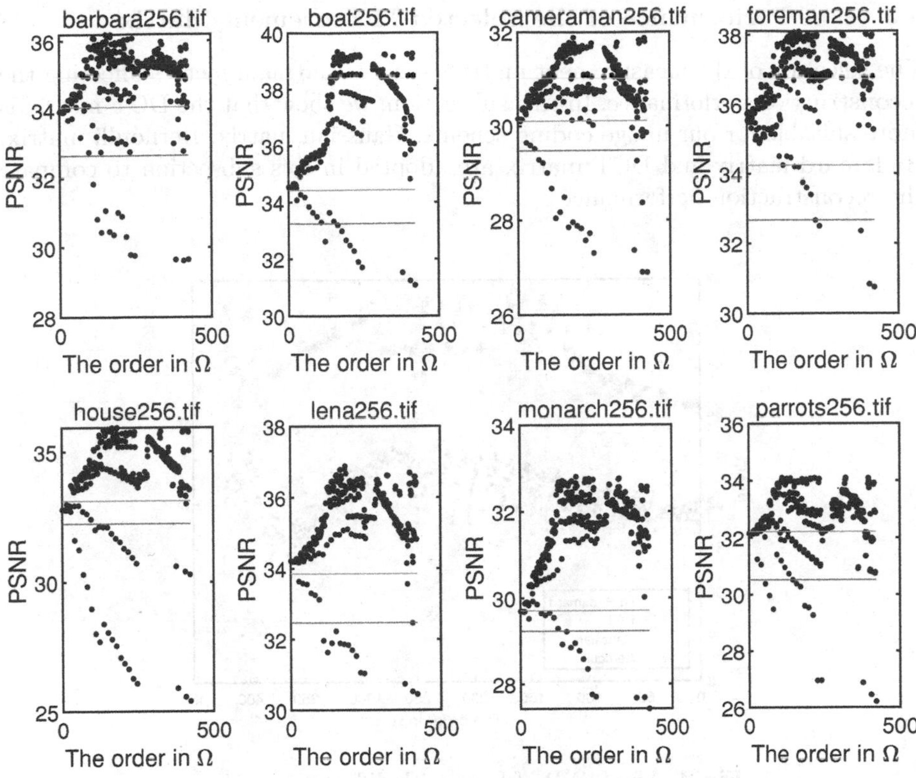

Fig. 3. The PSNR values of the reconstruction images. The red line represents the P1 value and the green line represents the P2 value.

Table 2. The reconstruction quality of the proposed algorithm and other algorithms.

Algorithm	PSNR
Proposed scheme	**36.8792 dB**
[6] (Sampling ratio : 56.25%, Quantization with 8 bpp)	25.9997 dB
[8] (Quantization with 8 bpp)	24dB–25 dB
[7] (Quantization with 8 bpp)	27.5466 dB
[9] (Quantization with 8 bpp)	28.4862 dB
[10] (Quantization with 8 bpp)	29 dB–30 dB
[11] (Without quantization)	32.5546 dB

reconstruction quality in most cases. In addition, we compare the reconstruction performance with some existing image encryption works in Table 2.

In brief, the proposed image coding scheme can achieve better R-D performance.

4.3 The Performance of the Selected Measurement Matrix

The selection of the measurement matrix is one of the main factors affecting the reconstruction performance. In this subsection, we show that the DCT matrix is more suitable for our image coding scheme. Gaussian matrix, Bernoulli matrix, Hadamard matrix and DCT matrix are adopted in this subsection to compare the reconstruction performance.

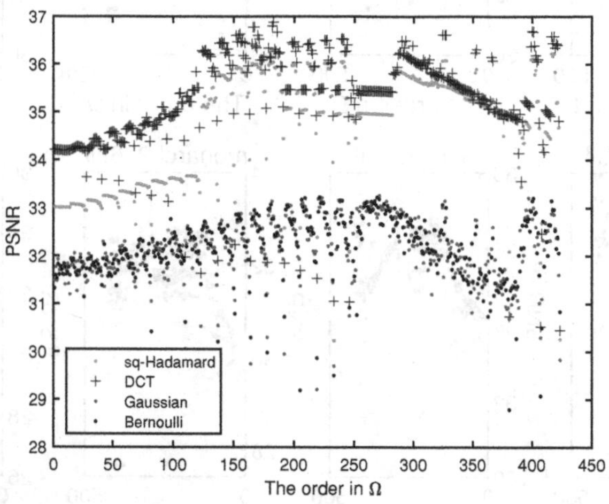

Fig. 4. The PSNR of Lena with different matrixes.

From Fig. 4, the DCT matrix and Hadamard matrix can achieve a higher reconstruction performance. The performance of the matrix whose energy is not distributed evenly can result in a good R-D performance. When the energy is more concentrated in the upper part of the matrix, the reconstruction performance can be better. Therefore, the DCT matrix outperforms the Hadamard matrix. In our image coding scheme, the DCT matrix is adopted as the measurements matrix.

4.4 Security Analysis

In order to prevent the attackers from inferring information from the ciphertext image, the secure image coding scheme should have the ability to resist the brute force attack, the statistical attack and the differential attack.

To resist the brute-force attack and exhaustive attack. The key space must be larger than 2^{100} [20] and the proposed scheme must be sensitive to the secret keys.

The secret keys are control parameters (r_1, r_2, r_3) and initial state values (z_1, z_2, z_3) of Logistic-Tent map. The overall key space is related to the key

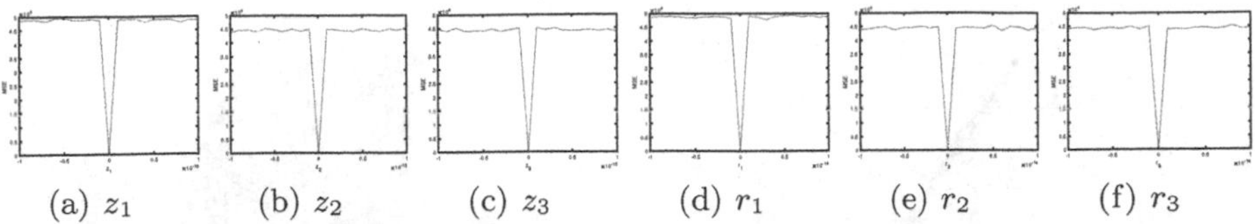

(a) z_1 (b) z_2 (c) z_3 (d) r_1 (e) r_2 (f) r_3

Fig. 5. MSE curves.

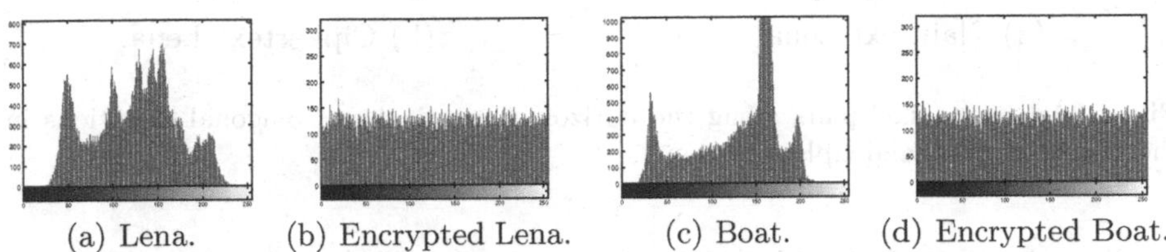

(a) Lena. (b) Encrypted Lena. (c) Boat. (d) Encrypted Boat.

Fig. 6. Histograms.

space of each key which can be calculated with mean absolute error (MAE). MAE is defined by

$$\mathrm{MAE}(\gamma, \tilde{\gamma}) = \frac{1}{N} \sum_{i=1}^{N} |\gamma_i - \tilde{\gamma}_i|, \tag{3}$$

where N is the length of the chaotic sequence, γ_i and $\tilde{\gamma}_i$ are the sequences generated with the initial state z_0 and $z_0 + \Delta$. The key space of z_0 can be described as $\frac{1}{\Delta^*}$, where Δ^* is one of the values Δ for $\mathrm{MAE}(\gamma, \tilde{\gamma}) = 0$. By detail numerical calculations, the key space of z_1, z_2, z_3, r_1, r_2 and r_3 are 10^{17}, 10^{17}, 10^{17}, 10^{16}, 10^{16} and 10^{16}, respectively. Thus, the overall key space is $10^{17} \times 10^{17} \times 10^{17} \times 10^{16} \times 10^{16} \times 10^{16} \times 10 \times 10 \times 10 = 10^{102} \approx 2^{338}$, which is larger than 2^{100}. Therefore, the proposed image coding scheme has the ability to resist brute-force attacks.

To analyze the sensitivity of the cryptoscheme to the secret keys, we utilize the mean square error (MSE) to evaluate the differences between the decrypted image with tiny changed keys and the original image, and it is given by

$$MSE = \frac{1}{H \times L} \sum_{i}^{H} \sum_{j}^{L} \left(\hat{\mathbf{X}}(i,j) - \mathbf{X}(i,j)\right)^2, \tag{4}$$

where $H \times L$ is the size of the image, $\hat{\mathbf{X}}$ and $\mathbf{X}$ are the decrypted image and the plaintext image. Figure 5 displays the MSE curves of the decrypted images with tiny changed keys. The changed keys of $z_1 \sim z_3$ and $r_1 \sim r_3$ ranges from $z + (-10^{-15} \sim 10^{-15})$ and $r + (-10^{-14} \sim 10^{-14})$, respectively. The MSE values of the error keys are significantly different from the MSE value of the correct keys. Accordingly, the proposed scheme is sensitive to the secret keys. It means that the proposed scheme can resist the exhaustive search of the keys.

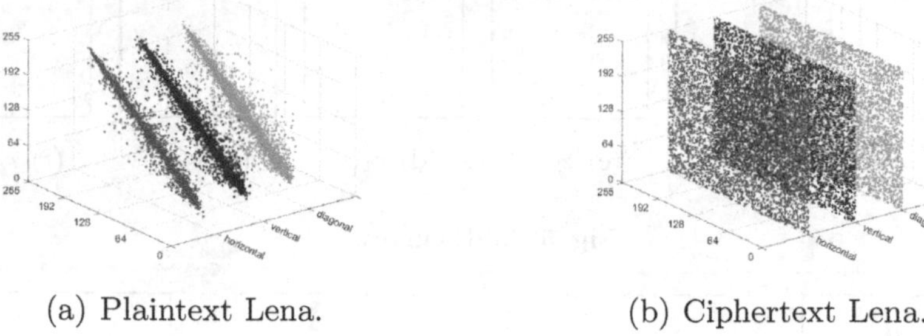

(a) Plaintext Lena. (b) Ciphertext Lena.

Fig. 7. Adjacent pixel pairs along the horizontal, vertical and diagonal directions in the plaintext Lena and ciphertext Lena.

To resist statistical analysis, the proposed scheme should have the ability to resist the histogram analysis and the correlation coefficient analysis.

To frustrate the histogram analysis attack, the distribution of the ciphertext image pixels must be close to uniform. In Fig. 6, we can observe that the histograms of the plaintext image and ciphertext image are totally different. The nearly uniform-shaped histograms of the encrypted Lena and Boat mean that the proposed scheme is able to resist the histogram analysis.

To frustrate the correlation coefficient analysis, the correlation of encrypted image is expected to be close to 0. To make a quantified analysis, the correlation coefficients can be computed by

$$C = \frac{\sum_{i=1}^{L}(x_i - \bar{x})(y_i - \bar{y})}{\sqrt{(\sum_{i=1}^{L}(x_i - \bar{x})^2)(\sum_{i=1}^{L}(y_i - \bar{y})^2)}} \tag{5}$$

where $\bar{x} = \frac{1}{N}\sum_{i=1}^{L} x_i$, $\bar{y} = \frac{1}{N}\sum_{i=1}^{L} y_i$. The 5000 adjacent pixel pairs of Lena image and its corresponding ciphertext image in horizontal, vertical and diagonal directions are selected randomly, respectively. The correlation coefficients of adjacent pixels of the plaintext Lena are 0.9721, 0.9439 and 0.9167, respectively. After coding, the correlation coefficients of adjacent pixels of the ciphertex Lena are 0.0066, −0.0092 and −0.0068, respectively. Refer to the sharply dropping correlation coefficients and Fig. 7, we can notice that the correlation of the ciphertext image is close to 0. In brief, the attackers cannot obtain effective information by using the correlation coefficient analysis.

In order to demonstrate the plaintext sensitivity of the proposed scheme, a pixel of the original Lena is randomly changed to 0, which is shown in Fig. 8 (a). In Fig. 8 (d), the pattern of the differential image between the encrypted original image and the encrypted tiny changed image is nearly noise. Therefore, the proposed scheme which is sensitive enough to the change of the original image can resist the differential attack.

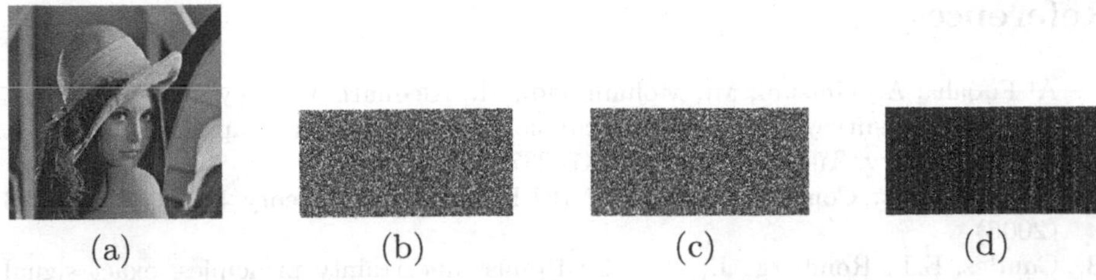

Fig. 8. Plaintext sensitivity analysis. (a) The image "Lena" got by setting a random pixel to 0. (b) The ciphertext image of the original "Lena" image. (c) The encrypted image with the same keys using the image in (a). (d) The differential image between (b) and (c).

Table 3. Information entropies of all the test images and all the corresponding encrypted test images with the same keys.

	Babara	Boat	Cameraman	Foreman	House	Lena	Monarch	Parrots
Plaintext	7.5252	7.1456	7.0097	7.0083	6.4930	7.4442	7.4716	7.4141
Ciphertext	7.9937	7.9944	7.9946	7.9950	7.9939	7.9937	7.9941	7.9947

The image entropy can be calculated by

$$H = \sum_{i=0}^{L} p(i)\log_2(p(i)) \tag{6}$$

where L is the number of gray levels of an image and $p(i)$ is the probability of the gray value i. The theoretical value of information entropy is 8 with 256 gray levels. Table 3 shows that the information entropies of the ciphertext images are all higher than 7.9937 and close to 8, which performs better than [7]. That means the encrypted images are nearly distributed evenly and the attacker cannot infer the effective visual information from the ciphertext images.

5 Conclusion

In this paper, a secure image coding scheme is proposed. Specifically, we elaborately design the encoder to improve the R-D performance of the secure image coding scheme. By exploiting the correlation among the measurements, we can increase the sampling ratio and decrease the quantization steps to achieve higher R-D performance. Experimental results verify the feasibility, higher R-D performance and security of the proposed scheme.

Acknowledge. The work was supported by the National Key R&D Program of China (Grant no. 2020YFB1805401), the National Natural Science Foundation of China (Grant No. 62072063) and the Project Supported by Graduate Student Research and Innovation Foundation of Chongqing, China (Grant No. CYB 21062).

References

1. Al-Fuqaha, A., Guizani, M., Mohammadi, M., Aledhari, M., Ayyash, M.: Internet of Things: a survey on enabling technologies, protocols, and applications. IEEE Commun. Surv. Tutorials **17**(4), 2347–2376 (2015)
2. Donoho, D.L.: Compressed sensing. IEEE Trans. Inf. Theory **52**(4), 1289–1306 (2006)
3. Candès, E.J., Romberg, J., Tao, T.: Robust uncertainty principles: exact signal reconstruction from highly incomplete frequency information. IEEE Trans. Inf. Theory **52**(2), 489–509 (2006)
4. Zhou, N., Zhang, A., Zheng, F., Gong, L.: Novel image compression-encryption hybrid algorithm based on key-controlled measurement matrix in compressive sensing. Optics Laser Technol. **62**, 152–160 (2014)
5. Zhou, N., Li, H., Wang, D., Pan, S., Zhou, Z.: Image compression and encryption scheme based on 2D compressive sensing and fractional Mellin transform. Optics Commun. **343**, 10–21 (2015)
6. Zhou, N., Pan, S., Cheng, S., Zhou, Z.: Image compression-encryption scheme based on hyper-chaotic system and 2D compressive sensing. Optics Laser Technol. **82**, 121–133 (2016)
7. Li, L., Wen, G., Wang, Z., Yang, Y.: Efficient and secure image communication system based on compressed sensing for IoT monitoring applications. IEEE Trans. Multimedia **22**(1), 82–95 (2019)
8. Hu, G., Xiao, D., Wang, Y., Xiang, T.: An image coding scheme using parallel compressive sensing for simultaneous compression-encryption applications. J. Vis. Commun. Image Represent. **44**, 116–127 (2017)
9. Luo, Y., et al.: A robust image encryption algorithm based on Chua's circuit and compressive sensing. Signal Process. **161**, 227–247 (2019)
10. Zhu, L., Song, H., Zhang, X., Yan, M., Zhang, L., Yan, T.: A novel image encryption scheme based on nonuniform sampling in block compressive sensing. IEEE Access **7**, 22161–22174 (2019)
11. Niu, Z., Zheng, M., Zhang, Y., Wang, T.: A new asymmetrical encryption algorithm based on semitensor compressed sensing in WBANs. IEEE Internet Things J. **7**(1), 734–750 (2019)
12. Li, L., Liu, L., Peng, H., Yang, Y., Cheng, S.: Flexible and secure data transmission system based on semitensor compressive sensing in wireless body area networks. IEEE Internet Things J. **6**(2), 3212–3227 (2018)
13. Zhang, Y., Xiang, Y., Zhang, L.Y., Yang, L.X., Zhou, J.: Efficiently and securely outsourcing compressed sensing reconstruction to a cloud. Inf. Sci. **496**, 150–160 (2019)
14. Zhang, Y., He, Q., Chen, G., Zhang, X., Xiang, Y.: A low-overhead, confidentiality-assured, and authenticated data acquisition framework for IoT. IEEE Trans. Industr. Inf. **16**(12), 7566–7578 (2020)
15. Wang, L., Wu, X., Shi, G.: Binned progressive quantization for compressive sensing. IEEE Trans. Image Process. **21**(6), 2980–2990 (2012)
16. Chen, Z., Hou, X., Qian, X., Gong, C.: Efficient and robust image coding and transmission based on scrambled block compressive sensing. IEEE Trans. Multimedia **20**(7), 1610–1621 (2017)
17. Chen, Z., et al.: Compressive sensing multi-layer residual coefficients for image coding. IEEE Trans. Circuits Syst. Video Technol. **30**(4), 1109–1120 (2019)

18. Mun, S., Fowler, J.E.: Block compressed sensing of images using directional transforms. In: 2009 16th IEEE international conference on image processing (ICIP), pp. 3021–3024. IEEE, Cairo (2009)
19. Candes, E.J., Plan, Y.: A probabilistic and RIPless theory of compressed sensing. IEEE Trans. Inf. Theory **57**(11), 7235–7254 (2011)
20. Alvarez, G., Li, S.: Some basic cryptographic requirements for chaos-based cryptosystems. Int. J. Bifurcat. Chaos **16**(08), 2129–2151 (2006)

Black-Box Audio Adversarial Example Generation Using Variational Autoencoder

Wei Zong(✉), Yang-Wai Chow(✉), and Willy Susilo

Institute of Cybersecurity and Cryptology, School of Computing and Information Technology, University of Wollongong, Wollongong, NSW, Australia
{wzong,caseyc,wsusilo}@uow.edu.au

Abstract. Automatic speech recognition (ASR) applications are ubiquitous these days. A variety of commercial products utilize powerful ASR capabilities to transcribe user speech. However, as with other deep learning models, the techniques underlying ASR models suffer from adversarial example (AE) attacks. Audio AEs resemble non-suspicious audio to the casual listener, but will be incorrectly transcribed by an ASR system. Existing black-box AE techniques require excessive requests sent to a targeted system. Such suspicious behavior can potentially trigger a threat alert on the system. This paper proposes a method of generating black-box AEs in a way that significantly reduces the required amount of requests. We describe our proposed method and presents experimental results demonstrating its effectiveness in generating word-level and sentence-level AEs that are incorrectly transcribed by an ASR system.

Keywords: Adversarial example · Automatic speech recognition · Deep learning · Machine learning · Variational autoencoder

1 Introduction

Automatic speech recognition (ASR) applications, such as Google Assistant, play an important role in our daily lives. Modern ASR systems are commonly based on deep learning. However, deep neural networks can be fooled by adversarial examples (AEs). AEs were first investigated in the image domain [21]. In general, AEs that look indistinguishable from their original images can be generated by adding small perturbations to the original input images. Despite appearing to be indistinguishable to the human visual system, these AEs will be misclassified by deep learning models.

While much of the research community has focused on investigating AEs in the image domain [7,14,16], there is less research on AEs in the audio domain. Audio AEs can be classified as targeted and non-targeted. The aim of non-targeted audio AEs is to make an ASR model incorrectly transcribe speech in input audio, while the aim of targeted audio AEs is to cause an ASR model to output a specific transcription injected by an adversary. This paper focuses on non-targeted audio AEs.

D. Gao et al. (Eds.): ICICS 2021, LNCS 12919, pp. 142–160, 2021.
https://doi.org/10.1007/978-3-030-88052-1_9

To date, many audio AE generation techniques adopt a white-box threat model, whereby an adversary knows the internal workings of the target ASR model [4,18,20]. However, a white-box threat model is not practical in the real-world, since commercial ASR application developers do not typically reveal the internal workings of their systems. Thus, black-box audio AE generation techniques are a more practical alternative. Under a black-box assumption, an adversary can only probe the ASR system with input audio and analyze the resulting transcription. Given this challenging problem, there are few studies on generating black-box audio AEs [2,12,22]. These black-box AE generation techniques are all based on the use of genetic algorithms.

Techniques for generating white-box audio AEs are usually formulated as an optimization problem, where input audio is optimized in the direction of the gradient of the loss function [4,18]. This is different for black-box audio AEs, since no internal information can be used to guide the generation process. As such, current black-box audio AEs employ the powerful searching capabilities of genetic algorithms to explore a large target space [2,12,22]. However, genetic algorithms are inefficient due to their non-deterministic nature, as they necessitate making many requests to a target ASR system. This may not be feasible in practice, as such suspicious behavior can be used to trigger a threat alert on the targeted system to block further requests.

This paper proposes a method to efficiently generate black-box audio AEs. The generation exploits the gap between the recognition capabilities of humans and machines. In particular, we interpolate two audio signals in the latent space of a variational autoencoder (VAE) [13] to a point at which the ASR model incorrectly transcribes the speech, but humans can still understand it. This is useful in the situation where users do not want an ASR system to automatically eavesdrop on a conversation. This paper discusses our method for generating word-level and sentence-level audio AEs. Our experiments demonstrate that generating audio AEs using the proposed method requires a low number of probing requests to the target ASR system as compared with other existing audio AE methods. In addition, our sentence-level audio AEs can circumvent temporal dependency detection, which is able to efficiently detect state-of-the-art audio AEs [25].

2 Variational Autoencoder

Variational autoencoder (VAE) is a probabilistic generative model [13] that constructs a relationship between random latent variables $z \sim p_\theta(z)$ and observations $x \sim p_\theta(x|z)$, where the prior $p_\theta(z)$ and conditional likelihood $p_\theta(x|z)$ are parameterized by θ. The marginal likelihood $p_\theta(x)$ and posterior $p_\theta(z|x)$ are intractable, as they both require the integral $\int p_\theta(x|z)p_\theta(z)dz$ to be calculated. As a solution, VAE introduces a recognition model $q_\phi(z|x)$ to approximate the posterior $p_\theta(z|x)$. Thus, $\log p_\theta(x)$ can be rewritten as shown in Eq. 1, where $\mathcal{L}(\theta, \phi; x)$ is the variational lower bound to optimize.

The prior $p_\theta(z)$ is assumed to be centered isotropic multivariate Gaussian $\mathcal{N}(z; 0, I)$, where I is an identity matrix. This is because by using a sufficiently complicated function, we can map a set of d normally distributed variables to any d-dimensional distribution. Besides, both the generative model $p_\theta(x|z)$ and recognition model $q_\phi(z|x)$ are considered as diagonal Gaussian distributions. Neural networks are used to calculate their mean and covariance.

$$\begin{aligned}\log p_\theta(x) &= KL[q_\phi(z|x)||p_\theta(z|x)] + \mathcal{L}(\theta, \phi; x)\\ &\geq \mathcal{L}(\theta, \phi; x)\\ &= -KL[q_\phi(z|x)||p_\theta(z)] + \mathbb{E}_{q_\phi(z|x)}[\log p_\theta(x|z)]\end{aligned} \tag{1}$$

In practice, VAE introduces the reparameterization trick to make the networks differentiable. First, ϵ is sampled from $\mathcal{N}(0, I)$. Then, sampling z from $\mathcal{N}(\mu, \sigma^2 I)$ is transformed as $z = \mu + \sigma \odot \epsilon$, where $\odot$ represents element-wise product.

3 Problem Definition

This study investigates a method of generating non-targeted word-level and sentence-level audio AEs. In word-level AEs, each audio only contains a single spoken word, whereas sentence-level AEs contain a spoken sentence or phrase with multiple words. The aim is for the target ASR model to incorrectly transcribe these audio AEs, while humans can still understand the speech.

Formally, given a speech waveform x, the ground truth transcription y and the target ASR model $f(.)$, our objective is to generate an AE x' by interpolating x in the latent space of VAE, so that x' is perceived to be similar to x by humans, while y' (i.e. the transcription of x') is different from y, where $y' = f(x')$ and $y = f(x)$.

A successful word-level AE requires the edit distance (also known as Levenshtein distance) between y and y' to be larger than a predefined value. Edit distance refers to the minimum number of operations, including deletions, insertions and substitutions, needed to modify letters of a transcribed AE text to match the ground truth transcription. Similarly, a successful sentence-level AE requires the word error rate (WER) between y and y' to exceeds a predefined value. WER is defined as the total number of operations, including deletions, insertions and substitutions, needed to change words of a transcribed AE sentence to match the ground truth transcription, divided by the number of words in the ground truth transcription.

To quantify the difference in human perception of x and x', we compute the Euclidean distance of log-scaled mel spectrograms between them. This distance gives an indication of the similarity of the audio x and x' to a human. The smaller the distance, the more similar the audio will sound to a human.

Threat Model and Assumptions. The proposed method assumes a black-box threat model, in which an adversary has no knowledge of the internal workings of the target ASR model. To probe the ASR system, an adversary can only input audio into the target ASR model and receive the corresponding transcriptions in text format. No other information is available to the adversary. In addition, we assume an over the line attack. This means that digital files are sent directly to the target ASR system for transcription, as opposed to playing back audio files over the air through speakers. We also assume that an adversary cannot probe the target system over thousands of times within a short period of time, since this suspicious behavior will be noticed by the system.

The Target ASR Model. To test the proposed method, DeepSpeech [10] was used as the target ASR model due to its state-of-the-art performance. Note that even though we have access to the internal workings of this open source model, the method proposed in this study treats it as a black-box. DeepSpeech version 0.6.1 was used in the experiments, as it was the most recent version at the time, and no language model was deployed, since related research [4,22,24] did not report on the use of any language models.

4 Related Work

Most current research on generating audio AEs assume a white-box threat model. Early work on white-box audio AEs can be found in [6], in which the authors successfully generated non-targeted audio AEs. However, their proposed method performed unsatisfactorily on targeted audio AEs, because target phrases are required to sound similar to the input audio. This limitation was overcome in [4], who examined targeted attacks where the input audio could be transcribed by DeepSpeech to certain target phrases. In their approach, the connectionist temporal classification loss [8] of the target phrase and the perturbed audio was minimized until DeepSpeech produced the desired transcription. In addition, [18] incorporated expectation over transform [3] into the generation process.

In contrast to white-box audio AEs, there is limited work in the area of black-box audio AEs. Previous work was conducted to fool a light-weight keyword spotting model using genetic algorithms [2]. This work was subsequently extended by targeting the DeepSpeech ASR model [22]. However, the methods presented in both of these studies accessed the prediction scores or logits of the targeted model. Such information is not normally available in commercial ASR products. Thus, as asserted in [12] the audio AEs generated in [2] and [22] are not strictly black-box models.

Black-box audio AEs based on resulting transcripts from the target ASR model using multi-objective evolutionary optimization was proposed in [12]. The fitness function adopted in their method contained two objectives: Euclidean distance of Mel-Frequency Cepstral Coefficients (MFCCs) for measuring the similarity of audio samples, and edit distance for measuring the similarity of transcriptions. When generating non-targeted audio AEs, a large edit distance from the original audio is preferrable, while a small edit distance between the AE transcription and the desired transcription is more appropriate in the generation of targeted audio AEs. The generating of black-box audio AEs using genetic algorithms [2,12,22] necessitates making a large number of requests to the target ASR model, due to the non-deterministic property of these algorithms. This unusual behavior can be used by such systems to detect an attack. Although the method proposed in this paper focuses on non-targeted audio AEs, the generation process requires much fewer requests. Recent work in [1] also investigated black-box untargeted audio AEs. They decomposed audio via singular spectrum

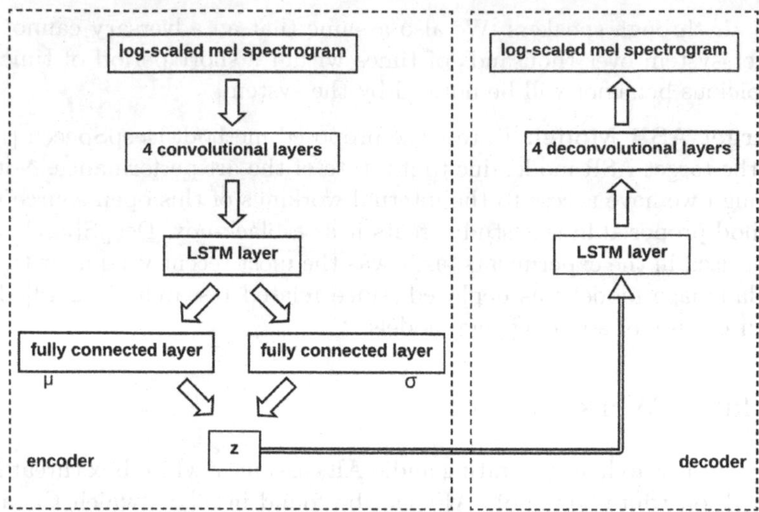

Fig. 1. Conceptual depiction of the VAE architecture.

analysis and discrete Fourier transforms. Audio AEs were then generated by removing components under thresholds.

There has also been an interest in the use of deep probabilistic generative models and VAE [13] in the audio domain. This is because the interpolation of audio in the latent space of VAE can results in meaningful samples. This property was exploited to smoothly interpolate audio samples [11].

5 Proposed Method

Audio Preprocessing. The audio data is first segmented based on word boundaries by forced alignment using corresponding transcriptions. Since we want the generated audio AEs to be similar to the input audio, we utilize log-scaled mel spectrograms as audio features. The commonly used MFCCs in ASR models is not suitable because it discards pitch variation. After alignment, each single-word audio is transformed into mel spectrograms with dimensions $D_t \times D_m$, where D_t is the number of time steps and D_m is the number of mel bands. In our experiments, we set $D_m = 80$ and round D_t down to a multiple of 8.

Model Architecture. In the proposed method, the VAE architecture from Hsu et al. [11] was extended by adding Long Short-Term Memory (LSTM) and extra convolutional layers. The reason for the LSTM layers is because audio data is sequence data, and LSTM is capable of learning temporal dependency in audio. In addition, extra convolutional layers were introduced to further down-sample the audio in the time dimension. In this manner, there are less time steps in the LSTM layers and the training is faster.

A conceptual depiction of the architecture for our VAE is provided in Fig. 1. The VAE is divided into encoder and decoder sections. There are 4 convolutional

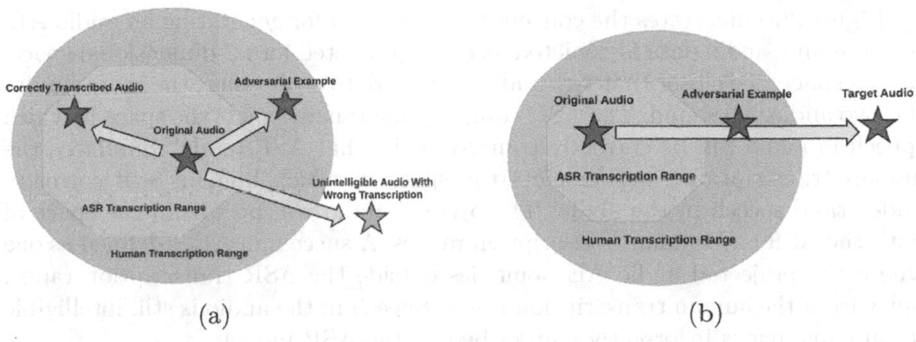

Fig. 2. Generating an audio AE. (a) A successful audio AE should be outside the ASR transcription range, but within the human transcription range. (b) Proposed AE generation method, where an AE is generated by interpolating between an original audio and a target audio in the latent space of VAE.

layers in the encoder. The number of filters for these layers are 64, 128, 256, and 256, respectively. The first convolutional layer has a $1 \times (D_m - 7)$ filter size with a 1×1 stride. The other 3 convolutional layers have a 3×3 filter size with a 2×2 stride. No padding is applied to the first layer, whereas the same padding was applied to the other layers.

The dimensions of the input log-scaled mel spectrogram is $D_t \times D_m$ so after the 4 convolutional layers, the audio is downsampled to $(D_t/8) \times 1 \times 256$. Specifically, $D_t/8$ is the time steps while 1×256 is the dimension of features. Then, a LSTM layer with hidden dimension $D_h = 128$ is applied to this down-sampled audio. The last hidden state with dimension D_h is passed to the Gaussian layer via fully connected layers. The mean value with dimension D_h output from the Gaussian layer is considered as a latent representation of the input audio and the corresponding space with dimension D_h is the latent space.

The decoder section of the architecture mirrors the stages in the encoder. First, a latent representation with dimension D_h is sampled using the mean and covariance output by the Gaussian layer. This sampled latent representation is replicated $(D_t/8)$ times and passed to a LSTM layer with hidden dimension equaling to 256 to reconstruct the $(D_t/8) \times 1 \times 256$ audio. Then, this audio is up-sampled using 4 deconvolutional layers until a log-scaled mel spectrogram with dimension $D_t \times D_m$ is reconstructed. After some experimentation, we found that the model performs well when the convolutional and deconvolutional layers used Leaky ReLU as activation functions, while the tanh activation function was adopted in the LSTM layers.

5.1 Generating Word-Level Adversarial Examples

This section describes our method for generating non-targeted audio AEs at word-level. The purpose of the method is to modify audio that contains a spoken word to a point at which the target ASR model incorrectly transcribes it, while humans can still correctly understand the word.

Figure 2(a) illustrates the concept that was used for generating an audio AE. In the figure, audio data is depicted as being projected into 2-dimensional space. In this space, the closer that two audio points are to each other, the more similar the two audio will sound. The ASR transcription range depicts the space in which speech in audio will be correctly transcribed by that ASR model. Similarly, the human transcription range depicts the space in which humans will correctly understand speech in the audio. The original audio will be within the space of both the ASR and human transcription ranges. A successful AE is defined as one where the projected audio AE point lies outside the ASR transcription range, but within the human transcription range. Speech in the audio is still intelligible to humans, but is incorrectly transcribed by the ASR model.

Black-box AE generation [12,22] makes use of genetic algorithms to randomly modify audio until a successful AE is obtained. The drawback of this non-deterministic method is that it requires the generation of many random samples. Each sample must be sent to the ASR model for transcription to determine whether or not the sample falls within the ASR transcription range. This typically results in a large number of transcription requests being sent to probe the ASR system, which may not be feasible in practice as the shear number of similar transcription requests can alert a system of such an attack.

In contrast, the purpose of our method is to significantly reduce the number of required samples by interpolating between two audio in the latent space of VAE. This is illustrated in Fig. 2(b), where the original audio, which contains a spoken word, is within the ASR and human transcription ranges. Audio which contains a different spoken word is then selected, i.e. the target audio. As the target audio contains a different spoken word, it will definitely lie outside both the ASR and human transcription ranges of the original audio. By interpolating between the original audio and the target audio in the latent space of VAE, the resulting audio will be somewhere in-between the two. The projected location of the resulting audio depends on the interpolation strength. By increasing the interpolation strength, the resulting audio will move closer to the target audio. An audio AE is successfully generated when the resulting audio moves outside the ASR transcription range, but remains within the human transcription range. In this way, the guided approach in our proposed method is more efficient than a genetic algorithm's random sampling.

Formally, let A_W be audio that contains a single spoken word. Our goal is to generate an AE, A'_W, such that A'_W will still be interpreted as A_W by a human, but with $Dist(ASR(A_W), ASR(A'_W)) \geq t$, where $ASR()$ represents the output of the ASR model, $Dist()$ is the function to compute the edit distance between transcribed audio, and t is a predefined threshold that indicates minimum error in the transcription.

Let M_W be the log-scaled mel spectrogram of A_W with dimension $D_t \times D_m$. Let L_W be the latent representation of M_W with dimension D_l. Thus, $L_W = Enc(M_W)$, where $Enc()$ is the encoding function of the VAE, which accepts the log-scaled mel spectrogram as input, and outputs the latent representation with dimension D_l. Let A_T be a target audio that contains a spoken word that is different from A_W. The procedure for generating A'_W by interpolating between A_W and A_T is described as follows. Let M_T and $L_T = Enc(M_T)$ be the log-scaled mel spectrogram and latent representation of A_T, respectively. The interpolated latent representation: L'_W, is calculated using linear interpolation $L'_W = L_W \times (1-s) + L_T \times s$, where strength s is a real number within $[0, 1]$ that controls the extent of the interpolation. Let $M'_W = Dec(L_{W'})$ be the reconstructed log-scaled mel spectrogram given $L_{W'}$, where $Dec()$ is the decoding function of the VAE, which accepts a latent representation of dimension D_l as input, and outputs the reconstructed log-scaled mel spectrogram with dimension $D_t \times D_m$. A'_W is reconstructed from M'_W by using Griffin-Lim spectrogram inversion [9].

A'_W is considered to be a successful audio AE if the word is incorrectly transcribed, i.e. $Dist(ASR(A_W), ASR(A'_W)) \geq t$. It should be mentioned that increasing the value of s will increase the likelihood that the ASR model will incorrectly transcribe A'_W, because it will increase the difference between the original audio A_W and the modified audio A'_W. However, a successful AE also requires that A'_W sounds similar to A_W from the perspective of human auditory perception, and that a human will interpret the word in A'_W as the same word in A_W. Thus, the value of s should only be as large as it needs to be for the ASR to incorrectly transcribe A'_W. If the resulting A'_W does not satisfy the conditions of a successful AE, either increase the value of s or a different target word can be used for A_T.

A naive way of selecting A_T and s is to sequentially select different audio from a dataset and to gradually increase the value of s. However, this potentially results in a large number of requests to the ASR system. In general, it is better to specify the minimum value of s, and select A_T from a set of different words. Then, only increase the value of s if each word in the set fails to produce a successful AE.

Algorithm 1 in the Appendix details the word-level AE generation procedure that was described above. Given a set of predetermined s values, it finds the minimum value of s that will produce a successfully AE. Let A_{Ti}, where $i \in \{1, 2, ..., n\}$, be a audio set that contain spoken words, and let s_j where $j \in \{1, 2, ..., m\}$, be a set of values for s with increasing strength. The input to the algorithm is an original audio, A_W, the set of target audio, A_{Ti}, the set of interpolation strengths, s_j, and the predefined minimum error threshold, t. For a given set of target audio and interpolation strengths, if a successful AE cannot be found, the algorithm can be repeated on a different set of target audio.

5.2 Generating Sentence-Level Adversarial Examples

This section describes our method for generating sentence-level AEs. An important point to highlight is that simply concatenating the word-level AEs of each word in a sentence, in an attempt to produce a sentence-level AE will not work. This is because state-of-the-art ASR models employ deep learning to learn temporal dependencies in audio. This means that ASR models apply a holistic approach to transcribing an entire sentence, as opposed to independently transcribing each word. In the word-level AE generation approach described above, temporal dependency does not have to be considered as the ASR model is only supplied with a single word without any context. However, for sentence-level AE generation to be successful, this has to be taken into account.

To describe the sentence-level AE generation method, let A_S be audio containing a sentence of spoken words. Let $(A_{w1}, A_{w2}, ..., A_{wp})$ represent all words in the sentence, and let $(M_{w1}, M_{w2}, ..., M_{wp})$ be the corresponding log-scaled mel spectrograms of the respective words, where p is the total number of words in the sentence. Let $WER()$ be the function to calculate the word error rate, which represents the transcription error in a sentence, and t_S be a predefined value indicating the minimum required transcription error. Our goal of generating a sentence-level AE, $A'_S \equiv (A'_{w1}, A'_{w2}, ..., A'_{wp})$, is to produce an A'_S such that $WER(ASR(A'_S), ASR(A_S)) \geq t_S$, while the words in A'_S are still interpreted by a human as being the same as the words in A_S.

Words in the sentence are sequentially replaced with modified audio, while ensuring that the transcription error increases. To describe the method for generating A'_S, the method starts with $A_S \equiv (A_{w1}, A_{w2}, ..., A_{wp})$, where p is the total number of words in the sentence. The audio of each word A_{wi} in A_S is replaced with a modified audio A'_{wi} in a sequential manner, where $i \in \{1, 2, ..., p\}$. The method for generating A'_{wi} is based on the word-level AE generation method described in the previous section. Given a set of audio that each contain a spoken word that is different from A_{wi}, A_{Tj} where $j \in \{1, 2, ..., n\}$, and a set of interpolation strengths, s_k where $k \in \{1, 2, ..., m\}$, A_{wi} and A_{Tj} are interpolated based on s_k to produce A'_{wi}. The value of s_k is within the range $[0, 1]$, and determines the degree of interpolation between A_{wi} and A_{Tj}.

Let $A_{Si} \equiv (A'_{w1}, ..., A'_{wi}, ..., A_{wp})$ represent a sentence in which the audio of the ith word and all words preceding the ith word, have been replaced with corresponding A'_{wi}. In other words, the audio of each word in the sentence have been sequentially replaced with a modified audio up until the ith word. We consider the inclusion of each A'_{wi} to be successful if $ASR(A_{Si}) \neq ASR(A_{Si-1})$ and $WER(ASR(A_{Si}), ASR(A_S)) \geq WER(ASR(A_{Si-1}), ASR(A_S))$. This means that the modification of the audio for the ith word is deemed to have succeeded if the ASR model produces different transcriptions for A_{Si} and A_{Si-1}, and the transcription error has increased, or is at least the same, with the modification of the ith word. Note that to initialize the transcription error, A_{S0} is set as A_S, hence, initially $WER(ASR(A_{S0}), ASR(A_S)) = 0$. Finally, the generating of the sentence-level AE is deemed to be successful if $WER(ASR(A'_S), ASR(A_S)) \geq t_S$. The procedure for generating sentence-level AE is detailed in Algorithm 2 in the Appendix.

6 Results

In this section, we first show that when compared with the original audio, distortion in the reconstructed audio increases as the interpolation strength increases. We then present results demonstrating word-level and sentence-level audio AEs generated using our method. Finally, we show that the audio AEs generated

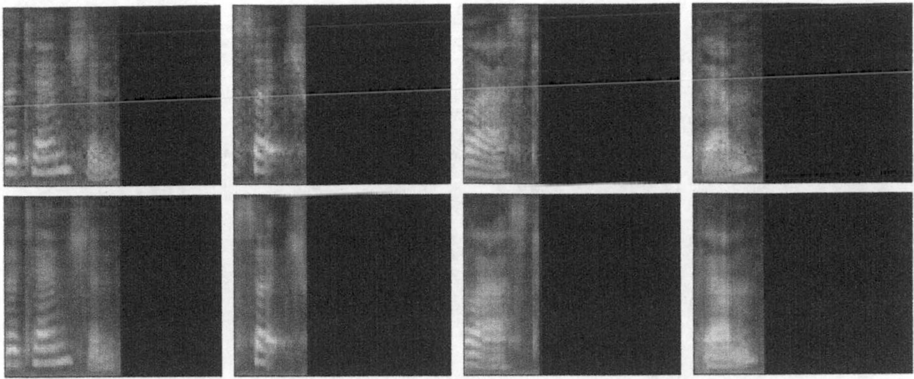

Fig. 3. Reconstructed mel spectrograms without interpolation; first row: mel spectrograms of original audio; second row: the corresponding reconstructed mel spectrograms.

using our proposed method can succeed in thwarting the AE detection method proposed in Yang et al. [25] and transformation defense.

The LibriSpeech [17] dataset was the audio dataset used in the experiments. This dataset contains approximately 1,000 h of read English speech, where the speech duration of a single speaker is usually longer than 20 min. In experiments presented in this paper, all audio data from speaker number 19 in LibriSpeech was used to train the VAE model as well as to generate the AEs. In addition, we used the LibriSpeech alignments produced by Lugosch et al. [15].

The version of DeepSpeech used in experiments is 0.6.1. To improve the performance of DeepSpeech, we deployed the language model, which can be downloaded together with the pre-trained DeepSpeech model.

6.1 Distortion vs Interpolation Strength

A key assumption in our method is that the smaller the interpolation strength, the less distortion produced in reconstructed audio. In this manner, the generation of AEs should use as small an interpolation strength as possible. To investigate the correctness of this assumption, we interpolate randomly selected audio of spoken words with all other words in the dataset using various interpolation strengths. We determined the amount of distortion by calculating the median Euclidean distance between log-scaled mel spectrograms of the original and reconstructed audio.

First, we randomly selected and plotted reconstructed log-scaled mel spectrograms without interpolation to show that the model has been well trained. As shown in Fig. 3, the reconstructed mel spectrogram highly resembles the original ones. This indicates successful training of the model. Then, three randomly selected audio of spoken words were interpolated with the audio of all other spoken words in the dataset. The three words were: “attention”, “such” and “last”.

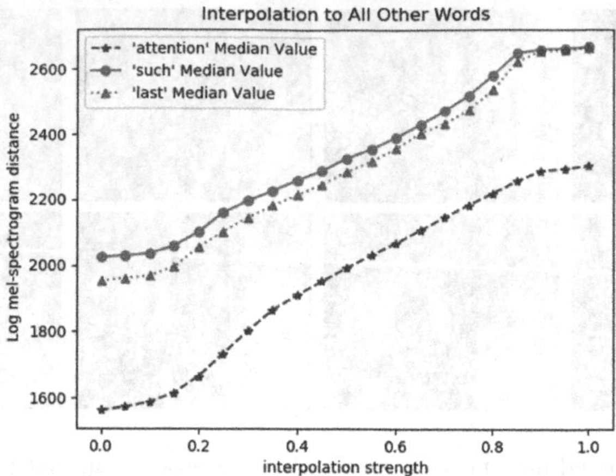

Fig. 4. Example distortion in reconstructed audio as a result of interpolation strength.

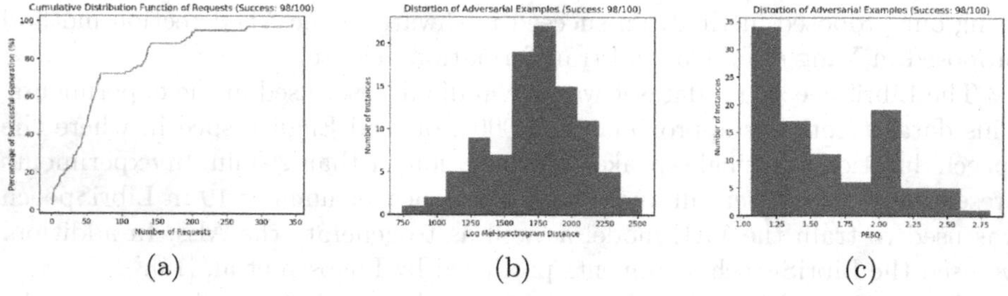

Fig. 5. (a) CFD of requests made to DeepSpeech. (b) Distribution of distortion in audio AEs based on log-scaled mel spectrogram distance. (c) Distribution of distortion in audio AEs based on PESQ.

The results of this are shown in Fig. 4. We can see that the distortion increases as the interpolation strength increases for all these words. This is intuitive in the sense that audio is distorted more and more as the interpolation strength increases, and with a large enough interpolation strength, the modified audio will eventually be more similar to the target audio than the original audio. Overall, the results presented in Fig. 4 show that smaller interpolation strength leads to less distortion in the reconstructed audio.

6.2 Word-Level Adversarial Examples

To make the non-targeted AEs non-trivial, we generate AEs for spoken words which are correctly transcribed by DeepSpeech. In addition, their corresponding reconstructed audio without interpolation must also be correctly transcribed by DeepSpeech. This is to verify the effectiveness of the proposed method. We applied Algorithm 1 to at most five different subsets of the LibriSpeech [17]

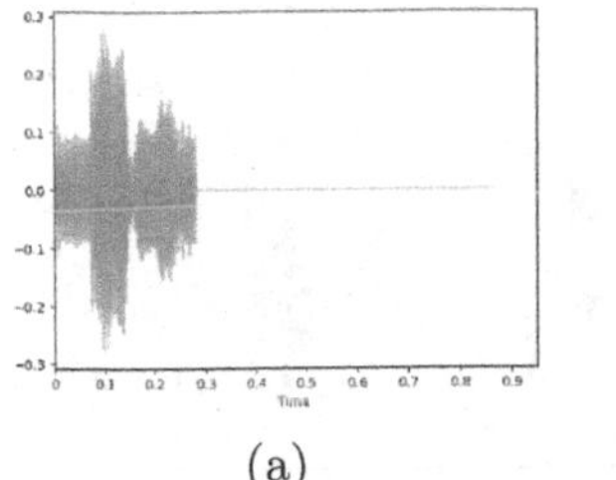
(a)

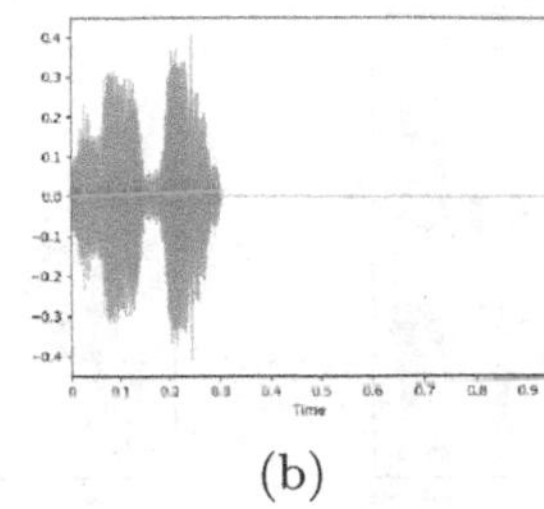
(b)

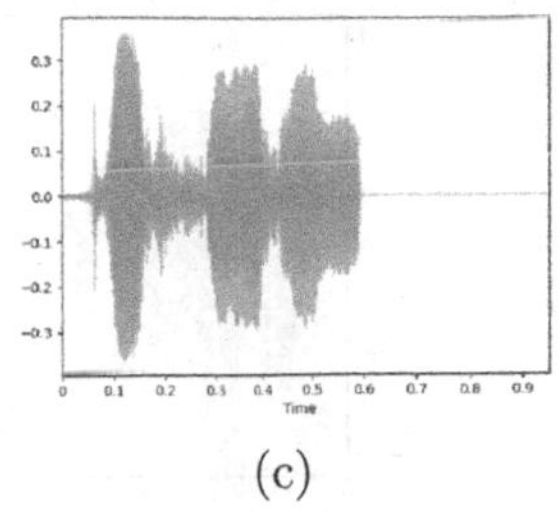
(c)

Fig. 6. Example depicting resulting audio for word-level AEs; original audio (blue), corresponding AE (orange). (a) DeepSpeech could not transcribe the AE for the word "many"; (b) DeepSpeech could not transcribe the AE for the word "never"; (c) The AE for the word "perceiving" was incorrectly transcribed as "curving". (Color figure online)

dataset. Of the key parameters that were used in the experiments, the number of words in A_{Ti} was 10, the values in s_j were {0.017, 0.033, 0.050, 0.067, 0.083, 0.100, 0.117} and the value of the threshold t was set as half the length of the input word.

In Fig. 5(a), we show a cumulative distribution function (CDF) of requests made to DeepSpeech in order to generate 100 AEs. The success rate of AE generation was 98/100, with the majority of AEs successfully generated by making in the order of tens of requests to DeepSpeech. A small number of AEs required requests in the order of hundreds of requests. In comparison, Taori et al. [22] reported that their AE approach requires thousands of iterations on average to generate one audio AE. Hence, our approach achieves its purpose of reducing the number of required requests. Wang et al. [24] pointed out that the method proposed by Khare et al. [12] did not consider success rates and the number of queries. As such, a comparison with that method could not be done adequately. Figure 5(b) and 5(c) in turn show the distortion distribution of the generated AEs. In addition to the distance of log-scaled mel spectrogram, we also measured Perceptual Evaluation of Speech Quality (PESQ), which was proposed as an automatic evaluation metric for measuring speech degradation in the context of telephony [19]. We can see that the log-scaled mel spectrogram distance is centered around 1800, while most PESQ values are between 1.0 to 2.2. It should be noted that we can potentially lower the distortion by making more requests to DeepSpeech. Specifically, we can increase the number of samples in each subset so that a successful AE is more likely to be generated with smaller s.

We present examples showing visual comparisons between original audio and their corresponding audio AEs in Fig. 6. It can be seen from Fig. 6 that waveforms of the audio AEs resemble the waveforms of their original audio. This suggests the acoustic similarity between the AEs and their respective original audio. The AEs either cannot be transcribed by DeepSpeech, or are transcribed as different words. For example, in Fig. 6(a) and 6(b), the AEs for the words "many" and "never" could not be transcribed by the ASR model, whereas in Fig. 6(c), the AE for the word "perceiving" was incorrectly transcribed as "curving".

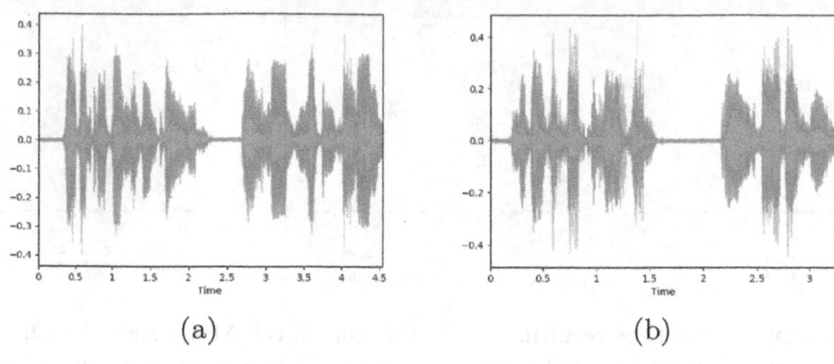

Fig. 7. Example depicting resulting audio for sentence-level AEs; original audio (blue), corresponding AE (orange). (a) AE sentence "hated confinement and cleanliness and loved nothing so well as" was transcribed as "kate could find mental cleanliness came loves nothing said well"; (b) AE sentence "she brought herself to read them and though there seemed" was transcribed as "to put herself to madam watho that she". (Color figure online)

6.3 Sentence-Level Adversarial Examples

In this section, we present experimental results obtained from generating sentence-level AEs. As mentioned in Sect. 5.2, simply concatenating word-level AEs into a sentence will not result to a successful sentence-level AE. This is because temporal dependencies in the audio data will help ASR models in correctly transcribing the sentence. In the experiments, the same parameters for word-level AEs generation were used for sentence-level AEs generation.

We selected 30 sentences, which contain at most 10 words, to demonstrate the effectiveness of our method. The results show that the mean WER is 0.75, with the minimum and maximum values equal to 0.4 and 1.0, respectively. If we set the minimal WER for success to 0.7, the success rate is 77%. The mean PESQ value of these 30 audio AEs is 1.37. On average, it needs 38.8 queries for each word in a sentence. It means there are expected to be only 390 queries needed for a sentence with 10 words. This is less than the thousands of queries required by the method in Taori et al. [22].

Two example experiment results are presented in Fig. 7. We can see that the waveforms of these AEs resemble their original audio. Both sentences shown in Fig. 7(a) and 7(b) were incorrectly transcribed with WER both equal to 0.8. It should be mentioned that we did not modify words with a duration of less than 15 ms, e.g., words such as "a" and "an". This is because these short words do not convey important information and they are too short to be successfully modified without overly distorting the resulting audio. Moreover, experiment results show that modifying words before or after such short words are sufficient to cause short words to be incorrectly transcribed. This is also due to temporal dependency in the audio data. In addition, skipping the modification of such short words also reduces the number of requests made to the ASR system.

6.4 Circumventing Temporal Dependency Detection

A recent audio AE detection method based on temporal dependency has been shown to be efficient in detecting state-of-the-art audio AEs [25]. This detection is based on the observation that previous audio AEs generation methods do not preserve temporal dependency. The detection procedure is briefly described as follows. First, only a portion of a spoken sentence, of length k, is fed into the ASR model and transcribed into transcription $T_{\{k\}}$. Then, the whole sentence is fed into the ASR model and transcribed. The portion of the whole sentence transcription that corresponds to length k is extracted as $T'_{\{k\}}$, and compared with $T_{\{k\}}$. An audio AE is detected if $T_{\{k\}}$ is significantly different from $T'_{\{k\}}$.

Since word-level AEs do not have temporal dependency, we only discuss how our sentence-level AEs circumvent temporal dependency detection. This is because in our proposed method, every time a word in the sentence is modified our method computes the error of the whole sentence, not just a portion of the sentence. Hence, temporal dependency in the modified sentence is preserved.

To demonstrate this, we extract various portions from the original audios and audio AEs in the same way as in [25], e.g. $k = \frac{1}{2}, \frac{2}{3}, \frac{3}{4}, \frac{4}{5}, \frac{5}{6}$. We then send all of these sub-sentences to be transcribed by the ASR system to see whether temporal dependency is preserved. Table 3 in the Appendix presents an example demonstrating this. It can be seen that the generated AE has a similar temporal dependency property as the original audio, because the preceding transcribed words are the same even when the number of words in the sub-sentence is increased. This indicates that the detection method proposed in [25] will not work on the sentence-level AEs generated using our proposed method, because no matter the value of k in $T_{\{k\}}$, the result of $T'_{\{k\}}$ will be consistent with $T_{\{k\}}$.

We implement the temporal detection method to detect the 30 sentence-level AEs generated in Sect. 6.3. The results in Table 1 suggest that the sentence-level AEs can successfully circumvent temporal dependency detection due to low AUC values.

6.5 Robustness Against Transformation

In addition to temporal dependency, preprocessing input audio using various transformations has also been shown to be an effective defense against audio AEs [5]. We conducted experiments to determine whether transformation would recover the original transcripts of our 30 sentence-level audio AEs. The following transformations were considered: Gaussian noise with different standard deviation, filtering by high pass filters with different cutoff frequencies and resampling the input audio at different rates. Experimental results are shown in Table 2. As mentioned above, the mean WER of our 30 sentence-level audio AEs is originally 0.75. We can see that the transformation cannot recover the original transcripts of the audio because the average WER only decreases slightly.

Table 1. Detection of our audio AEs through temporal dependency.

	WER	CER	LCP
$k = \frac{1}{2}$	0.728	0.735	0.593
$k = \frac{2}{3}$	0.728	0.716	0.593
$k = \frac{3}{4}$	0.567	0.557	0.589
$k = \frac{4}{5}$	0.592	0.623	0.644
$k = \frac{5}{6}$	0.629	0.635	0.638

Table 2. Robustness against transformation

	Gaussian noise			High pass filtering			Resampling		
	1e−4	1e−3	1e−2	200 Hz	300 Hz	400 Hz	8000	10000	12000
Mean WER	0.72	0.67	0.69	0.61	0.60	0.68	0.74	0.75	0.75

7 Limitations and Future Work

There are two main limitations in our proposed method. First, our method heavily relies on techniques to accurately align the lengths of spoken words in audio. Although alignment of speech is a well studied problem [15], it would be more efficient in future work if unaligned speech could be used directly. Another limitation of our proposed method is that some generated AEs may not be easily interpreted by a human due to the noise introduced in the resulting AE. This is a consequence of the black-box model, because unlike a white-box model, a black-box model assumes no knowledge of the internals workings of an ASR system. In future work, we will incorporate psychoacoustics and the use of a vocoder, such as Wavenet [23], to increase the quality of the reconstructed audio.

Furthermore, VAE trained in this paper is only based on a single speaker. It should be mentioned that VAE can be speaker-independent by integrating speech from various speakers in the training set. However, this would result in significantly more effort to successfully train a VAE that can produce clear speech. The complexity of the proposed architecture may also increase. We leave speaker-independent VAE as an investigation for future work.

8 Conclusion

This paper presents a novel black-box non-targeted audio AE generation method. The proposed method makes use of a VAE model to produce black-box audio AEs. This black-box generation process relies solely on transcription results produced by an ASR model, without requiring any information about the internal workings of the ASR model. Methods for generating both word-level AEs and sentence-level AEs are described. In addition, this paper presents experiment results demonstrating that our method can successfully generate audio

AEs using a smaller number of requests to an ASR system as compared with other methods that rely on the use of non-deterministic genetic algorithms.

Appendix

Table 3. Example of circumventing temporal dependency detection.

k	Original audio transcription	AE transcription
$\frac{1}{2}$	Her mother was a woman of	It mother let alone
$\frac{2}{3}$	Her mother was a woman of useful	It mother let alone useful
$\frac{3}{4}$	Her mother was a woman of useful plan	It mother let alone useful
$\frac{4}{5}$	Her mother was a woman of useful plans	It mother let alone useful and
$\frac{5}{6}$	Her mother was a woman of useful plain	It mother let alone useful in
1	Her mother was a woman of useful plain sense with	It mother let alone useful insense what

Algorithm 1. Word-level AE generation

Input: original audio, A_W; a set of target audio, A_{Ti} (where $i \in \{1, 2, ..., n\}$); a set of interpolation strengths, s_j (where $j \in \{1, 2, ..., m\}$); and a minimum edit distance, t
Output: word-level AE, A'_W

```
For each s_j, where j ∈ {1, 2, ..., m}, do
   For each A_Ti, where i ∈ {1, 2, ..., n}, do
      M_W ← log-scaled mel spectrogram for A_W
      M_T ← log-scaled mel spectrogram for A_Ti
      M'_W ← interpolate between M_W and M_T by s_j
      A'_W ← reconstruct audio from M'_W using
                 Griffin-Lim spectrogram inversion
// check whether AE generation succeeded (i.e. if resulting
// edit distance above threshold)
      If Dist(ASR(A_W), ASR(A'_W)) ≥ t
         return A'_W
      End If
   End For
End For
// if AE generation unsuccessful, use a different set of
// target audio
```

Algorithm 2. Sentence-level AE generation

Input: original audio containing a sentence, A_S; a set of target audio, A_{Tj} (where $j \in \{1, 2, ..., n\}$); a set of interpolation strengths, s_k (where $k \in \{1, 2, ..., m\}$)
Output: sentence-level AE, A'_S

WordLoop:
For each word A_{wi} in sentence A_S do
  For each s_k, where $k \in \{1, 2, ..., m\}$, do
    For each A_{Tj}, where $i \in \{1, 2, ..., n\}$, do
      $M_{wi} \leftarrow$ log-scaled mel spectrogram of A_{wi}
      $M_{Tj} \leftarrow$ log-scaled mel spectrogram of A_{Tj}
      $M'_{wi} \leftarrow$ interpolate between M_{wi} and M_{Tj} by s_k
      $A'_{wi} \leftarrow$ reconstruct audio from M'_{wi} using
          Griffin-Lim spectrogram inversion
// check whether the transcription of the modified
// sentence is different from the previous sentence
// and that the error has not decreased
      If $ASR(A_{Si}) \neq ASR(A_{Si-1})$ and
        $WER(ASR(A_{Si}), ASR(A_S)) \geq$
          $WER(ASR(A_{Si-1}), ASR(A_S))$
// save the modified sentence, and proceed to modify
// the next word in the sentence
          $A'_S \leftarrow A_{Si}$
          goto WordLoop
      End If
    End For
  End For
End For
// verify the sentence-level AE
If $WER(ASR(A'_S), ASR(A_S)) \geq t_S$
  return A'_S
End If

References

1. Abdullah, H., et al.: Hear "no evil", see "kenansville": efficient and transferable black-box attacks on speech recognition and voice identification systems. In: 2021 IEEE Symposium on Security and Privacy (SP), Los Alamitos, CA, USA, May 2021, pp. 142–159. IEEE Computer Society (2021)
2. Alzantot, M., Balaji, B., Srivastava, M.B.: Did you hear that? Adversarial examples against automatic speech recognition. CoRR, abs/1801.00554 (2018)
3. Athalye, A., Engstrom, L., Ilyas, A., Kwok, K.: Synthesizing robust adversarial examples. In: Proceedings of the 35th International Conference on Machine Learning, ICML 2018, Stockholmsmässan, Stockholm, Sweden, 10–15 July 2018, pp. 284–293 (2018)
4. Carlini, N., Wagner, D.A.: Audio adversarial examples: targeted attacks on speech-to-text. In: 2018 IEEE Security and Privacy Workshops, SP Workshops 2018, San Francisco, CA, USA, 24 May 2018, pp. 1–7 (2018)

5. Chen, G., et al.: Who is real bob? Adversarial attacks on speaker recognition systems. CoRR, abs/1911.01840 (2019)
6. Cissé, M., Adi, Y., Neverova, N., Keshet, J.: Houdini: fooling deep structured visual and speech recognition models with adversarial examples. In: Advances in Neural Information Processing Systems 30: Annual Conference on Neural Information Processing Systems 2017, Long Beach, CA, USA, 4–9 December 2017, pp. 6977–6987 (2017)
7. Goodfellow, I.J., Shlens, J., Szegedy, C.: Explaining and harnessing adversarial examples. In: 3rd International Conference on Learning Representations, ICLR 2015, San Diego, CA, USA, 7–9 May 2015, Conference Track Proceedings (2015)
8. Graves, A., Fernández, S., Gomez, F.J., Schmidhuber, J.: Connectionist temporal classification: labelling unsegmented sequence data with recurrent neural networks. In: Machine Learning, Proceedings of the Twenty-Third International Conference (ICML 2006), Pittsburgh, Pennsylvania, USA, 25–29 June 2006, pp. 369–376 (2006)
9. Griffin, D., Lim, J.: Signal estimation from modified short-time Fourier transform. IEEE Trans. Acoust. Speech Signal Process. **32**(2), 236–243 (1984)
10. Hannun, A.Y., et al.: Deep speech: scaling up end-to-end speech recognition. CoRR, abs/1412.5567 (2014)
11. Hsu, W., Zhang, Y., Glass, J.R.: Learning latent representations for speech generation and transformation. In: Interspeech 2017, 18th Annual Conference of the International Speech Communication Association, Stockholm, Sweden, 20–24 August 2017, pp. 1273–1277 (2017)
12. Khare, S., Aralikatte, R., Mani, S.: Adversarial black-box attacks for automatic speech recognition systems using multi-objective genetic optimization. CoRR, abs/1811.01312 (2018)
13. Kingma, D.P., Welling, M.: Auto-encoding variational Bayes. In: 2nd International Conference on Learning Representations, ICLR 2014, Banff, AB, Canada, 14–16 April 2014, Conference Track Proceedings (2014)
14. Kurakin, A., Goodfellow, I.J., Bengio, S.: Adversarial examples in the physical world. In: 5th International Conference on Learning Representations, ICLR 2017, Toulon, France, 24–26 April 2017, Workshop Track Proceedings (2017)
15. Lugosch, L., Ravanelli, M., Ignoto, P., Tomar, V.S., Bengio, Y.: Speech model pre-training for end-to-end spoken language understanding. CoRR, abs/1904.03670 (2019)
16. Moosavi-Dezfooli, S., Fawzi, A., Fawzi, O., Frossard, P.: Universal adversarial perturbations. In: 2017 IEEE Conference on Computer Vision and Pattern Recognition, CVPR 2017, Honolulu, HI, USA, 21–26 July 2017, pp. 86–94 (2017)
17. Panayotov, V., Chen, G., Povey, D., Khudanpur, S.: LibriSpeech: an ASR corpus based on public domain audio books. In: 2015 IEEE International Conference on Acoustics, Speech and Signal Processing, ICASSP 2015, South Brisbane, Queensland, Australia, 19–24 April 2015, pp. 5206–5210 (2015)
18. Qin, Y., Carlini, N., Cottrell, G.W., Goodfellow, I.J., Raffel, C.: Imperceptible, robust, and targeted adversarial examples for automatic speech recognition. In: Proceedings of the 36th International Conference on Machine Learning, ICML 2019, Long Beach, California, USA, 9–15 June 2019, pp. 5231–5240 (2019)
19. Rix, A.W., Beerends, J.G., Hollier, M.P., Hekstra, A.P.: Perceptual evaluation of speech quality (PESQ)-a new method for speech quality assessment of telephone networks and codecs. In: IEEE International Conference on Acoustics, Speech, and Signal Processing, ICASSP 2001, Salt Palace Convention Center, Salt Lake City, Utah, USA, 7–11 May, 2001, Proceedings, pp. 749–752. IEEE (2001)

20. Schönherr, L., Kohls, K., Zeiler, S., Holz, T., Kolossa, D.: Adversarial attacks against automatic speech recognition systems via psychoacoustic hiding. In: 26th Annual Network and Distributed System Security Symposium, NDSS 2019, San Diego, California, USA, 24–27 February 2019 (2019)
21. Szegedy, C., et al.: Intriguing properties of neural networks. In: 2nd International Conference on Learning Representations, ICLR 2014, Banff, AB, Canada, 14–16 April 2014, Conference Track Proceedings (2014)
22. Taori, R., Kamsetty, A., Chu, B., Vemuri, N.: Targeted adversarial examples for black box audio systems. In: 2019 IEEE Security and Privacy Workshops, SP Workshops 2019, San Francisco, CA, USA, 19–23 May 2019, pp. 15–20 (2019)
23. van den Oord, A., et al.: WaveNet: a generative model for raw audio. In: The 9th ISCA Speech Synthesis Workshop, Sunnyvale, CA, USA, 13–15 September 2016, p. 125 (2016)
24. Wang, Q., Zheng, B., Li, Q., Shen, C., Ba, Z.: Towards query-efficient adversarial attacks against automatic speech recognition systems. IEEE Trans. Inf. Forensics Secur. **16**, 896–908 (2021)
25. Yang, Z., Li, B., Chen, P., Song, D.: Characterizing audio adversarial examples using temporal dependency. In: 7th International Conference on Learning Representations, ICLR 2019, New Orleans, LA, USA, 6–9 May 2019 (2019)

Security Analysis

Security Analysis of Even-Mansour Structure Hash Functions

Shiwei Chen(✉), Ting Cui, and Chenhui Jin

The PLA SSF Information Engineering University, Zhengzhou, China

Abstract. In this paper, we mainly focus on the security of Even-Mansour structure hash functions, including preimage attack resistance and multi-block collision attack resistance.

Firstly, we focus on the Even-Mansour structure hash function with two iterations. Basing on the permutation used in the Even-Mansour structure hash function we construct two new functions f_1 and f_2, and find the partial invariables of input-output in one function f_1. Then using the partial invariables of input-output and the meet-in-the-middle techniques, we present a preimage attack on the Even-Mansour structure hash function with two iterations, with the time complexity of $2^{a(2^a-1)}+2^a+2^{n-2a}$ functional operations of f_1 or f_2 and the memory is 2^a a-bit values, where $a2^a \leq n$ and n is the size of hash value.

Secondly, we extend the Even-Mansour structure hash function to the one with arbitrary iterations. Utilizing the property that the beginning and the ending of every iteration in the Even-Mansour structure both need XOR the message or the transform result of the message, we construct many chaining values with relations in each iteration, which makes that the number of the final chaining values is equal to the product of the number of output chaining values in each iteration, and thereby propose our multi-block collision attack on the Even-Mansour structure hash functions with the time complexity of $t2^{\frac{s}{2t}}$ queries of F permutation and memory complexity of $O(2^{s/2})$, where t is the block number of collision message and s is the size of truncated hash value.

Keywords: Hash function · Even-Mansour structure hash function · Preimage attack · Multi-block collision attack · Partial invariables of input-output · Meet-in-the-middle technique

1 Introduction

Hash functions are an important class of primitive in modern cryptography, mainly used in many cryptographic protocols, message authentication, etc. A hash function H transfers a message M with arbitrary length into a fixed-length message digest *h called hash value.* If the length of the hash value is n bits, we call the hash function a *n-bit hash function.* To guarantee the security of the applications, a hash function H needs to satisfy the following three basic security principles, that is, preimage resistance, second preimage resistance and collision resistance. For a n-bit hash function, if the computational complexity of finding a second preimage or a preimage is less than 2^n,

D. Gao et al. (Eds.): ICICS 2021, LNCS 12919, pp. 163–173, 2021.
https://doi.org/10.1007/978-3-030-88052-1_10

then the hash function is considered not to be second preimage resistance or preimage resistance, and if the computational complexity of finding a collision is less than $2^{n/2}$, then the hash function is considered not to be collision resistance.

In one hash function, the inputs include one message and one fixed initial chaining value, and the output is the fixed-length hash value. Correspondingly, in one block cipher, its inputs are one plaintext and one key, and output is the ciphertext. Since these two structures are similar, cryptographers usually regard the key in the block cipher as the message in the hash function, and thereby construct hash functions based on block ciphers. Preneel [1] proposed 11 kinds of methods of constructing hash functions based on block cipher, which include Davies-Meyer (DM) construction used in the MD family hash functions.

Furthermore, there is one important construction in block cipher, that is, Even-Mansour (EM for short) structure. The EM structure was proposed by Even and Mansour [2] in 1997, which allows to construct block cipher from a permutation F. In this construction, the plaintext firstly XORs the key K_1, then bypass F, and finally XORs the key K_2, i.e., the ciphertext is computed by $c = F(p \oplus K_1) \oplus K_2$. In 2012, Dunkelaman and Shamir [3] proved that the EM construction remains the same security level even if $K_1 = K_2$. Meanwhile, Bogdanov et al. [4] generalized the EM structure into ones with more than one rounds, where different permutations are utilized in separated round, and they pointed out the security bound of the distinguishing attack. In 2017, Isobe [5] used the meet-in-the-middle technique to present the key recovery attack on the two variants, one of which is $E_K^{(2)}(x)$, that is,

$$E_K^{(2)}(x) = P_2(P_1(x \oplus K) \oplus \pi(K)) \oplus K$$

where P_1, P_2, P are n-bit permutation, K is n-bit key and π is an simple key schedule. In 2019, Leurent and Sibleyras [6] presented Low-Memory attacks against two-round Even-Mansour using the 3-XOR problem.

Though the Even-Mansour block cipher and hash function have the similar structure, the messages in Even-Mansour structure hash function could be chosen and different message blocks are used in different iterations. In 2013, Yiyuan Luo and Xuejia Lai [7] proposed the EM structure hash functions, and proposed one two-block collision attack with the time complexity of $2^{s/4+1}$(s is the size of hash value). In 2015, the Kupyna hash function was approved as the new Ukrainian standard DSTU 7564:2014 [12], which uses the Davies-Meyer compression function based on the Even-Mansour scheme. Furthermore, in the design of some new hash functions, the compression functions are based on permutations, such as SHA-3 [8], light-weight hash function PHOTON [9], JH hash function [10], etc. In this paper, we will research on the security of the EM hash function, including preimage attack resistance and multi-block collision attack resistance.

Our Contributions. For the Even-Mansour structure hash function with two iterations, we firstly construct two new functions f_1 and f_2 based on the permutation F, and then find the partial invariables of input-output in one function f_1. Then, using the partial invariables of input-output and the meet-in-the-middle techniques, we present a preimage attack on Even-Mansour structure hash functions with two iterations, and analyse the computational complexity of our preimage attack.

Then, for the EM structure hash functions with more iterations, we utilize the property that the beginning and the end of every iteration in Even-Mansour structure both need XOR the message or the transform result of message, to construct many chaining values with relations in each iteration, which makes that the number of the final chaining values is equal to the product of the number of output chaining values in each iteration, and thereby proposes our multi-block collision attack on the Even-Mansour structure hash functions and analyse the computational complexity of our multi-block collision attack.

Outline. The remainder of this paper is organized as follows. In Sect. 2, we describe the EM structure hash functions and some notations. In Sect. 3, we present our preimage attack on Even-Mansour structure hash functions with two iterations and analyse the computational complexity. And then we propose our Multi-block collision attack on Even-Mansour structure hash function with arbitrary iterations and analyse the computational complexity in Sect. 4. In Sect. 5, we conclude our work and propose the future work.

2 Preliminaries

2.1 Description of the Even-Mansour Structure Hash Functions

Even-Mansour structure was proposed by Even and Mansour [2] in 1997 to construct a scheme for a block cipher, which uses a fixed n-bit permutation. The n-bit plaintext is firstly XORed with n-bit K_1, and the result is the input of the permutation. The output of the permutation is XORed with n-bit K_2, and the result is the ciphertext. In [3], Dunkelman and Shamir showed that the original two-key Even-Mansour structure is not minimal since it can be simplified into a single key structure with $K_1 = K_2 = K$.

Since the structure of a hash function is quite similar to that of a block cipher, we can learn the designing of hash functions from mature designed block ciphers. In 2017, Isobe et al. [5] presented one variants of the two-round Even-Mansour structure block cipher, that is,

$$E_K^{(2)}(x) = P_2(P_1(x \oplus K) \oplus K) \oplus K$$

If the K and x are replaced by message and chaining value respectively, then we obtain the EM structure hash function with two iterations.

Let F be a n-bit random permutation, m_1, m_2 be two n-bit input messages, and $h_i (1 \leq i \leq 2)$ be the output chaining value after the ith iteration, $h_0 = IV$ be a fixed constant, n be the size of the hash value. Then the Even-Mansour structure hash function with two iterations $EM_n^{(2)}(IV, m_1, m_2)$ is described as follows:

Step1. Set $h_0 = IV$. For i from 1 to 2, compute

$$h_i = F(h_{i-1} \oplus m_i) \oplus m_i$$

Step2. Output the h_2 as the hash value.

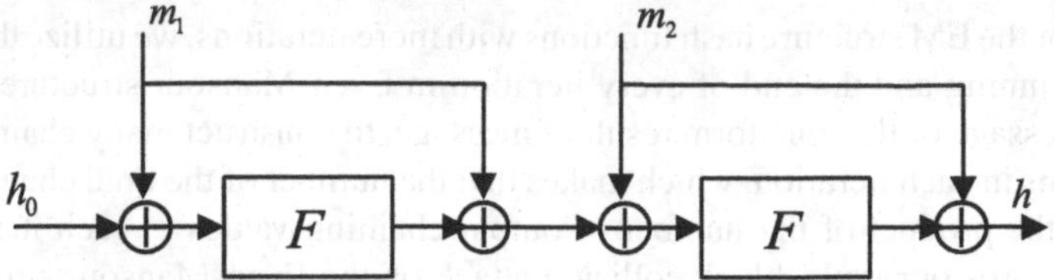

Fig. 1. The workflow of Even-Mansour structure hash function with two iterations

2.2 Notations

In this paper, we mainly focus on the security of the Even-Mansour structure hash function with s-bit hash value, t block n-bit input message $m_1, m_2, \cdots, m_t$ and initial chaining value IV, which is noted as $EM_s^{(t)}(IV, m_1, m_2, \cdots, m_t)$. If not specified, the notations used in this paper is described as follows:

F: the n-bit permutation used in EM structure hash function;

m_i: the n-bit message used in the ith iteration;

$Tur_a(x)$: the most a bits of the variable x;

$x||y$: the concatenation of x and y, that is, for $x \in \{0, 1\}^a, y \in \{0, 1\}^{n-a}, x||y = 2^{n-a}x \oplus y$;

x_a, x_{n-a}: the most a bits and the least (n-a) bits of variable x respectively, that is $x = x_a||x_{n-a}$;

u_i, v_i: the input and output respectively of the permutation F in the i-th iteration;

3 Our Preimage Attack on Even-Mansour Structure Hash Functions

In [5], Isobe et al. proposed the key recovery attack on the $E_K^{(2)}(x)$, in which the single key is used, so they need to guarantee the consistency of the two rounds. However, in the EM structure hash functions, different message blocks are used in different rounds and the message block could be chosen, which increases the degree of freedom for searching. In this section, utilizing the permutation F, we construct two new functions f_1 and f_2, and then outline the method to find the partial invariables of input-output in the f_1 and f_2 functions. Using the partial invariables of input-output in f_1 and the meet-in-the-middle techniques, we present a new preimage attack on the EM structure hash functions with two iterations.

3.1 Construction of the Partial Invariables of Input-Output in the Functions

Let $f : \{0, 1\}^m \times \{0, 1\}^n \rightarrow \{0, 1\}^n$ be a function from $M \times X$ to Y. Then the partial invariables and target partial invariables of inputs and outputs in f are defined as follows.

Definition 1 [11] **.** Let $x \in X, y \in Y$. If for any $m \in M$, there is $f(m, x) = y$. Then (x, y) is called *the invariable pair of input-output*. If there exists one $y' \in \{0,1\}^a (a < n)$ such that for any $m \in M$, we have $Tur_a(f(m, x)) = y'$, then (x, y') is called *the partial invariable pair of a-bit input-output*. If the y' of (x, y') is fixed, then (x, y') is called *target invariable pair of a-bit input-output*.

Let $f : \{0, 1\}^a \times \{0, 1\}^n \to \{0, 1\}^n$ from $M' \times X$ to Y. Then finding one partial invariable pair of a-bit input-output according to the following procedure:

Step1. Randomly choose one $x \in \{0, 1\}^n$;

Step2. Choose one $m_a \in \{0, 1\}^a$, compute $y_1 = f(m_a, x)$, and store $y' = Tur_a(y_1)$;

Step3. Choose another new $m'_a \in \{0, 1\}^a$, such that $m'_a \neq m_a$, and compute

$$y_2 = f(m'_a, x);$$

Step4. Check whether $y' = Tur_a(y_2)$ or not. If yes, then return to Step 3. If all m'_a in $\{0, 1\}^a$ are passed, then output (x, y'); or else, return to step1.

Then we analyse the time complexity of finding one partial invariable pair of a-bit input-output (x, y')。

In Step 4, the probability of $y' = Tr_a(y_2)$ is 2^{-a}, so the probability of $2^a - 1$ m'_a all passing is $(2^{-a})^{2^a-1}$. Therefore the time complexity of finding one partial invariable pair of a-bit input-output (x, y') is $2^{a(2^a-1)}$ functional operations of f.

3.2 Our Preimage Attack on Even-Mansour Structure Hash Functions

In every compression function of EM structure hash function, the message block is different. Each message block is firstly XORed to the chaining variable, and then is XORed to the result of the random n-bit permutation F. The output is the input chaining variable of the next compression function. So, to obtain the preimage of EM structure hash function with two iterations, the key point is finding one two-block message, which could keep consistency in the two-round compression function.

3.2.1 Our Preimage Attack on Even-Mansour Structure Hash Functions with Two Iterations

Let m_{1a} and $m_{1(n-a)}$ be respectively the most a bits and the least $n - a$ bits of m_1, and $m_1 \oplus IV$ be the XOR of the first message block m_1 and the initial chaining variable IV. Then we have

$$m_1 \oplus IV = (m_{1a} \oplus IV_a)||(m_{1(n-a)} \oplus IV_{n-a})$$

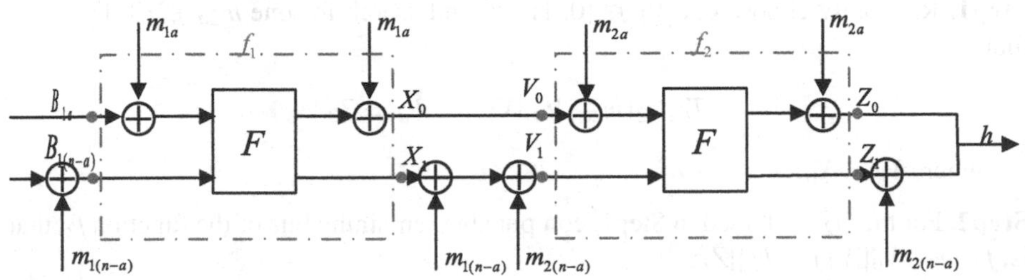

Fig. 2. The workflow of our preimage attack

The function f_1 is constructed as described in Fig. 2.

Let $B_1 = B_{1a}||B_{1(n-a)} = IV_a||(IV_{n-a} \oplus m_{1(n-a)})$ be the input chaining variable of f_1. Then we have

$$f_1(m_{1a}, B_1) = F(B_1 \oplus (m_{1a}||0_{n-a})) \oplus (m_{1a}||0_{n-a}) \triangleq X_0||X_1$$

where $X_0 \in \{0,1\}^a, X_1 \in \{0,1\}^{n-a}$. From the above expression, we know that it only depends on the message m_{1a}, which is helpful to find the partial invariable pair of input-output in the function f_1.

Let $V = V_0||V_1$ be the input chaining variable of the function f_2 as described in Fig. 3. Then we have.

$$V_0 = X_0,\ f_2(m_{2a}, V) = F(V \oplus (m_{2a}||0_{n-a})) \oplus (m_{2a}||0_{n-a}) \triangleq Z_0||Z_1.$$

Next we firstly seek for the partial input-output fixed-point of the function f_1, and use the different values of the remaining output of f_1 to obtain more values to be chosen. Then compute backward from the given hash value and utilizing the meet-in-the-middle technique and the property of the EM structure hash function, we obtain one preimage M of the given hash value h *for* $EM_n^{(2)}(IV, m_1, m_2)$. *The whole process is divided into two phases, that is, online phase and offline phase.*

Offline Phase:

Step1 Utilizing the algorithm described in Sect. 3.1, we could obtain one pair of partial *invariable pair* input-output fixed-point (B_1, X_0) of the function f_1, that is, for any $m_{1a} \in \{0,1\}^a$, the pair (B_1, X_0) satisfies:

$$Tur_a(f_1(m_{1a}, B_1)) = X_0;$$

Step2 For all the $m_{1a} \in \{0,1\}^a$, compute the remaining bits of the function f_1, that is,

$$f_1(m_{1a}^{(i)}, B_1) = X_0||X_1^{(i)}, i = 0, 1, \cdots, 2^a - 1$$

Compute $m_{1(n-a)} = IV_{n-a} \oplus B_{1(n-a)}$ and then $m_{1(n-a)} \oplus X_1^{(i)}$. Store $(m_{1a}^{(i)}, m_{1(n-a)} \oplus X_1^{(i)})$, $i = 0, 1, \cdots, 2^a - 1$ in table T_1.

Online Phase:

Step1. Randomly choose one $V_1 \in \{0,1\}^{n-a}$, and search for one $m_{2a} \in \{0,1\}^a$, such that

$$Tr_a(f_2(m_{2a}, V_0||V_1)) = h_a = Z_0$$

where $V_0 = X_0$;

Step2. For the m_{2a} obtained in Step1, compute the remaining bits of the function f_2, that is, $f_2(m_{2a}, V_0||V_1) = h_a||Z_1$;

Step3. Compute $m_{2(n-a)} = Z_1 \oplus h_{n-a}$, and judge whether $m_{2(n-a)} \oplus V_1$ is equal to one element $m_{1(n-a)} \oplus X_1^{(i)}$ in table T_1 or not. If yes, output $m_{2a}, m_{2(n-a)}, m_{1(n-a)}$ and $m_{1a}^{(i)}$ corresponding to $m_{1(n-a)} \oplus X_1^{(i)}$ in table T_1; Or else, return to Step1.

3.2.2 The Complexity of Our Preimage Attack

In this section, we analyze the time complexity and memory of our preimage attack proposed in Sect. 3.2.1.

The Complexity of the Offline Phase. In Step1, according to the algorithm described in Sect. 3.1, we know that the time complexity of finding one pair of partial a-bit input-output fixed-point (B_1, X_0) of the function f_1 is $2^{a(2^a-1)}$ functional operations of f_1. Since $B_{1a} = IV_a$ is fixed, there are only 2^{n-a} values of B_1 to choose. Hence, the condition $2^{a(2^a-1)} \leq 2^{n-a}$ needs to be satisfied, that is $a2^a \leq n$; In Step2, the time complexity of computing the values of f_1 for all the $m_{1a} \in \{0, 1\}^a$ is 2^a functional operations of f_1. Hence, the time complexity of the offline phase is $2^{a(2^a-1)}+2^a$ functional operations of f_1 and the memory is $2^a a$-bit values.

The Complexity of the Online Phase. In Step1, the time complexity of searching for $m_{2a} \in \{0, 1\}^a$ such that $Tr_a(f_2(m_{2a}, V_0||V_1)) = h_a = Z_0$ is 2^a functional operations of f_2; In Step2, we need to compute the remaining bits of the function f_2 for one m_{2a}, so the time complexity is one functional operations of f_2, which can be ignored; In Step3, since there are 2^a different values of $m_{1(n-a)} \oplus X_1^{(i)}$ in table T_1, the probability that $m_{2(n-a)} \oplus V_1$ is equal to one element $m_{1(n-a)} \oplus X_1^{(i)}$ in table T_1 *is* $2^{-(n-2a)}$, and, so we need to process the Step1–3 2^{n-2a} times to obtain one pair of $(V_1, X_1^{(i)})$ satisfying $m_{2(n-a)} \oplus V_1 = m_{1(n-a)} \oplus X_1^{(i)}$. Hence, the time complexity is about 2^{n-2a} functional operations of f_2.

In a word, the time complexity of our preimage attack is $2^{a(2^a-1)}+2^a + 2^{n-2a}$ functional operations of f_1 or f_2 and the memory is $2^a a$-bit values, where $a2^a \leq n$.

4 Multi-block Collision Attack on Even-Mansour Structure Hash Function

In this section, we extend the EM structure hash function with two iterations to the one with arbitrary iterations, that is $EM_s^{(t)}(IV, m_1, m_2, \cdots, m_t)(t \geq 2)$.

Let F be a n-bit random permutation, $m_1, m_2, \cdots, m_t(t \geq 2)$ be n-bit input messages, and $h_i(1 \leq i \leq t)$ be the output chaining value after the ith iteration, $h_0 = IV$ be a fixed constant, L_1 and L_2 be two transformations from $\{0, 1\}^n$ to $\{0, 1\}^n$, $s(s \leq n)$ be the size of the hash value. Then the Even-Mansour structure hash function $EM_s^{(t)}(IV, M)$ is described as follows (See Fig. 3):

Step1. Set $h_0 = IV$. For i from 1 to t, compute

$$h_i = F(h_{i-1} \oplus m_i) \oplus L_1(m_i) \oplus L_2(h_{i-1})$$

Step2. Output the most s bits of h_t as the hash value.

In 2013, Yiyuan Luo and Xuejia Lai [7] proposed two-block collision attack on the Even-Mausour structure hash functions, with the time complexity of $2^{s/4+1}$ of F, and they did not analyse the memory. Next we present one multi-block collision attack on the Even-Mausour structure hash function, and analyse the time complexity and memory.

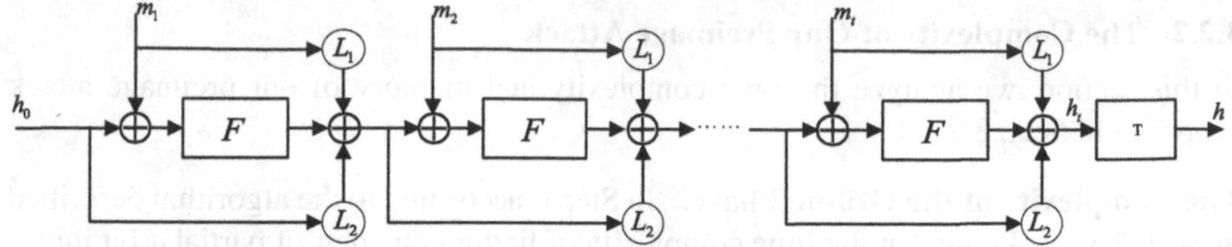

Fig. 3. The workflow of EM structure hash function with t-iteration

In every iteration of the Even-Mausour structure hash function, the input of the permutation F is related to the message, and the output of the permutation F is Xored into the message, which is the input of the second iteration. Hence, we could firstly have access to the permutation F, and use the result to compute the messages and the output chaining values. For each chaining value, use the same way to compute the message and the output chaining values in the next iteration. In this section, we present our multi-block collision attack on $EM_s^{(t)}(IV, M)$, which is an Even-Mansour structure hash function with s-bit hash value. We are to find two different t-block ($t \geq 2$) message $M = m_1||m_2||\cdots||m_t$ and $M' = m_1'||m_2'||\cdots||m_t'$, such that

$$EM_s^{(t)}(IV, M) = EM_s^{(t)}(IV, M')$$

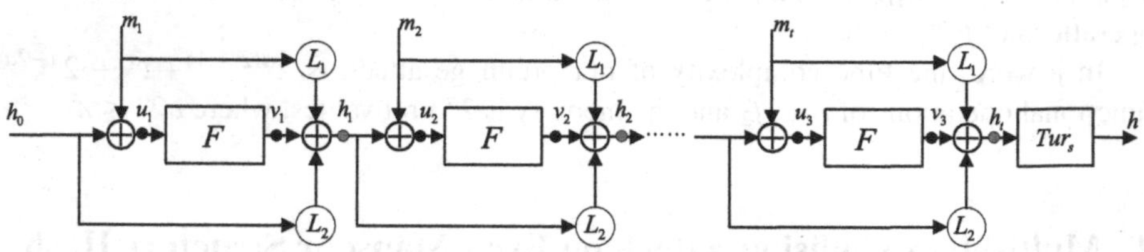

Fig. 4. The workflow of our multi-block collision attack

4.1 Our Multi-block Collision Attack on the Even-Mansour Structure Hash Function

Let F be one random permutation, $(m_1, m_2, \cdots, m_t)(t \geq 2)$ be t-block input message, h_i be n-bit chaining variable, and $h_0 = IV$, $(u_i, v_i)(1 \leq i \leq t)$ be the pair of input-output of the F in the i-th iteration. Then our multi-block collision attack on the Even-Mansour structure hash function is described as follows:

Step1. In the first iteration, randomly choose r_1 different values $u_1^{(1)}, u_1^{(2)}, \cdots, u_1^{(r_1)}$, and respectively visit the permutation F, and thereby obtain r_1 pairs of input-output $(u_1^{(1)}, v_1^{(1)}), (u_1^{(2)}, v_1^{(2)}), \cdots, (u_1^{(r_1)}, v_1^{(r_1)})$。Since $h_1 = v_1 \oplus L_1(m_1) \oplus L_2(IV)$, we could obtain r_1 random values of h_1。Store the r_1 quads $(\Phi, u_1^{(j)}, v_1^{(j)}, h_1^{(j)})(1 \leq j \leq r_1)$;

Step2. In the second iteration, randomly choose r_2 different values $u_2^{(1)}, u_2^{(2)}, \cdots, u_2^{(r_2)}$, and respectively visit the permutation F, and thereby obtain r_2 pairs of input-output $(u_2^{(1)}, v_2^{(1)}); (u_2^{(2)}, v_2^{(2)}), \cdots, (u_2^{(r_2)}, v_2^{(r_2)})$;

Step3. For every $(u_2^{(j)}, v_2^{(j)})(1 \le j \le r_2)$, compute $m_2 = u_2^{(j)} \oplus h_1$ and $h_2 = v_2^{(j)} \oplus L_1(m_2) \oplus L_2(h_1)$.

Since we obtain r_1 random values of h_1 in Step1, for each $(u_2^{(j)}, v_2^{(j)})(1 \le j \le r_2)$, we could obtain r_1 random (m_2, h_2)。And since we have r_2 $(u_2^{(j)}, v_2^{(j)})$ in Step2, we could obtain $r_1 r_2$ random (m_2, h_2)。Store $r_1 r_2$ quads

$$(h_1^{(k)}, u_2^{(j)}, v_2^{(j)}, h_2^{(j)})(1 \le k \le r_1, 1 \le j \le r_2);$$

Step4. In the i-th iteration, randomly choose r_i different values $u_i^{(1)}, u_i^{(2)}, \cdots, u_i^{(r_i)}$ and respectively visit the random permutation, and thereby obtain r_i pairs of input-output $(u_i^{(1)}, v_i^{(1)}), (u_i^{(2)}, v_i^{(2)}), \cdots, (u_i^{(r_2)}, v_i^{(r_2)})$。For every $(u_i^{(j)}, v_i^{(j)})(1 \le j \le r_i)$, compute

$$m_i = u_i^{(j)} \oplus h_{i-1} \text{ and } h_i = v_i^{(j)} \oplus L_1(m_i) \oplus L_2(h_{i-1}).$$

Since in the $(i-1)$-st iteration, we obtain $r_1 r_2 \cdots r_{i-1}$ random values of h_{i-1}, for every $(u_i^{(j)}, v_i^{(j)})(1 \le j \le r_i)$, we obtain $r_1 r_2 \cdots r_{i-1}$ random (m_2, h_2)。Store $r_1 r_2 \cdots r_{i-1} r_i$ quads $(h_{i-1}^{(k)}, u_i^{(j)}, v_i^{(j)}, h_i^{(j)})(1 \le k \le r_1 \cdots r_{i-1}, 1 \le j \le r_i)$;

Step5. Do as above up to the t-th iteration, and we could obtain $r_1 r_2 \cdots r_{t-1} r_t$ random (m_t, h_t)。Store $r_1 r_2 \cdots r_t$ quads $(h_{t-1}^{(k)}, u_t^{(j)}, v_t^{(j)}, h_t^{(j)})(1 \le k \le r_1 \cdots r_{t-1}, 1 \le j \le r_t)$;

Step6. If the size of the hash value is s, then according to the birthday attack, we have that if $r_1 r_2 \cdots r_{t-1} r_t = 2^{s/2}$, then the pair $h_t^{(p)}$ and $h_t^{(q)}$ satisfying $h_t^{(p)} = h_t^{(q)}$ could be found with the probability of 0.39. Then searching for the table of the t-th iteration, we could obtain the quads corresponding to the $h_t^{(p)}$ and $h_t^{(q)}$, that is,$(h_{t-1}^{(k_1)}, u_t^{(p)}, v_t^{(p)}, h_t^{(p)})$ and $(h_{t-1}^{(k_2)}, u_t^{(q)}, v_t^{(q)}, h_t^{(q)})$。Then compute

$$m_t^{(p)} = h_{t-1}^{(k_1)} \oplus u_t^{(p)} \text{ and } m_t^{(q)} = h_{t-1}^{(k_2)} \oplus u_t^{(q)}.$$

Continue to search for the table of the (t-1)-*st* iteration to obtain the quads corresponding to $h_{t-1}^{(k_1)}$ and $h_{t-1}^{(k_2)}$, and then compute the pair of message used in the (t-1)-*st* iteration. Look forward for the two t-block collision messages.

4.2 Analysis of the Computational Complexity

The computational complexity of our algorithm includes time complexity and memory. Firstly, we analyze the time complexity of our multi-block collision attack.

In Step1 and Step2, we need to visit the permutation F r_1 times and r_2 times respectively; In Step3, the computation of (m_2, h_2) could be ignored, and we need to visit the permutation F r_i times. Hence, the time complexity of our multi-block collision attack is $\sum_{i=1}^{t} r_i$ times of visiting permutation F, where $r_1 r_2 \cdots r_{t-1} r_t = 2^{s/2}$.

Due to the Geometric inequality

$$\frac{1}{t}\sum_{i=1}^{t} r_i \ge \sqrt[t]{r_1 r_2 \cdots r_t}$$

if and only if $r_1 = r_2 = \cdots = r_t$, the equality is guaranteed. Therefore, when $r_1 = r_2 = \cdots = r_t = 2^{\frac{s}{2t}}$, the time complexity reaches the minimal, that is, $t2^{\frac{s}{2t}}$.

Next we analyze the memory of our algorithm.

Since we need to look forward to obtain the two t-block collision messages, the results in Step1–5 need to be stored. In Step1, we need store the r_1 pairs of input-output $(u_1^{(1)}, v_1^{(1)}), (u_1^{(2)}, v_1^{(2)}), \cdots, (u_1^{(r_1)}, v_1^{(r_1)})$ and the corresponding $h_1^{(1)}, h_1^{(2)}, \cdots, h_1^{(r_1)}$, that is, r_1 triples $(u_1^{(j)}, v_1^{(j)}, h_1^{(j)})(1 \le j \le r_1)$; In Step2–3, for every $h_1^{(j)}(1 \le j \le r_1)$, we need store r_2 triples $(u_2^{(j)}, v_2^{(j)}, h_2^{(j)})(1 \le j \le r_2)$, hence we need store $r_1 r_2$ triples $(u_2^{(j)}, v_2^{(j)}, h_2^{(j)})(1 \le j \le r_2)$; In Step4, for every $h_{i-1}^{(j)}(1 \le j \le r_1 r_2 \cdots r_{i-1})$, we need store r_i triples $(u_i^{(j)}, v_i^{(j)}, h_i^{(j)})(1 \le j \le r_i)$. Hence, the memory complexity of our multi-block collision attack is $r_1 + r_1 r_2 + r_1 r_2 r_3 + \cdots + r_1 r_2 \cdots r_t$. When the time complexity reaches the minimal, that is,$r_1 = r_2 = \cdots = r_t = 2^{\frac{s}{2t}}$, the memory complexity is

$$r_1 + r_1 r_2 + r_1 r_2 r_3 + \cdots + r_1 r_2 \cdots r_t = (2^{\frac{s}{2t}})^{t+1} - 1 = O(2^{s/2})$$

In a word, the time complexity of our t-block collision attack is $t2^{\frac{s}{2t}}$ times of visiting the permutation F, and the memory complexity is about $O(2^{s/2})$.

5 Conclusion

In this paper, we analyse the security of the Even-Mansour structure hash function, mainly using the property that the message both needs to be XORed to the beginning and the end of every iteration. Firstly, utilizing the partial invariables of input-output of one function f_1 based on the permutation F and the meet-in-the-middle techniques, we firstly present a preimage attack on Even-Mansour structure hash functions with two iterations, of which the time complexity is $2^{a(2^a-1)}+2^a+2^{n-2a}$ functional operations of f_1 or f_2 and the memory is $2^a a$-bit values, where n is the size of hash value and $a2^a \le n$. Secondly, utilizing the property that the beginning and the end of every iteration in Even-Mansour structure both need XOR the message or the transform result of message, we propose our multi-block collision attack on Even-Mansour structure hash functions with the time complexity of $t2^{\frac{s}{2t}}$ queries of F permutation and memory complexity of $O(2^{s/2})$, where t is the block number of collision message and s is the size of hash value. In the future work, we would like to apply our attack on the hash functions with EM structure.

Acknowledgment. We-are grateful to the anonymous referees for their valuable comments. The work in this paper is supported by the National Natural Science Foundation of China (Grant No: 61802438 and 61772547).

References

1. Preneel, B., Govaerts, R., Vandewalle, J.: Hash functions based on block ciphers: a synthetic approach. In: Stinson, D.R. (ed.) CRYPTO 1993. LNCS, vol. 773, pp. 368–378. Springer, Heidelberg (1994). https://doi.org/10.1007/3-540-48329-2_31

2. Even, S., Mansour, Y.: A construction of a cipher from a single pseudorandom permutation. J. Cryptol. **10**(3), 151–161 (1997). https://doi.org/10.1007/s001459900025
3. Dunkelman, O., Keller, N., Shamir, A.: Minimalism in cryptography: the even-Mansour scheme revisited. In: Pointcheval, D., Johansson, T. (eds.) EUROCRYPT 2012. LNCS, vol. 7237, pp. 336–354. Springer, Heidelberg (2012). https://doi.org/10.1007/978-3-642-29011-4_21
4. Bogdanov, A., Knudsen, L.R., Leander, G., Standaert, F.-X., Steinberger, J., Tischhauser, E.: Key-alternating ciphers in a provable setting: encryption using a small number of public permutations. In: Pointcheval, D., Johansson, T. (eds.) EUROCRYPT 2012. LNCS, vol. 7237, pp. 45–62. Springer, Heidelberg (2012). https://doi.org/10.1007/978-3-642-29011-4_5
5. Isobe, T., Shibutani, K.: New key recovery attacks on minimal two-round even-Mansour ciphers. Asiacrypt 2017, Part I, LNCS 10624, pp. 244–263 (2017)
6. Leurent, G., Sibleyras, F.: Low-memory attacks against two-round even-mansour using the 3-XOR problem. In: Boldyreva, A., Micciancio, D. (eds.) CRYPTO 2019. LNCS, vol. 11693, pp. 210–235. Springer, Cham (2019). https://doi.org/10.1007/978-3-030-26951-7_8
7. Luo, Y.Y., Lai, X.J.: Attacks on JH, Grøstl and SMASH Hash Functions. http://eprint.iacr.org/2013/233.pdf
8. Dworkin, M.: SHA-3 Standard: Permutation-Based Hash and Extendable-Output Functions, Federal Inf. Process. Stds. (NIST FIPS), National Institute of Standards and Technology, Gaithersburg, MD. https://doi.org/10.6028/NIST.FIPS.202
9. Guo, J., Peyrin, T., Poschmann, A.: The PHOTON family of lightweight hash function. CRYPTO 2011, LNCS 6841, pp. 222–239 (2011)
10. Wu, H.J.: The hash function JH (2011). http://www3.ntu.edu.sg/home/wuhj/research/jh/jhround3.pdf
11. Isobe, T.: A single-key attack on the full GOST block cipher. J. Cryptol. **26**(1), 172–189 (2013)
12. Oliynykov, R., et al.: A new standard of Ukraine: The Kupyna hash function. Cryptology ePrint Archive, Report 2015/885 (2015). http://eprint.iacr.org/2015/885References

Rare Variants Analysis in Genetic Association Studies with Privacy Protection via Hybrid System

Mohammed Shujaa Aldeen[1,2] and Chuan Zhao[1,2,3(✉)]

[1] School of Information Science and Engineering, University of Jinan, Jinan 250022, China
ise_zhaoc@ujn.edu.cn

[2] Shandong Provincial Key Laboratory of Network-Based Intelligent Computing, Jinan 250022, China

[3] Shandong Provincial Key Laboratory of Software Engineering, Jinan, China

Abstract. Genomic data are becoming widely used for diagnosis and treatment. Researchers require to study a significant number of genomes in order to analyze patient genomes to figure out some disease-gene associations. Cost-efficient commercial cloud computing services can host genomic data and conduct genome-wide association studies on-demand at considerably lower cost and high availability and scalability. Due to privacy and security issues, genomic data providers are unwilling to send their sensitive data to the cloud service providers without applying any privacy-preserving measures. This paper proposes a novel hybrid privacy-preserving framework that utilizes twofold cryptographic protocols and minimal perfect hash functions to reach maximum efficiency and security for outsourcing genomic data with the least time overhead. Our framework leverages a trusted execution environment (i.e. software guard extensions) to perform rare variant case-control association tests securely. Also, the genomic data outsourced from multiple data providers are encrypted through additive homomorphic encryption. We perform the Weighted-Sum Statistic (WSS) test, a rare variant association test, and we show that our scheme achieves high accuracy results without an increase of computational complexity or time overhead.

Keywords: Genome-wide association study · Rare variants · Minimal perfect hash · Additively homomorphic encryption · Intel-SGX · Privacy-preserving

1 Introduction

Genomic studies have expanded significantly in recent years due to the remarkable developments made possible by Next Generation Sequencing (NGS) [1]. The advances in this area have contributed to the large availability of genomic data today [2]. The decreasing cost of genome sequencing results in a high availability of genomic data that provide new possibilities to scientific research in

D. Gao et al. (Eds.): ICICS 2021, LNCS 12919, pp. 174–191, 2021.
https://doi.org/10.1007/978-3-030-88052-1_11

medicine, such as improving the health care system and discovering new treatments for various diseases [3]. Each individual's genome is 99.9% identical, and rest 0.1% determining peoples' unique characteristics, a single nucleotide polymorphism (SNP) is the difference between people at a single position in the genome. A genome-wide association study (GWAS) examines the statistical association between SNPs and diseases to determine which SNPs are associated with a particular disease.

Despite the extensive discovery of trait and disease-associated common variants, much of the genetic contribution to complex traits remains unexplained. Rare variants can explain additional disease risk or trait discrepancy. Rare variant association tests analyze different genetic structures for common diseases than common variants. In fact, studies have demonstrated that rare variants can lead to more common diseases than common variants [4], which is the primary motivation for choosing rare variants for this study.

The amount of comprehensive genomic data is massive and demands a considerable volume of storage capacity. Cost-efficient commercial cloud computing services can host data and conduct required analysis on-demand at considerably lower cost with high availability and scalability. Nevertheless, cloud servers are exposed to security attacks, and an adversary may gain access to data residing on the servers. One research study revealed that cloud service providers certainly are not expected to preserve the privacy of information [5]. Genomic data cannot be processed as in other types of data due to their unique aspects. A genome can contain private details about a person. For instance, access to genome data may facilitate surname recovery [6], re-identification attack [7], and restoration of facial and voice features [8,9] and can cause abusive repercussions for both individuals and their families [10].

Leading to the security and privacy concerns associated with cloud service providers, genomic data providers are concerned about the privacy of their outsourced data. The optimal solution is to establish a secure genome database, which encrypts the genomic data to provide a security layer to the operations framework for the data analysis procedure. Nonetheless, performing computations on encrypted genomic data imposes a performance drawback due to the inefficiency of these security primitives compared to their plaintext counterparts. Scalability is another issue, as the high memory requirements imposed by these security protocols can make the process impractical. Indeed, GWAS may include up to 300,000 SNPs and thousands of subjects [11], requiring a considerable time until accessing the final results. Thus, in this paper, we propose a framework to balance between privacy and efficiency of the rare variants computation, and as the number of genomes increases, we used minimal perfect hashing to speed up the GWAS results.

1.1 Our Contributions

This paper proposes a novel hybrid secure GWAS statistical analysis that can be used for various rare variants analysis, including iterative studies that focused on vast sets of genotypes given by multiple data providers (i.e. WSS association test). Our proposed system enables different data providers to encrypt their genomic data and outsource them to the cloud service provider. The main contributions of this work are summarized threefold as follows:

- We designed a novel hybrid architecture that utilized additively homomorphic encryption for combining all ciphertexts from different data providers and Intel SGX to perform a secure rare variants GWAS statistical test (i.e. WSS association tests) on plaintext data reducing the computational and communicational overhead.
- Our scheme leverage minimal perfect hashing functions to improve access efficiency over large number of records, and each record can be accessed at a constant time.
- Our experiments show that our framework is fast and efficient, making it suitable for real-world large genomic datasets.

2 Related Work

Various studies have been proposed to protect genomic data by using several privacy-preserving techniques. Uhlerop et al. [12] proposed aggregated GWAS data using differential privacy (DP), which involves adding random noise to genomic data. They solve the chi-square statistics test of minor allele frequency (MAF) in common variants. However, the noise inserted into the original data reduces its efficiency in computations making accurate statistical studies even more difficult. Our work considers rare variants association tests and encrypted data will be decrypted inside the secured enclave of SGX, and statistical studies (WSS in our case) will be performed on plaintext with low computational and more accurate results.

Another approach Kim et al. [13] utilizes Fully Homomorphic Encryption (FHE) to calculate chi-square statistics and MAF over encrypted genetic data. They evaluated the efficiency of YASHE and BGV homomorphic encryption techniques in their model. Nevertheless, the chi-square statistics computation were performed after decrypting the data. They considered homomorphically computing only the allele counts. Our framework provides more security than theirs by using the SGX enclave to perform GWAS computation inside securely.

Sadat et al. [14] proposed a hybrid scheme for computing different GWAS statistical tests (LD, HWE, CATT, FET) on encrypted genomic data that combined the partially homomorphic encryption and Intel-SGX. This approach used the additive feature of Paillier homomorphic cryptosystem to obtain the total counts of all ciphertexts, which significantly decreased the computing overhead associated with decrypting all of the different ciphertexts received from different data providers. Following that, they performed statistical computations using the SGX-enclave. Even though their scheme reached a high level of efficiency and privacy, it lacks the flexibility of our system. Our scheme presents minimal perfect hashing to speed up the process of matching and computation. Unlike their work, our scheme does not depend on a trusted third party to manage key exchange between the essential parties with the cloud service provider. Additionally, their scheme does not address the privacy of the researcher's query, and they even stated that the privacy of results is protected if the researcher is semi-honest, which is vulnerable to adversary attack.

Until now, all the proposed techniques considered only a single SNP, where each (SNP) is evaluated independently. These studies are ineffective against rare variants due to their low strength; thus, none of them introduced a strategy to conduct the rare variant at the gene level, which is our primary purpose in this work.

3 Model Design Overview

3.1 System Architecture

Figure 1 illustrates an outline of our proposed system. Our system consists of three entities: *Data providers (D)*, *Cloud Service Provider (CSP)*, and *Researcher (R)*. Here is the functionality of each one:

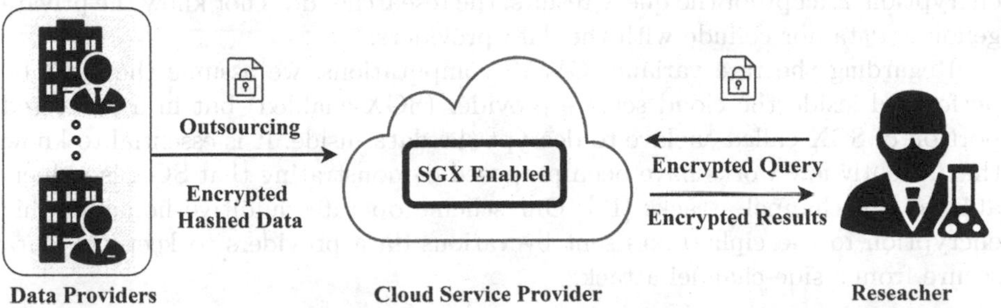

Fig. 1. System architecture

- *Data Providers (D):* an entity that posses genomic data and aims to securely outsource the sensitive data to the *Cloud service provider* for storage and analysis. They control transferring the encrypted data to the *CSP*, where the researcher can execute queries.
- *Cloud Service Provider (CSP):* Cloud server keeps the encrypted data inside for long-term storage, responding to more queries from researcher and responsible for communicating with other entities in the system. It is also an SGX-enabled server for secure WSS computation and transforms the results into ciphertext that can be decrypted locally from the researcher side. It executes the queries from the researcher and sends the encrypted results back to the researcher.
- *Researcher (R):* Who passes the remote attestation from the SGX and holds queries about the gene in interest to request over genomic databases. The *R* sends an encrypted query to the *CSP* and receives encrypted results from the *CSP*, which can be decrypted locally using the private key.

3.2 Threat Model

Firstly, our scheme goal is to preserve the privacy of the genomic data outsourced from various data providers. We assume that the data providers encrypt their sensitive data with the enclave public key, where each data provider will perform remote attestation individually with the SGX. Similarly, the researcher encrypts his queries with the enclave public key and generates his public and private keys to decrypt the encrypted results. We also presume that the cloud service provider is a semi-honest [15,16] entity, which indicates that the cloud server maintains the security protocol ultimately as specified and does not manipulate any information data about the client. Nevertheless, the cloud needs to collect some information about the computation before or after the protocol execution.

Secondly, we presume that the cloud server does not collude with any other entity throughout the computation process. Hence, we aim to ensure that the cloud service only knows public information to help with the process and does not learn anything about private genomic data. In case the cloud service provider colludes with one of the parties, it will not be able to identify anything about the private data, given that each data provider uses the enclave public key for encryption. Except for the query results, the researcher does not know the private genomic data nor collude with the data providers.

Regarding the rare variants GWAS computations, we assume they will be performed inside the cloud service provider (SGX-enabled) but in a protected portion of SGX called enclave to decrypt the data inside. It is essential to know that recently few works have been proposed demonstrating that SGX is vulnerable to side-channel attacks [17]. Our scheme operates additive homomorphic encryption to the ciphertexts sent by various data providers to keep the data secure from a side-channel attack.

4 Background

This section mentions details of homomorphic encryption, minimal perfect hash, Intel SGX, and weighted sum statistic algorithm.

4.1 Homomorphic Encryption

Homomorphic Encryption (HE) is a cryptographic algorithm that enables arithmetic operations such as addition and multiplication to be performed on encrypted data without decryption. In this paper, we have used paillier cryptosystem [18], which is additively homomorphic encryption enables us to homomorphically combine all ciphertexts together. Here is the detailed algorithm for additively homomorphic encryption:

Definition 1. *Public key additively homomorphic encryption (PHE) technique consist of tuple of poly time algorithms. (**ParmGen, KeyGen, Enc, Dec, Add, DecAd**):*

- pp $\leftarrow$ ***ParmGen*** (1^{λ}): *Given a security parameter* λ, *which outputs a public parameter pp which is inherently fed in the following algorithms.*
- $(pk, sk) \leftarrow$ ***Keygen*** (1^{λ}): *Outputs public key pk and a private key sk.*
- $C \leftarrow$ ***Enc*** (pk, m): *Encryption algorithm produces C as the ciphertext of message m.*
- $m \leftarrow$ ***Dec*** (sk, C): *Decryption algorithm returns message m from ciphertext C.*
- ***Add*** $(C, C^{'})$: *Given ciphertexts C and* $C^{'}$ *outputs the encryption of plaintext addition* C_{add}
- ***DecAd*** (sk, C_{add}): *Using sk to decrypt* C_{add} *to get the final plaintexts of the addition result.*

4.2 Minimal Perfect Hash Function

Minimal perfect hash functions (MPH) are utilized to give fast access to the values of high sets of keys in S. They are widely applied for memory-efficient storage and fast retrieval of static set objects. Unlike other hashing schemes, MPH avoids entirely the issue of wasted space and wasted time dealing with collisions [19]. Tables built with MPH are usually smaller than standard hash tables since there are no vacant memory slots in the table, and constructing MPH is not expensive. Because collisions are resolved, table lookups are quicker, resulting in an $O(1)$ lookup in the worst-case scenario. The $O(1)$ lookup time can yield a 10x speedup for in-memory cache lookups and MPH functions only require one disk access for on-disk data. The most crucial part is that the most compressed MPH functions need barely 2.07 bits per key [20]. Since traditional hash tables store the keys directly, it can cause extensive memory usage. We construct our minimal perfect hash function on our data as explained in detail in Subsect. 5.1.

4.3 Overview of Intel SGX

Intel Software Guard Extensions (SGX) [21] is an extension to provide a Trusted Execution Environment (TEE) in which applications can protect sensitive code and data against privileged systems that are malicious such as operating system, kernel, hyper-visor, BIOS, etc. In the SGX terminology, the trusted portion of the program is referred to as an enclave. The essential point is that data runs in plaintext within the enclave code but is encrypted outside. The enclave confines sensitive data and computations, preventing leaks if privileged modules become potentially malicious, vulnerable to attacks, or compromised due to the content within the enclave cannot be altered or modified from outside. Thus by using SGX, applications can establish a trusted execution environment over compromised hosts, and the clients who wrote the code for the enclave are still accountable for preserving the privacy of secrets managed by the enclave.

SGX also supports remote attestation [22] and sealing, which ensures that code inside an enclave will have messages signed with a pre-processor private key. As a result, other parties will validate that the messages originated from a legitimate enclave with a particular code and data specification. In other words, it communicates with a third-party provider to verify the code and data loaded into the enclave.

4.4 Weighted Sum Statistic Computation

Weighted sum statistic (WSS) is typically utilized in rare variant association tests that use sequence data on cases and controls to determine if there is an association between a phenotype and rare variants in a specific area of the genome (e.g., a gene) [23]. It proposes a weighting concept to highlight alleles with a low frequency in controls. Once scores for all samples are ordered, WSS is computed as the sum of ranks for cases.

The WSS algorithm requires first defining genomic positions within the gene where variants of interest exist, then developing a genetic score to every person depending on their genotypes at these various genomic positions (P_1, P_2), and comparing these genetic scores between cases and controls. Table 1 shows WSS table that will be used as an input of the WSS computation where $N_{i,j}$ represents genotype frequency such that if the individual is heterozygous, homozygous or homozygous recessive. Let us consider one gene that contains v genomic positions where there are variants of interest. The minor allele frequency then weights the number of rare alleles possessed by the person at each of the v variants at a control group position to obtain genetic scores as a linear combination. The aim is to assign the least frequent variants more weight because they are most likely to be more harmful and more expected to be associated with a disease.

To explain WSS computation's complexity, here is a four-step iterative method to illustrate the details:

1. For each variant $i \in \{1, 2, ..., v\}$, weight w_i should be calculated which depends on the frequency of alleles

$$\hat{w}_i = \sqrt{b_i \cdot k_i(1 - k_i)} \tag{1}$$

   where b_i is the number of individuals genotyped (cases and controls) for the i_{th} variant, $k_i = \frac{u_i+1}{2n_i+2}$ where n_i is the number of control group genotyped for the i_{th} variant, and u_i is the number of (mutant) minor alleles observed at the i_{th} variant in the control group.
2. A genetic score is computed for each individual j:

$$T_j = \sum_{j=1}^{v} \frac{g_{i,j}}{w_i} \tag{2}$$

   where $g_{i,j}$ is the genotype of individual j in the variant i.
3. Individuals are ranked based on their genetic scores T_j and the rank total s for cases (affected) individuals is determined

$$s = \sum_{j \in Cases} rank\,(T_j) \tag{3}$$

Table 1. Representation of WSS table

Variant	Positions	
	P_1	P_2
v_1	N_{11}	N_{12}
v_2	N_{21}	N_{22}
Status	Case	Control

4. An empirical $p-value$ is computed using a generic permutation test. Therefore, for all individuals cases and controls are permuted, and from step 1 to 3 are repeated q times to obtain q rank sums $s_1, s_2, ..., s_q$. These values are compared to the observe rank sum s, and the number of permutations q_0 where it exceeds s are determined to obtain the $p-value$:

$$p-value = \frac{q_0 + 1}{q + 1} \tag{4}$$

where q_0 is the number of permutations that give a rank sum s_l at least as extreme as s, and q is the total number of permutations which gives us the maximum level of significance that can be reached.

5 Method

This section describes methods used to encode and generate minimal perfect hash tables for the genomic data. We also illustrate the exact nature of the proposed approach with details.

5.1 Encoding of Genomic Data and Hash Generation

Genetic Data. The genomic data used in the genetic association contain multiple genotype information entries, where each of them consists of a chromosome identifier (CHROM), position within a chromosome (POS), locus (ID), reference (REF), alternate (ALT), and name of the gene (GENE). Also, the genotypes for the sample of individuals are listed, given an integer at a given position. For example, "0" denotes the reference allele is located on both chromosomes of this individual, "1" denotes the patient is heterozygous within one REF and one ALT allele, and "2" denotes the patient is homozygous for two ALT alleles. The genomic data representation is illustrated in Table 2.

Encoding of Genetic Data. Encoding the genotype as integers makes the homomorphic computation much more efficient. First, we represent the common SNPs by integer numbers since computing their counts and variations over integers is simple. For instance, the common SNPs will be presented by two binary numbers and encode them according to their order as follows (Table 3):

$$A \rightarrow 00$$
$$C \rightarrow 01$$
$$G \rightarrow 10$$
$$T \rightarrow 11$$

Table 2. The format of genomic data

Variant	Genomic data records						Genotypes	
	CHROM	POS	ID	*REF*	ALT	GENE	P_1	P_2
v_1	1	68598733	rs2820486	A	G	NRXN1	0	0
v_2	1	147398763	rs149024466	A	C	NRXN1	2	1
v_3	1	178099359	rs116823951	T	C	NRXN1	0	1
v_4	1	200184533	rs35656575	G	A	NRXN1	2	1
v_5	1	212394205	rs7515645	C	T	NRXN1	1	1

Table 3. The Encoding structure

Variant	Genomic data records				Genotypes	
	CHROM	POS	REF	ALT	P_1	P_2
v_1	6	720797	G	A	2	1
001	00110	0111001. . . .11	10	00	10	01

Generating Minimal Perfect Hash. Minimal perfect hash (MPH) is used to map a number of input records from genomic data records into a number of consecutive integers i.e. $[0, n-1]$ without collisions. Let f be a minimal perfect hash function, and D_i represents the data providers, where each data provider has multiple records. We calculate the hash reference $f(D_i)$ and use $f(D_i)$ as a reference on slot of H in a hash table. We denote $H = f(D_i)$ a set of all block numbers that $f(D_i)$ refers on. Figure 2 shows the details of this process.

Besides, we use FCH algorithm, which was introduced by Fox, Chen and Heath [24] in our scheme. This algorithm is often used to generate minimal perfect hash functions that need below 4 bits per key to be processed, and the corresponding MPHs are compressed significantly and very effective at evaluation time.

5.2 Proposed Framework

The design workflow consists of four significant phases: preprocessing, outsourcing, combining and sealing, researcher query execution, and query result. Figure 3 depicts the overall workflow, and we describe each phase of our scheme in detail.

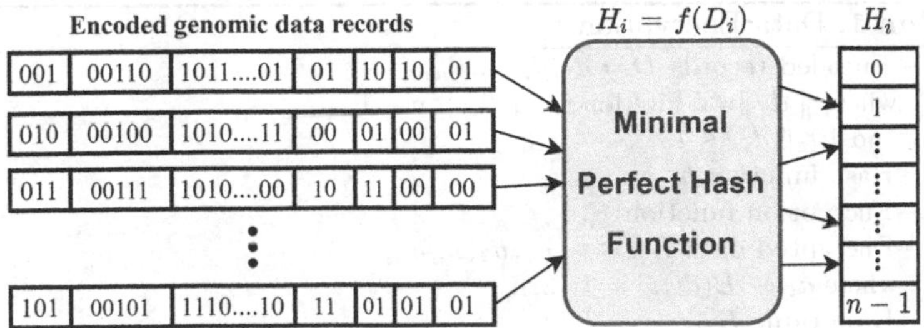

Fig. 2. Minimal perfect hash function generation

We describe each phase of our scheme in detail. The key generation protocol is shown in the Setup algorithm below:

- **Setup(1^λ)**: let N, Z be sets of all natural numbers and all real numbers, respectively. Upon the input of the security parameter $\lambda \in N$ with two prime numbers p, q with λ bits length ($2^{\lambda-1} < p, q < 2^\lambda$), let $N = qp^2$. The enclave (e) generates its public key and private key as a pair (Pk_e, Sk_e). The cryptosystem uses an asymmetric encryption scheme where Pk_e is used for encrypting the data, and Sk_e to decrypt the data inside the enclave. The researcher generates his public key and private key as a pair (Pk_r, Sk_r). The length of the keys $s + (\lambda - 1)$ where $s \in Z^+$ the space of all positive real numbers.

Phase 1 - Preprocessing: At first, each data provider needs to perform a remote attestation procedure to ensure that the enclave runs on top of a trusted hardware platform with legitimate code from a trusted cloud service provider. Similarly, the researcher performs the remote attestation with the secured enclave to exchange their public keys. For instance, the researcher passes his public key to the enclave, and the enclave shares its public key with the researcher for secure query encryption. Then, data provider encode their genomic data records, as described in Subsect. 5.1. After that, the data providers perform minimal perfect hash function upon the encoded records as illustrated in Subsect. 5.1.

Phase 2 - Outsourcing: Following the preprocessing phase, each data provider encrypts his genomic data and the generated minimal perfect hash tables using the public key of the enclave $\mathbf{Enc}(Pk_e, (E(D), H_D))$ according to Algorithm 1.

From Algorithm 1, the encoded data D is stored in encrypted form as $E(D) = E(d_1)E(d_2)...E(d_n) = a_1, a_2, ...a_n$ where a_i denotes an encrypted block number i of l bits length. For any d_i from $R_{1,l}(d_i)$. From the hash function h, we first calculate $h(E(u))$ for any $u \in R_{1,l}(d_i)$ and use it as a reference on slot of H in the hash table where we place a block number i. We indicate $H(h(E(u)))$ a set of all block numbers that $h(E(u))$ refers on. Therefore, if $c \leftarrow h(E(u))$ for any $u \in R_{1,l}(d_i)$, then $i \in H(c)$. After that, the data providers outsource the ciphertexts $C_e^i \leftarrow \mathbf{Enc}(Pk_e, ((E(D_i), H_{D_i})))$ to the cloud service provider.

Algorithm 1. Data Encryption

Input: – Encoded records $D = d_1, d_2, ..., d_n$,
where $\| d_i \| = l$ bits for $i = 1, 2, ..., n-1$
and $1 \leq \| d_i \| \leq l$.
–Hash function h.
–Encryption function E.

Output: –Encrypted data $E(D) \leftarrow a_1, a_2, ..., a_n$,
where $a_i \leftarrow E(d_i), i = 1, ..., n$
–Hash table H_D.

for $i \in \{0, 1, \ldots, |H_D| - 1\}$ **do**
    $H_D(i) \leftarrow \emptyset$
end for
while $i \leq n$ **do**
    for u **from** $R_{1,l}(d_i)$ **do**
        $c \leftarrow h(E(u))$
        $H_D(c) \leftarrow H_D(c) \cup \{i\}$
    end for
    $i \leftarrow i + 1$
end while
return $E(D), H_D$

Phase 3 - Combining and Sealing: After receiving all the ciphertexts from different data providers, which were encrypted under the secure enclave public key Pk_e, the cloud service provider performs additively homomorphic encyrption over the ciphertexts in order to combine all hashed tables and encrypted data. Given ciphertexts $C_e^1((D_1), (H_{D_1}))$ and $C_e^2((D_2), (H_{D_2}))$, the cloud service perform homomorphic addition as $C_e(D_1 + D_2, H_{D_1} + H_{D_2})$. Let the total number of encrypted records with their hashing index $C_eT = \sum_{i=1}^{N} C_e((D_1 + D_2 + ...), H_{D_1} + H_{D_2} + ...)$ and let case groups be C_eT_{cas} and the control group be C_eT_{con}. Based on that, a contingency table needs to be constructed for WSS association tests, which is described in Subsect. 4.4. This table is then sent to the enclave, where all these cases and controls at their positions are decrypted for further computation.

Furthermore, the enclave seals the encrypted data outside the SGX for extended storage and responds to more queries from the researcher after combining encrypted data and hashed tables. Considering the data is kept outside the enclave, the cloud service provider might reorder the data or send previous versions of the data to the enclave for unsealing, which can be regarded as a replay attack. As a result, we set the message authentication code (MAC) and data providers' information with the sealed data to prevent this type of attack.

Phase 4 - Researcher Query: In this step, the researcher sends a query to perform a WSS computation for a specific gene in order to know if its latter is associated with a phenotype. Like the data providers, the researcher needs to encode the query initially with the same encoding method as described in Subsect. 5.1, the minimal perfect hash function to the query to obtain the hash

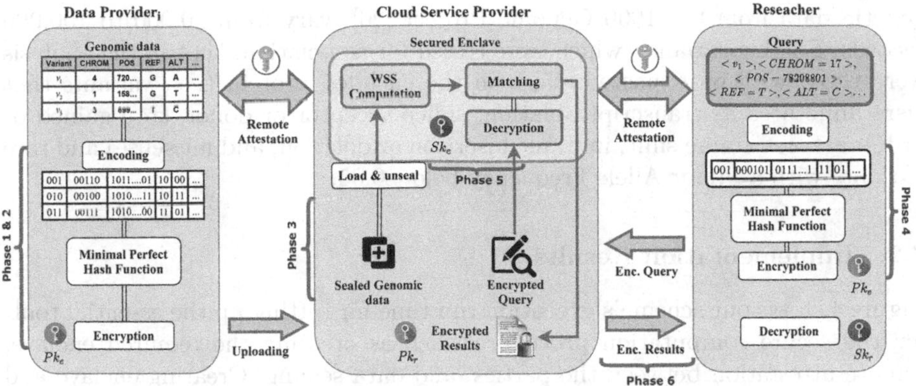

Fig. 3. The workflow of our proposed framework

value with the same method described in Subsect. 5.1. After that, the researcher encrypts the query with the enclave's public key and sends the encrypted query to the cloud service provider. The enclave then decrypts the query using its own private key Sk_e and unseals the required data from the cloud.

Phase 5 - Secure WSS Computation: According to the researcher's query, the cloud server loads the WSS table with both C_eT_{cas} and C_eT_{con} to the enclave to be decrypted inside using $\mathbf{Dec}(Sk_e, C_eT)$. The enclave performs the queried gene's WSS computation test based on the case/control data represented on WSS Table 1 using the four iterative steps mentioned in Subsect. 4.4. Then, the enclave encrypts the result of the computation inside the enclave using the researcher public key Pk_r. Assume y be the result, the enclave encrypts the result y with $\mathbf{Eec}(Pk_r, y) \rightarrow C_y$.

Phase 6 - Query Result: The enclave sends the encrypted results under the researcher's public key. The researcher then uses his private key Sk_r to decrypt the computation results using $\mathbf{Dec}(Sk_r, C_y) \rightarrow y$. Figure 3 depicts the workflow of each phase.

6 Experimental Results and Analysis

6.1 Experiment Setup

Our experiment was conducted on a PC with Intel(R) Core(TM) i7-9700KF CPU with 3.60 GHz and 32 GB of RAM. The prototype is funding with eight cores multi-threading and SGX-hardware enabled. The data providers and the cloud service provider communicate using a Secure Sockets Layer (SSL) channel built based on the OpenSSL library [25]. Experiments were performed using genetic data from the 1000 Genome Project [26], vary from 10,000 to 100,000 records. Eligible variants, which were tested for association, kept in the analysis were those with an expected effect on the encoded protein (i.e., variants that were annotated as transcript ablation, splice acceptor or donor, stop gained or lost, start lost, frame shift, in frame insertion or deletion, and missense) and rare variants with a Minor Allele Frequency below 0.05.

6.2 Implementation Results

Figure 4 shows our scheme's execution run time for setting up the essential tools for the secure computation procedure, such as creating the required enclave, remote attestation between the parties, and data sealing. Creating enclave and remote attestation are both involve to verify the parties; therefore, the run time is stable regardless of the data size. Unlike Data sealing, the time is increasing linearly to the data size.

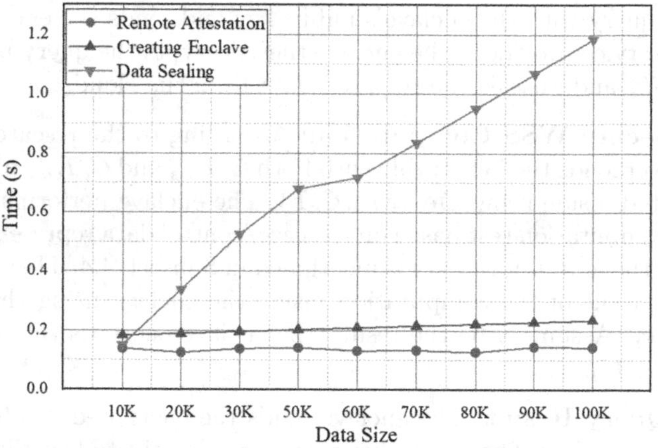

Fig. 4. Run time for setting up the environment

Table 4 shows the execution run time results for each operation in the system for different data sizes. The encoding and hash generation steps are performed on the data providers' side, while the rest of the operations are executed on the cloud server-side. From Fig. 5, the run time of WSS computation is relatively stable for different data sizes because inside the computation enclave is run on plaintext over the contingency table.

Table 4. Execution time (in seconds) for each step

Size	Encoding	MPH generation	WSS computation
10 K	0.029	1.350	3.453
50 K	0.106	7.245	3.863
100 K	0.214	16.571	3.961

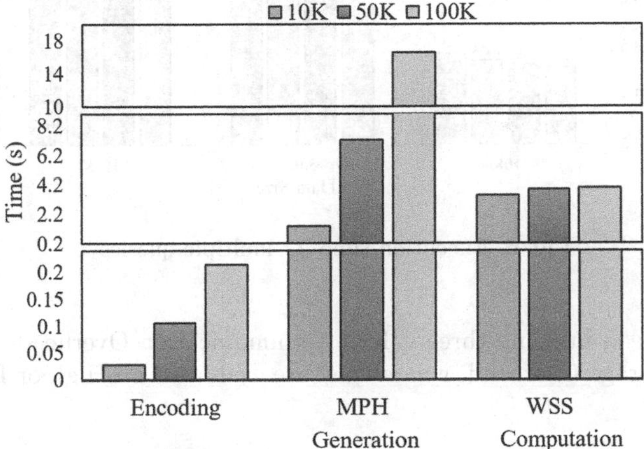

Fig. 5. Run time measured for different data sizes for each operation

Since querying is only for the specific gene of interest, it takes the least time among all steps based on our experiments, as illustrated in Fig. 6. As a result, it supports multiple queries, which can be persistent. The cloud requires only 4.022 s to match four queries within 100K records, including unsealing, query matching, loading and WSS computation, which means our scheme's MPH is very efficient.

On the other hand, the time consumption for other operations is linear to the data size. We notice that MPH generation is the most time-consuming step; however, it is only a one-time method.

6.3 Comparison with Existing Methods

Different works in genome privacy have been proposed; however, each work does not always secure the same process, and there are not many works on rare variants. Consequently, we compare the secure versions of the same feature to non-secure versions. We use a variety of measures to capture various facets regarding security and performance as motivated by [27]. We quantify the related works'

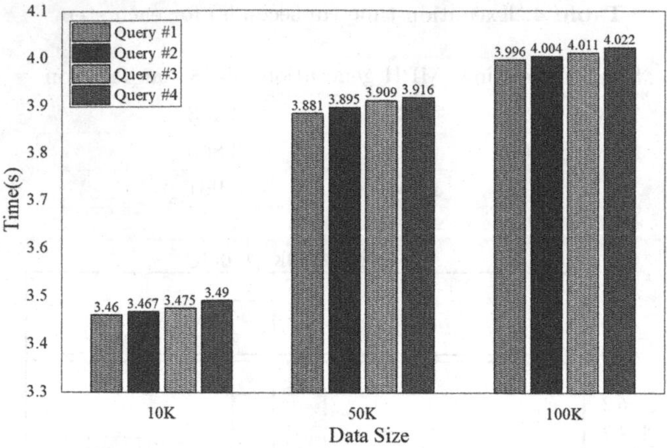

Fig. 6. Execution time for multiple queries

privacy overhead utilizing three values: Communication Overhead, Time Overhead, and Storage Overhead, where they are evaluated on High or Low costs.

Table 5. Comparison of our scheme with other schemes in terms of performance criteria

Benchmarks	Lu et al. [11]	Sei et al. [28]	Cho et al. [29]	Princess [30]	Our scheme
Cryptosystem	Homomorphic encryption	Differential privacy	Secret sharing	Paillier, SGX	MPH, SGX
Communication Overhead	High	Low	Low	Low	Low
Time overhead	High	Low	High	Low	Low
Storage overhead	High	Low	Low	Low	Low
GWAS algorithm	X^2 statistic	X^2 statistic	CATT	TDT	WSS

We choose to compare different methods used to solve genome-wide association studies, as shown in Table 5. Lu et al. [11] utilized homomorphic encryption to solve GWAS, yet it cost high computational and storage overheads, which makes it impractical for real-world applications [31]. Sei et al. [28] used differential privacy which induces an impact on the accuracy of association tests results because differential privacy basically adds noises to the data to preserve the privacy. Cho et al. [29] applied secret sharing [32] to their work, which constitutes a better option due to its lower computational overhead. On the other hand, secret sharing requires additional communication overhead and is not proper for the client-server architecture. Princess [30] leveraged SGX to compute global Transmission Disequilibrium Test (TDT). Although this work shows promising results on communication, time, and storage overheads, our framework has a much lower time overhead since we used MPH, which helps in fast look-up tables. In addition to that, their approach is computationally intense and has been limited to analyzing only the associated SNPs. Not only that, our framework preserves the accuracy of the association tests results because no noises were added to the data, such as [28], but also it can conduct the WSS algorithm without the need for additional communication as required in [29].

7 Conclusion

This paper has proposed a new hybrid framework that combined additively homomorphic encryption with Intel-SGX to conduct WSS association tests for rare variants. It mainly relies on first constructing MPH in order to make fast look-up tables to match queries inside the cloud. Second, using additively homomorphic encryption allows us to combine all different records from different data providers inside the cloud without any information leakage. Last, based on the query, Intel-SGX performs WSS association tests securely inside the enclave and ensures the sensitive data in WSS input tables are kept confidential. Not only is our scheme suitable for secure WSS association studies, but it can also be efficiently applied to some other GWAS statistical algorithms that use the same type of data. For instance, CAST, SKAT [33], and SKAT-OT [34] are rare variant association tests and common variants tests such as LD, HWE, CATT and FET that can be included in our system. This is the first framework that combines MPH, additive homomorphic encryption, and Intel-SGX to perform GWAS computation on genomic data.

Acknowledgement. This work is supported by National Natural Science Foundation of China (No. 61702218, 61672262), Shandong Provincial Key Research and Development Project (No. 2019GGX101028), Natural Science Foundation of Shandong Province (No. ZR2019LZH015), Shandong Province Higher Educational Science and Technology Program (No. J18KA349), Project of Independent Cultivated Innovation Team of Jinan City (No. 2018GXRC002).

References

1. Behjati, S., Tarpey, P.S.: What is next generation sequencing? Arch. Disease Childhood Educ. Pract. **98**(6), 236–238 (2013)
2. Wetterstrand, K.A.: DNA Sequencing Costs: Data-National Human Genome Research Institute (NHGRI) (2019)
3. Ginsburg, G.S., Willard, H.F.: Genomic and personalized medicine: foundations and applications. Transl. Res. **154**(6), 277–287 (2009)
4. Pierre, A.S., Génin, E.: How important are rare variants in common disease? Brief. Funct. Genomics **13**(5), 353–361 (2014)
5. Chen, J., Geyer, W., Dugan, C., Muller, M., Guy, I.: Make new friends, but keep the old: recommending people on social networking sites. In: Proceedings of the SIGCHI Conference on Human Factors in Computing Systems, pp. 201–210 (2009)
6. Gymrek, M., McGuire, A.L., Golan, D., Halperin, E., Erlich, Y.: Identifying personal genomes by surname inference. Science **339**(6117), 321–324 (2013)

7. Lin, Z., Owen, A.B., Altman, R.B.: Genomic research and human subject privacy (2004)
8. Claes, P., et al.: Modeling 3d facial shape from DNA. PLoS Genet. **10**(3), e1004224 (2014)
9. Lippert, C., et al.: Identification of individuals by trait prediction using whole-genome sequencing data. Proc. Natl. Acad. Sci. **114**(38), 10166–10171 (2017)
10. Kupersmith, J.: The privacy conundrum and genomic research: re-identification and other concerns. Health Affairs, Project HOPE (2013)
11. Lu, W.-J., Yamada, Y., Sakuma, J.: Privacy-preserving genome-wide association studies on cloud environment using fully homomorphic encryption. BMC Med. Inform. Decis. Mak. **15**, 1–8 (2015)
12. Uhlerop, C., Slavković, A., Fienberg, S.E.: Privacy-preserving data sharing for genome-wide association studies. J. Priv. Confid. **5**(1), 137 (2013)
13. Kim, M., Lauter, K.: Private genome analysis through homomorphic encryption. BMC Med. Inform. Decis. Mak. **15**, S3 (2015)
14. Sadat, Md.N., Al Aziz, Md.M., Mohammed, N., Chen, F., Wang, S., Jiang, X.: SAFETY: secure gwAs in federated environment through a hybrid solution with intel SGX and homomorphic encryption. arXiv preprint arXiv:1703.02577 (2017)
15. Lindell, Y., Pinkas, B.: An efficient protocol for secure two-party computation in the presence of malicious adversaries. In: Naor, M. (ed.) EUROCRYPT 2007. LNCS, vol. 4515, pp. 52–78. Springer, Heidelberg (2007). https://doi.org/10.1007/978-3-540-72540-4_4
16. Zhao, Q., Zhao, C., Cui, S., Jing, S., Chen, Z.: PrivateDL: privacy-preserving collaborative deep learning against leakage from gradient sharing. Int. J. Intell. Syst. **35**(8), 1262–1279 (2020)
17. Shih, M.-W., Lee, S., Kim, T., Peinado, M.: Eradicating controlled-channel attacks against enclave programs. In: NDSS, T-SGX (2017)
18. Nishide, T., Sakurai, K.: Distributed Paillier cryptosystem without trusted dealer. In: Chung, Y., Yung, M. (eds.) WISA 2010. LNCS, vol. 6513, pp. 44–60. Springer, Heidelberg (2011). https://doi.org/10.1007/978-3-642-17955-6_4
19. Manegold, S., Boncz, P.A., Kersten, M.L.: Optimizing database architecture for the new bottleneck: memory access. VLDB J. **9**(3), 231–246 (2000)
20. Botelho, F.C., Lacerda, A., Menezes, G.V., Ziviani, N.: Minimal perfect hashing: a competitive method for indexing internal memory. Inf. Sci. **181**(13), 2608–2625 (2011)
21. Costan, V., Devadas, S.: Intel SGX explained. IACR Cryptol. ePrint Arch. **2016**(086), 1–118 (2016)
22. Anati, I., Gueron, S., Johnson, S., Scarlata, V.: Innovative technology for CPU based attestation and sealing. In: Proceedings of the 2nd International Workshop on Hardware and Architectural Support for Security and Privacy, vol. 13, p. 7. ACM, New York (2013)
23. Madsen, B.E., Browning, S.R.: A groupwise association test for rare mutations using a weighted sum statistic. PLoS Genet. **5**(2), e1000384 (2009)
24. Fox, E.A., Chen, Q.F., Heath, L.S.: A faster algorithm for constructing minimal perfect hash functions. In: Proceedings of the 15th Annual International ACM SIGIR Conference on Research and Development in Information Retrieval, pp. 266–273 (1992)
25. The OpenSSL Project. OpenSSL: The open source toolkit for SSL/TLS, April 2003. www.openssl.org

26. Clarke, L., et al.: The international genome sample resource (IGSR): a worldwide collection of genome variation incorporating the 1000 genomes project data. Nucleic Acids Res. **45**(D1), D854–D859 (2017)
27. Mittos, A., Malin, B.,De Cristofaro, E.: Systematizing genome privacy research: a privacy-enhancing technologies perspective. arXiv preprint arXiv:1712.02193 (2017)
28. Sei, Y., Ohsuga, A.: Privacy-preserving chi-squared testing for genome SNP databases. In: 2017 39th Annual International Conference of the IEEE Engineering in Medicine and Biology Society (EMBC), pp. 3884–3889. IEEE (2017)
29. Cho, H., Wu, D.J., Berger, B.: Secure genome-wide association analysis using multiparty computation. Nature Biotechnol. **36**(6), 547–551 (2018)
30. Chen, F., et al.: Princess: privacy-protecting rare disease international network collaboration via encryption through software guard extensions. Bioinformatics **33**(6), 871–878 (2017)
31. Naehrig, M., Lauter, K., Vaikuntanathan, V.: Can homomorphic encryption be practical? In: Proceedings of the 3rd ACM Workshop on Cloud Computing Security Workshop, pp. 113–124 (2011)
32. Zhao, C., et al.: Secure multi-party computation: theory, practice and applications. Inf. Sci. **476**, 357–372 (2019)
33. Wu, M.C., Lee, S., Cai, T., Li, Y., Boehnke, M., Lin, X.: Rare-variant association testing for sequencing data with the sequence kernel association test. Am. J. Hum. Genet. **89**(1), 82–93 (2011)
34. Lee, S., et al.: Optimal unified approach for rare-variant association testing with application to small-sample case-control whole-exome sequencing studies. Am. J. Hum. Genet. **91**(2), 224–237 (2012)

Rotational-Linear Attack: A New Framework of Cryptanalysis on ARX Ciphers with Applications to Chaskey

Yaqi Xu[1,2], Baofeng Wu[1,2](✉), and Dongdai Lin[1,2]

[1] State Key Laboratory of Information Security, Institute of Information Engineering, Chinese Academy of Sciences, Beijing, China
{xuyaqi,wubaofeng,ddlin}@iie.ac.cn

[2] School of Cyber Security, University of Chinese Academy of Sciences, Beijing, China

Abstract. In this paper, we formulate a new framework of cryptanalysis called rotational-linear attack on ARX ciphers. We firstly build an efficient distinguisher for the cipher E consisted of the rotational attack and the linear attack together with some intermediate variables. Then a key recovery technique is introduced with which we can recover some bits of the last whitening key in the related-key scenario. To decrease data complexity of our attack, we also apply a new method, called bit flipping, in the rotational cryptanalysis for the first time and the effective partitioning technique to the key-recovery part.

Applying the new framework of attack to the MAC algorithm Chaskey, we build a full-round distinguisher over it. Besides, we have recovered 21 bits of information of the key in the related-key scenario, for keys belonging to a large weak-key class based on 6-round distinguisher. The data complexity is $2^{38.8}$ and the time complexity is $2^{46.8}$. Before our work, the rotational distinguisher can only be used to reveal key information by checking weak-key conditions. This is the first time it is applied in a last-rounds key-recovery attack. We build a 17-round rotational-linear distinguisher for ChaCha permutation as an improvement compared to single rotational cryptanalysis over it.

Keywords: Rotational-linear attack · ARX cipher · Partitioning · Key recovery · Chaskey · ChaCha permutation

1 Introduction

Symmetric cryptographic algorithms have significant security-relevant applications and play influential roles in modern cryptography. Among various kinds of lightweight symmetric primitives, one class of design-structure called ARX has been adopted frequently because of its efficient software and hardware performance.

D. Gao et al. (Eds.): ICICS 2021, LNCS 12919, pp. 192–209, 2021.
https://doi.org/10.1007/978-3-030-88052-1_12

ARX Ciphers. The ARX (Addition-Rotation-XOR) structure is an attractive candidate for designing lightweight cryptographic algorithms. In such a structure, confusion and diffusion can be obtained with low consumption using three simple operations, namely, modular addition ($\boxplus$), rotation ($\lll$) and XOR ($\oplus$). ARX-based designs are not only applied to stream-ciphers, but also to the design of efficient block ciphers and message authentication codes (MAC). There are some stream-ciphers, e.g., Salsa20 [5] and ChaCha [3]. Unlike SPN ciphers, whose nonlinear part consists of S-boxes, the nonlinear operation within ARX ciphers is modular addition. The ARX-based lightweight symmetric primitives can also serve as alternatives of the SPN structure which are used in the design of many block ciphers such as the advanced encryption standard (AES). Besides, message authentication code algorithms can also use ARX-designs to achieve strong diffusion. For example, Chaskey [19] is an efficient MAC algorithm which processes a message m and a secret key K to generate a tag τ for micro controllers, using the ARX-design approach.

Due to their good confusion and diffusion properties, many classical cryptanalysis methods on symmetric ciphers are not efficient enough for ARX ciphers. For example, we generally cannot obtain differential [7] or linear [18] distinguishers with high probabilities for long enough rounds. To improve attacks on ARX ciphers, some combined cryptanalysis methods based on differential and linear attacks are often considered, such as the boomerang attack [20] and the differential-linear attack [15].

Differential-Linear Cryptanalysis. Differential-linear cryptanalysis was introduced by Langford and Hellman [15] for the first time. A cipher E is divided into two sub-ciphers E_1 and E_2, i.e., $E = E_2 \circ E_1$. The two parts are assumed to be independent. Then a differential distinguisher with probability p for E_1 and a linear distinguisher with correlation q for E_2 are combined to a differential-linear distinguisher with correlation pq^2. The assumption that E_1 and E_2 are independent may cause wrong estimates. To perform this attack, the cipher E is often divided into three parts, a differential part, a linear part, and a connective part. This attack has good performances in attacking ARX ciphers by carefully arranging rounds for these three parts, especially the ARX ciphers based on permutations like ChaCha [3] and Chaskey [14].

Last-Rounds Key Recovery and Partitioning Technique. In the key recovery phase of an analysis of a symmetric cipher, Matsui's Algorithm 2 is a basic choice. It depends on a distinguisher on certain rounds of a cipher and a partial decryption on last few rounds by guessing some bits of sub-keys. After the partial decryption we can obtain the intermediate value to recover some bits of the key by detecting whether the distinguisher is satisfied or not. For ARX ciphers, applying partitioning technique is analogous to partial decryption during key recovery. The partitioning technique is proposed in [6] to improve linear cryptanalysis of ARX ciphers by finding a special relationship among two inputs and output on a modular addition, avoiding the impact of the carry information after selecting a set of inputs. Partitioning technique has also been applied to differential-linear attacks [16] to reduce the data complexity. In our work, we will apply partitioning technique in the key-recovery part based on the rotational-linear distinguisher.

Motivation of Our Work. Differential-linear attack is an important kind of combined attack and has been widely applied to many symmetric ciphers. However, the existing attacks still have some drawbacks, for example, the differential trail is limited by the connective part which increases the overall complexity obviously. Rotational attack is a specific kind of cryptanalysis which was applied to ARX ciphers primarily. This kind of distinguisher sometimes can hold with higher probability than the differential distinguisher for the same number of rounds for some ARX ciphers. However, key-recovery is usually infeasible and information of keys can only be revealed by checking certain weak-key conditions before. There is no article achieving key-recovery beyond weak keys under rotational distinguisher in prior of our work.

Motivated by the idea of differential-linear attack, we consider how to combine rotational attack and linear attack in this paper, aiming to obtain more efficient key recovery attacks on some ARX ciphers in addition to building a new kind of distinguisher. We call this attack a rotational-linear attack.

Our Contribution. We build the framework of rotational-linear cryptanalysis and analyze the complexity to perform this attack. A cipher E to be attacked is also divided into three parts: the rotational part, the linear part and the connective part. Since the connectivity between rotational and linear part only effects the choice of input mask of linear part, which means it has no limit on the rotational part, and we can obtain more efficient distinguishers under our framework. We obtained a 12-round distinguisher for Chaskey with probability $2^{-60.38}$ in the related-key scenario, which is an improvement compared with the work in [14]. Besides, we show how to take advantage of the partitioning technique to recover partial bits of the key. In Table 1, we present different kinds of attacks applying to the MAC cipher Chaskey, including differential-linear attack with key recovery, rotational attacks and our rotational-linear attacks with corresponding data and time complexities. It turns out that the rotational-linear attack exhibits advantages compared to other kinds of attacks. Rotational-linear attack also gives guidelines when designing ARX ciphers, especially the key schedule.

Table 1. Review of different kinds of attacks applied to Chaskey.

Different kinds of attacks	Rounds	Time	Data	Ref.
Differential-linear attack with key recovery	7	2^{67}	2^{48}	[16]
Differential-linear attack with key recovery	7	$2^{51.21}$	$2^{40.21}$	[4]
Weak-key related-key rotational distinguishing attack	6		2^{42}	[14]
Weak-key related-key rotational attack, forge a valid tag	12		2^{86}	[14]
Related-key rotational-linear distinguishing attack	12		$2^{60.38}$	This paper
Related-key rotational-linear key-recovery attack	7	$2^{46.8}$	$2^{38.8}$	This paper

Relationship with the Work in [17]**.** Recently, Liu et al. proposed the framework of rotational-XOR differential-linear (R-DL) attack in [17], which degenerated to our rotational-linear attack when setting the rotational-XOR differences to be 0. We have to point out that our work is a parallel and independent one with [17] rather than a follow-up of it. Actually, combining the rotational/rotational-XOR distinguisher with the linear distinguisher is a natural idea, and the key problem lies in whether one can obtain successful attacks for specific ciphers.

In [17] the authors paid main attention to distinguishing attacks on some permutation based ciphers, while we are focused on key-recovery attacks in this paper. In addition, our rotational-linear distinguisher is different with Liu et al.'s. First, we add the connective part within the distinguisher experimentally. The hamming weight of two output masks for the distinguisher in [17] is set to 1 with rotational relationship. Because of the connective part, we can choose linear masks for the linear part without these limits in our work. Second, we use a method, that is bit flipping, in the rotational cryptanalysis for the first time to decrease the data complexity. Third, we combine the partitioning technique to the key recovery whereas the rotational/rotational-XOR cryptanalysis only applied to build distinguishers before our work. It is a natural problem to extended our key-recovery techniques to the R-DL framework, which will be left as a further work.

Organization. The rest of this paper is organized as follows. We give some relevant preliminaries in Sect. 2 and a review of the rotational attack in Sect. 3. The new framework of attack, i.e., the rotational-linear attack is presented in Sect. 4. Precise processes of our attack on Chaskey are given in Sect. 5. Conclusions are given in Sect. 6. Finally, an extended application of rotational-linear cryptanalysis to ChaCha permutation is presented in Appendix A.

2 Preliminaries

2.1 Notations

We denote an n-bit vector by $x = (x[n-1], ..., x[1], x[0])$, where $x[i]$ denotes the i-th bit of x. Let $x[i_l, \dots, i_1]$ denote $\oplus_{j=1}^{l} x[i_j]$. The i-th unit vector is denoted by $[i] \in \mathbb{F}_2^n$. We denote the basic operations in ARX ciphers by $\boxplus$ (modular addition), $\oplus$ (XOR) and $\lll$ (rotation). A left rotation by the amount γ is denoted by $x \lll \gamma$. We also use $x = (x_0, x_1, \dots, x_l)$ to represent an n-bit vector which splits into l m-bit sub-vectors, and the rotation of x is denoted by $\overleftarrow{x}^{\gamma} = (x_0 \lll \gamma, x_1 \lll \gamma, \dots, x_l \lll \gamma)$. Let x, y be two n-bit vectors, $\langle x, y \rangle$ denotes the inner product of x and y. Given a set $\mathcal{S} \subseteq \mathbb{F}_2^n$ and a Boolean function $f : \mathbb{F}_2^n \to \mathbb{F}_2$, we define the correlation of f by $Cor_{x \in \mathcal{S}}[f(x)] := \frac{1}{|\mathcal{S}|} \sum_{x \in \mathcal{S}} (-1)^{f(x)}$.

2.2 Partitioning Technique for Modular Additions

Partition is to find a special relationship between the two inputs and output of a modular addition avoiding the impact of carry information after selecting a set of the inputs. The following lemmas display the partitioning technique which are applied in the key recovery. Assume there is a function $F : \mathbb{F}_2^{2m} \to \mathbb{F}_2^{2m}$ such that $F(a, b) = (s, b)$ where $s = a \boxplus b$. The partition could be used after selecting a set of the outputs as the following lemmas show from another point of view.

Lemma 1 ([4]). *Let* $i \geq 2$, $a, b \in \mathbb{F}_2^m$, $s = a \boxplus b$ *and* $\mathcal{S}_1 := \{(x_1, x_0) \in \mathbb{F}_2^{2m} \mid x_0[i-1] \neq x_1[i-1]\}$, $\mathcal{S}_2 := \{(x_1, x_0) \in \mathbb{F}_2^{2m} \mid x_0[i-1] = x_1[i-1]$ *and* $x_0[i-2] \neq x_1[i-2]\}$. *Then,*

$$a[i] = \begin{cases} b[i] \oplus s[i] \oplus b[i-1] \oplus 1 & \text{if } (s, b) \in \mathcal{S}_1, \\ b[i] \oplus s[i] \oplus b[i-2] \oplus 1 & \text{if } (s, b) \in \mathcal{S}_2. \end{cases}$$

Lemma 2 ([4]). *Let* $i \geq 2$, $a, b \in \mathbb{F}_2^m$, $s = a \boxplus b$ *and* $\mathcal{S}_3 := \{(x_1, x_0) \in \mathbb{F}_2^{2m} \mid x_0[i-1] = x_1[i-1]\}$, $\mathcal{S}_4 := \{(x_1, x_0) \in \mathbb{F}_2^{2m} \mid x_0[i-1] \neq x_1[i-1]$ *and* $x_0[i-2] \neq x_1[i-2]\}$. *Then,*

$$a[i] \oplus a[i-1] = \begin{cases} b[i] \oplus s[i] & \text{if } (s, b) \in \mathcal{S}_3, \\ b[i] \oplus s[i] \oplus b[i-1] \oplus b[i-2] \oplus 1 & \text{if } (s, b) \in \mathcal{S}_4. \end{cases}$$

2.3 Description of Chaskey

Chaskey is a lightweight MAC algorithm for 32-bit micro-controllers using an ARX structure in an Even-Mansour construction. A tag τ is extracted from the last state $K' \oplus F(M \oplus K)$. Chaskey splits a message m into l message blocks $m_1, m_2, \ldots, m_l$ of 128 bits each (after padding if needed). It employs a 12-round permutation π with 128-bit key K. If the message m is 128 bits, we can have $\tau = \pi(m \oplus K \oplus K_1) \oplus K_1$. Here the subkey K_1 is generated from the master key K. If $K[127]$ equals 0, then $K_1 = K \lll 1 \oplus 0^{128}$. If not, $K_1 = K \lll 1 \oplus 0^{120}10000111$. The permutation π is showed in Fig. 1.

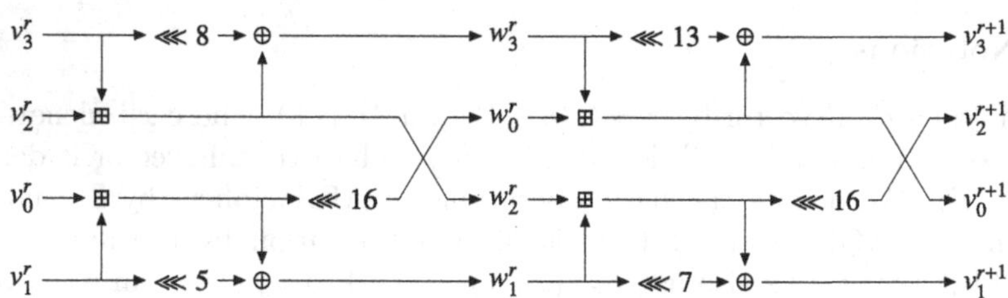

Fig. 1. The round function of Chaskey.

3 Rotational Cryptanalysis

Rotational cryptanalysis, presented in [12] for the first time, takes advantage of the high probability rotational relation propagated through the ARX operations and was applied to the reduced version of Threefish. In [12] the authors presented a method based on counting the number of additions in the scheme to get a universal upper bound on the probability of the distinguisher. However, it was showed in [13] that the rotational probabilities of ARX ciphers depends not only on the number of additions but also on their positions. An explicit formula to compute the rotational probability of chained modular additions is presented in [13]. In this section, we present the translation of rotational relations through different operations in ARX ciphers firstly.

Modular Addition. The following proposition provides a general way to compute the propagation of a rotational relation through a single modular addition.

Proposition 1 ([10]). *For $x, y \in \mathbb{F}_2^m$ and $0 < \gamma < m$, we have*

$$\Pr[(x \boxplus y) \lll \gamma = (x \lll \gamma) \boxplus (y \lll \gamma)] = (1 + 2^{\gamma-m} + 2^{-\gamma} + 2^{-m})/4.$$

The probability is maximized to $2^{-1.415}$ when m is large and $\gamma = 1$. However, it was found in [13] this assumption is actually not true and the method to compute the probability is presented by the following lemma.

Lemma 3. ([13]). *Let $a_1, ..., a_l$ be m-bit vectors chosen at random and let l be a positive integer with $0 < l < m$. Then*

$$\begin{aligned}
&\Pr([(a_1 \boxplus a_2) \lll \gamma = (a_1 \lll \gamma) \boxplus (a_2 \lll \gamma)] \wedge \\
&\ldots \\
&\wedge[(a_1 \boxplus \cdots \boxplus a_l) \lll \gamma = (a_1 \lll \gamma) \boxplus \cdots \boxplus (a_l \lll \gamma)]) \\
&= \frac{1}{2^{ml}} \binom{l + 2^{\gamma} - 1}{2^{\gamma} - 1} \binom{l + 2^{m-\gamma} - 1}{2^{m-\gamma} - 1}.
\end{aligned}$$

XOR Operation. Assume that $x, y \in \mathbb{F}_2^m$ are random variables and $c \in \mathbb{F}_2^m$ is a constant. We can obtain the rotational relation $(x \oplus y) \lll \gamma = (x \lll \gamma) \oplus (y \lll \gamma)$ with probability 1 and $(x \lll \gamma) \oplus c = (x \oplus c) \lll \gamma$ if and only if $c = c \lll \gamma$.

Rotation. For the rotation operation, we have $\Pr[(x \lll a) \lll \gamma = (x \lll \gamma) \lll a] = 1$.

In the remaining part of this paper the rotational value γ will be set to 1 and we denote $x \lll 1$ by $\overleftarrow{x}$. For parallel applications of a cipher E, if the input pair (x, x') have the relation $x' = \overleftarrow{x}$, we say that (x, x') is a *rotational pair.* The input pairs together with the sub-key pairs (k_r, k_r') XORed with intermediate values should be rotational pairs when building the rotational distinguisher. Obviously it is a kind of related-key attack. For this, we denote the transformation between master keys K and $\widetilde{K}$, such that their sub-key pairs (k_r, k_r') are rotational pairs, by $\widetilde{K} = f(K)$.

4 Rotational-Linear Attacks on ARX Ciphers

In this section, we will introduce the new framework of our attack combining the rotational and linear attacks, called rotational-linear attack. An entire cipher E is divided into two sub-ciphers E_1 and E_2 representing rotational and linear parts respectively and the intermediate states are showed in Fig. 2. For parallel applications of cipher E, we assume the input pairs are rotational pairs $(x, \overleftarrow{x})$. For two masks β^1 and β^0, we study correlation of linear approximations $Cor_{x\in\mathbb{F}_2^n}[\langle\beta^1, E(x)\rangle \oplus \langle\beta^0, E(\overleftarrow{x})\rangle]$. Making use of the distinguisher and the partition technique mentioned in [4,16], we can recover partial bits of the key for last rounds.

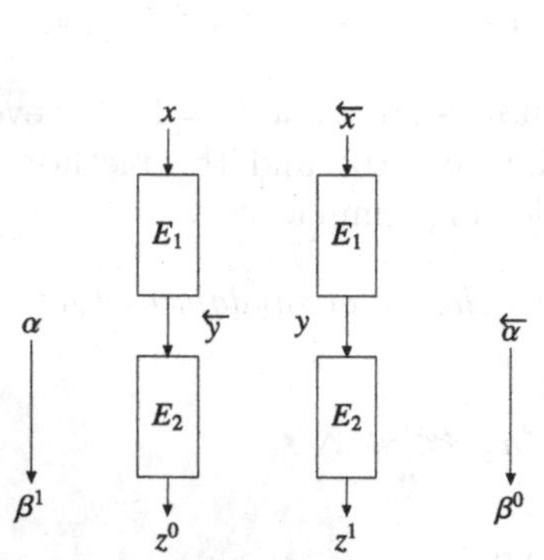

Fig. 2. Basic rotational-linear distinguisher with linear trails for linear part E_2.

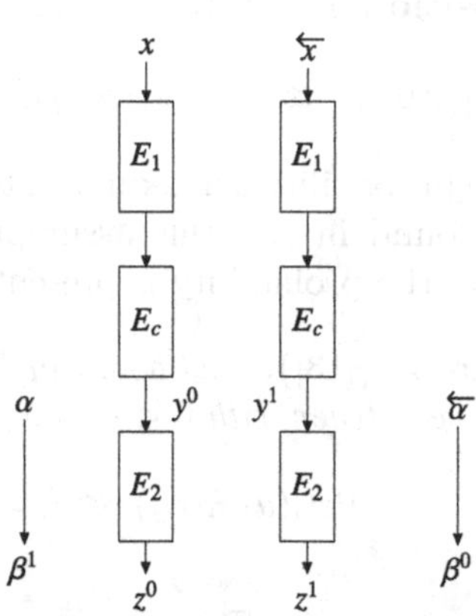

Fig. 3. The structure of rotational-linear distinguisher with a connective part E_c.

4.1 Correlation of Linear Approximations

After the rotational part E_1, we denote the rotational probability by $\Pr_{x\in\mathbb{F}_2^n}[\overleftarrow{E_1(x)} = E_1(\overleftarrow{x})] = p$, and we need to compute the correlation $Cor_{x\in\mathbb{F}_2^n}[\langle\beta^1, E(x)\rangle \oplus \langle\beta^0, E(\overleftarrow{x})\rangle]$. First we assume that E_1 is independent with E_2. Given a mask α, we have $\langle\alpha, E_1(x)\rangle = \langle\overleftarrow{\alpha}, E_1(\overleftarrow{x})\rangle$ if $\overleftarrow{E_1(x)} = E_1(\overleftarrow{x})$ after the rotational part. Then we need to find two linear trails for E_2 with the input masks α and $\overleftarrow{\alpha}$. The correlation of linear trails for the parallel are q_1 and q_0 respectively.

Now we can compute the correlation of the distinguisher as follows:

$$\begin{aligned}&Cor_{x\in\mathbb{F}_2^n}[\langle\beta^1, E(x)\rangle \oplus \langle\beta^0, E(\overleftarrow{x})\rangle]\\ &= Cor_{x\in\mathbb{F}_2^n}[\langle\beta^1, E_2\circ E_1(x)\rangle \oplus \langle\beta^0, E_2\circ E_1(\overleftarrow{x})\rangle]\\ &= Cor_{y\in\mathbb{F}_2^n}[\langle\beta^1, E_2(y)\rangle \oplus \langle\beta^0, E_2(\overleftarrow{y})\rangle]\cdot Pr_{x\in\mathbb{F}_2^n}[\overleftarrow{E_1(x)} = E_1(\overleftarrow{x})].\end{aligned}$$

Assume $\langle \beta^1, E_2(y)\rangle \oplus \langle \alpha, y\rangle$ and $\langle \beta^0, E_2(\overleftarrow{y})\rangle \oplus \langle \overleftarrow{\alpha}, \overleftarrow{y}\rangle$ are independent and $\langle \alpha, y\rangle = \langle \overleftarrow{\alpha}, \overleftarrow{y}\rangle$. By the Piling-up lemma we have the correlation of the distinguisher is pq_0q_1. Assume the data complexity of the rotational part is N_r, which is asymptotically $O(p^{-2})$. By preparing $N_r \cdot \delta(q_0q_1)^{-2}$ pairs of chosen plaintexts $(x, \overleftarrow{x})$, where $\delta \in \mathbb{N}$ is a small constant, one can distinguish the cipher from a pseudo random permutation.

4.2 The Connective Part

The assumption that E_1 and E_2 are independent might be a problem with wrong estimates for the correlation of linear approximations. The wrong estimate under differential-linear attacks has been testified in [2]. In rotational-linear cryptanalysis we also add a connective part as a simple solution (showed in Fig. 3). The correlation $p_c = Cor_{x\in\mathcal{S}}[\langle \alpha, E_c(x)\rangle \oplus \langle \overleftarrow{\alpha}, E_c(\overleftarrow{x})\rangle]$ can be evaluated experimentally where $\mathcal{S}$ denotes a set of random samples. Then the whole correlation of the linear approximation of the distinguisher is computed as $Cor_{x\in\mathbb{F}_2^n}[\langle \beta^1, E(x)\rangle \oplus \langle \beta^0, E(\overleftarrow{x})\rangle] = pp_cq_0q_1$.

4.3 Decrease the Data Complexity

Inspired by the work in [4], we want to construct many right pairs with probability (close to) 1 given a right pair satisfying rotational relationship. If we have a chained addition operation $s = a_0 \boxplus a_1 \boxplus a_2$ for $a_0, a_1, a_2 \in \mathbb{F}_2^m$, we denote the carry-bit vectors of $a_0 \boxplus a_1$ and $(a_0 \boxplus a_1) \boxplus a_2$ by c_1 and c_2 respectively. Note that $(a_0 \boxplus a_1 \boxplus a_2) \lll 1 = (a_0 \lll 1) \boxplus (a_1 \lll 1) \boxplus (a_2 \lll 1)$ and $(a_0 \boxplus a_1) \lll 1 = (a_0 \lll 1) \boxplus (a_1 \lll 1)$ if and only if the following conditions are satisfied:

$$\begin{aligned} c_2[m-1] = 0,\ c_1[m-1] = 0, \\ a_0[m-1] + a_1[m-1] + a_2[m-1] < 2. \end{aligned} \tag{1}$$

We flip a few bits of one input and assume it is a_0 without loss of generality. Write $s^r = a_0^r \boxplus a_1 \boxplus a_2$ where a_0^r is the flipped input. If the conditions in (1) can also be satisfied, then we obtain a new right pair for free. However, the conditions for a cipher is more complicated. Let us denote $\mathcal{R}$ as the set consisting of right data satisfying the rotational relation before and after an ARX permutation E_1, i.e., $\mathcal{R} = \{x \in \mathbb{F}_2^n \mid \overleftarrow{E_1(x)} = E_1(\overleftarrow{x})\}$. We assume that $\mathcal{R}$ contains an affine subspace $\mathcal{A} = a \oplus \mathcal{U}$. Instead of choosing random plaintexts from $\mathbb{F}_2^n$, we could generate a subset of $x \in \mathcal{A}$ to augment the correlation of the rotational-linear distinguisher. Now we can generate right data for the rotational part E_1 through a statistical model presented in Algorithm 1.

The number of flipping-bit candidates, namely, $|\mathcal{U}|$ getting from Algorithm 1, are not only related to the structure of E_1 but also to the number of rounds in E_1. The number of flipping-bit candidates needs to be sufficiently large to fulfill the data complexity of the remaining part of the attack. If the number of rounds in E_1 is beyond our expect, we can split E_1 into two parts $E_1 = E_{10} \circ E_{11}$ with rotational probabilities p_0 and p_1 respectively. Then the rotational probability of

Algorithm 1. Find the candidates of flipping-bits

Input: Permutation $E : \mathbb{F}_2^n \to \mathbb{F}_2^n$, a set $\mathcal{S} = \{x \mid x \in \mathbb{F}_2^n\}$ of N samples
Output: Probabilistic list of flipping-bit candidates $\mathcal{U}$, threshold ρ.

Let $r = 0$ and $t_j = 0$ for $j \in \{0, \ldots, n-1\}$
for $i = 0$ to N **do**
  Pick one element $x \in \mathcal{S}$, compute $E(x)$ and $E(\overleftarrow{x})$ respectively
  if $\overleftarrow{E(x)} = E(\overleftarrow{x})$ **then**
    $r \leftarrow r + 1$
    for $j \in \{0, \ldots, n-1\}$ **do**
      Prepare $x' = x \oplus 2^j$, $E(x')$ and $E(\overleftarrow{x'})$
      if $\overleftarrow{E(x')} = E(\overleftarrow{x'})$ **then**
        $t_j \leftarrow t_j + 1$
for $j \in \{0, \ldots, n-1\}$ **do**
  if $t_j / r > \rho$ **then**
    Save j as a flipping-bit candidate

E_1 is $p = p_0 p_1$. After applying Algorithm 1 to E_{10}, we can get a list of flipping-bit candidates with average probability p_a. If the result meets requirements for the remaining part of our attack, we can decrease the data complexity N_r of E_1 from $\mathcal{O}((p_0 p_1)^{-2})$ to $\mathcal{O}(p_0^{-1}(p_a p_1)^{-2})$.

4.4 Key Recovery

In this section, we present a method to recover part of the last whitening key k based on a rotational-linear distinguisher. The rotational pair $\{(x, \overleftarrow{x}) \mid x \in \mathbb{F}_2^n\}$ are inputs for the cipher E. Using the rotational-linear distinguisher built in Sect. 3 we have the correlation $Cor_{x \in \mathbb{F}_2^n}[\langle \beta^1, E(x) \rangle \oplus \langle \beta^0, E(\overleftarrow{x}) \rangle] = q$. The set of input pairs for the linear part is denoted by $\mathcal{D} := \{(y, \widetilde{y}) \mid y = E_c \circ E_1(x),\ \widetilde{y} = E_c \circ E_1(\overleftarrow{x})$ and $E_1(\overleftarrow{x}) = \overleftarrow{E_1(x)}$ for $x \in \mathbb{F}_2^n\}$. We denote the right pairs after cipher E by $\mathcal{D}_{out} := \{(z, \tilde{z}) \mid z = E_2(y),\ \tilde{z} = E_2(\tilde{y})$ for $(y, \tilde{y}) \in \mathcal{D}\}$ as the input pairs for F. In Matsui's last rounds attack in [18] one gathers some bits of key information with partial decryption of the last rounds. Because of the modular addition operation, we need to do some changes for the key-recovery work.

On the basis of correlation of the linear approximation $Cor_{(z,\tilde{z}) \in \mathcal{D}_{out}}[\langle \beta^1, z \rangle \oplus \langle \beta^0, \tilde{z} \rangle]$, we split β^ι into $\beta_0^\iota, \ldots, \beta_{l-1}^\iota$ for $\iota \in \{0, 1\}$ such that every β_i^ι is in the form of one or two consecutive active bits defined as a *partition point* [4] and the correlated linear approximation is $Cor_{(z,\tilde{z}) \in \mathcal{D}_{out}}[\langle \beta_i^1, z \rangle \oplus \langle \beta_j^0, \tilde{z} \rangle] = q_{i,j}$. The overall structure of key recovery is presented in Fig. 4. Applying the partition technique [4,16] to the outputs of F, we can generate several linear trails $\beta_i^1 \to \mu_{i,i_1}^1$ and $\beta_j^0 \to \mu_{j,j_1}^0$ corresponding to special partition $\mathcal{P}$ with high correlations

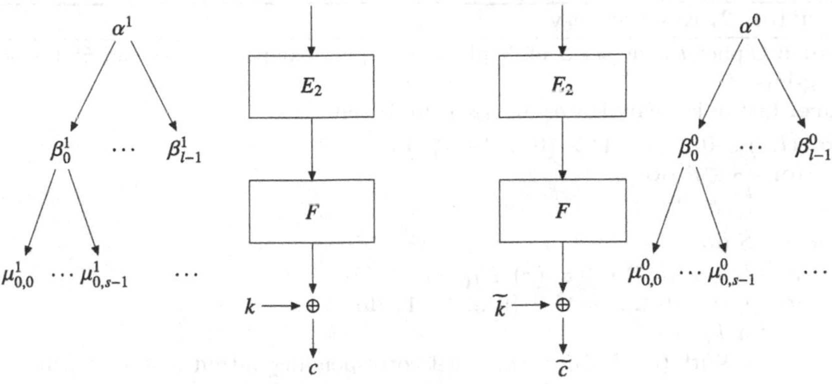

Fig. 4. To recover partial key, output mask of E_2, i.e., β^ι, is partitioned to *partition points* $\beta_0^\iota, \dots, \beta_{l-1}^\iota$, $\iota \in \{0,1\}$. For every partition points we will find linear trails $\beta_i^\iota \to \mu_{i,j}^\iota$ after partition, $i \in \{0,\dots,l-1\}$ and $j \in \{0,\dots,s-1\}$.

denoted by ϵ_{i,i_1}^1 and ϵ_{j,j_1}^0 for $i,j \in \{0,\dots,l-1\}$ and $i_1, j_1 \in \{0,\dots,s-1\}$. Then we have

$$\begin{aligned} &Cor_{\substack{(z,\widetilde{z})\in\mathcal{D}_{out} \text{ s.t.} \\ k\oplus c\in\mathcal{P},\ \widetilde{k}\oplus\widetilde{c}\in f(\mathcal{P})}} [\langle \mu_{i,i_1}^1, k\oplus c\rangle \oplus \langle \mu_{j,j_1}^0, \widetilde{k}\oplus\widetilde{c}\rangle] \\ &= Cor_{\substack{((z,\widetilde{z})\in\mathcal{D}_{out} \text{ s.t.} \\ k\oplus c\in\mathcal{P},\ \widetilde{k}\oplus\widetilde{c}\in f(\mathcal{P})}} [\langle \beta_i^1, z\rangle \oplus \langle \beta_j^0, \widetilde{z}\rangle] = q_{i,j}\epsilon_{i,i_1}^1\epsilon_{j,j_1}^0. \end{aligned}$$

Partitioning the outputs of F is equivalent to partitioning the set $\{(k\oplus c, \widetilde{k}\oplus\widetilde{c}) \mid (z,\widetilde{z}) \in \mathcal{D}_{out}$ s.t. $k\oplus c = F(z),\ \widetilde{k}\oplus\widetilde{c} = F(\widetilde{z})\}$. We denote $\mathcal{P}$ as the set of bits relevant to partitioning technique. Moreover we represent k as $k_\mathcal{P} \oplus k_\mu \oplus k'$ where $k_\mathcal{P} \in \mathcal{P}$, k_μ is the set of bits related to the masks $\mu^1 \oplus \mu^0$ while k' is the remaining bits we need to guess. The whole process of the key-recovery is demonstrated in Algorithm 2.

Build the Counter. Building a special counter is a significant speed-up in the key-recovery under the framework of differential-linear attack [4]. For our rotational-linear attack, we need to find the relations between active bits of β_j^0 and k before building a valid counter to recover the partial bits of the key, that is

$$\begin{aligned} &Cor_{\substack{(z,\widetilde{z})\in\mathcal{D}_{out} \text{ s.t.} \\ k\oplus c\in\mathcal{P},\ \widetilde{k}\oplus\widetilde{c}\in f(\mathcal{P})}} [\langle \mu_{i,i_1}^1, c\oplus k\rangle \oplus \langle \mu_{j,j_1}^0, \widetilde{c}\oplus\widetilde{k}\rangle] \\ =& \sum_{\substack{(z,\widetilde{z})\in\mathcal{D}_{out} \text{ s.t.} \\ k\oplus c\in\mathcal{P},\ \widetilde{k}\oplus\widetilde{c}\in f(\mathcal{P})}} (-1)^{\langle \mu_{i,i_1}^1, c\rangle \oplus \langle \mu_{j,j_1}^0, \widetilde{c}\rangle \oplus \langle \mu_{i,i_1}^1, k\rangle \oplus \langle f^{-1}(\mu_{j,j_1}^0), k\rangle} \\ =& (-1)^{\langle \mu_{i,i_1}^1 \oplus f^{-1}(\mu_{j,j_1}^0), k\rangle} \sum_{\substack{(z,\widetilde{z})\in\mathcal{D}_{out} \text{ s.t.} \\ k\oplus c\in\mathcal{P},\ \widetilde{k}\oplus\widetilde{c}\in f(\mathcal{P})}} (-1)^{\langle \mu_{i,i_1}^1, c\rangle \oplus \langle \mu_{j,j_1}^0, \widetilde{c}\rangle}. \end{aligned}$$

Algorithm 2. Key recovery

Require: Cipher E, the set $\mathcal{S}$ of N plaintext-ciphertext pairs, threshold Θ, the set of flipping-bits $\mathcal{U}$

Ensure: List of key candidates for $n_{\mathcal{P}} + \dim W$ bits of k.

- **for** $(i,j) \in \{0,...,l-1\} \times \{0,...,l-1\}$ **do**
  - **for** $k_{\mathcal{P}} \in \mathcal{P}$ **do**
    - $\nu_{i,j}^{k_{\mathcal{P}}} \leftarrow 0$
- **for** $a \in \mathcal{S}$ **do**
  - $x \xleftarrow{\$} \mathcal{U} \oplus a$, $(c, \tilde{c}) \leftarrow (E_k(x), E_{f(k)}(x \lll 1))$
  - **for** $(i,j) \in \{0,...,l-1\} \times \{0,...,l-1\}$ **do**
    - **for** $k_{\mathcal{P}}$ **do**
      - With $(c \oplus k_{\mathcal{P}}, \tilde{c} \oplus f(k_{\mathcal{P}}))$ get corresponding output masks μ_{i,i_1}^1 and μ_{j,j_1}^0
      - $\nu_{i,j}^{k_{\mathcal{P}}} \leftarrow \nu_{i,j}^{k_{\mathcal{P}}} + \sum_{i_1=0}^{s-1} \sum_{j_1=0}^{s-1} (-1)^{\langle \mu_{i,i_1}^1, c\rangle \oplus \langle \mu_{j,j_1}^0, \tilde{c}\rangle}$
- **for** $k_{\mathcal{P}} \in \mathcal{P}$ **do**
  - Compute $\mathcal{C}(k_{\mathcal{P}}, k_\mu)$ using the Fast Walsh-Hadamard Transform
  - **if** $\mathcal{C}(k_{\mathcal{P}}, k_\mu) > \Theta$ **then**
    - Save $(k_{\mathcal{P}}, k_\mu)$ as a key candidate

The value of k only impacts the sign of the correlation of linear approximation. Following the previous work we define an intermediate variable $\alpha_{i,j}$ by

$$\begin{aligned}
\alpha_{i,j} &= (-1)^{sgn(\epsilon_{i,i_1}^1 \epsilon_{j,j_1}^0 q_{i,j})} \sum_{\substack{(z,\tilde{z}) \in \mathcal{D}_{out} \text{ s.t.} \\ k \oplus c \in \mathcal{P},\ \tilde{k} \oplus \tilde{c} \in f(\mathcal{P})}} (-1)^{\langle \mu_{i,i_1}^1, k \oplus c\rangle \oplus \langle \mu_{j,j_1}^0, \tilde{k} \oplus \tilde{c}\rangle} \\
&= (-1)^{sgn(\epsilon_{i,i_1}^1 \epsilon_{j,j_1}^0 q_{i,j})} \sum_{\substack{(z,\tilde{z}) \in \mathcal{D}_{out} \text{ s.t.} \\ k \oplus c \in \mathcal{P},\ \tilde{k} \oplus \tilde{c} \in f(\mathcal{P}) \text{ and } \tilde{k} = f(k)}} (-1)^{\langle \mu_{i,i_1}^1, c\rangle \oplus \langle \mu_{j,j_1}^0, \tilde{c}\rangle \oplus \langle \mu_{j,j_1}^1, k\rangle \oplus \langle \mu_{j,j_1}^0, f(k)\rangle} \\
&= (-1)^{\langle \mu_{i,i_1}^1 \oplus f^{-1}(\mu_{j,j_1}^0), k_\mu\rangle} \left| \sum_{\substack{(z,\tilde{z}) \in \mathcal{D}_{out} \text{ s.t.} \\ c \in k \oplus \mathcal{P},\ \tilde{c} \in f(k \oplus \mathcal{P})}} (-1)^{\langle \mu_{i,i_1}^1, c\rangle \oplus \langle \mu_{j,j_1}^0, \tilde{c}\rangle} \right|,
\end{aligned}$$

where $sgn(r) = \begin{cases} 0 & \text{if } r \geq 0 \\ 1 & \text{if } r < 0 \end{cases}$. We define $W = Span\{\mu_{i,i_1}^1 \oplus f^{-1}(\mu_{j,j_1}^0) \mid i,j \in \{0,\ldots,l-1\}$ and $i_1, j_1 \in \{0,\ldots,j-1\}\}$ and

$$\mathcal{C}(k_{\mathcal{P}}, k_\mu) := \sum_{\mu \in W} (-1)^{\langle \mu, k_\mu\rangle} \sum_{\substack{(i,j) \text{ s.t.} \\ \mu_{i,i_1}^1 \oplus f^{-1}(\mu_{j,j_1}^0) = \mu}} \nu_{i,j}.$$

We need to guess bits of k corresponding to active bits of output masks. Let $n_{\mathcal{P}}$ denote the number of elements in $\mathcal{P}$. Then the number of bits we can get in the key-recovery process is $n_{\mathcal{P}} + \dim W$. The fast Walsh-Hadamard transform [8] can be used during the key-recovery. Therefore, the whole running time of the key-recovery decreases to $2^{n_{\mathcal{P}}}(2N + \dim W \cdot 2^{\dim W})$ [4].

4.5 A Simple Toy Example

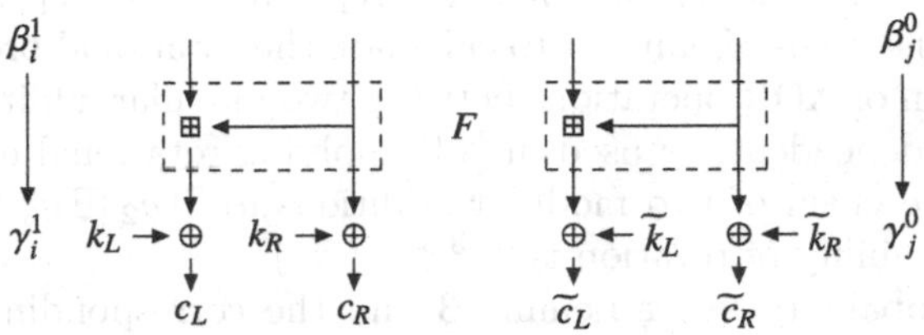

Fig. 5. A toy example of key recovery where the key-recovery part F only contains a modular addition.

In Fig. 5 there is a function $F : \mathbb{F}_2^{2m} \to \mathbb{F}_2^{2m}$ such that $F(a, b) = (s, b)$ where $s = a \boxplus b$. The input masks for F are denoted by β_i^1 and β_j^0. To simplify the key-recovery process, we suppose $\widetilde{k} = k \lll 1$ and the input masks for F are $(\beta^1, \beta^0) = ([i], [i+1, i])$ where β^0 is the rotation of β^1. If we denote $k = k^L||k^R = (k_{m-1}^L, \ldots, k_0^L)||(k_{m-1}^R, \ldots, k_0^R)$, then we have $\widetilde{k} = \widetilde{k}^L||\widetilde{k}^R = (k_{m-2}^L, \ldots, k_0^L, k_{m-1}^R)||(k_{m-2}^R, \ldots, k_0^R, k_{m-1}^L)$.

To apply the partitioning technique to find linear trails with high correlations, we need to obtain the values $k_{i-1}^L \oplus c_L[i-1] \oplus k_{i-1}^R \oplus c_R[i-1]$, $k_{i-2}^L \oplus c_L[i-2] \oplus k_{i-2}^R \oplus c_R[i-2]$, $\widetilde{k}_i^L \oplus \widetilde{c}_L[i] \oplus \widetilde{k}_i^R \oplus \widetilde{c}_R[i]$ and $\widetilde{k}_{i-1}^L \oplus \widetilde{c}_L[i-1] \oplus \widetilde{k}_{i-1}^R \oplus \widetilde{c}_R[i-1]$. If $i \geq 2$, we only need to guess two bits $k^L[i-1] \oplus k^R[i-1]$ and $k^L[i-2] \oplus k^R[i-2]$ before partitioning. Then we can find four trails, i.e.,

$$\beta_0^1 = ([i], []),\ \mu_0^1 = ([i, i-1], [i]),\ \text{if } (k_L \oplus c_L, k_R \oplus c_R) \in \mathcal{S}_1,$$
$$\beta_1^1 = ([i], []),\ \mu_1^1 = ([i, i-2], [i]),\ \text{if } (k_L \oplus c_L, k_R \oplus c_R) \in \mathcal{S}_2,$$
$$\beta_0^0 = ([i+1, i], []),\ \mu_0^0 = ([i], [i]),\ \text{if } (\widetilde{k}_L \oplus \widetilde{c}_L, \widetilde{k}_R \oplus \widetilde{c}_R) \in \mathcal{S}_3,$$
$$\beta_1^0 = ([i+1, i], []),\ \mu_1^0 = ([i, i-1, i-2], [i]),\ \text{if } (\widetilde{k}_L \oplus \widetilde{c}_L, \widetilde{k}_R \oplus \widetilde{c}_R) \in \mathcal{S}_4,$$

all with correlations 1 or -1. Then we obtain $W = \{(\mu_i^1 \oplus \mu_j^0) \mid i, j \in \{0, 1\}\} = \{([], []), ([i-1], []), ([i-2], []), ([i-1, i-2], [])\}$ and could recover four bits of information of the key, namely, $k^L[i-1]$, $k^L[i-2]$, $k^L[i-1] \oplus k^R[i-1]$ and $k^L[i-2] \oplus k^R[i-2]$.

5 Application to Chaskey

5.1 Attack Against 7-Round Chaskey

The process of our key-recovery attack applying to Chaskey covers 7 rounds splitting into four parts, including 2.5-round rotational part E_1, 3-round connective part E_c and 0.5-round linear part E_2, with 1-round key-recovery part F.

Rotational Part. In this part, we need to calculate the rotational probability of E_1 using Lemma 3. For Chaskey, we need that the input pairs $(m \oplus K \oplus K_1, \widetilde{m} \oplus \widetilde{K} \oplus \widetilde{K_1})$ have the relation $\widetilde{m} \oplus \widetilde{K} \oplus \widetilde{K_1} = \overleftarrow{m \oplus K \oplus K_1}$. For the chained modular additions we use Lemma 3 to calculate the rotational probability and if there are rotation or XOR operations between two modular additions we assume that they are independent, as used in [14] applying rotational cryptanalysis to Chaskey. For one chain of two modular additions $a_1 \boxplus a_2 \boxplus a_3$ with block size $n = 32$, the probability of rotation is $2^{-3.585}$.

Expected probability using Lemma 3 and the corresponding experimental probability of the rotational attack applied to chained modular additions presented in [12] are very close to each other. So the rotational probability for our E_1 part is reliable and the expected probability of 2.5-round E_1 is $2^{-17.17}$. We split the rotational part E_1 into E_{11} and E_{10}, where the E_{10} part includes the first 1.5 rounds and a modular addition $(w_1^1 \boxplus w_2^1)$. There are one modular addition and three double-addition so the rotational probability of E_{10} is $2^{-12.17}$. We apply Algorithm 1 to the E_{10} part with a set of random samples $\mathcal{S}$ which has 2^{32} elements. Then we collected 24 flipping bits with probability greater than 0.97 by experiments and the set of them is denoted by $\mathcal{U}$ from which we can generate 2^{24} right pairs $(a \oplus u, \overleftarrow{a \oplus u})$ for $u \in \mathcal{U}$ and a known right pair $(a, \overleftarrow{a})$. We can obtain the average probability with flipping-bits presented in Table 2, that is,

$$\Pr_{\substack{u \in \mathcal{U} \\ x \in \mathbb{F}_2^n}} [\overleftarrow{E_{10}(x \oplus u)} = E_{10}(\overleftarrow{x \oplus u}) \mid E_{10}(\overleftarrow{x}) = \overleftarrow{E_{10}(x)}] = 0.991.$$

This means if we have a right pair $(x, \overleftarrow{x})$, we can generate another right pair with probability 0.991 after E_{10}. These flipping bits can satisfy the data complexity for the later part and we can decrease the data complexity from $2^{34.34}$ to $2^{12.17+5\times 2} \times (0.991)^{-2}$, that is $2^{22.195}$.

Table 2. Candidates of flipping-bit applying Algorithm 1 to E_{10}.

The vector to flip	Index	Probability
v_0^0	0, 1, 2, 3, 4, 5	>0.97
v_1^0	0, 1, 2, 3	>0.97
v_2^0	0, 1, 2, 3, 4, 5, 6, 7, 8	>0.97
v_3^0	0, 1, 2, 3, 4	>0.97

Middle Part. After the rotational part E_1, we have the rotational relation $\overleftarrow{E_1(x)} = E_1(\overleftarrow{x})$, then we set the connective part E_c covering three rounds of Chaskey. We need to find input masks $(\alpha, \overleftarrow{\alpha})$ such that $\langle \alpha, E_c \circ E_1(x) \rangle \oplus \langle \overleftarrow{\alpha}, E_c \circ E_1(\overleftarrow{x}) \rangle$ has high correlation. On account of the limitation of computing capacity, we only search the masks α in the form of $[i]$. We observed for $\alpha = ([], [], [11], [])$, the correlation is $Cor_{x \in \mathcal{S}}[\langle \alpha, E_c(x) \rangle \oplus \langle \overleftarrow{\alpha}, E_c(\overleftarrow{x}) \rangle] = 2^{-1.73}$. Assume that the correlation obeys a normal distribution and the standard deviation of the normal distribution is 2^{12}. Using a set $\mathcal{S}$ consisting 2^{24} random samples to estimate is enough.

Linear Part and Key Recovery. Assume the input-mask pair for parallel E_2 is $(\alpha, \overleftarrow{\alpha}) = (\omega_1^5[11], \omega_1^5[12])$. After E_2 we have

$$\begin{aligned}\beta^1 &= \nu_0^6[24] \oplus \nu_0^6[11,10] \oplus \omega_2^6[0] \oplus \omega_3^6[0],\\ \beta^0 &= \nu_0^6[25,24] \oplus \nu_0^6[12] \oplus \omega_2^6[1,0] \oplus \omega_3^6[1,0],\end{aligned}$$

with the experimental correlation $2^{-3.187}$ over the set $\mathcal{S}$ consisting of 2^{26} random samples of ω^2. In the key-recovery part F, we need to partition the set of $(c \oplus K_1)$ and $(\widetilde{c} \oplus \widetilde{K}_1)$ to obtain the linear trails. Linear trails based on the partition technique are relevant to two chained modular additions. So we adopt the method in [4] and using the average of the absolute values of correlations of linear trails covering F, i.e., $2^{-0.83}$. Since it is difficult to evaluate the correlation $q_{i,j}$ after partition experimentally, we assume the correlations are equal for every partition, i.e., $q_{i,j} = 2^{-4.745}$ for all i and j.

In E_1 part the key $K \oplus K_1$ and $\widetilde{K} \oplus \widetilde{K_1}$ should satisfy $\widetilde{K} \oplus \widetilde{K_1} = \overleftarrow{K \oplus K_1}$. We denote values of the keys by

$$\begin{aligned}K &= ab{*_0},\ \ fg{*_1},\ \ kl{*_2},\ \ pq{*_3}; \quad & K_1 &= b *_0 f,\ \ g *_1 k,\ \ l *_2 p,\ \ (q *_3 a) \oplus \star;\\ \widetilde{K} &= b *_0 a,\ \ g *_1 f,\ \ l *_2 k,\ \ q *_3 p; \quad & \widetilde{K}_1 &= {*_0}ag,\ \ {*_1}fl,\ \ {*_2}kq,\ \ ({*_3}pb) \oplus \star,\end{aligned}$$

where $*_i \in \{0,1\}^{30}$ for $i \in \{0,1,2,3\}$ and $\star \in \mathbb{F}_2^{32}$ denotes the vector 0^{32} or $0^{24}||10000110$ decided by the value of $K[127]$ and $\widetilde{K}[127]$. For the rotational relation, we need to set $a = b = 0$ to let $\star = 0^{32}$. However, to have $\widetilde{K_1} = \overleftarrow{K_1}$, we need to set $a = b = f = g = k = l = p = q$. Then we obtain the weak-key class containing 2^{120} keys.

β^1 is split to $\beta_0^1 = \nu_0^6[24]$, $\beta_1^1 = \nu_0^6[11,10]$ and $\beta_2^1 = \omega_2^6[0] \oplus \omega_3^6[0]$. β^0 is split to $\beta_0^0 = \nu_0^6[25,24]$, $\beta_1^0 = \nu_0^6[12]$ and $\beta_2^0 = \omega_2^6[1,0] \oplus \omega_3^6[1,0]$. After the partition of outputs of F, presented in Table 3, we obtain linear trails $\beta_i^\iota \to \mu_i^\iota$ for $\iota \in \{0,1\}$ and $i \in \{0,1,2\}$. Because of the weak-key class, $k_i[31] = k_i[0] = \widetilde{k}_i[1] = \widetilde{k}_i[0] = 0$ for $i \in \{0,1,2,3\}$. Furthermore, the corresponding partition to $(c \oplus K_1)$ and $(\widetilde{c} \oplus \widetilde{K}_1)$ is decided by $k_{\mathcal{P}}$ with $k_{\mathcal{P}_1} = k_1[15] \oplus k_0[25] \oplus k_0[30]||(k_0 \oplus k_3)[30]||(k_0 \oplus k_3)[26]||(k_0 \oplus k_3)[25]$ and $k_{\mathcal{P}_0} = k_1[28] \oplus k_0[11] \oplus k_0[6]||(k_0 \oplus k_3)[12]||(k_0 \oplus k_3)[11]||(k_0 \oplus k_3)[7]||(k_0 \oplus k_3)[6]$.

From the set $\{(\mu_{i,i_1}^1 \oplus \mu_{j,j_1}^0) \mid i,j \in \{0,\ldots,l-1\} \text{ and } i_1, j_1 \in \{0,\ldots,s-1\}\}$, we can see k_μ consists $k_0[26] \oplus k_0[25]$, $k_0[7] \oplus k_0[6]$, $k_0[12] \oplus k_0[11]$, $k_0[30]$, and $\dim(W) = 4$. Summing up the above analysis, we can recover $13 + 8$, that is 21 bits of the master key K.

Data and Time Complexities and Success Probability. The way to recover partial key bits is based on the correlation of linear approximations. Our

Table 3. The outputs of F corresponding to partitioning technique. That is for every $\mathcal{P}$ in the table, we want to partition the set of ciphertexts to obtain the corresponding subset of it will belong to the $\{p \oplus k_{\mathcal{P}}$ for $\forall p \in \mathcal{P}\}$ after guessing partial bits of k.

Input mask	$\mathcal{P}$	Sub-key
β_1^1	$p_1[15] \oplus p_0[25] \oplus p_0[30] \Vert (p_0 \oplus p_3)[30] \Vert (p_0 \oplus p_3)[26] \Vert (p_0 \oplus p_3)[25]$	$k_{\mathcal{P}_1}$
β_1^0	$\tilde{p}_1[16] \oplus \tilde{p}_0[26] \oplus \tilde{p}_0[31] \Vert (\tilde{p}_0 \oplus \tilde{p}_3)[31] \Vert (\tilde{p}_0 \oplus \tilde{p}_3)[27] \Vert (\tilde{p}_0 \oplus \tilde{p}_3)[26]$	
β_0^1	$p_1[28] \oplus p_0[11] \oplus p_0[6] \Vert (p_0 \oplus p_3)[12] \Vert (p_0 \oplus p_3)[11] \Vert (p_0 \oplus p_3)[7] \Vert (p_0 \oplus p_3)[6]$	$k_{\mathcal{P}_0}$
β_0^0	$\tilde{p}_1[29] \oplus \tilde{p}_0[12] \oplus \tilde{p}_0[7] \Vert (\tilde{p}_0 \oplus \tilde{p}_3)[13] \Vert (\tilde{p}_0 \oplus \tilde{p}_3)[12] \Vert (\tilde{p}_0 \oplus \tilde{p}_3)[8] \Vert (\tilde{p}_0 \oplus \tilde{p}_3)[7]$	

method to build the counter is same as [4], so we use the same proposition used in it which is summarized in Appendix B to analyze the data and time complexity. The success probability is set to 0.978. Due to the E_1 part we need to run Algorithm 1 for $N_r = 2^{22.195}$ times to generate right pairs with expected probability $\frac{1}{2}$. The average correlation of connective part and linear part is $2^{-4.017}$. Use N data samples with the threshold defined as $\Theta = \sqrt{N^*} \times \Phi^{-1}\left(1 - \frac{2^{-22.195}}{2^{13}}\right)$ in Algorithm 2 where N^* is the data complexity corresponding to valid partitions.

We can compute that $N = \frac{4}{3}N^* = 2^{14.652}$. The data complexity is $2N_r \cdot N = 2^{22.195+14.652+1} = 2^{38.85}$. The major parts impacting on the time complexity are the ergodicity of key-guessing for $k_{\mathcal{P}}$, the collection of data samples and the Walsh-Hadamard transform during the computation of $\mathcal{C}(k_{\mathcal{P}}, k_\mu)$. The running time is estimated as $N_r \cdot 2^{n_{\mathcal{P}}}(2N + \text{dim}W \cdot 2^{\text{dim}W}) = 2^{22.195} \times 2^9 \times (2 \times 2^{14.652} + 4 \times 2^4) = 2^{46.8}$.

5.2 Distinguisher and Experimental Result

Under rotational-linear cryptanalysis with E_c and E_2 presented in Sect. 5.1, we implement toy versions of Chaskey with 4 and 5 rounds to have an additional experimental confirmation of the correctness of our framework and we build a full-round distinguisher with correlation $2^{-60.38}$.

To lunch the experiment we use a set of random samples $\mathcal{S} = \{x \mid x \in \mathbb{F}_2^{128}\}$ as input pairs $(x, \overleftarrow{x})$ and compute the correlation of $\langle \beta^1, E(x)\rangle \oplus \langle \beta^0, E(\overleftarrow{x})\rangle$ with linear masks β_1 and β_0 presented in Sect. 5.1. The 4-round distinguisher is composed of 0.5-round E_1, 3-round E_c and 0.5-round E_2. There are two modular additions in E_1 with the rotational probability $2^{-2.83}$, E_c and E_2 are presented in Sect. 5.1 where the correlations are $2^{-1.73}$ and 2^{-2} respectively. So we can obtain that the expected probability of the 4-round distinguisher is $2^{-6.56}$. And the corresponding experimental probability is $2^{-6.4}$. The expected probability and experimental probability for 5-round distinguisher are $2^{-13.74}$ and $2^{-12.1}$.

6 Conclusion

In this paper, we build a new framework of attack, called the rotational-linear attack. As a new combination of different kinds of attacks, we establish the key-recovery framework based on rotational cryptanalysis, which is mainly used in distinguishing attacks before. We also present a valid way to reduce the data complexity for the rotational part of our rotational-linear attack, called *bit flipping*. Our method is applied to Chaskey successfully. We built a full-round distinguisher for Chaskey and recovered partial bits of key under related-key attack, for keys belonging to a large weak-key class based on a 6-round distinguisher. It should be noted that although related-key attacks exists for any Even-Mansour ciphers [9], differentials of the whiting keys are considered before, while in our attack keys are related in a rotational manner.

The simple requirement that a cipher is suitable to rotational-linear attacks is that the rotational cryptanalysis can be applied to it. So rotational-linear attacks can be applied to many ARX ciphers, like Threefish and BLAKE2 [1]. And we hope that our framework of attack can be applied to other ARX ciphers to understand the constructing of rotational and linear cryptanalysis better. There still exist some possible improvements to our results. First, the connective part between rotational and linear parts is a little different from the differential-linear connectivity. Maybe one could construct a more exact connective part. Second, multidimensional linear cryptanalysis [11] maybe a way to improve the linear part of our attack.

A Application to ChaCha Permutation

The stream cipher ChaCha is an improvement of Salsa20 [5]. Each round of ChaCha uses 4 *Quarter Round Functions*, denoted by $QR(v_a^{(r)}, v_b^{(r)}, v_c^{(r)}, v_d^{(r)})$, to permute the 4×4 state matrix, denoted by $V^{(r)}$. Every word $v_i^{(r)}$ in $V^{(r)}$ is 32 bits, $i \in \{0, \ldots, 15\}$. For odd rounds, $V^{(r+1)}$ is calculated by selecting 4 columns, i.e., $(v_0^{(r)}, v_4^{(r)}, v_8^{(r)}, v_{12}^{(r)})$, $(v_1^{(r)}, v_5^{(r)}, v_9^{(r)}, v_{13}^{(r)})$, $(v_2^{(r)}, v_6^{(r)}, v_{10}^{(r)}, v_{14}^{(r)})$ and $(v_3^{(r)}, v_7^{(r)}, v_{11}^{(r)}, v_{15}^{(r)})$ as the inputs for QR functions. For even rounds, $V^{(r+1)}$ is computed by selecting 4 diagonals $(v_0^{(r)}, v_5^{(r)}, v_{10}^{(r)}, v_{15}^{(r)})$, $(v_1^{(r)}, v_6^{(r)}, v_{11}^{(r)}, v_{12}^{(r)})$, $(v_2^{(r)}, v_7^{(r)}, v_8^{(r)}, v_{13}^{(r)})$, $(v_3^{(r)}, v_4^{(r)}, v_9^{(r)}, v_{14}^{(r)})$ as the inputs for QR functions. The round function QR is presented in Fig. 6. In [3], the authors applied rotational cryptanalysis to the underlying permutation of ChaCha. They presented a rotational distinguisher for 17-round ChaCha permutation with probability greater than 2^{-488} whereas the probability of random permutation with same input size

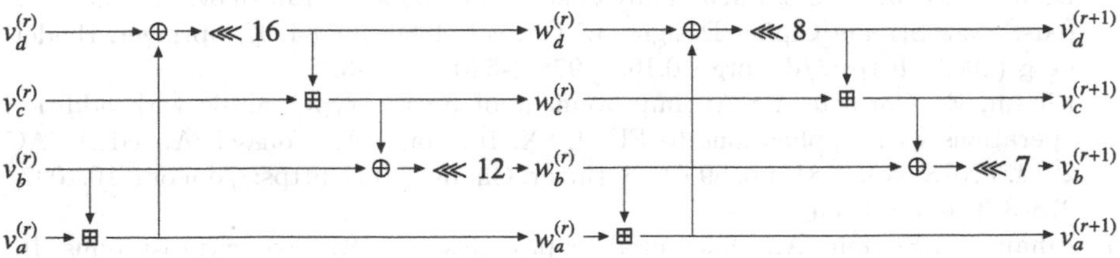

Fig. 6. The QR function of ChaCha.

is 2^{-511}. It declares that the underlying permutation of ChaCha doesn't behave as a random permutation.

The extended application of rotational-linear cryptanalysis is presented as follows. We build a rotational-linear distinguisher for 17-round ChaCha permutation with 15-round rotational part E_1, 1-round connective part E_c and 1-round linear part E_2. The lower bound for the probability of E_1 is $2^{-430.2}$, given by [3]. The correlation of E_c is 2^{-2} with the masks $\alpha = \nu_{15}^{15}[0]$ and $\overleftarrow{\alpha} = \nu_{15}^{15}[1]$. For linear part E_2, the two output trails are $\beta_1 = (\nu_0^{16}[16,0] \oplus \nu_5^{16}[7] \oplus \nu_{10}^{16}[0] \oplus \nu_{15}^{16}[24])$ and $\beta_0 = (\nu_0^{16}[17,1,0] \oplus \nu_5^{16}[8] \oplus \nu_{10}^{16}[1] \oplus \nu_{15}^{16}[25])$ with corresponding correlation 2^{-1}. In conclusion, the correlation of rotational-linear distinguisher for 17-round ChaCha permutation is greater than 2^{-433}. Compared to rotational cryptanalysis, the rotational-linear attack exhibits advantages.

B The Proposition used When Recovering Partial Key

Proposition 2 ([4]). *After running Algorithm 1 for N_r times, the probability that the correct key is among the key candidates is*

$$p_{success} \geq \frac{1}{2}\Pr(\mathcal{C}(k_\mu, k_\mathcal{P}) \geq \Theta) = \frac{1}{2}\left(1 - \Phi\left(\frac{\Theta - N \cdot cor}{\sqrt{N}}\right)\right).$$

References

1. Aumasson, J.-P., Neves, S., Wilcox-O'Hearn, Z., Winnerlein, C.: BLAKE2: simpler, smaller, fast as MD5. In: Jacobson, M., Locasto, M., Mohassel, P., Safavi-Naini, R. (eds.) ACNS 2013. LNCS, vol. 7954, pp. 119–135. Springer, Heidelberg (2013). https://doi.org/10.1007/978-3-642-38980-1_8
2. Bar-On, A., Dunkelman, O., Keller, N., Weizman, A.: DLCT: a new tool for differential-linear cryptanalysis. In: Ishai, Y., Rijmen, V. (eds.) EUROCRYPT 2019. LNCS, vol. 11476, pp. 313–342. Springer, Cham (2019). https://doi.org/10.1007/978-3-030-17653-2_11
3. Barbero, S., Bellini, E., Makarim, R.H.: Rotational analysis of chacha permutation. CoRR abs/2008.13406 (2020)
4. Beierle, C., Leander, G., Todo, Y.: Improved differential-linear attacks with applications to ARX ciphers. In: Micciancio, D., Ristenpart, T. (eds.) CRYPTO 2020. LNCS, vol. 12172, pp. 329–358. Springer, Cham (2020). https://doi.org/10.1007/978-3-030-56877-1_12
5. Bernstein, D.J.: The Salsa20 family of stream ciphers. In: Robshaw, M., Billet, O. (eds.) New Stream Cipher Designs. LNCS, vol. 4986, pp. 84–97. Springer, Heidelberg (2008). https://doi.org/10.1007/978-3-540-68351-3_8
6. Biham, E., Carmeli, Y.: An improvement of linear cryptanalysis with addition operations with applications to FEAL-8X. In: Joux, A., Youssef, A. (eds.) SAC 2014. LNCS, vol. 8781, pp. 59–76. Springer, Cham (2014). https://doi.org/10.1007/978-3-319-13051-4_4
7. Biham, E., Shamir, A.: Differential cryptanalysis of DES-like cryptosystems. In: Menezes, A.J., Vanstone, S.A. (eds.) CRYPTO 1990. LNCS, vol. 537, pp. 2–21. Springer, Heidelberg (1991). https://doi.org/10.1007/3-540-38424-3_1

8. Carlet, C., Crama, Y., Hammer, P.L.: Boolean functions for cryptography and error-correcting codes. In: Crama, Y., Hammer, P.L. (eds.) Boolean Models and Methods in Mathematics, Computer Science, and Engineering, pp. 257–397. Cambridge University Press (2010)
9. Cogliati, B., Seurin, Y.: On the provable security of the iterated even-Mansour cipher against related-key and chosen-key attacks. In: Oswald, E., Fischlin, M. (eds.) EUROCRYPT 2015. LNCS, vol. 9056, pp. 584–613. Springer, Heidelberg (2015). https://doi.org/10.1007/978-3-662-46800-5_23
10. Daum, M.: Cryptanalysis of Hash functions of the MD4-family. Ph.D. thesis, Ruhr University Bochum (2005)
11. Hermelin, M., Cho, J.Y., Nyberg, K.: Multidimensional linear cryptanalysis. J. Cryptol. **32**(1), 1–34 (2019)
12. Khovratovich, D., Nikolić, I.: Rotational cryptanalysis of ARX. In: Hong, S., Iwata, T. (eds.) FSE 2010. LNCS, vol. 6147, pp. 333–346. Springer, Heidelberg (2010). https://doi.org/10.1007/978-3-642-13858-4_19
13. Khovratovich, D., Nikolić, I., Pieprzyk, J., Sokołowski, P., Steinfeld, R.: Rotational cryptanalysis of ARX revisited. In: Leander, G. (ed.) FSE 2015. LNCS, vol. 9054, pp. 519–536. Springer, Heidelberg (2015). https://doi.org/10.1007/978-3-662-48116-5_25
14. Kraleva, L., Ashur, T., Rijmen, V.: Rotational cryptanalysis on MAC algorithm Chaskey. In: Conti, M., Zhou, J., Casalicchio, E., Spognardi, A. (eds.) ACNS 2020. LNCS, vol. 12146, pp. 153–168. Springer, Cham (2020). https://doi.org/10.1007/978-3-030-57808-4_8
15. Langford, S.K., Hellman, M.E.: Differential-linear cryptanalysis. In: Desmedt, Y.G. (ed.) CRYPTO 1994. LNCS, vol. 839, pp. 17–25. Springer, Heidelberg (1994). https://doi.org/10.1007/3-540-48658-5_3
16. Leurent, G.: Improved differential-linear cryptanalysis of 7-round Chaskey with partitioning. In: Fischlin, M., Coron, J.-S. (eds.) EUROCRYPT 2016. LNCS, vol. 9665, pp. 344–371. Springer, Heidelberg (2016). https://doi.org/10.1007/978-3-662-49890-3_14
17. Liu, Y., Sun, S., Li, C.: Rotational cryptanalysis from a differential-linear perspective: practical distinguishers for round-reduced FRIET, Xoodoo, and Alzette. Cryptology ePrint Archive, Report 2021/189 (2021). https://eprint.iacr.org/2021/189
18. Matsui, M.: Linear cryptanalysis method for DES cipher. In: Helleseth, T. (ed.) EUROCRYPT 1993. LNCS, vol. 765, pp. 386–397. Springer, Heidelberg (1994). https://doi.org/10.1007/3-540-48285-7_33
19. Mouha, N., Mennink, B., Van Herrewege, A., Watanabe, D., Preneel, B., Verbauwhede, I.: Chaskey: an efficient MAC algorithm for 32-bit microcontrollers. In: Joux, A., Youssef, A. (eds.) SAC 2014. LNCS, vol. 8781, pp. 306–323. Springer, Cham (2014). https://doi.org/10.1007/978-3-319-13051-4_19
20. Wagner, D.: The Boomerang attack. In: Knudsen, L. (ed.) FSE 1999. LNCS, vol. 1636, pp. 156–170. Springer, Heidelberg (1999). https://doi.org/10.1007/3-540-48519-8_12

A Novel Approach for Supervisor Synthesis to Enforce Opacity of Discrete Event Systems

Nour Elhouda Souid(✉) and Kais Klai(✉)

LIPN Research Lab, University Sorbonne Paris Nord, Paris, France
{souid,kais.klai}@lipn.univ-paris13.fr

Abstract. Opacity is a property of information flow that characterizes the ability of a system to keep its secret information hidden from a third party called an attacker. In the state-of-the-art, opacity of Discrete Event Systems (DES) has been investigated using a variety of techniques. Methods based on Supervisory Control Theory (SCT) emerge as an efficient approach for enforcing this property. In this paper, we address the problem of enforcing the opacity of a DES through the definition of a supervisor whose role is to restrain the behavior of the system keeping "good" runs only i.e., executions that exactly correspond to the opaque subset of the system's state space. The proposed approach is based on Symbolic Observation Graph: a hybrid graph where nodes are subsets of reachable states linked with unobservable actions. Encoding such nodes symbolically using binary decision diagrams allows to tackle the state space explosion problem.

We designed a reduced-cost algorithm that synthesizes an optimal supervisor (at design time) to ensure the opacity of the system (at runtime). Moreover, we implemented our approach in C++ language and we validated our proposition using a real-life case study.

Keywords: Information flow security · Formal verification · Discrete event systems · Supervisory Control Theory · Opacity · Symbolic Observation Graph

1 Introduction

The performance and safety requirements that systems face nowadays in different fields such as transportation, banking, e-voting systems, healthcare, communication, etc., make these systems increasingly complex with the rising integration of automation. This brings new challenges in terms of engineering, notably for critical systems for security where the slightest failure or error can lead to significant human, material or financial damages. For such services, naturally subject to malicious attacks, methods to certify their security are crucial. In this context there has been a lot of research to develop formal methods for the design of secure systems and a growing interest in the formal verification of security properties (e.g.,

D. Gao et al. (Eds.): ICICS 2021, LNCS 12919, pp. 210–227, 2021.
https://doi.org/10.1007/978-3-030-88052-1_13

[18,31]). However, these techniques are limited for applications on large systems, as the problem of combinatorial explosion of the system's state space arises.

In this paper, we investigate a specific class of information flow security properties, namely *opacity* [25], which aims at controlling the way information can flow between different entities of a system. Several security properties of information flow have been proposed for discrete event systems (DES). Non-interference [26] and opacity [8] are the most important examples. Opacity is an information flow security property capturing a system's ability to keep a subset of its behavior hidden from passive, but knowledgeable, observers. It is a confidentialiy property that generalizes several security properties such as non-interference and anonymity [8]. Considering a secret predicate on the system behavior (a set of secret states or secret execution traces), this predicate is said to be opaque if for every behavior satisfying the considered predicate, there is (at least) another behavior, not satisfying the predicate and such that both behaviors are indistinguishable by the attacker [16]. However, verifying this property requires the exploration of the state space of the considered system which generally leads to the combinatorial state space explosion problem. Previous work [3,5] has led to the development of efficient approaches for the verification of opacity based on an abstraction of the state space called the Symbolic Observation Graph (SOG) [17]. Inline with this work, we present in this paper a novel approach based on the same abstraction formalisms (SOG) to design a supervisor (also called a controller) for the opacity property. Such controller applies on the executions of the original DES and determines which actions have to be enabled/disabled to enforce the opacity of the system. Thus, we adopt a Supervisory Control Theory-based approach to reach this goal. Supervisory Control Theory (SCT) is a formal framework for modeling and control of discrete-event systems (DESs). Given a system, the objective of the SCT is to synthesize a supervisor γ in such a way that the system coupled with γ behaves according to various constraints. In this framework, the system is assumed to evolve spontaneously and the controller can prevent some events (those leading to the violation of the security property) from occurring. The objective is to disable the minimal number of events and hence allowing the system to run according to its intended behavior. This is a key concept in SCT and is called "maximum permissiveness": let the system behave as freely as possible as far as the security property is guaranteed.

In this paper, we consider a Labeled Transition System $\mathcal{T}$, a secret predicate ϕ on the system's behavior, and an attacker partially observing its behavior and attempting to infer secret information from his observation. Our aim is to synthesize a partial observation supervisor that can only control a subset of the actions it observes (controllable events). Based on the construction of the SOG, we detect the violation of the opacity on-the-fly, and proceed by backtracking in order to disable the closest controllable action leading to the disclosure of the secret information. We prove that the built supervisor leads to the largest possible behavior of the system satisfying the opacity property. We implemented our approach using C/C++ language[1].

[1] Further details on the implementation can be found in our github repository "https://github.com/NourSouid/Opacity-Supervision".

This paper is structured as follows. Section 2 introduces some preliminaries needed to develop our approach. Related work is presented in Sect. 3. Our approach is outlined in the fourth Section. A use case is introduced in Sect. 4 to validate our approach and to demonstrate how the theoretical concepts can be applied to a real life case study. Our conclusion and some perspectives are drawn in the final section.

2 Preliminaries

Discrete event systems (DESs) are event driven dynamic systems with a discrete and potentially infinite reachable set of states. Such systems can be modeled with Labeled Transition Systems. Note that, in this paper, we deal with finite state space systems only. In this section, we recall main formalisms and definitions used through the paper.

2.1 Labeled Transition System (LTS)

A Labeled Transition System (Definition 1), denoted by $\mathcal{T}$, is a discrete transition structure that can be viewed as a generalization of an automaton with outputs.

Definition 1. ***Labeled transition system***
A Labeled Transition System (LTS) is a four-tuple $\mathcal{T} = (X, \Sigma, f_t, X_0)$ *where:*

- X *is a set of states;*
- Σ *is a set of actions;*
- $f_t : X \times \Sigma \rightarrow X$ *is a transition relation;*
- $X_0 \subseteq X$ *is a subset of initial states.*

A transition from a state s to a state $s\prime$ by an event or action e over a LTS $\mathcal{T}$ is denoted by $s \xrightarrow{e} s\prime$. A run of a LTS Γ is a finite sequence of transitions from an initial state $s_0 \in X_0$. The trace of a run $\pi = s_0 \xrightarrow{e1} s_1 \ldots \xrightarrow{e_n} s_n$, denoted by $tr(\pi)$, is the finite sequence of actions/events $\sigma = e_1 \ldots e_n$. We denote by $s \xrightarrow{\sigma} s\prime$ the fact that s' is reachable from s by the sequence σ. Given two traces α and β, $\alpha.\beta$ denotes the trace built by the concatenation of α and β. By extension, given to languages L_1 and L_2, $L_1.L_2$ denotes the set of traces $\alpha.\beta$ where $\alpha \in L_1$ and $\beta \in L_2$. The language of a LTS $\mathcal{T}$ is defined as the set of its traces i.e. $L(\mathcal{T}) := \{tr(\pi) \in \Sigma^* \mid \pi \text{ is a run of } \mathcal{T}\}$. Finally, ε denotes the empty trace.

2.2 The Opacity Property

Opacity is a security property defined w.r.t a secret predicate (a set of secret states or runs) and an observer considered as an attacker. We assume that the attacker has a complete knowledge of the structure of the system and partially observes its actions. Before defining this security property, we introduce the notion of **projection function** on a subset of observable actions $\Sigma_o \subseteq \Sigma$.

Definition 2. ***Projection Function***
The projection operation $P_{\Sigma_o}: \Sigma^* \rightarrow \Sigma_o^*$

$$P_{\Sigma_o}(\varepsilon) = \varepsilon; \quad P_{\Sigma_o}(a\sigma) = \begin{cases} a.P(\sigma) & \text{if } a \in \Sigma_o \\ P(\sigma) & \text{if } a \notin \Sigma_o \end{cases}$$

Intuitively, a projection takes a word from Σ^* and erases each action that do not belong to Σ_O. In this work we use Σ_a to denote the set of actions observed by the attacker, and P_{Σ_a} the corresponding projection function.

Consider a LTS $\mathcal{T} = (X, \Sigma, ft, X_0)$, a regular predicate $\phi \subseteq \Sigma^*$ and a subset of actions Σ_a. The predicate ϕ is opaque if no attacker can ever conclude from its provided interface that the current **run** r of the system satisfies ϕ, denoted by $r \models \phi$ (i.e. the trace of r belongs to ϕ). We say that a **state** $s \in X$ satisfies the predicate ϕ, denoted by $s \models \phi$, when it is reachable by a trace belonging to ϕ. A set of states X_S is said to be satisfying ϕ, denoted by $X_S \models \phi$, when all its states do. In this context, the secret of the system can be indistinguishably represented by a set of traces $\phi \subseteq \Sigma^*$ or a set of states X_S (containing any state reachable by a secret trace in ϕ).

Definition 3. ***Opacity***
A LTS $\mathcal{T}$ is said to be opaque w.r.t. a A secret predicate ϕ and a subset of observable actions Σ_a iff $\forall r \in L(\mathcal{T})$ such that $r \models \phi$, there exists $r' \in L(\mathcal{T})$ such that $(P_{\Sigma_a}(r) = P_{\Sigma_a}(r')) \wedge (r' \not\models \phi)$.

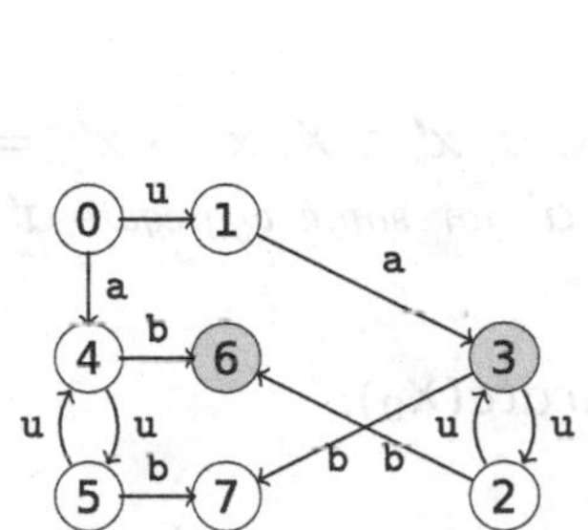

Fig. 1. A LTS $\mathcal{T}$

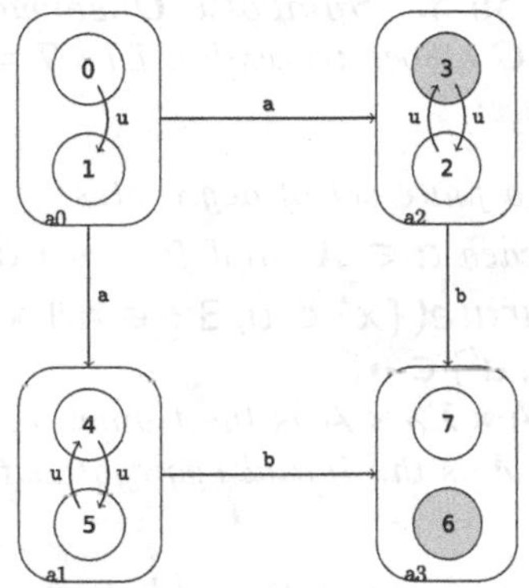

Fig. 2. The SOG of $\mathcal{T}$

Let us consider the LTS of Fig. 1 where the observation of the attacker is $\Sigma_a = \{a, b\}$, the set of unobservable actions is $\Sigma_u = \{u\}$, and $X_S = \{3, 6\}$ is the set of states satisfying a secret predicate ϕ. The system is opaque w.r.t to ϕ and Σ_a. In fact, for each trace $u.a.(u)^{2.n}$ leading to the secret state 3, there exists a trace a, having the same projection on Σ_a and leading to the non secret state 4. The same holds for the traces leading to the secret state 6 i.e. any trace of type $a.(u)^{2n}.b$ or $u.a.(u)^{2n+1}.b$. For both types of traces, any trace of the form $a.(u)^{2n+1}.b$ has the same projection $(a.b)$ on Σ_a while leading to not secret state (7).

2.3 Symbolic Observation Graph (SOG)

The **Symbolic Observation Graph (SOG)** [17] is defined as a *deterministic* graph where each node is a set of states linked by unobservable actions and each arc is labeled with an observable action. Nodes of the SOG are called aggregates and are represented and managed efficiently using decision diagram techniques (e.g., BDDs [12]). In [17], authors have introduced the SOG as an abstraction of the reachability graph of concurrent systems and showed that the verification of an action-based formula of LTL\ X (Linear-time Temporal Logic minus the next operator) on the SOG is equivalent to the verification on the original reachability graph. The construction of the SOG is guided by the set of actions occurring in the formula to be checked (observable actions). In this paper, we build the SOG under the observation of the attacker.

Definition 4. ***Aggregate***
Let $\mathcal{T} = (X, \Sigma, f_t, X_0)$ *be a LTS* $\Sigma = \Sigma_a \dot{\cup} \Sigma_u$*: s.t* Σ_a *is the set of observable actions and* Σ_u *the set of unobservable actions. An aggregate* a *is a non empty set of states satisfying:* $\forall s \in X,\ s \in a \iff Saturate(s) \subseteq a$; *where* $Saturate(s) = \{s' \in X : \exists \sigma \in (\Sigma_u)^* \mid s \xrightarrow{\sigma} s'\}$

Saturate is extended to sets of states as follows: $Saturate(S) = \bigcup_{s \in S} Saturate(s)$.

Definition 5. ***Symbolic Observation Graph (SOG)***
A SOG **G** *associated with a LTS* $\mathcal{T} = (X, \Sigma_u \cup \Sigma_a, f_t, X_0)$ *is a LTS (***A***,* Σ_a*,* $\rightarrow$*,* a_0*) where:*

- **A** *is a finite set of aggregates;*
- *For each* $a \in$ **A***, and for each* $o \in \Sigma_a$*,* $\exists x \in a,\ x' \in X$*:* $x \xrightarrow{o} x' \implies$ *:* $Saturate(\{x' \notin a, \exists x \in a \mid x \xrightarrow{e} x'\}) = a'$ *for some aggregate* a' *s.t.* $(a, o, a') \in \rightarrow$*;*
- $\rightarrow \subseteq A \times \Sigma_a \times A$ *is the transition relation;*
- $a_0 \in$ **A** *is the initial aggregate s.t.* $a_0 = Saturate(X_0)$*;*

Since a single state can belong to several aggregates, the complexity of the size of a SOG is expected to be exponential. However, due to the small number of actions in a typical formula (observable actions) and to symbolic representation of the aggregates using BDDs, the SOG has a very moderate size in practice (see [17,22,23] for experimental results). The verification of different variants of the opacity using SOGs has been investigated in [3,6,7] by building the SOG under the observation of the attacker. In this way, the language of the SOG coincides with the observation of the attacker (projections of complete traces). For the simple opacity (which we consider here), it has been proven that a SOG is opaque iff no aggregate is included in the set of secret states (which can be checked on-the-fly during the construction of the SOG and in an efficient manner thanks to BDDs). In fact, an aggregate a, that is reachable with a trace

σ, includes all the states that are reachable, in the corresponding LTS, by a trace in $P_{\Sigma_a}^{-1}(\sigma)$. Thus, if a is included in the set of secret states, then any trace in $P_{\Sigma_a}^{-1}(\sigma)$ leads to a secret state which violates the opacity property. This is captured by Definition 6 and Theorem 1.

Definition 6. ***Opacity of a SOG [6]***
Given a LTS $\mathcal{T} = (X, \Sigma_u \cup \Sigma_a, f_t, X_0)$, an attacker observing the subset of actions Σ_a and the set of secret states X_S, the corresponding SOG $(\mathbf{A}, \Sigma_a, \rightarrow, a_0)$ is opaque iff $\forall a \in A, a \nsubseteq X_S$.

Theorem 1. (Opacity verification [6]**).** *Let $\mathcal{T}$ be a LTS, X_S a subset of secret states, $\Sigma_a \subseteq \Sigma$ is the set of observable actions, and Γ the SOG of $\mathcal{T}$ w.r.t. Σ_a, then, $\mathcal{T}$ is opaque w.r.t. X_S and Σ_a if and only if Γ is opaque.*

Figure 2 illustrates the SOG associated with the LTS of Fig. 1 where none of its aggregates is included in the secret set of states, which proves the opacity of the underlying system.

2.4 Supervisory Control Background

The Supervisory Control Theory [28] (SCT) is a formal framework for modeling and control of Discrete Event Systems (DESs). Given a system modeled by a LTS $\mathcal{T}$, the objective of the SCT is to synthesize a supervisor (also called a controller) in such a way that the controller can prevent some actions from occurring to enforce security properties. We consider $K \subseteq L(\mathcal{T})$, the desired behavior of the system $\mathcal{T}$.

In this paper, K represents the opaque behavior of $\mathcal{T}$. Assuming that the supervisor **observes** a subset of actions $\Sigma_m \subseteq \Sigma$ and **controls** only a subset of its observed actions $\Sigma_c \subseteq \Sigma_m$, its role is to enforce the behavior K on the system $\mathcal{T}$ by enabling or disabling each action in Σ_c. $\Sigma_u = \Sigma \setminus \Sigma_m$ is the set of **unobservable** actions (by the controller) and $\Sigma \setminus \Sigma_c$ is the set of **uncontrollable** actions. In the following, we introduce some key properties regarding the targeted language K where the languages of the considered systems (as well as K) are supposed to be *prefix-closed* (i.e., any prefix α of $\sigma \in L(\mathcal{T})$ belongs to $L(\mathcal{T})$). We start by defining the controllability of a prefix-closed language (Definition 7). Intuitively, a language K is controllable if any extension of its traces with uncontrollable actions leads to traces that are in K as well (as long as they belong to $L(\mathcal{T})$). Formally, $\forall s \in K, \forall u \in (\Sigma \setminus \Sigma_c), s.u \in L(\mathcal{T}) \implies s.u \in K$.

Definition 7. ***Controllability of a Prefix-Closed Language K***
A language K is controllable w.r.t. $L(\mathcal{T})$ and Σ_c iff, $K.(\Sigma \setminus \Sigma_c) \cap L(\mathcal{T}) \subseteq K$.

Another key property SCT is **Observability**. Such a property is equivalent to another important one namely *normality* [13] when $\Sigma_c \subseteq \Sigma_m$ (which is our assumption in this paper). Intuitively, a language is observable if it can exactly be deduced from its projection P_{Σ_m}. Specifically, when a controller disables a controllable action c after the execution of a trace σ, then c has to be disabled after all execution traces equivalent to σ w.r.t P_{Σ_m}.

Definition 8. ***Observability of a Language*** *[14]*
A language K is observable w.r.t. $L(\mathcal{T})$ *and* Σ_m *iff* $P_{\Sigma_m}^{-1}[P_{\Sigma_m}(K)] \cap L(\mathcal{T}) \subseteq K$

The purpose of the SCT is to find the "largest" sublanguage of $L(\mathcal{T})$ that is controllable, observable, and s.t the specification (here, opacity) is respected; where "largest" is in terms of set inclusion. Such language is called *Supremal* and it has been proved that it always exists when $\Sigma_c \subseteq \Sigma_m$ [14].

Definition 9. ***Supremal Language***
A language K is supremal if $\nexists L \subseteq L(\mathcal{T})$ *s.t* L *is a prefix-closed controllable, observable, respects the specification (opacity), and* $K \subset L$.

3 Security Approach with Supervisory Control

This section presents the core contribution of the paper. Given a LTS $\mathcal{T}$, we propose a SOG-based approach to synthesize a supervisor of the system regarding the opacity property. First the supervisor behavior is defined through a supervision function γ. Then, we prove that the obtained supervisor language K is *controllable, observable, supremal* and ensures the opacity of $\mathcal{T}$. Finally, we propose an algorithm based on an on-the-fly construction of the system's SOG that builds the supervisor.

3.1 Supervisor Synthesis

Let $K \subseteq L(\mathcal{T})$ be the legal language that represents the authorized (or desired) part of the system's behavior i.e. the opaque behavior. A supervisor or controller (or monitor), with a partial observation Σ_m containing some controllable actions $\Sigma_c \subseteq \Sigma_m$, is a function that acts on $\mathcal{T}$ by enabling or disabling controllable actions in order to obtain the opaque language K. The supervisor is defined as a function, namely γ, that operates on each trace of $L(\mathcal{T})$ and gives the set of controllable actions in Σ to be disabled (to guarantee opacity).

In this paper, and for sake of simplicity, we assume that the attacker has the same observation as the supervisor i.e., $\Sigma_a = \Sigma_m$.

Under this assumption, we consider the SOG $\mathcal{G}$ associated with the system's LTS $\mathcal{T}$ w.r.t. $\Sigma_a = \Sigma_m$. Then, the definition of the aimed supervisor γ of $\mathcal{T}$ is defined through an intermediate supervisor γ_o of $\mathcal{G}$.

Definition 10. *Observed Trace-Based Supervision Function*
Let $\mathcal{T} = (X, \Sigma, f_t, X_0)$ *be a LTS. Let* ϕ *be a secret predicate and let* $\mathcal{G}$ *be the SOG of* $\mathcal{T}$ *under the observation of* Σ_m*. The observed trace-based supervision function is defined as follows:* γ_o: $P_{\Sigma_m}[L(\mathcal{T})] \rightarrow 2^{\Sigma_c}$.

$\forall \sigma \in P_{\Sigma_m}[L(\mathcal{T})], \gamma_o(\sigma) = \{e \in \Sigma_c \mid \exists \alpha \in (\Sigma_m \setminus \Sigma_c)^* : R(\sigma.e.\alpha) \models \phi\}$, *where* $R(\sigma.e.\alpha)$ *denotes the aggregate reachable, in* $\mathcal{G}$ *by the trace* $\sigma.e.\alpha$ *from the initial aggregate.*

Function γ_O is defined on observable traces of the system $\mathcal{T}$ and returns a set of actions to be disabled after the observation of a trace σ. Given an observable trace σ and a controllable action e, e is disabled iff the path induced by $\sigma.e$ in the SOG can be completed with a sequence of uncontrollable actions α to reach an aggregate a that satisfies the secret predicate ϕ.

Now, we can extend the supervision function to the complete traces of $\mathcal{T}$ as follows: The actions to be disabled after the occurrence of a complete trace $tr \in L(\mathcal{T})$ is the same as the set of actions disabled by the application of γ_O on its projection $P_{\Sigma_m}(tr)$.

Definition 11. *Supervision Function*
Let $\mathcal{T} = (X, \Sigma, f_t, X_0)$ *be a LTS, let* ϕ *be a secret predicate, let* $\mathcal{G}$ *be the SOG of* $\mathcal{T}$ *under the observation of* Σ_m *and let* $tr \in L(\mathcal{T})$ *be a trace of the system. The supervision function is defined as follows:*
$\gamma : L(\mathcal{T}) \to 2^{\Sigma_c}$
$\gamma(tr) = \gamma_O(P_{\Sigma_m}(tr))$.

3.2 Properties of the Language Induced by Supervision

In this section, we prove that the language of the system controlled by the supervisor defined in the previous section is *prefix-closed, supremal, observable, controllable* and guarantees the opacity of the underlying system. Such a language, denoted by K, is obtained by applying the supervision function γ on all the traces of the system (abusively denoted by $\gamma(L(\mathcal{T}))$.

Theorem 2. *Let* $\mathcal{T}$ *be a LTS with the set of controllable action* Σ_c, *the set of controller observation action* Σ_m, *and the set of attacker actions* Σ_a. *Assume that* $\Sigma_c \subseteq \Sigma_m = \Sigma_a$. *Then, the language* $K = \{\sigma \in L(\mathcal{T}) \mid \nexists(\alpha, c) \in L(\mathcal{T}) \times \Sigma_c : (\alpha.c \text{ is a prefix of } \sigma) \wedge c \in \gamma(\alpha)\}$ *is prefix-closed, controllable, observable, supremal and ensures the opacity of* $\mathcal{T}$.

Proof. For lack of place, the proof of the above theorem can be found in Appendix A.1.

3.3 SOG-Based Approach for Opacity Supervision

In this section we propose an algorithm, based on the SOG construction, that allows to synthesize the supervisor previously defined.

Algorithm 1 aims to build the SOG $\mathcal{G}$ of the system $\mathcal{T}$ w.r.t $\Sigma_a = \Sigma_m$.

We start by verifying if the first aggregate violates the opacity (Line 3 → Line 5). Then, we build the rest of the SOG (Line 7 → Line 26) and for each built aggregate we verify if it is included in the secret set of states, namely X_S. In this case, the supervisor, defined in Function *OpacifyByControl*, needs to act in order to reinforce the opacity (Line 18 → Line 22).

The purpose of Function *OpacifyByControl* is to disable -if possible- the last controllable transition, if any, that led to the opacity violation (Line 8 → 10).

Algorithm 1. SOG-Based Opacification

```
1: function SOG-OPACIFICATION((X^G, X^G_init, Σo ∪ Σuo, δ), Σo, Σc, Xs) : Bool
2: Begin
3:    a ← Saturate( {x_init});
4:    if a ⊆ Xs then
5:        return False;
6:    V ← {a}; E ← ∅ ;
7:    st.push (a, EnableObs(a));
8:    while (st ≠ ∅) do
9:        (a, enb) ← st.Top();
10:       if (enb = ∅) then
11:           st.Pop();
12:       else
13:           t ← RemoveLast(st.Top.Second());
14:           a′ ← Saturate(Img(a, t));
15:           if Treated(a′) then
16:               E ← E ∪ {t};
17:               Save(a −t→ a′);
18:           else if (a′ ⊆ Xs) then
19:               src← Enable(a, t);
20:               dest← Img(src, t)∩ a′ ;
21:               if !(OpacifyByControl(st, src, dest, t, a′, S)) then
22:                   return False;
23:           else
24:               V ← V∪ {a′}; E ← E ∪ {t};
25:               Save(a −t→ a′);
26:               st.Push(a′, EnableObs(a′));
27:   return True;
```

Such an action is searched by *Backtracking* (Line 12 → 20). To illustrate such a situation, let's consider Fig. 3 and Fig. 4. In Fig. 3, we have $A \in \Sigma_c$ and $b \in \Sigma_m \setminus \Sigma_c$, the third aggregate $a_3 \subseteq X_S = \{4\}$ which makes the system non opaque. To enforce the opacity of the system, the supervisor could only disables the event A because b is not controllable, which is illustrated by Fig. 4.

If Function *OpacifyByControl* returns True (Line 20 and 10), then the supervisor is updated and we continue the construction of the SOG. Otherwise, the SCT opacity reinforcement is impossible in this case (Line 22 and 24). When an aggregate is totally included in the set of secret states, it needs to be deleted totally with all its already constructed branches (Line 3 → Line 5). It should be noted that during backtracking, the crossed aggregates are reduced by removing the states involved in the opacity violation (Line 16). However, this causes modifications to the already built SOG. For this reason, the branches already built from this aggregate are reduced (*SlimOldBranches*) or completely removed (*CutOldBranches*), as the case may require.

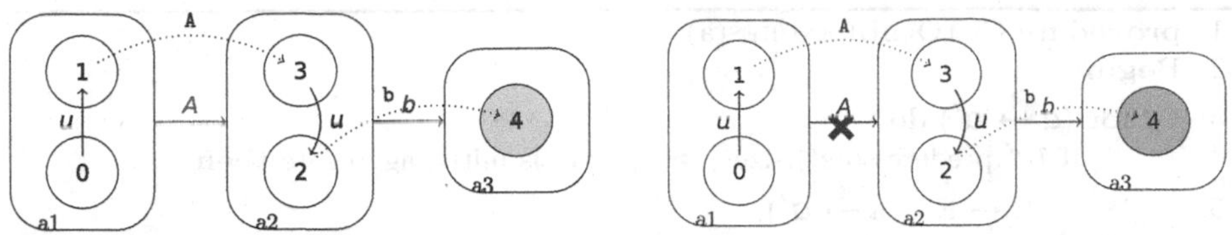

Fig. 3. A non opaque system

Fig. 4. Supervision of the system

```
1: function OpacifyByControl(st, src, dest, t, α′, S): Bool
2: Begin
3:     if (α′ ⊆ X_S) then
4:         CutOldBranches(α′);
5:         free(α′);
6:     else
7:         SlimOldBranches(a′);
8:     if (t ∈ Σ_C) then
9:         Desactivate(trace, t);
10:        return True;
11:    else
12:        if (st.size()>1) then
13:            a← pop(st);
14:            t←getTrans(st.Top(), a);
15:            dest← SaturatePreImg(src)∩ a;
16:            a′ ← a \ (dest ∪ src);
17:            src← PreImg (dest, t)∩ st.Top();
18:            if OpacifyByControl(st, src, dest, t, α′, S) then
19:                st.push(α′, EnableObs(α′));
20:                return True;
21:            else
22:                return False;
23:        else
24:            return False;
```

Procedure *CutOldBranches* checks if each successor (a') of the considered aggregate (a) has other predecessors. In this case, we simply delete the transition from a to a' (Line 3→5). Otherwise, a' will be deleted (Line 7→Line 9). Figure 5 presents a non opaque system s.t the aggregate $a_4 \subseteq X_S, X_S = \{3, 4\}$ and $A \in \Sigma_C$. Hence, the supervisor is given by $\gamma(u.b.u) = A$. By disabling A, we reduce the aggregate a_2 which becomes included in X_S. Therefore, we "Cut Old Branches" of a_2. As a result, the aggregate a_3 will be deleted (cannot be reached from another aggregate). The aggregate a_2 will be deleted as well (Fig. 6 and 7).

Procedure *SlimOldBranches* will be called with reduced aggregates. Each successor a' of an aggregate a, is analyzed. If a' is no longer compatible with this reduction (Line 5 → 15), we need to verify if it violates the opacity (Line 6→ 8) and if not we update it (Line 9 → 15). To help understand this function, let us consider the example illustrated in Fig. 8 which represents a non opaque system

```
procedure CutOldBranches(a)
Begin
    for (a --t--> a') do
        if (a'.predecessors().size() > 1) or a' is initial aggregate then
            E ← E \ (a --t--> a');
        else
            CutOldBranches(a')
            if (a') then
                free(a');
```

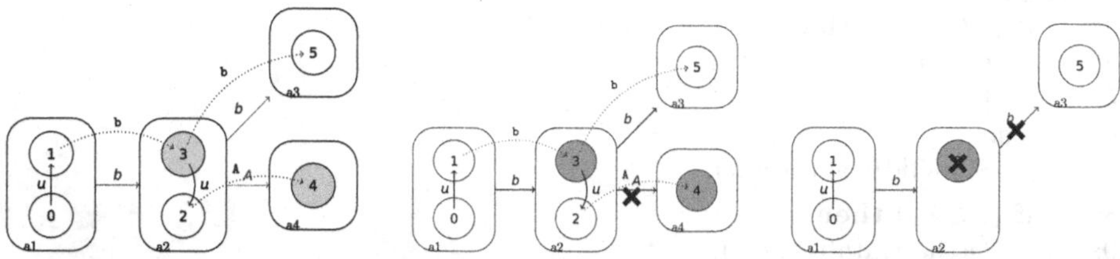

Fig. 5. A non opaque system $\mathcal{G}$

Fig. 6. Supervision of the system $\mathcal{G}$

Fig. 7. System $\mathcal{G}$ after opacification

since the aggregate a_4, obtained after the occurrence of the event $B \subseteq \Sigma_c$, is included in the secret set of states. The supervisor is defined by $\gamma(u) = B$. As a result, a_1 will be reduced (SlimOldBranches), a_2 and a_4 will be removed (CutOldBranches) and a_3 will persist, because reachable from state $\mathbf{1}$ (Figs. 9 and 10).

```
procedure SlimOldBranches(a)
Begin
    for (a --t--> a') do
        a'' ← Saturate(a, t);
        if (a' ≠ a'') then
            if a'' ⊆ X_S then
                CutOldBranches(a')
                free(a');
            else
                if (a'.predecessors().size() > 1) then /*a' is elsewhere accessible*/
                    E←E \ (a --t--> a');
                    save(a --t--> a'');
                else
                    a' ← a'';
                    SlimOldBranches(a');
```

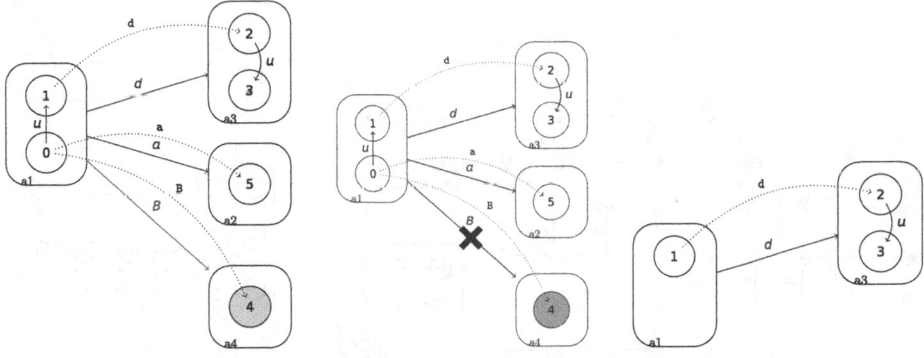

Fig. 8. A non opaque system $\mathcal{G}$

Fig. 9. Supervision of $\mathcal{G}$

Fig. 10. Reinforced opacity of $\mathcal{G}$

4 Implementation and Application to an IoT Maze Case Study

The case study that we propose in our work is illustrated in Fig. 13 in Appendix A.2. It represents an IoT labyrinth of a building, containing some secret rooms, and observed by an attacker trying to find out if a tracked object/person is in a secret room. The attacker observes only a subset of actions $\Sigma_a = \{t_0, t_8, t_9, t_{10}, t_{11}, t_{12}, t_{13}, t_{14}, t_{15}\} \subseteq \Sigma$ and his observation is obtained thanks to sensors (colored in blue). We propose to synthesize an optimal supervisor to enforce the opacity of this system. We assume that the supervisor and the attacker have the same observation of the system ($\Sigma_a = \Sigma_m$). We assume that the supervisor controls a subset of controllable actions $\Sigma_c = \{t_{11}, t_{13}\} \subseteq \Sigma_m$. This building is considered opaque if and only if for every path leading to a secret room, there exists another path, observably equivalent, that do not. This makes the intruder uncertain if the tracked object/person is in a secret location or not. To describe the behavior of the system, we use a Labelled Transition System. Figure 11 gives the LTS of the IoT labyrinth (observable actions are in blue, and secret states/rooms in red). As we can see, every trace leading to a secret room does not necessarily have an other one, observably equivalent, not leading to the secret. For instance, the trajectory leading to the secret room represented by state 10 in Fig. 11 does not have an observably equivalent path not leading to a secret. It is worth noting that this LTS is generated from a Petri net model [27] of the maze (see Fig. 14 in Appendix A.2). Thus, in our approach, the SOG w.r.t Σ_a, is not built from the LTS but from the Petri net model (which allows to tackle the state space explosion problem). The synthesis of the optimal supervisor is then performed on-the-fly during the construction of the SOG. Figure 12 illustrates the SOG of the considered IoT maze. Clearly, the SOG is not opaque ($a_8 \subseteq X_S$ following Theorem 1). Let us assume that aggregate a_8 has been reached first from a_1 by firing transition t_{13}. Once this aggregate is built and checked as non opaque, it

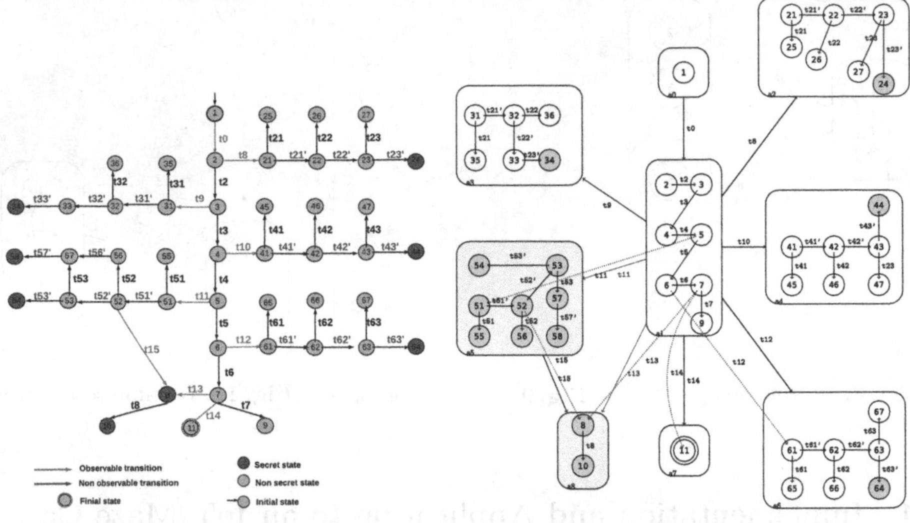

Fig. 11. LTS of the maze

Fig. 12. SOG of the maze use case

will be removed from the SOG. Also, since t_{13} is controllable, the value of the supervision function for any trace whose projection is equal to t_0 is saved (i.e. action $\gamma_o(t_0) = \{t_{13}\}$ is disabled). However, when a_8 is reached again from a_5 by transition t_{15}, the behavior of our algorithm will be different: since t_{15} is not controllable, a_5 will be reduced by removing internal states 52 and its proper predecessors (and successors). Here, all the states of a_5 are removed which lead to remove the aggregate a_5 and disable t_{11} (which is a controllable transition) for any trace whose projection is equal to t_0 (i.e., $\gamma_o(t_0) = \{t_{13}, t_{11}\}$). The reduced SOG of the system obtained by removing aggregates a_3 and a_5 and blue arcs.

- $\gamma(t_0.\sigma) = \{t_{11}, t_{13}\}$ for any prefix σ of $t_2.t_3.t_4.t_5.t_6$,
- $\gamma(s) = \emptyset$ for any other trace s.

The presented case study contains a limited number of states since the objective is to illustrate the application of our approach in this context. Nevertheless, the proposed approach can be used in the general case. The whole approach is implemented with C++ language. All the source code and description of our prototype is available on (https://github.com/NourSouid/Opacity-Supervision). The necessary material to produce the results on the Maze case study, or to check other examples are available there.

5 Related Work

Research efforts on opacity are centered around the efficient verification of various notions of opacity [6,10,11,20,29–32], the enforcement of this property (for non opaque systems) [4] using a variety of techniques, and the quantification [2,5] which suggests that the opacity is not necessary a binary property. Much of work in this context has been carried out using **Petri nets** modeling formalism [10,11]. In [9], authors extended the notion of opacity to **LTS**s and generalized this property to represent information flow concepts (anonymity and non interference). Here, we focus on existing approaches to enforce systems' opacity (which is the goal of this paper) and particularly those based on SCT.

In such approaches, we assume that the intruder (eventually more than one attacker) observes only a subset of the system's events that is previously fixed. Let Σ_a, Σ_m and Σ_c be respectively the set of observable events of the intruder, observable events of the controller and controllable events. In [15] authors have shown that an optimal control always exists and provided sufficient conditions under which it is regular and effectively computable. Using the SCT, researchers in [33] presented a reduced-complexity approach to verify the opacity of modular systems, and proposed a method for computing a local supervisor to each module. Moreover, in [1] authors assumed that the system is associated with partial observers, each one having it predefined secret, and proved that an optimal control always exists but is not generally regular.

To sum up, there exist multiple approaches to ensure and enforce opacity. However, these techniques suffer from practical limitations since most of them do not provide any implementation. In fact, the implementation of any new approach in this field offers a testing environment, allowing a better vision and tangible results of the proposed solution. For the verification of opacity there exist tools such as **Takos** [19], **Umdes** [24] and the **SOG** [21]. However, to the best of our knowledge, there exists no accessible tools for the supervision of opacity. In this paper, the proposed approach uses the implementation of the **SOG** to reinforce the opacity based on the **SCT**.

6 Conclusion and Future Work

In this work, we investigated the problem of enforcing the opacity of a non opaque systems. We proposed a novel methodology to calculate a supervisor using an on-the-fly construction of a symbolic graph (SOG). The use of this graph guarantees a smaller number of states, since it is an abstraction of the state space. Nevertheless, our work clearly has a limitation: the assumption that the supervisor observation coincides with the observation of the attacker. One of the perspectives of this work is to study the different possible relationships between the set of controllable actions Σ_c, the observation of the attacker Σ_a and the observation of the controller Σ_m in order to propose an optimal supervision function. An other extension of our approach is to consider more than one attacker, each has his own observation and the case where more than one supervisor is controlling the system (with possibly different observations and different controllable sets): *Decentralized Supervisory Control*. Furthermore, we aim to validate the scalability of our approach using more realistic case studies.

A Appendix

A.1 Proof of Theorem 2

Proof. 1. K is prefix-closed i.e. the prefix of each element in K is an element of K:
Let $\sigma \in K$ and let α be a prefix of σ. Let us prove that $\alpha \in K$.
Assume $\alpha \notin K$. Then, there exists $(\alpha_1, c) \in L(\mathcal{T}) \times \Sigma_c$ s.t. $\alpha_1.c$ is a prefix of α and $c \in \gamma(\alpha_1)$. Since α_1 is a prefix of α and α is a prefix of σ, α_1 is a prefix of σ as well. This is not possible, otherwise it contradicts, by definition, the membership of σ in K. Thus, $\alpha \in K$.

2. K is controllable i.e. $K.(\Sigma \setminus \Sigma_c) \cap L(\mathcal{T}) \subseteq K$:
Let $\sigma \in K$ and let $u \in (\Sigma \setminus \Sigma_c) \cap L(\mathcal{T})$. Let us prove that $\sigma.u \in K$.
Assume the opposite. Then, there exists $(\alpha_1, c) \in L(\mathcal{T}) \times \Sigma_c$ s.t. $\alpha_1.c$ is a prefix of $\sigma.u$ and $c \in \gamma(\alpha_1)$. Since $c \neq u$ ($c \in \Sigma_c$ while $u \in \sigma \setminus \sigma_c$), $\alpha_1.c$ is a prefix of σ which contradicts, by definition, the membership of σ in K. Thus, $\sigma.u \in K$.
3. K is observable i.e., $P_{\Sigma_m}^{-1}[P_{\Sigma_m}(K)] \cap L(\mathcal{T}) \subseteq K$.
Let $\sigma_1 \in K$ and let $\sigma_2 \in L(\mathcal{T})$ s.t. $P_{\Sigma_m}(\sigma_1) = P_{\Sigma_m}(\sigma_2)$. Assume that $\sigma_2 \notin K$. Then, there exists $(\alpha_2, c) \in L(\mathcal{T}) \times \Sigma_c$ s.t. $\alpha_2.c$ is a prefix of $\sigma_2.u$ and $c \in \gamma(\alpha_2)$. Let α_1 be the prefix of σ_1 s.t. $P_{\Sigma_m}(\alpha_1) = P_{\Sigma_m}(\alpha_2)$. The fact that $c \in \gamma(\alpha_2)$ implies that the aggregate reached by $P_{\Sigma_m}(\alpha_2).c$ is included in the set of secret states. However, such an aggregate is also reached by $P_{\Sigma_m}(\alpha_1).c$ while $c \notin \gamma(\alpha_1)$ otherwise σ_1 would not belong to K. Thus, $\sigma_2 \in K$.
4. K is supremal i.e. $\nexists K \subset L \subseteq L(\mathcal{T})$ s.t. L is a prefix-closed language that is controllable, observable and opaque w.r.t. the secret predicate φ and the attacker observation Σ_a.
Assume that such a language exists. Let $\sigma \in L \setminus K$. Then, there exists $(\alpha, c) \in L(\mathcal{T}) \times \Sigma_c$ s.t. $\alpha.c$ is a prefix of σ and $c \in \gamma(\alpha)$. Thus, by definition, the aggregate reached by the trace $\alpha.c$ is included in the set of secret states. This contradicts the membership of α in L since L is a prefix-closed language. Thus, K is supremal.
5. K ensures the opacity of the system. This is guaranteed by construction of the supervisor and by using the result of [6] stating that a $\mathcal{T}$ is opaque iff the corresponding SOG does not contain any aggregate included in the set of secret states. □

A.2 Plan of the Maze

Figure 13 represents a building, observed by an attacker trying to find out if a tracked object/person is in a secret room. Secret rooms are marked by a little red circle (and white cross). These rooms can be dedicated to patients with contagious diseases in a hospital or rooms containing strongboxes or valuable possessions in any company or private household. Sensors are represented in blue and provide the interface of the attacker and the supervisor.

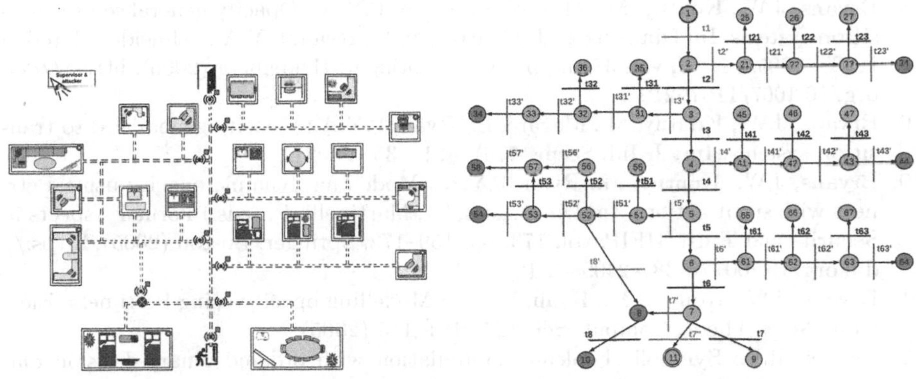

Fig. 13. A plan of the maze (Color figure online)

Fig. 14. Petri net of the maze

Figure 14 represents the Petri net of our use case. It is worth mentioning that the input of our implementation is a Petri net since the SOG implementation has been made using this model. However, the proposed algorithm is general and the implementation can be made using another model provided that it define an initial set of states and a transition function.

References

1. Badouel, E., Bednarczyk, M.A., Borzyszkowski, A.M., Caillaud, B., Darondeau, P.: Concurrent secrets. Discrete Event Dyn. Syst. **17**(4), 425–446 (2007)
2. Bérard, B., Mullins, J., Sassolas, M.: Quantifying opacity. In: QEST 2010, Seventh International Conference on the Quantitative Evaluation of Systems, Williamsburg, Virginia, USA, pp. 263–272. IEEE Computer Society, 15–18 September 2010
3. Bourouis, A., Klai, K., El Touati, Y., Hadj-Alouane, N.B.: Opacity preserving abstraction for web services and their composition using sogs. In: 2015 IEEE International Conference on Web Services, pp. 313–320 (2015)
4. Bourouis, A., Klai, K., Hadj-Alouane, N.B.: Measuring opacity in web services. In: Proceedings of the 19th International Conference on Information Integration and Web-Based Applications & Services, iiWAS 2017, New York, NY, USA, pp. 530–534. Association for Computing Machinery (2017)
5. Bourouis, A., Klai, K., Hadj-Alouane, N.B.: Measuring opacity for non-probabilistic DES: a SOG-based approach. In: 24th International Conference on Engineering of Complex Computer Systems, ICECCS 2019, Guangzhou, China, 10–13 November, pp. 242–247. IEEE (2019)
6. Bourouis, A., Klai, K., Hadj-Alouane, N.B., El Touati, Y.: On the verification of opacity in web services and their composition. IEEE Trans. Serv. Comput. **10**(1), 66–79 (2017)
7. Bourouis, A., Klai, K., El Touati, Y., Hadj-Alouane, N.B.: Checking opacity of vulnerable critical systems on-the-fly. IJITWE **10**(1), 1–30 (2015)

8. Bryans, J.W., Koutny, M., Mazaré, L., Ryan, P.Y.A.: Opacity generalised to transition systems. In: Dimitrakos, T., Martinelli, F., Ryan, P.Y.A., Schneider, S. (eds.) FAST 2005. LNCS, vol. 3866, pp. 81–95. Springer, Heidelberg (2006). https://doi.org/10.1007/11679219_7
9. Bryans, J.W., Koutny, M., Mazaré, L., Ryan, P.Y.A.: Opacity generalised to transition systems. Int. J. Inf. Secur. **7**(6), 421–435 (2008)
10. Bryans, J.W., Koutny, M., Ryan, P.Y.A.: Modelling dynamic opacity using Petri nets with silent actions. In: Dimitrakos, T., Martinelli, F. (eds.) Formal Aspects in Security and Trust. IIFIP, vol. 173, pp. 159–172. Springer, Boston (2005). https://doi.org/10.1007/0-387-24098-5_12
11. Bryans, J.W., Koutny, M., Ryan, P.Y.A.: Modelling opacity using Petri nets. Electron. Notes Theor. Comput. Sci. **121**, 101–115 (2005)
12. Bryant, R.E.: Symbolic boolean manipulation with ordered binary-decision diagrams. ACM Comput. Surv. **24**(3), 293–318 (1992)
13. Cassandras, C.G., Lafortune, S.: Introduction to Discrete Event Systems, 2nd edn. Springer, New York (2010)
14. Dubreil, J., Darondeau, P., Marchand, H.: Opacity enforcing control synthesis. In: 9th International Workshop on Discrete Event Systems, pp. 28–35, May 2008
15. Dubreil, J.: Monitoring and supervisory control for opacity properties. (Vérification et Synthèse de Contrôleur pour des Propriétés de Confidentialité). Ph.D. thesis, University of Rennes 1, France (2009)
16. Falcone, Y., Marchand, H.: Enforcement and validation (at runtime) of various notions of opacity. Discrete Event Dyn. Syst. **25**(4), 531–570 (2014). https://doi.org/10.1007/s10626-014-0196-4
17. Haddad, S., Ilié, J.-M., Klai, K.: Design and evaluation of a symbolic and abstraction-based model checker. In: Wang, F. (ed.) ATVA 2004. LNCS, vol. 3299, pp. 196–210. Springer, Heidelberg (2004). https://doi.org/10.1007/978-3-540-30476-0_19
18. Hadj-Alouane, N., Lafrance, S., Lin, F., Mullins, J., Yeddes, M.: On the verification of intransitive noninterference in mulitlevel security. IEEE Trans. Syst., Man, Cybern., Part B, Cybern. **35**(5), 948–958 (2005)
19. Takos (2010). http://toolboxopacity.gforge.inria.fr/
20. Jacob, R., Lesage, J.-J., Faure, J.-M.: Overview of discrete event systems opacity: models, validation, and quantification. Annu. Rev. Control. **41**, 135–146 (2016)
21. Klai, K., Hamdi, N., BenHadj-Alouane, N.: An on-the-fly approach for the verification of opacity in critical systems. In: 2014 IEEE 23rd International WETICE Conference, WETICE 2014, Parma, Italy, 23–25 June, pp. 345–350. IEEE Computer Society (2014)
22. Klai, K., Petrucci, L.: Modular construction of the symbolic observation graph. In 8th International Conference on Application of Concurrency to System Design (ACSD 2008), Xi'an, China, 23–27 June, pp. 88–97. IEEE (2008)
23. Klai, K., Poitrenaud, D.: MC-SOG: an LTL model checker based on symbolic observation graphs. In: van Hee, K.M., Valk, R. (eds.) PETRI NETS 2008. LNCS, vol. 5062, pp. 288–306. Springer, Heidelberg (2008). https://doi.org/10.1007/978-3-540-68746-7_20
24. Software library (2009). http://www.eecs.umich.edu/umdes/toolboxes.html
25. Mazaré, L.: Decidability of opacity with non-atomic keys. In: Dimitrakos, T., Martinelli, F. (eds.) Formal Aspects in Security and Trust. IIFIP, vol. 173, pp. 71–84. Springer, Boston (2005). https://doi.org/10.1007/0-387-24098-5_6

26. O'Halloran, C.: A calculus of information flow. In: ESORICS 90 - First European Symposium on Research in Computer Security, Toulouse, France, 24–26 October, pp. 147–159. AFCET (1990)
27. Petri, C.A.: Concepts of net theory. In: MFCS 1973. Mathematical Institute of the Slovak Academy of Sciences (1973)
28. Ramadge, P.J., Wonham, W.M.: The control of discrete event systems. Proc. IEEE Spec. Issue Dyn. Discrete Event Syst. **77**(1), 81–98 (1989)
29. Saboori, A., Hadjicostis, C.N.: Verification of initial-state opacity in security applications of DES. In: 2008 9th International Workshop on Discrete Event Systems, pp. 328–333 (2008)
30. Saboori, A.: Verification and enforcement of state-based notions of opacity in discrete event systems. Ph.D. thesis, University of Illinois at Urbana-Champaign (2011)
31. Saboori, A., Hadjicostis, C.: Verification of k-step opacity and analysis of its complexity. Autom. Sci. Eng. **8**, 549–559 (2011)
32. Saboori, A., Hadjicostis, C.N.: Verification of infinite-step opacity and complexity considerations. IEEE Trans. Autom. Control. **57**(5), 1265–1269 (2012)
33. Zinck, G., Ricker, L., Marchand, H., Hélouët, L.: Enforcing opacity in modular systems. In: IFAC 2020, Ifac world Congress, pp. 1–8, November 2020

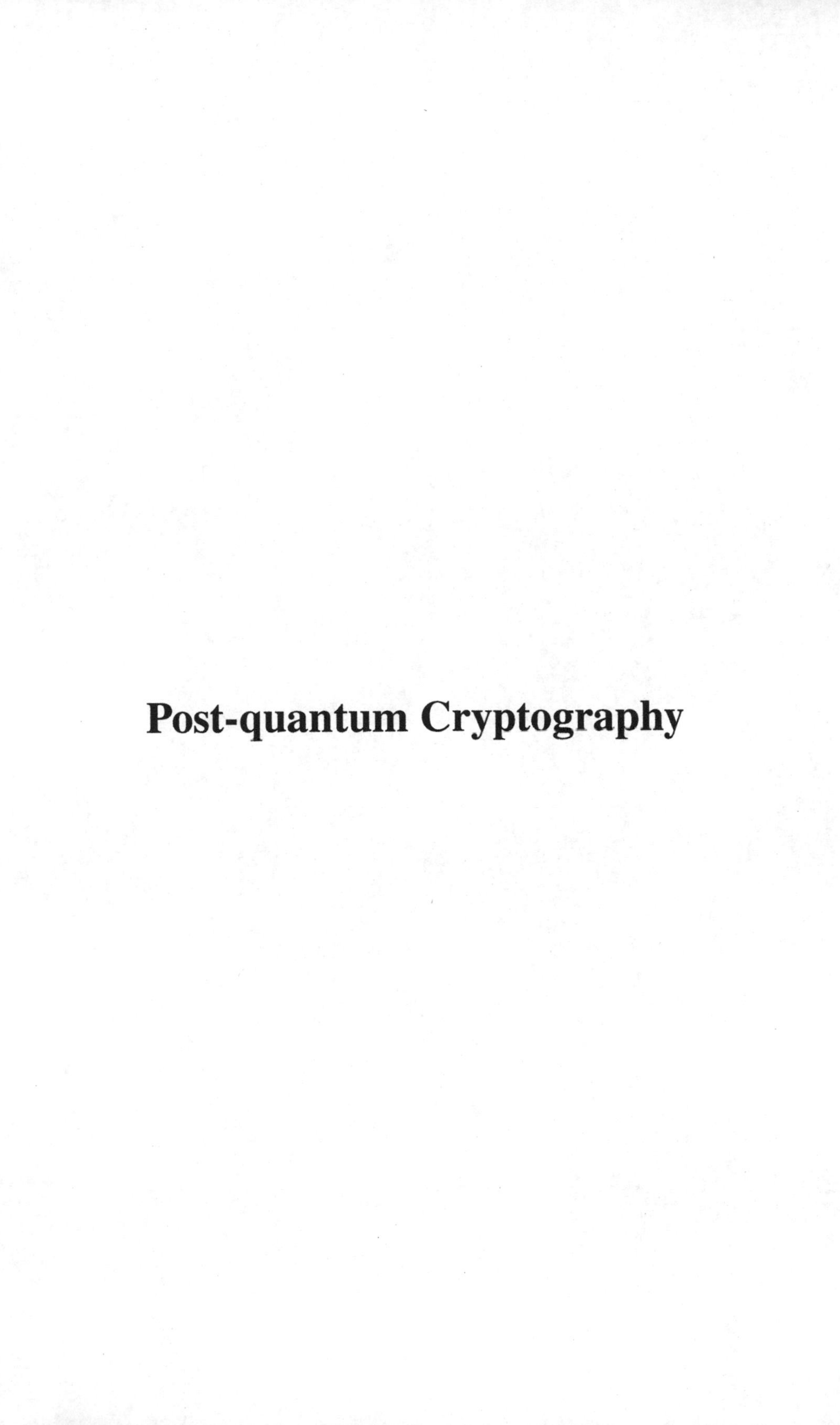

Post-quantum Cryptography

Lattice-Based Secret Handshakes with Reusable Credentials

Zhiyuan An[1,2], Zhuoran Zhang[1,2], Yamin Wen[2,3], and Fangguo Zhang[1,2](✉)

[1] School of Computer Science and Engineering, Sun Yat-sen University, Guangzhou 510006, China
{anzhy,zhangzhr26}@mail2.sysu.edu.cn, isszhfg@mail.sysu.edu.cn
[2] Guangdong Province Key Laboratory of Information Security Technology, Guangzhou 510006, China
[3] School of Statistics and Mathematics, Guangdong University of Finance and Economics, Guangzhou 510320, China
wenyamin@gdufe.edu.cn

Abstract. Secret handshake, as a fundamental privacy-preserving primitive, allows members in the same organization to anonymously authenticate each other. Since its proposal in 2003, numerous schemes have been presented in terms of various security, efficiency, and functionality. Unfortunately, all of the contemporary designs are based on number theoretic assumptions and will be fragile in the setting of quantum computations. In this paper, we fill this gap by presenting the first lattice-based secret handshake scheme with reusable credentials. More precisely, we utilize the verifier-local revocation techniques for member secession, such that users' credentials support reusability rather than one-time usage. To build an interactive authentication protocol, we subtly modify a Stern-type zero-knowledge argument by use of a key exchange protocol, which enables users to negotiate a session key for further communication. The security of our scheme relies on the Short Integer Solution (SIS) and Learning With Errors (LWE) assumptions.

Keywords: Secret handshake · Lattice cryptography · Zero-knowledge · Privacy-preserving · Mutual authentication

1 Introduction

Secret Handshake Scheme, firstly introduced by Balfanz *et al.* [5], is designed for realizing mutually anonymous authentication. In secret handshakes, potential users form different groups and one will reveal his/her affiliation to another if and only if both of them belong to the same organization. Thus the interactive protocol run between users from different groups will leak nothing about their identities and affiliations. Moreover, members keep responsible for the handshakes they execute since a tracing algorithm will identify them should the need occurs. Following the initial work in [5], many secret handshake schemes have been proposed based on different cryptography techniques. Some of them used one-time

D. Gao et al. (Eds.): ICICS 2021, LNCS 12919, pp. 231–248, 2021.
https://doi.org/10.1007/978-3-030-88052-1_14

pseudonyms in their constructions [7,14,26,29,33]. Whereas, a more efficient design for unlinkability is to use reusable credentials. For better efficiency, Xu and Yung [30] presented the first such scheme with somewhat weaker unlinkability. Ateniese *et al.* [4] proposed an improved unlinkable secret handshake scheme secure in the standard model. Subsequently, Jarecki and Liu [15] proposed a practical unlinkable secret handshake scheme achieving both traceability and revocation with reusable certificates. From then on, many unlinkable secret handshake schemes achieving more requirements were proposed [13,17,25,28]. Some practical applications of secret handshakes in social networks were also exploited, such as online dating, anonymous services of e-commerce and e-healthcare [12].

Since the integrated systems offering authentication interface always maintain high staff turnover, one desirable functionality of secret handshake is the support for membership revocation, i.e., users can leave or be revoked from the group. Early attempts to capture this property need the whole system to be re-initialized (including group public keys and users' secret keys), which obviously bring unsuitable workloads to all involved parties. Another flexible approach, verifier-local revocation (VLR), is formalized by Boneh and Shacham [6] and allows revoking a group member in a simpler manner. It only requires the corresponding verifiers to download an updatable revocation list. Jarecki and Liu [15] first employed a VLR group signature to design a secret handshake. Although their construction shows a heuristic relation between the VLR group signature and secret handshake, the aforementioned scheme employed an additional technique, i.e., a private Conditional Oblivious Transfer for relations on discrete logarithm representations. Besides, as pointed out in [27], their scheme only provided a generic construction and may be too complicated to be implemented. The above unsatisfactory situation encourages us to design a more compact scheme with flexible user management.

In addition, nearly all the known secret handshake schemes are designed on the hardness of factoring integers or the discrete logarithm problem. These constructions will be insecure once quantum computers become a reality. To our best knowledge, the only known post-quantum secret handshake scheme was proposed by Zhang *et al.* [32] using one-time pseudonyms from coding theory. However, we observe that due to improper adaptation of Stern's identification system, challenges used in their scheme are independent of the commitments generated from user's secrets. Therefore an adversary, who has no valid group credential, can always utilize simulated zero-knowledge proof to forge an authentication code, so as to conduct a successful handshake. As for other post-quantum candidates, lattice-based cryptography is considered to be very promising and enjoys provable security under worst-case hardness assumptions. Further, we observe that group signature, another privacy-preserving primitive analogous to secret handshake, has made some inspiring breakthroughs in lattice theory [18,19,21]. Thus, it is worthwhile to explore the area of lattice-based secret handshakes. To fill this deficiency, we may need some adaptive and insightful ideas.

Our Contributions and Techniques. Inspired by the VLR group signature [18], we introduce the first lattice-based secret handshake scheme with reusable credentials.

Consider the system having $N = 2^\ell$ members for each group, user's identity ID is represented by a binary index $d \in \{0,1\}^\ell$. To generate a reusable group credential, the identity is embedded into the user's secret key $\mathsf{usk} := \mathbf{x} \in \mathbb{Z}^{(2\ell+1)m}$ by setting $\mathbf{x}_k^{d[k]} := \mathbf{0}^m$ for $k \in [\ell]$. Indeed, $\mathbf{x}$ is a β-bounded solution to the ISIS instance determined by the Bonsai signature, holding that $\mathbf{A} \cdot \mathbf{x} = \mathbf{u}$, where $\mathbf{A} = [\mathbf{A}_0|\mathbf{A}_1^0|\mathbf{A}_1^1|\ldots|\mathbf{A}_\ell^0|\mathbf{A}_\ell^1|]$ specifies the structure of a Bonsai tree. Furthermore, user's revocation token (urt) is constructed via the root element of $\mathbf{A}$ and $\mathbf{x}$, i.e., $\mathsf{urt} := \mathbf{A}_0 \cdot \mathbf{x}_0$, according to VLR feature. The above realization guarantees the secrecy of user's credential, such that it can be reusable instead of one-time usage for one handshake.

The major difficulty we have overcome lies in how to modify the zero-knowledge argument to fit our handshake protocol. Generally, a Stern-like zero-knowledge argument system has three components: three commitments $cmt = (c_1, c_2, c_3)$, a challenge $ch = \mathcal{H}_0(cmt, \cdot) \in \{1,2,3\}$ and a response rsp, which is used to recover and verify 2 of 3 commitments according to the value of ch (e.g., check (c_2, c_3) for $ch = 1$). Since a secret handshake scheme is a mutual anonymous authentication protocol, we need to cut off the functionality of directly verifying the generated argument for the receiver. Therefore, instead of sending cmt, we dispatch a partial commitment value $\overline{cmt}$, consisting of 1/3 of commitments that can not be checked by the corresponding response (e.g., $\overline{cmt} = c_1$ for $ch = 1$). Next, we change the challenge ch as $ch := ch \oplus \mathbf{m}$, where $\mathbf{m}$ is a hidden message utilized to conduct an LWE-based key exchange [8]. After the above adjustment, both participants can first calculate the reserved 2/3 of commitments[1] via received responses rsp, and then recover the original cmt combining $\overline{cmt}$. Further, they can retrieve the hidden message $\mathbf{m} := ch \oplus \mathcal{H}_0(cmt, \cdot)$ to produce a session key $\mathbf{K}$. In the end, a message authentication code $\mathsf{V} = \mathcal{H}_2(\mathbf{K}\|\mathbf{m}, \cdot)$ is used to determine the result (0 or 1) of a handshake. In this way, we also fix the flaw of Zhang *et al.*'s scheme [32]. We elaborate more details on this strategy in algorithm Handshake of our scheme.

To summarize, by employing the setting of VLR, our scheme supports reusable credentials and it only requires active users to download the published revocation token list for group updates. The whole revocation tokens will serve as a tracing secret key kept by group authority. Besides, we mask a secret message with a modified Stern-type zero-knowledge argument [18], which ensures that the interactive handshake protocol can negotiate a session key for both participants and also prevents the attack of detection.

ORGANIZATION. The remainder of this paper is organized as follows. In Sect. 2, we recall our preliminaries including some lattice techniques and the underlying argument system. Model and security requirements of secret handshakes are reviewed in Sect. 3. In Sect. 4, we describe our secret handshake scheme. The security and performance analysis are depicted in Sect. 5.

[1] Note that they can not verify these commitments since they do not have the original ones.

2 Preliminaries

Notations. Vectors will be denoted in bold lower-case letters and matrices will be denoted in bold upper-case letters. We assume that all vectors are column vectors. Let $\|\cdot\|$ and $\|\cdot\|_\infty$ denote the Euclidean norm (ℓ_2) and infinity norm (ℓ_∞) of a vector respectively. The concatenation of vectors $\mathbf{x} \in \mathbb{R}^m$ and $\mathbf{y} \in \mathbb{R}^k$ is denoted by $(\mathbf{x}\|\mathbf{y})$, and the concatenation of matrices $\mathbf{A} \in \mathbb{R}^{n\times m}$ and $\mathbf{B} \in \mathbb{R}^{n\times k}$ is denoted by $[\mathbf{A}|\mathbf{B}]$. For a positive integer n, let $[n]$ denote the set $\{1, \ldots, n\}$. If S is a finite set, $y \xleftarrow{\$} \mathsf{S}$ means that y is chosen uniformly at random from S. For $a \in \mathbb{R}$, use $\log a$ and $\exp(a)$ to denote the logarithm and the power of a with base 2 and e, respectively.

2.1 Background on Lattices

Let $n, m, q \in \mathbb{Z}^+$ with $q > 2$. For $\mathbf{A} \in \mathbb{Z}_q^{n\times m}$, define two lattices as $\Lambda^\perp(\mathbf{A}) = \{\mathbf{x} \in \mathbb{Z}^m \mid \mathbf{A}\cdot\mathbf{x} = \mathbf{0} \mod q\}$ and $\Lambda^{\mathbf{u}}(\mathbf{A}) = \{\mathbf{x} \in \mathbb{Z}^m \mid \mathbf{A}\cdot\mathbf{x} = \mathbf{u} \mod q\}$.

Gaussians over Lattices. For any positive real σ and n-dimensional lattice Λ, the n-dimensional Gaussian function and the discrete Gaussian distribution over Λ are defined as: $\forall \mathbf{x} \in \mathbb{R}^n, \rho_\sigma(\mathbf{x}) = \exp(-\pi\|\mathbf{x}\|^2/\sigma^2)$; $\forall \mathbf{x} \in \Lambda, D_{\Lambda,\rho}(\mathbf{x}) = \frac{\rho_\sigma(\mathbf{x})}{\rho_\sigma(\Lambda)}$.

Lemma 1 ([9]). *Let n and $q \geq 2$ be integers. Let $m \geq 2n\log q$, and $\sigma \geq \omega(\sqrt{\log m})$.*

1. *For all but a $2q^{-n}$ fraction of all $\mathbf{A} \in \mathbb{Z}_q^{n\times m}$, for $\mathbf{x} \hookleftarrow D_{\mathbb{Z}^m,\sigma}$, the distribution of $\mathbf{u} = \mathbf{A}\cdot\mathbf{x} \mod q$ is statistically close to uniform over $\mathbb{Z}_q^n$.*
2. *For $\beta = \lceil\sigma\cdot\log m\rceil$, and $\mathbf{x} \hookleftarrow D_{\mathbb{Z}^m,\sigma}$, $\Pr[\|\mathbf{x}\|_\infty > \beta]$ is negligible.*

Computational Lattice Problems. The following are the definitions and hardness results of SIS, ISIS (ℓ_∞ norm) and LWE, which will be used in this work.

Definition 1 ([1,9]). *The $\mathsf{SIS}^\infty_{n,m,q,\beta}$ and $\mathsf{ISIS}^\infty_{n,m,q,\beta}$ with parameters (n, m, q, β) are as follows: Given a uniformly random matrix $\mathbf{A} \in \mathbb{Z}_q^{n\times m}$, and a uniformly random vector $\mathbf{u} \in \mathbb{Z}_q^n$,*

- $\mathsf{SIS}^\infty_{n,m,q,\beta}$: *to find a non-zero vector $\mathbf{x} \in \Lambda^\perp(\mathbf{A})$ such that $\|\mathbf{x}\|_\infty \leq \beta$.*
- $\mathsf{ISIS}^\infty_{n,m,q,\beta}$: *to find a vector $\mathbf{x} \in \Lambda^{\mathbf{u}}(\mathbf{A})$ such that $\|\mathbf{x}\|_\infty \leq \beta$.*

The hardness of the SIS and ISIS problems is given by a worst-case to average-case reduction from standard lattice problems, such as SIVP.

Definition 2 ([23]). *Let $n, m \geq 1, q \geq 2$, and let χ be a probability distribution over $\mathbb{Z}$. For $\mathbf{s} \in \mathbb{Z}_q^n$, let $A_{\mathbf{s},\chi}$ be the distribution obtained by sampling $\mathbf{a} \xleftarrow{\$} \mathbb{Z}_q^n$ and $e \hookleftarrow \chi$, and outputting the pair $(\mathbf{a}, \mathbf{a}^\top\cdot\mathbf{s} + e) \in \mathbb{Z}_q^n \times \mathbb{Z}_q$. The $\mathsf{LWE}_{n,q,\chi}$ problem is to distinguish m samples from $A_{\mathbf{s},\chi}$ (let $\mathbf{s} \xleftarrow{\$} \mathbb{Z}_q^n$) and m samples chosen according to the uniform distribution over $\mathbb{Z}_q^n \times \mathbb{Z}_q$.*

If q is a prime power, $\beta \geq \sqrt{n}\mathcal{O}(\log n), \gamma = \widetilde{\mathcal{O}}(nq/\beta)$, and χ is a β-bounded distribution (i.e., $\chi = D_{\mathbb{Z}_m,\sigma}$), $\mathsf{LWE}_{n,q,\chi}$ problem is as least as hard as SIVP_γ.

Lattice Algorithms. The following facts describe two fundamental tools in lattice-based cryptography: the trapdoor generation and the preimage sampling algorithms. We use them to generate group/user keys in our scheme.

Lemma 2 **([2,3,20]).** *Given integers $n \geq 1$, $q \geq 2$, and $m \geq 2n \log q$. There is a* PPT *algorithm* $\mathsf{GenTrap}(n, m, q)$ *that outputs a matrix $\mathbf{A} \in \mathbb{Z}_q^{n\times m}$ and a trapdoor $\mathbf{R_A}$, such that $\mathbf{A}$ is statistically close to uniform in $\mathbb{Z}_q^{n\times m}$ and $\mathbf{R_A}$ is a basis for $\Lambda^\perp(\mathbf{A})$. Moreover, for any vector $\mathbf{u} \in \mathbb{Z}_q^n$ and $\sigma = \omega(\sqrt{n \log q \log n})$, there is a* PPT *algorithm* $\mathsf{SamplePre}(\mathbf{R_A}, \mathbf{A}, \mathbf{u}, \sigma)$ *that outputs $\mathbf{x} \in \Lambda^{\mathbf{u}}(\mathbf{A})$ from a distribution that is with negligible distance from $D_{\Lambda^{\mathbf{u}}(\mathbf{A}),\sigma}$.*

2.2 Zero-Knowledge Arguments of Knowledge

In a zero-knowledge argument of knowledge (ZKAoK) system, a prover proves his/her possession of some witness for an NP relation to a verifier, without revealing any additional information. Generally, a secure ZKAoK must satisfy three requirements: *completeness, proof of knowledge* and *zero knowledge* [10].

In [18], Langlois et al. proposed a Stern-type ZKAoK over lattices for the following relation:

$$\begin{cases} d = d[1]\ldots d[\ell] \in \{0,1\}^\ell,\ \mathbf{e} \in \mathbb{Z}^m; \\ \mathbf{x}_k^{1-d[k]} = \mathbf{0}^m,\ \ \forall k \in [\ell],\ \mathbf{x} = (\mathbf{x}_0\|\mathbf{x}_1^0\|\mathbf{x}_1^1\|\ldots\|\mathbf{x}_\ell^0\|\mathbf{x}_\ell^1) \in \mathbb{Z}^{(2\ell+1)m}; \\ \mathbf{A}\cdot\mathbf{x} = \mathbf{u} \mod q,\ \ \|\mathbf{x}\|_\infty \leq \beta; \\ \mathbf{W}\cdot(\mathbf{A}_0\cdot\mathbf{x}_0) + \mathbf{e} = \mathbf{w} \mod q,\ \ \|\mathbf{e}\|_\infty \leq \beta, \end{cases} \tag{1}$$

where the tuple $(d, \mathbf{x}, \mathbf{e})$ is the secret witness and $(\mathbf{A}, \mathbf{W}, \mathbf{u}, \mathbf{w})$ is the public input. The above protocol has perfect completeness, soundness error 2/3 with a statistical simulator, and an efficient knowledge extractor. Further, by use of Fiat-Shamir heuristic, it can be transformed into an NIZKAoK termed as a triple

$$\Pi = (\{cmt^k\}_{k=1}^t, \{ch^k\}_{k=1}^t, \{rsp^k\}_{k=1}^t), \tag{2}$$

where $cmt^k = \langle cmt^k(1), cmt^k(2), cmt^k(3)\rangle$ for $k \in [t]$ and $\{ch^k\}_{k=1}^t = \mathcal{H}_0(\mathbf{A}, \mathbf{W}, \mathbf{u}, \mathbf{w}, \{cmt^k\}_{k=1}^t) \in \{1,2,3\}^t$. We utilize this protocol as an underlying building block and refer readers to [18, Sec. 4] for a more detailed description. Security of the aforementioned ZKAoK is under the hardness assumption of SIS.

3 Model and Security Properties of Secret Handshake

In this section, we review the model and security definitions for a secret handshake scheme (SHS). An SHS involves several entities: a group authority GA that manages members' enrollment and revocation, as well as tracing users' malicious behaviors, and s set of users who are potential group members. Based on the previous definitions in [5,7], an SHS consists of the following algorithms:

- Setup: On input security parameter λ, this algorithm generates the public parameters par, which is common to all subsequently established groups.
- CreateGroup: It is a key generation algorithm executed by GA to create a group G. On input par, this algorithm outputs group public key and secret key (gpk, gsk).
- AddMember: It is a two-party algorithm run by GA, which certifies a user to become a legitimate group member. After verifying the user's real identity, GA issues the user's group credential Cred (including group identity ID).
- Handshake: This algorithm is a mutual authentication protocol between two active members (A, B). It outputs 1 and produces a session key for both parties if and only if A and B belong to the same group.
- TraceMember: It is a polynomial time algorithm executed by GA. When a transcript T of a secret handshake between user A and B is submitted, GA outputs the identities of user A and B via secret key gsk.
- RemoveMember: It is a polynomial time algorithm authorized by GA. Taking the current credential revocation list ($\mathcal{CRL}$) and the target user's credential as input, it outputs an up-to-date list $\mathcal{CRL}$ to revoke an active member.

As considered in [4,5], an SHS must satisfy some security requirements: *completeness*, *impersonator resistance*, *detector resistance*, *unlinkability*. They are stated via the corresponding experiments below, respectively. Use CoU and CoG to denote the corruption list of users and groups, respectively. The involved oracles are listed as follows:

KeyP(par): this oracle simulates to create a new group and returns gpk to $\mathcal{A}$.
AddM(U, G): this oracle adds a puppet user U to the chosen group G. Then it returns the user's credential Cred to $\mathcal{A}$ and adds ID to corruption list Cor, which is initialized as $\emptyset$.
CorU(ID, G): this oracle returns user's Cred whose identity in group G is ID to $\mathcal{A}$, then it adds (ID, G) to list CoU.
KeyG(par): this oracle returns secret key gsk of some group G and adds G to CoG, implying that G is under the control of $\mathcal{A}$.
HS(ID): this oracle simulates a two-party handshake by generating the interactive transcripts. In particular, the adversary can request the hash functions and valid NIZKAoK used in algorithm Handshake on any random witness.
Trace(T): this oracle returns the identities of users involved in the handshake transcript T. Note that this oracle is only allowed to be queried for transcripts that are not generated from the game between $\mathcal{A}$ and the challenger.

Completeness makes sure that the secret handshake protocol always outputs 1 when the interactive participants belong to the same group, and that algorithm TraceMember can always identify the involved users.

Impersonator resistance demands that an adversary, who attempts to impersonate a legitimate member of an uncorrupted group, can only succeed with a negligible probability.

Definition 3. *Impersonator resistance is achieved if, for any* PPT *adversary, the following experiment returns 1 with negligible probability.*
Experiment: $\mathbf{Exp}_{\mathcal{A}}^{\mathsf{IR}}(\lambda)$

$\mathsf{par} \leftarrow \mathsf{Setup}(\lambda)$, CoG, $\mathsf{CoU} := \emptyset$.
$(\mathsf{gpk}) \leftarrow \mathcal{A}^{\mathsf{KeyP}}(\mathsf{par})$.
Return 0 if gpk is not well-formed.
$(\mathsf{ID}^*, G^*) \leftarrow \mathcal{A}^{\mathsf{AddM,CorU,KeyG,HS,Trace}}(\mathsf{gpk})$.
Return 1 if $\mathsf{Handshake}(\mathcal{A}, \mathsf{ID}^*) = 1 \wedge G^* \notin \mathsf{CoG} \wedge (\,\cdot, G^*) \notin \mathsf{CoU}$.

Detector resistance requires that an adversary will only succeed with a negligible probability when he activates a handshake protocol with an honest user to identify his/her affiliation. Namely, it's infeasible to detect a user's affiliation without the corresponding group secret key.

Definition 4. *Detector resistance is achieved if, for any* PPT *adversary, the absolute difference of probability of outputting 1 between experiment* $\mathbf{Exp}_{\mathcal{A}}^{\mathsf{DR}-1}$ *and* $\mathbf{Exp}_{\mathcal{A}}^{\mathsf{DR}-0}$ *is negligible.*
Experiment: $\mathbf{Exp}_{\mathcal{A}}^{\mathsf{DR}-\mathsf{b}}(\lambda)$

$\mathsf{par} \leftarrow \mathsf{Setup}(\lambda)$, CoG, $\mathsf{CoU} := \emptyset$.
$(\mathsf{gpk}) \leftarrow \mathcal{A}^{\mathsf{KeyP}}(\mathsf{par})$.
Return 0 if gpk is not well-formed.
$(\mathsf{ID}^*, G^*) \leftarrow \mathcal{A}^{\mathsf{AddM,CorU,KeyG,HS,Trace}}(\mathsf{gpk})$, holding $G^* \notin \mathsf{CoG} \wedge (\,\cdot, G^*) \notin \mathsf{CoU}$.
if $b = 0:$ $\mathsf{Handshake}(\mathcal{A}, \mathsf{ID}^*)$;
if $b = 1:$ $\mathsf{Handshake}(\mathcal{A}, \mathsf{ID}_r)$. ID_r is an arbitrary active user (not ID^*).
$b^* \leftarrow \mathcal{A}^{\mathsf{AddM,CorU}(\neg\{\mathsf{ID}^*,\mathsf{ID}_r\}),\mathsf{KeyG}(\neg\{G^*,G_r\}),\mathsf{HS,Trace}}(\mathsf{gpk})$.
Return 1 if $b^* = b$ else return 0.

Unlinkability ensures that no adversary can distinguish whether two executions of secret handshake protocol involve the same honest and active user with a non-negligible probability.

Definition 5. *Unlinkability is achieved if, for any* PPT *adversary, the absolute difference of probability of outputting 1 between experiment* $\mathbf{Exp}_{\mathcal{A}}^{\mathsf{Unlink}-1}$ *and* $\mathbf{Exp}_{\mathcal{A}}^{\mathsf{Unlink}-0}$ *is negligible.*
Experiment: $\mathbf{Exp}_{\mathcal{A}}^{\mathsf{Unlink}-\mathsf{b}}(\lambda)$

$\mathsf{par} \leftarrow \mathsf{Setup}(\lambda)$, CoG, $\mathsf{CoU} := \emptyset$.
$(\mathsf{gpk}) \leftarrow \mathcal{A}^{\mathsf{KeyP}}(\mathsf{par})$.
Return 0 if gpk is not well-formed.
$(\mathsf{ID}_0, G_0, \mathsf{ID}_1, G_1) \leftarrow \mathcal{A}^{\mathsf{AddM,CorU,KeyG,HS,Trace}}(\mathsf{gpk})$,
holding that $G_i \notin \mathsf{CoG} \wedge (\mathsf{ID}_i, G_i) \notin \mathsf{Cor} \cup \mathcal{CRL}$ for $i \in \{0, 1\}$.
if $b = 0:$ $\mathsf{Handshake}(\mathcal{A}, \mathsf{ID}_0)$, $\mathsf{Handshake}(\mathcal{A}, \mathsf{ID}_0)$;
if $b = 1:$ $\mathsf{Handshake}(\mathcal{A}, \mathsf{ID}_0)$, $\mathsf{Handshake}(\mathcal{A}, \mathsf{ID}_1)$.

$b^* \leftarrow \mathcal{A}^{\mathsf{AddM},\mathsf{CorU}(\neg\{\mathsf{ID}_0,\mathsf{ID}_1\}),\mathsf{KeyG}(\neg\{G_0,G_1\}),\mathsf{HS},\mathsf{Trace}}(\mathsf{gpk})$.
Return 1 if $b^* = b$ else return 0.

4 Our Lattice-Based Secret Handshake Scheme

In this section, we describe how to, relying on the technique of VLR, modify and apply the Stern-like ZKAoK [18] to construct a lattice-based SHS with reusable credentials, which satisfies the security requirements in Sect. 3. As the setting in [18], we assume that the group of our scheme has a maximum number of members N. Procedures for building our scheme are depicted as follows.

- Setup: Given a security parameter λ, this algorithm specifies the following:
  - A maximum number of group members $N = 2^\ell = \mathsf{poly}(\lambda)$.
  - Dimension $n = \mathcal{O}(\lambda)$, prime modulus $q = \omega(n^2 \log n)$ and matrix dimension $m \geq 2n \log q$.
  - Matrix dimensions $m_1 = \mathsf{poly}(n)$, integer modulus $q_1 \leq 2^{\mathsf{poly}(n)}$, and an integer $\theta \geq 2\lambda/(nm_1)$ for the session key exchange.
  - Gaussian parameter $\sigma = \omega(\sqrt{n \log q \log n})$ and integer norm bound $\beta = \lceil \sigma \cdot \log m \rceil$.
  - A β-bounded distribution $\chi = D_{\mathbb{Z}_m,\sigma}$ for the LWE function.
  - Discrete Gaussian distribution χ_1 over $\mathbb{Z}$ with standard deviation $\sigma_1 > \sqrt{2n/\pi}$.
  - A random matrix $\mathbf{K} \in \mathbb{Z}_{q_1}^{n \times m_1}$.
  - An injective map $F : \mathbb{Z}_{q_1}^{n \times m_1} \to \{1,2,3\}^t$, where $t = \omega(\log n)$ is the number of argument repetitions. F^{-1} is the inverse of F.
  - Two random oracles: $\mathcal{H}_0 : \{0,1\}^* \to \{1,2,3\}^t$ and $\mathcal{H}_1 : \{0,1\}^* \to \mathbb{Z}_q^{m \times n}$. A secure hash function $\mathcal{H}_2 : \{0,1\}^* \to \mathbb{Z}_q^n$.

The algorithm outputs global public parameters

$$\mathsf{par} = (N, \ell, n, q, m, m_1, q_1, \theta, \sigma, \beta, \chi, \chi_1, \sigma_1, \mathbf{K}, F, F^{-1}, t, \mathcal{H}_0, \mathcal{H}_1, \mathcal{H}_2).$$

- CreateGroup: GA takes par as input to create a group G. GA works as follows:
  - Run $\mathsf{GenTrap}(n, m, q)$ to get $\mathbf{A}_0 \in \mathbb{Z}^{n \times m}$ and trapdoor $\mathbf{R}$.
  - Sample $\mathbf{u} \xleftarrow{\$} \mathbb{Z}_q^n$, and $\mathbf{A}_i^b \xleftarrow{\$} \mathbb{Z}^{n \times m}$ for all $b \in \{0,1\}$ and $i \in [\ell]$. Then define the matrix

$$\mathbf{A} = [\mathbf{A}_0 | \mathbf{A}_1^0 | \mathbf{A}_1^1 | \ldots | \mathbf{A}_\ell^0 | \mathbf{A}_\ell^1] \in \mathbb{Z}_q^{n \times (2\ell+1)m}. \quad (3)$$

  - For group user with index $d \in [N]$, let $d[1] \ldots d[l] \in \{0,1\}^\ell$ denote the binary representation of d, and do the following:
    - Sample vectors $\mathbf{x}_1^{d[1]}, \ldots, \mathbf{x}_\ell^{d[\ell]} \hookleftarrow D_{\mathbb{Z}^m,\sigma}$, and then compute $\mathbf{z} = \sum_{i=1}^{\ell-1} \mathbf{A}_i^{d[i]} \cdot \mathbf{x}_i^{d[i]} \bmod q$. Run $\mathsf{SamplePre}(\mathbf{R}, \mathbf{A_0}, \mathbf{u} - \mathbf{z}, \sigma)$ to get $\mathbf{x}_0 \in \mathbb{Z}^m$. Let $\mathbf{x}_1^{1-d[1]}, \ldots, \mathbf{x}_\ell^{1-d[\ell]}$ be zero-vectors $\mathbf{0}^m$, and define $\mathbf{x}^{(d)} = (\mathbf{x}_0 \| \mathbf{x}_1^0 \| \mathbf{x}_1^1 \| \ldots \| \mathbf{x}_\ell^0 \| \mathbf{x}_\ell^1) \in \mathbb{Z}^{(2\ell+1)m}$. If $\|\mathbf{x}^{(d)}\|_\infty > \beta$ with negligible probability then repeat this step.

- Set the user secret key as $\mathsf{usk}[d] = \mathbf{x}^{(d)}$, and the revocation token as $\mathsf{urt}[d] = \mathbf{A}_0 \cdot \mathbf{x}_0 \in \mathbb{Z}_q^n$.

Finally GA sets the group public and secret key as $\mathsf{gpk} = (\mathbf{A}, \mathbf{u})$, $\mathsf{gsk} = (\mathbf{R}, \{\mathsf{usk}[d], \mathsf{urt}[d]\}_{d=1}^N)$, respectively. Then GA builds users' identities $\mathsf{ID} = \{d\}_{d=1}^N$, revocation list $\mathcal{CRL} = \{\emptyset\}$ and member list $\mathcal{L} = \{\emptyset\}$.

- AddMember: When a user U wants to join the group G, GA chooses a spare d_u as user's ID_u and issues U's credential as $\mathsf{Cred}_u = (\mathsf{ID}_u, \mathsf{usk}[d_u], \mathsf{urt}[d_u])$. Then GA sends Cred_u to the user and adds (U, ID_u) to $\mathcal{L}$.
- Handshake: Suppose a member A from group G_1 with $\mathsf{gpk}_1 = (\mathbf{A}, \mathbf{u}_1)$, $\mathsf{Cred}_a = (d_a, \mathsf{usk}_a, \mathsf{urt}_a)$, credential revocation list $\mathcal{CRL}_1$, and another member B from group G_2 with $\mathsf{gpk}_2 = (\mathbf{B}, \mathbf{u}_2)$, $\mathsf{Cred}_b = (d_b, \mathsf{usk}_b, \mathsf{urt}_b)$, credential revocation list $\mathcal{CRL}_2$, engage in a handshake protocol.
  1. $A \to B : (\mathtt{PROOF}_a)$
     (a) A samples a private key $\mathbf{S}_a \hookleftarrow \chi(\mathbb{Z}_{q_1}^{n_3 \times m_1})$ and a small noise $\mathbf{E}_a \hookleftarrow \chi(\mathbb{Z}_{q_1}^{n_3 \times m_1})$. Then A computes $\mathbf{C}_a = \mathbf{K} \cdot \mathbf{S}_a + \mathbf{E}_a \in \mathbb{Z}_{q_1}^{n_3 \times m_1}$.
     (b) A samples $\mathbf{e}_a \hookleftarrow \chi^m$ and $\rho_a \xleftarrow{\$} \{0,1\}^n$. Then A computes $\mathbf{W}_a = \mathcal{H}_1(\mathbf{A}, \mathbf{u}_1, \mathbf{K}, \rho_a) \in \mathbb{Z}_q^{m \times n}$ and $\mathbf{w}_a = \mathbf{W}_a \cdot \mathsf{urt}_a + \mathbf{e}_a \mod q$.
     (c) A repeats t times the underlying ZKAoK protocol [18, Sec. 4.1] with public parameter $(\mathbf{A}, \mathbf{u}_1, \mathbf{W}_a, \mathbf{w}_a)$ and witness $(d_a, \mathsf{usk}_a, \mathbf{e}_a)$, then makes it non-interactive with the Fiat-Shamir heuristic as a triple $\Pi_a = (\{cmt_a^k\}_{k=1}^t, ch_a, \{rsp_a^k\}_{k=1}^t)$, where

$$ch_a = (\{ch_a^k\}_{k=1}^t) = \mathcal{H}_0(\mathbf{A}, \mathbf{u}_1, \mathbf{W}_a, \mathbf{w}_a, \{cmt_a^k\}_{k=1}^t) \oplus F(\mathbf{C}_a). \quad (4)$$

     (d) Denote the commitment values which will not be checked as $\overline{cmt_a} = (\overline{cmt_a^1}, \ldots, \overline{cmt_a^t})$. Namely, A sets

$$\overline{cmt_a^k} = \begin{cases} \langle cmt_a^k(1) \rangle, & ch_a^k = 1; \\ \langle cmt_a^k(2) \rangle, & ch_a^k = 2; \\ \langle cmt_a^k(3) \rangle, & ch_a^k = 3. \end{cases} \quad (5)$$

     (e) A sets $\mathtt{PROOF}_a = (\overline{cmt_a}, ch_a, \{rsp_a^k\}_{k=1}^t, \rho_a, \mathbf{w}_a)$ and sends it to B.
  2. $B \to A : (\mathtt{PROOF}_b, \mathtt{V}_b)$
     (a) B sets $\mathbf{W}_a' = \mathcal{H}_1(\mathbf{B}, \mathbf{u}_2, \mathbf{K}, \rho_a)$. Then for each $\mathbf{v}_i \in \mathcal{CRL}_2$, B computes $\mathbf{e}_i' = \mathbf{w}_a - \mathbf{W}_a' \cdot \mathbf{v}_i$. If there exists an index i such that $\|\mathbf{e}_i'\|_\infty \leq \beta$, B sends A a random pair $(\mathtt{PROOF}_b, \mathtt{V}_b)$ and aborts.
     (b) B samples his ephemeral key $\mathbf{S}_b \hookleftarrow \chi(\mathbb{Z}_{q_1}^{m_1 \times n_3})$ and a small noise $\mathbf{E}_b \hookleftarrow \chi(\mathbb{Z}_{q_1}^{m_1 \times n_3})$. Then B computes $\mathbf{C}_b = \mathbf{K} \cdot \mathbf{S}_b + \mathbf{E}_b \in \mathbb{Z}_{q_1}^{m_1 \times n_3}$.
     (c) B computes the checked value $cmt_a^* = (cmt_a^{*1}, \ldots, cmt_a^{*t})$ for $k \in [t]$ from corresponding rsp_a^k and ch_a^k. Namely, B computes

$$cmt_a^{*k} = \begin{cases} \langle cmt_a^{*k}(2), cmt_a^{*k}(3) \rangle, & ch_a^k = 1; \\ \langle cmt_a^{*k}(1), cmt_a^{*k}(3) \rangle, & ch_a^k = 2; \\ \langle cmt_a^{*k}(1), cmt_a^{*k}(2) \rangle, & ch_a^k = 3. \end{cases} \quad (6)$$

     Details of the above calculations are depicted in [18, Sec. 4.1].

(d) By proper concatenations and rearrangements of cmt^*_a and $\overline{cmt_a}$ according to ch_a, B recovers the original commitments cmt'_a (e.g., set $cmt'^k_a = (cmt^{*k}_a(2), \overline{cmt}^k_a, cmt^{*k}_a(3))$ if $ch^k_a = 2$). Then B retrieves the hidden message $\mathbf{C}'_a = F^{-1}(ch_a \oplus \mathcal{H}_0(\mathbf{B}, \mathbf{u}_2, \mathbf{W}'_a, \mathbf{w}_a, cmt'_a))$.

(e) B computes $\mathbf{w}_b = \mathbf{W}_b \cdot \mathsf{urt}[d_b] + \mathbf{e}_b \mod q$, where $\rho_b \xleftarrow{\$} \{0,1\}^n$, $\mathbf{W}_b = \mathcal{H}_1(\mathbf{B}, \mathbf{u}_2, \mathbf{K}, \rho_b)$ and $\mathbf{e}_b \hookleftarrow \chi^m$.

(f) Similarly with public input $(\mathbf{B}, \mathbf{u}_2, \mathbf{W}_b, \mathbf{w}_b)$ and witness $(d_b, \mathsf{usk}[d_b], \mathbf{e}_b)$, B runs the underlying ZKAoK to get a triple $\Pi_b = (\{cmt^k_b\}^t_{k=1}, ch_b, \{rsp^k_b\}^t_{k=1})$, where

$$ch_b = (\{ch^k_b\}^t_{k=1}) = \mathcal{H}_0(\mathbf{B}, \mathbf{u}_2, \mathbf{W}_b, \mathbf{w}_b, \{cmt^k_b\}^t_{k=1}) \oplus F(\mathbf{C}^\top_b). \quad (7)$$

(g) B also sets each element of $\overline{cmt_b} = (\overline{cmt}^1_b, \ldots, \overline{cmt}^t_a)$ as

$$\overline{cmt}^k_b = \begin{cases} \langle cmt^k_b(1) \rangle, & ch^k_b = 1; \\ \langle cmt^k_b(2) \rangle, & ch^k_b = 2; \\ \langle cmt^k_b(3) \rangle, & ch^k_b = 3. \end{cases} \quad (8)$$

(h) B samples another noise $\tilde{\mathbf{E}}_b \hookleftarrow \chi(\mathbb{Z}^{m_1 \times m_1}_{q_1})$ and computes an auxiliary matrix $\mathbf{V}_b = \mathbf{S}_b \cdot \mathbf{C}'_a + \tilde{\mathbf{E}}_b$. Then B generates the reconciliation matrix $\mathbf{M} \in \mathbb{Z}^{m_1 \times m_1}_2$ holds that

$$\mathbf{M}[i,j] = \lfloor \frac{2^{\theta+1}}{q_1} \cdot \mathbf{V}_b[i,j] \rfloor \mod 2, \quad \forall\, i,j \in [m_1], \quad (9)$$

where each entry of V_b is viewed as an integer in $[-q_1/2, q_1/2-1]$[2].

(i) B generates the shared session key $\mathbf{K}_b \in \mathbb{Z}^{m_1 \times m_1}_{2^\theta}$ by rounding the θ most significant bits from each entry of $\mathbf{V}_b$, i.e., the (i,j)-th entry of $\mathbf{K}_b$ is:

$$\mathbf{K}_b[i,j] = \lfloor \frac{2^\theta}{q_1} \cdot \mathbf{V}_b[i,j] \rceil \mod 2^\theta, \quad (10)$$

where entries of $\mathbf{V}_b$ are also viewed as integers in $[-q_1/2, q_1/2-1]$.

(j) B sets $\mathtt{PROOF}_b = (\overline{cmt_b}, ch_b, \{rsp^k_b\}^t_{k=1}, \rho_b, \mathbf{w}_b, \mathbf{M})$ and authentication code $\mathtt{V}_b = \mathcal{H}_2(\mathbf{K}_b \| \mathbf{C}_b \| \mathbf{0})$. Then he sends $(\mathtt{PROOF}_b, \mathtt{V}_b)$ to A.

Remark 1. There is one pivotal modification of the above interactive algorithm: the transported tuple $\mathtt{PROOF}_a$ is a partial $\mathsf{NIZKAoK}$ compared with the original one generated in [18]. Namely, B can recover 2/3 part (cmt'_a) of the whole commitments cmt_a from ch_a and rsp_a, yet the validity of cmt'_a cannot be verified since he only received the rest 1/3 contents $(\overline{cmt_a})$. In this way, the only information B can get is the retrieved message $\mathbf{C}'_a$. Therefore, B is unable to detect which group A belongs to in this flow, and has to symmetrically send his proof (masking his message $\mathbf{C}_b$) of group credential to A. This strategy also fix the flaw of Zhang *et al.*'s scheme [32].

[2] This can be done by setting $V_b[i,j]' = V_b[i,j] - \alpha q_1$ where $\alpha = 1$ if $V_b[i,j] > \frac{q_1}{2} - 1$ and $\alpha = 0$ otherwise.

3. $A \to B : (\mathtt{V}_a)$
   (a) A sets $\mathbf{W}'_b = \mathcal{H}_1(\mathbf{A}, \mathbf{u}_1, \mathbf{K}, \rho_b)$. Then for each $\mathbf{v}_j \in \mathcal{CRL}_1$, A computes $\mathbf{e}'_j = \mathbf{w}_b - \mathbf{W}'_b \cdot \mathbf{v}_j$. If there exist an index j such that $\|\mathbf{e}'_j\|_\infty \leq \beta$, A chooses a random value $\mathtt{V}_a \xleftarrow{\$} \{0,1\}^{q_1}$, outputs 0 and aborts.
   (b) A also computes the checked value $cmt^*_b = (cmt^{*1}_b, \ldots, cmt^{*t}_b)$ for $k \in [t]$ from corresponding rsp^k_a and ch^k_a as follows:

$$cmt^{*k}_b = \begin{cases} \langle cmt^{*k}_b(2), cmt^{*k}_b(3) \rangle, \ ch^k_b = 1; \\ \langle cmt^{*k}_b(1), cmt^{*k}_b(3) \rangle, \ ch^k_b = 2; \\ \langle cmt^{*k}_b(1), cmt^{*k}_b(2) \rangle, \ ch^k_b = 3. \end{cases} \tag{11}$$

   Then with identical operations A recovers the original cmt'_b and computes the masked matrix $\mathbf{C'}^\top_b = F^{-1}(ch_b \oplus \mathcal{H}_0(\mathbf{A}, \mathbf{u}_1, \mathbf{W}'_b, \mathbf{w}_b, cmt'_b))$.
   (c) A computes an assistant matrix $\mathbf{V}_a = \mathbf{C}'_b \cdot \mathbf{S}_a$. Next, she extracts the shared session key $\mathbf{K}_a \in \mathbb{Z}_{2^\theta}^{m_1 \times m_1}$ from $\mathbf{V}_a$ via a reconciliation technique, i.e., using the check field $\mathbf{M}$ to apply the rounding. The (i,j)-th entry of $\mathbf{K}_a$ is:

$$\mathbf{K}_a[i,j] = \lfloor \frac{2^\theta}{q_1} \cdot \mathbf{V}_a[i,j] + \frac{1}{4} \cdot (2\mathbf{M}[i,j] - 1) \rceil \mod 2^\theta, \tag{12}$$

   where each entry of V_b is also viewed as an integer in $[-q_1/2, q_1/2 - 1]$.
   (d) A verifies that $\mathtt{V}_b \stackrel{?}{=} \mathcal{H}(\mathbf{K}_a \| \mathbf{C}'_b \| \mathbf{0})$. If so, A outputs 1 and sends $\mathtt{V}_a = \mathcal{H}_2(\mathbf{K}_a \| \mathbf{C}_a \| \mathbf{1})$ to B. Otherwise, A outputs 0 and responds a random $\mathtt{V}_a$.
   (e) B verifies $\mathtt{V}_a$ through a similar equation $\mathtt{V}_a \stackrel{?}{=} \mathcal{H}(\mathbf{K}_b \| \mathbf{C}'_a \| \mathbf{1})$. B outputs 1 if the equation holds, else he outputs 0.

- TraceMember: When a dispute happens, firstly GA will retrieve the handshake transcripts of A and B. Then for $d \in [N]$, GA computes $\mathbf{e}_d = \mathbf{w} - \mathbf{W} \cdot \mathsf{urt}[d]$ and outputs the first index d^* such that $\|\mathbf{e}_{d^*}\|_\infty \leq \beta$, otherwise outputs $\perp$ indicating that the involved participant is a malicious outsider.
- RemoveMember: GA maintains and updates the information of $\mathcal{CRL}$ and $\mathcal{L}$ after tracing a malicious group member or receiving a logout request. To remove a member U from group G, GA first looks up and removes the member's UserSecret $= (U, \mathsf{ID}_u)$ from $\mathcal{L}$. Then GA adds $\mathsf{urt}[d_u]$ to $\mathcal{CRL}$, and distributes the updated list $\mathcal{CRL}$ to every other group members via an authenticated anonymous channel.

5 Security and Performance Analysis of the Scheme

5.1 Security

Completeness: We first demonstrate that the scheme is complete with overwhelming probability if both active users belong to the same group

($\mathsf{gpk}_1 = \mathsf{gpk}_2$), based on the perfect completeness of the underlying Stern-like protocol.

Note that the interactive message PROOF generated by an honest and active user is always valid, i.e., the receiver can rightly recover the original commitments holding that $cmt' = cmt$. Thus, such a receiver can always retrieve the hidden matrix $\mathbf{C}'$ equals to $\mathbf{C}$. In this way, it can be deduced from [8, A.1.4] that $\mathbf{K}_a \neq \mathbf{K}_b$ with negligible probability. Therefore, both authentication codes (V_a and V_b) would be successfully verified, and consequently the handshake protocol outputs 1 for A and B. Moreover, the tracing algorithm TraceMember will get $\mathbf{e}_{d^*} = \mathbf{w} - \mathbf{W} \cdot \mathsf{urt}[d^*] = \mathbf{e}^*$ for $d^* = d_a$ or d_b, where $\mathbf{e}^*$ is sampled from a β-bounded distribution such that $\|\mathbf{e}^*\|_\infty \leq \beta$ holds with overwhelming probability. So both users can always be traced when disputes happen.

Privacy: We now prove that our scheme satisfies the privacy requirements listed in Sect. 3 through Theorems 1–3 below, for which some proofs are deferred to Appendix 1.

Theorem 1. *In the random oracle model, impersonator resistance holds for our scheme under the* SIS *assumption.*

Theorem 2. *In the random oracle model, detector resistance holds for our scheme under the* LWE *assumption.*

Theorem 3. *In the random oracle model, unlinkability holds for our scheme under the* LWE *assumption.*

Proof. The proof is similar to that of Theorem 2. Based on the security of utilized ZK protocol and the $\mathsf{LWE}_{n,q,\chi}$ assumption, we can build a sequence of games to argue that $|\Pr[\mathbf{Exp}_{\mathcal{A}}^{\mathsf{Unlink}-1} = 1] - \Pr[\mathbf{Exp}_{\mathcal{A}}^{\mathsf{Unlink}-0} = 1]| = \mathsf{negl}(\lambda)$.

5.2 Performance

From Theorem 1, 2 and 3 we know that our scheme's provable security depends on the $\mathsf{LWE}_{n,q,\chi}$ and $\mathsf{SIS}^{\infty}_{n,(\ell+1)\cdot m,q,2\beta}$ (implying $\mathsf{SIS}^{2}_{n,(\ell+1)\cdot m,q,2\beta\sqrt{(\ell+1)\cdot m}}$) assumptions. Recently Yang *et al.* [31] gave a concrete technique to estimate and derive parameters for hardness theorems over lattices. They examine the root Hermite factor (RHF) and summarize the required RHF for these problems as follows:

$$\mathrm{RHF} = \begin{cases} \exp(\frac{\log^2 \beta}{4n \log q}), & \text{for } \mathsf{SIS}^2_{n,m,q,\beta}; \\ \exp(\frac{\log^2 \frac{\sigma\cdot\sqrt{2\pi}}{5.31q}}{4n\log q}), & \text{for } \mathsf{LWE}_{n,q,\chi}. \end{cases} \tag{13}$$

We adopt this method and set RHF as 1.0048 to achieve an 80-bit security. In this way, we get $n = 471$ from the above equations. Then we set

$$(q, m, \sigma, \beta, m_1, q_1, \theta, \sigma_1) = (1961767, 19654, 296, 389, 6, 2^{13}, 4, 2309),$$

according to the asymptotic bounds of these scheme parameters. To make soundness error of the ZK protocol negligible, we set repetitions $t = 137$. Besides, we set $N = 2^{19}$ for efficient group management.

- **Communication Cost:** In $\mathsf{Addmember}$, GA sends Cred_u to the user, where $\mathsf{ID}_u = d_u$ is a binary string of size ℓ, $(\mathsf{usk}[d_u], \mathsf{urt}[d_u])$ comprises an element of $\mathbb{Z}^{(2\ell+1)m}$ holding $\|\mathsf{usk}[d_u]\|_\infty \leq \beta$ and an element of $\mathbb{Z}_q^n$, respectively. So the communication cost in this step is less than $\ell + (\ell+1)m \log \beta + n \log q$ bits ≈579 KB. In $\mathsf{Handshake}$, each member finally needs to transmit a pair $(\mathtt{PROOF}, \mathtt{V})$ in two rounds. $\mathtt{PROOF}$ comprises partial commitments $\overline{cmt}$ with bit-size $tn \log q$, a challenge value ch having $2t$ bits, t responses rsp with no more than $3tm \log \beta(4\ell + 4 + 2(\ell+1) \log q)$ bits and an LWE function output $\mathbf{w} \in \mathbb{Z}_q^m$, so the total length is about 7.79 GB (user B sends an extra matrix $\mathbf{M} \in \mathbb{Z}_2^{m_1 \cdot m_1}$ having bit-size 36). The authentication code $\mathtt{V}$ has length $n \log q$ bits. Thus, the communication cost in $\mathsf{Handshake}$ for each participant is about 7.8 GB.
- **Computational Cost:** In $\mathsf{CreateGroup}$, GA generates all the potential users' credentials, the main computation cost here is the polynomial-time algorithms $\mathsf{GenTrap}$ and $\mathsf{SamplePre}$ which can be pre-computed. In $\mathsf{Handshake}$, the main operations here are the multiplications of matrices and vectors in $\mathcal{O}(n^2)$ and a polynomial-time commitment scheme COM [16] used in ZK protocol, whose runtime is on the order of milliseconds using libraries like GMP [11] and NTL [24]. Thus the computational cost of $\mathsf{Handshake}$ is considered to be very small. While the step of revocation check runs in the size of list $\mathcal{CRL}$, as it seems unavoidable for the setting of VLR.

6 Conclusion

This paper aims to propose the first secret handshake scheme from lattices, which supports reusable credentials and membership revocation. With some subtle modifications, we transform a Stern-like ZKAoK system into a mutual authentication protocol. It's intriguing to consider whether this design is a generic framework, e.g., can apply to other types of ZKAoK like Fiat-Shamir with abort ones [21,31]. To achieve traceability and unlinkability with ease, we utilize the VLR structure to generate revocation tokens with group identities encoded in a Bonsai tree. We believe that, our construction - while not being entirely novel - would certainly help to exploit the area of post-quantum secret handshakes. One interesting future work is to build secret handshakes supporting more functionalities such as backward unlinkability or full dynamicity through more efficient lattice-based techniques.

Acknowledgements. This work is supported by Guangdong Major Project of Basic and Applied Basic Research (2019B030302008) and the National Natural Science Foundation of China (No. 61972429) and Guangdong Basic and Applied Basic Research Foundation (No. 2019A1515011797) and the Opening Project of Guangdong Provincial Key Laboratory of Information Security Technology (2020B1212060078-09).

Appendix 1. Impersonator Resistance (Proof of Theorem 1)

Proof. Suppose that $\mathcal{A}$ succeeds in experiment $\mathbf{Exp}_{\mathcal{A}}^{\mathsf{IR}}$ with non-negligible advantage ϵ. Then we can build a PPT algorithm $\mathcal{F}$ that solves $\mathsf{SIS}_{n,(l+1)\cdot m,q,2\beta}^{\infty}$ problem with non-negligible probability.

Given an SIS instance $\mathbf{C} = [\mathbf{C}_0|\mathbf{C}_1|\ldots|\mathbf{C}_\ell] \in \mathbb{Z}_q^{n\times(\ell+1)m}$, the goal of $\mathcal{F}$ is to find a non-zero vector $\mathbf{y} \in \mathbb{Z}^{(\ell+1)\cdot m}$ such that $\mathbf{C}\cdot\mathbf{y} = \mathbf{0} \mod q$ and $\|\mathbf{y}\|_\infty \leq 2\beta$. Toward this goal, $\mathcal{F}$ first generates the public parameters par as we do in Setup, and proceeds as described in experiment $\mathbf{Exp}_{\mathcal{A}}^{\mathsf{IR}}$. Note that $\mathcal{F}$ can consistently answer all the oracle queries made by $\mathcal{A}$. In particular, $\mathcal{F}$ randomly picks $i \in [q_G]$ where q_G is the number of queries to oracle KeyP, then it performs the following steps at the i-th query to oracle KeyP to bulid a group $G^{(i)}$:

- Sample vector $\mathbf{z} = (\mathbf{x}_0|\mathbf{x}_1|\ldots|\mathbf{x}_\ell) \in \mathbb{Z}^{(\ell+1)\cdot m}$ from $D_{\mathbb{Z}^{(\ell+1)\cdot m},\sigma}$. If $\|\mathbf{z}\|_\infty > \beta$, repeat the sampling. Otherwise, compute $\mathbf{u} = \mathbf{C}\cdot\mathbf{z} \mod q$.
- Get ℓ pairs $\{(\mathbf{F}_i, \mathbf{R}_i)\}_{i\in[\ell]}$ by invoking algorithm $\mathsf{GenTrap}(n, m, q)$ for ℓ times.
- Choose a target identity $d^* \xleftarrow{\$} \{0,1\}^\ell$, and define $\mathbf{A} = [\mathbf{A}_0|\mathbf{A}_1^0|\mathbf{A}_1^1|\ldots|\mathbf{A}_\ell^0|\mathbf{A}_\ell^1] \in \mathbb{Z}_q^{n\times(2\ell+1)m}$ by setting $\mathbf{A}_0 = \mathbf{C}_0$, $\mathbf{A}_i^{d^*[i]} = \mathbf{C}_i$ and $\mathbf{A}_i^{1-d^*[i]} = \mathbf{F}_i$ for $i \in [\ell]$.
- Define the secret key and revocation token of member d^* as follows:
  - i: $\mathsf{usk}[d^*] = (\mathbf{x}_0\|\mathbf{x}_1^0\|\mathbf{x}_1^1\|\ldots\|\mathbf{x}_\ell^0\|\mathbf{x}_\ell^1) \in \mathbb{Z}^{(2\ell+1)m}$, where $\mathbf{x}_0 = \mathbf{z}_0$, $\mathbf{x}_i^{d^*[i]} = \mathbf{z}_i$ and $\mathbf{x}_i^{1-d^*[i]} = \mathbf{0}^m$ for all $i \in [\ell]$.
  - ii: $\mathsf{urt}[d^*] = \mathbf{A}_0\cdot\mathbf{x}_0 \mod q \in \mathbb{Z}_q^n$.
- For member's identity $d \neq d^*$, generate its secret key and revocation token as follows:
  1. Since $d \neq d^*$, there exists an index p being the first index of LTR-order such that $d[p] \neq d^*[p]$. Then it holds that $\mathbf{A}_p^{d[p]} = \mathbf{A}_p^{1-d*[p]} = \mathbf{F}_p$.
  2. Sample ℓ vectors $\mathbf{x}_0, \mathbf{x}_1^{d[1]}, \ldots, \mathbf{x}_{p-1}^{d[p-1]}, \mathbf{x}_{p+1}^{d[p+1]}, \ldots, \mathbf{x}_\ell^{d[\ell]} \hookleftarrow D_{\mathbb{Z}^m,\sigma}$, and set $\mathbf{s}^{(d)} = \mathbf{u} - (\mathbf{A}_0\cdot\mathbf{x}_0 + \sum_{i\in[\ell],i\neq b}(\mathbf{A}_i^{d[i]}\cdot\mathbf{x}_i^{d[i]})) \mod q$.
  3. Sample $\mathbf{x}_p^{d[p]} \hookleftarrow \mathsf{SamplePre}(\mathbf{R}_p, \mathbf{F}_p, \mathbf{s}^{(d)}, \sigma)$.
  4. Set $\mathbf{x}^{(d)} = (\mathbf{x}_0\|\mathbf{x}_1^0\|\mathbf{x}_1^1\|\ldots\|\mathbf{x}_\ell^0\|\mathbf{x}_\ell^1) \in \mathbb{Z}^{(2\ell+1)m}$, where $\mathbf{x}_i^{1-d[i]} = \mathbf{0}^m$ for all $i \in [\ell]$. Repeat the sampling if $\|\mathbf{x}^{(d)}\|_\infty > \beta$. Otherwise, let $\mathsf{usk}[d] = \mathbf{x}^{(d)}$ and $\mathsf{urt}[d] = \mathbf{A}_0\cdot\mathbf{x}_0 \mod q$.
- Set $\mathsf{gpk} = (\mathbf{A}, \mathbf{u})$, $\mathsf{gsk} = (\mathbf{R}_i, \mathsf{grt})$, and $\mathsf{usk} = \{\mathsf{usk}[k]\}_{k=1}^N$. Note that, by construction, the distribution of $(\mathsf{gpk}, \mathsf{grt}, \mathsf{usk})$ is statistically close to that of the real scheme, and the choice of d^* is hidden from the adversary.

Eventually, $\mathcal{A}$ wins with its output $\mathtt{PROOF}^* = (\overline{cmt}^*, ch^*, \{rsp_k^*\}_{k=1}^t, \rho^*, \mathbf{w}^*)$. Since the involved user outputs 1 after a handshake with $\mathcal{A}$, we know that he must have retrieved the right hidden matrix $\mathbf{C}^*$. This fact also means that the recovered commitments cmt'^* is equal to the original one cmt^*. Now it can be deduced that the NIZKAoK $(cmt^*, ch^*, \{rsp_k^*\}_{k=1}^t)$ is a valid one generated by $\mathcal{A}$ via the underlying ZK protocol. Then we can argue that $\mathcal{A}$ must have queried

$\mathcal{H}_0$ on input $(\mathbf{A}, \mathbf{u}, \mathbf{W}^*, \mathbf{w}^*, cmt^*)$ (denoted as η^*), as otherwise, the probability that $ch^* = \mathcal{H}_0(\eta^*)$ is at most 3^{-t}. Thus, with probability at least $\epsilon - 3^{-t}$, there exists some $\kappa^* \leq q_{\mathcal{H}}$ such that the κ^*-th hash query involves the tuple η^*, where $q_{\mathcal{H}}$ is the number of queries to random oracle $\mathcal{H}_0$.

To employ the Improved Forking Lemma [22], $\mathcal{F}$ reinvokes $\mathcal{A}$ polynomial times with the same random tape and input as in the original run, until the κ^* query, that is, from the κ^* query onwards, $\mathcal{F}$ answers $\mathcal{A}$ with fresh and independent values $\rho_{\kappa^*}, \ldots, \rho_{q_{\mathcal{H}}} \xleftarrow{\$} \{1,2,3\}^t$. By the aforementioned Forking Lemma, with probability $\geq \frac{1}{2}$, $\mathcal{F}$ obtains 3-fork $\{\rho^1_{\kappa^*}, \rho^2_{\kappa^*}, \rho^3_{\kappa^*}\}$ involving the same tuple η^* after less than $32 \cdot q_{\mathcal{H}}/(\epsilon - 3^{-t})$ executions of $\mathcal{A}$. Then we have $\{\rho^1_{\kappa^*}(i), \rho^2_{\kappa^*}(i), \rho^3_{\kappa^*}(i)\} = \{1,2,3\}$ for some $i \in [t]$ with probability $1 - (\frac{7}{9})^t$. Having such index i, $\mathcal{F}$ can parse the 3 forgeries from the fork branches to obtain 3 valid responses $(rsp^*_i(1), rsp^*_i(2), rsp^*_i(3))$ w.r.t. 3 different challenges for the same commitment cmt^*_i. By Theorem 1 in [18], we can extract vectors $\mathbf{x} = (\mathbf{x}_0\|\mathbf{x}^0_1\|\mathbf{x}^1_1\|\ldots\|\mathbf{x}^0_\ell\|\mathbf{x}^1_\ell) \in \mathbb{Z}^{(2\ell+1)m}$ and $\mathbf{e}^* \in \mathbb{Z}^m$ such that:

1. $\|\mathbf{x}\|_\infty \leq \beta$, the following ℓ blocks are zero-blocks $\mathbf{0}^m$: $\mathbf{x}^{1-d[1]}_1, \ldots, \mathbf{x}^{1-d[\ell]}_\ell$ for some $d \in \{0,1\}^\ell$;
2. $\mathbf{A} \cdot \mathbf{x} = \mathbf{u} \mod q$;
3. $\|\mathbf{e}'\|_\infty \leq \beta$ and $\mathbf{w}^* = \mathbf{W}^* \cdot (\mathbf{A}_0 \cdot \mathbf{x}_0) + \mathbf{e}^* \mod q$.

Now we consider two cases:

- If G^* is not created at the i-th query to oracle KeyP or $d \neq d^*$, which happens with probability at most $\frac{N \cdot q_G - 1}{N \cdot q_G}$, then algorithm $\mathcal{F}$ fails and aborts.
- If $d = d^*$ belongs to $G^{(i)}$, set $\mathbf{x}^* = (\mathbf{x}_0\|\mathbf{x}^{d[1]}_1\|\ldots\|\mathbf{x}^{d[\ell]}_\ell) \in \mathbb{Z}^{(\ell+1)m}$. Then by construction it holds that $\mathbf{C} \cdot \mathbf{x}^* = \mathbf{A} \cdot \mathbf{x} = \mathbf{u} \mod q$. Furthermore, experiment $\mathbf{Exp}^{\mathsf{IR}}_{\mathcal{A}}$ ensures that $\mathcal{A}$ has never requested the user secret key $\mathsf{usk}[d^*]$, so that $\mathbf{z}$ is unknown to $\mathcal{A}$. In this case, because $\mathbf{z}$ has large min-entropy given $\mathbf{u}$ (see Lemma 1), we have $\mathbf{x}^* \neq \mathbf{z}$ with overwhelming probability.

  Now let $\mathbf{y} = \mathbf{x}^* - \mathbf{z}$, then we get the following facts: i) $\mathbf{y} \neq \mathbf{0}$; ii) $\mathbf{C} \cdot \mathbf{y} = \mathbf{0} \mod q$; iii) $\|\mathbf{y}\|_\infty \leq \|\mathbf{x}^*\|_\infty + \|\mathbf{z}\|_\infty \leq \beta + \beta = 2\beta$. So $\mathcal{F}$ finally outputs the vector $\mathbf{y}$, which is a solution to the related $\mathsf{SIS}^\infty_{n,(l+1)\cdot m,q,2\beta}$ problem.

In summary, the probability that $\mathcal{F}$ does not abort and solve the $\mathsf{SIS}^\infty_{n,(l+1)\cdot m,q,2\beta}$ assumption is larger than $(1 - (\frac{7}{9})^t)/2(N \cdot q_G)$. This concludes the proof.

Appendix 2. Detector Resistance (Proof of Theorem 2)

Proof. We define a sequence of hybrid games where the first is $\mathbf{Exp}^{\mathsf{DR}-0}_{\mathcal{A}}$ and the last is $\mathbf{Exp}^{\mathsf{DR}-1}_{\mathcal{A}}$. Then we prove that these games are indistinguishable. For i-th game, denote the output of $\mathcal{A}$ by R_i. The concrete games are described as follows.

Game 0: This is exactly the original game $\mathbf{Exp}_{\mathcal{A}}^{\mathsf{DR}-0}$.
Game 1: This game is the same as Game 0 except that it generates a simulated proof for the interactive handshake between $\mathcal{A}$ and the chosen user ID^*, via running the simulator of the underlying argument for every repetition, and then generates the corresponding challenge via oracle $\mathcal{H}_0$. Since the hidden vector $\mathbf{C}$ is also generated randomly by an LWE function, the view of adversary $\mathcal{A}$ is statistically indistinguishable between Game 1 and Game 2 by zero-knowledge property of underlying ZK protocol. So $\Pr[R_1 = 1] \approx \Pr[R_2 = 1]$.
Game 2: This game is the same as Game 1 with only one modification: for token embedding, we compute the LWE function using a random nonce $\mathbf{s}$ instead of the revocation token $\mathsf{urt}[\mathsf{ID}^*]$, namely, $\mathbf{w} = \mathbf{W} \cdot \mathbf{s} + \mathbf{e}^* \mod q$ where $\mathbf{s} \xleftarrow{\$} \mathbb{Z}_q^n$. Recall that the token $\mathsf{urt}[\mathsf{ID}^*] = \mathbf{A}_0 \cdot \mathbf{x}_0$ is statistically close to uniform over $\mathbb{Z}_q^n$. In this way, we have $\Pr[R_2 = 1] \approx \Pr[R_1 = 1]$.
Game 3: This game follows Game 2 with one change: we make $\mathbf{w}$ uniformly sampled from $\mathbb{Z}_q^m$. Note that in the previous game, $\mathbf{W}$ is uniformly random over $\mathbb{Z}_q^{m \times n}$, so the pair $(\mathbf{W}, \mathbf{w})$ is a valid $\mathsf{LWE}_{n,q,\chi}$ instance and its distribution is computationally close to the uniform distribution over $\mathbb{Z}_q^{m \times n} \times \mathbb{Z}_q^m$. Thus, it holds that $\Pr[R_3 = 1] - Pr[R_2 = 1] = \mathsf{negl}(\lambda)$.
Game 4: This game switches back to use a random nonce to produce $\mathbf{w}$, and this LWE function is for an arbitrary user ID_r, i.e., $\mathbf{w} = \mathbf{W} \cdot \mathbf{s} + \mathbf{e}_r \mod q$. Since $\mathbf{e}_r \hookleftarrow \chi^m$ is β-bounded, the output $\mathtt{PROOF}$ is computationally close to that in Game 3. Hence we have $\Pr[R_4 = 1] - Pr[R_3 = 1] = \mathsf{negl}(\lambda)$.
Game 5: In this game, we generate $\mathbf{w}$ with another user's revocation token $\mathsf{urt}[\mathsf{ID}_r]$, namely, $\mathbf{w} = \mathbf{W} \cdot \mathsf{urt}[\mathsf{ID}_r] + \mathbf{e}_r \mod q$. Since $\mathsf{urt}[\mathsf{ID}_r]$ is statistically close to uniform over $\mathbb{Z}_q^n$, this change makes no difference to the view of $\mathcal{A}$. Therefore, it holds that $\Pr[R_5 = 1] \approx \Pr[R_4 = 1]$.
Game 6: This game is exactly the experiment $\mathbf{Exp}_{\mathcal{A}}^{\mathsf{DR}-1}$. We generate the real argument for the handshake between $\mathcal{A}$ and ID_r, the transcript is statistically indistinguishable from that of Game 5 by the zero-knowledge property of the utilized ZKAoK. In this way, we have $\Pr[R_6 = 1] \approx \Pr[R_5 = 1]$.

Combining the above analysis, we have that $|\Pr[\mathbf{Exp}_{\mathcal{A}}^{\mathsf{DR}-1} = 1] - \Pr[\mathbf{Exp}_{\mathcal{A}}^{\mathsf{DR}-0} = 1]| = \mathsf{negl}(\lambda)$. This concludes the proof.

References

1. Ajtai, M.: Generating hard instances of lattice problems (extended abstract). In: Miller, G.L. (ed.) STOC 1996, pp. 99–108. ACM (1996). https://doi.org/10.1145/237814.237838
2. Ajtai, M.: Generating hard instances of the short basis problem. In: Wiedermann, J., van Emde Boas, P., Nielsen, M. (eds.) ICALP 1999. LNCS, vol. 1644, pp. 1–9. Springer, Heidelberg (1999). https://doi.org/10.1007/3-540-48523-6_1
3. Alwen, J., Peikert, C.: Generating shorter bases for hard random lattices. Theory Comput. Syst. **48**(3), 535–553 (2011). https://doi.org/10.1007/s00224-010-9278-3
4. Ateniese, G., Kirsch, J., Blanton, M.: Secret handshakes with dynamic and fuzzy matching. In: NDSS 2007. The Internet Society (2007)

5. Balfanz, D., Durfee, G., Shankar, N., Smetters, D.K., Staddon, J., Wong, H.: Secret handshakes from pairing-based key agreements. In: S&P 2003, pp. 180–196. IEEE Computer Society (2003). https://doi.org/10.1109/SECPRI.2003.1199336
6. Boneh, D., Shacham, H.: Group signatures with verifier-local revocation. In: Atluri, V., Pfitzmann, B., McDaniel, P.D. (eds.) CCS 2004, pp. 168–177. ACM (2004). https://doi.org/10.1145/1030083.1030106
7. Castelluccia, C., Jarecki, S., Tsudik, G.: Secret handshakes from CA-oblivious encryption. In: Lee, P.J. (ed.) ASIACRYPT 2004. LNCS, vol. 3329, pp. 293–307. Springer, Heidelberg (2004). https://doi.org/10.1007/978-3-540-30539-2_21
8. ETSI: ETSI TR 103 570: CYBER; Quantum-Safe Key Exchange, 1.1.1 edn. (2017)
9. Gentry, C., Peikert, C., Vaikuntanathan, V.: Trapdoors for hard lattices and new cryptographic constructions. In: Dwork, C. (ed.) STOC 2008, pp. 197–206. ACM (2008). https://doi.org/10.1145/1374376.1374407
10. Goldwasser, S., Micali, S., Rackoff, C.: The knowledge complexity of interactive proof-systems (extended abstract). In: Sedgewick, R. (ed.) STOC 1985, pp. 291–304. ACM (1985). https://doi.org/10.1145/22145.22178
11. Granlund, T.: The GMP Development Team: GNU MP: The GNU Multiple Precision Arithmetic Library, 6.1.2 edn. (2016). http://gmplib.org/
12. He, D., Kumar, N., Wang, H., Wang, L., Choo, K.R., Vinel, A.V.: A provably-secure cross-domain handshake scheme with symptoms-matching for mobile healthcare social network. IEEE Trans. Dependable Secur. Comput. **15**(4), 633–645 (2018). https://doi.org/10.1109/TDSC.2016.2596286
13. Hou, L., Lai, J., Liu, L.: Secret handshakes with dynamic expressive matching policy. In: Liu, J.K., Steinfeld, R. (eds.) ACISP 2016. LNCS, vol. 9722, pp. 461–476. Springer, Cham (2016). https://doi.org/10.1007/978-3-319-40253-6_28
14. Jarecki, S., Kim, J., Tsudik, G.: Group secret handshakes or affiliation-hiding authenticated group key agreement. In: Abe, M. (ed.) CT-RSA 2007. LNCS, vol. 4377, pp. 287–308. Springer, Heidelberg (2006). https://doi.org/10.1007/11967668_19
15. Jarecki, S., Liu, X.: Private mutual authentication and conditional oblivious transfer. In: Halevi, S. (ed.) CRYPTO 2009. LNCS, vol. 5677, pp. 90–107. Springer, Heidelberg (2009). https://doi.org/10.1007/978-3-642-03356-8_6
16. Kawachi, A., Tanaka, K., Xagawa, K.: Concurrently secure identification schemes based on the worst-case hardness of lattice problems. In: Pieprzyk, J. (ed.) ASIACRYPT 2008. LNCS, vol. 5350, pp. 372–389. Springer, Heidelberg (2008). https://doi.org/10.1007/978-3-540-89255-7_23
17. Kulshrestha, P., Pal, A.: A new secret handshakes scheme with dynamic matching based on ZSS. IJNSA **7**(1), 67–78 (2015)
18. Langlois, A., Ling, S., Nguyen, K., Wang, H.: Lattice-based group signature scheme with verifier-local revocation. In: Krawczyk, H. (ed.) PKC 2014. LNCS, vol. 8383, pp. 345–361. Springer, Heidelberg (2014). https://doi.org/10.1007/978-3-642-54631-0_20
19. Libert, B., Ling, S., Nguyen, K., Wang, H.: Zero-knowledge arguments for lattice-based accumulators: logarithmic-size ring signatures and group signatures without trapdoors. In: Fischlin, M., Coron, J.-S. (eds.) EUROCRYPT 2016. LNCS, vol. 9666, pp. 1–31. Springer, Heidelberg (2016). https://doi.org/10.1007/978-3-662-49896-5_1
20. Micciancio, D., Peikert, C.: Trapdoors for lattices: simpler, tighter, faster, smaller. In: Pointcheval, D., Johansson, T. (eds.) EUROCRYPT 2012. LNCS, vol. 7237, pp. 700–718. Springer, Heidelberg (2012). https://doi.org/10.1007/978-3-642-29011-4_41

21. del Pino, R., Lyubashevsky, V., Seiler, G.: Lattice-based group signatures and zero-knowledge proofs of automorphism stability. In: Lie, D., Mannan, M., Backes, M., Wang, X. (eds.) CCS 2018, pp. 574–591. ACM (2018). https://doi.org/10.1145/3243734.3243852
22. Pointcheval, D., Vaudenay, S.: On provable security for digital signature algorithms. Technical report LIENS-96-17 of the Laboratoire d'Informatique de Ecole Normale Superieure, November 1996
23. Regev, O.: On lattices, learning with errors, random linear codes, and cryptography. In: Gabow, H.N., Fagin, R. (eds.) STOC 2005, pp. 84–93. ACM (2005). https://doi.org/10.1145/1060590.1060603
24. Shoup, V.: A Tour of NTL, 11.4.3 edn. http://www.shoup.net/ntl/
25. Tian, Y., Li, Y., Zhang, Y., Li, N., Yang, G., Yu, Y.: DSH: deniable secret handshake framework. In: Su, C., Kikuchi, H. (eds.) ISPEC 2018. LNCS, vol. 11125, pp. 341–353. Springer, Cham (2018). https://doi.org/10.1007/978-3-319-99807-7_21
26. Tsudik, G., Xu, S.: A flexible framework for secret handshakes. In: Danezis, G., Golle, P. (eds.) PET 2006. LNCS, vol. 4258, pp. 295–315. Springer, Heidelberg (2006). https://doi.org/10.1007/11957454_17
27. Wen, Y., Zhang, F.: A new revocable secret handshake scheme with backward unlinkability. In: Camenisch, J., Lambrinoudakis, C. (eds.) EuroPKI 2010. LNCS, vol. 6711, pp. 17–30. Springer, Heidelberg (2011). https://doi.org/10.1007/978-3-642-22633-5_2
28. Wen, Y., Zhang, F.: Delegatable secret handshake scheme. J. Syst. Softw. **84**(12), 2284–2292 (2011). https://doi.org/10.1016/j.jss.2011.06.046
29. Wen, Y., Zhang, F., Xu, L.: Secret handshakes from id-based message recovery signatures: a new generic approach. Comput. Electr. Eng. **38**(1), 96–104 (2012). https://doi.org/10.1016/j.compeleceng.2011.11.020
30. Xu, S., Yung, M.: k-anonymous secret handshakes with reusable credentials. In: Atluri, V., Pfitzmann, B., McDaniel, P.D. (eds.) CCS 2004, pp. 158–167. ACM (2004). https://doi.org/10.1145/1030083.1030105
31. Yang, R., Au, M.H., Zhang, Z., Xu, Q., Yu, Z., Whyte, W.: Efficient lattice-based zero-knowledge arguments with standard soundness: construction and applications. In: Boldyreva, A., Micciancio, D. (eds.) CRYPTO 2019. LNCS, vol. 11692, pp. 147–175. Springer, Cham (2019). https://doi.org/10.1007/978-3-030-26948-7_6
32. Zhang, Z., Zhang, F., Tian, H.: CSH: a post-quantum secret handshake scheme from coding theory. In: Chen, L., Li, N., Liang, K., Schneider, S. (eds.) ESORICS 2020. LNCS, vol. 12309, pp. 317–335. Springer, Cham (2020). https://doi.org/10.1007/978-3-030-59013-0_16
33. Zhou, L., Susilo, W., Mu, Y.: Three-round secret handshakes based on ElGamal and DSA. In: Chen, K., Deng, R., Lai, X., Zhou, J. (eds.) ISPEC 2006. LNCS, vol. 3903, pp. 332–342. Springer, Heidelberg (2006). https://doi.org/10.1007/11689522_31

When NTT Meets Karatsuba: Preprocess-then-NTT Technique Revisited

Yiming Zhu[1,2], Zhen Liu[1,2,3], and Yanbin Pan[1,2](✉)

[1] Key Laboratory of Mathematics Mechanization, Academy of Mathematics and Systems Science, Chinese Academy of Sciences, Beijing 100190, China
panyanbin@amss.ac.cn

[2] School of Mathematical Sciences, University of Chinese Academy of Sciences, Beijing 100049, China
{zhuyiming17,liuzhen16}@mails.ucas.ac.cn

[3] Faculty of Mathematics and Statistics, Hubei Key Laboratory of Applied Mathematics, Hubei University, Wuhan 430062, China

Abstract. The Number Theoretic Transform (NTT) technique is widely used to implement cryptographic schemes based on the Ring Learning With Errors problem(RLWE), since it provides efficient algorithm for multiplication of polynomials over the finite field. However, the module in NTT must be big enough such that the finite field has some special root of unity, which makes the corresponding schemes a bit less efficient. At Inscrypt 2018, Zhou *et al.* proposed a technique called Preprocess-then-NTT to relax the constraint for the modulus while keeping NTT work, at the cost of time complexity. In this paper, we improve the Preprocess-then-NTT technique by mixing it with Karatsuba multiplication such that the time complexity is better than the original NTT algorithm asymptotically. The claim was also verified in our experiments. As a result, our new algorithm not only relaxes the constraint for modulus but also improves efficiency in practice. In addition, we also present some advantages and applications of our new algorithm.

Keywords: NTT · Ring Learning With Errors · Polynomial · Multiplication

1 Introduction

In recent years, there have been a substantial amount of researches in quantum computers. If quantum computers are ever built, the public-key cryptosystems currently in use, based on the hardness of solving (elliptic curve) discrete logarithm or factoring large integers, will be broken efficiently [21]. To avoid this

This work is supported by National Key Research and Development Program of China (No. 2018YFA0704705, 2020YFA0712300), National Natural Science Foundation of China (No. 62032009).

D. Gao et al. (Eds.): ICICS 2021, LNCS 12919, pp. 249–264, 2021.
https://doi.org/10.1007/978-3-030-88052-1_15

problem, many post-quantum cryptosystems have been proposed. Among them, lattice-based cryptography is widely believed to be a promising candidate.

The shortest vector problem is one of the most famous hard problem for lattices and its hardness is usually seen as the foundation of lattice-based cryptosystems. However, compared with the shortest vector problem, the learning with errors problem (LWE) [20] and its variants, such as the Ring-Learning With Errors problem (RLWE) [14] or the Module-Learning With Errors problem (MLWE) [5,22], appear to be much more versatile in the construction of cryptographic schemes.

Moreover, compared with the plain LWE, both RLWE and MLWE usually employ the polynomial ring $\mathbb{Z}_q[x]/(x^n+1)$, to compress the size of sample, which leads to much more efficient cryptosystems. Hence they are widely used in the construction of public-key encryption, digital signature, key exchange and so on, such as [3,4,12,14]. To further improve the efficiency of these schemes, complicated discrete Gauss distribution is usually replaced with some other discrete distribution that is easy to be sampled. Hence, the most time-consuming operation in the implementation of RLWE (or MLWE)-based schemes becomes the polynomial multiplication in the ring.

Many algorithms have been proposed to improve the efficiency of the polynomial multiplication, such as Karatsuba algorithm [9,10], Toom-Cook algorithm [6,23] and Fast Fourier Transform (FFT) algorithm [7]. To multiply two polynomials with degree n, Karatsuba algorithm needs $O(n^{\log 3})$ arithmetic multiplications whereas FFT needs $O(n \log n)$ asymptotically. It can be seen that FFT works much better for the polynomials with big degree. Typically, an FFT algorithm to compute the product of polynomials f and g consists of three steps: computing the Fourier transformations $\hat{f}$ and $\hat{g}$ of f, g respectively first, then computing the point-wise multiplication of $\hat{f}$ and $\hat{g}$ and lastly computing the Fourier inverse transformations of the product to obtain the final polynomial.

For RLWE or MLWE, since the coefficient ring of the polynomial ring is usually a residue class ring, such as $\mathbb{Z}_q$, an FFT-analogy called Number Theoretic Transform (NTT) was proposed by using the root of unity in the residue class ring instead of the field of complexity number. For example, considering the polynomial multiplication in the ring $R_q = \mathbb{Z}_q[x]/(x^n + 1)$ widely used in cryptographic constructions where q is a prime and n is some power of 2, the product can be efficiently computed by NTT when there exists $2n$-th root of unity in $\mathbb{Z}_q$, which is equivalent to $2n|(q-1)$ [13]. As a result, applying the NTT algorithm significantly improves the efficiency of corresponding schemes.

However, since the modulus q is required to satisfy $2n|(q-1)$ in NTT, a large enough q is usually chosen for the R(M)LWE-based cryptographic schemes, which obviously enlarges the key size and decreases the efficiency. We would also like to point out that we can use NTT to speedup polynomial multiplication over $R_{q'}$ regardless of whether $2n|(q'-1)$ or not, if there exists an NTT modulus q such that $2n|(q-1)$ and q is sufficiently larger than q'. However, this will increase the time for the coefficients multiplication since it operates over $\mathbb{Z}_q$ instead of $\mathbb{Z}_{q'}$. Hence a smaller q will be more welcome.

A way to overcome the issue is the mixed basis FFTs introduced by Moenck [16], which shows how to compute the multiplication of two polynomials in $\mathbb{Z}[x]/(x^n - 1)$ by FFT with a 2^k-th primitive root of unity w where $n = 2^k \cdot l$. The basic idea is exploiting FFT to split the multiplication into 2^k multiplications in $\mathbb{Z}[x]/(x^l - w^i)$ for $i = 0, 1, \cdots, 2^k - 1$ and then compute the 2^k component-wise products by classical polynomial multiplication algorithms. Letting $l = 2$ and generalizing the idea for NTT in $\mathbb{Z}_q[x]/(x^n + 1)$, KYBER [4] reduced the size of q in their Round 2 submission to the NIST post-quantum cryptography standardization since in their algorithm, only n-th primitive root of unity in $\mathbb{Z}_q$ is needed, that is, $n|(q-1)$. However, $n/2$ component-wise products of linear polynomials should be computed when multiplying two polynomials, which can be done by classical method. Moreover, the idea of mixed basis FFTs was also used to speedup the multiplication in $R_q = \mathbb{Z}_{7681}[x]/(x^{768} - x^{384} + 1)$ in [15] with $l = 3$ to improve the efficiency of NTRU [8]. Replacing the classical method in component-wise multiplication in [4,15] with Karatsuba's algorithm, Alkim *et al.* [1] improved the time complexity of polynomial multiplication with NTT.

At Inscrypt 2018, Zhou *et al.* [24] achieve the same purpose of reducing the size of q in a different way by introducing the technique called preprocess-then-NTT (PtNTT). Their basic idea is employing the well-known even–odd splitting method to divide the polynomial into some new polynomials with lower degrees and then applying the NTT to these new polynomials respectively. They proposed two versions of preprocess-then-NTT algorithm, 1-Round PtNTT (1PtNTT) and 2-Round PtNTT(2PtNTT), depending on how they split the polynomial. Moreover, 1PtNTT requires $n|(q-1)$ and the time complexity is approximately $\frac{7}{6}$ times of the original NTT, whereas 2PtNTT requires $\frac{n}{2}|(q-1)$ and its time complexity is approximately $\frac{5}{4}$ times of the original NTT.

Although PtNTT algorithm seems less efficient than the NTT algorithm in [1,4] while they all reduce the size of modulus, we think it still has some advantages, such as to implement it we do not need change the original NTT algorithm but just add an implementation of the component-wise polynomial multiplication, whereas in Kyber's NTT [4] or [1], we have to change both the original NTT a bit and the component-wise polynomial multiplication. Since PtNTT just invokes the original NTT as its subroutine, any improvement on NTT can also be applied to PtNTT. Moreover, we can run PtNTT algorithm in parallel easily. Hence, we think it makes sense to improve the PtNTT algorithm.

In this paper, we propose a new algorithm called KNTT to improve PtNTT. First of all we present a quite simple high-level framework that enables us to exploit the NTT algorithm over some ring $\mathcal{R}$ to multiply two polynomials in its polynomial ring $\mathcal{R}[x]$. This technique is also known as Nussbaumer's trick [17]. With this point of view, PtNTT can be easily gotten. Then, we choose Karatsuba's algorithm to multiply polynomials in $\mathcal{R}[x]$ and finally improve PtNTT algorithm. A theoretical analysis shows that the time complexity of our KNTT algorithm is as the same as the algorithm in [1], which is better than the original NTT, and our experiments also verified it.

Hence, KNTT not only weakens the limitation of the modulus q but also is more efficient than the original NTT algorithm. Moreover, KNTT obviously has the advantage shared by PtNTT that it just invokes the original NTT algorithm, which means we do not need to change NTT when implementing KNTT and any improvement of NTT can be used to speedup KNTT, and KNTT is easy to be parallelized.

We would also like to point out that at Inscrypt 2020, Liang *et al.* [11] made a systematic and comprehensive study of NTT and its variants including KNTT algorithm (which was public in ePrint in 2019 [25]) and NTT in [1], corrected some mistakes in the analysis of time complexity, clarified the computational equivalence of the two algorithms, generalized NTT further and derived the optimal bounds for the generalizations.

Roadmap. The remainder of the paper is organized as follows. In Sect. 2 we present some preliminaries. In Sect. 3 we present our KNTT algorithm. In Sect. 4 we give a short conclusion.

2 Preliminaries

2.1 Karatsuba Algorithm

Karatsuba [9,10] introduced a method to perform multiplication of large numbers in fewer operations than the usual direct multiplication. The idea can also be used in computing the product of two polynomials.

Denote by $f(x)$, $g(x)$ two polynomials of degree bounded by n. Karatsuba algorithm first divides them into polynomials of lower degrees as follows:

$$f = f_0 + x^{\frac{n}{2}} f_1, g = g_0 + x^{\frac{n}{2}} g_1.$$

Then the product can be computed as follows:

$$\begin{aligned} h &= f \cdot g \\ &= (f_0 + x^{\frac{n}{2}} f_1) \cdot (g_0 + x^{\frac{n}{2}} g_1) \\ &= f_0 \cdot g_0 + x^n f_1 \cdot g_1 + x^{\frac{n}{2}} (f_1 \cdot g_0 + f_0 \cdot g_1) \\ &= f_0 \cdot g_0 - f_1 \cdot g_1 + x^{\frac{n}{2}} ((f_0 + f_1) \cdot (g_0 + g_1) - f_0 \cdot g_0 - f_1 \cdot g_1) \end{aligned}$$

Thus by using Karatsuba algorithm we only need to compute products of polynomials of lower degrees for 3 times to compute the original product. Repeating the process until the degree of the polynomial is zero, the complexity of multiplication operations for the final algorithm is shown to be $O(n^{\log 3})$.

2.2 Number Theoretic Transform

The Number Theoretic Transform (NTT) [7] is a specialized version of the Fast Fourier Transform (FFT) over a finite field, which employs the root of unity in the finite field instead of the field of complex number.

In lattice-based cryptography, we usually use the polynomial ring $R_q = \mathbb{Z}_q[x]/(x^n+1)$ where n is some power of 2, and q is a prime satisfying $2n|(q-1)$. Next we consider NTT in this ring.

Let ω be an n-th primitive root of unity in $\mathbb{Z}_q$, and f be any element of R_q. Then for $0 \le i \le n-1$, we define the forward transformation $\hat{f} = NTT(f)$ by $\hat{f}_i = \sum_{j=0}^{n-1} f_j \cdot \omega^{ij} \mod q$, and the inverse transformation $f = NTT^{-1}(\hat{f})$ is given by $f_i = n^{-1}\sum_{j=0}^{n-1} \hat{f}_j \cdot \omega^{-ij} \mod q$. Notice that $f = NTT^{-1}(NTT(f))$ holds.

Let f, g be elements of R_q. Computing $h = f \cdot g \mod x^n + 1$ would require applying the NTT of length $2n$ at the first glance. Then h is given by $NTT^{-1}(\hat{f} \circ \hat{g}) \mod x^n + 1$, where $\circ$ is the component-wise product. However, this method will require the computation of a reduction modulo $x^n + 1$ and it seems not necessary to use a $2n$-point NTT since the degree of h is at most $n-1$. In order to avoid this, an algorithm was introduced in [13], which behaves as follows. Denote by γ the $2n$-th primitive root of unity in $\mathbb{Z}_q$ such that $\gamma = \sqrt{\omega}$. Note that the condition $2n|(q-1)$ guarantees the existence of γ. Let $\tilde{f} = (f_0, \gamma f_1, \cdots, \gamma^{n-1} f_{n-1})$ and $\tilde{g} = (g_0, \gamma g_1, \cdots, \gamma^{n-1} g_{n-1})$, then h is given by $(1, \gamma^{-1}, \cdots, \gamma^{1-n}) \circ NTT^{-1}(NTT(\tilde{f}) \circ NTT(\tilde{g}))$.

More precisely, one can use the view of isomorphism to implement the algorithm. See [2] for a nice survey. Note that $x^n + 1$ can be factored over $\mathbb{Z}_q$ as $x^n + 1 = (x^{n/2} - \gamma^{n/2}) \cdot (x^{n/2} + \gamma^{n/2})$. Thus we have an isomorphism

$$\mathbb{Z}_q[x]/(x^n+1) \cong \mathbb{Z}_q[x]/(x^{n/2} - \gamma^{n/2}) \times \mathbb{Z}_q[x]/(x^{n/2} + \gamma^{n/2}),$$

and the map is easy to compute just with $\frac{n}{2}$ multiplications, $\frac{n}{2}$ additions and $\frac{n}{2}$ subtractions. Concretely let $f = f_0 + f_1 x + \cdots + f_{n-1}x^{n-1} \in R_q$. We will have

$$\begin{aligned} f \mod (x^{n/2} - \gamma^{n/2}) &= (f_0 + \gamma^{n/2} f_{n/2}) + \cdots + (f_{n/2-1} + \gamma^{n/2} f_{n-1})x^{n/2-1}, \\ f \mod (x^{n/2} + \gamma^{n/2}) &= (f_0 - \gamma^{n/2} f_{n/2}) + \cdots + (f_{n/2-1} - \gamma^{n/2} f_{n-1})x^{n/2-1} \end{aligned}$$

We call the above process the first level. Since we have $2n$-th primitive root of unity in $\mathbb{Z}_q$ we can repeat this until splitting the ring into n factors as follows:

$$\mathbb{Z}_q[x]/(x^n+1) \cong \mathbb{Z}_q[x]/(x-\gamma) \times \mathbb{Z}_q[x]/(x-\gamma^3) \times \cdots \times \mathbb{Z}_q[x]/(x-\gamma^{2n-1}).$$

Then the product of polynomials in R_q can be computed through computing this map (i.e. the forward NTT transformation), then computing the component-wise multiplications in $\mathbb{Z}_q$, and finally the inverse of the map (i.e. the inverse NTT transformation).

Since each level consists of $\frac{n}{2}$ multiplications, $\frac{n}{2}$ additions and $\frac{n}{2}$ subtractions, and there are $\log n$ levels totally, the total cost of the forward NTT transformation consists of $\frac{n}{2}\log n$ multiplications, $\frac{n}{2}\log n$ additions and $\frac{n}{2}\log n$ subtractions, which holds similarly for the inverse NTT transformation except there is additional n multiplications for inverse NTT. We just focus on the number of arithmetic multiplications, and have that

Property 1. To compute the product of two polynomials in $R_q = \mathbb{Z}_q[x]/(x^n + 1)$ where n is some power of 2, and q is a prime, the NTT algorithm in [13] needs $2n|(q-1)$ and $(\frac{3}{2}n\log n + 2n)$ multiplications in $\mathbb{Z}_q$.

2.3 NTT for $\mathbb{Z}_q[x]/(x^n + 1)$ Without $2n$-th Root

Note that the modulus q is required to satisfy $2n|(q-1)$ in NTT above, which obviously restricts the choice of q and n. There are already some work dedicated to weaken the restriction while using NTT, which can be roughly divided into two classes.

Kyber's NTT. Kyber is one of the candidates in Round 3 of the NIST post-quantum cryptography standardization. It employs a technique to weaken the restriction of modulus q, whose idea can date back to the mixed basis FFT introduced by Moenck [16].

More precisely, Kyber chooses parameters $n = 256, q = 3329$ for their scheme. Notice that the base field $\mathbb{Z}_q$ only contains primitive 256-th roots of unity but not 512-th roots since q doesn't satisfy $2n|(q-1)$. Hence the polynomial $x^{256}+1$ can only be factored into irreducible quadratic polynomials

$$x^{256} + 1 = f_1(x) \times \cdots \times f_{128}(x) \mod q,$$

So they consider the isomorphism

$$\mathbb{Z}_q[x]/(x^{256} + 1) \cong \mathbb{Z}_q[x]/f_1(x) \times \cdots \times \mathbb{Z}_q[x]/f_{128}(x),$$

and use the component-wise multiplication defined by the linear polynomials multiplication in the corresponding $\mathbb{Z}_q[x]/f_i(x)$. In fact, note that the original NTT in Sect. 2.3 has $\log n$ levels, Kyber's NTT has just $\log n - 1$ levels.

What's more, Kyber claimed that using a q such that $n|(q-1)$ (and maybe even $\frac{n}{2}|(q-1)$) is enough to achieve equal (or even slightly better) performance by their technique compared with the original NTT algorithm. However they didn't give much more details about this.

By replacing the component-wise multiplication in Kyber's NTT with Karatsuba algorithm, Alkim *et al.* [1] improves the efficiency further. In addition, they also consider the case for $\frac{n}{2}|(q-1)$ and $\frac{n}{4}|(q-1)$, and showed that

Property 2. To compute the product of two polynomials in $R_q = \mathbb{Z}_q[x]/(x^n + 1)$ where n is some power of 2, and q is a prime, the $(\log n - 2)$-level NTT mixed with Karatsuba algorithm in [1] needs $\frac{n}{2}|(q-1)$, and $(\frac{3}{2}n\log n + \frac{5n}{4})$ multiplications in $\mathbb{Z}_q$, whereas the $(\log n - 3)$-level algorithm needs $\frac{n}{4}|(q-1)$, and $(\frac{3}{2}n\log n + \frac{15n}{8})$ multiplications in $\mathbb{Z}_q$.

Preprocess-then-NTT. Zhou *et al.* [24] proposed the Preprocess-then-NTT (PtNTT) technique to weaken the restriction of modulus for computing the product of two polynomials in $R_q = \mathbb{Z}_q[x]/(x^n + 1)$ where n is some power of 2, and q is a prime. Next, we will describe it in details.

Recall that we let $\tilde{f} = (f_0, \gamma f_1, \cdots, \gamma^{n-1} f_{n-1})$, $\tilde{g} = (g_0, \gamma g_1, \cdots, \gamma^{n-1} g_{n-1})$. For simplicity, denote by $\widehat{NTT}(f) = NTT(\tilde{f})$ for any polynomial $f \in R_q$, and $\widehat{NTT}^{-1}(\cdot) = (1, \gamma, \cdots, \gamma^{n-1}) \circ NTT^{-1}(\cdot)$.

When $n|q-1$, denote x^2 by y. The 1-Round Preprocess-then-NTT(1PtNTT) algorithm used the even-indexed and odd-indexed coefficients of $f(x) \in R_q$ separately to define two new polynomials $f_{even}(y)$ and $f_{odd}(y)$ whose degrees are bounded by $\frac{n}{2}$:

$$f_{even}(y) = f_0 + f_2 \cdot y + f_4 \cdot y^2 + \cdots + f_{n-2} \cdot y^{n/2-1} \in \mathbb{Z}_q[y]/(y^{n/2} + 1),$$
$$f_{odd}(y) = f_1 + f_3 \cdot y + f_5 \cdot y^2 + \cdots + f_{n-1} \cdot y^{n/2-1} \in \mathbb{Z}_q[y]/(y^{n/2} + 1).$$

Then the 1PtNTT algorithm is presented as follows:

Step 1: (Separation) $f(x) = f_{even}(x^2) + x \cdot f_{odd}(x^2)$, $g(x) = g_{even}(x^2) + x \cdot g_{odd}(x^2)$, where the degrees of $f_{even}, f_{odd}, g_{even}, g_{odd}$ are bounded by $\frac{n}{2}$.

Step 2: (Multiplication) Compute $h_{even}(y), h_{odd}(y) \in \mathbb{Z}_q[y]/(y^{n/2} + 1)$ as in the following, where $\vec{g}_{odd}(y) = y \cdot g_{odd}(y) \in \mathbb{Z}_q[y]/(y^{n/2} + 1)$:

$$\begin{aligned} h_{even}(y) &= f_{even}(y) \cdot g_{even}(y) + f_{odd}(y) \cdot \vec{g}_{odd}(y) \\ &= \widehat{NTT}^{-1}(\widehat{NTT}(f_{even}(y)) \circ \widehat{NTT}(g_{even}(y)) \\ &\quad + \widehat{NTT}(f_{odd}(y)) \circ \widehat{NTT}(\vec{g}_{odd}(y))) \\ h_{odd}(y) &= f_{even}(y) \cdot g_{odd}(y) + f_{odd}(y) \cdot g_{even}(y) \\ &= \widehat{NTT}^{-1}(\widehat{NTT}(f_{odd}(y)) \circ \widehat{NTT}(g_{even}(y)) \\ &\quad + \widehat{NTT}(f_{even}(y)) \circ \widehat{NTT}(g_{odd}(y))). \end{aligned}$$

Step 3: (Gatheration) Compute h in R_q as following:

$$h(x) = h_{even}(x^2) + x \cdot h_{odd}(x^2).$$

It can be easily to generalize the algorithm above to α-round preprocess-then-NTT algorithm (αPtNTT), which divides each polynomial into 2^α parts, and then transform the original multiplication into several multiplications of polynomials of lower degrees. In [24], they only showed the results for $\alpha = 1$ and $\alpha = 2$.

Property 3. To compute the product of two polynomials in $R_q = \mathbb{Z}_q[x]/(x^n + 1)$ where n is some power of 2, and q is a prime, the 1PtNTT algorithm in [24] needs $n|(q-1)$, and $(\frac{7}{4} n \log n + \frac{5n}{4})$ multiplications in $\mathbb{Z}_q$, whereas 2PtNTT needs $\frac{n}{2}|(q-1)$, and $(\frac{15}{8} n \log n + \frac{5n}{4})$ multiplications in $\mathbb{Z}_q$.

For general α, we can show that it needs $\frac{n}{2^{\alpha-1}}|(q-1)$, and $(2-\frac{1}{2^{\alpha+1}})n\log n+(2^\alpha-2\alpha+\frac{\alpha}{2^{\alpha+1}}+1)n$ multiplications in $\mathbb{Z}_q$. Notice that the complexity of the algorithm grows while the number of round increases. That is why Zhou *et al.* only consider the cases when $\alpha=1$ and $\alpha=2$, since the efficiency loss can not be tolerated when the number of round is somehow large.

3 Preprocess-then-NTT with Karatsuba (KNTT)

Although PtNTT algorithm seems less efficient than the NTT algorithm in [1,4] while they all reduce the size of modulus, we think it still has some advantages, such as to implement it we do not need change the original NTT algorithm but just add an implementation of the component-wise polynomial multiplication, whereas in Kyber's NTT [4] or [1], we have to change both the original NTT a bit and the component-wise polynomial multiplication. Since PtNTT just invokes the original NTT as its subroutine, any improvement on NTT can also be generalized to PtNTT. Moreover, we can run PtNTT algorithm in parallel easily. Hence, we revisit the PtNTT algorithm and try to improve its efficiency.

Surprisingly, we find there is a quite simple high-level framework to cover the idea of PtNTT, based on which we can improve its efficiency easily.

The idea is quite simple. Roughly speaking, to multiply two polynomials in $\mathbb{Z}_q[x]/(x^n+1)$, before we usually take $\mathbb{Z}_q[x]/(x^n+1)$ as a polynomial ring over the base ring $\mathbb{Z}_q$. Hence, to employ NTT, we ask $\mathbb{Z}_q$ to have some root of unity. However, we can change the base ring of $\mathbb{Z}_q[x]/(x^n+1)$ to some ring $\mathcal{R}$ that admits NTT. Then the polynomial multiplication in $\mathbb{Z}_q[x]/(x^n+1)$ can be improved by NTT in $\mathcal{R}$. This technique is also known as Nussbaumer's trick [17].

Taking 1PtNTT as an example, we want to compute the product of two polynomials in $\mathbb{Z}_q[x]/(x^n+1)$ where n is some power of 2, and q is a prime just satisfying $n|(q-1)$. We consider the case that there is no $2n$-th primitive root of unity in $\mathbb{Z}_q$ and hence NTT is not available for $\mathbb{Z}_q[x]/(x^n+1)$.

Note that we have isomorphism

$$\mathbb{Z}_q[x]/(x^n+1)\cong(\mathbb{Z}_q[y]/(y^{\frac{n}{2}}+1))[x]/(x^2-y).$$

We can take $\mathcal{R}=\mathbb{Z}_q[y]/(y^{\frac{n}{2}}+1)$ which obviously admits NTT. Then the polynomial in $\mathbb{Z}_q[x]/(x^n+1)$ can be seen as the polynomial over $\mathcal{R}$ and the multiplication can be done with the help of NTT algorithm in $\mathcal{R}$.

More precisely, denote by η a $2n$-th primitive complex root of unity and by $\zeta=\eta^2$ an n-th primitive complexity root of unity. Then we can view $\mathbb{Z}_q[x]/(x^n+1)$ as $\mathbb{Z}_q[\eta]$ and view $\mathbb{Z}_q[y]/(y^{\frac{n}{2}}+1)$ as $\mathcal{R}=\mathbb{Z}_q[\zeta]$ for simplicity by the map $x\mapsto\eta$ and $y\mapsto\zeta$ respectively. We have

$$\mathbb{Z}_q[\eta]\cong\mathcal{R}[x]/(x^2-\zeta)=\mathcal{R}[\eta].$$

Note that for any $f=\sum_{0\le i<n}f_i\eta^i$ in $\mathbb{Z}_q[\eta]$, we can efficiently express it as $f=f^{(0)}+\eta f^{(1)}$, where $f^{(0)}=\sum_{0\le i<\frac{n}{2}}f_{2i}\zeta^i\in\mathcal{R}$, and $f^{(1)}=\sum_{0\le i<\frac{n}{2}}f_{2i+1}\zeta^i\in\mathcal{R}$, which is exactly as the same as f_{even} and f_{odd} in 1PtNTT algorithm.

Similarly, for $g \in \mathbb{Z}_q[\eta]$, we can efficiently write it as $g = g^{(0)} + \eta g^{(1)}$, and have

$$fg = (f^{(0)}g^{(0)} + \zeta f^{(1)}g^{(1)}) + \eta(f^{(1)}g^{(0)} + f^{(0)}g^{(1)}). \tag{1}$$

The products $f^{(i)}g^{(j)}$ can be computed just in $\mathbb{Z}_q[\zeta]$, and NTT can be used to speedup the computation.

For the case αPtNTT, we can easily consider the following isomorphism,

$$\mathbb{Z}_q[x]/(x^n + 1) \cong (\mathbb{Z}_q[y]/(y^{\frac{n}{2^\alpha}} + 1))[x]/(x^{2^\alpha} - y),$$

or equivalently,

$$\mathbb{Z}_q[\eta] \cong \mathbb{Z}_q[\zeta'][x]/(x^{2^\alpha} - \zeta'),$$

where $\zeta' = \eta^{2^\alpha}$ is a $\frac{n}{2^{\alpha-1}}$-th complex root of unity.

3.1 Improving PtNTT with Karatsuba Algorithm

Due to the observation above, it can be seen that the polynomial multiplication in $R_q = \mathbb{Z}_q[x]/(x^n + 1)$ involves two multiplication operations: the polynomial multiplication in $\mathcal{R}[\eta]$, and the multiplication in $\mathcal{R}$. Note that we can speedup the multiplication in $\mathcal{R}$ with NTT. We focus on improving the polynomial multiplication in $\mathcal{R}[\eta]$ with Karatsuba's algorithm, which is the key idea of our following 1KNTT algorithm to improve 1PtNTT algorithm.

Step 1: (Map and split) Take f and g as the elements in $\mathbb{Z}_q[\eta]$ and find $f^{(0)}$, $f^{(1)}$, $g^{(0)}$, $g^{(1)} \in \mathbb{Z}_q[\zeta]$, such that

$$f = f^{(0)} + \eta f^{(1)}, \quad g = g^{(0)} + \eta g^{(1)}.$$

Step 2: (Multiplication) Note that by Karatsuba's algorithm, we have

$$\begin{aligned} fg &= (f^{(0)}g^{(0)} + \zeta f^{(1)}g^{(1)}) + \eta(f^{(1)}g^{(0)} + f^{(0)}g^{(1)}) \\ &= (f^{(0)}g^{(0)} + \zeta f^{(1)}g^{(1)}) + \eta((f^{(0)} + f^{(1)})(g^{(0)} + g^{(1)}) - f^{(0)}g^{(0)} - f^{(1)}g^{(1)}). \end{aligned}$$

So we need to compute $f^{(0)}g^{(0)} + \zeta f^{(1)}g^{(1)}$ and $f^{(1)}g^{(0)} + f^{(0)}g^{(1)}$ in $\mathbb{Z}_q[\zeta]$. In the original PtNTT algorithm, they need to compute $\widehat{NTT}(f^{(0)})$, $\widehat{NTT}(f^{(1)})$, $\widehat{NTT}(g^{(0)})$, $\widehat{NTT}(g^{(1)})$ and $\widehat{NTT}(\zeta g^{(1)})$. However, notice that we can precompute $\widehat{NTT}(\zeta)$ at first. Then it is enough for us to compute the following 4 forward NTT operations

$$\widehat{NTT}(f^{(0)}), \widehat{NTT}(f^{(1)}), \widehat{NTT}(g^{(0)}), \widehat{NTT}(g^{(1)}).$$

Moreover, by Karatsuba's algorithm, we need 4 point-wise multiplications

$$\begin{aligned} P_1 &= \widehat{NTT}(f^{(0)}) \circ \widehat{NTT}(g^{(0)}), \\ P_2 &= \widehat{NTT}(f^{(1)}) \circ \widehat{NTT}(g^{(1)}), \\ P_3 &= (\widehat{NTT}(f^{(0)}) + \widehat{NTT}(f^{(1)})) \circ (\widehat{NTT}(g^{(0)}) + \widehat{NTT}(g^{(1)})), \\ P_4 &= \widehat{NTT}(\zeta) \circ P_2, \end{aligned}$$

and 2 inverse NTT operations:

$$Q_1 = \widehat{NTT}^{-1}(P_1 + P_4),$$
$$Q_2 = \widehat{NTT}^{-1}(P_3 - P_1 - P_2).$$

Step 3: (Inverse) Compute $fg = Q_1(\zeta) + \eta Q_2(\zeta)$ in $\mathbb{Z}_q[\eta]$ and invert it as a polynomial in R_q by the map $\eta \mapsto x$.

As discussed above, 1KNTT algorithm consists of 4 forward NTT transformations, 2 inverse NTT transformations and 4 point-wise multiplications. Then the number of multiplication operations is given by

$$4 \cdot \frac{n}{4} \log \frac{n}{2} + 2 \cdot (\frac{n}{4} \log \frac{n}{2} + \frac{n}{2}) + 4 \cdot \frac{n}{2} = \frac{3}{2} n \log n + \frac{3n}{2}.$$

As a result, we have the following property.

Property 4. To compute the product of two polynomials in $R_q = \mathbb{Z}_q[x]/(x^n + 1)$ where n is some power of 2, and q is a prime, the 1KNTT algorithm needs $n|(q-1)$, and $(\frac{3}{2} n \log n + \frac{3n}{2})$ multiplications in $\mathbb{Z}_q$.

3.2 α-Round Preprocess-then-NTT with Karatsuba (αKNTT)

We can easily generalize 1KNTT to αKNTT for $\alpha > 1$ when we just have $\frac{n}{2^{\alpha-1}}|q-1$. Consider the following isomorphism,

$$\mathbb{Z}_q[\eta] \cong \mathbb{Z}_q[\zeta'][x]/(x^{2^\alpha} - \zeta').$$

where $\zeta' = \eta^{2^\alpha}$ is a $\frac{n}{2^{\alpha-1}}$-th complex root of unity. Then we have the αKNTT algorithms as follows.

Step 1: (Map and split) Take f and g as the elements in $\mathbb{Z}_q[\eta]$ and express them as

$$f = \sum_{i=0}^{2^\alpha - 1} \eta^i \cdot f^{(i)}, \text{ and } g = \sum_{j=0}^{2^\alpha - 1} \eta^j \cdot g^{(j)},$$

where $f^{(i)}, g^{(j)}$ are in $\mathbb{Z}_q[\zeta']$.

Step 2: (Multiplication) Compute $fg = \sum_{k=0}^{2^\alpha-1} \eta^k \cdot Q^{(k)}$ in $\mathbb{Z}_q[\eta]$, where

$$Q^{(k)} = \sum_{l=0}^{k} f^{(l)} \cdot g^{(k-l)} + \sum_{l=k+1} \zeta' \cdot f^{(l)} \cdot g^{(2^\alpha + k - l)},$$

can be computed in $\mathbb{Z}_q[\zeta']$ with NTT.

Again, we can precompute $\widehat{NTT}(\zeta')$ at first and then we just need to compute the $2^{\alpha+1}$ forward NTT transformations

$$(\widehat{NTT}(f^{(i)}))_{i=0,1,\cdots,2^\alpha-1}, (\widehat{NTT}(g^{(j)}))_{i=0,1,\cdots,2^\alpha-1}.$$

By Karatsuba's algorithm, we first compute the following 2^α point-wise multiplications:

$$P_{i,i} = \widehat{NTT}(f^{(i)}) \circ \widehat{NTT}(g^{(i)}), \text{ for } i = 0, 1, \cdots, 2^\alpha - 1.$$

Then for $0 \le i < j \le 2^\alpha - 1$, we compute the following $2^{\alpha-1}(2^\alpha - 1)$ point-wise multiplications:

$$\widetilde{P}_{i,j} = (\widehat{NTT}(f^{(i)}) + \widehat{NTT}(f^{(j)})) \circ (\widehat{NTT}(g^{(i)}) + \widehat{NTT}(g^{(j)}));$$
$$P_{i,j} = \widetilde{P}_{i,j} - P_{i,i} - P_{j,j}.$$

Note that $P_{i,j} = \widehat{NTT}(f^{(i)}g^{(j)} + f^{(j)}g^{(i)})$.

Then, for every $Q^{(k)}$ $(k = 0, 1, \cdots, 2^\alpha - 2)$, we need compute one more point-wise multiplication:

$$Z_k = \widehat{NTT}(\zeta') \circ \sum_{\substack{i \le j \\ i+j=2^\alpha+k}} P_{i,j}.$$

Hence we need compute $2^\alpha - 1$ point-wise multiplications for compute Z_k's.

Then we have

$$Q^{(k)} = \widehat{NTT}^{-1}(\sum_{\substack{i<j \\ i+j=k}} P_{i,j} + Z_k),$$

via 2^α inverse NTT.

Step 3: (Inverse) Compute $fg = \sum_{k=0}^{2^\alpha-1} \eta^k \cdot Q^{(k)}$ in $\mathbb{Z}[\eta]$ and invert it as a polynomial in R_q by the map $\eta \mapsto x$.

As discussed above, αKNTT algorithm needs $2^{\alpha+1}$ forward NTT transformations, 2^α inverse NTT transformations and $2^{\alpha-1}(2^\alpha + 3) - 1$ point-wise multiplications. Then the number of multiplication operations is given by

$$\begin{aligned} & 2^{\alpha+1} \cdot \frac{n}{2^{\alpha+1}} \log \frac{n}{2^\alpha} + 2^\alpha \cdot (\frac{n}{2^{\alpha+1}} \log \frac{n}{2^\alpha} + \frac{n}{2^\alpha}) + (2^{\alpha-1}(2^\alpha + 3) - 1) \cdot \frac{n}{2^\alpha} \\ = & \frac{3}{2} n \log n + (2^{\alpha-1} - \frac{3}{2}\alpha - \frac{1}{2^\alpha} + \frac{5}{2})n. \end{aligned}$$

As a result, we have the following property.

Property 5. To compute the product of two polynomials in $R_q = \mathbb{Z}_q[x]/(x^n + 1)$ where n is some power of 2, and q is a prime, the αKNTT algorithm needs $\frac{n}{2^{\alpha-1}} | (q - 1)$, and $\frac{3}{2} n \log n + (2^{\alpha-1} - \frac{3}{2}\alpha - \frac{1}{2^\alpha} + \frac{5}{2})n$ multiplications in $\mathbb{Z}_q$.

Remark 1. We would like to point out that we can run PtNTT algorithm in parallel easily. More precisely, suppose we have 2^α processors for αKNTT algorithm. Note that $(\widehat{NTT}(f^{(i)}))_{i=0,1,\cdots,2^\alpha-1}, (\widehat{NTT}(g^{(j)}))_{i=0,1,\cdots,2^\alpha-1}$ can be computed independently, then the point multiplication for $P_{i,i}$ can also be computed independently and then so can $\tilde{P}_{i,j}$, Z_k and then the 2^α inverse NTT. It can be concluded easily that every processor computes 2 forward NTT transformations, 1 inverse NTT transformations and less than or equal to $2^{\alpha-1}+2$ point-wise multiplications. Then the number of multiplication operations for every processor is given by

$$\begin{aligned}&2\cdot\frac{n}{2^{\alpha+1}}\log\frac{n}{2^\alpha}+(\frac{n}{2^{\alpha+1}}\log\frac{n}{2^\alpha}+\frac{n}{2^\alpha})+(2^{\alpha-1}+2)\cdot\frac{n}{2^\alpha}\\=&\frac{3}{2^{\alpha+1}}n\log n+(\frac{1}{2}-\frac{3}{2^{\alpha+1}}\alpha+\frac{3}{2^\alpha})n,\end{aligned}$$

which dominates the time complexity of the parallel algorithm and is roughly $\frac{1}{2^\alpha}$ of the time for αKNTT with just single processor regardless of the communication cost between the processors.

3.3 Experiment Results

We implemented KNTT algorithm, 1PtNTT algorithm and the original NTT algorithm for the ring $\mathbb{Z}_q[x]/(x^n+1)$. Our C implementation was compiled with gcc-8.2.0 on a 3.70GHZ Inter(R) Core(TM) i3-4170 processor. Note that all the algorithms invokes the original NTT algorithms as their subroutine. It is reasonable to compare their performance with the same implementation of original NTT algorithm that may be not optimized.

Note that 1PtNTT and αKNTT ($\alpha=1,2,3$) can deal with some parameters that are not suitable for the original NTT. However, to compare the efficiency more fairly, we test the computational cost of NTT, 1PtNTT and αKNTT with the same parameters that are suitable for all the algorithms. For every fixed (n,q), we uniformly randomly generated 100000 pairs of polynomial f and g, then recorded the average time to compute their products with the three kinds of algorithms respectively. The results are listed in Table 1.

Table 1. Results of our C implementation (average of 100000 runs)

Algorithm	Parameters		
	Time (ms)		
	n = 256, q = 7681	n = 512, q = 12289	n = 1024, q = 12289
NTT [13]	0.030100	0.065920	0.145280
1PtNTT [24]	0.034720	0.074260	0.164420
1KNTT (this work)	0.029410	0.063820	0.140260
2KNTT (this work)	0.025840	0.057630	0.128060
3KNTT (this work)	0.024460	0.055020	0.123140

It is easy to demonstrate the improvement of αKNTT on the efficiency, since 1KNTT costs about 97%, 2KNTT costs 87%, and 3KNTT costs about 84%, of the time for the original NTT whereas 1PtNTT costs 113% of the time forthe original NTT. Hence, replacing the polynomial multiplication with the original NTT algorithm in some cryptosystem, such as NewHope [19], with our KNTT algorithm, will improve the efficiency directly.

Moreover, by our KNTT algorithm, we can choose smaller q such that R_q admits fast polynomial multiplication, which can improve the efficiency of corresponding cryptosystem further. Taking NewHope with the ring $\mathbb{Z}_q[x]/(x^{1024}+1)$ as an example again, q is set to be 12289 in NewHope and we can choose q as 3329 due to our 3KNTT algorithm in a similar RLWE-based cryptosystem TALE [18], since we relax the constraints for q. With the new parameters in [18], the key size and ciphertext size can be reduced by about 12% and 19% respectively, and the time cost in key generation, encapsulation and decapsulation can be reduced by 39% compared with non-optimized reference implementation of NewHope.

3.4 Theoretical Comparison and Further Discussion

For completeness, we compare our KNTT algorithm with PtNTT and the algorithm in [1] in theory. Although these two algorithms only presents some results for special α, we can easily generalize them for any α. We list our results for $\alpha < 5$ in Table 2.

Table 2. The number of multiplication operations in known algorithms

α	1	2	3	4
NTT in [1]	$\frac{3}{2}n\log n+\frac{3}{2}n$	$\frac{3}{2}n\log n+\frac{5}{4}n$	$\frac{3}{2}n\log n+\frac{15}{8}n$	$\frac{3}{2}n\log n+\frac{71}{16}n$
PtNTT	$\frac{7}{4}n\log n+\frac{5}{4}n$	$\frac{15}{8}n\log n+\frac{5}{4}n$	$\frac{31}{16}n\log n+\frac{51}{16}n$	$\frac{63}{32}n\log n+\frac{73}{8}n$
KNTT (this work)	$\frac{3}{2}n\log n+\frac{3}{2}n$	$\frac{3}{2}n\log n+\frac{5}{4}n$	$\frac{3}{2}n\log n+\frac{15}{8}n$	$\frac{3}{2}n\log n+\frac{71}{16}n$

It is easy to check that the number of multiplications in KNTT is smallest when $\alpha = 2$. Moreover, it's obvious that the numbers of multiplications in KNTT for $\alpha \leq 3$ are less than the original NTT algorithm that needs $\frac{3}{2}n\log n+2n$ multiplications, which illustrates that they are more efficient than NTT. Since PtNTT is worse than the original NTT, KNTT behaves better than PtNTT. However, there is still a question that we cannot answer, that is, why 3KNTT is more efficient in practice than 2KNTT though the former has more multiplication operations than the latter in theory.

Compared with the NTT in [1], we find that the numbers of multiplications are exactly the same. The computational equivalence can also be specified in [11], which means that the advantage of NTT in [1] over other algorithms can also be achieved by our algorithm. However, we think there are still some advantages for KNTT compared to the NTT in [1], such as

- To implement KNTT we do not need change the original NTT algorithm but just add an implementation of the component-wise polynomial multiplication, whereas in [1], we have to change both the original NTT a bit and the component-wise polynomial multiplication. Therefore, it is very easy to implement KNTT with the program or device at hand that implements the original NTT, where in [1] we have to change the program or device. In addition, we would like to point out that the H-NTT algorithm presented in [11] has the advantage in employing the program or device designed for Kyber's NTT [1] instead of the original NTT, since it also utilizes the upper dividing approach as in our KNTT algorithm.
- Since KNTT just invokes the original NTT as its subroutine, any improvement or optimization on NTT can also be generalized to KNTT directly.
- We can run PtNTT algorithm in parallel easily as explained in Remark 1. It seems that just the point-wise multiplications can be parallelized easily for NTT in [1], which means that we can improve our implementation much more with multi-core CPU.

Furthermore, we believe there are some applications of our point of view, such as

- We can also apply the Karatsuba's idea to the polynomial multiplication in $\mathbb{Z}[x]$ using FFT. As a consequence, we may improve the efficiency of the algorithm too.
- Our point of view can also give a way to choose more rings that admits NTT for RLWE or MLWE-based cryptographic schemes, which makes the parameter selection more flexible and improves the efficiency of the scheme in practice. For example, a typical ring for RLWE-based cryptosystem is $\mathbb{Z}_q[x]/(x^n+1)$ where n is some power of 2 and q is a prime satisfying $2n|(q-1)$. Choosing n to be the power of 2 brings NTT to speedup the multiplications but restricts the parameter choice heavily. In fact, we can enlarges the choice of n while keeping the efficiency of multiplications by the idea of KNTT as follows. Suppose $\mathcal{R} = \mathbb{Z}_q[x]/(x^m+1)$ is a ring that admits NTT, then we can construct a ring $R = \mathcal{R}[y]/(f(y))$ where $f(y)$ is some polynomial over $\mathcal{R}$ with degree l. Then we can speedup the multiplication in R with the help of NTT in $\mathcal{R}$ and the corresponding degree $n = m \cdot l$ that is not necessarily a power of 2.

4 Conclusion

We present an improved NTT algorithm (i.e. KNTT), which not only weakens the restriction of modulus q but also has a better performance in efficiency when compared with the original NTT algorithm.

Acknowledgements. Thank the anonymous referees very much for their helpful comments. Thank Prof. Yunlei Zhao very much for his valuable suggestions on improving this paper and directing us to Nussbaumer's trick [17]. Thank Renzhang Liu for his help on the programming.

References

1. Alkım, E., Bilgin, Y.A., Cenk, M.: Compact and simple RLWE based key encapsulation mechanism. In: Schwabe, P., Thériault, N. (eds.) LATINCRYPT 2019. LNCS, vol. 11774, pp. 237–256. Springer, Cham (2019). https://doi.org/10.1007/978-3-030-30530-7_12
2. Bernstein, D.J.: Multidigit multiplication for mathematicians (2001). http://cr.yp.to/papers.html#m3
3. Bos, J.W., Costello, C., Naehrig, M., Stebila, D.: Post-quantum key exchange for the TLS protocol from the ring learning with errors problem. In: 2015 IEEE Symposium on Security and Privacy, pp. 553–570. IEEE (2015)
4. Bos, J., et al.: CRYSTALS-Kyber: a CCA-secure module-lattice-based KEM. In: IEEE European Symposium on Security and Privacy, pp. 353–367. IEEE (2018)
5. Brakerski, Z., Gentry, C., Vaikuntanathan, V.: Fully homomorphic encryption without bootstrapping. In: Innovations in Theoretical Computer Science, pp. 309–325 (2012)
6. Cook, S., Aanderaa, S.: On the minimum computation time of functions. Trans. Am. Math. Soc. **142**, 291–314 (1969)
7. Cooley, J.W., Tukey, J.W.: An algorithm for the machine calculation of complex Fourier series. Math. Comput. **19**(90), 297–301 (1965)
8. Hoffstein, J., Pipher, J., Silverman, J.H.: NTRU: a ring-based public key cryptosystem. In: Buhler, J.P. (ed.) ANTS 1998. LNCS, vol. 1423, pp. 267–288. Springer, Heidelberg (1998). https://doi.org/10.1007/BFb0054868
9. Karatsuba, A.: Multiplication of multidigit numbers on automata. Sov. Phys. Dokl. **7**, 595–596 (1963)
10. Karatsuba, A.A., Ofman, Y.: Multiplication of many-digital numbers by automatic computers. In: Doklady Akademii Nauk, vol. 145, pp. 293–294. Russian Academy of Sciences (1962)
11. Liang, Z., et al.: Number theoretic transform: generalization, optimization, concrete analysis and applications. In: Wu, Y., Yung, M. (eds.) Inscrypt 2020. LNCS, vol. 12612, pp. 415–432. Springer, Cham (2021). https://doi.org/10.1007/978-3-030-71852-7_28
12. Lyubashevsky, V.: Lattice signatures without trapdoors. In: Pointcheval, D., Johansson, T. (eds.) EUROCRYPT 2012. LNCS, vol. 7237, pp. 738–755. Springer, Heidelberg (2012). https://doi.org/10.1007/978-3-642-29011-4_43
13. Lyubashevsky, V., Micciancio, D., Peikert, C., Rosen, A.: SWIFFT: a modest proposal for FFT hashing. In: Nyberg, K. (ed.) FSE 2008. LNCS, vol. 5086, pp. 54–72. Springer, Heidelberg (2008). https://doi.org/10.1007/978-3-540-71039-4_4
14. Lyubashevsky, V., Peikert, C., Regev, O.: On ideal lattices and learning with errors over rings. In: Gilbert, H. (ed.) EUROCRYPT 2010. LNCS, vol. 6110, pp. 1–23. Springer, Heidelberg (2010). https://doi.org/10.1007/978-3-642-13190-5_1
15. Lyubashevsky, V., Seiler, G.: NTTRU: truly fast NTRU using NTT. IACR Trans. Cryptogr. Hardw. Embed. Syst. **2019**(3), 180–201 (2019)
16. Moenck, R.T.: Practical fast polynomial multiplication. In: Proceedings of the Third ACM Symposium on Symbolic and Algebraic Computation, pp. 136–148. ACM (1976)
17. Nussbaumer, H.J.: Fast polynomial transform algorithms for digital convolution. IEEE Trans. Acoust. Speech Sig. Process. **28**, 205–215 (1980)
18. Pan, Y., Li, H., Xie, T., Liu, Z., Yang, Z., Zhu, Y.: TALE: a lattice-based public key encryption scheme (2020). https://sfjs.cacrnet.org.cn/upload/5db41c6543be3.rar

19. Pöppelmann, T., Alkim, E., Ducas, L., Schwabe, P.: NewHope: algorithm specifications and supporting documentation (version 1.0.3). NIST Post-Quantum Cryptography Standardization Process (2019)
20. Regev, O.: On lattices, learning with errors, random linear codes, and cryptography. J. ACM (JACM) **56**(6), 34 (2009)
21. Shor, P.W.: Algorithms for quantum computation: discrete logarithms and factoring. In: 35th Annual Symposium on Foundations of Computer Science - FOCS, pp. 124–134 (1994)
22. Langlois, A., Stehlé, D.: Worst-case to average-case reductions for module lattices. Des. Codes Crypt. **75**(3), 565–599 (2014). https://doi.org/10.1007/s10623-014-9938-4
23. Toom, A.: The complexity of a scheme of functional elements realizing the multiplication of integers. Dokl. Akad. Nauk SSSR **3**(3), 496–498 (1963)
24. Zhou, S., et al.: Preprocess-then-NTT technique and its applications to Kyber and NewHope. In: Guo, F., Huang, X., Yung, M. (eds.) Inscrypt 2018. LNCS, vol. 11449, pp. 117–137. Springer, Cham (2019). https://doi.org/10.1007/978-3-030-14234-6_7
25. Zhu, Y., Liu, Z., Pan, Y.: When NTT meets Karatsuba: preprocess-then-NTT technique revisited. Cryptology ePrint Archive: Report 2019/1079 (2019). https://eprint.iacr.org/2019/1079.pdf

Predicting the Concrete Security of LWE Against the Dual Attack Using Binary Search

Shuaigang Li[1,2,3], Xianhui Lu[1,2,3](✉), Jiang Zhang[2], Bao Li[1,3], and Lei Bi[1,3]

[1] SKLOIS, Institute of Information Engineering, CAS, Beijing, China
{lishuaigang,luxianhui}@iie.ac.cn
[2] State Key Laboratory of Cryptology, P.O. Box 5159, Beijing 100878, China
[3] School of Cyber Security, University of Chinese Academy of Sciences, Beijing, China

Abstract. The dual attack is widely used in the concrete security estimation of the learning with errors (LWE) problem. Predicting the concrete security of LWE against the dual attack, i.e., the minimal cost of the dual attack, is a constrained optimization problem. However, there is no complete theoretical analysis. We fill in this gap by proving that, for almost all LWE instances used in the design of public-key cryptographic schemes, the cost of the dual attack can be considered as a U-shape function. Therefore, we can predict the minimal cost with binary search. We use the binary search to predict the concrete security of all LWE-based algorithms in NIST-PQC and the experimental results demonstrate the accuracy of the binary search.

Keywords: Concrete security of LWE · Dual attack · Binary search

1 Introduction

The learning with errors (LWE) problem [34] is widely used in the design of nearly all types of lattice-based cryptographic schemes. The concrete security estimation of LWE is one of the most important tasks in the research and standardization of lattice-based cryptographic schemes. There are many attacks used in the concrete security estimation of LWE, including the algebraic attack [3,12], combinatorial attack [6,16,26,28], decoding attack [31], dual attack [2,10,32], primal attack [7,14] and hybrid attack [19,27,35]. For LWE instances $(\mathbf{A}, \mathbf{b} = \mathbf{As} + \mathbf{e}) \in \mathbb{Z}_q^{m\times n} \times \mathbb{Z}_q^m$ with a large n, it's almost impossible to run a real attack. Therefore, predicting the concrete security of LWE against a specific attack, i.e., the minimal cost of the attack, is very necessary. In this paper, we focus on the dual attack, which is one of the most efficient attacks [4,10]. Considering that the dual attack doesn't exploit the algebraic structure of RLWE and MLWE, we regard them as LWE.

The dual attack reduces the Decision-LWE problem to the (Inhomogeneous) Short Integer Solution ((I)SIS) problem [1], which can be solved by lattice reduction algorithms (e.g., BKZ). The dual attack has two categories: Micciancio and

D. Gao et al. (Eds.): ICICS 2021, LNCS 12919, pp. 265–282, 2021.
https://doi.org/10.1007/978-3-030-88052-1_16

Regev dual attack (MR dual attack) [32], and Albrecht dual attack [2]. Each dual attack consists of the following two steps:

1. Construct a lattice which reduces the Decision-LWE problem to the (I)SIS problem.
2. Run BKZ to find a set of short lattice vectors which are used to solve the (I)SIS problem.

The cost of the dual attack is determined by the parameters of the lattice and BKZ. The lattice is relevant to the scaling factor[1] c and the dimension d of the lattice. According to the Core-SVP model introduced in [10], the cost of BKZ is determined by the block size β. In addition, to guarantee the dual attack is meaningful, d and β must satisfy certain constraints. Consequently, predicting the minimal cost of each dual attack is a constrained optimization problem of which the cost and constraints are shown in Table 1.

Table 1. The cost and constraints of each dual attack.

Attack	Cost	Constraints
MR dual attack	$T(d, \beta)$	$\beta \leq d,\ d > n,\ d \in \mathbb{Z}^+,\ \beta \in \mathbb{Z}^+$
Albrecht dual attack	$T(c, d, \beta)$	

To predict the minimal costs, there exist some works about c, d and β. Given LWE instances $(\mathbf{A}, \mathbf{b} = \mathbf{A}\mathbf{s} + \mathbf{e})$, c was chosen to balance the effects of $\mathbf{e}$ and $\mathbf{s}$ in [2]. Zhang et al. [36] also considered $c = \sigma_{\mathbf{e}}/\sigma_{\mathbf{s}}$ to balance the effects of $\mathbf{e}_i$ and $\mathbf{s}_i$, where $\sigma_{\mathbf{e}}$ (resp., $\sigma_{\mathbf{s}}$) is the standard deviation of $\mathbf{e}$ (resp., $\mathbf{s}$). To find the optimal integers d and β, one estimator [10] searches d and β exhaustively. However, another estimator [8] simplifies each cost by using the conclusion introduced in [32] that the optimal d is a function of β.

It's still a problem of providing a complete theoretical analysis to predict the minimal cost of each dual attack.

1.1 Our Contributions

In this paper, under some conditions (see Sect. 2), we predict the minimal cost of each dual attack using binary search by proving that the cost can be considered as a U-shape function of the BKZ block size β.

We obtain the U-shape functions by the following steps:

1. We prove that the optimal c is $\sigma_{\mathbf{e}}/\sigma_{\mathbf{s}}$ in Albrecht dual attack. Therefore, according to Table 1, each cost is a function of β and d.
2. We further prove that each cost can be considered as a U-shape function of β under the conditions above.

[1] The scaling factor c only appears in Albrecht dual attack.

We illustrate the second step by taking Albrecht dual attack and Kyber [13] as an example:

1. For a fixed β, the cost is a U-shape function of d (see Fig. 1).
2. The lowest points of U-shape functions form a U-shape function of β (see Fig. 2).

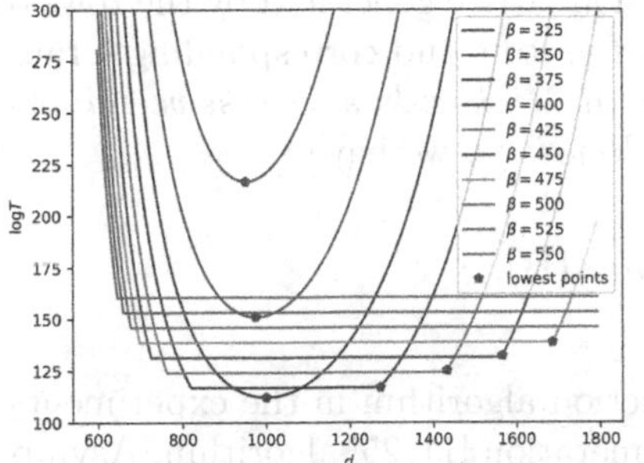

Fig. 1. The cost of MR dual attack with Kyber's parameters ($n = 512$, $q = 3329$, $\sigma_{\mathbf{e}} = \sigma_{\mathbf{s}} = 1$).

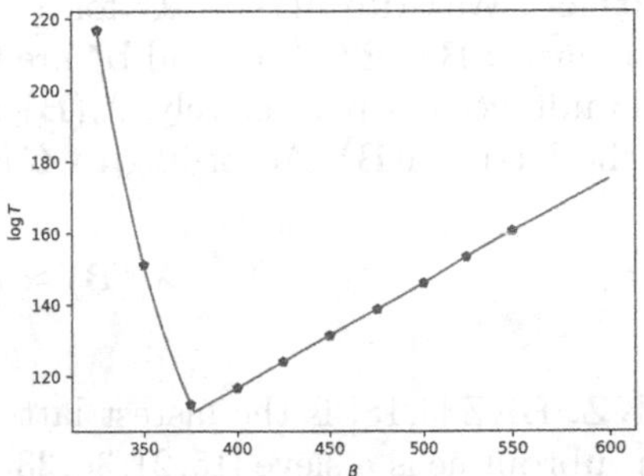

Fig. 2. The U-shape function of MR dual attack with Kyber's parameters.

Depending on the U-shape functions, we can predict the minimal costs using binary search. Moreover, we compare the minimal costs of MR and Albrecht dual attacks in certain situations.

We use the binary search to predict the concrete security of all LWE-based algorithms in NIST-PQC. The experimental results show that the minimal costs obtained by binary search are almost always the same as those obtained by exhaustive search, which demonstrates the rationality of the conditions (see Sect. 2) and the accuracy of the binary search.

1.2 Roadmap

Some relevant preliminaries are shown in Sect. 2. In Sect. 3, we provide the theoretical analysis of predicting the minimal cost of each dual attack. We compare the costs of the two dual attacks in Sect. 4. In Sect. 5, we provide the binary search to predict the concrete security of LWE.

2 Preliminaries

Logarithms are based on 2 and ln represents the natural logarithm. We denote vectors in lower-case bold letters (e.g., $\mathbf{a}$) and matrices in upper-case bold letters (e.g., $\mathbf{A}$). We write $\mathbf{a}^T$ and $\mathbf{A}^T$ for the transpose of vector $\mathbf{a}$ and matrix $\mathbf{A}$ respectively. We denote by $\mathbf{A}^{-1}$ (resp., $\mathrm{Vol}(\mathbf{A})$) the inversion (resp., determinant) of matrix $\mathbf{A}$. We write $\mathbf{A}_{a:b}$ for the rows $a, \cdots, b$ of matrix $\mathbf{A}$. $\langle \mathbf{v}, \mathbf{w} \rangle$ is the inner product of vectors $\mathbf{v}$ and $\mathbf{w}$. For a function f of x, f'_x or f' is the derivative of f. We write BKZ-β for BKZ with the block size β.

LWE. LWE instances $(\mathbf{A}, \mathbf{b} = \mathbf{As} + \mathbf{e}) \in \mathbb{Z}_q^{m \times n} \times \mathbb{Z}_q^m$ are sampled by choosing $\mathbf{A}$ uniformly at random and sampling $\mathbf{s}$ and $\mathbf{e}$ from two fixed distributions.

Search-LWE is to find $\mathbf{s}$, Decision-LWE is to distinguish LWE instances and the uniformly random one.

Lattice. We write $\Lambda(\mathbf{B}) \in \mathbb{R}^n$ for a d-dimension lattice generated by the rows of the matrix $\mathbf{B} \in \mathbb{R}^{n \times d}$. $\mathbf{b}_i$ and $\mathbf{b}_i^*$ are the basis vectors and corresponding Gram-Schmidt vectors respectively. $\lambda_i(\mathbf{B})$ is the i-th *Minkowski's successive minima* of the lattice $\Lambda(\mathbf{B})$. According to *Gaussian Heuristic*, we have

$$\lambda_1(\mathbf{B}) \approx \sqrt{\frac{n}{2\pi e}} \mathrm{Vol}^{\frac{1}{d}}(\mathbf{B}).$$

BKZ. BKZ [5,18] is the fastest lattice reduction algorithm in the experiments. Its subroutine is a sieve [15,21,30,33] or enumeration [11,25] algorithm. Asymptotically, the sieve algorithm is faster than enumeration algorithm, thus we consider sieve algorithm as the subroutine. The cost of β-dimension sieve algorithm is $2^{a\beta}$, where $a = 0.292$ [15] in the classical model and $a = 0.265$ [29] in the quantum model. According to the Core-SVP model [10], the cost of BKZ-β is $2^{a\beta}$ and BKZ provides $2^{0.2075\beta}$ short vectors which have the same length

$$\delta_0^d \mathrm{Vol}^{\frac{1}{d}}(\Lambda),$$

where δ_0 is the root-Hermite factor and d is the dimension of the lattice Λ. Chen [17] provided an approximate formula of δ_0 after running BKZ-β:

$$\delta_0 = (\frac{\beta}{2\pi e}(\pi\beta)^{\frac{1}{\beta}})^{\frac{1}{2(\beta-1)}}.$$

In certain cases, to clearly show the range of some parameters, we use the simplified formula[2] $\delta_0 = (\frac{\beta}{2\pi e})^{\frac{1}{2\beta}}$.

Lemma 1. *The dual attack can solve the Decision-LWE problem with advantage* $\epsilon = 4e^{-2\pi^2(\frac{\langle \mathbf{v}, \mathbf{b} \rangle}{q})^2}$, *where* $\mathbf{v}$ *is a short lattice vector obtained by BKZ-*β. *To amplify* ϵ *to at least* 0.5, *according to [10], one needs to repeat BKZ*

$$N = \max(1, \frac{1}{2^{0.2075\beta}\epsilon^2})$$

times[3]. *Consequently, the logarithm of the cost of the dual attack is*

$$\log T = \log(N \cdot 2^{a\beta}) = \max(a\beta, (a - 0.2075)\beta - 2\log\epsilon).$$

[2] The gap between the two formulas of δ_0 is very small (see Fig. 3 in Appendix A).

[3] In fact, the accurate value of N is $\max(1, \lceil \frac{1}{2^{0.2075\beta}\epsilon^2} \rceil)$. The gap of the concrete security obtained by these two numbers is at most 1 bit, therefore, we omit this gap.

Our Conditions. In Sect. 3, to simplify the theoretical analysis, we propose the following conditions:

1. d and β are positive real numbers and d is unlimited.
2. $\beta \geq 2\pi e^{2.5}$.
3. For each dual attack, we provide other conditions shown in Table 2.

Table 2. The attacks and corresponding conditions ($c = \sigma_{\mathbf{e}}/\sigma_{\mathbf{s}}$).

Attack	Conditions	Asymptotically
MR	$q^2 \geq \max(\frac{n \ln q}{274.5\sigma_{\mathbf{e}}^2 \ln(4\sigma_{\mathbf{e}} q)}, \frac{\sigma_{\mathbf{e}}^2 n \ln q}{\ln \frac{q}{4\sigma_{\mathbf{e}}}})$ and $q \geq \max(\frac{0.530}{\sigma_{\mathbf{e}}}, 8.5\sigma_{\mathbf{e}})$	$q^2 \geq O(n)$
Albrecht	$q^2 \geq \max(\frac{nc^4 \ln \frac{q}{c}}{274.5\sigma_{\mathbf{e}}^2 \ln \frac{4\sigma_{\mathbf{e}} q}{c^2}}, \frac{\sigma_{\mathbf{e}}^2 n \ln \frac{q}{c}}{\ln \frac{q}{4\sigma_{\mathbf{e}}}})$ and $q \geq \max(\frac{0.530c^2}{\sigma_{\mathbf{e}}}, 8.5\sigma_{\mathbf{e}})$	

Next, we analyze the rationality and necessity of the conditions above:

1. The first condition is often used to simplify the theoretical analysis. However, to predict the concrete security of LWE accurately, we don't use this condition in the actual prediction (see Sect. 5).
2. If the optimal β is smaller than $2\pi e^{2.5} \approx 77$, the concrete security of the algorithm is lower than 23 bits. This condition is proposed to guarantee that certain functions (e.g., $(\delta_0)'_\beta$) of β are monotonic.
3. The conditions in Table 2 can be asymptotically simplified as $q^2 \geq O(n)$ satisfied in almost all LWE instances used in the design of public-key cryptographic schemes.

3 Predicting the Minimal Cost of the Dual Attack

In this section, based on the conditions in Sect. 2, we prove that the cost of each dual attack can be considered as a U-shape function of β. Therefore, we can minimize each cost using binary search. As a side contribution, we find that the heuristic scaling factor $c = \frac{\sqrt{m}\sigma_{\mathbf{e}}}{\sqrt{n}\sigma_{\mathbf{s}}}$ is not optimal in Albrecht dual attack [2], which overestimates the cost of Albrecht dual attack.

The dual attack reduces the Decision-LWE problem to the (I)SIS problem. Specifically, given instances $(\mathbf{A}, \mathbf{b}) \in \mathbb{Z}_q^{m \times n} \times \mathbb{Z}_q^m$, where $\mathbf{b} = \mathbf{A}\mathbf{s} + \mathbf{e} \mod q$ or $\mathbf{b}$ is uniformly random, the dual attack can distinguish the two cases by finding short vectors

$$\mathbf{v} \in \{\mathbf{x} \in \mathbb{Z}^m | \mathbf{x}\mathbf{A} = \mathbf{0} \mod q\} \text{ or } (\mathbf{v}, \mathbf{w}) \in \{(\mathbf{x}, \mathbf{y}) \in \mathbb{Z}^m \times \frac{\mathbb{Z}^n}{c} | \mathbf{x}\mathbf{A} = c\mathbf{y} \mod q\}.$$

If $\mathbf{b} = \mathbf{A}\mathbf{s} + \mathbf{e} \mod q$ and the variances of $\mathbf{s}_i$ and $\mathbf{e}_i$ are small, then $\langle \mathbf{v}, \mathbf{b} \rangle = \mathbf{v}\mathbf{A}\mathbf{s} + \langle \mathbf{v}, \mathbf{e} \rangle \mod q$ is small. If $\mathbf{b}$ is uniformly random, then $\langle \mathbf{v}, \mathbf{b} \rangle \mod q$ is random and thus large.

The dual attack has two categories: MR dual attack [32] and Albrecht dual attack [2]. The lattice used in MR dual attack is

$$\Lambda_q^{\perp}(\mathbf{A}) = \{\mathbf{x} \in \mathbb{Z}^m | \mathbf{x}\mathbf{A} = \mathbf{0} \mod q\},$$

of which the basis is denoted by

$$\begin{pmatrix} q\mathbf{I}_n & \mathbf{0} \\ -\mathbf{A}_{n+1:m}\mathbf{A}_{1:n}^{-1} & \mathbf{I}_{m-n} \end{pmatrix}.$$

The dimension and volume of $\Lambda_q^{\perp}(\mathbf{A})$ are $d = m$ and q^n respectively. According to Lemma 1, the logarithm of the cost of MR dual attack is:

$$\log T = \max(a\beta, (a - 0.2075)\beta + 4\pi^2\sigma_{\mathbf{e}}^2(\log e)\delta_0^{2d}q^{\frac{2(n-d)}{d}} - 4). \qquad (1)$$

We can see that the cost of MR dual attack is irrelevant to $\mathbf{s}$, therefore, Albrecht dual attack [2] is proposed to balance the impacts of $\mathbf{s}$ and $\mathbf{e}$. The lattice used in Albrecht dual attack is

$$\Lambda_q^{\perp}(\mathbf{A}, c) = \{(\mathbf{x}, \mathbf{y}) \in \mathbb{Z}^m \times \frac{\mathbb{Z}^n}{c} | \mathbf{x}\mathbf{A} = c\mathbf{y} \mod q\},$$

of which the basis [24] is

$$\begin{pmatrix} \mathbf{0} & \frac{q}{c}\mathbf{I}_n \\ \mathbf{I}_m & \frac{\mathbf{A}}{c} \end{pmatrix}.$$

The dimension and volume of $\Lambda_q^{\perp}(\mathbf{A}, c)$ are $d = m + n$ and $(\frac{q}{c})^n$ respectively. According to Lemma 1, the logarithm of the cost of Albrecht dual attack is:

$$\log T_1 = \max(a\beta, (a - 0.2075)\beta + 4\pi^2\frac{((d-n)\sigma_{\mathbf{e}}^2 + nc^2\sigma_{\mathbf{s}}^2)\delta_0^{2d}}{q^2 d}(\frac{q}{c})^{\frac{2n}{d}}\log e - 4).$$

Moreover, for each dual attack, the following constraints hold:

1. $\beta \leq d$, which is required in BKZ.
2. $d > n$. If $d \leq n$, the lattice is $q\mathbf{I}_d$ (resp., $\frac{q}{c}\mathbf{I}_d$) in MR (resp., Albrecht) dual attack. In either case, the lattice will be irrelevant to LWE instances.

Based on the constraints above, to predict the minimal costs, we need to find the optimal c, d and β. There are analyses on c and d:

1. Due to $\langle \mathbf{v}, \mathbf{b} \rangle = \langle \mathbf{w}, c\mathbf{s} \rangle + \langle \mathbf{v}, \mathbf{e} \rangle \mod q$, $c = \frac{\sqrt{m}\sigma_{\mathbf{e}}}{\sqrt{n}\sigma_{\mathbf{s}}}$ was chosen to make $|\langle \mathbf{w}, c\mathbf{s} \rangle| \approx |\langle \mathbf{v}, \mathbf{e} \rangle|$ in [2]. Meanwhile, $c = \frac{\sigma_{\mathbf{e}}}{\sigma_{\mathbf{s}}}$ was also considered to make $\frac{|\langle \mathbf{w}, c\mathbf{s} \rangle|}{n} \approx \frac{|\langle \mathbf{v}, \mathbf{e} \rangle|}{m}$ in [36].
2. In MR dual attack [32], the optimal d was proved to be $\sqrt{\frac{n \ln q}{\ln \delta_0}}$ without considering the constraints above.

Following their works, we simplify the costs by two steps:

1. In Sect. 3.1, we prove that $c = \frac{\sigma_{\mathbf{e}}}{\sigma_{\mathbf{s}}}$ is optimal. Therefore, the cost of Albrecht dual attack can be simplified as a function of d and β.
2. Considering the constraints above, under the conditions in Sect. 2 we prove each cost can be regarded as a U-shape function of β in Sect. 3.2. Consequently, we can predict the minimal costs using binary search.

3.1 The Optimal Scaling Factor

In this Section, we prove that the optimal c is $\frac{\sigma_e}{\sigma_s}$.

The cost of Albrecht dual attack is $T_1 = 2^{\max(a\beta, f_A(c,d,\beta))}$, where

$$f_A = (a - 0.2075)\beta + 4\pi^2 \frac{((d-n)\sigma_e^2 + nc^2\sigma_s^2)\delta_0^{2d}}{q^2 d} (\frac{q}{c})^{\frac{2n}{d}} \log e - 4.$$

Defining $f_{A1} = 4\pi^2 \frac{\delta_0^{2d} \log e}{q^2 d} q^{\frac{2n}{d}}$, we have

$$(f_A)'_c = 2n(d-n) f_{A1} c^{\frac{-2n}{d}-1} (c^2\sigma_s^2 - \sigma_e^2)/d.$$

Therefore, for any fixed β and d, the optimal c is $c^* = \frac{\sigma_e}{\sigma_s}$. In this case, the logarithm of the cost can be simplified as a function of β and d:

$$\log T_1 = \max(a\beta, (a - 0.2075)\beta + 4\pi^2\sigma_e^2(\log e)\delta_0^{2d} q^{\frac{2(n-d)}{d}} (c^*)^{\frac{-2n}{d}} - 4). \quad (2)$$

3.2 The Optimal Dimension and Block Size

In this section, we prove each cost can be considered as a U-shape function of β under the conditions in Sect. 2. Therefore, we can predict their minimal costs using binary search.

To show how the costs change with d and β, we take Albrecht dual attack and Kyber algorithm as an example. From the experimental results, we observe that:

1. For a fixed β, the cost is a U-shape function of d (see Fig. 1).
2. The lowest points of U-shape functions form a U-shape function of β (see Fig. 2).

Based on the observations, we present the complete analysis in Theorem 1 and 2 under the conditions. These conditions and their rationality are shown in Sect. 2. Based on the analysis, we prove the costs can be considered as U-shape functions of β and we can predict the minimal costs using binary search.

Theorem 1. *Given LWE instances $(\mathbf{A}, \mathbf{b}) \in \mathbb{Z}_q^{m\times n} \times \mathbb{Z}_q^m$, based on the conditions in Sect. 2, we can predict the minimal cost of MR dual attack*

$$T_{min} = 2^{a\beta^*}$$

using binary search when $d = \sqrt{\frac{n \ln q}{\ln \delta_0}}$, where β^* is the unique zero of the monotonically decreasing function

$$4\pi^2\sigma_e^2(\log e)\delta_0^{4d}/q^2 - 0.2075\beta - 4.$$

Proof. Predicting the minimum of the cost

$$\log T = \max(a\beta, (a - 0.2075)\beta + 4\pi^2\sigma_e^2(\log e)\delta_0^{2d} q^{\frac{2(n-d)}{d}} - 4) \triangleq \max(a\beta, f(d,\beta))$$

is a constrained optimization problem. We can solve it by the following steps:

1. To compare $a\beta$ and $f(d,\beta)$, we first find d^* (the optimal d) without considering the constraints, where d^* is a function of β.
2. When $\beta \in (\beta_1, \beta_2]$, where $d^*(\beta_1) = n$ and $d^*(\beta_2) = \beta_2$, we prove $d^*(\beta)$ satisfies the constraints above.
3. For $\beta \in (\beta_1, \beta_2]$, based on the conditions in Sect. 2, we prove that the cost is a U-shape function of β, therefore, we can obtain the local minimum T^l_{min} using binary search.
4. When $\beta \leq \beta_1$ and $\beta > \beta_2$, we prove that the cost is bigger than T^l_{min}.

Therefore, the global minimum T_{min} is T^l_{min}. In the following, we interpret the above four steps in details:

Step 1. Since $f'_d = 4\pi^2\sigma_{\mathbf{e}}^2(\log e)\delta_0^{2d} q^{\frac{2(n-d)}{d}}(2\ln\delta_0 - \frac{2n}{d^2}\ln q)$, we have $d^* = \sqrt{\frac{n\ln q}{\ln\delta_0}}$ is the optimal, i.e.,

$$q^{\frac{n}{d^*}} = \delta_0^{d^*}. \tag{3}$$

Step 2. Since δ_0 is a decreasing function of β (see Lemma 2), we have d^* is an increasing function of β. Therefore, for $\beta \in (\beta_1, \beta_2]$, we have $d^*(\beta) > d^*(\beta_1) = n$, i.e., the first constraint can be satisfied. For the second constraint, defining

$$h(\beta) = \frac{d^*}{\beta} = \sqrt{\frac{n\ln q}{\beta^2\ln\delta_0}},$$

we have $h(\beta_2) = 1$. Because $\beta^2\ln\delta_0$ is an increasing function of β (see Lemma 3), we have h is a decreasing function of β. Therefore, for $\beta \in (\beta_1, \beta_2]$, we have $h(\beta) \geq h(\beta_2) = 1 \iff d^*(\beta) \geq \beta$, i.e., the second constraint is satisfied.

Step 3. To compare $a\beta$ and $f(d^*,\beta)$, we define $g_1 = f(d^*,\beta)$ and $g = g_1 - a\beta$. According to Eq. (3), we have

$$g = 4\pi^2\sigma_{\mathbf{e}}^2(\log e)\delta_0^{2d^*} q^{\frac{2n}{d^*}-2} - 0.2075\beta - 4 = 4\pi^2\sigma_{\mathbf{e}}^2(\log e) q^{\frac{4n}{d^*}-2} - 0.2075\beta - 4.$$

Because d^* is an increasing function of β, we have g is a decreasing function of β. Based on the conditions in Table 2, we prove (see Lemmas 4 and 5)

$$g(\beta_1) > 0 \text{ and } g(\beta_2) < 0.$$

Consequently, there exists a unique $\beta^* \in (\beta_1, \beta_2)$ such that $g(\beta^*) = 0$ and

$$\log T = \begin{cases} g_1(\beta) & \beta_1 \leq \beta < \beta^* \\ a\beta & \beta^* \leq \beta \leq \beta_2 \end{cases}.$$

When $\beta \in [2\pi e^{2.5}, \beta^*)$ where $2\pi e^{2.5} \leq \beta_1$, g_1 is a decreasing function of β (see Lemma 7) and $a\beta$ is an increasing function of β. Therefore, for $\beta \in (\beta_1, \beta_2]$, the cost is a U-shape function of β and we can obtain the local minimum $T^l_{min} = 2^{a\beta^*}$ using binary search.

Step 4. When $\beta \leq \beta_1$, we have $d^*(\beta) \leq n$, i.e., the first constraint can't be satisfied. Consequently, the optimal d is $n+1$ and

$$f(n+1,\beta) > f(d^*(\beta),\beta) = g_1(\beta) > g_1(\beta^*) = a\beta^*.$$

When $\beta > \beta_2$, $T \geq 2^{a\beta} > 2^{a\beta^*} = T^l_{min}$. Therefore, the local minimum T^l_{min} is the global minimum. □

In conclusion, we can predict the minimal cost of MR dual attack using binary search. In the same way, we analyze Albrecht dual attack in Theorem 2.

Theorem 2. *Given LWE instances* $(\mathbf{A},\mathbf{b}) \in \mathbb{Z}_q^{m\times n} \times \mathbb{Z}_q^m$, *based on the conditions in Sect. 2, we can predict the minimal cost of Albrecht dual attack*

$$2^{a\beta_A^*}$$

using binary search when $c = \frac{\sigma_{\mathbf{e}}}{\sigma_{\mathbf{s}}}$ *and* $d_A = \sqrt{\frac{n \ln \frac{q}{c}}{\ln \delta_0}}$, *where* β_A^* *is the unique zero of the monotonically decreasing function*

$$4\pi^2\sigma_{\mathbf{e}}^2(\log e)\delta_0^{4d_A}/q^2 - 0.2075\beta - 4.$$

4 Theoretical Comparison Between the Costs of MR Dual Attack and Albrecht Dual Attack

In this section, we compare the costs of the two dual attacks in Theorem 3 and 4 without using the conditions in Sect. 2. Specifically, we prove Albrecht dual attack isn't slower than MR dual attack when $\sigma_{\mathbf{s}} \leq \sigma_{\mathbf{e}}$ and MR dual attack isn't slower than Albrecht dual attack in certain situations. Thus one dual attack is not definitely faster than the other.

To accurately compare the costs of the two dual attacks, we use the accurate costs in Eq. 1 and 2, i.e., the logarithm of the cost of MR dual attack is

$$\log T_{MR} = \max(a\beta_{MR}, (a-0.2075)\beta_{MR} + 4\pi^2\sigma_{\mathbf{e}}^2(\log e)\delta_0^{2d_{MR}}q^{\frac{2(n-d_{MR})}{d_{MR}}} - 4)$$

and the logarithm of the cost of Albrecht dual attack is

$$\log T_A = \max(a\beta_A, (a-0.2075)\beta_A + 4\pi^2\sigma_{\mathbf{e}}^2(\log e)\delta_0^{2d_A}q^{\frac{2(n-d_A)}{d_A}}(c^*)^{\frac{-2n}{d_A}} - 4).$$

We compare the two costs in Theorem 3 and 4.

Theorem 3. *Albrecht dual attack isn't slower than MR dual attack when* $\sigma_{\mathbf{s}} \leq \sigma_{\mathbf{e}}$.

Proof. We assume that attackers can get m_{max} LWE samples, where m_{max} is a constant or $m_{max} = +\infty$. For any dimension d_{MR} and block size β_{MR} in MR dual attack, where $d_{MR} \in [n+1, m_{max}]$ and $\beta_{MR} \leq d_{MR}$, Albrecht dual attack can obtain the same dimension d_{MR} and block size β_{MR} because $d_A \in [n+1, m_{max}+n]$ and $\beta_A \leq d_A$. Then

$$\sigma_{\mathbf{s}} \leq \sigma_{\mathbf{e}} \Longleftrightarrow c^* \geq 1 \Longleftrightarrow T_{MR}(d_{MR},\beta_{MR}) \geq T_A(d_{MR},\beta_{MR}).$$

Therefore, Albrecht dual attack isn't slower than MR dual attack. □

Suppose that d^*_{MR} and β^*_{MR} are the optimal dimension and block size in MR dual attack when the number of LWE samples is unlimited.

Theorem 4. *MR dual attack isn't slower than Albrecht dual attack when $\sigma_{\mathbf{s}} > \sigma_{\mathbf{e}}$ and attackers can obtain $d^*_{MR} - n$ LWE samples.*

Proof. When attackers obtain $d^*_{MR} - n$ LWE samples, the dimension of the lattice can be d^*_{MR} in MR dual attack. Assuming that d^*_A and β^*_A are the optimal parameters in Albrecht dual attack, we have

$$\sigma_{\mathbf{s}} > \sigma_{\mathbf{e}} \Longleftrightarrow c^* < 1 \Longleftrightarrow T_A(d^*_A, \beta^*_A) \geq T_{MR}(d^*_A, \beta^*_A) \geq T_{MR}(d^*_{MR}, \beta^*_{MR}).$$

Therefore, MR dual attack isn't slower than Albrecht dual attack. □

For the other situation that $\sigma_{\mathbf{s}} > \sigma_{\mathbf{e}}$ and the number of LWE samples obtained by attackers is less than d^*_1, which dual attack is the fastest depends on the number of LWE samples that attackers can obtain.

In conclusion, given LWE samples, which dual attack is the fastest depends on $\frac{\sigma_{\mathbf{e}}}{\sigma_{\mathbf{s}}}$ and the number of LWE samples that attackers can obtain.

5 Experiments

In the binary search in Sect. 3, we assume that integers β and d are real numbers and d is unlimited. Consequently, in Appendix **C**, we fine-tuned the binary search to make it more accurate. We use the binary search to predict the concrete security of all LWE-based algorithms in NIST-PQC and the experimental results demonstrate the accuracy of the binary search.

In this section, we take the classical attack model and NIST algorithms (RLizard [20], Saber [23], Kyber, NewHope [9] and Dilithium [22]) as examples to show the accuracy of the binary search by the following two steps:

1. Verify whether the scaling factor $c^* = \frac{\sigma_{\mathbf{e}}}{\sigma_{\mathbf{s}}}$ is optimal in Sect. 5.1.
2. Verify whether the output of the binary search is accurate in Sect. 5.2.

We write m_{max}, β^*, m^* and t^* for the number of LWE samples that attackers can obtain, the optimal β, the optimal m and the minimal cost respectively.

5.1 The Optimal Scaling Factor

To compare the two heuristic choices of c ($\frac{\sigma_{\mathbf{e}}}{\sigma_{\mathbf{s}}}$ and $\frac{\sqrt{m}\sigma_{\mathbf{e}}}{\sqrt{n}\sigma_{\mathbf{s}}}$), we take RLizard as an example. In experiments, we also choose some other c's and then obtain each minimal cost by searching all possible β's and m's. The experimental results (see Table 3) verify the correctness of the theoretical analysis on c:

1. The cost is a U-shape function of c and the optimal c is $\frac{\sigma_{\mathbf{e}}}{\sigma_{\mathbf{s}}}$.
2. The heuristic choice $\frac{\sqrt{m}\sigma_{\mathbf{e}}}{\sqrt{n}\sigma_{\mathbf{s}}}$ overestimates the minimal cost. As for RLizard ($n = q = 2048$), the minimal cost is overestimated by 3.5 bits.

Table 3. Verify the optimal scaling factor with RLizard parameter.

n	q	σ_s	σ_e	m_{max}	c	Model	β^*	m^*	t^*(bits)
2048	2048	0.283	1.12	2048	$0.2 \cdot \sigma_e/\sigma_s$	Albrecht	1920	1230	560.6
					$0.6 \cdot \sigma_e/\sigma_s$		1684	950	491.7
					$1 \cdot \sigma_e/\sigma_s$		**1656**	**988**	**483.6**
					$1.4 \cdot \sigma_e/\sigma_s$		1666	978	486.5
					$1.8 \cdot \sigma_e/\sigma_s$		1685	921	492.0
					$\frac{\sqrt{m}\sigma_e}{\sqrt{n}\sigma_s}$		**1668**	**1053**	**487.1**

5.2 The Output of the Binary Search

We use the binary search to predict the concrete security of all LWE-based algorithms in NIST-PQC. The experimental results show that the minimal costs obtained by binary search are the same as those obtained by exhaustive search. In this section, we take Kyber, Saber, NewHope and Dilithium as examples to show the accuracy of the binary search.

The experimental results are shown in Table 4, 5, 6 and 7, where the blue results are obtained by searching all possible β's and m's, and the magenta results are obtained by the binary search. Through the experimental results, we find

1. The blue results and the magenta results are the same, i.e., the parameters (β and m) obtained by the binary search are the optimal and the output of the binary search is the minimal cost.
2. In our experiments, Albrecht dual attack is faster than MR dual attack under the situation $\sigma_s \le \sigma_e$, which accords with Theorem 3.

Table 4. The security of Kyber.

n	q	σ_s	σ_e	m_{max}	Model	β^*	m^*	t^*(bits)
512	3329	1	1	768	MR	422/422	768/768	123.2/123.2
					Albrecht	377/377	470/470	110.1/110.1
768	3329	1	1	1024	MR	766/766	1024/1024	223.7/223.7
					Albrecht	617/617	692/692	180.4/180.4
1024	3329	1	1	1280	MR	1151/1151	1280/1280	336.1/336.1
					Albrecht	866/866	837/837	252.9/252.9

Table 5. The security of Saber.

n	q	σ_s	σ_e	m_{max}	Model	β^*	m^*	t^*(bits)
512	8192	1.58	1.58	512	Albrecht	378/378	508/508	110.4/110.4
768	8192	1.41	1.41	768	Albrecht	602/602	724/724	175.8/175.8
1024	8192	1.22	1.22	1024	Albrecht	816/816	946/946	238.3/238.3

Table 6. The security of NewHope.

n	q	σ_s	σ_e	m_{max}	Model	β^*	m^*	t^*(bits)
512	12289	2	2	1024	MR	382/382	1017/1017	111.5/111.5
					Albrecht	380/380	570/570	111.0/111.0
1024	12289	2	2	2048	MR	879/879	2032/2032	256.7/256.7
					Albrecht	879/879	1008/1008	256.7/256.7

Table 7. The security of Dilithium.

n	q	σ_s	σ_e	m_{max}	Model	β^*	m^*	t^*(bits)
768	8380417	3.74	3.74	1024	MR	596/596	1024/1024	174.0/174.0
					Albrecht	340/340	840/840	99.3/99.3
1024	8380417	3.16	3.16	1280	MR	968/968	1280/1280	282.9/282.9
					Albrecht	482/482	1128/1128	140.7/140.7
1280	8380417	2	2	1536	MR	1209/1209	1536/1536	353.0/353.0
					Albrecht	595/595	1267/1267	173.8/173.8

6 Conclusion

In this paper, we prove that, for almost all LWE instances used in the design of public-key cryptographic schemes, the cost of each dual attack can be considered as a U-shape function of the block size. Therefore, we can predict their minimal costs using binary search. We use the binary search to predict the concrete security of all LWE-based algorithms in NIST-PQC and the experimental results demonstrate the accuracy of the binary search and the correctness of our theoretical analysis.

Acknowledgements. We thank the anonymous reviewers for their helpful comments and suggestions. Xianhui Lu and Shuaigang Li are supported by the National Natural Science Foundation of China (Grant No. 61972391). Jiang Zhang is supported by the National Natural Science Foundation of China (Grant Nos. 62022018, 61932019), the National Key Research and Development Program of China (Grant No. 2018YFB0804105).

A Comparison of δ_0 and the Simplified δ_0

B The Proof of Some Lemmas

Lemma 2. *δ_0 is a decreasing function when $\beta \geq 2\pi e^{2.5}$.*

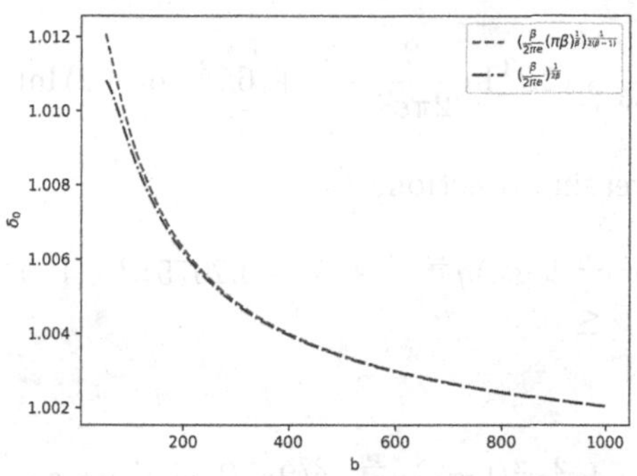

Fig. 3. Comparison of δ_0 and the simplified δ_0.

Proof. When $\beta \geq 2\pi e^{2.5}$, we have

$$(\ln \delta_0)'_\beta = \frac{1}{2(\beta-1)^2}(\ln \frac{2\pi e^2}{\beta} - \frac{1+(2\beta-1)\ln(\pi\beta)}{\beta^2}) < 0,$$

thus δ_0 is a decreasing function. □

Lemma 3. *$\beta^2 \ln \delta_0$ is an increasing function when $\beta \geq 2\pi e^{2.5}$.*

Proof. When $\beta \geq 2\pi e^{2.5}$, we have

$$(\beta^2 \ln \delta_0)'_\beta = \frac{\beta^2}{2(\beta-1)^2}(\frac{\beta-2}{\beta}\ln\frac{\beta}{2\pi e} + 1 - \frac{1+\ln(\pi\beta)}{\beta^2}) > 0,$$

thus $\beta^2 \ln \delta_0$ is an increasing function. □

Lemma 4. *$g(\beta_1) > 0$ when $q^2 \geq \frac{n \ln q}{274.5\sigma_{\mathbf{e}}^2 \ln(4\sigma_{\mathbf{e}} q)}$ and $q \geq \frac{0.530}{\sigma_{\mathbf{e}}}$.*

Proof. Define $a = \frac{4\pi^2(\log e)\sigma_{\mathbf{e}}^2 q^2 - 4}{0.2075} \approx 274.5\sigma_{\mathbf{e}}^2 q^2$. We have

$$q \geq \frac{0.530}{\sigma_{\mathbf{e}}} \Longrightarrow a \geq 2\pi e^{2.5},$$

$$q^2 \geq \frac{n \ln q}{274.5\sigma_{\mathbf{e}}^2 \ln(4\sigma_{\mathbf{e}} q)} \geq \frac{2n \ln q}{274.5\sigma_{\mathbf{e}}^2 \ln \frac{a}{2\pi e}}, \text{ i.e., } h(a) \approx \sqrt{\frac{2n \ln q}{a \ln \frac{a}{2\pi e}}} \leq 1.$$

Since $h(a) \leq 1 = h(\beta_2)$ and h is a decreasing function of β, therefore, we have

$$a \geq \beta_2 \Longrightarrow a > \beta_1 \Longleftrightarrow g(\beta_1) = 4\pi^2\sigma_{\mathbf{e}}^2 q^2 \log e - 0.2075\beta_1 - 4 > 0.$$ □

Lemma 5. *$g(\beta_2) < 0$ when $q^2 \geq \frac{\sigma_{\mathbf{e}}^2 n \ln q}{\ln \frac{q}{4\sigma_{\mathbf{e}}}}$ and $q > 8.5\sigma_{\mathbf{e}}$.*

Proof. This proof is similar to that of Lemma 4.

Lemma 6. *$(\delta_0)'_\beta$ is an increasing function when $\beta \geq 2\pi e^{2.5}$.*

Proof. When $\beta \geq 2\pi e^{2.5}$, we have

$$(\ln \delta_0)''_{\beta\beta} = \frac{1}{2(\beta-1)^3\beta^3}(2\beta^3 \ln \frac{\beta}{2\pi e^2} - \beta^3 + (6\beta^2 - 6\beta + 2)\ln(\pi\beta) - \beta^2 + 7\beta - 3) > 0,$$

thus $(\delta_0)'_\beta$ is an increasing function. □

Lemma 7. *$g_1 = 4\pi^2\sigma_{\mathbf{e}}^2(\log e)q^{\frac{4n}{d^*}-2} + (a - 0.2075)\beta - 4$ is a decreasing function of β when $2\pi e^{2.5} \leq \beta \leq \beta^*$.*

Proof. Compute

$$(g_1)'_\beta = 4\pi^2\sigma_{\mathbf{e}}^2(\log e)q^{\frac{4n}{d^*}-2}(2d^*(\ln \delta_0)'_\beta) + a - 0.2075,$$

$$(g_1)''_{\beta\beta} = 4\pi^2\sigma_{\mathbf{e}}^2(\log e)q^{\frac{4n}{d^*}-2}(2d^*(\ln \delta_0)'_\beta)((2d^* - \frac{1}{2\ln \delta_0})(\ln \delta_0)'_\beta + \frac{(\ln \delta_0)''_{\beta\beta}}{(\ln \delta_0)'_\beta}).$$

Since $(\ln \delta_0)'_\beta < 0$ (see Lemma 2), $(\ln \delta_0)''_{\beta\beta} > 0$ (See Lemma 6) and

$$2d^* - \frac{1}{2\ln \delta_0} = \frac{4d^* \ln \delta_0 - 1}{2\ln \delta_0} \overset{d^* \geq \beta}{>} \frac{(\beta/(2\pi e))^2 - 1}{2\ln \delta_0} > 0,$$

we have $(g_1)''_{\beta\beta} > 0$, i.e., $(g_1)'_\beta$ is an increasing function. Furthermore, for $\beta \in [2\pi e^{2.5}, \beta^*]$, we have

$$(g_1)'_\beta(\beta) < (g_1)'_\beta(\beta^*) < -0.2075\frac{d^*}{\beta^*}\ln \frac{\beta^*}{2\pi e^2} + a - 0.2075 < 0.$$

Consequently, for $2\pi e^{2.5} \leq \beta \leq \beta^*$, g_1 is a decreasing function of β. □

C The Binary Search

Based on the conditions in Sect. 2, Theorem 1 and 2 provide the binary search to predict the minimal costs of dual attacks. However, the first condition makes the binary search inaccurate. Therefore, we fine-tuned the binary search and obtain the more accurate binary search **Search-2** by the following steps:

1. Propose the binary search **Search-1** which doesn't rely on the conditions: d and β are real numbers.
2. Based on **Search-1**, propose the binary search **Search-2** which doesn't rely on the condition: d is unlimited.

We write β^* and d^* for the optimal β and d respectively in Theorem 1 and 2. To obtain the minimal costs accurately, we use the costs in Eq. 1 and 2, the cost of MR or Albrecht dual attack is

$$T = 2^{\max(f+a\beta, a\beta)},$$

where

$$f = 4\pi^2(\log e)\sigma_{\mathbf{e}}^2\delta_0^{2d}q^{\frac{2(n-d)}{d}} - 0.2075\beta - 4 \text{ or}$$
$$f = 4\pi^2(\log e)\sigma_{\mathbf{e}}^2\delta_0^{2d}q^{\frac{2(n-d)}{d}}(c^*)^{\frac{-2n}{d}} - 0.2075\beta - 4.$$

Moreover, we denote the optimal β and d by β_0^* and d_0^* (resp., β_1^* and d_1^*) when attackers can obtain unlimited (resp., m_{max}) LWE samples and define

$$f_0 = f(\beta, \lfloor d^*(\beta) \rfloor), f_1 = f(\beta, \lceil d^*(\beta) \rceil), T_0 = 2^{\max(f_0+a\beta, a\beta)} \text{ and } T_1 = 2^{\max(f_1+a\beta, a\beta)}.$$

Step 1. The binary search **Search-1** includes the following steps:

1. For each dual attack, we find the integers β_{i0} and β_{i1} ($i = 0, 1$) using binary search, which satisfy $\beta_{i0} - \beta_{i1} = 1$ and $f_i(\beta_{i0})f_i(\beta_{i1}) \leq 0$.
2. For each dual attack, the minimal cost is $T_0^{min} = 2^{t_{min}}$, where
$$t_{min} = \min(T_0(\beta_{00}), T_0(\beta_{01}), T_1(\beta_{10}), T_1(\beta_{11})).$$
Therefore, we obtain β_0^* and d_0 to minimize each cost.
3. We have $d_0^* = d_0$, when
$$\log T_0^{min} = \max(f(\beta_0^*, d_0) + a\beta_0^*, a\beta_0^*) = f(\beta_0^*, d_0) + a\beta_0^*.$$
Otherwise, the integer d_0^* is the smallest d satisfying $f(\beta_0^*, d) \leq 0$ and can be obtained using binary search because $f(\beta_0^*, d)$ is a decreasing function of d when $d < d_0$.

Consequently, if attackers can obtain unlimited number of LWE samples, we can obtain the minimal cost T_0^{min} and the optimal parameters (β_0^* and d_0^*) by the binary search **Search-1**.

Step 2. To obtain **Search-2**, we provide the following two lemmas. We denote the maximum of the dimension d by d_{max} and define $h = f(\beta, d_{max})$, $g = h + a\beta$.

Lemma 8. *For each attack, the optimal d is d_{max} when $d_{max} < d_0^*$.*

Proof. Define $d^*(\beta') = d_{max}$, we have $\beta_0^* > \beta'$ because $d_{max} < d_0^* \approx d^*(\beta_0^*)$. For $\beta > \beta'$, attackers can't obtain $d_0^*(\beta)$ LWE samples, in this case, d_{max} is the optimal d. For $\beta < \beta'$, attackers can't obtain the minimal cost. □

Lemma 9. *When $d_{max} < d_0^*$, we can obtain the logarithm of the minimal cost of each dual attack*

$$\log T_1^{min} = \begin{cases} g(\beta_2) & h(\beta_2) \geq 0 \\ \min(g(\beta_0), a\beta_1) & \textit{Otherwise} \end{cases}$$

using binary search, where $\beta_2 = d_{max}$, integers β_0 and β_1 satisfy $h(\beta_0)h(\beta_1) \leq 0$ and $\beta_0 - \beta_1 = 1$.

Proof. For each dual attack, h is a decreasing function of β. If $h(\beta_2) \geq 0$, we prove g is a decreasing function of β when $\beta \in (2\pi e^{2.5}, \beta_2]$, therefore, we have $\log T_1^{min} = g(\beta_2)$. If $h(\beta_2) < 0$, there is a real number $\beta'' \in [2\pi e^{2.5}, \beta_2)$ making $h(\beta'') = 0$. In this case, g is also a decreasing function[4] of β when $\beta \in [2\pi e^{2.5}, \beta'']$. Consequently, we can obtain $\log T_1^{min} = \min(g(\beta_1), a\beta_0)$ by finding the β_0 and β_1 using binary search. □

According to Lemma 9, we provide the binary search **Search-2**:

1. If $d_0^* \leq d_{max}$, T_0^{min} is also the minimal cost when attackers obtain m_{max} LWE samples.
2. If $d_0^* > d_{max}$, according to Lemma 9, we can obtain the minimal cost T_1^{min} and the optimal parameters (d_{max} and β_1^*).
3. When $d_0^* > d_{max}$, d_{max} may not be the unique optimal d to minimize the cost. Just like **Search-1**, we can obtain d_1^* (the smallest d to minimize the cost) using binary search.

References

1. Ajtai, M.: Generating hard instances of lattice problems (extended abstract). In: STOC, pp. 99–108. ACM (1996)
2. Albrecht, M.R.: On dual lattice attacks against small-secret LWE and parameter choices in HElib and SEAL. In: Coron, J.-S., Nielsen, J.B. (eds.) EUROCRYPT 2017. LNCS, vol. 10211, pp. 103–129. Springer, Cham (2017). https://doi.org/10.1007/978-3-319-56614-6_4
3. Albrecht, M.R., Cid, C., Faugère, J., Fitzpatrick, R., Perret, L.: Algebraic algorithms for LWE problems. ACM Commun. Comput. Algebra **49**(2), 62 (2015)
4. Albrecht, M.R., et al.: Estimate all the LWE, NTRU schemes! In: Catalano, D., De Prisco, R. (eds.) SCN 2018. LNCS, vol. 11035, pp. 351–367. Springer, Cham (2018). https://doi.org/10.1007/978-3-319-98113-0_19
5. Albrecht, M.R., Ducas, L., Herold, G., Kirshanova, E., Postlethwaite, E.W., Stevens, M.: The general sieve kernel and new records in lattice reduction. In: Ishai, Y., Rijmen, V. (eds.) EUROCRYPT 2019. LNCS, vol. 11477, pp. 717–746. Springer, Cham (2019). https://doi.org/10.1007/978-3-030-17656-3_25
6. Albrecht, M.R., Faugère, J.-C., Fitzpatrick, R., Perret, L.: Lazy modulus switching for the BKW algorithm on LWE. In: Krawczyk, H. (ed.) PKC 2014. LNCS, vol. 8383, pp. 429–445. Springer, Heidelberg (2014). https://doi.org/10.1007/978-3-642-54631-0_25
7. Albrecht, M.R., Göpfert, F., Virdia, F., Wunderer, T.: Revisiting the expected cost of solving uSVP and applications to LWE. In: Takagi, T., Peyrin, T. (eds.) ASIACRYPT 2017. LNCS, vol. 10624, pp. 297–322. Springer, Cham (2017). https://doi.org/10.1007/978-3-319-70694-8_11
8. Albrecht, M.R., Player, R., Scott, S.: On the concrete hardness of learning with errors. J. Math. Cryptol. **9**(3), 169–203 (2015)
9. Alkim, E., et al.: Newhope. Technical report, NIST (2019). https://csrc.nist.gov/projects/post-quantum-cryptography/round-2-submissions

[4] This proof is similar to Lemma 7.

10. Alkim, E., Ducas, L., Pöppelmann, T., Schwabe, P.: Post-quantum key exchange - a new hope. In: USENIX Security Symposium, pp. 327–343. USENIX Association (2016)
11. Aono, Y., Nguyen, P.Q.: Random sampling revisited: lattice enumeration with discrete pruning. In: Coron, J.-S., Nielsen, J.B. (eds.) EUROCRYPT 2017. LNCS, vol. 10211, pp. 65–102. Springer, Cham (2017). https://doi.org/10.1007/978-3-319-56614-6_3
12. Arora, S., Ge, R.: New algorithms for learning in presence of errors. In: Aceto, L., Henzinger, M., Sgall, J. (eds.) ICALP 2011. LNCS, vol. 6755, pp. 403–415. Springer, Heidelberg (2011). https://doi.org/10.1007/978-3-642-22006-7_34
13. Avanzi, R., et al.: Crystals-kyber. Technical report, NIST (2019). https://csrc.nist.gov/projects/post-quantum-cryptography/round-2-submissions
14. Bai, S., Galbraith, S.D.: Lattice decoding attacks on binary LWE. In: Susilo, W., Mu, Y. (eds.) ACISP 2014. LNCS, vol. 8544, pp. 322–337. Springer, Cham (2014). https://doi.org/10.1007/978-3-319-08344-5_21
15. Becker, A., Ducas, L., Gama, N., Laarhoven, T.: New directions in nearest neighbor searching with applications to lattice sieving. In: SODA, pp. 10–24. SIAM (2016)
16. Blum, A., Kalai, A., Wasserman, H.: Noise-tolerant learning, the parity problem, and the statistical query model. J. ACM **50**(4), 506–519 (2003)
17. Chen, Y.: Réduction de réseau et sécurité concrete du chiffrement completement homomorphe. Ph.D. thesis, Paris 7 (2013)
18. Chen, Y., Nguyen, P.Q.: BKZ 2.0: better lattice security estimates. In: Lee, D.H., Wang, X. (eds.) ASIACRYPT 2011. LNCS, vol. 7073, pp. 1–20. Springer, Heidelberg (2011). https://doi.org/10.1007/978-3-642-25385-0_1
19. Cheon, J.H., Hhan, M., Hong, S., Son, Y.: A hybrid of dual and meet-in-the-middle attack on sparse and ternary secret LWE. IEEE Access **7**, 89497–89506 (2019)
20. Cheon, J.H., et al.: Lizard. Technical report, NIST (2019). https://csrc.nist.gov/projects/post-quantum-cryptography/round-2-submissions
21. Ducas, L.: Shortest vector from lattice sieving: a few dimensions for free. In: Nielsen, J.B., Rijmen, V. (eds.) EUROCRYPT 2018. LNCS, vol. 10820, pp. 125–145. Springer, Cham (2018). https://doi.org/10.1007/978-3-319-78381-9_5
22. Ducas, L., et al.: Crystals-dilithium. Technical report, NIST (2019). https://csrc.nist.gov/projects/post-quantum-cryptography/round-2-submissions
23. D'Anvers, J.P., Karmakar, A., Roy, S.S., Vercauteren, F.: Saber. Technical report, NIST (2019). https://csrc.nist.gov/projects/post-quantum-cryptography/round-2-submissions
24. Espitau, T., Joux, A., Kharchenko, N.: On a dual/hybrid approach to small secret LWE. In: Bhargavan, K., Oswald, E., Prabhakaran, M. (eds.) INDOCRYPT 2020. LNCS, vol. 12578, pp. 440–462. Springer, Cham (2020). https://doi.org/10.1007/978-3-030-65277-7_20
25. Gama, N., Nguyen, P.Q., Regev, O.: Lattice enumeration using extreme pruning. In: Gilbert, H. (ed.) EUROCRYPT 2010. LNCS, vol. 6110, pp. 257–278. Springer, Heidelberg (2010). https://doi.org/10.1007/978-3-642-13190-5_13
26. Guo, Q., Johansson, T., Stankovski, P.: Coded-BKW: solving LWE using lattice codes. In: Gennaro, R., Robshaw, M. (eds.) CRYPTO 2015. LNCS, vol. 9215, pp. 23–42. Springer, Heidelberg (2015). https://doi.org/10.1007/978-3-662-47989-6_2
27. Howgrave-Graham, N.: A hybrid lattice-reduction and meet-in-the-middle attack against NTRU. In: Menezes, A. (ed.) CRYPTO 2007. LNCS, vol. 4622, pp. 150–169. Springer, Heidelberg (2007). https://doi.org/10.1007/978-3-540-74143-5_9

28. Kirchner, P., Fouque, P.-A.: An improved BKW algorithm for LWE with applications to cryptography and lattices. In: Gennaro, R., Robshaw, M. (eds.) CRYPTO 2015. LNCS, vol. 9215, pp. 43–62. Springer, Heidelberg (2015). https://doi.org/10.1007/978-3-662-47989-6_3
29. Laarhoven, T.: Search problems in cryptography: from fingerprinting to lattice sieving. Ph.D. thesis, Eindhoven University of Technology (2015)
30. Laarhoven, T.: Sieving for shortest vectors in lattices using angular locality-sensitive hashing. In: Gennaro, R., Robshaw, M. (eds.) CRYPTO 2015. LNCS, vol. 9215, pp. 3–22. Springer, Heidelberg (2015). https://doi.org/10.1007/978-3-662-47989-6_1
31. Lindner, R., Peikert, C.: Better key sizes (and attacks) for LWE-based encryption. In: Kiayias, A. (ed.) CT-RSA 2011. LNCS, vol. 6558, pp. 319–339. Springer, Heidelberg (2011). https://doi.org/10.1007/978-3-642-19074-2_21
32. Micciancio, D., Regev, O.: Lattice-based cryptography. In: Bernstein, D.J., Buchmann, J., Dahmen, E. (eds.) Post-Quantum Cryptography, pp. 147–191. Springer, Heidelberg (2009). https://doi.org/10.1007/978-3-540-88702-7_5
33. Micciancio, D., Voulgaris, P.: Faster exponential time algorithms for the shortest vector problem. In: SODA, pp. 1468–1480. SIAM (2010)
34. Regev, O.: On lattices, learning with errors, random linear codes, and cryptography. In: STOC, pp. 84–93. ACM (2005)
35. Wunderer, T.: Revisiting the hybrid attack: improved analysis and refined security estimates. IACR Cryptology ePrint Archive 2016/733 (2016). http://eprint.iacr.org/2016/733
36. Zhang, J., Yu, Yu., Fan, S., Zhang, Z., Yang, K.: Tweaking the asymmetry of asymmetric-key cryptography on lattices: KEMs and signatures of smaller sizes. In: Kiayias, A., Kohlweiss, M., Wallden, P., Zikas, V. (eds.) PKC 2020. LNCS, vol. 12111, pp. 37–65. Springer, Cham (2020). https://doi.org/10.1007/978-3-030-45388-6_2

Small Leaks Sink a Great Ship: An Evaluation of Key Reuse Resilience of PQC Third Round Finalist NTRU-HRSS

Xiaohan Zhang[1,2,3], Chi Cheng[1,2,3(✉)], and Ruoyu Ding[1,2,3]

[1] School of Computer Science, China University of Geosciences, Wuhan 430074, China
chengchi@cug.edu.cn

[2] State Key Laboratory of Cryptology, P.O. Box 5159, Beijing 100878, China

[3] Guangxi Key Laboratory of Trusted Software, Guilin University of Electronic Technology, Guilin 541004, China

Abstract. NTRU is regarded as an appealing finalist due to its long history against all known attacks and relatively high efficiency. In the third round of NIST competition, the submitted NTRU cryptosystem is the merger of NTRU-HPS and NTRU-HRSS. In 2019, Ding et al. have analyzed the case when the public key is reused for the original NTRU scheme. However, NTRU-HRSS selects coefficients in an arbitrary way, instead of fixed-weight sample spaces in the original NTRU and NTRU-HPS. Therefore, their method cannot be applied to NTRU-HRSS. To address this problem, we propose a full key mismatch attack on NTRU-HRSS. Firstly, we find a longest chain which helps us in recovering the following coefficients. Next, the most influential interference factors are eliminated by increasing the weight of targeted coefficients. In this step, we adaptively select the weights according to the feedbacks of the oracle to avoid errors. Finally, experiments show that we succeed in recovering all coefficients of the secret key in NTRU-HRSS with a success rate of 93.6%. Furthermore, we illustrate the trade-off among the success rate, average number of queries, and average time. Particularly, we show that when the success rate is 93.6%, it has the minimum number of queries at the same time.

Keywords: Post-quantum cryptography · Lattice based cryptography · NTRU · Public key reuse · Key mismatch attack

1 Introduction

Under the threat of rapid development of quantum computers [16], the current public key algorithms which base their security on number theoretic problems will no longer be safe. For example, the RSA and DH algorithms relying on integer factorization and discrete logarithm problems could be broken as shown in Shor's pioneer paper [30]. To thwart attacks from quantum computers, the

D. Gao et al. (Eds.): ICICS 2021, LNCS 12919, pp. 283–300, 2021.
https://doi.org/10.1007/978-3-030-88052-1_17

cryptography community has prompted to look for a new cryptosystem, which is called post-quantum cryptography (PQC) [7].

The National Institute of Standards and Technology (NIST) has started a project to select and evaluate PQC algorithms against both classical and quantum computers ever since 2016 [22]. The second round NIST PQC standardization process has been completed on July, 2020 [1]. On the finalists, the lattice-based public key encryption (PKE) or key encapsulation mechanism (KEM) algorithms draw significant attention, since there are 3 out of 4 candidates, KYBER [3], SABER [12], and NTRU [6]. NIST aims to standardize at most one of them when the third round ends. Among them, NTRU has been regarded as a compelling one due to its long history against known attacks and relatively high efficiency [1].

Currently, it can be noted that in the widely adopted Internet standards, the key reuse mode is commonly used. For example, in the released Transport Layer Security (TLS) 1.3 [29], the key pair in the pre-shared key mode is reused. However, key reuse may cause attacks in lattice-based key exchange [19]. In general, key reuse attacks can be divided into signal leakage attacks [8,13] and key mismatch attacks [10]. The main reason for the signal leakage attack is that if the key is reused, the relevant signal information used for key recovery leaks the relevant information of the secret key. Meanwhile, the key mismatch attack is to query the two communication parties whether the shared keys match or not, analyzing the feedbacks to recover the secret key.

Nowadays, a series of key mismatch attacks have been successively proposed. In [10], a key mismatch attack was proposed by Ding et al. on the one pass case of [11], in which no information leaked by the signal function was used. Later, Bauer et al. [5] proposed a key mismatch attack against a PQC second round candidate NewHope [2]. In [24], Qin et al. showed that the recovery in Bauer et al. was incomplete, and then proposed an effective key recovery scheme. Okada et al. followed closely, and in [23] they further improved Qin et al.'s method. Later, the work of [15] gave a key mismatch attack on another PQC second round candidate LAC. In [25], a key mismatch attack is proposed against Kyber. Băetu et al. proposed a classical key mismatch attack as well as a quantum key recovery [4]. In [26] Qin et al. gave a systematic approach to find bounds of key mismatch attacks against all the NIST candidate KEMs.

Unlike the protocols based on Ring Learning with Errors (RLWE) problem [21] or Modular Learning with Errors (MLWE) problem [20], the NTRU cryptosystem submitted to the NIST [6] is operated in a different polynomial ring which modulo $x^n - 1$. Therefore, these attacks proposed by Ding et al. [10], Qin et al. [24] or Okada et al. [23] cannot be directly applied to the NTRU cryptosystem [6]. The main reason is that NTRU lacks the structure of affine transformation, making it difficult to recover the secret key using the previous method.

In 2019, Ding et al. [9] proposed a key mismatch attack on the original NTRU scheme [17]. As we know, the coefficients of the secret key in NTRU belong to $\{-1, 0, 1\}$ and there is a longest chain of consequent coefficients that consists of either consecutive 1's or consecutive –1's of a secret key at least. With the longest chain, they proposed an elegant method, which is claimed to recover all the coefficients in the secret key.

However, their method cannot be directly applied to the current whole NTRU cryptosystem [6]. The NTRU cryptosystem submitted to the third round of NIST competition [6] is a merger of NTRU-HPS [17] and NTRU-HRSS [18]. One of the most important differences is that they compute on cyclotomic polynomials $\mathbf{\Phi}_1 = x - 1$ and $\mathbf{\Phi}_n = x^{n-1} + x^{n-2} + \cdots + 1$, instead of $x^n - 1$ in the original NTRU. Another important difference is that NTRU-HPS is similar to the original NTRU scheme, which still selects coefficients from fixed-weight sample spaces. While NTRU-HRSS selects coefficients in an arbitrary way. Therefore, Ding et al.'s method still works for NTRU-HPS, but cannot be applied to NTRU-HRSS.

Contributions. In this paper, we propose a complete key mismatch attack on NTRU-HRSS. The main contributions of this paper include:

1. We investigate the resilience of the NTRU-HRSS KEM under a misuse case: we assume that the same key is reused for multiple key establishments and an attacker can use a key mismatch oracle.
2. Unlike the direct recovery of secret key in Ding et al.'s method, we recover the product of a secret key and a cyclotomic polynomial, which is also the reason why Ding et al.'s method cannot be applied directly. Specifically, we first find a longest chain. After that, we increase the weight of targeted coefficients to eliminate the most influence of disturbances. Considering that the introduction of weight may lead to the errors in the recovery, we adaptively select the weights according to the feedbacks of the oracle to avoid errors.
3. As verified by the experiments, our improved method can recover all the coefficients in the secret key with a probability of 93.6%. Moreover, by evaluating the trade-off between the success rate and average number of queries, we can achieve minimum number of queries with a success rate of 93.6% at the same time. Furthermore, as shown in [28], we can utilize side-channel assisted our proposed method to attack the CCA-secure NTRU-HRSS KEM.

Organization of this Paper. In Sect. 2, we introduce the basic notions and describe the NTRU-HRSS KEM. In Sect. 3, we propose an improved key mismatch attack on NTRU-HRSS KEM. We give the experimental results and illustrate the trade-off among the success rate, average number of queries, average time in Sect. 4. Finally, the conclusion is given in Sect. 5.

2 Preliminaries

2.1 Notations

In NTRU, n, p and q are coprime integers. We denote the i-th cyclotomic polynomial by $\mathbf{\Phi}_i$. Specifically, $\mathbf{\Phi}_n = x^{n-1} + x^{n-2} + \cdots + 1$, $\mathbf{\Phi}_1 = x - 1$, and $\mathbf{\Phi}_1\mathbf{\Phi}_n = x^n - 1$. $\mathbb{Z}_q$ represents the integer ring modulo q. Let $\mathbb{Z}_q[x]$ represent a polynomial ring, in which all polynomial coefficients are selected from $\mathbb{Z}_q$.

We further define the polynomial rings $\mathcal{R}_q = \mathbb{Z}_q[x]/(x^n-1)$, $\mathcal{R}'_q = \mathbb{Z}_q[x]/(\boldsymbol{\Phi}_n)$, and $\mathcal{R}'_p = \mathbb{Z}_p[x]/(\boldsymbol{\Phi}_n)$. Here, all polynomials are in bold. A polynomial $\mathbf{P}$ in $\mathcal{R}_q$ is of degree at most $n-1$ with coefficients in $\mathbb{Z}_q$. If a polynomial $\mathbf{P}'$ belongs to $\mathcal{R}'_q$, it is a polynomial of degree of $n-2$ with coefficients $\mathbf{P}'[i]$ belonging to the set $\mathbb{Z}_q$, where $\mathbf{P}'[i]$ $(0 \le i \le n-2)$ represents the ith coefficient of the polynomial $\mathbf{P}'$. $\mathbf{P}$ and $\mathbf{P}'$ can also be represented as a vector with n and $n-1$ coordinates, respectively. For a real number x, the operation $\lceil x \rceil$ represents the smallest integer not less than x.

NTRU was originally presented as a probabilistic public key encryption (PPKE) scheme in [17]. In the third round NTRU submission, PPKE is replaced with the deterministic public key encryption (DPKE) scheme and all aspects of the designs are unified except for the use of fixed-weight sampling. Specifically, the probability of occurrence of –1, 0 and 1 are $\frac{85}{256}$, $\frac{86}{256}$, $\frac{85}{256}$, and we can easily sample them from $(\sum_{i=0}^{7} 2^i b_i) \bmod 3$. Here b_i is randomly selected from $\{0, 1\}$.

2.2 NTRU-HRSS KEM

Table 1. The CPA version of the NTRU-HRSS KEM

Alice		Bob
$\mathbf{f} \in \mathbf{F}_+$, $\mathbf{g} \in \mathbf{F}_+$		
$\mathbf{f}_q \leftarrow \mathbf{f}^{-1} \in \mathcal{R}'_q$		
$\mathbf{f}_p \leftarrow \mathbf{f}^{-1} \in \mathcal{R}'_p$		
$\mathbf{h} \leftarrow p\mathbf{g}\boldsymbol{\Phi}_1\mathbf{f}_q \in \mathcal{R}_q$		
$\mathbf{h}_q \leftarrow \mathbf{h}^{-1} \in \mathcal{R}'_q$	$\xrightarrow{\mathbf{h}}$	$\mathbf{r} \in \mathcal{R}'_p$, $\mathbf{m} \in \mathcal{R}'_p$
$\mathbf{a} \leftarrow \mathbf{c}\mathbf{f} \in \mathcal{R}_q$	$\xleftarrow{\mathbf{c}}$	$\mathbf{c} \leftarrow \mathbf{r}\mathbf{h} + \mathrm{Lift}(\mathbf{m}) \in \mathcal{R}_q$
$\mathbf{m}' \leftarrow \mathbf{a}\mathbf{f}_p \in \mathcal{R}'_p$		
$\mathbf{r}' \leftarrow (\mathbf{c} - \mathrm{Lift}(\mathbf{m}'))\mathbf{h}_q \in \mathcal{R}'_q$		
if $(\mathbf{r}', \mathbf{m}') \in \mathcal{R}'_p \times \mathcal{R}'_p$		
Return$(\mathbf{r}', \mathbf{m}', 0)$;		
else		
Return$(0, 0, 1)$;		

The most important definitions in the NTRU-HRSS KEM are shown as below.

Definition 1. *The Lift function Lift:* $\mathcal{R}'_p \to \mathcal{R}_q$ *is defined as* $\boldsymbol{P}' = \mathrm{Lift}(\boldsymbol{m})$,

$$\boldsymbol{P}' = \boldsymbol{m}(\boldsymbol{\Phi}_1^{-1} \bmod (p, \boldsymbol{\Phi}_n))\boldsymbol{\Phi}_1. \tag{1}$$

Definition 2. *Non-negative-correlation:*

$$\mathbf{F}_+ = \{\mathbf{P} \in \mathcal{R}'_p : \langle x\mathbf{P}, \mathbf{P} \rangle \geq 0\}. \tag{2}$$

In NTRU-HRSS, $n = 701$, $q = 8192$, and $p = 3$ are employed. It consists of three parts:

(1) Alice selects $\mathbf{f}$ and $\mathbf{g}$ uniformly at random from $\mathbf{F}_+$. Then she computes the inverses of $\mathbf{f}$ in $\mathcal{R}'_q$ and $\mathcal{R}'_p$ as $\mathbf{f}_q$ and $\mathbf{f}_p$. Next she computes the public key $\mathbf{h} \leftarrow p\mathbf{g}\boldsymbol{\Phi}_1\mathbf{f}_q$ and the inverse of $\mathbf{h}$ in $\mathcal{R}'_q$. Finally, she sends $\mathbf{h}$ to Bob.
(2) After receiving $\mathbf{h}$, Bob selects $\mathbf{r}$ and the shared key $\mathbf{m}$ uniformly at random from $\mathcal{R}'_p$. Then he calculates the ciphertext $\mathbf{c} \leftarrow \mathbf{rh} + \mathrm{Lift}(\mathbf{m})$. Subsequently, he sends $\mathbf{c}$ to Alice.
(3) When Alice receives $\mathbf{c}$, she calculates $\mathbf{a} \leftarrow \mathbf{cf}$, $\mathbf{m}' \leftarrow \mathbf{af}_p$ and $\mathbf{r}' \leftarrow (\mathbf{c} - \mathrm{Lift}(\mathbf{m}'))\mathbf{h}_q$. In the end, she checks whether $(\mathbf{r}', \mathbf{m}')$ in message space or not.

2.3 The Key Mismatch Attack Oracle $\mathcal{O}$

Algorithm 1: The Oracle $\mathcal{O}$

Input: $\mathbf{c}, \mathbf{m}$
Output: 1 or 0
$\mathbf{a} \leftarrow \mathbf{cf} \in \mathcal{R}_q$
$\mathbf{m}' \leftarrow \mathbf{af}_p \in \mathcal{R}'_p$
$\mathbf{r}' \leftarrow (\mathbf{c} - \mathrm{Lift}(\mathbf{m}'))\mathbf{h}_q) \in \mathcal{R}'_q$
if $(r', m') \in \mathcal{R}'_p \times \mathcal{R}'_p$ *and* $m = m'$ **then**
    Return 1
else
    Return 0

In the process of key mismatch attack on NTRU-HRSS, Alice is an honest server and the adversary $\mathcal{A}$ acts as Bob. For convenience, we build the Oracle $\mathcal{O}$ that plays the role of Alice. In addition, we suppose that public key $\mathbf{h}$ is reused and $\mathcal{A}$ has access to the Oracle $\mathcal{O}$ many times. The inputs of oracle $\mathcal{O}$ are $\mathbf{c}$ and $\mathbf{m}$. Afterwards, $\mathcal{O}$ calculates $\mathbf{a}$, $\mathbf{m}'$ and $\mathbf{r}'$ as depicted in Algorithm 1. Next, $\mathcal{O}$ first checks whether $(\mathbf{r}', \mathbf{m}')$ in the message space and then checks whether $\mathbf{m} = \mathbf{m}'$ holds. If both of them are yes, $\mathcal{O}$ outputs 1, and 0 otherwise. That is, when $\mathcal{O}$ outputs 1, $\mathbf{m}$ and $\mathbf{m}'$ match, otherwise $\mathbf{m}$ and $\mathbf{m}'$ mismatch. By observing the outputs of $\mathcal{O}$, $\mathcal{A}$ can get information about the secret key.

3 Our Proposed Attack

In this section, we propose an attack on NTRU-HRSS KEM. Firstly, we introduce the parameter choices of the adversary, then propose improvements in two following subsections, finally describe the complete attack.

3.1 Parameter Choices of the Adversary

We recover $\mathbf{G} = \mathbf{g}\mathbf{\Phi}_1$ instead of $\mathbf{g}$ in Ding et al.'s method, and we say that $\mathcal{A}$ succeeds if he recovers any equivalent of $\mathbf{G}$, which is denoted as $\mathbf{G}'$.

The equivalent of G. $\mathbf{G}'$ can differ from $\mathbf{G}$ by a sign $s \in \{-1, 1\}$ and a shifting of its coefficients. The relationship between $\mathbf{G}'$ and $\mathbf{G}$ is shown as follows, for some integer $v \in \mathbb{N}$,

$$\begin{aligned} \mathbf{G}' &= s\sum_{i=0}^{n-1} \mathbf{G}[(i+v) \bmod n]x^i \\ &= sx^v \sum_{i=0}^{n-1} \mathbf{G}[i]x^i \\ &= sx^v\mathbf{G}. \end{aligned} \tag{3}$$

To launch this attack, $\mathcal{A}$ sets $\mathbf{m}$ as $\mathbf{0}$ and selects the proper $\mathbf{r}$. Then, $\mathcal{A}$ calculates $\mathbf{c}$. And $\mathbf{c}$ and $\mathbf{m}$ are sent to the oracle $\mathcal{O}$.

After receiving the inputs $\mathbf{c}$ and $\mathbf{m}$, $\mathcal{O}$ first calculates

$$\begin{aligned} \mathbf{a} &\equiv \mathbf{cf} & \pmod q \\ &\equiv \mathbf{rhf} + \mathrm{Lift}(\mathbf{m})\mathbf{f} & \pmod q \\ &\equiv \mathbf{rhf} & \pmod q \\ &\equiv p\mathbf{rg}\mathbf{\Phi}_1\mathbf{f}_q\mathbf{f} & \pmod q. \end{aligned} \tag{4}$$

Since $\mathbf{f}_q \in \mathcal{R}_q'$, $\mathbf{f}_q\mathbf{f} = (1 + \mathbf{t}\mathbf{\Phi}_n)$, where $t \in \mathbb{Z}$. Further, we have

$$\begin{aligned} \mathbf{a} &\equiv p\mathbf{rg}\mathbf{\Phi}_1(1 + \mathbf{t}\mathbf{\Phi}_n) & \pmod q \\ &\equiv p\mathbf{rg}\mathbf{\Phi}_1 & \pmod q \\ &\equiv p\mathbf{rG} & \pmod q \end{aligned} \tag{5}$$

For $i = 0, 1, \ldots, n-1$, $t \in \mathbb{Z}$, we get

$$\mathbf{a}[i] = \begin{cases} p(\mathbf{rG})[i] & \text{if } p(\mathbf{rG})[i] \in \left[-\frac{q}{2}, \frac{q}{2}\right], \\ p(\mathbf{rG})[i] - tq & \text{otherwise.} \end{cases} \tag{6}$$

Then we have

$$\begin{aligned} \mathbf{m}'[i] &\equiv (\mathbf{a}\mathbf{f}_p)[i] & \pmod p \\ &\equiv (\mathbf{a}[0]\mathbf{f}_p[i] + \cdots \mathbf{a}[n-1]\mathbf{f}_p[(i+1) \bmod n]) & \pmod p. \end{aligned} \tag{7}$$

Next, if all $p(\mathbf{rG})[i] \in \left[-\frac{q}{2}, \frac{q}{2}\right]$, the corresponding $\mathbf{m}'[i]$ is equal to

$$\begin{aligned} \mathbf{m}'[i] &\equiv p(\mathbf{rG})[0]\mathbf{f}_p[i] + \cdots p(\mathbf{rG})[n-1]\mathbf{f}_p[(i+1) \bmod n] \pmod p \\ &\equiv 0 \pmod p. \end{aligned} \tag{8}$$

Otherwise, if there is one $p(\mathbf{rG})[j] \notin \left[-\frac{q}{2}, \frac{q}{2}\right]$, for $j \in [0, n-1]$, then

$$\mathbf{m}'[i] \equiv -tq\mathbf{f}_p[(i-j) \bmod n] \not\equiv 0 \pmod{p}. \quad (9)$$

Since we set $\mathbf{m} = 0$, Eq. (9) means that $\mathbf{m}' \neq \mathbf{m}$ and the corresponding $\mathcal{O}$ outputs 0. Therefore, in order to recover the coefficients of $\mathbf{G}$, we only need to make $p(\mathbf{rG})[j] \notin [-\frac{q}{2}, \frac{q}{2}]$ by setting the proper coefficients of $\mathbf{r}$. Then, according to the output of $\mathcal{O}$, we can recover $\mathbf{G}$.

3.2 Finding a Longest Chain

After that, the remaining problem is how to recover $\mathbf{G}$ according to the output of $\mathcal{O}$. In NTRU-HRSS, the most crucial issue is finding a longest chain. To illustrate this issue, we first discuss the range of coefficients in $\mathbf{G}$.

$$\begin{aligned}\mathbf{G} &= \mathbf{g}\mathbf{\Phi}_1 \\ &= (\mathbf{g}[n-1] - \mathbf{g}[0]) + (\mathbf{g}[0] - \mathbf{g}[1])x + \cdots + (\mathbf{g}[n-2] - \mathbf{g}[n-1])x^{n-1},\end{aligned} \quad (10)$$

and for $i = 0, 1, \ldots n-1$,

$$\mathbf{G}[i] = \begin{cases} \mathbf{g}[n-1] - \mathbf{g}[0] & \text{if } i = 0, \\ \mathbf{g}[i-1] - \mathbf{g}[i] & \text{otherwise.} \end{cases} \quad (11)$$

According to Eq. (11), the sum of d consecutive coefficients in $\mathbf{G}$ is

$$\mathbf{G}[i] + \cdots + \mathbf{G}[i+d-1] = \begin{cases} \mathbf{g}[n-1] - \mathbf{g}[d-1] & \text{if } i = 0, \\ \mathbf{g}[i-1] - \mathbf{g}[i+d-1] & \text{otherwise,} \end{cases} \quad (12)$$

where $d \in [2, n]$.

For $i \in [0, n-1]$, $\mathbf{g}[i] \in [-1, 1]$, according to Eq. (11), $\mathbf{G}[i] \in [-2, 2]$. And according to Eq. (12), we can get $(\mathbf{G}[i] + \cdots + \mathbf{G}[i+d-1]) \in [-2, 2]$.

Specifically, when $d = 2$, $(\mathbf{G}[i] + \mathbf{G}[i+1]) \in [-2, 2]$. By simply adding the two consecutive coefficients, we can draw the first conclusion:

(1) In $\mathbf{G}$, $(\mathbf{G}[i], \mathbf{G}[i+1])$ isn't in {(1,2), (2,1), (–1, –2), (–2, –1), (–2,–2), (2,2)}. When $d = 3$, $(\mathbf{G}[i] + \mathbf{G}[i+1] + \mathbf{G}[i+2]) \in [-2, 2]$, i.e. $(\mathbf{G}[i], \mathbf{G}[i+1], \mathbf{G}[i+2])$ cannot be (1,1,1) or (–1, –1, –1). Therefore, we can similarly conclude that:

(2) There are at most two consecutive 1's or –1's in $\mathbf{G}$.

By denoting a chain $(2, -2, \ldots, 2 * (-1)^{k-1})$ with length k the k-chain, we have the following result.

Theorem 1. *When $k \leq 701$, the average number of times a k-chain occurs in G is $(\frac{85}{256})^k * (702 - k)$.*

Proof. From the second observation, we cannot find a longest chain consisting of consecutive 1's or –1's. Therefore, a longest k-chain consists of consecutive coefficients as $(2, -2, \ldots, 2 * (-1)^{k-1})$ in $\mathbf{G}$.

According to Eq. (11), for $i = 0, 1, \ldots n-1$, we note that when $\mathbf{G}[i] = 2$, it should be the case that $\mathbf{g}[i-1] = 1$, $\mathbf{g}[i] = -1$. Corresponding to this, when

$\mathbf{G}[i] = -2$, we have $\mathbf{g}[i-1] = -1$, $\mathbf{g}[i] = 1$. Thus, the occurrence probability of $(2, -2, \ldots, 2*(-1)^{k-1})$ in $\mathbf{G}$ is the same as that of $(-1, 1, \ldots, (-1)^{k-1})$ in $\mathbf{g}$. As we mentioned above, the probabilities of occurrences of –1, 0 and 1 are $\frac{85}{256}$, $\frac{86}{256}$, $\frac{85}{256}$, respectively.

Let $\mathcal{X}$ denote the event that a k-chain $(2, -2, \ldots, 2*(-1)^{k-1})$ occurs in $\mathbf{G}$. To calculate the average number of times a k-chain occurs in $\mathbf{G}$, we try to get the corresponding expectation $E_k(\mathcal{X})$. By dividing $\mathcal{X}$ into the subevents $\mathcal{X}_i$ $i = 0, \ldots, n-k$, where each $\mathcal{X}_i$ denotes the event that a k-chain $(2, -2, \ldots, 2*(-1)^{k-1})$ occurs in the i-th position of $\mathbf{G}$. Since $E_k(\mathcal{X}_i) = (\frac{85}{256})^k$ and recall that $n = 701$, from the property of Expectation, we have

$$E_k(\mathcal{X}) = \sum_{i=0}^{n-k} E_k(\mathcal{X}_i) = (\frac{85}{256})^k * (702 - k). \tag{13}$$

Table 2. The relationship between k and $E_k(\mathcal{X})$

k	2	3	4	5	6	7
$E_k(\mathcal{X})$	77.171	25.587	8.483	2.813	0.933	0.309

In Table 2, we show the relationship between k and $E_k(\mathcal{X})$, where k is selected from the set {2,3,4,5,6,7}. As we can see when $k = 6$, $E_k(\mathcal{X})$ is near 1. The results show that we can find a longest chain that consists of consecutive coefficients such as $(2, -2, \ldots, 2*(-1)^{k-1})$ in $\mathbf{G}$ when $k = 6$ with a high probability. Afterwards, we use the chain as an anchor to recover $\mathbf{G}$.

3.3 The Selection of Parameter r

In addition, in order to recover $\mathbf{G}$, the adversary $\mathcal{A}$ directly sets all coefficients of $\mathbf{r}$ as 0 except for the first few coefficients of $\mathbf{r}$. In NTRU-HRSS, while setting $\mathbf{r}$, we need to increase the weight of targeted coefficients.

As we stated above, the coefficients of $\mathbf{G}$ range from –2 to 2, and there are many disturbances to prevent us from recovering coefficients of $\mathbf{G}$ correctly. We take two adjacent coefficients of $\mathbf{G}$ as an illustration, including $5^2 = 25$ tuples. According to the first conclusion above, the tuples of the set {(1,2), (2,1), (–1, –2), (–2, –1), (–2, –2), (2,2)} do not exist in $\mathbf{G}$. Then, we can classify the remaining tuples in accordance with the summation of the two adjacent coefficients in Table 3. The tuples of equal summation interfere with each other's recovery. Concretely, when the summation is –2, the tuples (–2,0) and (0,–2) disturb the recovery of the tuple (–1, –1). Therefore, we need to make the sum of these tuples unequal to eliminate the disturbance by increasing the weight of some coefficients. Obviously, increasing the weight of 0 is useless, and increasing the weight of 1 or –1 is ineffective since 2 or –2 can get the double weight. Finally, we can only increase the weight of coefficients 2 and –2, which has proved to be effective.

Table 3. Different summation of the two adjacent coefficients

Summation	Tuple1	Tuple2	Tuple3	Tuple4	Tuple5
–2	(–2,0)	(0, –2)	(–1, –1)		
–1	(–2,1)	(1, –2)	(–1,0)	(0, –1)	
0	(–2,2)	(2, –2)	(–1,1)	(1, –1)	(0,0)
1	(–1,2)	(2, –1)	(0,1)	(1,0)	
2	(0,2)	(2,0)	(1,1)		

Additionally, the tuples of different summation can also interfere each other's recovery in Table 4. To recover the coefficients of $\mathbf{G}$ correctly, when $\mathbf{G}[i] = 0$, if $\mathbf{r}[i-1] \geq 0$, we set $\mathbf{r}[i] > 0$, and if $\mathbf{r}[i-1] < 0$, we set $\mathbf{r}[i] < 0$.

Table 4. Interference between tuples of different summation

Recovered tuple	Interference tuple1	Interference tuple2
(–2,0)	(–2,2)	(–2,1)
(0, –2)	(1, –2)	(2, –2)
(2,0)	(2, –2)	(2, –1)
(0,2)	(–1,2)	(–2,2)

For convenience, we define some symbols. Let num_1 denote the number of recovered coefficients with absolute value of 1 in $\mathbf{G}$, then num_2 denote the number of recovered coefficients with absolute value of 2 in $\mathbf{G}$ and w is the weight of whose absolute value is 2 in recovered coefficients of $\mathbf{G}$. G_s denotes the weighted sum of recovered coefficients in $\mathbf{G}$, which can be computed as $G_s = 2 * num_2 * w + 1 * num_1$. r_u denotes the unit value of $\mathbf{r}$ and $r_u > 0$.

If w is too large, the mismatch appears prematurely, and if it is too small, it is not enough to recover the target coefficients. To take a balance, we set the initial value of w to 4.

3.4 The Full Attack

In this subsection, we introduce our method to recover $\mathbf{G}$. Recall that we suppose the length of a longest chain that consists of consecutive coefficients such as $(2, -2, \ldots, 2 * (-1)^{k-1})$ in $\mathbf{G}$ is k.

The key mismatch attack consists of three steps. And the adversary $\mathcal{A}$ always sets $\mathbf{m}$ as $\mathbf{0}$ in each step.

Step 1: In this step, the adversary $\mathcal{A}$ recovers $(\mathbf{G}[0], \cdots, \mathbf{G}[k-1])$ and decides the value of k. For this purpose, he needs to find a longest chain in $\mathbf{G}$.

The parameter selections of $\mathbf{r}$ is shown as below.

For $l \geq 2$, $0 \leq i \leq l-1$, $\mathcal{A}$ sets $\mathbf{r} = (\mathbf{r}[0], \ldots, \mathbf{r}[l-1], 0, \ldots, 0)$,

$$\mathbf{r}[i] = \begin{cases} \left\lceil \dfrac{q}{2p * 2l} \right\rceil & \text{if } i \text{ is even,} \\ -\left\lceil \dfrac{q}{2p * 2l} \right\rceil & \text{if } i \text{ is odd.} \end{cases} \tag{14}$$

Since $\mathbf{a} \equiv p\mathbf{r}\mathbf{G} \pmod q$, for $i = 0, 1, \ldots n-1$,

$$\begin{aligned} \mathbf{a}[i] &\equiv p(\mathbf{r}[0]\mathbf{G}[i] + \cdots \mathbf{r}[n-1]\mathbf{G}[(i+1) \bmod n]) && \pmod q \\ &\equiv p(\mathbf{r}[0]\mathbf{G}[i] + \cdots \mathbf{r}[l-1]\mathbf{G}[(i-l+1) \bmod n]) && \pmod q. \end{aligned} \tag{15}$$

Note that when $l \leq k$, $|\mathbf{a}[i]| \equiv p * \left\lceil \frac{q}{2p*2l} \right\rceil * 2l > \frac{q}{2}$, which means $\mathcal{O}$ outputs 0, and when $l = k+1$, $|\mathbf{a}[i]| \equiv p * \left\lceil \frac{q}{2p*2(k+1)} \right\rceil * (2k+1) < \frac{q}{2}$, which means $\mathcal{O}$ outputs 1. Therefore, when $\mathcal{O}$ outputs 1, $\mathcal{A}$ can get $k = l - 1$.

Step 2: The adversary $\mathcal{A}$ has recovered $(\mathbf{G}[0], \ldots, \mathbf{G}[k-1])$ and he needs to recover $\mathbf{G}[k]$ in this step.

Algorithm 2: Find-w-1

Input: num_1, num_2
Output: w
Set $w = 4$, $G_s = \text{NULL}$, $temp = \text{NULL}$;
for $i := 1$ *to* 3 **do**
  $G_s = 2 * (num_2 + 1) * w + num_1$;
  $temp = \lceil \frac{q}{G_s * 2p} \rceil$;
  if $temp * (G_s - 2*w) * p \geq \frac{q}{2}$ *or* $\lceil \frac{\frac{q}{2} - temp*(G_s - 2*w)*p}{temp*p} \rceil < 2*w$ **then**
    $w = w - 1$;
  end
  else
    break;
  end
end
Return w

Step 2.1: The adversary $\mathcal{A}$ judges whether $(\mathbf{G}[k], \mathbf{G}[k+1])$ is (0,2) or (0, –2).

First of all, $\mathcal{A}$ sets the proper w in Algorithm 2. In this step, when $\mathcal{O}$ outputs 0, which demonstrates that $(\mathbf{G}[k], \mathbf{G}[k+1])$ is (0,2) or (0,–2). Hence, $\mathcal{A}$ needs to keep $\mathcal{O}$ output 1 before adding the tuple (0,2) or (0, –2). Also, the absolute value of the sum of two coefficients in the tuple must be 2. Otherwise, $\mathcal{A}$ needs to decrease w.

Then $\mathcal{A}$ computes the value of G_s. Since the recovered coefficients of $\mathbf{G}$ are $(\mathbf{G}[0], \mathbf{G}[1], \cdots, \mathbf{G}[k-1])$, and $(\mathbf{G}[k], \mathbf{G}[k+1])$ is (0,2) or (0, –2). Therefore, $num_2 = k+1$, $num_1 = 0$, $G_s = 2 * (k+1) * w$.

Next, $\mathcal{A}$ sets $\mathbf{r} = (\mathbf{r}[0], \ldots, \mathbf{r}[k-1], \mathbf{r}[k], \mathbf{r}[k+1], 0, \ldots, 0)$. For $0 \leq i \leq k-1$,

$$\mathbf{r}[i] = \begin{cases} \left\lceil \dfrac{q}{2p * G_s} \right\rceil * w & \text{if } \mathbf{G}[i] = 2, \\ -\left\lceil \dfrac{q}{2p * G_s} \right\rceil * w & \text{if } \mathbf{G}[i] = -2. \end{cases} \tag{16}$$

Specifically, $\mathcal{A}$ sets $\mathbf{r}[k]$ and $\mathbf{r}[k+1]$ as follows.

(1) When $\mathbf{G}[k-1] = -2$, $(\mathbf{G}[k], \mathbf{G}[k+1]) = (0{,}2)$, $\mathbf{r}[k] = \left\lceil \frac{q}{2p*G_s} \right\rceil$, $\mathbf{r}[k+1] = \left\lceil \frac{q}{2p*G_s} \right\rceil * w$. If $\mathcal{O}$ outputs 0, $\mathcal{A}$ recovers $(\mathbf{G}[k], \mathbf{G}[k+1])$ as (0,2). Otherwise $(\mathbf{G}[k], \mathbf{G}[k+1])$ isn't (0,2).

(2) When $\mathbf{G}[k-1] = 2$, $(\mathbf{G}[k], \mathbf{G}[k+1]) = (0,-2)$, $\mathbf{r}[k] = -\left\lceil \frac{q}{2p*G_s} \right\rceil$, $\mathbf{r}[k+1] = -\left\lceil \frac{q}{2p*G_s} \right\rceil * w$. If $\mathcal{O}$ outputs 0, $\mathcal{A}$ recovers $(\mathbf{G}[k], \mathbf{G}[k+1])$ as $(0, -2)$. Otherwise $(\mathbf{G}[k], \mathbf{G}[k+1])$ isn't $(0, -2)$.

When $(\mathbf{G}[k], \mathbf{G}[k+1])$ is neither (0,2) nor (0, –2), according to Eq. (11),

$$\mathbf{G}[k] = \mathbf{g}[k-1] - \mathbf{g}[k], \tag{17}$$

and $\mathbf{g}[k-1]$ is known, so the adversary $\mathcal{A}$ recovers $\mathbf{G}[k]$ in {-1,0} or {1,0} in turn. Specifically, when $\mathbf{G}[k-1] = 2$, $\mathbf{g}[k-1] = -1$, $\mathbf{g}[k] \in \{-1, 0, 1\}$, according to Eq. (17), $\mathbf{G}[k] \in \{0, -1, -2\}$. Since the length of a longest chain that consists of consecutive coefficients such as $(2, -2, \ldots, 2*(-1)^{k-1})$ in $\mathbf{G}$ is k, then $\mathbf{G}[k] \neq -2$, $\mathbf{G}[k] \in \{-1, 0\}$. Similarly, when $\mathbf{G}[k-1] = -2$, $\mathbf{G}[k] \in \{1, 0\}$.

Step 2.2: When $(\mathbf{G}[k], \mathbf{G}[k+1])$ is neither (0,2) nor (0,–2), $\mathcal{A}$ recovers $\mathbf{G}[k]$ in {-1,0} or {1,0} in turn.

Algorithm 3: Find-w-2

Input: num_1, num_2
Output: w

Set $w = 4$, $G_{s_1} = \text{NULL}$, $G_{s_2} = \text{NULL}$;
for $i := 1$ *to* 3 **do**
  $G_{s_1} = 2 * num_2 * w + num_1 + 1$;
  $G_{s_2} = 2 * num_2 * w + num_1 + 2$;
  if $\lceil \frac{q}{G_{s_1}*2p} \rceil = \lceil \frac{q}{G_{s_2}*2p} \rceil$ *or* $\lceil \frac{q}{G_{s_1}*2p} \rceil * (G_{s_1} - 1) * p \geq \frac{q}{2}$ **then**
    $w = w - 1$;
  end
  else
    break;
  end
end
Return w

Firstly, $\mathcal{A}$ sets the proper w according to Algorithm 3. Then $\mathcal{A}$ computes the value of G_s, since the recovered coefficients of $\mathbf{G}$ are $(\mathbf{G}[0], \mathbf{G}[1], \cdots, \mathbf{G}[k-1])$, and $\mathbf{G}[k] \in \{-1, 0\}$ or $\{1, 0\}$. Therefore, $num_2 = k$, $num_1 = 1$, $G_s = 2k * w + 1$. Next, $\mathcal{A}$ sets $\mathbf{r} = (\mathbf{r}[0], \ldots, \mathbf{r}[k-1], \mathbf{r}[k], 0, \ldots, 0)$. For $0 \le i \le k-1$, he sets according to Eq. (16). Afterward, we discuss the parameter selection of $\mathbf{r}[k]$ in cases {-1,0} and {1,0}, respectively.

(1) When $\mathbf{G}[k-1] = 2$, i.e. $\mathbf{G}[k] \in \{-1, 0\}$, $\mathbf{r}[k] = -\left\lceil \frac{q}{2p*G_s} \right\rceil$. If the output of $\mathcal{O}$ related to the selection of $\mathbf{r}$ is 0, $\mathbf{G}[k] = -1$, otherwise $\mathbf{G}[k] = 0$.
(2) When $\mathbf{G}[k-1] = -2$, then $\mathbf{G}[k] \in \{1, 0\}$, $\mathbf{r}[k] = \left\lceil \frac{q}{2p*G_s} \right\rceil$. If $\mathcal{O}$'s output associated with the selection of $\mathbf{r}$ is 0, $\mathbf{G}[k] = 1$, otherwise $\mathbf{G}[k] = 0$.

Step 3: Suppose that $\mathcal{A}$ has recovered $(\mathbf{G}[0], \ldots, \mathbf{G}[k-1], \mathbf{G}[k], \cdots, \mathbf{G}[k+t-1])$, then $\mathcal{A}$ needs to recover $\mathbf{G}[k+t]$, where $t \in [1, n-k-1]$.

Recall that $(\mathbf{G}[0], \ldots, \mathbf{G}[k-1])$ is denoted as a k-chain, we denote a chain $(\mathbf{G}[0], \cdots, \mathbf{G}[k-1], \mathbf{G}[k], \cdots, \mathbf{G}[z-1])$ with length z the z-chain, which is the extension of the k-chain. Here $\mathbf{G}[k], \cdots, \mathbf{G}[z-1]$ can be arbitrary coefficients and z is a fixed number. Through experiments we find that by setting $z = 15$ we can get the best results.

Step 3.1: $\mathcal{A}$ needs to determine whether $(\mathbf{G}[k+t], \mathbf{G}[k+t+1])$ is in the set {(0,2), (2,0), (0, –2), (–2,0)}.

Firstly, $\mathcal{A}$ selects the proper w in Algorithm 2 and computes the value of G_s according to $G_s = 2 * num_2 * w + num_1$. Then, according to Eq. (11),

$$\mathbf{G}[k+t] = \mathbf{g}[k+t-1] - \mathbf{g}[k+t], \tag{18}$$

and $\mathbf{g}[k+t-1]$ is known, thus $\mathcal{A}$ can recover $(\mathbf{G}[k+t], \mathbf{G}[k+t+1])$ in the set {(0,2), (2,0)} or {(0,–2), (–2,0)}, respectively.

Specifically, when $\mathbf{g}[k+t-1] = -1$, $(\mathbf{G}[k+t], \mathbf{G}[k+t+1])$ is in the set {(0,–2), (–2,0)}. When $\mathbf{g}[k+t-1] = 1$, $(\mathbf{G}[k+t], \mathbf{G}[k+t+1])$ is in {(0,2), (2,0)}.

After that, $\mathcal{A}$ sets $\mathbf{r} = (\mathbf{r}[0], \ldots, \mathbf{r}[z-1], 0, \ldots, 0, \mathbf{r}[k+t], \mathbf{r}[k+t+1], 0, \ldots, 0)$. For $0 \le i \le z-1$,

$$\mathbf{r}[i] = \begin{cases} \left\lceil \dfrac{q}{2p * G_s} \right\rceil * w * \dfrac{\mathbf{G}[i]}{2} & \text{if } |\mathbf{G}[i]| = 2, \\ \left\lceil \dfrac{q}{2p * G_s} \right\rceil * \mathbf{G}[i] & \text{if } |\mathbf{G}[i]| = 1, \\ \left\lceil \dfrac{q}{2p * G_s} \right\rceil & \text{if } \mathbf{G}[i] = 0 \text{ and } \mathbf{r}[i-1] \ge 0, \\ -\left\lceil \dfrac{q}{2p * G_s} \right\rceil & \text{if } \mathbf{G}[i] = 0 \text{ and } \mathbf{r}[i-1] < 0. \end{cases} \tag{19}$$

And $\mathcal{A}$ sets $\mathbf{r}[k+t]$ and $\mathbf{r}[k+t+1]$ as follows.

(1) When $\mathbf{g}[k+t-1] = -1$, $(\mathbf{G}[k+t], \mathbf{G}[k+t+1])$ is in {(0, –2), (–2,0)}. Firstly, $\mathcal{A}$ sets $\mathbf{r}[k+t]$ and $\mathbf{r}[k+t+1]$ as:
1) (–2,0): $\mathbf{r}[k+t] = -\left\lceil \frac{q}{2p*G_s} \right\rceil * w$, $\mathbf{r}[k+t+1] = -\left\lceil \frac{q}{2p*G_s} \right\rceil$,

2) (0,-2): $\mathbf{r}[k+t] = -\left\lceil \frac{q}{2p*G_s} \right\rceil$, $\mathbf{r}[k+t+1] = -\left\lceil \frac{q}{2p*G_s} \right\rceil * w$.

$\mathcal{A}$ recovers $(\mathbf{G}[k+t], \mathbf{G}[k+t+1])$ as (–2,0) if $\mathcal{O}$'s output associated with the first choice of $\mathbf{r}$ is 0, otherwise $\mathcal{A}$ continues to set in the order. If the output of $\mathcal{O}$ associated with the second choice of $\mathbf{r}$ is 0, $\mathcal{A}$ recovers $(\mathbf{G}[k+t], \mathbf{G}[k+t+1])$ as (0,–2). Finally, if $\mathcal{O}$ does not output 0, which demonstrates $(\mathbf{G}[k+t], \mathbf{G}[k+t+1])$ is neither (–2,0) nor (0, –2).

(2) When $\mathbf{g}[k+t-1] = 1$, $(\mathbf{G}[k+t], \mathbf{G}[k+t+1])$ is in {(0,2), (2,0)}. At the outset, $\mathcal{A}$ sets $\mathbf{r}[k+t]$ and $\mathbf{r}[k+t+1]$ as:
1) (0,2): $\mathbf{r}[k+t] = \left\lceil \frac{q}{2p*G_s} \right\rceil$, $\mathbf{r}[k+t+1] = \left\lceil \frac{q}{2p*G_s} \right\rceil * w$,
2) (2,0): $\mathbf{r}[k+t] = \left\lceil \frac{q}{2p*G_s} \right\rceil * w$, $\mathbf{r}[k+t+1] = \left\lceil \frac{q}{2p*G_s} \right\rceil$.

Similarly, $\mathcal{A}$ sets $\mathbf{r}[k+t]$ and $\mathbf{r}[k+t+1]$ in the order and when $\mathcal{O}$ outputs 0, $\mathcal{A}$ recovers $\mathbf{G}[k+t], \mathbf{G}[k+t+1]$ as the corresponding tuple. In the end, if $\mathcal{O}$ does not output 0, $(\mathbf{G}[k+t], \mathbf{G}[k+t+1])$ is neither (0,2) nor (2,0).

Step 3.2: When $(\mathbf{G}[k+t], \mathbf{G}[k+t+1])$ isn't in {(0,2), (2,0), (0,–2), (–2,0)}, $\mathcal{A}$ recovers $\mathbf{G}[k+t]$ in {0,–1,–2}, {1,0,–1} or {2,1,0} in turn.

Table 5. The two outputs of $\mathcal{O}$ corresponding to $\mathbf{G}[k+t]$ in three sets

$\mathbf{G}[k+t]$ \ $\mathcal{O}$ / Set	(0,0)	(0,1)	(1,1)	(1,0)
{0,-1,-2}	-2	-1	0	
{1,0,-1}	1	1	0	-1
{2,1,0}	2	1	0	

Specifically, when $\mathbf{g}[k+t-1] = -1$, $\mathbf{g}[k+t] \in \{-1, 0, 1\}$, according to Eq. (18), $\mathbf{G}[k+t] \in \{0, -1, -2\}$. When $\mathbf{g}[k+t-1] = 0$, $\mathbf{G}[k+t] \in \{1, 0, -1\}$. And when $\mathbf{g}[k+t-1] = 1$, $\mathbf{G}[k+t] \in \{2, 1, 0\}$.

Next, we discuss the parameter selections of $\mathbf{r}$ in cases {0, –1, –2}, {1,0, –1} and {2,1,0}, respectively. The two outputs of $\mathcal{O}$ corresponding to $\mathbf{G}[k+t]$ are shown in Table 5.

(1) When $\mathbf{g}[k+t-1] = -1$, then $\mathbf{G}[k+t] \in \{0, -1, -2\}$. $\mathcal{A}$ first selects w according to Algorithm 3. Then $\mathcal{A}$ computes $G_s = 2 * num_2 * w + num_1 + 1$. Next, $\mathcal{A}$ sets $\mathbf{r} = (\mathbf{r}[0], \ldots, \mathbf{r}[z-1], 0, \ldots, 0, \mathbf{r}[k+t], 0, \ldots, 0)$, for $0 \le i \le z-1$, he sets according to Eq. (19) and $\mathbf{r}[k+t] = -\left\lceil \frac{q}{2p*G_s} \right\rceil$.
Afterward, $\mathcal{A}$ sets $\mathbf{r} = (\mathbf{r}[0], \ldots, \mathbf{r}[z-1], 0, \ldots, 0, \mathbf{r}[k+t], 0, \ldots, 0]$, for $0 \le i \le z-1$,

$$\mathbf{r}[i] = \begin{cases} \left\lceil \frac{q}{2p*(G_s+1)} \right\rceil * w * \frac{\mathbf{G}[i]}{2} & \text{if } |\mathbf{G}[i]| = 2, \\ \left\lceil \frac{q}{2p*(G_s+1)} \right\rceil * \mathbf{G}[i] & \text{if } |\mathbf{G}[i]| = 1, \\ \left\lceil \frac{q}{2p*(G_s+1)} \right\rceil & \text{if } \mathbf{G}[i] = 0 \text{ and } \mathbf{r}[i-1] \geq 0, \\ -\left\lceil \frac{q}{2p*(G_s+1)} \right\rceil & \text{if } \mathbf{G}[i] = 0 \text{ and } \mathbf{r}[i-1] < 0. \end{cases} \tag{20}$$

and $\mathbf{r}[k+t] = -\left\lceil \frac{q}{2p*(G_s+1)} \right\rceil$.
If the only output of $\mathcal{O}$ related to the first choice of $\mathbf{r}$ is 0, $\mathbf{G}[k+t] = -1$. And if both of the two outputs of $\mathcal{O}$ are 0, $\mathbf{G}[k+t] = -2$. Then if both of the two outputs of $\mathcal{O}$ are 1, $\mathbf{G}[k+t] = 0$.

(2) When $\mathbf{g}[k+t-1] = 1$, $\mathbf{G}[k+t] \in \{2,1,0\}$. Similarly, $\mathcal{A}$ first selects the proper w and calculates G_s. Then, for $0 \leq i \leq z-1$, $\mathcal{A}$ sets $\mathbf{r}$ according to Eq. (19) and $\mathbf{r}[k+t] = \left\lceil \frac{q}{2p*G_s} \right\rceil$. Subsequently, for $0 \leq i \leq z-1$, $\mathcal{A}$ sets $\mathbf{r}$ according to Eq. (20) and $\mathbf{r}[k+t] = \left\lceil \frac{q}{2p*(G_s+1)} \right\rceil$. If the only $\mathcal{O}$'s output associated with the first choice of $\mathbf{r}$ is 0, $\mathbf{G}[k+t] = 1$. And if $\mathcal{O}$ outputs 0 twice, $\mathbf{G}[k+t] = 2$. Then if $\mathcal{O}$ outputs 1 twice, $\mathbf{G}[k+t] = 0$.

(3) When $\mathbf{g}[k+t-1] = 0$, $\mathbf{G}[k+t] \in \{1,0,-1\}$. $\mathcal{A}$ similarly selects w according to Algorithm 3 except judging whether $\lceil \frac{q}{G_{s_1}*2p} \rceil = \lceil \frac{q}{G_{s_2}*2p} \rceil$ holds. Then $\mathcal{A}$ computes the value of G_s by $G_s = 2 * num_2 * w + num_1 + 1$. Next, $\mathcal{A}$ sets $\mathbf{r} = (\mathbf{r}[0], \ldots, \mathbf{r}[z-1], 0, \ldots, 0, \mathbf{r}[k+t], 0, \ldots, 0)$, for $0 \leq i \leq z-1$. After that, he sets $\mathbf{r}[k+t] = -\left\lceil \frac{q}{2p*G_s} \right\rceil$.

If the only $\mathcal{O}$'s output related to the first choice of $\mathbf{r}$ is 0, $\mathbf{G}[k+t] = 1$. And if $\mathcal{O}$ only outputs 0 on the second choice of $\mathbf{r}$, $\mathbf{G}[k+t] = -1$. Then if $\mathcal{O}$ outputs 1 twice, $\mathbf{G}[k+t] = 0$. In addition, if $\mathcal{O}$ outputs 0 twice, which demonstrates there are at least two chains of length z in $\mathbf{G}$. In order to recover the unique $\mathbf{G}$, $\mathcal{A}$ simply assigns $\mathbf{G}[k+t]$ as 1, and he sets $\mathbf{r}[k+t]$ in recovering the remaining coefficients of $\mathbf{G}$ later.

Finally, $\mathcal{A}$ repeats **Step 3** until all the coefficients of $\mathbf{G}$ are recovered.

3.5 Attacking CCA-Secure NTRU-HRSS KEM Using Side Channel Information with Proposed Method

In the above results, we focus on CPA-secure NTRU-HRSS KEM, and the CCA version induces some differences with the previously discussed scheme, which deserves being analyzed. In a CCA-secure NTRU-HRSS KEM, by applying the Fujisaki-Okamoto (FO) transformation [14], Alice first decrypts and then re-encrypts the result of decryption, checking whether the re-encrypted result matches the received ciphertext to reject the malicious ciphertext. Thus our proposed attack cannot directly work on CCA-secure NTRU-HRSS KEM.

However, Ravi et al. [28] showed that side channel attack could gain useful information from decryption of chosen ciphertexts, and they utilized these information to successfully attack some CCA-secure KEMs. In addition, the key idea of their chosen ciphertexts attack is almost identical to key mismatch attack, apart from that the adversary $\mathcal{A}$ actively accesses to real-world devices used for decapsulation, obtaining the match or mismatch information depending on side channel attack. Therefore, our proposed method can be directly applied to attack CCA-secure NTRU-HRSS KEM with the help of side channel information.

In [27], Ravi proposed a method against Streamlined NTRU Prime, and the method is also applicable to NTRU-HRSS. In the method of Ravi, recovering a single coefficient needs 4 chosen-ciphertext queries, that is, 4 side-channel traces, and $n = 701$, thus the total number of traces for NTRU-HRSS is 2804. By applying our improved method to the side channel-assisted attacks against CCA-secure NTRU-HRSS KEM, we only need 1844 traces on average, decreasing the number of traces by 34.23%.

4 Experiments and Analysis

In this section, we introduce our experiments and the results show the correctness and efficiency of our proposed attack. We run our code on an Intel Xeon E5-2620 at 2.1 GHz and a 64 GB RAM. Our code is made public[1].

To make our experiments more convincing, we generate 10,000 secret keys using the code submitted to NIST [6] by the designers of NTRU-HRSS. Recall that z denotes the length of z-chain, and w is the weight whose absolute value is 2 in recovering coefficients of $\mathbf{G}$. In NTRU-HRSS, the parameters $(n, q, p) = (701, 8192, 3)$. Then we implement our proposed method to recover all coefficients of the secret key in NTRU-HRSS, where we try different z in the set {5,7,9,11,13,15,17,19}.

Table 6. Performance comparison when increasing the value of z

z	Success rate (%)	Average #queries	Average time (s)
5	50.0	1884	12.652
7	70.0	1879	11.744
9	90.0	1855	11.471
11	92.4	1866	11.586
13	92.9	1856	11.853
15	93.6	1844	11.983
17	92.7	1867	11.858
19	90.0	1945	11.965

[1] https://github.com/AHaQY/Key-Mismatch-Attack-on-NIST-KEMs/tree/master/ntruhrss701_key_mismatch_attack.

The results are shown in Table 6, where we illustrate the trade-off among the success rate, average number of queries, and average time. We also represent the relationship between the success rate and z in Fig. 1. It is notable that our proposed attack can achieve the success rate of 93.6% when $z = 15$. The results show that among 10,000 secret keys, all coefficients of 9360 secret keys can be recovered. Meanwhile, when $z = 15$, it also represents the least number of queries. Therefore, we choose $z = 15$ in the final.

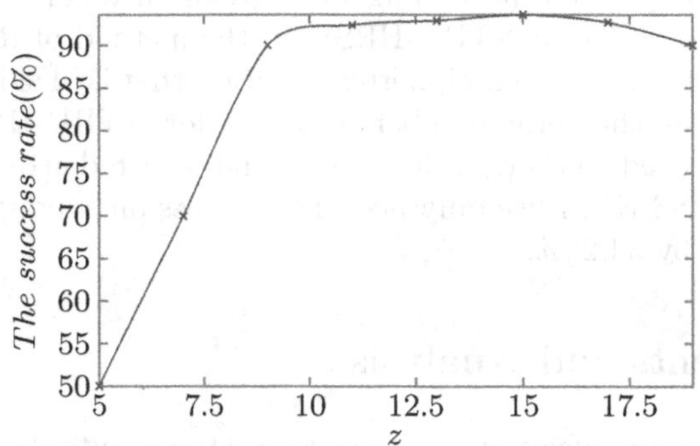

Fig. 1. The relationship between z and the success rate

And when $z > 15$, we need to set a smaller weight w, which prevents us from distinguishing some coefficients. Thus, the success rate continues decreasing as depicted in Fig. 1. In addition, when the weight $w = 1$, we cannot continue decreasing w as required in Algorithm 2 or Algorithm 3. Otherwise the value of w is 0, which is the reason why the success rate cannot be 100%.

5 Conclusion

In this paper, we propose a key mismatch attack on NTRU-HRSS KEM. Furthermore, we illustrate the trade-off among the success rate, average number of queries, and the average running time. As a result, we can achieve minimum number of queries with a success rate of 93.6% at the same time. NTRU-HRSS KEM submitted to NIST is CCA-secure, so our proposed key mismatch attack does not harm the NTRU-HRSS designers' security goals. However, as shown in [28], we can further combine our proposed method with side-channel attacks to attack the CCA-secure NTRU-HRSS.

Acknowledgments. The research in this paper was partially supported by the National Natural Science Foundation of China (NSFC) under Grant no. 61672029, and Guangxi Key Laboratory of Trusted Software (no. KX202038).

References

1. Alagic, G., et al.: Status Report on the Second Round of the NIST Post-Quantum Cryptography Standardization Process. US Department of Commerce, National Institute of Standards and Technology (2020)
2. Alkim, E., et al.: Newhope. Submission to the NIST Post-Quantum Cryptography standardization project, Round 2 (2019)
3. Avanzi, R., et al.: Algorithm specifications and supporting documentation, version 2.0, nist pqc round 2. Tech. rep. (2019)
4. Băetu, C., Durak, F.B., Huguenin-Dumittan, L., Talayhan, A., Vaudenay, S.: Misuse attacks on post-quantum cryptosystems. In: Annual International Conference on the Theory and Applications of Cryptographic Techniques, pp. 747–776. Springer (2019)
5. Bauer, A., Gilbert, H., Renault, G., Rossi, M.: Assessment of the key-reuse resilience of NewHope. Topics in Cryptology – CT-RSA 2019 , pp. 272–292 (2019). https://doi.org/10.1007/978-3-030-12612-4_14
6. Chen, C, et al.: NTRU: algorithm specifications and supporting documentation (2019)
7. Chen, L., et al.: Report on Post-quantum Cryptography. US Department of Commerce, National Institute of Standards and Technology (2016)
8. Ding, J., Alsayigh, S., Saraswathy, R., Fluhrer, S., Lin, X.: Leakage of signal function with reused keys in RLWE key exchange. In: 2017 IEEE International Conference on Communications (ICC), pp. 1–6. IEEE (2017)
9. Ding, J., Deaton, J., Schmidt, K., Vishakha, Zhang, Z.: A simple and efficient key reuse attack on NTRU cryptosystem (2019)
10. Ding, J., Fluhrer, S., Rv, S.: Complete attack on RLWE key exchange with reused keys, without signal leakage. In: Australasian Conference on Information Security and Privacy, pp. 467–486. Springer (2018)
11. Ding, J., Xie, X., Lin, X.: A simple provably secure key exchange scheme based on the learning with errors problem. IACR Cryptol. EPrint Arch. **2012**, 688 (2012)
12. D'Anvers, J.P., Karmakar, A., Roy, S.S., Vercauteren, F.: Saber: Mod-LWR based KEM (round 2 submission). Tech. Rep. (2019)
13. Fluhrer, S.R.: Cryptanalysis of ring-LWE based key exchange with key share reuse. IACR Cryptol. ePrint Arch. (2016)
14. Fujisaki, E., Okamoto, T.: Secure integration of asymmetric and symmetric encryption schemes. In: Wiener, M. (ed.) CRYPTO 1999. LNCS, vol. 1666, pp. 537–554. Springer, Heidelberg (1999). https://doi.org/10.1007/3-540-48405-1_34
15. Greuet, A., Montoya, S., Renault, G.: Attack on LAC key exchange in misuse situation. IACR Cryptol. ePrint Arch. **2020**, 63 (2020)
16. Gyongyosi, L., Imre, S.: A survey on quantum computing technology. Comput. Sci. Rev. **31**, 51–71 (2019)
17. Hoffstein, J., Pipher, J., Silverman, J.H.: NTRU: a ring-based public key cryptosystem. In: Buhler, J.P. (ed.) ANTS 1998. LNCS, vol. 1423, pp. 267–288. Springer, Heidelberg (1998). https://doi.org/10.1007/BFb0054868
18. Hülsing, A., Rijneveld, J., Schanck, J.M., Schwabe, P.: NTRU-HRSS-KEM: algorithm specifications and supporting documentation (2017)
19. Kirkwood, D., Lackey, B.C., McVey, J., Motley, M., Solinas, J.A., Tuller, D.: Failure is not an option: standardization issues for post-quantum key agreement. In: Workshop on Cybersecurity in a Post-Quantum World, p. 21 (2015)

20. Langlois, A., Stehlé, D.: Worst-case to average-case reductions for module lattices. Designs, Codes and Cryptography **75**(3), 565–599 (2014). https://doi.org/10.1007/s10623-014-9938-4
21. Lyubashevsky, V., Peikert, C., Regev, O.: On ideal lattices and learning with errors over rings. In: Cryptology - EUROCRYPT, pp. 1–23 (2010)
22. Moody, D.: Post-quantum cryptography standardization: announcement and outline of NIST's call for submissions (2016)
23. Okada, S., Wang, Y., Takagi, T.: Improving key mismatch attack on newhope with fewer queries. In: Liu, J.K., Cui, H. (eds.) ACISP 2020. LNCS, vol. 12248, pp. 505–524. Springer, Cham (2020). https://doi.org/10.1007/978-3-030-55304-3_26
24. Qin, Y., Cheng, C., Ding, J.: A complete and optimized key mismatch attack on NIST candidate newhope. In: Sako, K., Schneider, S., Ryan, P.Y.A. (eds.) ESORICS 2019. LNCS, vol. 11736, pp. 504–520. Springer, Cham (2019). https://doi.org/10.1007/978-3-030-29962-0_24
25. Qin, Y., Cheng, C., Ding, J.: An efficient key mismatch attack on the NIST second round candidate kyber. IACR Cryptol. ePrint Arch. **2019**, 1343 (2019)
26. Qin, Y., Cheng, C., Zhang, X., Pan, Y., Hu, L., Ding, J.: A Systematic Approach and Analysis of Key Mismatch Attacks on CPA-Secure Lattice-Based NIST Candidate KEMs. Cryptology ePrint Archive, Report 2021/123 (2021)
27. Ravi, P., Ezerman, M.F., Bhasin, S., Chattopadhyay, A., Roy, S.S.: Generic Side-Channel Assisted Chosen-Ciphertext Attacks on Streamlined NTRU Prime. Cryptology ePrint Archive, Report 2021/718 (2021)
28. Ravi, P., Roy, S.S., Chattopadhyay, A., Bhasin, S.: Generic side-channel attacks on CCA-secure lattice-based PKE and KEMs. In:IACR Transactions on Cryptographic Hardware and Embedded Systems, pp. 307–335 (2020)
29. Rescorla, E.: The transport layer security (TLS) protocol version 1.3. Tech. rep. (2018)
30. Shor, P.W.: Polynomial-time algorithms for prime factorization and discrete logarithms on a quantum computer. SIAM Rev. **41**(2), 303–332 (1999)

Efficient and Fully Secure Lattice-Based IBE with Equality Test

Zhenghao Wu, Jian Weng(✉), Anjia Yang, Lisha Yao, Xiaojian Liang, Zike Jiang, and Jinghang Wen

College of Cyber Security, Jinan University, Guangdong 510632, China

Abstract. Identity-based encryption with equality test (IBEET), derived from public key encryption with equality test (PKEET), allows the equality test algorithm on two ciphertexts without decrypting the messages and simplifies the certificate management of PKEET. In response to the explosive growth of quantum computing, recently, some IBEET schemes based on the learning with errors (LWE) problem were proposed, which could survive under the quantum attacks. However, there are several unsatisfactory performances on either efficiency or security due to the key size and the security loss. In this work, we construct an efficient and fully secure IBEET scheme from the LWE problem in the standard model. Our construction favors *weakly compact key size*, which refers that our key size is independent of the bit length of identity ℓ and only depends on a smaller value (i.e., the seed length λ of pseudo-random function (PRF)). Moreover, we achieve full security in the standard model without abort-resistant hash functions in security proof compared with prior adaptively secure lattice-based IBEET schemes, which reduces the losses of efficiency and security.

Keywords: Identity-based encryption · Equality test · Learning with errors · Full security

1 Introduction

Identity-based encryption with equality test (IBEET), an interesting primitive introduced by Ma et al. [24], is designed to support the equality test algorithm between two ciphertexts encrypted with same or different identities while keeping the messages secret. It is derived from the concept of identity-based encryption (IBE) and public key encryption with equality test (PKEET) [12,25,34]. Accordingly, IBEET by itself could simplify the certificate management. As one of the most promising candidates to effective encrypted data management, IBEET has a considerable amount of applications, e.g., the e-mail spam filtering in encrypted systems [23], malware detection and verifiability of encrypted data [3], data management in resource-restricted devices [14] and so on.

In 2016, Lee et al. [20] proposed a generic IBEET construction. Later, a lot of works appeared successively from different motivations. Some were dedicated

D. Gao et al. (Eds.): ICICS 2021, LNCS 12919, pp. 301–318, 2021.
https://doi.org/10.1007/978-3-030-88052-1_18

to higher efficiency and security [4,19,22,33], while others intended to extend IBEET with more attractive features [10,21,30]. However, these aforementioned schemes are based on classical number-theoretic assumptions, which are vulnerable under quantum attacks. Recently, several works [13,27,31] have tried to build quantum-resistant IBEET schemes relying on lattice problems. But the constructions [13,27] suffered from efficiency issues (e.g., the key size grows linearly with the bit length of identity ℓ) and the losses in security reduction due to the necessity of abort-resistant hash functions. Susilo et al. [31] only achieved selective security despite the efficiency of their IBEET.

Related Work. We mainly focus on the IBEET schemes from lattices in this part. As described, Lee et al. [20] proposed a generic IBEET construction, which exploits three different cryptographic primitives: hierarchical identity-based encryption (HIBE) scheme, one-time signature (OTS) scheme, and collision-resistant hash function (CRHF). Their construction was proved to be fully secure in the standard model and could be adapted to the lattice setting. Duong et al. [13] provided the instantiation over the integer lattice later. Besides, they also introduced a new and direct approach to construct an IBEET based on the learning with errors (LWE) problem, which is a well-known quantum-resistant problem on lattices. Specifically, they took advantage of the adaptively secure IBE scheme from Agrawal et al. [1] and CRHF to build a corresponding adaptively secure IBEET scheme. However, the lattice-based IBEET scheme still lacks a kind of flexible authorization allowing users (identities) to control who could perform the equality test algorithm on their ciphertexts. Consequently, Nguyen et al. [27] extended IBEET with flexible authorization (IBEET-FA) by allowing the user more customized controls (e.g., the identity control, the specific ciphertext control, and so on) on ciphertexts. But these schemes were still impractical and unaffordable due to the great cost of algorithms (e.g., the space consumption of rather large key size and the cost of Gaussian sampling). To address these issues, Susilo et al. [31] proposed an efficient and selectively secure IBEET, where the sizes of public key and ciphertext are smaller as well. Their construction employed much more efficient trapdoor sampling algorithms from Micciancio and Peikert [26] and the equality test mechanism from Duong et al. [13].

Our Contribution. In this work, we propose a new and efficient LWE-based IBEET with weakly compact key size, which is proved to be fully secure in the standard model.

The core idea is adapting the techniques of fully secure IBE by Tsabary [32] to construct a fully secure IBEET scheme. One of the biggest challenges is to optimize the key size for better efficiency while achieving full security in the meantime. Besides, the security proof would be also challenging. Note that the parameter setting is always a fundamental but complicated process in lattice-based construction, which is closely related to the analysis of correctness and security.

Table 1. Storage and security comparison

Properties*	Scheme			
	Ours	Duong et al. [13]	Nguyen et al. [27]	Susilo et al. [31]
Trapdoor matrix	$n \times 2 \cdot m'$, $m' = (n+1)\lceil \log q \rceil + 2\lambda$	$n \times 2 \cdot m'$, $m' \geq 6n\lceil \log q \rceil$	$n \times 2 \cdot m'$, $m' \geq 6n\lceil \log q \rceil$	$m \times 2 \cdot m'$, $m' = n\lceil \log q \rceil, m \geq n\lceil \log q \rceil$
Function matrix	$n \times m \cdot \lambda$, $m = n\lceil \log q \rceil$	$n \times m \cdot \ell$, $m \geq 6n\lceil \log q \rceil$	$n \times m \cdot \ell$, $m \geq 6n\lceil \log q \rceil$	$n \times (4 \cdot m' + 2 \cdot m)$
Public key	$n \times (2 \cdot m' + m \cdot \lambda + t)$	$n \times (2 \cdot m' + m \cdot (\ell+1) + t)$	$n \times (2 \cdot m' + m \cdot (\ell+1) + t)$	$n \times (4 \cdot m' + 2 \cdot m)$
Full security	✓	✓	✓	✗

* The trapdoor ($n \times m'$)-matrix is generated by TrapGen algorithm, the function ($n \times m$)-matrix used to encode the user identity is selected uniformly at random, ℓ is the bit length of identity and the input length of PRF, λ is the length of PRF seed, and k is the output length of PRF, t is the bit length of messages.

As shown in Table 1, we compare our scheme with three other state-of-the-art constructions [13,27,31] from lattices in terms of efficiency and security performance. The sizes of trapdoor matrix, function matrix and public key are smaller than Duong et al. [13] and Nguyen et al. [27] and are independent of the bit length of identity ℓ. Although the construction of Susilo et al. [31] has a smaller function matrix, it comes at the cost of security. In a word, our scheme achieves full security with smaller parameters and thus enjoys the better performance. Specifically:

1. Our proposed IBEET features weakly compact key size since the size of the public key is independent of the bit length of identity ℓ instead of selecting ℓ ($n \times m$)-matrices as in Duong et al. [13] and Nguyen et al. [27]. This allows a wider scope of applications with different length of identity in which it only needs to switch to a new PRF with an equal length of the input. Therefore, it also contributes to simplifying the key management infrastructure.
2. The sizes of the trapdoor matrix and function matrix corresponding to the secret key and public key respectively are smaller in our proposed IBEET. Besides, the size of ciphertext could also be fairly small since it only depends on the length of PRF seed λ, which we could easily control by choosing a suitable PRF with a certain short PRF seed (e.g. $\lambda < \ell$).
3. Our proposed IBEET offers full security without the requirement for abort-resistant hash functions in security proof compared with prior adaptively secure lattice-based IBEET schemes, which reduces the losses of efficiency and security.

Paper Organization. Some necessary preliminaries, such as lattice background and PRF, are shown in Sect. 2. In Sect. 3, we give a formal definition and security model of IBEET. In Sect. 4, we construct an efficient and fully secure IBEET scheme from the LWE problem as well as its correctness analysis and security proof. Finally, Sect. 5 concludes this paper.

2 Preliminaries

In this section, we first introduce the notation used in our paper and then recall necessary definitions, theorems, lemmas and corollaries.

Notation. Let $\mathcal{M}$ and $\mathcal{I}$ denote the message space and identity space, respectively. For a distribution or a random variable X, we denote uniformly sampling a random x according to X by $x \xleftarrow{\$} X$. Let $D_{\mathbb{Z}^m,\tau}$ denote the discrete Gaussian distribution over $\mathbb{Z}^m$ with parameter τ. And let $U(S)$ denote the uniform distribution over the set S. We use bold-face letters (e.g. $\mathbf{v}$) to denote vectors and use bold-face capital letters (e.g. $\mathbf{M}$) to denote matrices. Let $\mathbf{A}_\tau^{-1}$ denote the τ-trapdoor for $\mathbf{A}$ and let $\mathbf{A}_\tau^{-1}(\mathbf{v})$ denote the random variable whose distribution is $D_{\mathbb{Z}^m,\tau}$ with the property that $\mathbf{A} \cdot \mathbf{A}_\tau^{-1}(\mathbf{v}) = \mathbf{v}$. And let $\|\mathbf{v}\|$ denote the ℓ_2 norm and $\|\mathbf{v}\|_\infty$ (resp. $\|\mathbf{M}\|_\infty$) denote the maximum absolute value of the entries of $\mathbf{v}$ (resp. $\|\mathbf{M}\|$).

2.1 Lattices

Lemma 1 **([29], Lemma 2.5).** *We have* $\Pr[\|\mathbf{x}\| > \tau\sqrt{m} : \mathbf{x} \leftarrow D_{\mathbb{Z}^m,\tau}] < 2^{-2m}$.

Lemma 2 (Leftover Hash Lemma). *Let* $q > 2$ *be a prime and* $m > (n+1)\log q + \omega(\log n)$, $k = poly(n)$, *we have that* $(\mathbf{A}, \mathbf{AR})$ *is distributed negligibly close to* $U(\mathbb{Z}_q^{n\times m} \times \mathbb{Z}_q^{n\times k})$ *if we sample uniformly* $\mathbf{A} \leftarrow \mathbb{Z}_q^{n\times m}$ *and* $\mathbf{R} \leftarrow \{-1, 0, 1\}^{m\times k}$ *at random.*

Definition 1 **([29], Decisional LWE** (DLWE)**).** *Let* n, m *be integers,* $q > 2$ *be a prime and let* χ *be a probability distribution over* $\mathbb{Z}$. *The* $DLWE_{n,q,\chi}$ *problem holds that* $(\mathbf{A}, \mathbf{sA} + \mathbf{e})$ *and* $(\mathbf{A}, \mathbf{u})$ *are computationally indistinguishable if* $\mathbf{A} \xleftarrow{\$} \mathbb{Z}_q^{n\times m}$, $\mathbf{s} \xleftarrow{\$} \mathbb{Z}_q^n$, $\mathbf{e} \xleftarrow{\$} \chi^m$, *and* $\mathbf{u} \xleftarrow{\$} \mathbb{Z}_q^m$.

Corollary 1 **([32], Corollary 6).** *For all* $\epsilon > 0$, $q = q(n)$, $\chi = \chi(n)$ *such that* χ *is* B*-bounded for some* $B = B(n)$, $q/b \geq 2^n$, $DLWE_{n,q,\chi}$ *is at least as hard as the classical hardness of* GapSVP_γ *and quantum hardness of* SIVP_γ *for* $\gamma = 2^{\Omega(n^\epsilon)}$.

Gadget Matrix. Let $n, q \in \mathbb{Z}$ and $m \geq n\lceil \log q \rceil$. A gadget matrix $\mathbf{G} \in \mathbb{Z}_q^{n\times m} = \mathbf{I}_n \oplus (1, 2, 4, \ldots, 2^{\lceil \log q \rceil - 1})$.

We use the following results of lattice trapdoor from Katsumata et al. [17] with subtle difference:

Theorem 1 **([17], Theorem 2.5).** *Lattice trapdoors have following properties.*

1. *For any* $\tau' \geq \tau$, *it is efficient to compute* $\mathbf{A}_{\tau'}^{-1}$ *with* $\mathbf{A}_\tau^{-1}$.
2. *For any* $\mathbf{B}$, *it is efficient to compute* $[\mathbf{A}\|\mathbf{B}]_\tau^{-1}$ *with* $\mathbf{A}_\tau^{-1}$.

3. *([32], Corollary 2.4) Given* $\mathbf{A} \in \mathbb{Z}_q^{n\times m'}$*, and* $\mathbf{R} \in \mathbb{Z}^{m'\times m}$ *with* $m = n\lceil \log q\rceil$*, it is efficient to compute* $[\mathbf{A}\|\mathbf{AR}+\mathbf{G}]_\tau^{-1}$ *for* $\tau = O(\sqrt{mm'}\|\mathbf{R}\|_\infty)$*.*
4. *There exists an efficient algorithm* TrapGen$(1^n, m, q)$ *that outputs* $(\mathbf{A}, \mathbf{A}_{\tau_0}^{-1})$ *where* $\mathbf{A} \in \mathbb{Z}_q^{n\times m}$ *for some* $m = O(n\log q)$ *is* 2^{-n}*-uniform and* $\tau_0 = O(\sqrt{n\log q\log n})$*.*
5. *For any* $\mathbf{A}_\tau^{-1}$ *and* $\mathbf{u} \in \mathbb{Z}_q^n$*, it follows* $\Pr[\|\mathbf{A}_\tau^{-1}(\mathbf{u})\|_\infty > \sqrt{m}\tau] = \mathsf{negl}(\lambda)$*.*

Theorem 2 **([32], Theorem 2.5).** *There exist efficient deterministic algorithms* EvalF *and* EvalFX *such that for all* $n, q, \ell \in \mathbb{N}$ *and* $m = n\lceil\log q\rceil$*, for any depth* d *boolean circuit* $f : \{0,1\}^\ell \to \{0,1\}^k$ *and matrix* $\mathbf{A} \in \mathbb{Z}_q^{n\times m\cdot\ell}$*, and for any input* $x \in \{0,1\}^\ell$*, the outputs* $\mathbf{H} \leftarrow \mathsf{EvalF}(f, \mathbf{A})$ *and* $\widehat{\mathbf{H}} \leftarrow \mathsf{EvalFX}(f, x, \mathbf{A})$ *are both in* $\mathbb{Z}_q^{m\cdot\ell\times m\cdot k}$ *and it holds* $\|\mathbf{H}\|_\infty, \|\widehat{\mathbf{H}}\|_\infty \le (2m)^d$ *and*

$$[\mathbf{A} - x \oplus G]\widehat{\mathbf{H}} = \mathbf{AH} - f(x) \oplus \mathbf{G} \pmod q)^1.$$

Moreover, for any pair of circuits $f : \{0,1\}^\ell \to \{0,1\}^k$*,* $g : \{0,1\}^k \to \{0,1\}^t$ *and any matrix* $\mathbf{A} \in \mathbb{Z}_q^{n\times m\cdot\ell}$*, the outputs* $\mathbf{H}_f \leftarrow \mathsf{EvalF}(f, \mathbf{A})$*,* $\mathbf{H}_g \leftarrow \mathsf{EvalF}(f, \mathbf{AH}_f)$ *and* $\mathbf{H}_{g\circ f} \leftarrow \mathsf{EvalF}(g\circ f, A)$ *satisfy* $\mathbf{H}_f\mathbf{H}_g = \mathbf{H}_{g\circ f}$*.*

2.2 Bounded Distributions

The following definitions and corollaries, taken from Brakerski and Vaikuntanathan [8], will contribute to the setting of parameters.

Definition 2. *A* (B,ϵ)*-bounded* χ *is a distribution over* $\mathbb{Z}$ *if* $\Pr_{x \xleftarrow{\$} \chi}[|x| > B] < \epsilon$*.*

Definition 3. *A* (B,ϵ)*-swallowing* $\tilde{\chi}$ *is a distribution over* $\mathbb{Z}$ *if it holds that* $\tilde{\chi}$ *and* $y + \tilde{\chi}$ *are within* ϵ *statistical distance for any* $y \in [-B, B] \cap \mathbb{Z}$*.*

Corollary 2. *For every* B, ϵ, δ*, there exists an efficient algorithm to sample from the distribution that is both* (B,ϵ)*-swallowing and* $(B\cdot\sqrt{\log(1/\delta)}/\epsilon, O(\delta))$*-bounded.*

Definition 4. *A* (χ,ϵ)*-swallowing* $\tilde{\chi}$ *is a distribution over* $\mathbb{Z}$ *if it holds that* $\tilde{\chi}$ *and* $\chi + \tilde{\chi}$ *are within* ϵ *statistical distance for* χ*. We sometimes omit the* ϵ *when it is clear from the correct.*

Corollary 3. *Let* $B(\lambda)$ *be some function and let* $\tilde{B}(\lambda) = B(\lambda)\cdot\lambda^{\omega(1)}$*, for any* $B(\lambda)$*-bounded and* $\tilde{B}(\lambda)$*-bounded* $\{\tilde{\chi}_\lambda\}_\lambda$*, if* $\tilde{\chi}$ *is* χ*-swallowing, then there exists an efficient algorithm to sample from the ensemble* $\{\tilde{\chi}_\lambda\}_\lambda$*.*

---

[1] For any $n \in \mathbb{Z}$ and $v \in \{0,1\}^n$ the term $v\oplus\mathbf{G}$ denotes a tensor product of the binary vector $v = (v_1, \ldots, v_n)$ and the gadget matrix $\mathbf{G}$. That is, $v\oplus\mathbf{G} = [v_1\cdot\mathbf{G}\|\ldots\|v_n\cdot\mathbf{G}]$.

2.3 Pseudo-random Function

Now we recall the definition of the PRF that contributes to the full security in our construction.

Definition 5 ((Standard) PRF). *A pseudo-random function (PRF) family consists of two probabilistic polynomial-time (*PPT*) algorithms where:*

- $\mathsf{P.Setup}(1^\lambda) \rightarrow \mathsf{P.sk}$: *Take as input a security parameter* λ *and output a secret key* $\mathsf{P.sk}$.
- $\mathsf{P.Eval}(\mathsf{P.sk}, x) \rightarrow r_x$: *Take as input a secret key* sk *and a string* $x \in \{0,1\}^\ell$, *and output a bit-string* $r_x \in \{0,1\}^k$.

Pseudorandomness. For any PPT *adversary* $\mathcal{A}$, *a PRF family is (adaptively) pseudorandom if it holds that*

$$\left|\Pr[\mathcal{A}^{\mathsf{P.Eval}(\mathsf{P.sk},\cdot)}(1^\lambda) = 1] - Pr[\mathcal{A}^{\mathcal{O}(\mathsf{P.sk},\cdot)}(1^\lambda)] = 1\right| = \mathsf{negl}(\lambda)$$

where $\mathsf{P.sk} \leftarrow \mathsf{P.Setup}(1^\lambda)$ *and* $\mathcal{O}(\mathsf{P.sk},\cdot)$ *is a random oracle.*

3 Identity-Based Encryption with Equality Test

In this section, we introduce the formal definition and security model of IBEET.

3.1 Formal Definition

Definition 6 (IBEET). *An identity-based encryption with equality test scheme consists of six* PPT *algorithms as below:*

- $\mathsf{Setup}(1^\lambda) \rightarrow (\mathsf{PP}, \mathsf{MSK})$: *Take as input a security parameter* λ *and output public parameters* PP *and a master secret key* MSK.
- $\mathsf{Enc}(\mathsf{PP}, m, \mathsf{id}) \rightarrow \mathsf{CT}$: *Take as input* PP, *a message* $m \in \mathcal{M}$ *and an identity* $\mathsf{id} \in \mathcal{I}$. *Output the corresponding ciphertext* CT.
- $\mathsf{KeyGen}(\mathsf{MSK}, \mathsf{id}) \rightarrow \mathsf{sk}_{\mathsf{id}}$: *Take as input* MSK *and* id *and output the secret key* $\mathsf{sk}_{\mathsf{id}}$.
- $\mathsf{Dec}(\mathsf{PP}, \mathsf{sk}_{\mathsf{id}}, \mathsf{CT}) \rightarrow m/\perp$: *Take as input public parameters* PP, $\mathsf{sk}_{\mathsf{id}}$ *and* CT *and output a message* m' *or* $\perp$.
- $\mathsf{Trapdoor}(\mathsf{sk}_{\mathsf{id}}) \rightarrow \mathsf{td}_{\mathsf{id}}$: *Take as input a secret key* $\mathsf{sk}_{\mathsf{id}}$ *and output a trapdoor* $\mathsf{td}_{\mathsf{id}}$.
- $\mathsf{Test}(\mathsf{CT}_A, \mathsf{td}_{\mathsf{id}_A}, \mathsf{CT}_B, \mathsf{td}_{\mathsf{id}_B}) \rightarrow \{0,1\}$: *Take as input ciphertexts* CT_A *and* CT_B *with their trapdoors* $\mathsf{td}_{\mathsf{id}_A}$ *and* $\mathsf{td}_{\mathsf{id}_B}$ *and output 1 if the underlying messages are the same, otherwise 0.*

Correctness. *We say the above IBEET is* correct *if the following conditions hold:*

(1) *For any security parameter* λ, *any* $\mathsf{id} \in \mathcal{I}$ *and any message* $m \in \mathcal{M}$, *it holds that*

$$\Pr[m = \mathsf{Dec}(\mathsf{PP}, \mathsf{KeyGen}(\mathsf{MSK}, \mathsf{id}), \mathsf{Enc}(\mathsf{PP}, m, \mathsf{id}))] = 1 - \mathsf{negl}(\lambda)$$

where $(\mathsf{PP}, \mathsf{MSK}) \leftarrow \mathsf{Setup}(1^\lambda)$.

(2) *For any security parameter* λ, *any identities* $\mathsf{id}_A, \mathsf{id}_B \in \mathcal{I}$, *and any messages* $m_A, m_B \in \mathcal{M}$, *it holds that*

$$\Pr\left[\mathsf{Test}(\mathsf{CT}_A, \mathsf{td}_{\mathsf{id}_A}, \mathsf{CT}_B, \mathsf{td}_{\mathsf{id}_B}) = 1 \;\middle|\; \begin{array}{c} (\mathsf{PP}, \mathsf{MSK}) \leftarrow \mathsf{Setup}(1^\lambda) \\ \mathsf{CT}_A \leftarrow \mathsf{Enc}(\mathsf{PP}, \mathsf{m_A}, \mathsf{id}_A) \\ \mathsf{CT}_B \leftarrow \mathsf{Enc}(\mathsf{PP}, \mathsf{m_B}, \mathsf{id}_B) \\ \mathsf{td}_{\mathsf{id}_A} \leftarrow \mathsf{Trapdoor}(\mathsf{sk}_{\mathsf{id}_A}) \\ \mathsf{td}_{\mathsf{id}_B} \leftarrow \mathsf{Trapdoor}(\mathsf{sk}_{\mathsf{id}_A}) \end{array}\right] = 1 - \mathsf{negl}(\lambda)$$

if $m_A = m_B$, *and the probability is negligible in* λ *for any ciphertext* $\mathsf{CT}_A, \mathsf{CT}_B$ *such that* $\mathsf{Dec}(\mathsf{sk}_{\mathsf{id}_A}, \mathsf{CT}_A) \neq \mathsf{Dec}(\mathsf{sk}_{\mathsf{id}_A}, \mathsf{CT}_B)$, *regardless of whether* $A = B$.

3.2 Security Model

Note that there are two types of adversaries under the IBEET setting inherited from the PKEET in the security model. To define the security model of IBEET, we need to introduce the following two types of adversaries:

- Type-I adversary: The adversaries belonging to Type-I can query any identity to get the corresponding trapdoor. In other words, the adversaries could perform the equality test algorithm on the challenge ciphertext. Their target is to find out the underlying message in the challenge ciphertext.
- Type-II adversary: The adversaries belonging to Type-II can query any identity except the target identity. In other words, the adversaries could not perform the equality test algorithm on challenge ciphertext. And their target is to distinguish which message, in the two candidates submitted by themselves, is encrypted in the challenge ciphertext.

Then, corresponding to the two types of adversaries, we define the security of one-wayness under chosen-identity attacks (**OW-ID-ATK**) and the security of indistinguishability under chosen-identity attacks (**IND-ID-ATK**) respectively, as below.

OW-ID-ATK Security Against Type-I Adversaries. The one-wayness security against adaptive attacks of an IBEET scheme between an adversary $\mathcal{A}^{ow}$ and a challenger $\mathcal{C}^{ow}$ is defined as follows, such that $\mathcal{A}^{ow}$ can have a trapdoor for all ciphertext including the targeted identity:

1. Setup: $\mathcal{C}^{ow}$ generates $(\mathsf{PP}, \mathsf{MSK}) \leftarrow \mathsf{Setup}(1^\lambda)$ and sends PP to $\mathcal{A}^{ow}$.
2. Query Phase I: $\mathcal{A}^{ow}$ adaptively issues the following queries for polynomially times.

- KeyGen Query $\mathcal{O}^{KG(\cdot)}$. $\mathcal{A}^{ow}$ submits an identity $\mathsf{id} \in \mathcal{I}$ and $\mathcal{C}^{ow}$ returns $\mathsf{sk}_{\mathsf{id}} \leftarrow \mathsf{KeyGen}(\mathsf{MSK}, \mathsf{id})$.
- Trapdoor Query $\mathcal{O}^{Td(\cdot)}$. $\mathcal{A}^{ow}$ submits an identity $\mathsf{id} \in \mathcal{I}$ and $\mathcal{C}^{ow}$ returns $\mathsf{td}_{\mathsf{id}} \leftarrow \mathsf{Trapdoor}(\mathsf{sk}_{\mathsf{id}})$.
- Decryption Query $\mathcal{O}^{Dec(\cdot,\cdot)}$. $\mathcal{A}^{ow}$ submits a ciphertext CT with an identity $\mathsf{id} \in \mathcal{I}$, and $\mathcal{C}^{ow}$ returns the corresponding decryption result $m \leftarrow \mathsf{Dec}(\mathsf{KeyGen}(\mathsf{MSK}, \mathsf{id}), \mathsf{CT})$ if **ATK=CCA**, otherwise $\mathcal{C}^{ow}$ returns $\perp$.

3. Challenge Phase: $\mathcal{A}^{ow}$ submits $\mathsf{id}^* \in \mathcal{I}$ as the challenge identity where all of key queries id in Query Phase I satisfy $\mathsf{id}^* \neq \mathsf{id}$. $\mathcal{C}^{ow}$ chooses a random message m^*, and computes $\mathsf{CT}^* \leftarrow \mathsf{Enc}(\mathsf{PP}, m^*, \mathsf{id}^*)$. It returns CT^* as the challenge ciphertext to $\mathcal{A}$.
4. Query Phase II: $\mathcal{A}^{ow}$ adaptively issues queries as Query Phase I except that it is not allowed to issue a keyGen query $\mathcal{O}^{KG}$ on input id^*, nor to issue a decryption query $\mathcal{O}^{Dec}$ $(\mathsf{CT}^*, \mathsf{id}^*)$ if **ATK=CCA**.
5. Guess: $\mathcal{A}^{ow}$ outputs m' and if $m' = m^*$, $\mathcal{A}^{ow}$ wins.

An IBEET scheme is **OW-ID-ATK** secure for **ATK** $\in$ {**CPA** (Chosen-plaintext attack), **CCA** (Chosen-ciphertext attack)} if for all PPT adversary $\mathcal{A}^{ow}$, the probability that $\mathcal{A}^{ow}$ wins in above game is negligible in λ.

Remark 1. Note that the message space should be large enough and have sufficient min-entropy. Only then could it prevent the attacks described in Duong et al. [13] since a Type-I adversary could perform the equality test algorithm on the challenge ciphertext with all other ciphertexts generated by the adversary himself.

IND-ID-ATK Security Against Type-II Adversaries. The indistinguishability security against adaptive attacks of an IBEET scheme between an adversary $\mathcal{A}^{ind}$ and a challenger $\mathcal{C}^{ind}$ is defined as follows, such that $\mathcal{A}^{ind}$ cannot perform the equality test algorithm on the challenge ciphertext:

1. Setup: Same as in **OW-ID-ATK** game.
2. Query Phase I: Same as in **OW-ID-ATK** game.
3. Challenge Phase: $\mathcal{A}^{ind}$ submits $\mathsf{id}^* \in \mathcal{I}$ as the challenge identity along with two equal-length messages $m_0, m_1 \in \mathcal{M}$. It is restricted that all of key queries id in Query Phase I satisfying $\mathsf{id}^* \neq \mathsf{id}$. $\mathcal{C}^{ind}$ choose randomly a bit b, and computes $\mathsf{CT}^* \leftarrow \mathsf{Enc}(\mathsf{PP}, m_b, \mathsf{id}^*)$. It returns CT^* as the challenge ciphertext to $\mathcal{A}^{ind}$.
4. Query Phase II: Same as **OW-ID-ATK** game, except that $\mathcal{A}^{ind}$ cannot ask any trapdoor query $\mathcal{O}^{Td(\cdot)}$ on input id^*.
5. Guess: $\mathcal{A}^{ind}$ outputs b' and if $b' = b$, $\mathcal{A}^{ind}$ wins.

An IBEET scheme is **IND-ID-ATK** secure for **ATK** $\in$ {**CPA**, **CCA**} if for all PPT adversaries $\mathcal{A}^{ind}$, the probability that $\mathcal{A}^{ind}$ wins in above game is negligible in λ.

4 Our Proposed IBEET

Here we first give a brief overview of our techniques in the proposed IBEET. Next, we give the concrete construction with weakly compact key size from the LWE problem. Moreover, the parameter setting, correctness analysis and security proof are carefully covered.

Technical Overview. Our idea is inspired by the latest techniques of fully secure schemes by Tsabary [32] in Crypto 2019.

Note that we split the input space of the PRF by adding an entry bit inspired by Katsumata et al. [17], where the additional bit is an identifier and the last ℓ bits serve as user's identity space $\mathsf{id} \in \mathcal{I} : \{0,1\}^{\ell}$. If it's a bit 0, then $(0\|\mathsf{id})$ denotes the user's identity that will be computed by the PRF for encryption; otherwise, let $(1\|\mathsf{id})$ denote the value that will be computed by PRF for equality test. Clearly, we denote $(0\|\mathsf{id})$ by X and $(1\|\mathsf{id})$ by X'. In a word, it's a trick to not only satisfy the requirement for security reduction but also reduce the size of the public key by getting rid of another PRF with the cost of only one bit, which simplifies the scheme remarkably. Another trick is to encode the fresh PRF seed σ' as $\mathsf{c}_{\sigma'}$ without sampling a Gaussian item since it is just an interval variable and will not be revealed to the others.

In addition, we recall some techniques from Tsabary [32] that are used in our construction:

- Identity $\mathsf{id} \in \{0,1\}^{\ell}$ is encoded as a matrix $\mathbf{A}_{\mathsf{id}}^{\mathsf{eval}}$ where $\mathbf{A}_{\mathsf{id}}^{\mathsf{eval}} = \mathbf{A}\mathbf{H}_{\sigma\to\mathsf{id}}$, $\mathbf{H}_{\sigma\to\mathsf{id}} \leftarrow \mathsf{EvalF}(U_{\sigma\to\mathsf{id}}, \mathbf{A})$, and $\mathbf{A}$ is a public function matrix, EvalF is a lattice evaluation algorithm, $U_{\sigma\to\mathsf{id}}$ denotes the circuit that takes as input σ and evaluates the PRF on the point id.
- In order to build a fully secure scheme on lattices, we need to apply the "tagging" technique [15] where every ciphertext contains a random tag r' and every secret key contains a random tag r. And the decryption algorithm proceeds with the condition that the identities are the same and $r' \neq r$.
- The lattice evaluation techniques from homomorphic encryption [6] were summarized succinctly by Tsabary [32] (see Theorem 2) and play a major role together with the PRF in our construction.

Nevertheless, the method to construct a fully secure IBE scheme only has a brief and conceptual description, and lacks concrete construction, parameter setting, and security proof. Our work begins with the above obstacles. Namely, we first try to adapt the techniques of fully secure IBE systems to support the equality test, which composes our IBEET scheme later. At this stage, we apply our tricks described above to avoid doubling the PRF and to reduce the cost of sampling from Gaussian distribution in the encryption algorithm respectively. Then, by the results of the hardness and reduction of the LWE problem [7,26, 28,29], we manage to choose the appropriate parameters. Furthermore, we give formal proofs of the **OW-ID-CPA** security and **IND-ID-CPA** security.

4.1 Construction

Let $\mathsf{P} = \{\mathsf{P.Setup}, \mathsf{P.Eval}\}$ be a PRF with input length $\ell+1$, seed length λ, and output length k. $U_{\sigma\to x}: \{0,1\}^\lambda \to \{0,1\}^k$ denotes the circuit that takes as input $\mathsf{P.sk}$ and computes $\mathsf{P.Eval}(\mathsf{P.sk}, \mathsf{id})$. Define the fully secure IBEET scheme based on the LWE problem as follows:

- $\mathsf{Setup}(1^\lambda)$: Take as input a security parameter λ and set the parameters $n, q, m', \tau, \chi, \tilde{\chi}$ as below and let $m = n\lceil \log q \rceil$.
  1. Sample $\mathsf{P.sk} \leftarrow \mathsf{P.Setup}(1^\lambda)$ and denote $\sigma = \mathsf{P.sk}$.
  2. Use $\mathsf{TrapGen}(1^n, m', q)$ to generate two uniformly random $(n \times m')$-matrices $\mathbf{B}, \mathbf{B}'$ (Trapdoor matrix) together with their trapdoors $\mathbf{B}^{-1}_{\tau_0}, \mathbf{B}'^{-1}_{\tau_0}$.
  3. Select a uniformly random $\mathbf{A} \xleftarrow{\$} \mathbb{Z}_q^{n\times m\cdot\lambda}$ (Function matrix).
  4. Select a uniformly random matrix $\mathbf{V} \xleftarrow{\$} \mathbb{Z}_q^{n\times t}$.
  5. $H: \{0,1\}^* \to \{0,1\}^t$ is a collision-resistant hash function.
  6. Output the public parameters and the master secret key
  $$\mathsf{PP} = (\mathbf{B}, \mathbf{B}', \mathbf{A}, \mathbf{V}, H), \mathsf{MSK} = (\mathbf{B}^{-1}_{\tau_0}, \mathbf{B}'^{-1}_{\tau_0}, \sigma).$$
- $\mathsf{Enc}(\mathsf{PP}, \mathbf{m}, \mathsf{id})$: Take as input a public parameters PP, a message $\mathbf{m} \in \{0,1\}^t$, an identity $\mathsf{id} \in \{0,1\}^\ell$. Let $x = (0\|\mathsf{id}), x' = (1\|\mathsf{id})$.
  1. Sample a random PRF key σ', and $\mathbf{s}, \mathbf{s}' \xleftarrow{\$} \mathbb{Z}_q^n$, $\mathbf{e}_1, \mathbf{e}_1' \xleftarrow{\$} \chi^t$, $\mathbf{e}_2, \mathbf{e}_2' \xleftarrow{\$} \chi^{m'}$, $\mathbf{e}, \mathbf{e}' \xleftarrow{\$} \tilde{\chi}^{m\cdot\lambda}$ and compute
  $$\mathsf{c}_1 = \mathbf{s}^T\mathbf{V} + \mathbf{e}_1^T + \mathbf{m}\lfloor q/2 \rceil, \qquad \mathsf{c}_1' = \mathbf{s}'^T\mathbf{V} + \mathbf{e}'^T_1 + H(\mathbf{m})\lfloor q/2 \rceil,$$
  $$\mathsf{c}_2 = \mathbf{s}^T\mathbf{B} + \mathbf{e}_2^T, \qquad \mathsf{c}_2' = \mathbf{s}'^T\mathbf{B}' + \mathbf{e}'^T_2,$$
  $$\mathsf{c}_x^{\mathsf{eval}} = \mathsf{c}_{\sigma'}\widehat{\mathbf{H}}_{\sigma'\to r_1'} + \mathbf{e}^T, \qquad \mathsf{c}_{x'}^{\mathsf{eval}} = \mathsf{c}_{\sigma'}'\widehat{\mathbf{H}}_{\sigma'\to r_2'} + \mathbf{e}'^T$$
  where $\mathsf{c}_{\sigma'} = \mathbf{s}^T[\mathbf{A} - \sigma' \oplus \mathbf{G}]$, $r_1' = \mathsf{P.Eval}(\sigma', x)$, $\widehat{\mathbf{H}}_{\sigma'\to r_1'} = \mathsf{EvalFX}(U_{\sigma'\to x}, \sigma', \mathbf{A})$ and samely for $\mathsf{c}_{\sigma'}'$, r_2', $\widehat{\mathbf{H}}_{\sigma'\to r_2'}$.
  2. Output the ciphertext $\mathbf{CT} = (r_1', r_2', \mathsf{c}_1, \mathsf{c}_1', \mathsf{c}_2, \mathsf{c}_2', \mathsf{c}_x^{\mathsf{eval}}, \mathsf{c}_{x'}^{\mathsf{eval}})$.
- $\mathsf{KeyGen}(\mathsf{MSK}, \mathsf{id})$: Take as input a master secret key $\mathsf{MSK} = (\mathbf{B}^{-1}_{\tau_0}, \mathbf{B}'^{-1}_{\tau_0}, \sigma)$, an identity $\mathsf{id} \in \{0,1\}^\ell$. Samely, let $x = (0\|\mathsf{id}), x' = (1\|\mathsf{id})$.
  1. Compute the matrix $\mathbf{H}_{\sigma\to x} \leftarrow \mathsf{EvalF}(U_{\sigma\to x}, \mathbf{A})$ and denote $\mathbf{A}_x^{\mathsf{eval}} = \mathbf{A}\mathbf{H}_{\sigma\to x}$.
  2. Compute $r_1 \leftarrow \mathsf{P.Eval}(\sigma, x)$ and let $I_{r_1}: \{0,1\}^k \to \{0,1\}$ be the function that on input r_1' returns 1 if and only if $r_1 = r_1'$.
  3. Compute $\mathbf{H}_{r_1} \leftarrow \mathsf{EvalF}(I_{r_1}, \mathbf{A}_x^{\mathsf{eval}})$, denote $\mathbf{A}^{\mathsf{eq}}_{x,r_1} = \mathbf{A}_x^{\mathsf{eval}}\mathbf{H}_{r_1}$.
  4. Use $\mathbf{B}^{-1}_{\tau_0}$ to compute $\mathbf{K} = [\mathbf{B}\|\mathbf{A}^{\mathsf{eq}}_{x,r_1}]^{-1}_\tau(\mathbf{V})$ such that $[\mathbf{B}\|\mathbf{A}^{\mathsf{eq}}_{x,r_1}] \cdot \mathbf{K} = \mathbf{V}$.
  5. Use $\sigma, x', \mathbf{A}, \mathbf{B}', \mathbf{B}'^{-1}_{\tau_0}$ to compute $r_2, \mathbf{A}_{x'}^{\mathsf{eval}}, \mathbf{A}^{\mathsf{eq}}_{x',r_2}$ and $\mathbf{K}'$ as above, such that $[\mathbf{B}'\|\mathbf{A}^{\mathsf{eq}}_{x',r_2}] \cdot \mathbf{K}' = \mathbf{V}$.
  6. Output $\mathsf{sk_{id}} = (r_1, \mathbf{K}, r_2, \mathbf{K}')$.

- $\mathsf{Dec}(\mathsf{PP}, \mathsf{sk_{id}}, \mathsf{CT})$: Take as input public parameters PP, a ciphertext CT, a secret key $\mathsf{sk_{id}}$.
  1. Parse $\mathsf{sk_{id}} = (r_1, \mathbf{K}, r_2, \mathbf{K}')$ and $\mathbf{CT} = (r_1', r_2', \mathsf{c}_1, \mathsf{c}_1', \mathsf{c}_2, \mathsf{c}_2', \mathsf{c}_x^{\mathsf{eval}}, \mathsf{c}_{x'}^{\mathsf{eval}})$.
  2. If $r_1 = r_1'$ or $r_2 = r_2'$ then abort. Otherwise, compute $\mathbf{A}_x^{\mathsf{eval}}$ as in KeyGen, and $\widehat{\mathbf{H}}_{r_1, r_1'} = \mathsf{EvalFX}(I_{r_1}, r_1', \mathbf{A}_x^{\mathsf{eval}})$.
  3. Compute $\mathbf{w} = \mathsf{c}_1 - [\mathsf{c}_2 \| \mathsf{c}_x^{\mathsf{eval}} \cdot \widehat{\mathbf{H}}_{r_1, r_1'}] \cdot \mathbf{K}$ and for each $i = 1, ..., t$, set $m_i = 1$ if and only if $|w_i| > q/4$, otherwise set $m_i = 0$. We then obtain the message $\mathbf{m}$.
  4. Compute $\mathbf{A}_{x'}^{\mathsf{eval}}$ as in KeyGen, and $\widehat{\mathbf{H}}_{r_2, r_2'} = \mathsf{EvalFX}(I_{r_2}, r_2', \mathbf{A}_{x'}^{\mathsf{eval}})$.
  5. Compute $\mathbf{h} = \mathsf{c}_1' - [\mathsf{c}_2' \| \mathsf{c}_{x'}^{\mathsf{eval}} \cdot \widehat{\mathbf{H}}_{r_2, r_2'}] \cdot \mathbf{K}'$ and for each $i = 1, ..., t$, set $h_i = 1$ if and only if $|h_i| > q/4$, otherwise set $h_i = 0$. We then obtain the value $\mathbf{h}$.
  6. If $H(\mathbf{m}) = \mathbf{h}$ then output $\mathbf{m}$, otherwise output $\perp$.
- $\mathsf{Trapdoor}(\mathsf{sk_{id}})$: Parse the identity's secret key $\mathsf{sk_{id}} = (r_1^{\mathsf{id}}, \mathbf{K}^{\mathsf{id}}, r_2^{\mathsf{id}}, \mathbf{K}'^{\mathsf{id}})$, it outputs a trapdoor $\mathsf{td}_i = (r_2^{\mathsf{id}}, \mathbf{K}'^{\mathsf{id}})$.
- $\mathsf{Test}(\mathsf{CT}_{\mathsf{id}_A}, \mathsf{td}_{\mathsf{id}_A}, \mathsf{CT}_{\mathsf{id}_B}, \mathsf{td}_{\mathsf{id}_B})$: Take as input trapdoors $\mathsf{td}_{\mathsf{id}_A} = (r_2^{\mathsf{id}_A}, \mathbf{K}'^{\mathsf{id}_A})$, $\mathsf{td}_B = (r_2^{\mathsf{id}_B}, \mathbf{K}'^{\mathsf{id}_B})$ and ciphertexts $\mathsf{CT}_{\mathsf{id}_A}$, $\mathsf{CT}_{\mathsf{id}_B}$ for users id_A, id_B respectively, compute
  1. For A (*resp.* B), do the following
     - Compute $\mathbf{A}_{x'}^{\mathsf{eval}}$ as in KeyGen, then compute
     $$\widehat{\mathbf{H}}_{r_2^{\mathsf{id}_A}, r_2'^{\mathsf{id}_A}} = \mathsf{EvalFX}(I_{r_2}^{\mathsf{id}_A}, r_2'^{\mathsf{id}_A}, \mathbf{A}_{x_A'}^{\mathsf{eval}}).$$
     - Compute $\mathbf{h}_k = \mathsf{c}_1'^{\mathsf{id}_A} - [\mathsf{c}_2^{\mathsf{id}_A} \| \mathsf{c}_{x_A'}^{\mathsf{eval}} \cdot \widehat{\mathbf{H}}_{r_2^{\mathsf{id}_A}, r_2'^{\mathsf{id}_A}}] \cdot \mathbf{K}'^{\mathsf{id}_A}$ and for each $k = 1, ..., t$, set $h_k = 1$ if and only if $|h_k| > q/4$, otherwise set $h_k = 0$. We then obtain the value $\mathbf{h}_A$ (*resp.* $\mathbf{h}_B$).
  2. Output 1 if $\mathbf{h}_A = \mathbf{h}_B$ and 0 otherwise.

Choice of Parameters. We follow the method in [[32], Sect. 4.1] to choose the parameters through the security and correctness analysis. Firstly, choose $k = \lambda$, let $d = poly(\lambda)$ denote the depth of $U_{\sigma \to \mathsf{id}}$. Choose $n \geq \lambda$ such that $(2n^2)^{d+3} \leq 2^{n^\epsilon}$, where $\epsilon \in (0, 1)$ is a security/efficiency tradeoff parameter. Moreover, $E' \leq 2^{n^\epsilon}$ where E' is as defined in Eq. 1. Choose q, B, χ according to Corollary 1 and note that $q/B \geq 2^{n^\epsilon}$ and that χ is B-bounded. Choose $m' = (n+1)\lceil \log q \rceil + 2\lambda$ and $\tau = max\{\tau_0, \tau'\}$, where τ_0 is as in item 2 of Theorem 1 and τ' is as in Eq. 2. Set $\tilde{\chi}$ to be a B'-swallowing distribution, where $B' = m'm\lambda B(2m)^d$. By Corollary 3, $\tilde{B}$ can be chosen such that it is $\tilde{B}$-bounded for some $\tilde{B} \in O(B', \lambda)$.

Remark 2. Here we suppose the existence of efficient lattice evaluation algorithms and PRF with low circuit depth, which are served as independent research interests. Notably, the former are benefited from the prosperous development of fully homomorphic encryption (FHE) and attribute-based encryption (ABE) [2,6,16,26]. In addition, many existing provably secure lattice-based PRF constructions are efficient and can be computed by circuits in NC^1 depth [5,11,18].

4.2 Correctness

Theorem 3. *Our IBEET construction above is correct if H is a collision-resistant hash function.*

Proof. We first take the part $(r_1', \mathsf{c}_1, \mathsf{c}_2, \mathsf{c}_x^{\mathsf{eval}})$ of ciphertext CT to check the correctness of message $\mathbf{m}$ and similarly, we could use the same method to verify the correctness of another part.

$$\begin{aligned}\mathsf{c}_x^{\mathsf{eval}} \cdot \widehat{\mathbf{H}}_{r_1,r_1'} &= (\mathsf{c}_{\sigma'}\widehat{\mathbf{H}}_{\sigma' \to r_1'} + \mathbf{e}^T) \cdot \widehat{\mathbf{H}}_{r_1,r_1'} \\ &= \mathbf{s}^T(\mathbf{A}_x^{\mathsf{eval}}\mathbf{H}_r - I_{r_1}(r_1') \oplus \mathbf{G}) + \mathbf{e}' \qquad \text{where } \mathbf{e}' = \mathbf{e}^T\widehat{\mathbf{H}}_{r_1,r_1'} \\ &= \mathbf{s}^T\mathbf{A}_{x,r_1}^{\mathsf{eq}} + \mathbf{e}'.\end{aligned}$$

Hence,

$$\begin{aligned}\mathsf{c}_1 - [\mathsf{c}_2 \| \mathsf{c}_x^{\mathsf{eval}} \cdot \widehat{\mathbf{H}}_{r_1,r_1'}] \cdot \mathbf{K} &= \mathbf{s}^T\mathbf{V} + \mathbf{e}_1^T + \mathbf{m}\lfloor q/2 \rceil - \mathbf{s}^T[\mathbf{B} \| \mathbf{A}_{x,r_1}^{\mathsf{eq}}] \cdot \mathbf{K} - [\mathbf{e}_2^T \| \mathbf{e}'] \cdot \mathbf{K} \\ &= \mathbf{m}\lfloor q/2 \rceil + \mathbf{e}_1^T - [\mathbf{e}_2^T \| \mathbf{e}'] \cdot \mathbf{K}.\end{aligned}$$

Note that $\|\mathbf{e}'\|_\infty \le m\lambda \|\mathbf{e}^T\|_\infty \|\widehat{\mathbf{H}}_{r,r'}\|_\infty \le m\lambda\tilde{B}$ and that $\|\mathbf{K}\|_\infty \le \tau\sqrt{(m+m')}$ with all but $2^{-(m'+m)} = negl(\lambda)$ probability according to Lemma 1 and item 4 of Theorem 1.

Therefore, if $m', k \in O(n, \lceil \log q \rceil)$, $\tilde{B} \in O(B, n)$ and $\tau \in O(k, \lambda, (2m)^{d+3})$, then with all but negligible probability

$$\begin{aligned}\|\mathbf{e}_1^T - [\mathbf{e}_2^T \| \mathbf{e}'] \cdot \mathbf{K}\|_\infty &\le \|\mathbf{e}_1^T\|_\infty + (\|\mathbf{e}_2^T\|_\infty + \|\mathbf{e}'\|_\infty) \cdot \|\mathbf{K}\|_\infty \\ &\le B + (B + m\lambda\tilde{B})\tau\sqrt{(m+m')} \\ &\le B \cdot poly(n, \lceil \log q \rceil) \cdot (2m)^{d+3}.\end{aligned}$$

Denote $E = B \cdot poly(n, \lceil \log q \rceil) \cdot (2m)^{d+3}$ and

$$E' = 4E/B = 4 \cdot poly(n, \lceil \log q \rceil) \cdot (2m)^{d+3}, \tag{1}$$

by our choice of parameters E' is bounded by q/B, and therefore $E = BE'/4$ is bounded by $q/4$. Therefore, if $m_i' = 0$ then $w_i \le q/4$ and if $m_i = 1$ then $w_i > q/4$. Thus, we could get the message $\mathbf{m}$ correctly. In the same way, we can obtain the correct value $\mathbf{h}$ through the part $(r_2', \mathsf{c}_1', \mathsf{c}_2', \mathsf{c}_{x'}^{\mathsf{eval}})$. Now, it is easy to see that if CT is a valid ciphertext of $\mathbf{m}$ by checking if $\mathbf{h} = H(\mathbf{m})$.

Moreover, if CT_{id_A} and CT_{id_B} are valid ciphertext of $\mathbf{m}_A$ and $\mathbf{m}_B$ of identities id_A and id_B respectively. Then it proceeds to check whether $H(\mathbf{m}_A) = H(\mathbf{m}_B)$. If so then it outputs 1, meaning that $\mathbf{m}_A = \mathbf{m}_B$, which is always correct with overwhelming probability since H is collision resistant.

Hence, combining the above results, our IBEET is correct.

4.3 Security Proof

In this section, we claim that our IBEET is **OW-ID-CPA** secure against Type-I adversaries and **IND-ID-CPA** secure against Type-II adversaries. Here we give a proof sketch of Theorem 4 and refer to Appendix for the full proof.

Theorem 4. *Our IBEET with parameters as above has **OW-ID-CPA** security against Type-I adversaries and **IND-ID-CPA** security against Type-II adversaries if it meets the following requirements:*

- *H is a collision-resistant hash function.*
- *$DLWE_{n,q,\chi}$ problem holds.*

The advantage of adversary $\mathcal{A}^{ow}$ that intends to attack the one-wayness and the advantage of $\mathcal{A}^{ind}$ that intends to attack the indistinguishability are negligible.

Proof (Sketch). We prove the security according to a sequence of security games. Technically, for **OW-ID-CPA** security, we follow the description in the part of the technical overview [17] and adapt the proof techniques [1,6,32] in the meantime. Firstly, we utilize the properties of the collision-resistant hash function to prove the underlying content (i.e., hash value $H(\mathbf{m})$ of message $\mathbf{m}$) of c_1' will not reveal the underlying content (message $\mathbf{m}$) of c_1. Next, recall that with the help of "tagging" technique and PRF, we can achieve full security. Specifically, we change to use the real PRF seed σ instead of sampling a fresh σ' in the challenge query relying on the adaptive pseudorandomness of PRF. As a result, the random tags associated with the secret key and challenge ciphertext for the same id are identical now. Then, we change slightly the way to generate the matrix $\mathbf{A}$ for the public parameters and the ciphertext for challenge query id*, which depends on the extended leftover hash lemma and swallowing property of Gaussian distribution $\bar{\chi}$ respectively. Moreover, we change the way to answer key queries by item 3 of Theorem 1 instead of the original trapdoor $\mathbf{B}_{\tau_0}^{-1}$ sampled from TrapGen. Finally, we could prove that the challenge ciphertext at this stage is indistinguishable with uniform one due to the $DLWE_{n,q,\chi}$ problem.

For **IND-ID-CPA** security, it is very similar to above except that the aim of adversaries is to attack the indistinguishability and the adversary itself submits two messages instead of choosing by the challenger. Hence, we omit here it for briefness.

5 Conclusion

In this work, we construct an efficient and fully secure IBEET scheme from the LWE problem. Our IBEET favors weakly compact key size and achieves full security without the requirement for abort-resistant hash functions. Note that we could get a fully CCA-secure IBEET through the well-known CHK transformation [9], although CPA security suffices for a lot of applications. Besides, it is worth mentioning that our IBEET is free to be extended to the one with resistance of insider attack, support of flexible authorization and other attractive properties. Moreover, the construction could be optimized by adapting more efficient PRF with lower circuit depth and lattice evaluation techniques. At last, we will leave it as a future work for building a practical and fully secure IBEET scheme with compact key size.

Acknowledgement. The authors would like to thank the anonymous reviewers for their valuable comments and suggestions. This work is supported by the Major Program of Guangdong Basic and Applied Research Project under Grant No. 2019B030302008, National Key Research and Development Plan of China under Grant Nos. 2020YFB1005600, National Natural Science Foundation of China (Grant Nos. 61825203, U1736203, 61732021, 62072215, 61702222), Key-Area Research and Development Program of Guangdong Province (Grant No. 2020B0101360001), and Special Funds for the Cultivation of Guangdong College Students' Scientific and Technological Innovation. ("Climbing Program" Special Funds.) (No. pdjh2021a0050).

Appendix

As the proof techniques of **IND-ID-CPA** security are quite similar to that of **OW-ID-CPA** security, we only present the full proof of **OW-ID-CPA** security in Theorem 4 for lack of space and briefness.

Proof. **OW-ID-CPA security.** Assume that there is a Type-I adversary $\mathcal{A}^{ow}$ who's aim is to break the **OW-ID-CPA** security of the IBEET scheme. And the proof consists of a sequence of properly designed security games from **Game 0** to **Game 9** with negligible distinguishability.

Game 0. This is the **OW-ID-CPA** game from Definition 6 between the **OW-ID-CPA** challenger $\mathcal{C}^{ow}$ and the Type-I adversaries $\mathcal{A}^{ow}$ against the scheme.

Game 1. We change the the way $\mathcal{C}^{ow}$ answers the challenge query. $\mathcal{C}^{ow}$ chooses two random messages $\mathbf{m}$ and $\mathbf{m}'$, and encrypt $\mathbf{m}$ in c_1 and $H(\mathbf{m}')$ in c_1'. The remains are identical to **Game 0**. As $\mathcal{A}^{ow}$ is Type-I adversaries who could ask any trapdoor query $\mathcal{O}^{Td(\cdot)}$ including id^*, $\mathcal{A}^{ow}$ is able to get $H(\mathbf{m}')$. At the end if $\mathcal{A}^{ow}$ outputs $\mathbf{m}'$ for $\mathbf{m}$, then $\mathcal{A}^{ow}$ has broken the one-wayness of the hash function H.

Thus, **Game 1** and **Game 0** are computationally indistinguishable.

Game 2. We change again how $\mathcal{C}^{ow}$ answers the challenge query that it explicitly generates $\mathsf{c}_x^{\mathsf{eval}}$ using the random tag r_1'. Recall that we denote $x = (0\|\mathsf{id})$ and $x' = (1\|\mathsf{id})$. In **Game 1**, the challenge ciphertexts are generated as

$$\mathsf{c}_x^{\mathsf{eval}*} = \mathsf{c}_{\sigma'}\widehat{\mathbf{H}}_{\sigma'\to r_1'} + \mathbf{e}^T = \mathbf{s}^T(\mathbf{A}\mathbf{H}_{\sigma\to x} - r_1' \oplus \mathbf{G}) + \mathbf{e}^T.$$

Instead of embedding the random PRF key σ' in the ciphertext directly, $\mathcal{C}^{ow}$ just computes $\mathbf{H}_{\sigma\to x} \leftarrow \mathsf{EvalF}(U_{\sigma\to x}, \mathbf{A})$ and $r' \leftarrow \mathsf{P.Eval}(\sigma', x)$. Sample an error term $\mathbf{e} \leftarrow \widetilde{\chi}^{m\cdot\lambda}$, then compute $\mathsf{c}_x^{\mathsf{eval}*} = \mathbf{s}^T(\mathbf{A}\mathbf{H}_{\sigma\to x} - r' \oplus \mathbf{G}) + \mathbf{e}^T$. And it generates $\mathsf{c}_{x'}^{\mathsf{eval}*}$ as above as well.

Apparently, this is statistically the same as in **Game 1**.

Game 3. We now change to use the real seed σ instead of sampling a fresh σ'. Note that the random tags associated with the secret key and challenge ciphertext for the same id are identical now.

Game 3 and **Game 2** are computationally indistinguishable since the adaptive pseudorandomness of the PRF.

Game 4. We then switch back to the real scheme where Enc algorithm first construct c_σ and c'_σ. The only difference is that σ is encoded rather than the random PRF seed σ'.

Thus, **Game 4** and **Game 3** are statistically indistinguishable.

Game 5. In contrast to **Game 4**, We slightly change how the matrix $\mathbf{A}$ generates for the public parameters. In **Game 5**, sample uniformly a matrix $\mathbf{R} \leftarrow \{-1, 0, 1\}^{m' \times m\lambda}$ and the matrix $\mathbf{A}$ is constructed as $\mathbf{A} = \mathbf{BR} + \sigma \oplus \mathbf{G}$.

Therefore, **Game 5** is statistically indistinguishable from **Game 4** according to $\mathbf{B}$ is statistically-close to uniform by Lemma 2 and item 4 of Theorem 1.

Game 6. We change the way $\mathcal{C}^{ow}$ answers the challenge query id*. The values $\mathbf{s} \xleftarrow{\$} \mathbb{Z}_q^n$, c_1^*, c_2^* will be generated as before, sample $\mathbf{e}_1 \xleftarrow{\$} \chi^t$, $\mathbf{e}_2 \xleftarrow{\$} \chi^{m'}$ and compute $c_1^* = \mathbf{s}^T\mathbf{V} + \mathbf{e}_1^T + \mathbf{m}\lfloor q/2 \rceil$ and $c_2^* = \mathbf{s}^T\mathbf{B} + \mathbf{e}_2^T$.

Recall that previously c_σ^* is computed as $c_\sigma = \mathbf{s}^T(\mathbf{A} - \sigma \oplus \mathbf{G})$. In this game, it will be computed as $c_\sigma = c_2^*\mathbf{R} = \mathbf{s}^T\mathbf{BR} + \mathbf{e}_2^T\mathbf{R}$. Note that now

$$\begin{aligned} c_{\mathsf{id}}^{\mathsf{eval}*} &= c_\sigma^* \widehat{\mathbf{H}}_{\sigma \to r_1} + \mathbf{e}^T \\ &= (\mathbf{s}^T\mathbf{BR} + \mathbf{e}_2^T\mathbf{R})\widehat{\mathbf{H}}_{\sigma \to r_1} + \mathbf{e}^T \\ &= \mathbf{s}^T\mathbf{BR}_{\mathsf{id}}^{\mathsf{eval}} + \mathbf{e}_2^T\mathbf{R}\widehat{\mathbf{H}}_{\sigma \to r_1} + \mathbf{e}^T \end{aligned}$$

where $\mathbf{R}_{\mathsf{id}}^{\mathsf{eval}} = \mathbf{R}\widehat{\mathbf{H}}_{\sigma \to r_1}$ and that

$$B' = \|\mathbf{e}_2^T\mathbf{R}\widehat{\mathbf{H}}_{\sigma \to r_1}\|_\infty \le m'm\lambda\|\mathbf{e}_2^T\|_\infty\|\mathbf{R}\|_\infty\|\widehat{\mathbf{H}}_{\sigma \to r_1}\|_\infty \le m'm\lambda B(2m)^d.$$

Therefore, if $\tilde{\chi}$ is B'-swallowing then this change is statistically indistinguishable with **Game 5**.

Game 7. We now change the way $\mathcal{C}^{ow}$ answers key queries. Note that

$$[\mathbf{A} - \sigma \oplus \mathbf{G}]\widehat{\mathbf{H}}_{\sigma \to r_1} = \mathbf{A}_x^{\mathsf{eval}} - r_1 \oplus \mathbf{G}$$

and since $I_{r_1}(r_1) = 1$,

$$[\mathbf{A}_x^{\mathsf{eval}} - r_1 \oplus \mathbf{G}]\widehat{\mathbf{H}}_{r_1, r_1'} = \mathbf{A}_x^{\mathsf{eval}}\mathbf{H}_r - \mathbf{G} = \mathbf{A}_{x,r_1}^{\mathsf{eq}} - \mathbf{G}.$$

Therefore, since $\mathbf{A} := \mathbf{BR} + \sigma \oplus \mathbf{G}$ holds that $\mathbf{BR}\widehat{\mathbf{H}}_{\sigma \to r_1}\widehat{\mathbf{H}}_{r_1, r_1'} = \mathbf{A}_{x,r_1}^{\mathsf{eq}} - \mathbf{G}$ and hence $[\mathbf{B}\|\mathbf{A}_{x,r_1}^{\mathsf{eq}}] = [\mathbf{B}\|\mathbf{BR}\widehat{\mathbf{H}}_{\sigma \to r_1}\widehat{\mathbf{H}}_{r_1, r_1'} + \mathbf{G}]$. Note that

$$\begin{aligned} \|\mathbf{R}\widehat{\mathbf{H}}_{\sigma \to r_1}\widehat{\mathbf{H}}_{r_1, r_1'}\|_\infty &\le m^2\lambda k\|\mathbf{R}\|_\infty\|\widehat{\mathbf{H}}_{\sigma \to r_1}\|_\infty\|\widehat{\mathbf{H}}_{r_1, r_1'}\|_\infty \\ &\le m^2\lambda k(2m)^{d+1} \end{aligned}$$

and by item 3 of Theorem 1, given $\mathbf{B}$ and $\mathbf{R}^{\mathsf{eq}}_{id,r_1} = \mathbf{R}\widehat{\mathbf{H}}_{\sigma\to r_1}\widehat{\mathbf{H}}_{r_1,r_1'}$, it is efficient to compute $[\mathbf{B}\|\mathbf{A}^{\mathsf{eq}}_{x,r_1}]^{-1}_{\tau'}$ for some

$$\tau' = O\left(\|\mathbf{R}\widehat{\mathbf{H}}_{\sigma\to r_1}\widehat{\mathbf{H}}_{r_1,r_1'}\|_\infty\right) = O(k, \lambda, (2m)^{d+3}). \tag{2}$$

Therefore, if $\tau > \tau'$ then $\mathcal{C}^{ow}$ can now sample from $[\mathbf{B}\|\mathbf{A}^{\mathsf{eq}}_{x,r_1}]^{-1}_{\tau}$ without $\mathbf{B}^{-1}_{\tau_0}$. Likewise, compute

$$[\mathbf{B}'\|\mathbf{A}^{\mathsf{eq}}_{x',r_2}] = [\mathbf{B}'\|\mathbf{B}\mathbf{R}\widehat{\mathbf{H}}_{\sigma\to r_2}\widehat{\mathbf{H}}_{r_2,r_2'} + \mathbf{G}].$$

But $\mathcal{C}^{ow}$ still samples from $[\mathbf{B}'\|\mathbf{A}^{\mathsf{eq}}_{x',r_2}]^{-1}_{\tau}$ as in the real construction with $\mathbf{B}'^{-1}_{\tau_0}$.

Note that when $\mathcal{A}^{ow}$ queries trapdoor query $\mathcal{O}^{Td(\cdot)}$ (including id^*), the trapdoor is still computed as in the real construction.

The distribution remains identical to the previous game, that **Game 6** and **Game 7** are statistically indistinguishable.

Game 8. We change the way $\mathbf{B}$ is generated. Instead of sampling it via $\mathsf{TrapGen}$, sample a uniformly $\mathbf{B} \leftarrow \mathbb{Z}_q^{n\times m'}$.

By item 4 of Theorem 1 this change is statistically indistinguishable with **Game 7**.

Game 9. We change again the way $\mathcal{C}^{ow}$ answers the challenge query. It now samples uniformly $\mathsf{c}_1, \mathsf{c}_1' \stackrel{\$}{\leftarrow} \mathbb{Z}_q^t$.

This change is computationally indistinguishable with **Game 8** under the $DLWE_{n,q,\chi}$ problem. At this step the challenger completely hides $\mathbf{m}$ and so $\mathcal{A}^{ow}$ has no advantage.

Hence combining the above results, we obtain that the advantage of $\mathcal{A}^{ow}$ is negligible in security parameter λ, which ends the proof.

References

1. Agrawal, S., Boneh, D., Boyen, X.: Efficient lattice (H)IBE in the standard model. In: Gilbert, H. (ed.) EUROCRYPT 2010. LNCS, vol. 6110, pp. 553–572. Springer, Heidelberg (2010). https://doi.org/10.1007/978-3-642-13190-5_28
2. Agrawal, S., Boneh, D., Boyen, X.: Lattice basis delegation in fixed dimension and shorter-ciphertext hierarchical IBE. In: Rabin, T. (ed.) CRYPTO 2010. LNCS, vol. 6223, pp. 98–115. Springer, Heidelberg (2010). https://doi.org/10.1007/978-3-642-14623-7_6
3. Alornyo, S., Asante, M., Hu, X., Kissi Mireku, K.: Encrypted traffic analytic using identity based encryption with equality test for cloud computing, pp. 1–4, August 2018. https://doi.org/10.1109/ICASTECH.2018.8507063
4. Alornyo, S., Zhao, Y., Zhu, G., Xiong, H.: Identity based key-insulated encryption with outsourced equality test. Int. J. Netw. Secur. (2019). https://doi.org/10.6633/IJNS.860
5. Banerjee, A., Peikert, C., Rosen, A.: Pseudorandom functions and lattices. In: Pointcheval, D., Johansson, T. (eds.) EUROCRYPT 2012. LNCS, vol. 7237, pp. 719–737. Springer, Heidelberg (2012). https://doi.org/10.1007/978-3-642-29011-4_42

6. Boneh, D., et al.: Fully key-homomorphic encryption, arithmetic circuit ABE and compact garbled circuits. In: Nguyen, P.Q., Oswald, E. (eds.) EUROCRYPT 2014. LNCS, vol. 8441, pp. 533–556. Springer, Heidelberg (2014). https://doi.org/10.1007/978-3-642-55220-5_30
7. Brakerski, Z., Langlois, A., Peikert, C., Regev, O., Stehlé, D.: Classical hardness of learning with errors. In: Proceedings of the 45th Annual ACM Symposium on Symposium on Theory of Computing (STOC 2013), p. 575. ACM Press, Palo Alto, California (2013). https://doi.org/10.1145/2488608.2488680
8. Brakerski, Z., Vaikuntanathan, V.: Circuit-ABE from LWE: unbounded attributes and semi-adaptive security. In: Robshaw, M., Katz, J. (eds.) CRYPTO 2016. LNCS, vol. 9816, pp. 363–384. Springer, Heidelberg (2016). https://doi.org/10.1007/978-3-662-53015-3_13
9. Canetti, R., Halevi, S., Katz, J.: Chosen-ciphertext security from identity-based encryption. In: Cachin, C., Camenisch, J.L. (eds.) EUROCRYPT 2004. LNCS, vol. 3027, pp. 207–222. Springer, Heidelberg (2004). https://doi.org/10.1007/978-3-540-24676-3_13
10. Cui, Y., Huang, Q., Huang, J., Li, H., Yang, G.: Ciphertext-policy attribute-based encrypted data equality test and classification. Comput. J **62**(8), 1166–1177 (2019). https://doi.org/10.1093/comjnl/bxz036
11. Davidson, A., Katsumata, S., Nishimaki, R., Yamada, S., Yamakawa, T.: Adaptively secure constrained pseudorandom functions in the standard model. In: Micciancio, D., Ristenpart, T. (eds.) CRYPTO 2020. LNCS, vol. 12170, pp. 559–589. Springer, Cham (2020). https://doi.org/10.1007/978-3-030-56784-2_19
12. Duong, D.H., Fukushima, K., Kiyomoto, S., Roy, P.S., Susilo, W.: A lattice-based Public key encryption with equality test in standard model. In: Information Security and Privacy, vol. 11547, pp. 138–155. Springer International Publishing, Cham (2019). https://doi.org/10.1007/978-3-030-21548-4_8
13. Duong, D.H., Le, H.Q., Roy, P.S., Susilo, W.: Lattice-based IBE with equality test in standard model. In: Steinfeld, R., Yuen, T.H. (eds.) ProvSec 2019. LNCS, vol. 11821, pp. 19–40. Springer, Cham (2019). https://doi.org/10.1007/978-3-030-31919-9_2
14. Elhabob, R., Zhao, Y., Eltayieb, N., Abdelgader, A.M.S., Xiong, H.: Identity-based encryption with authorized equivalence test for cloud-assisted IoT. Cluster Comput. **23**(2), 1085–1101 (2019). https://doi.org/10.1007/s10586-019-02979-1
15. Gentry, C.: Practical identity-based encryption without random oracles. In: Vaudenay, S. (ed.) EUROCRYPT 2006. LNCS, vol. 4004, pp. 445–464. Springer, Heidelberg (2006). https://doi.org/10.1007/11761679_27
16. Gorbunov, S., Vaikuntanathan, V., Wichs, D.: Leveled fully homomorphic signatures from standard lattices. In: Proceedings of the Forty-Seventh Annual ACM Symposium on Theory of Computing, pp. 469–477. ACM, Portland, June 2015. https://doi.org/10.1145/2746539.2746576
17. Katsumata, S., Nishimaki, R., Yamada, S., Yamakawa, T.: Adaptively secure inner product encryption from LWE. In: Moriai, S., Wang, H. (eds.) ASIACRYPT 2020. LNCS, vol. 12493, pp. 375–404. Springer, Cham (2020). https://doi.org/10.1007/978-3-030-64840-4_13
18. Kim, S.: Key-homomorphic pseudorandom functions from LWE with small modulus. In: Canteaut, A., Ishai, Y. (eds.) EUROCRYPT 2020. LNCS, vol. 12106, pp. 576–607. Springer, Cham (2020). https://doi.org/10.1007/978-3-030-45724-2_20
19. Lee, H.T., Ling, S., Seo, J.H., Wang, H.: Semi-generic construction of public key encryption and identity-based encryption with equality test. Inf. Sci. **373**, 419–440 (2016). https://doi.org/10.1016/j.ins.2016.09.013

20. Lee, H.T., Ling, S., Seo, J.H., Wang, H., Youn, T.Y.: Public key encryption with equality test in the standard model. Inf. Sci. **516**, 89–108 (2020). https://doi.org/10.1016/j.ins.2019.12.023
21. Lin, X.J., Wang, Q., Sun, L., Qu, H.: Identity-based encryption with equality test and datestamp-based authorization mechanism. Theoret. Comput. Sci. **861**, 117–132 (2021). https://doi.org/10.1016/j.tcs.2021.02.015
22. Ling, Y., Ma, S., Huang, Q., Li, X., Zhong, Y., Ling, Y.: Efficient group ID-based encryption with equality test against insider attack. Comput. J. **64**(4), 661–674 (2021). https://doi.org/10.1093/comjnl/bxaa120
23. Ma, S.: Identity-based encryption with outsourced equality test in cloud computing. Inf. Sci. **328**, 389–402 (2016). https://doi.org/10.1016/j.ins.2015.08.053
24. Ma, S., Huang, Q., Zhang, M., Yang, B.: Efficient public key encryption with equality test supporting flexible authorization. IEEE Trans. Inf. Foren. Secur. **10**(3), 458–470 (2015). https://doi.org/10.1109/TIFS.2014.2378592
25. Ma, S., Zhang, M., Huang, Q., Yang, B.: Public key encryption with delegated equality test in a multi-user setting. Comput. J. **58**(4), 986–1002 (2015). https://doi.org/10.1093/comjnl/bxu026
26. Micciancio, D., Peikert, C.: Trapdoors for lattices: simpler, tighter, faster, smaller. In: Advances in Cryptology – EUROCRYPT 2012, vol. 7237, pp. 700–718. Springer, Heidelberg (2012). https://doi.org/10.1007/978-3-642-29011-4_41
27. Nguyen, G.L.D., Susilo, W., Duong, D.H., Le, H.Q., Guo, F.: Lattice-based IBE with equality test supporting flexible authorization in the standard model. In: Bhargavan, K., Oswald, E., Prabhakaran, M. (eds.) INDOCRYPT 2020. LNCS, vol. 12578, pp. 624–643. Springer, Cham (2020). https://doi.org/10.1007/978-3-030-65277-7_28
28. Peikert, C.: Public-key cryptosystems from the worst-case shortest vector problem: extended abstract. In: Proceedings of the 41st Annual ACM Symposium on Symposium on Theory of Computing (STOC 2019), p. 333. ACM Press, Bethesda (2009). https://doi.org/10.1145/1536414.1536461
29. Regev, O.: On lattices, learning with errors, random linear codes, and cryptography. J. ACM (JACM) **56**, 84–93 (2005). https://doi.org/10.1145/1568318.1568324
30. Sun, J., Xiong, H., Zhang, H., Peng, L.: Mobile access and flexible search over encrypted cloud data in heterogeneous systems. Inf. Sci. **507**, 1–15 (2020). https://doi.org/10.1016/j.ins.2019.08.026
31. Susilo, W., Duong, D.H., Le, H.Q.: Efficient post-quantum identity-based encryption with equality test. In: 2020 IEEE 26th International Conference on Parallel and Distributed Systems (ICPADS), pp. 633–640, December2020. https://doi.org/10.1109/ICPADS51040.2020.00088
32. Tsabary, R.: Fully secure attribute-based encryption for t-CNF from LWE. In: Advances in Cryptology – CRYPTO 2019, vol. 11692, pp. 62–85. Springer International Publishing, Cham (2019). https://doi.org/10.1007/978-3-030-26948-7_3
33. Wu, T., Ma, S., Mu, Y., Zeng, S.: ID-based encryption with equality test against insider attack. In: Pieprzyk, J., Suriadi, S. (eds.) ACISP 2017. LNCS, vol. 10342, pp. 168–183. Springer, Cham (2017). https://doi.org/10.1007/978-3-319-60055-0_9
34. Yang, G., Tan, C.H., Huang, Q., Wong, D.S.: Probabilistic public key encryption with equality test. In: Pieprzyk, J. (ed.) CT-RSA 2010. LNCS, vol. 5985, pp. 119–131. Springer, Heidelberg (2010). https://doi.org/10.1007/978-3-642-11925-5_9

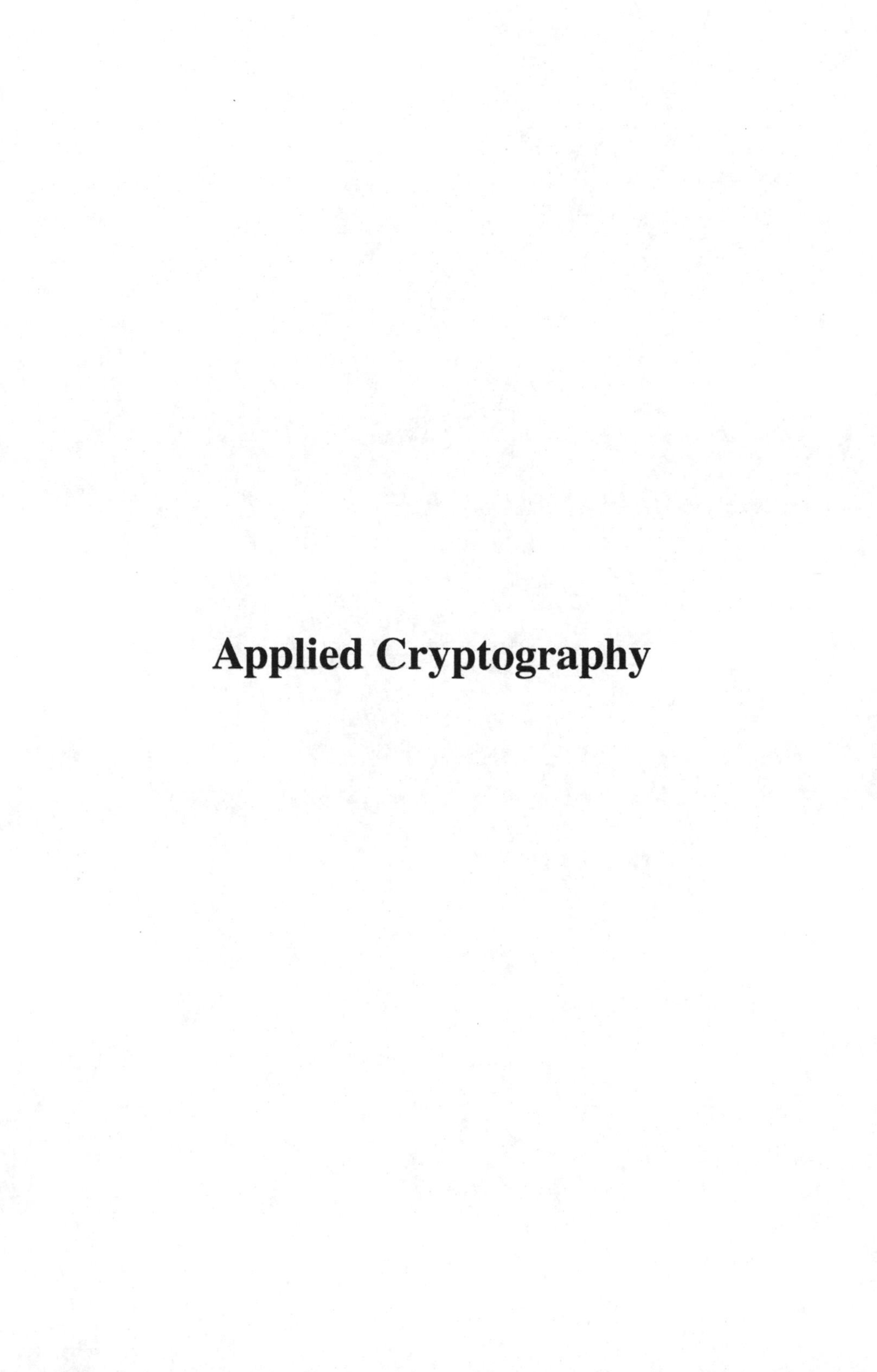

Applied Cryptography

Forward-Secure Revocable Identity-Based Encryption

Baodong Qin[1,2,3(✉)], Xue Bai[1], Dong Zheng[1,4(✉)], Hui Cui[5], and Yiyuan Luo[6,7,8]

[1] School of Cyberspace Security, Xi'an University of Posts and Telecommunications, Xi'an 710121, China
{qinbaodong,zhengdong}@xupt.edu.cn
[2] Science and Technology on Communication Security Laboratory, Chengdu 610041, China
[3] State Key Laboratory of Integrated Services Networks, Xidian University, Xi'an, China
[4] Westone Cryptologic Research Center, Beijing, China
[5] Discipline of IT, College of Arts, Business, Law and Social Sciences, Murdoch University, Murdoch, Western Australia, WA 6150, Australia
hui.cui@murdoch.edu.au
[6] School of Computer Science and Engineering, Huizhou University, Huizhou 516007, China
luoyy@hzu.edu.cn
[7] Henan Key Laboratory of Network Cryptography Technology, Zhengzhou, China
[8] Network and Data Security Key Laboratory of Sichuan Province, University of Electronic Science and Technology of China, Chengdu, China

Abstract. For identity-based encryption (IBE), if a user's private key is compromised, the security of his/her ciphertexts will fail completely. Revocation capability provides an effective way to mitigate above harm, so that the adversary cannot access to future ciphertexts anymore. However, current revocable IBE schemes do not provide any means to guarantee the security of the user's previous ciphertexts. In this paper, we propose a new cryptographic primitive, namely forward-secure revocable identity-based encryption (FS-RIBE), to address this issue. In FS-RIBE, when the event of full exposure of the user's current private key occurs, the forward security can guarantee that the user's private keys prior to this remain secure, while the revocation capability further guarantees that the adversary cannot obtain any valid decryption keys for future times. We provide formal definition and security model for FS-RIBE, and give a generic construction that is secure under the security model from (Hierarchical) IBE. Finally, we show some results of instantiations from various IBE and Hierarchical IBE schemes.

Keywords: Identity-based encryption · Revocation · Forward security · Decryption key exposure

D. Gao et al. (Eds.): ICICS 2021, LNCS 12919, pp. 321–340, 2021.
https://doi.org/10.1007/978-3-030-88052-1_19

1 Introduction

In 1984, Shamir initially proposed the primitive of Identity-Based Cryptosystem (IBC) and realized the first construction of Identity-Based Signature (IBS). But, the first Identity-based Encryption (IBE) scheme was realized until to 2001, by Boneh and Franklin [8], and Cocks [14] respectively. To date, a plentiful IBE/IBS schemes were proposed, e.g., [6,10,15–18,22,44], and they were extended to some high level cryptographic primitives, including fuzzy IBE [37], hierarchical IBE/IBS [7,13,19,25] and attribute-based cryptosystem [20,31]. In an IBC system, there is a Key Generation Center (KGC) to distribute private keys for users. An attractive feature of IBC is that a user can use any string, e.g., email address, as his/her public key. Hence, IBC removes the requirement of Public Key Infrastructure (PKI) used in traditional public-key cryptosystem. However, the absence of PKI results in the research on user/key revocation mechanism for IBC system. Indeed, we must provide an efficient way to remove a user from the IBC system once his secret key is expired or leaked.

In recent years, many works devoted to alleviate above issue in the setting of IBE via ciphertext update [21,40,42] or key update [5,26]. This paper focuses on the later technique, which is usually called revocable IBE. It applies a key update method to periodically update users' decryption keys, so that revoked users can not get their updated decryption keys. This provides an efficient way to prevent the basic and realistic (long-term) secret key exposure attacks on future ciphertexts. That is, once a user's key is exposed, the user will be fully removed from the system and can not decrypt any ciphertexts encrypted in the future time periods any more. In PKC 2013, Seo and Emura [38] considered a very realistic threats and attack scenarios: a user is not removed from the system, but his decryption keys may be exposed at some time periods. They called it Decryption Key Exposure (DKE) attacks and hoped that an exposure of a user's decryption key at some time period does not endanger the confidentiality of ciphertexts that are encrypted in other time periods. They showed that some previous RIBE schemes (e.g. [5]) can not resist against DKE attacks. Since the introduction of DKE security, many follow up works [23,24,26,32,34,43] have concerned RIBE schemes with DKE resistance. Currently, the security notions for RIBE schemes have captured as many realistic attack scenarios as possible, such as DKE security, adaptive security and post-quantum resistance. However, none of them consider forward security. That is, once a user's private key is leaked, current security notions provide no means to guarantee the confidentiality of the user's previous ciphertexts. To the best of our knowledge, only the work of [45] studied forward security of revocable IBS and gave a concrete construction based on the q-type Diffie-Hellman Exponent assumption. But, it is unknown how to extend it to the IBE setting in a generic way and how to give a post-quantum construction.

Our Contributions. This paper studies on forward-secure revocable IBE (FS-RIBE). In an FS-RIBE system (see Fig. 1), each user has two type of private keys: one is secret key that contains the user's all secret information and the other is decryption key that is only available to decrypt ciphertexts encrypted in a specified time period. User's secret key is associated with time periods and will be evolved by the user himself with time while keeping the public key fixed. The KGC periodically broadcasts (time-based) update keys to all system users, so that only non-revoked user can generate the corresponding time-based decryption key from update keys and his own time-based secret key.

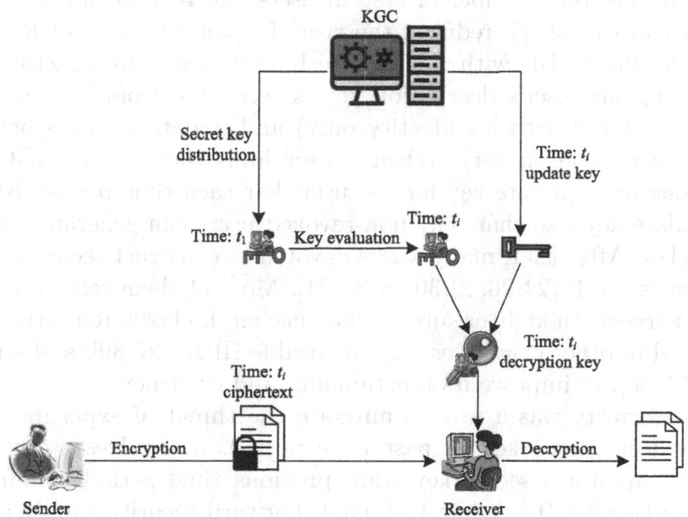

Fig. 1. The system model of FS-RIBE

Our contributions are summarized as follows:

- First, we provide the formal definition and security model for FS-RIBE system. It captures user revocation, decryption key exposure resistance and forward security simultaneously.
- Second, we introduce a generic construction of FS-RIBE scheme. It combines a hierarchical IBE (HIBE) scheme and a standard IBE scheme to form a forward-secure RIBE scheme. The underlying HIBE scheme will be used to generate user's initial time period secret key that can evolve to future time period, while the underlying IBE scheme will be used to generate time-based update keys via a complete subtree method.
- Third, we further replace the IBE scheme with the HIBE scheme to generate time-based update keys. This results in another generic construction of FS-RIBE scheme with more compact ciphertexts, if the underlying HIBE scheme has compact ciphertexts.
- Finally, we show that our generic method implies some new constructions of RIBE with both DKE resistance and forward security based on bilinear maps or lattices. We give an overview comparison of our instantiations with other related RIBE schemes with or without DKE resistance.

Related Work. User revocation is a basic requirement for identity-based encryption. Since the invention of the first IBE scheme, Boneh and Franklin [8] had already suggested to periodically issue a private key for any non-revoked user by combining his identity and time $\mathsf{ID}||t$ as public key. As the user's identities are in fact distinct from each other, the scheme already satisfies forward security. However, this method does not scale well, as the complexity of update keys is $O(N-R)$, which is linearly increased with the number of non-revoked users. Here, N and R are the total number of system users and revoked users respectively. Later, Boldyreva et al. [5] reduced the size of update keys to $O(R \cdot \log N/R)$, by combining fuzzy IBE with a complete binary tree data structure. In their RIBE scheme, each user's decryption key is generated from his long-term private key (associated with his identity only) and update keys (associated with time and the revocation list). When a user joins the system, KGC will distribute a long-term private key for the user. For each time period, KGC issues a set of update keys, so that only non-revoked users can generate current time decryption key. After that, many works devoted to construct secure and efficient RIBE schemes [11,12,24,26,29,30,34,38,41]. Most of them rely on either complete binary tree method [5] or subset difference method [26]. Recently, RIBE was also extended to other primitives, e.g., revocable HIBE [27,39], and server-aided RIBE [33,35,36], to improve its functionality and efficiency.

Forward security was a way to mitigate the threat of exposure of a secret (signing or decryption) key in past time period. It involves a key evolution paradigm to update a secret key from previous time period to current time period while keeping the public key fixed. Forward security can guarantee the security of previous secret keys, even the current key was exposed. Anderson [3] firstly proposed the idea of forward security, and later Bellare et al. [4], and Canetti et al. [9] formalized the definition and security model for forward-secure signature and forward-secure encryption respectively. In 2017, Wei et al. [45] first combined forward security with revocable IBS, to mitigate the threat of exposure of a user's long-term private key. However, till now, there is no work to solve this issue for revocable identity-based encryption.

2 Preliminary

Notations. For two binary string X and Y, we denote by $X\|Y$ their concatenate. For a k-vector $\vec{v} = (v_1, \ldots, v_k)$ and an element v_0, we denote by $v_0|\vec{v}$ the $(k+1)$-vector $(v_0, v_1, \ldots, v_k)$. If S is a finite set, then $s \leftarrow S$ denotes the operation of sampling an element s from S uniformly at random, and $s \xleftarrow{\chi} S$ denotes the operation of sampling an element s from S according to the distribution χ.

2.1 Syntax for (H)IBE

In an IBE system, it contains four PPT (probabilistic polynomial-time) algorithms:

- $(\mathsf{mpk}, \mathsf{msk}) \leftarrow \mathsf{Setup}(\lambda, \ell_{id})$: On input a security parameter λ and a parameter of identity space ℓ_{id} (it may be implicitly involved by the algorithm), it outputs a master public key mpk and a master secret key msk.
- $sk_{\mathsf{ID}} \leftarrow \mathsf{Extract}(\mathsf{mpk}, \mathsf{msk}, \mathsf{ID})$: On input a master public key mpk, a master secret key msk and an identity $\mathsf{ID} \in \{0,1\}^{\ell_{id}}$, it outputs a secret key sk_{ID} corresponding to the identity.
- $C_{\mathsf{ID}} \leftarrow \mathsf{Encrypt}(\mathsf{mpk}, \mathsf{ID}, M)$: On input a master public key mpk, an identity $\mathsf{ID} \in \{0,1\}^{\ell_{id}}$ and a message M (from the message space), it outputs a ciphertext C_{ID}.
- $M/\bot \leftarrow \mathsf{Decrypt}(sk_{\mathsf{ID}}, C_{\mathsf{ID}})$: On input a user's secret key sk_{ID}, and a ciphertext C_{ID}, it outputs a message M or a special symbol $\bot$ indicating the ciphertext is invalid.

In a HIBE system with maximum hierarchy depth d, each identity is viewed as a vector with dimension no more than d, e.g. $(\mathsf{ID}_1, \ldots, \mathsf{ID}_k)$. It has an additional algorithm, namely Derive, to derive secret keys for identities from secret keys corresponding to their prefix identities. Specifically, on input a secret key $\mathsf{sk}_{\mathsf{ID}_{|k-1}}$ for a $(k-1)$-dimension identity $\mathsf{ID}_{|k-1} = (\mathsf{ID}_1, \ldots, \mathsf{ID}_{k-1})$ and a k-dimension identity $\mathsf{ID}_{|k} = (\mathsf{ID}_1, \ldots, \mathsf{ID}_{k-1}, \mathsf{ID}_k)$, it outputs a secret key $sk_{\mathsf{ID}_{|k}}$ for the identity $\mathsf{ID}_{|k}$. Clearly, if the maximum depth of the hierarchy is 1, it is just the IBE system.

Next, we recall the IBE and HIBE adaptive indistinguishability against chosen-plaintext attacks (IND-CPA security). We consider a HIBE system with maximum hierarchy depth d (IBE is the case of $d = 1$). The security experiment is defined as follows.

1. **Setup:** The challenge $\mathcal{C}$ runs $(\mathsf{mpk}, \mathsf{msk}) \leftarrow \mathsf{Setup}(\lambda, \ell_{id}, d)$. It gives mpk to the adversary $\mathcal{A}$ and keeps msk in hand.
2. **Phase 1:** The adversary can adaptively make a polynomial number of the secret key queries. When $\mathcal{A}$ request a secret key for an identity $\mathsf{ID}_{|k}$ with dimension $k \leq d$, the challenger $\mathcal{C}$ computes a secret key $sk_{\mathsf{ID}_{|k}}$ by running algorithm $\mathsf{Extract}$, and sends it to the adversary. We require that $\mathsf{ID}_{|k}$ cannot be a prefix of the challenge identity $\mathsf{ID}^* = (\mathsf{ID}_1, \ldots, \mathsf{ID}_{k^*})$ as described in the challenge phase.
3. **Challenge:** When $\mathcal{A}$ submits two equal-length messages M_0, M_1 and a challenge identity vector $\mathsf{ID}^* = (\mathsf{ID}_1, \ldots, \mathsf{ID}_{k^*})$ with dimension $k^* \leq d$. $\mathcal{C}$ chooses a random bit b and runs $C^*_{\mathsf{ID}^*} \leftarrow \mathsf{Encrypt}(\mathsf{mpk}, \mathsf{ID}^*, M_b)$. It returns $C^*_{\mathsf{ID}^*}$ to $\mathcal{A}$.
4. **Phase 2:** The adversary can continuously and adaptively make a polynomial number of secret key queries on identities as in Phase 1, as long as the identity ID is not a prefix of the challenge identity ID^*.
5. **Guess:** Finally, $\mathcal{A}$ outputs a bit b' as the guess of b.
   The advantage of $\mathcal{A}$ in the above experiment is defined as:

$$\mathsf{Adv}^{\text{IND-CPA}}_{\text{(H)IBE},\mathcal{A}}(\lambda) = \left| \Pr[b' = b] - \frac{1}{2} \right|.$$

Definition 1 (IND-CPA security for (H)IBE). *For any PPT adversary $\mathcal{A}$, if the above advantage of $\mathcal{A}$ is negligible in λ, then the (H)IBE scheme is IND-CPA secure.*

Multi-ciphertext Security. In the challenge phase, if the adversary submits multiple challenge identities, e.g., $\mathsf{ID}_1^*, \ldots, \mathsf{ID}_n^*$, and obtains a multiple challenge ciphertexts, i.e., $C_i^* \leftarrow \mathsf{Encrypt}(\mathsf{mpk}, \mathsf{ID}_i^*, M_b)$, for $i = 1, \ldots, n$. By a hybrid argument, we can prove that the advantage of $\mathcal{A}$ to distinguish n challenge ciphertexts is no more than $n \cdot \mathsf{Adv}_{\text{(H)IBE},\mathcal{A}}^{\text{IND-CPA}}(\lambda)$.

2.2 The Node Selection Algorithm

The node selection algorithm will be used in our complete tree based user revocation method, to find the minimal number of nodes that can cover all non-revoked users. In a complete binary tree, each leaf node is associated with an identity of user. Let $\mathsf{Path}(\mathsf{ID})$ denote the set of nodes on the path from ID to the root. For each node x, let x_l and x_r denote its left and right child nodes respectively. On input a binary tree BT, an revocation list RL and a time period t, the node selection algorithm $\mathsf{KUNodes}(\mathsf{BT}, \mathsf{RL}, t)$ works as follows:

1. Initial two empty sets X and Y.
2. For each $(\mathsf{ID}_i, t_i) \in \mathsf{RL}$, if $t_i \leq t$, add $\mathsf{Path}(\mathsf{ID}_i)$ to X.
3. For each $x \in X$, if $x_l \notin X$, then add x_l to Y; if $x_r \notin X$, then add x_r to Y.
4. If $Y = \emptyset$, return the root node; else return Y.

Figure 2 gives an example of the node selection algorithm when no user is revoked or the user $\mathsf{ID} = 2$ is revoked. In Sect. 4, we assign each left edge and right edge of the binary tree BT with value 0 and 1 respectively. For each node, e.g., x_{10}, we denote by $v_{x_{10}}$ the bit string of the path values from the root node to node x_{10} (i.e., $v_{x_{10}} = 011$).

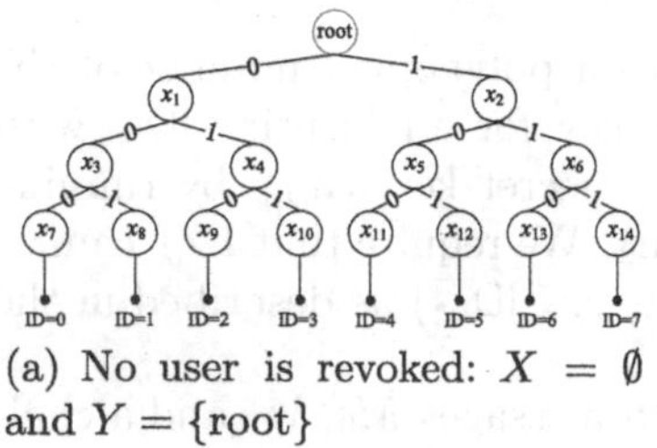

(a) No user is revoked: $X = \emptyset$ and $Y = \{\text{root}\}$

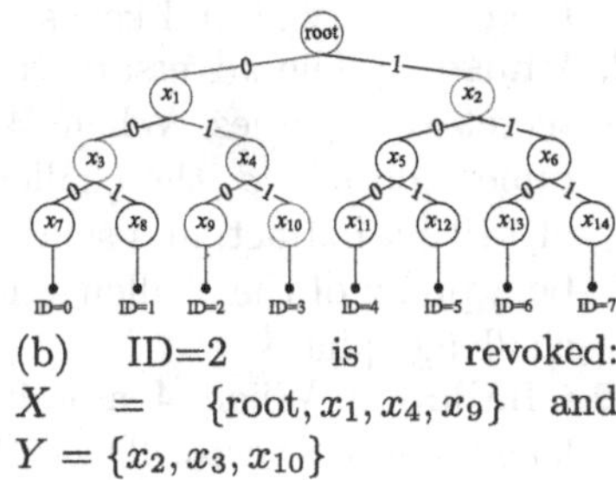

(b) ID=2 is revoked: $X = \{\text{root}, x_1, x_4, x_9\}$ and $Y = \{x_2, x_3, x_{10}\}$

Fig. 2. Example of node section algorithm

3 Syntax for FS-RIBE

A forward-secure revocable identity-based encryption (FS-RIBE) consists of the following eight algorithms. We assume that each user is distributed a secrete key for initialized time period when he joins the system. After that, the user generates secret keys of the following time periods by himself using algorithm SKEval.

- $(\mathsf{mpk}, \mathsf{msk}, \mathsf{ST}, \mathsf{RL}) \leftarrow \mathsf{Setup}(\lambda, \ell_{id}, \ell_{time})$: Let λ be the security parameter, $\{0,1\}^{\ell_{id}}$ be the identity space of users and $2^{\ell_{time}}$ be the number of time periods. This algorithm takes as input the parameters λ, ℓ_{id} and ℓ_{time}, and outputs a pair of master public/secret keys $(\mathsf{mpk}, \mathsf{msk})$ and two sets ST and RL initialized with empty. The set ST stores some (secret) information about users (e.g., the binary tree BT in our scheme) and is maintained by the key generator center. The set RL stores information about revoked users, including their identities and time periods when they were revoked.
- $sk_{\mathsf{ID}}^{(t_1)} \leftarrow \mathsf{KeyGen}(\mathsf{mpk}, \mathsf{msk}, \mathsf{ID}, \mathsf{ST})$: For any user with identity $\mathsf{ID} \in \{0,1\}^{\ell_{id}}$, this algorithm outputs a secret key $sk_{\mathsf{ID}}^{(t_1)}$ for initial time period $t_1 = 0^{\ell_{time}-1}1$.
- $sk_{\mathsf{ID}}^{(t)} \leftarrow \mathsf{SKEval}(\mathsf{mpk}, sk_{\mathsf{ID}}^{(t_1)}, t)$: For a time period $t > t_1$, this algorithm evaluates the user's secret $sk_{\mathsf{ID}}^{(t_1)}$ from time period t_1 to t, and outputs the new secret key $sk_{\mathsf{ID}}^{(t)}$. If $t = t_1$, the algorithm returns $sk_{\mathsf{ID}}^{(t_1)}$ directly.
- $uk_t \leftarrow \mathsf{DKUpdate}(\mathsf{mpk}, \mathsf{msk}, \mathsf{ST}, \mathsf{RL}, t)$: For the time period $t \in \{0,1\}^{\ell_{time}}$, this algorithm outputs a set of update keys uk_t.
- $dk_{\mathsf{ID},t} \leftarrow \mathsf{DKGen}(sk_{\mathsf{ID}}^{(t)}, uk_t)$: This algorithm takes as input user's secret key $\mathsf{ID}^{(t)}$ and update key uk_t for time period t, and outputs a decryption key $dk_{\mathsf{ID},t}$ for time period t.
- $C_{\mathsf{ID},t} \leftarrow \mathsf{Encrypt}(\mathsf{mpk}, \mathsf{ID}, t, M)$: For a message M, this algorithm encrypts it with identity ID and time period t, and outputs the ciphertext $C_{\mathsf{ID},t}$.
- $M/\bot \leftarrow \mathsf{Decrypt}(dk_{\mathsf{ID},t}, C_{\mathsf{ID},t})$: If the identity ID is not revoked at time period t, this algorithm decrypts the ciphertext $C_{\mathsf{ID},t}$ using the decryption key $dk_{\mathsf{ID},t}$, and outputs a message M. Otherwise, it outputs $\bot$.
- $\mathsf{RL} \leftarrow \mathsf{Revoke}(\mathsf{RL}, \mathsf{ID}, t)$: If the identity ID is revoked at time period t, the key authority adds (ID, t) to the revocation list, and outputs an updated revocation list RL.

Correctness. For any identity ID and message M, if the user is not revoked at time period t, then the following probability holds.

$$\Pr\left[M = M' : \begin{array}{l} (\mathsf{mpk}, \mathsf{msk}, \mathsf{ST}, \mathsf{RL}) \leftarrow \mathsf{Setup}(\lambda, \ell_{id}, \ell_{time}) \\ sk_{\mathsf{ID}}^{(t_1)} \leftarrow \mathsf{KeyGen}(\mathsf{mpk}, \mathsf{msk}, \mathsf{ID}, \mathsf{ST}) \\ sk_{\mathsf{ID}}^{(t)} \leftarrow \mathsf{SKEval}(\mathsf{mpk}, sk_{\mathsf{ID}}^{(t_1)}, t) \\ uk_t \leftarrow \mathsf{DKUpdate}(\mathsf{mpk}, \mathsf{msk}, \mathsf{ST}, \mathsf{RL}, t) \\ dk_{\mathsf{ID},t} \leftarrow \mathsf{DKGen}(sk_{\mathsf{ID}}^{(t)}, uk_t) \\ C_{\mathsf{ID},t} \leftarrow \mathsf{Encrypt}(\mathsf{mpk}, \mathsf{ID}, t, M) \\ M' \leftarrow \mathsf{Decrypt}(dk_{\mathsf{ID},t}, C_{\mathsf{ID},t}) \end{array} \right] = 1$$

IND-CPA-Security for FS-RIBE. The IND-CPA security of FS-RIBE is defined by the following experiment played between a challenger $\mathcal{C}$ and a PPT adversary $\mathcal{A}$.

1. **Setup:** $\mathcal{C}$ runs $\mathsf{Setup}(\lambda, \ell_{id}, \ell_{time})$ to obtain a master public key mpk, a master secret key msk, a state ST and a revocation list RL. It gives mpk to $\mathcal{A}$.

2. **Phase 1:** $\mathcal{A}$ can adaptively make a polynomial number of queries. The queries are proceeded as follows.
   - *Create key:* If $\mathcal{A}$ makes a create key query for identity $\mathsf{ID} \in \{0,1\}^{\ell_{id}}$ and time period $t \in \{0,1\}^{\ell_{time}}$, $\mathcal{C}$ first checks whether $t = 0^{\ell_{time}-1}1$ is the initial time period. If so, it runs $\mathsf{KeyGen}(\mathsf{mpk}, \mathsf{msk}, \mathsf{ID}, \mathsf{ST})$ to obtain an initial secret key $sk_{\mathsf{ID}}^{(t)}$, and stores the tuple $(\mathsf{ID}, t_1, sk_{\mathsf{ID}}^{(t_1)})$ into the key list KL. Otherwise, $\mathcal{C}$ checks whether there is a tuple $(\mathsf{ID}, t', sk_{\mathsf{ID}}^{(t')})$ in list KL such that $t' < t$. If so, it runs $\mathsf{SKEval}(\mathsf{mpk}, sk_{\mathsf{ID}}^{(t')}, t)$ to obtain a new secret key $sk_{\mathsf{ID}}^{(t)}$ for time period t, and replaces the tuple $(\mathsf{ID}, t', sk_{\mathsf{ID}}^{(t')})$ with $(\mathsf{ID}, t, sk_{\mathsf{ID}}^{(t)})$. If not, $\mathcal{C}$ aborts the response.
   - *Secret key:* If $\mathcal{A}$ makes a secret key query for identity $\mathsf{ID} \in \{0,1\}^{\ell_{id}}$ at time period $t \in \{0,1\}^{\ell_{time}}$, $\mathcal{C}$ checks whether there is tuple $(\mathsf{ID}, t, sk_{\mathsf{ID}}^{(t)})$ in list KL. If so, $\mathcal{C}$ returns $sk_{\mathsf{ID}}^{(t)}$ to $\mathcal{A}$; Otherwise, it returns $\perp$.
   - *Update key:* If $\mathcal{A}$ makes an update key query for time period t, $\mathcal{C}$ runs $\mathsf{DKUpdate}(\mathsf{mpk}, \mathsf{msk}, \mathsf{ST}, \mathsf{RL}, t)$ to obtain uk_t and returns it to $\mathcal{A}$.
   - *Decryption key:* If $\mathcal{A}$ makes a decryption key query for identity ID and time period t, $\mathcal{C}$ first retrieves from KL the tuple $(\mathsf{ID}, t', sk_{\mathsf{ID}}^{(t')})$ such that $t' \leq t$. If no such tuple, $\mathcal{C}$ aborts the response. Otherwise, $\mathcal{C}$ evaluates the secret key $sk_{\mathsf{ID}}^{(t')}$ from time period t' to t by running algorithm $\mathsf{SKEval}(\mathsf{mpk}, sk_{\mathsf{ID}}^{(t')}, t)$, and obtains the decryption $dk_{\mathsf{ID},t}$ by running algorithm $\mathsf{DKGen}(sk_{\mathsf{ID}}^{(t)}, uk_t)$. $\mathcal{C}$ returns $dk_{\mathsf{ID},t}$ to $\mathcal{A}$.
   - *Revocation:* If $\mathcal{A}$ makes a revocation query for identity ID at time period t, $\mathcal{C}$ adds (ID, t) to the revocation list RL with the restriction that $\mathcal{A}$ did not request the update key for time period t.
3. **Challenge:** When $\mathcal{A}$ submits a challenge identity ID^*, a challenge time period t^* and two equal-length messages M_0^*, M_1^*, $\mathcal{C}$ chooses a random bit $b \in \{0,1\}$, computes the challenge ciphertext $C^* \leftarrow \mathsf{Encrypt}(\mathsf{mpk}, \mathsf{ID}^*, t^*, M_b)$ and returns the challenge ciphertext to $\mathcal{A}$, with the following restriction:
   - $\mathcal{A}$ never request a decryption key for identity ID^* and time period t^*.
   - If $\mathcal{A}$ requests a secret key for ID^* and time period $t < t^*$, then the challenge identity must be revoked before time period t^*.
4. **Phase 2:** $\mathcal{A}$ may continue to adaptively make a polynomial number of queries with the restriction as in the challenge phase.
5. **Guess:** Finally, $\mathcal{A}$ outputs a bit b' as the guess of b.

In above experiment, we require that a secret key queried by the adversary is pre-created in the key list KL, otherwise, the adversary can ask the "*Create key*" oracle to generate it. The advantage of $\mathcal{A}$ in this experiment is defined by

$$\mathsf{Adv}_{\text{FS-RIBE},\mathcal{A}}^{\text{IND-CPA}}(\lambda) := \left| \Pr[b' = b] - \frac{1}{2} \right|.$$

Definition 2 (IND-CPA security). *An FS-RIBE scheme is IND-CPA secure if for any PPT adversary $\mathcal{A}$, the advantage of $\mathcal{A}$ in the above experiment is negligible in the security parameter λ. If the challenge identity and time period is initially specified, the scheme is selective IND-CPA (sIND-CPA) secure.*

About the Forward Security. In Definition 2, the adversary is allowed to query secret keys for the challenge identity ID^*, as long as the corresponding time period t is greater than the challenge time period t^*. This indicates that the exposure of a secret key at time period t does not compromise the security of secret keys before time period t. This is just the forward security as required by our security notion of FS-RIBE.

4 Generic Constructions

Let HIBE = (HIBE.Setup, HIBE.Extract, HIBE.Derive, HIBE.Encrypt, HIBE.Decrypt) be a hierarchical IBE scheme with maximum identity depth $\ell_{time} + 1$ over space $\{0,1\}^{\ell_{id}}$. Let IBE=(IBE.Setup, IBE.Extract, IBE.Encrypt, IBE.Decrypt) be an IBE scheme with identity space $\{0,1\}^{\ell_{time}+\ell_{id}}$. Assume that the message spaces of HIBE and IBE both are $\mathcal{M}$. Then, we can construct a forward secure RIBE scheme RIBE = (RIBE.Setup, RIBE.KeyGen, RIBE.SKEval, RIBE.DKUpdate, RIBE.DKGen, RIBE.Encrypt, RIBE.Decrypt, RIBE.Revoke) as described in Construction 1. Specifically, the identity space is $\{0,1\}^{\ell_{id}}$ and the time period space is $\{0,1\}^{\ell_{time}}$, and the message space is $\mathcal{M}$.

In the construction, each user's secret key is associated with a discrete time period. Let $T = \{0, 1, \ldots, 2^{\ell_{time}} - 1\}$ be the set of $2^{\ell_{time}}$ time periods. Each time period is viewed as a leaf node of a binary tree at depth ℓ_{time} in chronological order. Each node of the tree is arranged as bit "0" if it is the left child of its parent node and as "1" otherwise. In this case, a time period can be identified by an ℓ_{time}-bit integer $t = I_1 I_2 \cdots I_{\ell_{time}} \in \{0,1\}^{\ell_{time}}$, ordered from the top to the bottom of the tree. For each time period $t \in T$, we denote by $\mathcal{J}_t = \{J_{t,1}, J_{t,2}, \ldots, J_{t,\ell_{time}+1}\}$ a set of $\ell_{time} + 1$ identities and view each $J_{t,c}$ as an identity vector. For $c = 1, \ldots, \ell_{time} + 1$, the $J_{t,c}$ is defined as follows

$$J_{t,c} = \begin{cases} (I_1, I_2, \ldots, I_{c-1}, 1) & \text{if } 1 \le c \le \ell_{time} \text{ and } I_c = 0 \\ \perp & \text{if } 1 \le c \le \ell_{time} \text{ and } I_c = 1 \\ (I_1, I_2, \cdots, I_{\ell_{time}}) & \text{if } c = \ell_{time} + 1 \end{cases}.$$

As depicted in Fig. 3, for a number of $|T| = 2^4$ time periods and time $t = 0001$, the set $\mathcal{J}_1$ is given by $\{1, 01, 001, \perp, 0001\}$.

Without loss of generality, we also assume that the time period is begin by time $0^{\ell_{time}-1}1$.

4.1 The First Construction

Construction 1 (Forward-secure RIBE scheme). *Our first generic construction of FS-RIBE scheme is described as below.*

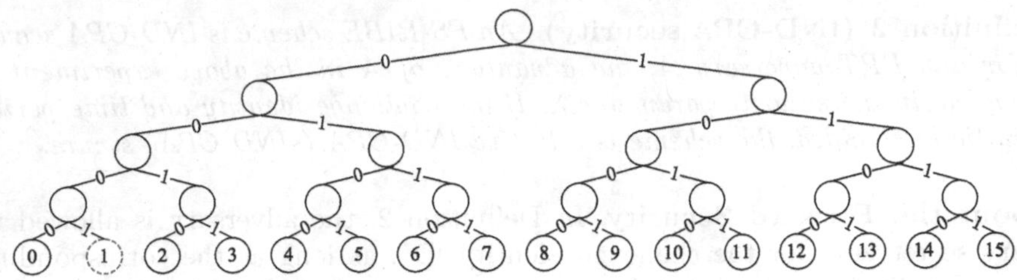

Fig. 3. An example for time period $t = 0001$

- $(\mathsf{mpk}, \mathsf{msk}, \mathsf{ST}, \mathsf{RL}) \leftarrow \mathsf{RIBE.Setup}(\lambda, \ell_{id}, \ell_{time})$: *It runs* $\mathsf{HIBE.Setup}(\lambda, \ell_{time} + 1)$ *and* $\mathsf{IBE.Setup}(\lambda, \ell_{time} + \ell_{id})$ *to obtain* $(\mathsf{mpk}_1, \mathsf{msk}_1)$ *and* $(\mathsf{mpk}_2, \mathsf{msk}_2)$ *respectively. It initializes a complete binary tree* BT *with depth* ℓ_{id}. *Each leaf node is associated with an identity. Finally, the algorithm returns* $\mathsf{mpk} = (\mathsf{mpk}_1, \mathsf{mpk}_2)$, $\mathsf{msk} = (\mathsf{msk}_1, \mathsf{msk}_2)$, $\mathsf{ST} = \mathsf{BT}$ *and an empty revocation list* RL.
- $sk_{\mathsf{ID}}^{(1)} \leftarrow \mathsf{RIBE.KeyGen}(\mathsf{mpk}, \mathsf{msk}, \mathsf{ID}, \mathsf{ST})$: *For any user with identity* $\mathsf{ID} \in \{0,1\}^{\ell_{id}}$, *the algorithm first computes the set* $\mathcal{J}_t = \{J_{t,1}, J_{t,2}, \cdots, J_{t,\ell_{time}+1}\}$ *for initial time period* $t = 0^{\ell_{time}-1}1$. *For each* $c = 1, \ldots, \ell_{time}+1$, *if* $J_{t,c} \neq \perp$, *it involves algorithm* $\mathsf{HIBE.Extract}(\mathsf{mpk}_1, \mathsf{msk}_1, \mathsf{ID}|J_{t,c})$ *to obtain a corresponding secret key* $K_{t,c}$, *where* $\mathsf{ID}|J_{t,c}$ *is an extended vector of* $J_{t,c}$ *with first element* ID, *as explained in notations in Sect. 2. If* $J_{t,c} = \perp$, *it sets* $K_{t,c} = \perp$. *Finally, it returns the secret key* $sk_{\mathsf{ID}}^{(1)} = \{1, (K_{t,1}, \ldots, K_{t,\ell_{time}+1})\}$.
- $sk_{\mathsf{ID}}^{(t_2)} \leftarrow \mathsf{RIBE.SKEval}(\mathsf{mpk}, sk_{\mathsf{ID}}^{(t_1)}, t_2)$: *For a time period* $t_2 > t_1$, *the algorithm first computes the two sets* $\mathcal{J}_{t_1}$ *and* $\mathcal{J}_{t_2}$ *respectively. For each* $c_2 \in \{1, \ldots, \ell_{time}+1\}$, *if* $J_{t_2,c_2} \neq \perp$, *there must exist a* $c_1 \in \{1, \ldots, \ell_{time}+1\}$ *so that* $(\mathsf{ID}, J_{t_1,c_1})$ *is a prefix of* $(\mathsf{ID}, J_{t_2,c_2})$. *It then involves algorithm* $\mathsf{HIBE.Derive}(\mathsf{mpk}_1, K_{t_1,c_1}, \mathsf{ID}|J_{t_2,c_2})$ *to obtain the corresponding key* K_{t_2,c_2}. *If* $J_{t_2,c_2} = \perp$, *it sets* $K_{t_2,c_2} = \perp$. *Finally, the algorithm returns* $sk_{\mathsf{ID}}^{(t_2)} = \{t_2, (K_{t_2,1}, \ldots, K_{t_2,\ell_{time}+1})\}$.
- $uk_t \leftarrow \mathsf{RIBE.DKUpdate}(\mathsf{mpk}, \mathsf{msk}, \mathsf{ST}, \mathsf{RL}, t)$: *For the time period* $t \in \{0,1\}^{\ell_{time}}$, *the algorithm first computes the cover set* $\mathsf{KUNodes}(\mathsf{BT}, \mathsf{RL}, t)$. *For each node* $x \in \mathsf{KUNodes}(\mathsf{BT}, \mathsf{RL}, t)$, *it involves algorithm* $\mathsf{IBE.Extract}(\mathsf{mpk}_2, \mathsf{msk}_2, t||v_x)$ *to obtain the key* L_x *corresponding to identity* $t||v_x$. *Here,* v_x *is the binary string as defined in the node selection algorithm. Finally, it returns the update key* $uk_t = \{t, \{L_x\}_{x \in \mathsf{KUNodes}(\mathsf{BT},\mathsf{RL},t)}\}$.
- $dk_{\mathsf{ID},t} \leftarrow \mathsf{RIBE.DKGen}(sk_{\mathsf{ID}}^{(t)}, uk_t)$: *Suppose that a user's current secret key is* $sk_{\mathsf{ID}}^{(t)} = \{t, (K_{t,1}, \ldots, K_{t,\ell_{time}+1})\}$ *and the current time period update key is* $uk_t = \{t, \{L_x\}_{x \in \mathsf{KUNodes}(\mathsf{BT},\mathsf{RL},t)}\}$. *If* ID *is not revoked at time period* t, *there must exist a common node* $x^* \in \mathsf{Path}(\mathsf{ID}) \cap \mathsf{KUNodes}(\mathsf{BT}, \mathsf{RL}, t)$. *The algorithm returns the corresponding decryption key* $dk_{\mathsf{ID},t} = (K_{t,\ell_{time}+1}, L_{x^*})$.
- $C_{\mathsf{ID},t} \leftarrow \mathsf{Encrypt}(\mathsf{mpk}, \mathsf{ID}, t, M)$: *For a message* $M \in \mathcal{M}$, *the algorithm first splits the message into two parts* $M_1, M_2 \in \mathcal{M}$ *so that* $M = M_1 \oplus M_2$. *Then, it computes* $C_1 \leftarrow \mathsf{HIBE.Encrypt}(\mathsf{mpk}_1, \mathsf{ID}|J_{t,\ell_{time}+1}, M_1)$, *and* $C_{2,x} \leftarrow$

IBE.Encrypt($\mathsf{mpk}_2, (t||v_x, M_2)$) *for each node* $x \in \mathsf{Path}(\mathsf{ID})$. *Finally, the algorithm returns ciphertexts* $C_{\mathsf{ID},t} = (C_1, \{C_{2,x}\}_{x \in \mathsf{Path(ID)}})$.

- $M/\perp \leftarrow$ Decrypt($dk_{\mathsf{ID},t}, C_{\mathsf{ID},t}$): *Suppose that* $C_{\mathsf{ID},t} = (C_1, \{C_{2,x}\}_{x \in \mathsf{Path(ID)}})$, *and* $dk_{\mathsf{ID},t} = (K_{t,\ell_{time}+1}, L_{x^*})$. *If the identity* ID *is not revoked at time period* t, *the node index* x^* *in* L_{x^*} *must belong to* Path(ID). *The algorithm computes* $M_1 \leftarrow$ HIBE.Decrypt($K_{t,\ell_{time}+1}, C_1$) *and* $M_2 \leftarrow$ IBE.Decrypt(L_{x^*}, C_{2,x^*}). *Finally, the algorithm returns* $M = M_1 \oplus M_2$. *If the identity is revoked at time period* t, *the algorithm returns* $\perp$ *directly.*
- RL $\leftarrow$ Revoke(RL, ID, t): *If the identity* ID *is revoked at time period* t, *the algorithm adds* (ID, t) *to the revocation list, and returns an updated revocation list* RL.

Correctness. The correctness of Construction 1 follows directly from the correctnesses of the underlying HIBE scheme and IBE scheme. That is, if identity ID is not revoked at time period t, $K_{t,\ell_{time}+1}$ is the decryption key corresponding to identity (ID, $J_{t,\ell_{time}+1}$) in the HIBE scheme, and L_{x^*} is the decryption key corresponding to identity $t||v_x$ in the IBE scheme. So, the two decryption algorithms IBE.Decrypt and HIBE.Decrypt can correctly recover the two parts M_1 and M_2 respectively, and hence the message $M = M_1 \oplus M_2$.

Security. The IND-CPA security of Construction 1 follows from the IND-CPA security of the underlying HIBE scheme and IBE scheme. Specifically, it is guaranteed by the following Theorem 1.

Theorem 1. *If the underlying HIBE and IBE schemes both are IND-CPA secure, then the FS-RIBE scheme in Construction 1 is IND-CPA secure.*

Outline of Proof. Here, we first highlight the idea of the security proof and then give the rigorous proof of security reduction. In the proof, we divide the adversary into two distinct types: (1) **Type-1** adversary is the one that can issue a secret key $sk_{\mathsf{ID}^*}^{(t)}$ of the challenge identity ID* at or before the challenge time period $t \leq t^*$. So, the identity must be revoked before time period t^*. (2) **Type-2** adversary never issues the above secret key. But, it can issue a decryption key of the challenge identity at any time period $t \neq t^*$, or issue a secret key of the challenge identity after the challenge time period t^*. The second type of adversary actually captures the scenario of *forward security.* For **Type-1** adversary, we will construct a simulator which holds the master secret key of the underlying HIBE, and reduces the IND-CPA security of the FS-RIBE scheme to the IND-CPA security of the underlying IBE scheme. For **Type-2** adversary, the simulator holds the master secret key of the underlying IBE scheme, and reduces the IND-CPA security of the FS-RIBE scheme to the IND-CPA security of the underlying HIBE scheme.

Proof. Let $\mathcal{A}$ be an adversary that breaks the IND-CPA security of the FS-RIBE scheme. Then, we construct a PPT simulator $\mathcal{S}$ to break the IND-CPA security of the underlying IBE scheme or the HIBE scheme. The simulator works as follows: It flips a bit b. If $b = 0$, $\mathcal{S}$ assumes $\mathcal{A}$ to be **Type-1** adversary; otherwise, it assumes $\mathcal{A}$ to be **Type-2** adversary. Thus, $\mathcal{S}$ correctly guesses the type of the adversary with probability exactly 1/2.

- For **Type-1** adversary, $\mathcal{S}$ is given a challenge master public key mpk_2 of the underlying IBE scheme. It simulates the experiment as follows:
  1. **Setup:** It generates the master public/secret key pair $(\mathsf{mpk}_1, \mathsf{msk}_1)$ of the underlying HIBE scheme by itself. $\mathcal{S}$ initializes a complete binary tree BT and an empty revocation list RL. It returns mpk_1 and mpk_2 to $\mathcal{A}$.
  2. **Phase 1:** As $\mathcal{S}$ knows the master secret key of HIBE scheme, it can answer $\mathcal{A}$'s create key query and secret key query by itself for any identity ID and time period t.
     When $\mathcal{A}$ requests an update key query for time period t, $\mathcal{S}$ first computes the cover set $\mathsf{KUNodes}(\mathsf{BT}, \mathsf{ST}, t)$. It then sends the set of identities $\{t||v_x\}_{x\in\mathsf{KUNodes}(\mathsf{BT},\mathsf{ST},t)}$ to the challenger of the underlying IBE scheme to obtain the corresponding update keys $\{L_x\}_{x\in\mathsf{KUNodes}(\mathsf{BT},\mathsf{ST},t)}$. Finally, $\mathcal{S}$ returns these update keys to $\mathcal{A}$. As $\mathcal{S}$ can get the corresponding update keys from its own challenger, it hence can answer $\mathcal{A}$'s decryption key queries.
  3. **Challenge:** When $\mathcal{A}$ submits a challenge identity ID^*, a challenge time period t^* and two equal-length messages M_0^*, M_1^*, $\mathcal{S}$ chooses a random message M' and sets $\overline{M}_0^* = M_0^* \oplus M'$ and $\overline{M}_1^* = M_1^* \oplus M'$. $\mathcal{S}$ sends the set of identities $\{t^*||v_x\}_{x\in\mathsf{Path}(\mathsf{ID}^*)}$ and the two equal-length messages $\overline{M}_0^*$ and $\overline{M}_1^*$ to its own challenge. $\mathcal{S}$ will obtain a set of challenge ciphertexts $\{C_{2,x}^*\}_{x\in\mathsf{Path}(\mathsf{ID}^*)}$ which is the encryption of either $\overline{M}_0^*$ or $\overline{M}_1^*$ under the identities $\{t^*||v_x\}_{x\in\mathsf{Path}(\mathsf{ID}^*)}$. Next, $\mathcal{S}$ computes the ciphertext $C_1^* = \mathsf{HIBE.Encrypt}(\mathsf{mpk}_1, \mathsf{ID}^*|J_{t^*,\ell_{time}+1}, M')$. Finally, $\mathcal{S}$ sets the challenge ciphertext C_{ID^*,t^*} as $(C_1^*, \{C_{2,x}^*\}_{x\in\mathsf{Path}(\mathsf{ID}^*)})$ and returns it to $\mathcal{A}$.
  4. **Phase 2:** $\mathcal{S}$ answers $\mathcal{A}$'s queries as in Phase 1.
  5. **Guess:** Finally, when $\mathcal{A}$ outputs a bit b', $\mathcal{S}$ outputs it as its own guess.

  Now, we discuss the success probability of $\mathcal{S}$. In the above simulated experiment, as the challenge identity ID^* has already be revoked before the challenge time period t^*, for any (even the challenge) time period t, the set of identities $\{t||v_x\}_{x\in\mathsf{KUNodes}(\mathsf{BT},\mathsf{ST},t)}$ never intersects with the set of identities $\{t^*||v_x\}_{x\in\mathsf{Path}(\mathsf{ID}^*)}$. Thus, the challenge identities $\mathcal{S}$ sent to its own challenger are valid. Clearly, if $\{C_{2,x}^*\}_{x\in\mathsf{Path}(\mathsf{ID}^*)}$ are encryptions of the IBE challenge message $\overline{M}_b^*$, then C_{ID^*,t^*} is the encryption of the FS-RIBE challenge message M_b^*. So, $\mathcal{S}$ has the same success probability to break the Multi-identity IND-CPA security of the underlying IBE scheme, as $\mathcal{A}$ to break the IND-CPA security of the FS-RIBE scheme. Thus, we have

  $$\mathsf{Adv}_{\text{FS-RIBE},\mathcal{A}}^{\text{IND-CPA}}(\lambda) = \mathsf{Adv}_{\text{IBE},\mathcal{S}}^{\text{M-IND-CPA}}(\lambda) \leq (\ell+1)\mathsf{Adv}_{\text{IBE},\mathcal{A}_1}^{\text{IND-CPA}}(\lambda)$$

  where $\mathcal{A}_1$ is any PPT adversary to attack the IND-CPA security of the underlying IBE scheme.
- For **Type-2** adversary, we can similarly construct a PPT algorithm $\mathcal{S}$ to simulate the experiment and reduces the IND-CPA security of the FS-RIBE

scheme to the IND-CPA security of the underlying HIBE scheme. In this case, $\mathcal{S}$ is given the challenge master public key of the HIBE scheme and generates the master public/secret key pair of IBE by itself.
$\mathcal{S}$ will answer $\mathcal{A}$'s create key queries and secret key queries with the help of its own HIBE challenger. Specifically, $\mathcal{A}$ may request the secret key for challenge identity after the challenge time period. $\mathcal{S}$ answers the update key queries by itself using the master secret key of the underlying IBE scheme. Hence, the simulator can answer decryption key queries, by constructing the decryption key using corresponding secret key and update key. To generate the challenge FS-RIBE ciphertext for challenge identity ID^*, challenge time period t^* and challenge messages M_0^*, M_1^*, $\mathcal{S}$ obtains the first part of the challenge ciphertext (i.e., C_1^*) by submitting the two challenge messages $\overline{M}_0^* = M_0^* \oplus M'$ and $\overline{M}_1^* = M_1^* \oplus M'$ along with the challenge identity $(\mathsf{ID}^*, J_{t^*,\ell_{time}+1})$ to the HIBE challenger. Recall that the secret key for identities prefix to $(\mathsf{ID}^*, J_{t^*,\ell_{time}+1})$ is never allowed to request by $\mathcal{A}$. So, the challenge identity submitted by $\mathcal{S}$ to the HIBE challenger is valid. Next, $\mathcal{S}$ generates the second part of the challenge ciphertext by computing $C_{2,x}^* = \mathsf{IBE.Enc}(\mathsf{mpk}_2, t^*||v_x, M')$ for each $x \in \mathsf{Path}(\mathsf{ID}^*)$. Thus, for **Type-2** adversary, we will have

$$\mathsf{Adv}_{\text{FS-RIBE},\mathcal{A}}^{\text{IND-CPA}}(\lambda) \leq \mathsf{Adv}_{\text{HIBE},\mathcal{A}_2}^{\text{IND-CPA}}(\lambda)$$

where $\mathcal{A}_2$ is any PPT adversary to attack the IND-CPA security of the underlying HIBE scheme.

Taking the above two cases together, it follows that

$$\mathsf{Adv}_{\text{FS-RIBE},\mathcal{A}}^{\text{IND-CPA}}(\lambda) \leq \frac{\ell_{id}+1}{2}\mathsf{Adv}_{\text{IBE},\mathcal{A}_1}^{\text{IND-CPA}}(\lambda) + \frac{1}{2}\mathsf{Adv}_{\text{HIBE},\mathcal{A}_2}^{\text{IND-CPA}}(\lambda).$$

This completes the proof of Theorem 1.

4.2 The Second Construction

In stead of using an IBE scheme to generate update keys, we replace it with a HIBE scheme in our second construction of FS-RIBE scheme. In addition, we view the value of each selected node in the node section algorithm as an identity vector of the underlying HIBE scheme. For example, if a selected node value is $v_{x_{10}} = 011$ as in Fig. 2, we denote by $\vec{v}_{x_{10}}$ the identity vector $(0, 1, 1)$. So, for a time period $t \in \{0,1\}^{\ell_{time}}$, $t|\vec{v}_{x_{10}}$ denotes the identity vector $(t, 0, 1, 1)$.

Construction 2 (Forward-secure RIBE scheme). *Our second construction is described as follows.*

- $(\mathsf{mpk}, \mathsf{msk}, \mathsf{ST}, \mathsf{RL}) \leftarrow \mathsf{RIBE.Setup}(\lambda, \ell_{id}, \ell_{time})$: *It runs twice the setup algorithm of HIBE scheme, i.e.,* $(\mathsf{mpk}_1, \mathsf{msk}_1) \leftarrow \mathsf{HIBE.Setup}(\lambda, \ell_{time}+1)$ *and* $(\mathsf{mpk}_2, \mathsf{msk}_2) \leftarrow \mathsf{HIBE.Setup}(\lambda, \ell_{id}+1)$. *It initializes a complete binary tree* BT *with depth* ℓ_{id}. *Each leaf node is associated with an identity. Finally, the algorithm returns* $\mathsf{mpk} = (\mathsf{mpk}_1, \mathsf{mpk}_2)$, $\mathsf{msk} = (\mathsf{msk}_1, \mathsf{msk}_2)$, $\mathsf{ST} = \mathsf{BT}$ *and an empty revocation list* RL.

- $sk_{\mathsf{ID}}^{(1)} \leftarrow \mathsf{RIBE.KeyGen}(\mathsf{mpk}, \mathsf{msk}, \mathsf{ID}, \mathsf{ST})$: *For any user with identity* $\mathsf{ID} \in \{0,1\}^{\ell_{id}}$, *the algorithm first computes the set* $\mathcal{J}_t = \{J_{t,1}, J_{t,2}, \ldots, J_{t,\ell_{time}+1}\}$ *for initial time period* $t = 0^{\ell_{time}-1}1$. *For each* $c = 1, \ldots, \ell_{time}+1$, *if* $J_{t,c} \neq \perp$, *it involves algorithm* $\mathsf{HIBE.Extract}(\mathsf{mpk}_1, \mathsf{msk}_1, \mathsf{ID}|J_{t,c})$ *to obtain a corresponding secret key* $K_{t,c}$. *If* $J_{t,c} = \perp$, *it sets* $K_{t,c} = \perp$. *Finally, it returns the secret key* $sk_{\mathsf{ID}}^{(1)} = \{1, (K_{t,1}, \ldots, K_{t,\ell_{time}+1})\}$.
- $sk_{\mathsf{ID}}^{(t_2)} \leftarrow \mathsf{RIBE.SKEval}(\mathsf{mpk}, sk_{\mathsf{ID}}^{(t_1)}, t_2)$: *For a time period* $t_2 > t_1$, *the algorithm first computes the two sets* $\mathcal{J}_{t_1}$ *and* $\mathcal{J}_{t_2}$ *respectively. For each* $c_2 = 1, \ldots, \ell_{time}+1$, *if* $J_{t_2,c_2} \neq \perp$, *there must exist a* $c_1 \in \{1, \ldots, \ell_{time}+1\}$ *so that* $(\mathsf{ID}, J_{t_1,c_1})$ *is a prefix of* $(\mathsf{ID}, J_{t_2,c_2})$. *It then involves algorithm* $\mathsf{HIBE.Derive}(\mathsf{mpk}_1, K_{t_1,c_1}, \mathsf{ID}|J_{t_2,c_2})$ *to obtain the corresponding key* K_{t_2,c_2}. *If* $J_{t_2,c_2} = \perp$, *it sets* $K_{t_2,c_2} = \perp$. *Finally, the algorithm returns* $sk_{\mathsf{ID}}^{(t_2)} = \{t_2, (K_{t_2,1}, \ldots, K_{t_2,\ell_{time}+1})\}$.
- $uk_t \leftarrow \mathsf{RIBE.DKUpdate}(\mathsf{mpk}, \mathsf{msk}, \mathsf{ST}, \mathsf{RL}, t)$: *For a time period* $t \in \{0,1\}^{\ell_{time}}$, *the algorithm first computes the cover set* $\mathsf{KUNodes}(\mathsf{BT}, \mathsf{RL}, t)$. *For each node* $x \in \mathsf{KUNodes}(\mathsf{BT}, \mathsf{RL}, t)$, *it involves algorithm* $\mathsf{HIBE.Extract}(\mathsf{mpk}_2, \mathsf{msk}_2, t|\vec{v}_x)$ *to obtain the key* L_x *corresponding to identity vector* $t|v_x$. *Finally, it returns the update key* $uk_t = \{t, \{L_x\}_{x \in \mathsf{KUNodes}(\mathsf{BT},\mathsf{RL},t)}\}$.
- $dk_{\mathsf{ID},t} \leftarrow \mathsf{RIBE.DKGen}(sk_{\mathsf{ID}}^{(t)}, uk_t)$: *Suppose that user's secret key is* $sk_{\mathsf{ID}}^{(t)} = \{t, (K_{t,1}, \ldots, K_{t,\ell_{time}+1})\}$ *and the corresponding time period update key is* $uk_t = \{t, \{L_x\}_{x \in \mathsf{KUNodes}(\mathsf{BT},\mathsf{RL},t)}\}$. *If* ID *is not revoked at time period* t, *there must exist a common node* $x^* \in \mathsf{Path}(\mathsf{ID}) \cap \mathsf{KUNodes}(\mathsf{BT}, \mathsf{RL}, t)$. *The node index* x^* *in* L_{x^*} *must belong to* $\mathsf{Path}(\mathsf{ID})$. *So,* $t|\vec{v}_{x^*}$ *must be a prefix of* $t|\vec{v}_{\mathsf{ID}}$. *The algorithm first runs* $\mathsf{HIBE.Derive}(\mathsf{mpk}_2, L_{x^*}, t|\vec{v}_{\mathsf{ID}})$ *to obtain the corresponding key* L_{ID}. *Finally, it returns the corresponding decryption key* $dk_{\mathsf{ID},t} = (K_{t,\ell_{time}+1}, L_{\mathsf{ID}})$.
- $C_{\mathsf{ID},t} \leftarrow \mathsf{Encrypt}(\mathsf{mpk}, \mathsf{ID}, t, M)$: *For a message* $M \in \mathcal{M}$, *the algorithm first splits the message into two parts* $M_1, M_2 \in \mathcal{M}$ *so that* $M = M_1 \oplus M_2$. *Then, it computes* $C_1 \leftarrow \mathsf{HIBE.Encrypt}(\mathsf{mpk}_1, \mathsf{ID}|J_{t,\ell_{time}+1}, M_1)$, *and* $C_2 \leftarrow \mathsf{HIBE.Encrypt}(\mathsf{mpk}_2, t|\vec{v}_{\mathsf{ID}}, M_2)$. *Finally, it returns ciphertexts* $C_{\mathsf{ID},t} = (C_1, C_2)$.
- $M/\perp \leftarrow \mathsf{Decrypt}(dk_{\mathsf{ID},t}, C_{\mathsf{ID},t})$: *Suppose that* $C_{\mathsf{ID},t} = (C_1, C_2)$, *and* $dk_{\mathsf{ID},t} = (K_{t,\ell_{time}+1}, L_{\mathsf{ID}})$. *The algorithm computes* $M_1 \leftarrow \mathsf{HIBE.Decrypt}(K_{t,\ell_{time}+1}, C_1)$ *and* $M_2 \leftarrow \mathsf{HIBE.Decrypt}(L_{\mathsf{ID}}, C_2)$. *Finally, the algorithm returns* $M = M_1 \oplus M_2$. *If the identity is revoked at time period* t, *the algorithm returns* $\perp$ *directly.*
- $\mathsf{RL} \leftarrow \mathsf{Revoke}(\mathsf{RL}, \mathsf{ID}, t)$: *If the identity* ID *is revoked at time period* t, *the algorithm adds* (ID, t) *to the revocation list, and returns an updated revocation list* RL.

Correctness. As in the analysis for the first generic construction, the correctness of Construction 2 follows directly from the correctnesses of the underlying two HIBE schemes. Different from Construction 1, L_{x^*} is the decryption key corresponding to identity vector $t|\vec{v}_x$ in the second HIBE scheme and the real decryption key L_{ID} is derived from L_{x^*} as $t|\vec{v}_x$ is a prefix identity vector of $t|\vec{v}_{\mathsf{ID}}$.

So, the two decryption algorithms of HIBE schemes can correctly recover the two parts M_1 and M_2 respectively, and hence the message $M = M_1 \oplus M_2$.

Security. The IND-CPA security of Construction 2 follows from the IND-CPA security of the underlying HIBE schemes. We have the following Theorem 2.

Theorem 2. *If the underlying HIBE schemes are IND-CPA secure, then the FS-RIBE scheme in Construction 2 is IND-CPA secure.*

Proof. The proof of Theorem 2 is identity to that of Theorem 1, with the exception that the update key is generated by a HIBE scheme rather than an IBE scheme. Here, we just give a highlight of the proof.

The adversary is also divided into two types as introduced in the proof of Theorem 1. For **Type-1** adversary, the simulator $\mathcal{S}$ generates the key pairs $(\mathsf{mpk}_1, \mathsf{msk}_1)$ of the first HIBE scheme by himself, and is given a challenge master public key mpk_2 of the second HIBE scheme. So, the simulator can answer all secret key queries for (ID, t). To answer update key queries at time period t, it applies node selection algorithm to obtain a set of identity vectors $\{t|\vec{v}_x\}_{x \in \mathsf{KUNodes(BT,ST},t)}$. It then sends this set of identity vectors to the challenger of the second HIBE scheme to obtain the corresponding update keys $\{L_x\}_{x \in \mathsf{KUNodes(BT,ST},t)}$. As the challenge identity ID^* is revoked at time period t^*, the challenge identity vector $t^*|\vec{v}_{\mathsf{ID}^*}$ involved in the encryption algorithm of the second part message never be a subfix of any identity vector used in generating update keys. So, the simulator can ask the challenger of the second HIBE scheme to obtain the challenge ciphertext of the second part message. This reduces the INC-CPA security of the underlying second HIBE scheme to the IND-CPA security of our FS-RIBE scheme (for **Type-1** adversary). Hence,

$$\mathsf{Adv}^{\text{IND-CPA}}_{\text{FS-RIBE},\mathcal{A}}(\lambda) = \mathsf{Adv}^{\text{IND-CPA}}_{\text{HIBE}_2,\mathcal{S}}(\lambda)$$

where $\mathcal{A}_1$ is any PPT adversary to attack the IND-CPA security of the underlying second HIBE scheme.

For **Type-2** adversary, we can similarly reduce the INC-CPA security of the underlying first HIBE scheme to the IND-CPA security of our FS-RIBE scheme (for **Type-2** adversary), i.e.,

$$\mathsf{Adv}^{\text{IND-CPA}}_{\text{FS-RIBE},\mathcal{A}}(\lambda) \leq \mathsf{Adv}^{\text{IND-CPA}}_{\text{HIBE}_1,\mathcal{A}_2}(\lambda)$$

where $\mathcal{A}_2$ is any PPT adversary to attack the IND-CPA security of the underlying first HIBE scheme.

Taking the above two cases together, it follows that

$$\mathsf{Adv}^{\text{IND-CPA}}_{\text{FS-RIBE},\mathcal{A}}(\lambda) \leq \frac{1}{2}\mathsf{Adv}^{\text{IND-CPA}}_{\text{HIBE}_1,\mathcal{A}_1}(\lambda) + \frac{1}{2}\mathsf{Adv}^{\text{IND-CPA}}_{\text{HIBE}_2,\mathcal{A}_2}(\lambda).$$

This completes the proof of Theorem 2.

Table 1. Comparison of RIBE schemes (with/without forward security) based on assumptions over bilinear maps. $|\mathsf{mpk}|$, $|sk_{\mathsf{ID}}|$, $|uk_t|$ and $|C|$ denotes the numbers of group elements in master public key, user's secret key, time-based update key and ciphertext respectively. Assume that the maximal number of time period and system users are T and N respectively. R is the number of revoked users and $L = R \cdot \log N/R$. "DKE" means decryption key exposure resistance, "FS" is forward security, "AID" stands for adaptive identity, and "SDM" stands for the standard model.

Schemes	$\|\mathsf{mpk}\|$	$\|sk_{\mathsf{ID}}\|$	$\|uk_t\|$	$\|C\|$	DKE	FS	AID	SDM
BF01[8]	$O(1)$	$O(1)$	$O(N-R)$	$O(1)$	Yes	Yes	Yes	No
BGK08 [5]	$O(1)$	$O(\log N)$	$O(L)$	$O(1)$	No	No	No	Yes
LV09 [29]	$O(\lambda)$	$O(\log N)$	$O(L)$	$O(1)$	No	No	Yes	Yes
SE13 [38]	$O(\lambda)$	$O(\log N)$	$O(L)$	$O(1)$	Yes	No	Yes	Yes
ML19-1 [30]	$O(1)$	$O(1)$	$O(L)$	$O(\log N)$	Yes	No	Yes	No
ML19-2 [30]	$O(\log N)$	$O(1)$	$O(L)$	$O(1)$	Yes	No	Yes	Yes
Con. 1+ [28]	$O(\log T)$	$O((\log T)^2)$	$O(L)$	$O(\log N)$	Yes	Yes	Yes	Yes
Con. 2+ [28]	$O(\log(TN))$	$O((\log T)^2)$	$O(L \cdot \log N)$	$O(1)$	Yes	Yes	Yes	Yes

5 Instantiations and Comparison

In this section, we give some instantiations of our generic construction from various (H)IBE schemes, and compare their efficiency with other related RIBE schemes with/without forward security.

We first instantiate Construction 1 using Lewko and Waters fully secure HIBE and IBE schemes [28]. It results in an adaptively secure FS-RIBE scheme (denoted by "Con. 1+[28]") with $O(\log N)$ group elements in ciphertext. Further, applying Lewko and Waters fully secure HIBE scheme to Construction 2, we obtain an adaptively secure FS-RIBE scheme (denoted by "Con. 2+[28]") with constant ciphertext size. These two instantiations are all based on bilinear map. We compare them with other bilinear map based RIBE schemes in Table 1. We omit the comparison with other RIBE schemes that are not from bilinear map or not use complete binary tree method to update keys. Prior to our work, only Boneh and Franklin's RIBE scheme achieved both forward security and DKER security. However, their scheme does not scale well, as its update key size is linear to the number of system users. Besides forward security, the scheme "Con. 2+[28]" also has other advantages as in previous RIBE schemes, including constant size ciphertext, DKE resistance and full security in the standard model. Its update key size has a factor $\log N$ than other binary-tree based key updating method. Because each update key in our scheme is actually a HIBE key which has $O(\log N)$ group elements. In all, our schemes achieve forward security, but still have competitive parameter sizes.

Besides pairing-based instantiations, we also instantiate our constructions under lattice based assumption, i.e., LWE assumption. We apply Agrawal, Boneh and Boyen LWE-based HIBE and IBE schemes [1] to our first generic construction. It gives an LWE-based FS-RIBE scheme in the standard model, i.e., "Con. 1+[1]" as shown in Table 2. If we instantiate it according to our second generic construction, however, the result does not have better parameter sizes

Table 2. Comparison of RIBE schemes (with/without forward security) based on LWE assumption. We measure the size of $|\mathsf{mpk}|$ in the number of matrices $\mathbb{Z}_q^{n\times m}$, the size of $|sk_{\mathsf{ID}}|$ and $|uk_t|$ in the number of vector $\mathbb{Z}^m$, and the size of $|C|$ in the numbers of vector $\mathbb{Z}_q^m$. Assume that the maximal number of time period and system users are T and N respectively. R is the number of revoked users and $L = R \cdot \log N/R$. "DKE" means decryption key exposure resistance, "FS" is forward security, "AID" stands for adaptive identity and "SDM" stands for the standard model.

Schemes	$\lvert\mathsf{mpk}\rvert(\#\mathbb{Z}_q^{n\times m})$	$\lvert sk_{\mathsf{ID}}\rvert(\#\mathbb{Z}^m)$	$\lvert uk_t\rvert(\#\mathbb{Z}^m)$	$\lvert C\rvert(\#\mathbb{Z}_q^m)$	DKE	FS	AID	SDM
CLLWN12 [11]	$O(1)$	$O(\log N)$	$O(L)$	$O(1)$	No	No	No	Yes
KMT19 [24]	$O(1)$	$O(m + \log N)$	$O(L)$	$O(1)$	Yes	No	No	Yes
Con. 1+ [1]	$O(\log T)$	$O(m \cdot \log T)$	$O(L)$	$O(\log(TN))$	Yes	Yes	No	Yes
Con. 2+ [1]	$O(\log(TN))$	$O(m \cdot \log T)$	$O(mL)$	$O(\log(TN))$	Yes	Yes	No	Yes
Con. 1+ [2]	$O(1)$	$O(m \cdot \log T)$	$O(L)$	$O(\log N)$	Yes	Yes	Yes	No
Con. 2+ [2]	$O(1)$	$O(m \cdot \log T)$	$O(mL)$	$O(1)$	Yes	Yes	Yes	No

than that of the first instantiation. To reduce the sizes of some parameters, we instantiate our generic constructions using the LWE-based HIBE scheme with short ciphertext [2]. The results both have constant size master public key. In addition, the scheme of "Con. 2+[2]" also has constant size ciphertext. Compared with other RIBE schemes, our schemes all achieve DKE resistance and forward security simultaneously, while none of previous schemes has forward security.

6 Conclusion

This paper proposed a primitive namely forward-secure revocable identity-based encryption (FS-RIBE). It aims to mitigate the threat of exposure of a user's long-term private key in a revocable IBE scheme. The paper formalized the definition of FS-RIBE and its IND-CPA security. It gave two generic constructions of FS-RIBE schemes by combining (H)IBE schemes. It instantiated the generic constructions from various (H)IBE schemes and compared them with previous RIBE schemes.

Acknowledgments. Baodong Qin is supported by the fund of Science and Technology on Communication Security Laboratory (No. 6142103190101) and the National Natural Science Foundation of China (No. 61872292). Dong Zheng is supported by the National Natural Science Foundation of China (No. 62072207). Yiyuan Luo is supported by National Natural Science Foundation of China (No. 62072207), Natural Science Foundation of Shanghai (No. 19ZR1420000), Henan Key Laboratory of Network Cryptography Technology (No. LNCT2020-A05), Open Foundation of Network and Data Security Key Laboratory of Sichuan Province (University of Electronic Science and Technology of China) (No. NDS2021-1), and Program for Innovative Research Team of Huizhou University.

References

1. Agrawal, S., Boneh, D., Boyen, X.: Efficient lattice (H)IBE in the standard model. In: Gilbert, H. (ed.) EUROCRYPT 2010. LNCS, vol. 6110, pp. 553–572. Springer, Heidelberg (2010). https://doi.org/10.1007/978-3-642-13190-5_28
2. Agrawal, S., Boneh, D., Boyen, X.: Lattice basis delegation in fixed dimension and shorter-ciphertext hierarchical IBE. In: Rabin, T. (ed.) CRYPTO 2010. LNCS, vol. 6223, pp. 98–115. Springer, Heidelberg (2010). https://doi.org/10.1007/978-3-642-14623-7_6
3. Anderson, R.: Two remarks on public key cryptology. Technical reports published by the University of Cambridge (1997)
4. Bellare, M., Miner, S.K.: A forward-secure digital signature scheme. In: Wiener, M. (ed.) CRYPTO 1999. LNCS, vol. 1666, pp. 431–448. Springer, Heidelberg (1999). https://doi.org/10.1007/3-540-48405-1_28
5. Boldyreva, A., Goyal, V., Kumar, V.: Identity-based encryption with efficient revocation. In: Ning, P., Syverson, P.F., Jha, S. (eds.) CCS 2008, pp. 417–426. ACM (2008)
6. Boneh, D., Boyen, X.: Efficient selective-ID secure identity-based encryption without random oracles. In: Cachin, C., Camenisch, J.L. (eds.) EUROCRYPT 2004. LNCS, vol. 3027, pp. 223–238. Springer, Heidelberg (2004). https://doi.org/10.1007/978-3-540-24676-3_14
7. Boneh, D., Boyen, X., Goh, E.-J.: Hierarchical identity based encryption with constant size ciphertext. In: Cramer, R. (ed.) EUROCRYPT 2005. LNCS, vol. 3494, pp. 440–456. Springer, Heidelberg (2005). https://doi.org/10.1007/11426639_26
8. Boneh, D., Franklin, M.: Identity-based encryption from the Weil pairing. In: Kilian, J. (ed.) CRYPTO 2001. LNCS, vol. 2139, pp. 213–229. Springer, Heidelberg (2001). https://doi.org/10.1007/3-540-44647-8_13
9. Canetti, R., Halevi, S., Katz, J.: A forward-secure public-key encryption scheme. In: Biham, E. (ed.) EUROCRYPT 2003. LNCS, vol. 2656, pp. 255–271. Springer, Heidelberg (2003). https://doi.org/10.1007/3-540-39200-9_16
10. Choon, J.C., Hee Cheon, J.: An identity-based signature from gap Diffie-Hellman groups. In: Desmedt, Y.G. (ed.) PKC 2003. LNCS, vol. 2567, pp. 18–30. Springer, Heidelberg (2003). https://doi.org/10.1007/3-540-36288-6_2
11. Chen, J., Lim, H.W., Ling, S., Wang, H., Nguyen, K.: Revocable identity-based encryption from lattices. In: Susilo, W., Mu, Y., Seberry, J. (eds.) ACISP 2012. LNCS, vol. 7372, pp. 390–403. Springer, Heidelberg (2012). https://doi.org/10.1007/978-3-642-31448-3_29
12. Cheng, S., Zhang, J.: Adaptive-ID secure revocable identity-based encryption from lattices via subset difference method. In: Lopez, J., Wu, Y. (eds.) ISPEC 2015. LNCS, vol. 9065, pp. 283–297. Springer, Cham (2015). https://doi.org/10.1007/978-3-319-17533-1_20
13. Chow, S.S.M., Hui, L.C.K., Yiu, S.M., Chow, K.P.: Secure hierarchical identity based signature and its application. In: Lopez, J., Qing, S., Okamoto, E. (eds.) ICICS 2004. LNCS, vol. 3269, pp. 480–494. Springer, Heidelberg (2004). https://doi.org/10.1007/978-3-540-30191-2_37
14. Cocks, C.: An identity based encryption scheme based on quadratic residues. In: Honary, B. (ed.) Cryptography and Coding 2001. LNCS, vol. 2260, pp. 360–363. Springer, Heidelberg (2001). https://doi.org/10.1007/3-540-45325-3_32
15. Döttling, N., Garg, S.: Identity-based encryption from the Diffie-Hellman assumption. In: Katz, J., Shacham, H. (eds.) CRYPTO 2017. LNCS, vol. 10401, pp. 537–569. Springer, Cham (2017). https://doi.org/10.1007/978-3-319-63688-7_18

16. Emura, K., Katsumata, S., Watanabe, Y.: Identity-based encryption with security against the KGC: a formal model and its instantiation from lattices. In: Sako, K., Schneider, S., Ryan, P.Y.A. (eds.) ESORICS 2019. LNCS, vol. 11736, pp. 113–133. Springer, Cham (2019). https://doi.org/10.1007/978-3-030-29962-0_6
17. Galindo, D., Herranz, J., Kiltz, E.: On the generic construction of identity-based signatures with additional properties. In: Lai, X., Chen, K. (eds.) ASIACRYPT 2006. LNCS, vol. 4284, pp. 178–193. Springer, Heidelberg (2006). https://doi.org/10.1007/11935230_12
18. Gentry, C.: Practical identity-based encryption without random oracles. In: Vaudenay, S. (ed.) EUROCRYPT 2006. LNCS, vol. 4004, pp. 445–464. Springer, Heidelberg (2006). https://doi.org/10.1007/11761679_27
19. Gentry, C., Halevi, S.: Hierarchical identity based encryption with polynomially many levels. In: Reingold, O. (ed.) TCC 2009. LNCS, vol. 5444, pp. 437–456. Springer, Heidelberg (2009). https://doi.org/10.1007/978-3-642-00457-5_26
20. Goyal, V., Pandey, O., Sahai, A., Waters, B.: Attribute-based encryption for fine-grained access control of encrypted data. In: Juels, A., Wright, R.N., di Vimercati, S.D.C. (eds.) CCS 2006, pp. 89–98. ACM (2006)
21. Green, M., Ateniese, G.: Identity-based proxy re-encryption. In: Katz, J., Yung, M. (eds.) ACNS 2007. LNCS, vol. 4521, pp. 288–306. Springer, Heidelberg (2007). https://doi.org/10.1007/978-3-540-72738-5_19
22. Hofheinz, D., Matt, C., Maurer, U.: Idealizing identity-based encryption. In: Iwata, T., Cheon, J.H. (eds.) ASIACRYPT 2015. LNCS, vol. 9452, pp. 495–520. Springer, Heidelberg (2015). https://doi.org/10.1007/978-3-662-48797-6_21
23. Ishida, Y., Shikata, J., Watanabe, Y.: CCA-secure revocable identity-based encryption schemes with decryption key exposure resistance. Int. J. Appl. Cryptogr. **3**(3), 288–311 (2017)
24. Katsumata, S., Matsuda, T., Takayasu, A.: Lattice-based revocable (hierarchical) IBE with decryption key exposure resistance. In: Lin, D., Sako, K. (eds.) PKC 2019. LNCS, vol. 11443, pp. 441–471. Springer, Cham (2019). https://doi.org/10.1007/978-3-030-17259-6_15
25. Langrehr, R., Pan, J.: Hierarchical identity-based encryption with tight multi-challenge security. In: Kiayias, A., Kohlweiss, M., Wallden, P., Zikas, V. (eds.) PKC 2020. LNCS, vol. 12110, pp. 153–183. Springer, Cham (2020). https://doi.org/10.1007/978-3-030-45374-9_6
26. Lee, K., Lee, D.H., Park, J.H.: Efficient revocable identity-based encryption via subset difference methods. Des. Codes Cryptogr. **85**(1), 39–76 (2017). https://doi.org/10.1007/s10623-016-0287-3
27. Lee, K., Park, S.: Revocable hierarchical identity-based encryption with shorter private keys and update keys. Des. Codes Cryptogr. **86**(10), 2407–2440 (2018)
28. Lewko, A., Waters, B.: New techniques for dual system encryption and fully secure HIBE with short ciphertexts. In: Micciancio, D. (ed.) TCC 2010. LNCS, vol. 5978, pp. 455–479. Springer, Heidelberg (2010). https://doi.org/10.1007/978-3-642-11799-2_27
29. Libert, B., Vergnaud, D.: Adaptive-ID secure revocable identity-based encryption. In: Fischlin, M. (ed.) CT-RSA 2009. LNCS, vol. 5473, pp. 1–15. Springer, Heidelberg (2009). https://doi.org/10.1007/978-3-642-00862-7_1
30. Ma, X., Lin, D.: Generic constructions of revocable identity-based encryption. In: Liu, Z., Yung, M. (eds.) Inscrypt 2019. LNCS, vol. 12020, pp. 381–396. Springer, Cham (2020). https://doi.org/10.1007/978-3-030-42921-8_22

31. Maji, H.K., Prabhakaran, M., Rosulek, M.: Attribute-based signatures. In: Kiayias, A. (ed.) CT-RSA 2011. LNCS, vol. 6558, pp. 376–392. Springer, Heidelberg (2011). https://doi.org/10.1007/978-3-642-19074-2_24
32. Mao, X., Lai, J., Chen, K., Weng, J., Mei, Q.: Efficient revocable identity-based encryption from multilinear maps. Secur. Commun. Netw. **8**(18), 3511–3522 (2015)
33. Nguyen, K., Wang, H., Zhang, J.: Server-aided revocable identity-based encryption from lattices. In: Foresti, S., Persiano, G. (eds.) CANS 2016. LNCS, vol. 10052, pp. 107–123. Springer, Cham (2016). https://doi.org/10.1007/978-3-319-48965-0_7
34. Park, S., Lee, K., Lee, D.H.: New constructions of revocable identity-based encryption from multilinear maps. IEEE Trans. Inf. Forensics Secur. **10**(8), 1564–1577 (2015)
35. Qin, B., Deng, R.H., Li, Y., Liu, S.: Server-aided revocable identity-based encryption. In: Pernul, G., Ryan, P.Y.A., Weippl, E. (eds.) ESORICS 2015. LNCS, vol. 9326, pp. 286–304. Springer, Cham (2015). https://doi.org/10.1007/978-3-319-24174-6_15
36. Qin, B., Liu, X., Wei, Z., Zheng, D.: Space efficient revocable IBE for mobile devices in cloud computing. Sci. China Inf. Sci. **63**(3), 1 (2020)
37. Sahai, A., Waters, B.: Fuzzy identity-based encryption. In: Cramer, R. (ed.) EUROCRYPT 2005. LNCS, vol. 3494, pp. 457–473. Springer, Heidelberg (2005). https://doi.org/10.1007/11426639_27
38. Seo, J.H., Emura, K.: Revocable identity-based encryption revisited: security model and construction. In: Kurosawa, K., Hanaoka, G. (eds.) PKC 2013. LNCS, vol. 7778, pp. 216–234. Springer, Heidelberg (2013). https://doi.org/10.1007/978-3-642-36362-7_14
39. Seo, J.H., Emura, K.: Revocable hierarchical identity-based encryption: history-free update, security against insiders, and short ciphertexts. In: Nyberg, K. (ed.) CT-RSA 2015. LNCS, vol. 9048, pp. 106–123. Springer, Cham (2015). https://doi.org/10.1007/978-3-319-16715-2_6
40. Sun, Y., Mu, Y., Susilo, W., Zhang, F., Fu, A.: Revocable identity-based encryption with server-aided ciphertext evolution. Theoret. Comput. Sci. **815**, 11–24 (2020)
41. Takayasu, A., Watanabe, Y.: Lattice-based revocable identity-based encryption with bounded decryption key exposure resistance. In: Pieprzyk, J., Suriadi, S. (eds.) ACISP 2017. LNCS, vol. 10342, pp. 184–204. Springer, Cham (2017). https://doi.org/10.1007/978-3-319-60055-0_10
42. Wang, C., Li, Y., Fang, J., Xie, J.: Cloud-aided scalable revocable identity-based encryption scheme with ciphertext update. Concurr. Comput. Pract. Exp. **29**(20) (2017)
43. Watanabe, Y., Emura, K., Seo, J.H.: New revocable IBE in prime-order groups: adaptively secure, decryption key exposure resistant, and with short public parameters. In: Handschuh, H. (ed.) CT-RSA 2017. LNCS, vol. 10159, pp. 432–449. Springer, Cham (2017). https://doi.org/10.1007/978-3-319-52153-4_25
44. Waters, B.: Efficient identity-based encryption without random oracles. In: Cramer, R. (ed.) EUROCRYPT 2005. LNCS, vol. 3494, pp. 114–127. Springer, Heidelberg (2005). https://doi.org/10.1007/11426639_7
45. Wei, J., Liu, W., Hu, X.: Forward-secure identity-based signature with efficient revocation. Int. J. Comput. Math. **94**(7), 1390–1411 (2017)

An Optimized Inner Product Argument with More Application Scenarios

Zongyang Zhang(✉), Zibo Zhou, Weihan Li, and Hongyu Tao

School of Cyber Science and Technology, Beihang University, Beijing, China
{zongyangzhang,zbzhou,leeweihan,taohongyu}@buaa.edu.cn

Abstract. The inner product argument is an effective tool to reduce communication complexity in many cryptographic protocols. Bootle et al. (EUROCRYPT'16) presented an inner product argument with a statement including two vector commitments to two vectors and the inner product of the two vectors equals to a public scalar. Bünz et al. (S&P'18) then presented an inner product argument with a statement including only one vector commitment to two vectors. In this paper, we first summarize the scenarios to use inner product arguments based on Bootle et al. and Bünz et al. Then we propose and implement an improved inner product argument for the same statement as Bootle et al. Our argument has a lower communication complexity of $4 \log_2 n$ which improves by about 30% when $n = 8192$. Moreover, as most existing inner product argument protocols have a recursive structure, we find the most appropriate recursive round that decides a better communication complexity.

Keywords: Inner product argument · Argument of knowledge · Vector commitment

1 Introduction

Informally, an inner product argument involves two parties, a prover and a verifier, and allows the prover to prove that the inner product of two vectors (usually hidden by group exponentiation based on the discrete logarithm assumption) is equal to a public scalar. Generally, an inner product argument has two properties, i.e., completeness and witness-extended emulation. Completeness ensures that an honest prover can convince the verifier with overwhelming probability. Witness-extended emulation ensures that if the prover convinces the verifier successfully, it does own the two right vectors. The inner product argument is an effective tool to reduce communication complexity of many cryptography primitives, such as zero knowledge proofs [1,5,10] and verifiable polynomial commitment schemes [3,14].

Bootle et al. [2] first introduced an inner product argument which is used as a subroutine to obtain a zero-knowledge arithmetic circuit satisfiability argument

Z. Zhang, Z. Zhou and W. Li contributed equally.

D. Gao et al. (Eds.): ICICS 2021, LNCS 12919, pp. 341–357, 2021.
https://doi.org/10.1007/978-3-030-88052-1_20

with logarithmic communication, i.e., $6 \log_2 n$, where n is the dimension of vectors. Note that the two vectors in this argument are committed separately. Bünz et al. [4] proposed an improved inner product argument with a communication complexity of $2 \log_2 n$, and then used it to obtain an efficient range proof and an arithmetic circuit satisfiability argument with better communication complexity. However, the two vectors are committed together in the latter argument, which leads to fewer application scenarios. In some scenarios one can only use the inner product argument of Bootle et al., whose communication cost may still be further optimized.

1.1 Our Contributions

We start from observations of the inner product arguments of Bootle et al. and Bünz et al. The statement of the former argument includes two public commitments to two vectors, respectively, while the statement of the latter argument includes only one public commitment to two vectors. This difference makes the former argument applicable in more scenarios. We propose an inner product argument protocol with a better communication complexity than Bootle et al. and a wider application range than Bünz et al. We argue that our inner product argument may replace the argument of Bootle et al. totally with a lower communication cost. The comparison of the three protocols is shown in Table 1.

Table 1. Comparison of inner product arguments with n the dimension of vectors. Notation: $\mathbb{G}$ means group elements, $\mathbb{F}$ means field elements, E means group exponentiations, M means field multiplications.

Protocol	Commitment structure	Communication complexity	Prover complexity	Verifier complexity
Bootle et al. [2]	Two commitments to two vectors	$(4 \log_2 n - 8)$ $\mathbb{G}$ $(2 \log_2 n + 4)$ $\mathbb{F}$	$(8n - 32)$ E $(6n - 24)$ M	$(4n + 4 \log_2 n - 16)$ E $\log_2 n$ M
Bünz et al. [4]	One commitment to two vectors	$(2 \log_2 n - 2)$ $\mathbb{G}$ 4 $\mathbb{F}$	$(8n + 2 \log_2 n - 18)$ E $(6n - 12)$ M	$(4n + 2 \log_2 n - 5)$ E 2 M
This work	Two commitments to two vectors	$(4 \log_2 n - 8)$ $\mathbb{G}$ 8 $\mathbb{F}$	$(8n + 2 \log_2 n - 36)$ E $(6n - 24)$ M	$(4n + 4 \log_2 n - 15)$ E 4 M

Inner product arguments of Bootle et al. and Bünz et al. both use a recursive construction to realize logarithmic communication complexity. This recursion works by halving original vectors and constructing a new inner product argument round by round. We argue that the recursion stopping at $n_0 = 1$ may not be the best choice, where n_0 is the dimension of vectors in the final round. We provide a function between the communication complexity and the number of recursive round and give a best choice accordingly.

Summary of Contributions. The contributions of this paper are as follows.

- We summarize the application scenarios of inner product arguments inspired by Bootle et al. and Bünz et al. Then we present our inner product argument

protocol with a communication complexity of $4 \log_2 n$ that is superior in certain application scenarios.
- We find the most appropriate recursive round that decides a better communication complexity, based on the recursive structure of inner product argument protocols.
- We implement our inner product argument protocol in Rust and evaluate its efficiency compared with Bootle et al.

1.2 Related Work

Bootle et al. [2] first presented an inner product argument protocol with logarithmic communication complexity, using which they made a major breakthrough on the arithmetic circuit satisfiability arguments merely based on the discrete logarithm assumption. Bünz et al. [4] reduced the communication complexity of the inner product argument of Bootle et al. by committing to the two vectors and the scalar in a single commitment meanwhile maintaining the halving structure of the argument. Using the improved inner product argument they greatly improved on the linear sized range proofs in existing proposals and further improved the arithmetic circuit satisfiability arguments through well-designed constraint reductions. Later, more and more researchers begin to study the inner product argument and use it to complete some proofs. Wahby et al. [14] made use of the inner product argument of Bünz et al. to reduce the communication complexity of their polynomial commitment scheme. Inspired by Wahby et al., Bowe et al. [3] presented a modified univariate polynomial commitment scheme based on the inner product arguments of Bootle et al. and Bünz et al. Moreover, they claimed that inner product arguments are also aggregatable. By exploiting the smooth structure of vectors, one can amortize away the cost of verifying many inner product arguments with the help of an untrusted third party. Recently, Attema and Cramer [1] provided an orthogonal generalization of the inner product argument and repurposed the inner product argument of Bünz et al. as a blackbox compression mechanism for standard sigma protocols handling zero knowledge proofs of general linear relations.

Some researchers consider applying the inner product argument under other assumptions and modifying it to become zero knowledge. Lai et al. [11] introduced an inner product argument for pairing-based languages under the SXDH assumption with $O(n)$ verifier computation, where n is the dimension of vectors. Hoffmann et al. [10] used the "redundancy/kernel" technique to devise zero-knowledge variants of the inner product arguments of Bootle et al. and Bünz et al. They constructed a commit-and-prove argument for satisfiability of a set of quadratic equations via their zero knowledge inner product argument.

Moreover, there are some works on reducing the verification cost of inner product arguments. Although the verification can be optimized through multi-exponentiation technique showed by Bünz et al., the verification complexity is still $O(n)$. Daza et al. [7] replaced the unstructured commitment key of the inner product argument of Bootle et al. by a structured one, which is also updateable. Then with the structured commitment key they proposed a new inner product argument with logarithmic verification complexity in the designated verifier setting relying on the discrete logarithm assumption, and their argument can be compiled to achieve public verifiability in asymmetric bilinear groups. However, their argument requires a communication complexity of $8\log_2 n$.

Bünz et al. [6] proposed a generalized inner product argument and provided a unified view of all prior related works, which enables simpler exposition and simpler security proofs. Their generalized argument can be used as long as the commitments are doubly homomorphic and the inner product maps are bilinear. Concretely, the bilinear inner product maps can be bewteen vectors of 1) group elements, 2) field elements or 3) group and field elements. Our inner product argument belongs to the second category while they mainly focus on the first category, which is also called inner pairing product. Using a structured reference string, they achieved an inner pairing product argument with logarithmic verification complexity over pairing-based languages, which is an improvement to Lai et al. Then they applied their inner pairing product argument to aggregate n Groth16 zkSNARKs [8] into a proof of size $O(\log n)$ and build the first polynomial commitment scheme with $O(\log d)$ verifier complexity, $O(\sqrt{d})$ prover complexity and CRS of size $O(\sqrt{d})$, where d is the degree of polynomials.

2 Preliminaries

In this section, we borrow a series of definitions and notations from Bootle et al. [2] and Bünz et al. [4]. In what follows, let $\mathbb{G}$ denote a cyclic group on Elliptic curves of prime order p with respect to the operations $\cdot$, let $\mathbb{Z}_p$ denote the field of integers modulo p with respect to the operations $+$ and $\cdot$, and let $\mathbb{Z}_p^*$ denote $\mathbb{Z}_p \backslash \{0\}$. Let $\mathbb{G}^n$ and $\mathbb{Z}_p^n$ be vector spaces of dimension n over $\mathbb{G}$ and $\mathbb{Z}_p$, respectively. We use lowercase bold font denote vectors, i.e. $\boldsymbol{a} \in \mathbb{Z}_p^n$ is a vector with elements $a_1, \ldots, a_n \in \mathbb{Z}_p$.

Furthermore, we write $\langle \boldsymbol{a}, \boldsymbol{b} \rangle = \sum_{i=1}^n a_i b_i$ and $\boldsymbol{a} \circ \boldsymbol{b} = (a_1 b_1, \ldots, a_n b_n)$ for denoting the inner product and the Hadamard product between two vectors $\boldsymbol{a}, \boldsymbol{b}$, respectively. For vectors $\boldsymbol{g} \in \mathbb{G}^n$, $\boldsymbol{a} \in \mathbb{Z}_p^n$ and $b, c \in \mathbb{Z}_p$, we write $\boldsymbol{g}^{\boldsymbol{a}} = \prod_{i=1}^n g_i^{a_i}, \boldsymbol{g}^b = (g_1^b, \ldots, g_n^b), c\boldsymbol{a} = (ca_1, \ldots, ca_n)$.

In this paper, we take security parameter λ as input. We will drop λ when it is implicit. We write $y = A(x; r)$ when the algorithm A takes x as input and r as randomness, then outputs y. We write $y \leftarrow A(x)$ for picking a randomness r and compute $A(x; r)$. We write $y \stackrel{\$}{\leftarrow} S$ for sampling y uniformly at random from set S. Given a function $\mu(\cdot) : \mathbb{N} \rightarrow \mathbb{N}$, we say $\mu(\cdot)$ is *negligible* if for every positive polynomial $p(\cdot)$ and all sufficiently large κ it holds that $\mu(\kappa) < \frac{1}{p(\kappa)}$. Given functions $f(\cdot), g(\cdot) : \mathbb{N} \rightarrow \mathbb{N}$, we say $f(\cdot) \approx g(\cdot)$ if $f(\cdot) - g(\cdot)$ is *negligible*.

2.1 Assumptions

Let $(p, \mathbb{G}, g) \leftarrow \mathsf{GGen}(1^\lambda)$ denote the generation of parameters in the group $\mathbb{G}$. Let a PPT adversary $\mathcal{A}$ be a probabilistic interactive Turing Machine which runs in polynomial time in λ. Our scheme relies on the discrete logarithm assumption and the discrete logarithm relation assumption defined as follows.

Definition 1 (Discrete Logarithm Assumption). *The discrete logarithm assumption holds relative to* GGen *if for all PPT adversaries* $\mathcal{A}$*, we have*

$$\Pr\left[(p, \mathbb{G}, g) \leftarrow \mathsf{GGen}(1^\lambda); h \xleftarrow{\$} \mathbb{G}; a \leftarrow \mathcal{A}(p, \mathbb{G}, g, h) : g^a = h\right] \approx 0$$

Definition 2 (Discrete Logarithm Relation Assumption). *For all* $n \geq 1$ *and all PPT adversaries* $\mathcal{A}$*, we have*

$$\Pr\left[\begin{array}{l}(p, \mathbb{G}, g) \leftarrow \mathsf{GGen}(1^\lambda); g_1, ..., g_n \xleftarrow{\$} \mathbb{G}; \\ a_1, ..., a_n \leftarrow \mathcal{A}(\mathsf{gp}, \{g_i\})\end{array} : \exists a_i \neq 0 \wedge \prod_{i=1}^{n} g_i^{a_i} = 1\right] \approx 0$$

We say such a product $\prod_{i=1}^{n} g_i^{a_i} = 1$ is a non-trivial discrete logarithm relation between $g_1, ..., g_n$. The discrete logarithm relation assumption states that it is hard for an adversary to find a non-trivial discrete logarithm relation between randomly chosen group elements.

2.2 Commitments

Definition 3 (Commitment). *A non-interacitve commitment scheme consists of a triple of probabilistic polynomial time algorithms* $(\mathsf{Setup}, \mathsf{Com}, \mathsf{Open})$*. The* Setup *algorithm* $\mathsf{pp} \leftarrow \mathsf{Setup}(1^\lambda)$ *generates public parameters* pp *for the scheme, for security parameter* λ*. The* Com *algorithm defines a function* $\mathsf{M_{pp}} \times \mathsf{R_{pp}} \rightarrow \mathsf{C_{pp}}$*, where the message space* $\mathsf{M_{pp}}$*, randomness space* $\mathsf{R_{pp}}$ *and commitment space* $\mathsf{C_{pp}}$ *are all determined by* pp*. The* Open *algorithm defines a function* $\mathsf{C_{pp}} \times \mathsf{R_{pp}} \rightarrow \mathsf{M_{pp}} \cup \{\perp\}$*. Specifically, for a message* $x \in \mathsf{M_{pp}}$*, a randomness* $r \in \mathsf{R_{pp}}$*, the commitment* cm *is computed as* $cm = \mathsf{Com_{pp}}(x; r)$*, and the open scheme is computed as* $\mathsf{Open_{pp}}(cm; r) = x$*. We will write* $\mathsf{Com} = \mathsf{Com_{pp}}$ *and* $\mathsf{Open} = \mathsf{Open_{pp}}$ *for ease of notation.*

Definition 4 (Pedersen Commitment [4]**)**

$\mathsf{M_{pp}}, \mathsf{R_{pp}} = \mathbb{Z}_p, \mathsf{C_{pp}} = \mathbb{G}$ *with order* p*.*
$\mathsf{Setup} : g, h \xleftarrow{\$} \mathbb{G}$
$\mathsf{Com}(x; r) = g^x h^r$
$\mathsf{Open}(\mathsf{Com}(x; r), r) = x$

Definition 5 (Pedersen Vector Commitment [4]**)**

$\mathsf{M_{pp}} = \mathbb{Z}_p^n, \mathsf{R_{pp}} = \mathbb{Z}_p, \mathsf{C_{pp}} = \mathbb{G}$ *with order* p*.*

$\mathsf{Setup} : \boldsymbol{g} = (g_1, ..., g_n) \xleftarrow{\$} \mathbb{G}^n, h \xleftarrow{\$} \mathbb{G}$
$\mathsf{Com}(\boldsymbol{x} = (x_1, ..., x_n); r) = \boldsymbol{g}^{\boldsymbol{x}} h^r = (\prod_{i=1}^{n} g_i^{x_i}) h^r$
$\mathsf{Open}(\mathsf{Com}(\boldsymbol{x}; r), r) = \boldsymbol{x}$

The Pedersen vector commitment is perfectly hiding and computationally binding under the discrete logarithm assumption, which are defined below.

Definition 6 (Perfect Hiding). *We say a commitment* (Setup, Com, Open) *is perfectly hiding if the commitment does not reveal the message. Formally, for all PPT adversaries $\mathcal{A}$, we have*

$$\left|\Pr\left[\begin{matrix}\mathsf{pp} \leftarrow \mathsf{Setup}(1^\lambda); (x_0, x_1) \leftarrow \mathcal{A}(\mathsf{pp}); \\ b \xleftarrow{\$} \{0,1\}; r \xleftarrow{\$} \mathsf{R_{pp}}; c \leftarrow \mathsf{Com}(x_b; r); b' \leftarrow \mathcal{A}(\mathsf{pp}, c)\end{matrix} : b = b'\right] - \frac{1}{2}\right| \approx 0$$

Definition 7 (Computational Binding). *We say a commitment* (Setup, Com,Open) *is computationally binding if the commitment can only be opened to one message. Formally, for all PPT adversaries $\mathcal{A}$, we have*

$$\Pr\left[\begin{matrix}\mathsf{pp} \leftarrow \mathsf{Setup}(1^\lambda) \\ (x_0, x_1, r_0, r_1) \leftarrow \mathcal{A}(\mathsf{pp})\end{matrix} : \mathsf{Com}(x_0, r_0) = \mathsf{Com}(x_1, r_1) \wedge x_0 \neq x_1\right] \approx 0$$

Since Pedersen commitment picks random group elements, it is perfectly hiding. On the other hand, breaking its binding property corresponds to breaking the discrete logarithm assumption. In addition, Pedersen commitment is homomorphic, which states that for all $x_1, x_2 \in \mathsf{M_{pp}}, r_1, r_2 \in \mathsf{R_{pp}}$, we have

$$\mathsf{Com}(x_1; r_1) \cdot \mathsf{Com}(x_2; r_2) = \mathsf{Com}(x_1 + x_2; r_1 + r_2)$$

2.3 Arguments of Knowledge

Our scheme is an argument of knowledge. An argument of knowledge is an interactive protocol where a prover $\mathcal{P}$ can convince a verifier $\mathcal{V}$ that $\mathcal{P}$ knows some statement u, where $\mathcal{P}$ is computationally bounded. In this paper, we consider arguments where $\mathcal{P}$ and $\mathcal{V}$ are all probabilistic polynomial time Turing Machines.

Let $\mathcal{R}$ be a binary relation which defines a NP language. For a statement u, we call w a witness for u iff $(u, w) \in \mathcal{R}$. We let $tr \leftarrow \langle \mathcal{P}(u, w), \mathcal{V}(u)\rangle$ denote the transcript produced by $\mathcal{P}$ and $\mathcal{V}$. We denote the output of $\langle \mathcal{P}(u, w), \mathcal{V}(u)\rangle$ by a bit b. If $b = 0$, the verifier accepts, otherwise the verifier rejects.

Definition 8 (Argument of Knowledge [9,12]**).** *The pair $(\mathcal{P}, \mathcal{V})$ is called an argument of knowledge for relation $\mathcal{R}$ if it satisfies the following two properties.*

- Perfect Completeness. $(\mathcal{P}, \mathcal{V})$ *has perfect completeness if for all PPT adversaries $\mathcal{A}$, we have*

$$\Pr\left[(u, w) \leftarrow \mathcal{A}(1^\lambda) : (u, w) \notin \mathcal{R} \vee \langle \mathcal{P}(u, w), \mathcal{V}(u)\rangle = 1\right] = 1$$

- Statistical witness-extended emulation. $(\mathcal{P}, \mathcal{V})$ *has statistical witness-extended emulation if for all deterministic polynomial time $\mathcal{P}^*$ there exists an expected polynomial time emulator $\mathcal{E}$ such that for all interactive adversaries $\mathcal{A}$, we have*

$$\Pr\left[(u, s) \leftarrow \mathcal{A}(1^\lambda); tr \leftarrow \langle \mathcal{P}^*(u, s), \mathcal{V}(u)\rangle : \mathcal{A}(tr) = 1\right]$$

$$\approx \Pr\left[\begin{matrix}(u, s) \leftarrow \mathcal{A}(1^\lambda); (tr, w) \leftarrow \mathcal{E}^{\langle \mathcal{P}^*(u,s), \mathcal{V}(u)\rangle}(u) : \\ \mathcal{A}(tr) = 1 \text{ and if } tr \text{ is accepting then } (u, w) \in \mathcal{R}\end{matrix}\right]$$

where the oracle called by $\mathcal{E}^{\langle \mathcal{P}^*(u,s),\mathcal{V}(u)\rangle}$ permits rewinding to a specific point and resuming with fresh randomness for the verifier from this point onwards.

In the definition, s can be interpreted as the state of $\mathcal{P}^*$, including the randomness. So, whenever $\mathcal{P}^*$ is able to make a convincing argument when in state s, $\mathcal{E}$ can extract a witness. This is why we call it an argument of knowledge.

3 Inner Product Argument

In this section, we first describe the application scenarios of inner product arguments inspired by Bootle et al. and Bünz et al. Then we present our inner product argument protocol formally and give its security analysis and theoretical efficiency analysis.

3.1 Application Scenarios

The inner product argument is mainly used as a component of whole protocols to reduce communication complexity from linear to logarithmic. The inner product argument of Bootle et al. allows the prover to prove the knowledge of two vectors $\boldsymbol{a}, \boldsymbol{b} \in \mathbb{Z}_p^n$, such that $A = \boldsymbol{g}^{\boldsymbol{a}}, B = \boldsymbol{h}^{\boldsymbol{b}}$ and $\langle \boldsymbol{a}, \boldsymbol{b} \rangle = z$, given the public $z \in \mathbb{Z}_p, A, B \in \mathbb{G}$ and $\boldsymbol{g}, \boldsymbol{h} \in \mathbb{G}^n$, where n is the dimension of vectors. More precisely, their inner product argument is an argument of knowledge for the following relation:

$$\left\{\left(\boldsymbol{g}, \boldsymbol{h} \in \mathbb{G}^n, A, B \in \mathbb{G}, z \in \mathbb{Z}_p; \boldsymbol{a}, \boldsymbol{b} \in \mathbb{Z}_p^n\right) : A = \boldsymbol{g}^{\boldsymbol{a}} \wedge B = \boldsymbol{h}^{\boldsymbol{b}} \wedge z = \langle \boldsymbol{a}, \boldsymbol{b} \rangle\right\} \tag{1}$$

where A and B are considered as two different Pedersen vector commitments to the witness $\boldsymbol{a}$ and $\boldsymbol{b}$ without randomness, respectively. However, the inner product argument of Bünz et al. is an argument of knowledge for another relation:

$$\left\{\left(\boldsymbol{g}, \boldsymbol{h} \in \mathbb{G}^n, C \in \mathbb{G}, z \in \mathbb{Z}_p; \boldsymbol{a}, \boldsymbol{b} \in \mathbb{Z}_p^n\right) : C = \boldsymbol{g}^{\boldsymbol{a}} \boldsymbol{h}^{\boldsymbol{b}} \wedge z = \langle \boldsymbol{a}, \boldsymbol{b} \rangle\right\} \tag{2}$$

where C is considered as one Pedersen vector commitment to both $\boldsymbol{a}$ and $\boldsymbol{b}$ without randomness.

The inner product argument is usually used to construct range proofs, arithmetic circuit satisfiability arguments, grand product arguments and so on. We summarize its application scenarios into the following structure.

The prover has some private vectors $(\boldsymbol{pv}_1, \ldots, \boldsymbol{pv}_t)$ and uses these vectors to construct two vectors $\boldsymbol{a}$ and $\boldsymbol{b}$ with public calculation formulas, such that the inner product of $\boldsymbol{a}$ and $\boldsymbol{b}$ is equal to a public scalar z. For example,

$$\boldsymbol{a} = k_1 \boldsymbol{pv}_1 + \cdots + k_t \boldsymbol{pv}_t \qquad \boldsymbol{b} = k_1' \boldsymbol{pv}_1 + \cdots + k_t' \boldsymbol{pv}_t$$

Then the prover intends to convince the verifier that 1) $\boldsymbol{a}$ and $\boldsymbol{b}$ are calculated correctly according to the public formulas, and 2) the inner product of $\boldsymbol{a}$ and $\boldsymbol{b}$ is exactly z. He first generates some commitments $(cm_1, \ldots, cm_t)$ to the vectors $(\boldsymbol{pv}_1, \ldots, \boldsymbol{pv}_t)$ with the same commitment keys, i.e., $\boldsymbol{g}$. Then the verifier computes $A = \prod_{i=1}^{t} cm_i^{k_i}$, $B = \prod_{i=1}^{t} cm_i^{k'_i}$. Now, the prover may send $\boldsymbol{a}$ and $\boldsymbol{b}$ directly to the verifier for verification. However, it requires linear communication complexity with respect to the dimension of vectors.

In order to achieve logarithmic communication complexity, the prover and the verifier may choose to engage in an inner product argument for relation (1) with the input as $(\boldsymbol{g}, \boldsymbol{g}, A, B, z; \boldsymbol{a}, \boldsymbol{b})$. Also, they may choose an inner product argument for relation (2). However, this requires that the above structure meet the following two constraints. First, both $\boldsymbol{a}$ and $\boldsymbol{b}$ do not have any common private vector $\boldsymbol{pv}_i$. Second, assume that $\boldsymbol{a} = k_1\boldsymbol{pv}_1 + \cdots + k_s\boldsymbol{pv}_s$ and $\boldsymbol{b} = k'_{s+1}\boldsymbol{pv}_{s+1} + \cdots + k'_t\boldsymbol{pv}_t$, then $(\boldsymbol{pv}_1, \ldots, \boldsymbol{pv}_s)$ and $(\boldsymbol{pv}_{s+1}, \ldots, \boldsymbol{pv}_t)$ should be committed with two independent commitment keys $\boldsymbol{g}$ and $\boldsymbol{h}$, respectively. Otherwise, the prover may convince the verifier of a false statement, and thus one can use the inner product argument of Bootle et al. instead of Bünz et al.

3.2 Main Idea

The inner product argument we present is an argument of knowledge for relation (1), which is applicable in more scenarios than that for relation (2). In the following section, we assume that the dimension n is a power of 2. If necessary, one may pad the vectors easily to ensure this assumption holds.

We first combine the last two constraints in relation (1) to get a new single constraint relying on Schwartz-Zippel lemma [13] and the discrete logarithm assumption. Then the prover and the verifier are engaged in an interactive argument protocol for a new relation. The new relation is described as follows:

$$\left\{(\boldsymbol{g}, \boldsymbol{h} \in \mathbb{G}^n, u, A, B \in \mathbb{G}; \boldsymbol{a}, \boldsymbol{b} \in \mathbb{Z}_p^n) : A = \boldsymbol{g}^{\boldsymbol{a}} \wedge B = \boldsymbol{h}^{\boldsymbol{b}} u^{\langle \boldsymbol{a}, \boldsymbol{b} \rangle}\right\} \tag{3}$$

In relation (3), the added value u is also certain part of the public statement, functioning as $\boldsymbol{g}$, $\boldsymbol{h}$ and independent of $\boldsymbol{h}$. When the prover and the verifier are engaged in the interactive argument protocol for relation (1), they both compute $\hat{B} = Bu^{cz}$ and $\hat{u} = u^c$, in which c is a random challenge chosen by the verifier. Then they are engaged in the interactive argument protocol for relation (3) with the input as public statement $\left(\boldsymbol{g}, \boldsymbol{h}, \hat{u}, A, \hat{B}\right)$ and witness $(\boldsymbol{a}, \boldsymbol{b})$. According to Schwartz-Zippel lemma and the discrete logarithm assumption, an interactive argument protocol for relation (3) gives an interactive argument protocol for relation (1) with the same complexity.

Now we describe the main idea and process of the interactive argument protocol for relation (3). The intuitive idea is to split every vector into two small sets. The prover takes the small sets of private vectors as exponent, the small sets of public vectors as base, and performs group exponentiation operations with four specific combinations. Then, the prover obtains four group elements and sends them to the verifier as one part of the proof. Then the verifier chooses a random challenge and sends it to the prover. Next, the prover computes two shorter vectors as response using the challenge and the small sets of private vectors. What is striking is that the form of the verification equations is exactly the same as the form of the original constraint equations. So the prover and the verifier recursively engage in the same interactive argument protocol as mentioned before for smaller statement and witness. After an appropriate number of recursion, the interactive argument protocol is concluded with the prover revealing a very small witness for a very small statement. In this way, the communication complexity of our protocol is reduced to $4\log_2 n$.

To be more specific, we set $\boldsymbol{g} = (\boldsymbol{g}_1, \boldsymbol{g}_2), \boldsymbol{h} = (\boldsymbol{h}_1, \boldsymbol{h}_2)$ and $\boldsymbol{a} = (\boldsymbol{a}_1, \boldsymbol{a}_2), \boldsymbol{b} = (\boldsymbol{b}_1, \boldsymbol{b}_2)$, where the length of each short vectors is $\frac{n}{2}$. Now we write A and B as follows:

$$A = \boldsymbol{g}_1^{\boldsymbol{a}_1} \cdot \boldsymbol{g}_2^{\boldsymbol{a}_2} \qquad B = \boldsymbol{h}_1^{\boldsymbol{b}_1} \cdot \boldsymbol{h}_2^{\boldsymbol{b}_2} \cdot u^{\langle \boldsymbol{a}_1, \boldsymbol{b}_1 \rangle + \langle \boldsymbol{a}_2, \boldsymbol{b}_2 \rangle}$$

In the interactive argument protocol, the prover first computes and sends the following items:

$$A_{-1} = \boldsymbol{g}_2^{\boldsymbol{a}_1} \qquad A_1 = \boldsymbol{g}_1^{\boldsymbol{a}_2} \qquad B_{-1} = \boldsymbol{h}_2^{\boldsymbol{b}_1} \cdot u^{\langle \boldsymbol{a}_2, \boldsymbol{b}_1 \rangle} \qquad B_1 = \boldsymbol{h}_1^{\boldsymbol{b}_2} \cdot u^{\langle \boldsymbol{a}_1, \boldsymbol{b}_2 \rangle}$$

After receiving the verifier's challenge e, the prover computes and sends the following items as response:

$$\boldsymbol{a}' = e\boldsymbol{a}_1 + e^2\boldsymbol{a}_2 \qquad \boldsymbol{b}' = e^{-1}\boldsymbol{b}_1 + e^{-2}\boldsymbol{b}_2$$

Now since the values $A, B, \boldsymbol{g}_1, \boldsymbol{g}_2, \boldsymbol{h}_1, \boldsymbol{h}_2$ are part of the statement, both the prover and the verifier compute the following items:

$$A' = A_{-1}^{e^{-1}} A A_1^{e} \qquad B' = B_{-1}^{e} B B_1^{e^{-1}} \qquad \boldsymbol{g}' = \boldsymbol{g}_1^{e^{-1}} \circ \boldsymbol{g}_2^{e^{-2}} \qquad \boldsymbol{h}' = \boldsymbol{h}_1^{e} \circ \boldsymbol{h}_2^{e^2}$$

After receiving the prover's response, the verifier checks whether the prover's witness is valid for the statement or not using $\boldsymbol{a}'$ and $\boldsymbol{b}'$. The verification equations are as follows:

$$A' = \boldsymbol{g}'^{\boldsymbol{a}'} \qquad B' = \boldsymbol{h}'^{\boldsymbol{b}'} u^{\langle \boldsymbol{a}', \boldsymbol{b}' \rangle}$$

Notice that the form of the verification equations is exactly the same as the form of the constraint equations in relation (3). Thus the prover and the verifier may engage in the same process again instead of prover's sending $\boldsymbol{a}'$ and $\boldsymbol{b}'$ as response, whose total length is n. And in the second round protocol, the total length of $\boldsymbol{a}'$ and $\boldsymbol{b}'$ is $\frac{n}{2}$, which is half the length of them in the first round protocol. The prover and the verifier continue repeating the above process recursively until the total length of $\boldsymbol{a}'$ and $\boldsymbol{b}'$ is 2, then the prover sends them directly to the verifier.

3.3 Complete Protocol

We first describe the formal and complete protocol for relation (3).
Statement: $(\boldsymbol{g}, \boldsymbol{h} \in \mathbb{G}^n, u, A, B \in \mathbb{G})$
Witness: $(\boldsymbol{a}, \boldsymbol{b} \in \mathbb{Z}_p^n)$
Let n_0 represent the dimension of vectors.

If $n_0 = 1$**:**

$P \rightarrow V$: a, b

V checks:

$$A = g^a \qquad B = h^b u^{\langle a,b \rangle}$$

If both equations are satisfied, it accepts; otherwise it rejects.

Else:

P computes:

$$A_{-1} = \boldsymbol{g}_2^{\boldsymbol{a}_1} \qquad A_1 = \boldsymbol{g}_1^{\boldsymbol{a}_2} \qquad B_{-1} = \boldsymbol{h}_2^{\boldsymbol{b}_1} \cdot u^{\langle \boldsymbol{a}_2, \boldsymbol{b}_1 \rangle} \qquad B_1 = \boldsymbol{h}_1^{\boldsymbol{b}_2} \cdot u^{\langle \boldsymbol{a}_1, \boldsymbol{b}_2 \rangle}$$

P → V: A_{-1}, A_1, B_{-1}, B_1

V → P: $e \xleftarrow{\$} \mathbb{Z}_p^*$

P computes:

$$\boldsymbol{a}' = e\boldsymbol{a}_1 + e^2\boldsymbol{a}_2 \qquad \boldsymbol{b}' = e^{-1}\boldsymbol{b}_1 + e^{-2}\boldsymbol{b}_2$$

P&V compute:

$$A' = A_{-1}^{e^{-1}} A A_1^e \qquad B' = B_{-1}^e B B_1^{e^{-1}} \qquad \boldsymbol{g}' = \boldsymbol{g}_1^{e^{-1}} \circ \boldsymbol{g}_2^{e^{-2}} \qquad \boldsymbol{h}' = \boldsymbol{h}_1^e \circ \boldsymbol{h}_2^{e^2}$$

Recursively run the protocol on statement $(\boldsymbol{g}', \boldsymbol{h}', u, A', B')$ and witness $(\boldsymbol{a}', \boldsymbol{b}')$.

We now describe the formal and complete protocol for relation (1).

Statement: $(\boldsymbol{g}, \boldsymbol{h} \in \mathbb{G}^n, u, A, B \in \mathbb{G}, z \in \mathbb{Z}_p)$

Witness: $(\boldsymbol{a}, \boldsymbol{b} \in \mathbb{Z}_p^n)$

V → P: $c \xleftarrow{\$} \mathbb{Z}_p^*$

P&V compute:

$$\hat{B} = Bu^{cz} \qquad \hat{u} = u^c$$

Run the above protocol for relation (3) on statement $\left(\boldsymbol{g}, \boldsymbol{h}, \hat{u}, A, \hat{B}\right)$ and witness $(\boldsymbol{a}, \boldsymbol{b})$.

Security Analysis

Theorem 1. *The interactive argument protocol for relation (1) presented in Sect. 3.3 has perfect completeness and statistical witness-extended emulation.*

Proof We first give a proof of perfect completeness, then we give a proof of statistical witness-extended emulation.

Perfect Completeness. If $(\boldsymbol{a}, \boldsymbol{b})$ is a valid witness for relation (1), i.e., $A = \boldsymbol{g}^{\boldsymbol{a}} \wedge B = \boldsymbol{h}^{\boldsymbol{b}} \wedge z = \langle \boldsymbol{a}, \boldsymbol{b} \rangle$, then for a random challenge c the following constraints are satisfied:

$$A = \boldsymbol{g}^{\boldsymbol{a}} \wedge Bu^{cz} = \boldsymbol{h}^{\boldsymbol{b}} u^{c\langle \boldsymbol{a}, \boldsymbol{b} \rangle},$$

which means $(\boldsymbol{a}, \boldsymbol{b})$ is a valid witness on statement $(\boldsymbol{g}, \boldsymbol{h}, u^c, A, Bu^{cz})$ in relation (3). In the first recursive round for relation (3), it holds that $A' = \boldsymbol{g}'^{\boldsymbol{a}'} \wedge B' = \boldsymbol{h}'^{\boldsymbol{b}'} u^{\langle \boldsymbol{a}', \boldsymbol{b}' \rangle}$. Indeed,

$$A' = A_{-1}^{e^{-1}} A A_1^e = (\boldsymbol{g}_2^{\boldsymbol{a}_1})^{e^{-1}} \boldsymbol{g}_1^{\boldsymbol{a}_1} \boldsymbol{g}_2^{\boldsymbol{a}_2} (\boldsymbol{g}_1^{\boldsymbol{a}_2})^e = \left(\boldsymbol{g}_1^{e^{-1}} \circ \boldsymbol{g}_2^{e^{-2}}\right)^{e\boldsymbol{a}_1 + e^2 \boldsymbol{a}_2} = \boldsymbol{g}'^{\boldsymbol{a}'}$$

$$B' = B_{-1}^e B B_1^{e^{-1}} = \left(\boldsymbol{h}_2^{\boldsymbol{b}_1} u^{\langle \boldsymbol{a}_2, \boldsymbol{b}_1 \rangle}\right)^e \boldsymbol{h}_1^{\boldsymbol{b}_1} \boldsymbol{h}_2^{\boldsymbol{b}_2} u^{\langle \boldsymbol{a}_1, \boldsymbol{b}_1 \rangle + \langle \boldsymbol{a}_2, \boldsymbol{b}_2 \rangle} \left(\boldsymbol{h}_1^{\boldsymbol{b}_2} u^{\langle \boldsymbol{a}_1, \boldsymbol{b}_2 \rangle}\right)^{e^{-1}}$$

$$= \left(\boldsymbol{h}_1^e \circ \boldsymbol{h}_2^{e^2}\right)^{e^{-1}\boldsymbol{b}_1 + e^{-2}\boldsymbol{b}_2} u^{\langle e\boldsymbol{a}_1 + e^2 \boldsymbol{a}_2, e^{-1}\boldsymbol{b}_1 + e^{-2}\boldsymbol{b}_2 \rangle} = \boldsymbol{h}'^{\boldsymbol{b}'} u^{\langle \boldsymbol{a}', \boldsymbol{b}' \rangle},$$

which means that $(\boldsymbol{g}', \boldsymbol{h}', u, A', B')$ is a valid statement and $(\boldsymbol{a}', \boldsymbol{b}')$ is the corresponding witness. Each recursive round leads to a valid reduced statement, thus the verifier will accept in the end.

Statistical Witness-extended Emulation. We first construct an extractor $\mathcal{X}_1$ which on input $(\boldsymbol{g}, \boldsymbol{h}, u, A, B)$ either extracts a witness for relation (3), or discovers a non-trivial discrete logarithm relation.

If $n = 1$, the prover sends witness (a, b) to the verifier directly, then the verifier verifies whether it is valid or not.

Next for each recursive step, we show that the extractor can extract a valid witness or a non-trivial discrete logarithm relation by rewinding the prover many times for the same A_{-1}, A_1, B_{-1}, B_1. After rewinding the prover with three different challenges e_1, e_2, e_3, the extractor can obtain three accepting transcripts $\{A_{-1}, A_1, B_{-1}, B_1, e_i, \boldsymbol{a}'_i, \boldsymbol{b}'_i\}_{i=1}^3$ that satisfy the following equations:

$$A_{-1}^{e_i^{-1}} A A_1^{e_i} = \left(\boldsymbol{g}_1^{e_i^{-1}} \circ \boldsymbol{g}_2^{e_i^{-2}}\right)^{\boldsymbol{a}'_i} \tag{4}$$

$$B_{-1}^{e_i} B B_1^{e_i^{-1}} = \left(\boldsymbol{h}_1^{e_i} \circ \boldsymbol{h}_2^{e_i^2}\right)^{\boldsymbol{b}'_i} u^{\langle \boldsymbol{a}'_i, \boldsymbol{b}'_i \rangle} \tag{5}$$

Using the three different challenges e_1, e_2, e_3 we compute $v_1, v_2, v_3, w_1, w_2, w_3, t_1, t_2, t_3$ such that the following holds:

$$\sum_{i=1}^{3} v_i e_i^{-1} = 1 \qquad \sum_{i=1}^{3} v_i = 0 \qquad \sum_{i=1}^{3} v_i e_i = 0$$

$$\sum_{i=1}^{3} w_i e_i^{-1} = 0 \qquad \sum_{i=1}^{3} w_i = 0 \qquad \sum_{i=1}^{3} w_i e_i = 1$$

$$\sum_{i=1}^{3} t_i e_i^{-1} = 0 \qquad \sum_{i=1}^{3} t_i = 1 \qquad \sum_{i=1}^{3} t_i e_i = 0$$

Then taking a linear combination of Eq. (4) and Eq. (5) with v_1, v_2, v_3 as powers, respectively, we compute $\boldsymbol{a}_{-1,1}$, $\boldsymbol{a}_{-1,2}$ and $\boldsymbol{b}_{1,1}$, $\boldsymbol{b}_{1,2}$, z_1 such that

$$A_{-1} = \boldsymbol{g}_1^{\boldsymbol{a}_{-1,1}} \boldsymbol{g}_2^{\boldsymbol{a}_{-1,2}} \qquad B_1 = \boldsymbol{h}_1^{\boldsymbol{b}_{1,1}} \boldsymbol{h}_2^{\boldsymbol{b}_{1,2}} u^{z_1}$$

Taking a linear combination of Eq. (4) and Eq. (5) with w_1, w_2, w_3 as powers, respectively, we compute $\boldsymbol{a}_{1,1}$, $\boldsymbol{a}_{1,2}$ and $\boldsymbol{b}_{-1,1}$, $\boldsymbol{b}_{-1,2}$, z_{-1} such that

$$A_1 = \boldsymbol{g}_1^{\boldsymbol{a}_{1,1}} \boldsymbol{g}_2^{\boldsymbol{a}_{1,2}} \qquad B_{-1} = \boldsymbol{h}_1^{\boldsymbol{b}_{-1,1}} \boldsymbol{h}_2^{\boldsymbol{b}_{-1,2}} u^{z_{-1}}$$

Taking a linear combination of Eq. (4) and Eq. (5) with t_1, t_2, t_3 as powers, respectively, we compute $\boldsymbol{a}_{0,1}$, $\boldsymbol{a}_{0,2}$ and $\boldsymbol{b}_{0,1}$, $\boldsymbol{b}_{0,2}$, z_0 such that

$$A = \boldsymbol{g}_1^{\boldsymbol{a}_{0,1}} \boldsymbol{g}_2^{\boldsymbol{a}_{0,2}} \qquad B = \boldsymbol{h}_1^{\boldsymbol{b}_{0,1}} \boldsymbol{h}_2^{\boldsymbol{b}_{0,2}} u^{z_0}$$

According to discrete logarithm relation assumption and the generation formula of $A_{-1}, A_1, B_{-1}, B_1, A, B$, we may deduce

$$\begin{aligned} &\boldsymbol{a}_{-1,1} = \boldsymbol{a}_{1,2} = \boldsymbol{b}_{-1,1} = \boldsymbol{b}_{1,2} = \boldsymbol{0} \\ &\boldsymbol{a}_{-1,2} = \boldsymbol{a}_{0,1} \qquad \boldsymbol{a}_{1,1} = \boldsymbol{a}_{0,2} \\ &\boldsymbol{b}_{-1,2} = \boldsymbol{b}_{0,1} \qquad \boldsymbol{b}_{1,1} = \boldsymbol{b}_{0,2} \end{aligned}$$

Next for each accepting transcript $\{A_{-1}, A_1, B_{-1}, B_1, e, \boldsymbol{a}', \boldsymbol{b}'\}$, it must satisfy the verification equations. We use the extracted values to represent A_{-1}, A_1, B_{-1}, B_1, A, B. Then we get the following equations:

$$\left(\boldsymbol{g}_1^{e^{-1}} \circ \boldsymbol{g}_2^{e^{-2}}\right)^{\boldsymbol{a}'} = A_{-1}^{e^{-1}} A A_1^{e} = \left(\boldsymbol{g}_1^{\boldsymbol{a}_{-1,1}} \boldsymbol{g}_2^{\boldsymbol{a}_{-1,2}}\right)^{e^{-1}} \boldsymbol{g}_1^{\boldsymbol{a}_{0,1}} \boldsymbol{g}_2^{\boldsymbol{a}_{0,2}} \left(\boldsymbol{g}_1^{\boldsymbol{a}_{1,1}} \boldsymbol{g}_2^{\boldsymbol{a}_{1,2}}\right)^{e}$$

$$\begin{aligned} \left(\boldsymbol{h}_1^{e} \circ \boldsymbol{h}_2^{e^2}\right)^{\boldsymbol{b}'} u^{\langle \boldsymbol{a}', \boldsymbol{b}' \rangle} &= B_{-1}^{e} B B_1^{e^{-1}} \\ &= \left(\boldsymbol{h}_1^{\boldsymbol{b}_{-1,1}} \boldsymbol{h}_2^{\boldsymbol{b}_{-1,2}} u^{z_{-1}}\right)^{e} \boldsymbol{h}_1^{\boldsymbol{b}_{0,1}} \boldsymbol{h}_2^{\boldsymbol{b}_{0,2}} u^{z_0} \left(\boldsymbol{h}_1^{\boldsymbol{b}_{1,1}} \boldsymbol{h}_2^{\boldsymbol{b}_{1,2}} u^{z_1}\right)^{e^{-1}} \end{aligned}$$

The two equations imply that

$$\boldsymbol{a}' = e\boldsymbol{a}_{0,1} + e^2 \boldsymbol{a}_{0,2} \quad \boldsymbol{b}' = e^{-1}\boldsymbol{b}_{0,1} + e^{-2}\boldsymbol{b}_{0,2} \quad \langle \boldsymbol{a}', \boldsymbol{b}' \rangle = e z_{-1} + z_0 + e^{-1} z_1,$$

otherwise we obtain a non-trivial discrete logarithm relation between $\{\boldsymbol{g}_1, \boldsymbol{g}_2\}$ or a non-trivial discrete logarithm relation between $\{\boldsymbol{h}_1, \boldsymbol{h}_2, u\}$. We define $\boldsymbol{a}_0 = (\boldsymbol{a}_{0,1}, \boldsymbol{a}_{0,2})$, $\boldsymbol{b}_0 = (\boldsymbol{b}_{0,1}, \boldsymbol{b}_{0,2})$. Now we show that the inner product of $\boldsymbol{a}_0, \boldsymbol{b}_0$ is exactly z_0, which means that the extracted $(\boldsymbol{a}_0, \boldsymbol{b}_0)$ is the valid witness in this recursive round.

$$\begin{aligned} e z_{-1} + z_0 + e^{-1} z_1 &= \langle \boldsymbol{a}', \boldsymbol{b}' \rangle \\ &= \left\langle e\boldsymbol{a}_{0,1} + e^2 \boldsymbol{a}_{0,2}, e^{-1}\boldsymbol{b}_{0,1} + e^{-2}\boldsymbol{b}_{0,2} \right\rangle \\ &= e \langle \boldsymbol{a}_{0,2}, \boldsymbol{b}_{0,1} \rangle + \langle \boldsymbol{a}_0, \boldsymbol{b}_0 \rangle + e^{-1} \langle \boldsymbol{a}_{0,1}, \boldsymbol{b}_{0,2} \rangle \end{aligned} \tag{6}$$

Let $F(x) = x z_{-1} + z_0 + x^{-1} z_1$, $G(x) = x \langle \boldsymbol{a}_{0,2}, \boldsymbol{b}_{0,1} \rangle + \langle \boldsymbol{a}_0, \boldsymbol{b}_0 \rangle + x^{-1} \langle \boldsymbol{a}_{0,1}, \boldsymbol{b}_{0,2} \rangle$ and $H(x) = F(x) - G(x)$. According to Schwartz-Zippel lemma, if $H(x)$ is a non-zero polynomial, then the probability that $H(e) = 0$ is at most $\frac{2}{p-1}$ for a challenge e sampled uniformly at random in $\mathbb{Z}_p^*$. Thus except with error probability $\frac{2}{p-1}$, Eq. (6) implies that $H(x)$ is a zero polynomial, which means $\langle \boldsymbol{a}_0, \boldsymbol{b}_0 \rangle = z_0$.

The extractor $\mathcal{X}_1$ recursively runs the above process and finally can extract the valid witness for relation (3) with $O(n^2)$ accepting transcripts.

Now we construct an extractor $\mathcal{X}$ to extract the witness for relation (1) using the extractor $\mathcal{X}_1$. The extractor $\mathcal{X}$ rewinds the prover many times with two different challenges c_1, c_2. Then $\mathcal{X}$ calls $\mathcal{X}_1$ two times on input $\left(\boldsymbol{g}, \boldsymbol{h}, \hat{u}_1, A, \hat{B}_1\right)$ and $\left(\boldsymbol{g}, \boldsymbol{h}, \hat{u}_2, A, \hat{B}_2\right)$, respectively, after which it obtains $\boldsymbol{a}, \boldsymbol{b}$ and $\boldsymbol{x}, \boldsymbol{y}$ such that

$$A = \boldsymbol{g}^{\boldsymbol{a}} \qquad Bu^{c_1 z} = \boldsymbol{h}^{\boldsymbol{b}} u^{c_1 \langle \boldsymbol{a}, \boldsymbol{b} \rangle}$$
$$A = \boldsymbol{g}^{\boldsymbol{x}} \qquad Bu^{c_2 z} = \boldsymbol{h}^{\boldsymbol{y}} u^{c_2 \langle \boldsymbol{x}, \boldsymbol{y} \rangle}$$

These equations imply that $\boldsymbol{a} = \boldsymbol{x}$, $\boldsymbol{b} = \boldsymbol{y}$, $\langle \boldsymbol{a}, \boldsymbol{b} \rangle = z$, otherwise we may get a non-trivial discrete logarithm relation. Thus the extracted values $\boldsymbol{a}$ and $\boldsymbol{b}$ are valid witness for relation (1).

The extractor $\mathcal{X}$ can extract the valid witness with $O(n^2)$ accepting transcripts, which is polynomial in λ. Using the forking lemma of Bootle et al., we conclude that the interactive argument protocol for relation (1) has statistical witness-extended emulation. □

Efficiency. We now discuss the efficiency of the aforementioned protocol. Observing that the efficiency of the protocol for relation (1) is dominated by the called protocol for relation (3), thus we mainly focus on the interactive argument protocol for relation (3).

For prover complexity, at each iteration, the main cost of the prover is computing A_{-1}, A_1, B_{-1}, B_1 and $\boldsymbol{g}', \boldsymbol{h}'$. The computation cost of all steps sums up to $O(n)$ group exponentiations and $O(n)$ field multiplications. Thus the prover complexity is $O(n)$.

For verifier complexity, the main cost of the verifier is computing $A', B', \boldsymbol{g}', \boldsymbol{h}'$ at each iteration and checking the verification equations in the end. The total complexity is $O(n)$. Inspired by Bünz et al., we may also optimize the computation complexity of the verifier by delaying all the computations until the last round.

For communication complexity, the group elements and the field elements are stored as different number of bytes depending on the specific implementation, we consider the total number of elements as communication complexity in this part. In Sect. 4 we discuss the communication complexity considering the number of bytes stored per element.

If the protocol is executed only one round, then the total length of $\boldsymbol{a}'$ and $\boldsymbol{b}'$ is n. Thus the communication overhead is 4 group elements and n field elements. For each additional round of recursion, the communication overhead will increase by 4 group elements and decrease by $\frac{n}{2}$ field elements. After logarithmic round recursion, the total length of $\boldsymbol{a}'$ and $\boldsymbol{b}'$ will be a small constant. Then the overall communication cost of our protocol is reduced to $O(\log n)$. To be more specific, suppose the recursion stops at $n_0 = 2^k$, the communication overhead is $f(k)$ such that

$$f(k) = 2^{k+1} - 4k + 4 \log_2 n$$

where k is an integer and $k \geq 0$. Then we conclude that the lowest communication overhead is $4\log_2 n$ with $4\log_2 n - 4$ group elements and 4 field elements when $k = 1$ or $4\log_2 n - 8$ group elements and 8 field elements when $k = 2$. However, the recursion stoping at $k = 2$, i.e., $n_0 = 4$ may reduce a round of recursion and bring lower computational complexity for both the prover and the verifier.

Now we describe the functions between the communication complexity and the number of recursive round of inner product arguments of Bootle et al. (we consider $m = 2$) and Bünz et al. Suppose the recursion stops at $n_0 = 2^k$, the communication overhead of Bootle et al. and Bünz et al. is $g(k)$ and $h(k)$, respectively, such that

$$g(k) = 2^{k+1} - 6k + 6\log_2 n, \qquad h(k) = 2^{k+1} - 2k + 2\log_2 n$$

where k is an integer and $k \geq 0$. Then we conclude that $g(k)$ takes the minimum value $6\log_2 n - 4$ when $k = 2$ and $h(k)$ takes the minimum value $2\log_2 n + 2$ when $k = 0$ or $k = 1$. For lower computational complexity, the recursion stopping at $k = 1$, i.e., $n_0 = 2$ is optimal for Bünz et al.

4 Implementation and Performance

To evaluate the performance of our inner product argument protocol for relation (1) in practice, we both implement the protocol of Bootle et al. and ours in Rust[1] under the same configuration. For consistency, we consider $m = 2$ of Bootle et al., i.e., every vector is split into two small sets per round. Our implementations are based on library libsecp256k1[2], which uses the elliptic curve secp256k1 with 128 bit security. Every field element is stored as 32 bytes and every secp256k1 point is stored as 32 bytes plus one bit using its compressed form. Observing that the group elements and the field elements are stored as almost the same number of bytes, by calculation we conclude that the communication complexity is lowest when the total number of communication elements is minimal. Combined with the conclusions in Sect. 3.3, we let the recursion stop at $n_0 = 4$ in our implementations, which brings the lowest communication complexity for inner product arguments of both Bootle et al. and ours. We create a virtual machine running CentOS 7 on Windows 10 to perform our experiments. The host computer has 2.20 GHz Intel i7-8750H CPU and 8 GB of RAM. The guest computer is allocated one processor and 1 GB of RAM.

Performance Comparison. To our best knowledge, among the inner product arguments for relation (1) in Sect. 3.1, the argument of Bootle et al. has the lowest communication cost, and the argument of Bünz et al. is for a different relation. So we mainly compare our protocol with Bootle et al.'s.

Figure 1 shows that the proof size of two protocols both grows logarithmically with respect to the dimension of vectors. The size difference is not obvious when the dimension is small. However, the dimension of vectors is greater than

[1] We refer to the bulletproof library at https://github.com/ZenGo-X/bulletproofs.
[2] https://github.com/rust-bitcoin/rust-secp256k1.

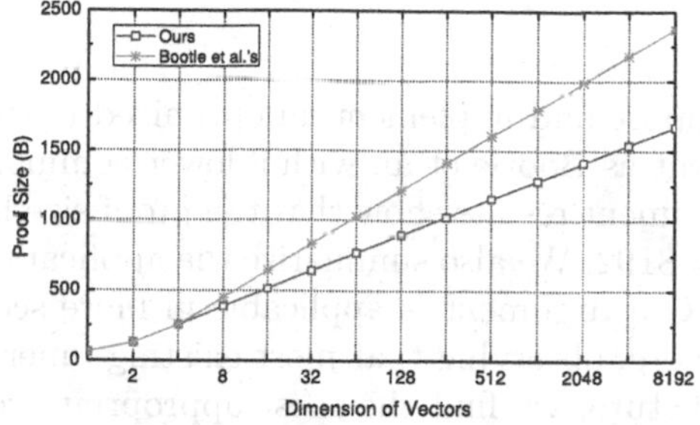

Fig. 1. Sizes for inner product arguments

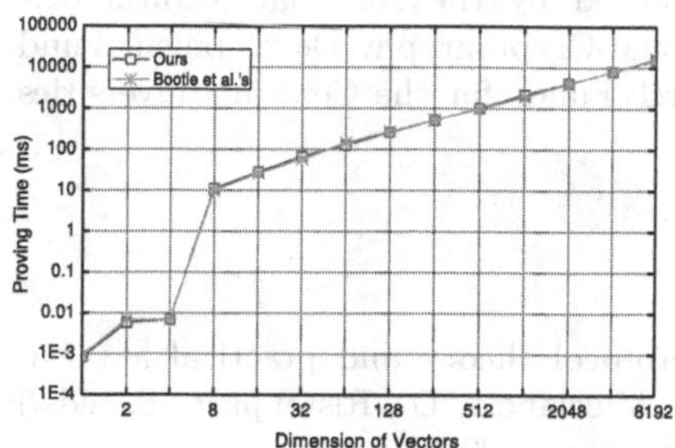

Fig. 2. Proving time for inner product arguments

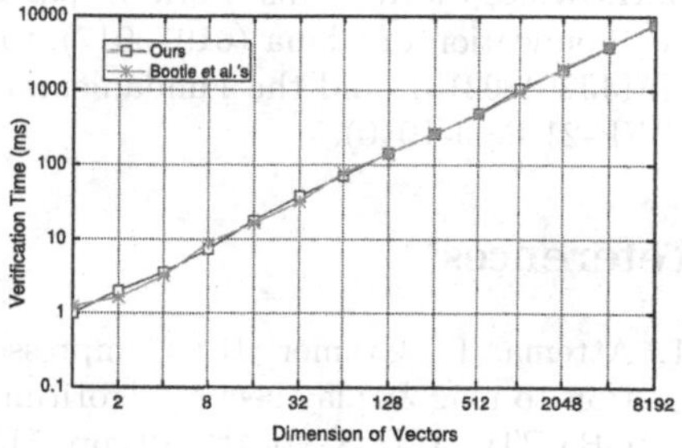

Fig. 3. Verification time for inner product arguments

512 in many specific applications using inner product arguments, such as matrix product, polynomial evaluation, image matching, shortest paths and gas simulation (refer to Table 2 of Bootle et al.). Furthermore, it reaches 8192 in proving knowledge of Pedersen hash preimage (refer to Table 3 of Bünz et al.). In these applications, the superiority of our protocol becomes more prominent. When the dimension is 8192, the proof size of Bootle et al.'s protocol is about 2400 bytes while the proof size of our protocol is only about 1670 bytes. It has been reduced by about 30%. Thus, our protocol is very competitive in terms of proof size.

Figure 2 shows that the two protocols have almost the same proving time. When the dimension of vectors is less than or equal to 4, the prover sends the witness to the verifier directly for the lowest communication complexity. Thus, the proving time is a small order of magnitude. When the dimension of vectors is greater than or equal to 8, the prover's complexity is dominated by computing the reduced statements and the proving time grows linearly. Figure 3 shows that the two protocols have almost the same verification time which grows linearly with respect to the dimension of vectors.

From the above comparison, we conclude that our inner product argument protocol is superior to that of Bootle et al. on communication complexity with almost no additional overhead for the prover and the verifier.

5 Conclusion

In this paper, we propose and implement an optimized inner product argument for the same statement as Bootle et al. with a lower communication complexity of $4\log_2 n$. Our experiment results show that the proof size has been reduced by about 30% when $n = 8192$. We also summarize the application scenarios of inner product arguments. Our argument is applicable in more scenarios than that of Bünz et al. Furthermore, observing that most existing inner product arguments have a recursive structure, we find the most appropriate recursive round that decides a better communication complexity.

Acknowledgment. This work is partly supported by the National Natural Science Foundation of China (61972017), the National Cryptography Development Fund (MMJJ20180215), and the Fundamental Research Funds for the Central Universities (YWF-21-BJ-J-1040).

References

1. Attema, T., Cramer, R.: Compressed Σ-protocol theory and practical application to plug & play secure algorithmics. In: Micciancio, D., Ristenpart, T. (eds.) CRYPTO. LNCS, vol. 12172, pp. 513–543. Springer (2020)
2. Bootle, J., Cerulli, A., Chaidos, P., Groth, J., Petit, C.: Efficient zero-knowledge arguments for arithmetic circuits in the discrete log setting. In: Fischlin, M., Coron, J.-S. (eds.) EUROCRYPT 2016. LNCS, vol. 9666, pp. 327–357. Springer, Heidelberg (2016). https://doi.org/10.1007/978-3-662-49896-5_12
3. Bowe, S., Grigg, J., Hopwood, D.: Recursive proof composition without a trusted setup. Cryptology ePrint Archive, Report 2019/1021 (2019)
4. Bünz, B., Bootle, J., Boneh, D., Poelstra, A., Wuille, P., Maxwell, G.: Bulletproofs: short proofs for confidential transactions and more. In: S&P, pp. 315–334. IEEE (2018)
5. Bünz, B., Chiesa, A., Mishra, P., Spooner, N.: Recursive proof composition from accumulation schemes. In: Pass, R., Pietrzak, K. (eds.) TCC 2020. LNCS, vol. 12551, pp. 1–18. Springer, Cham (2020). https://doi.org/10.1007/978-3-030-64378-2_1
6. Bünz, B., Maller, M., Mishra, P., Tyagi, N., Vesely, P.: Proofs for inner pairing products and applications. Cryptology ePrint Archive, Report 2019/1177 (2019)
7. Daza, V., Ràfols, C., Zacharakis, A.: Updateable inner product argument with logarithmic verifier and applications. In: Kiayias, A., Kohlweiss, M., Wallden, P., Zikas, V. (eds.) PKC 2020. LNCS, vol. 12110, pp. 527–557. Springer, Cham (2020). https://doi.org/10.1007/978-3-030-45374-9_18
8. Groth, J.: On the size of pairing-based non-interactive arguments. In: Fischlin, M., Coron, J.-S. (eds.) EUROCRYPT 2016. LNCS, vol. 9666, pp. 305–326. Springer, Heidelberg (2016). https://doi.org/10.1007/978-3-662-49896-5_11
9. Groth, J., Ishai, Y.: Sub-linear zero-knowledge argument for correctness of a shuffle. In: Smart, N. (ed.) EUROCRYPT 2008. LNCS, vol. 4965, pp. 379–396. Springer, Heidelberg (2008). https://doi.org/10.1007/978-3-540-78967-3_22
10. Hoffmann, M., Klooß, M., Rupp, A.: Efficient zero-knowledge arguments in the discrete log setting, revisited. In: Cavallaro, L., Kinder, J., Wang, X., Katz, J. (eds.) CCS, pp. 2093–2110. ACM (2019)

11. Lai, R.W.F., Malavolta, G., Ronge, V.: Succinct arguments for bilinear group arithmetic: Practical structure-preserving cryptography. In: Cavallaro, L., Kinder, J., Wang, X., Katz, J. (eds.) CCS, pp. 2057–2074. ACM (2019)
12. Lindell, Y.: Parallel coin-tossing and constant-round secure two-party computation. J. Cryptol. **16**(3), 143–184 (2003)
13. Schwartz, J.T.: Fast probabilistic algorithms for verification of polynomial identities. J. ACM **27**(4), 701–717 (1980)
14. Wahby, R.S., Tzialla, I., Shelat, A., Thaler, J., Walfish, M.: Doubly-efficient zksnarks without trusted setup. In: S&P, pp. 926–943. IEEE (2018)

Updatable All-But-One Dual Projective Hashing and Its Applications

Kai Zhang[1], Zhe Jiang[1], Junqing Gong[2(✉)], and Haifeng Qian[2]

[1] School of Computer Science and Technology, Shanghai University of Electric Power, Shanghai, China

[2] Software Engineering Institute, East China Normal University, Shanghai, China
jqgong@sei.ecnu.edu.cn

Abstract. Dual projective hashing is an extension of Cramer-Shoup projective hashing, which implies lossy trapdoor functions (LTDFs) and deterministic PKE schemes secure with respect to hard-to-invert auxiliary input. In this paper, we introduce the notion of *updatable all-but-one dual projective hashing* (UDPH) based on the all-but-one variant of dual projective hashing, which allows us to investigate the continuous leakage of invisible key update in the same context. In particular,

- we give a general construction of leakage-resilient all-but-one LTDFs via UDPH, which yields high efficiency compared with existed direct leakage-resilient all-but-one LTDFs constructions based on MDDH and SXDH. Concretely, our generic framework can be instantiated with k-LIN, DCR, QR and LWE assumptions in the standard model.
- we present a modular framework for leakage-resilient deterministic PKEs with hard-to-invert auxiliary input, which is proven secure under the introduced *continuous-leakage-resilient strong privacy indistinguishability-based* security model of invisible key update. Compared with the known MDDH/SXDH-based schemes, our constructions can be instantiated with more widely-accepted assumptions including k-LIN, DCR, QR and LWE.

Keywords: Dual projective hashing · Continuous leakage-resilient · Lossy trapdoor functions · Deterministic public key encryption

1 Introduction

(All-But-One) Dual Projective Hashing. The notion of dual projective hashing (DPH) introduced by Wee [1] is an extension of Cramer-Shoup smooth projective hashing function (SPHF) [2], which is completely dual to the structure of SPHF. Moreover, Zhang et al. [3] studied the all-but-one setting of DPH and formalized the all-but-one dual projective hashing (ABO DPH) notion. The main difference between SPHF and (ABO) DPH is that the usage of an instance u sampled from a NP language set is completely different.

D. Gao et al. (Eds.): ICICS 2021, LNCS 12919, pp. 358–374, 2021.
https://doi.org/10.1007/978-3-030-88052-1_21

- SMOOTH PROJECTIVE HASH FUNCTION [2]. The SPHF and its developed variants are promising cryptographic primitives, which are widely employed to construct chosen-ciphertext attack (CCA) secure PKE scheme [2], public key searchable encryption scheme [4], authenticated key exchange protocol [5] and leakage-resilient PKE scheme [6]. Technically, the SPHF contains a family of hash functions $\{\mathsf{H}_x(u) : \mathcal{U} \rightarrow \mathcal{Y}\}_{x \in \mathcal{X}}$ indexed by a hash key $x \in \mathcal{X}$, where u is an instance from a NP language set and $\mathsf{H}_x(u)$ is a smooth projective hash value. For any YES instance u, the hash function H_x can be computed from either a public evaluation algorithm $\mathsf{Pub}(u, w)$ with its witness w or a private evaluation algorithm $\mathsf{Priv}(u)$. Actually, the YES instance is used to yield a concrete construction, while the NO instance is used to guarantee the security of a scheme based on *smoothness* property.
- DUAL PROJECTIVE HASHING [1]. As a dual of SPHF, the structure of DPH [1] is behaved as $\{\Lambda_u(x) : \mathcal{X} \rightarrow \mathcal{Y}\}_{u \in \mathcal{U}}$ indexed by an instance u, where x is a hash key and $\Lambda_u(x)$ is a dual projective hash value. Different from SPHF, for any NO instance u, the hash key $x \in \mathcal{X}$ is recovered by a projection map $\alpha(\text{HP}, x)$ and a hash value $\Lambda_u(x)$, where HP is a public parameter. In DPH, the NO instance is used to construct a concrete scheme or a protocol, while the YES instance is used to provide the security guarantee of the construction based on the *invertibility* property.
- ALL-BUT-ONE DUAL PROJECTIVE HASHING [3]. As a generalized version of DPH, the ABO DPH is behaved as $\{\Lambda_u(\mathsf{tag}, x) : \text{TAG} \times \mathcal{X} \rightarrow \mathcal{Y}\}_{u \in \mathcal{U}}$ indexed by an instance u, where the hash value $\Lambda_u(\mathsf{tag}, x)$ is determined by a tag and a hash key x. Different from DPH for concerning the subset membership assumption (SMP) that it is hard to distinguish a NO instance from a YES instance, the ABO DPH considers the *hidden projective tag* (HPT) property that it is hard to distinguish a projective tag from a random tag. Technically, for any projective tag $\widehat{\mathsf{tag}} \in \text{TAG}$ and any instance u (as a public parameter) generated by $\mathsf{KeyGen}(\mathsf{mtd}, \widehat{\mathsf{tag}})$ where mtd is the master trapdoor, the *projective* property indicates that the hash value is determined by a projection map $\alpha(\text{HP}, x)$ and u with its witness w when $\mathsf{tag} = \widehat{\mathsf{tag}}$; while the *invertibility* property implies that the hash key x can be recovered by $\alpha(\text{HP}, x)$ and a hash value $\Lambda_u(\mathsf{tag}, x)$ when $\mathsf{tag} \neq \widehat{\mathsf{tag}}$.

In addition, Wee [1] and Zhang et al. [3] showed modular frameworks for constructing (ABO) LTDFs and deterministic PKE schemes based on the *invertibility* property of (ABO) DPH. These frameworks can be instantiated with some widely-accepted assumptions, such as Decisional Diffie-Hellman-based assumptions like k-LIN, number-theoretic assumptions like Quadratic Residuosity (QR), Decisional Composite Residuosity (DCR) and lattice-based assumptions like Learning with Error (LWE).

Leakage-Resilient Deterministic Public Key Encryption. The deterministic PKE introduced by Bellare et al. [7] has many promising applications in various scenarios but is also vulnerable to information leakage attacks. In the field of leakage-resilient cryptography, to deal with the internal private information leakage caused by side channel attacks, the *continuous memory leakage*

(CML) model was formalized by Brakerski et al. [8] and Dodis et al. [9], in which an adversary can get unbounded leakage information during system running. At the same time, the CML security model of "invisible key update" (the floppy model) [10] was introduced to design leakage-resilient (public key) traitor tracing schemes, which considers no leakage produced at key update phase but still allows an adversary to obtain unbounded leakage information. Note that the CML model of invisible key update is slightly weaker than the CML model but stronger than the bounded memory leakage (BML) model [11], where an adversary only obtains bounded leakage information and the secret key is not allowed to be updated in the BML security model.

In particular, the known deterministic PKEs [12] with leakage-resilient security are obtained from leakage-resilient ABO LTDFs, which seriously consider the continuous memory leakage during system running but still preserve required functionalities. However, their constructions [12] are not highly efficient and concise due to the use of bilinear pairings, whose security are reduced to specific DDH-based assumptions, such as matrix DDH (MDDH) and SXDH (external asymmetric Diffie-Hellman). To our best knowledge, there is no efficient general construction of deterministic PKEs with leakage-resilient security. Note that (ABO) DPH can provide a simple and general framework of deterministic PKEs and there are many efficient instantiations of (ABO) DPH [1,3], a natural question arises: "*Can we construct efficient leakage-resilient deterministic PKE schemes from (all-but-one) dual projective hashing in a modular way?*"

1.1 Our Contributions

To address the question, we introduce the *updatable all-but-one dual projective hashing* (UDPH) notion inspired by the work [3,6,12], which contains a family of hash function $\mathcal{H} = \{\Lambda_u(\mathsf{tag}, x) : \text{TAG} \times \mathcal{X} \rightarrow \mathcal{Y}\}_{u \in \mathcal{U}}$ indexed by an instance $u \in \mathcal{U}$ with inputs (tag, x). Our UDPH has the following properties (c.f. Sect. 3):

- (PROJECTIVE.) For any tag $\mathsf{tag} \in \text{TAG}$ and a projective tag $\widehat{\mathsf{tag}} \in \text{TAG}$, the hash value $\Lambda_u(\mathsf{tag}, x)$ is determined by an instance u with its witness w and a projective map $\alpha(\text{HP}, x)$ if $\mathsf{tag} = \widehat{\mathsf{tag}}$.
- (INVERTIBILITY.) For any tag $\mathsf{tag} \in \text{TAG}$ and a projective tag $\widehat{\mathsf{tag}} \in \text{TAG}$, the hash key $x \in \mathcal{X}$ can be recovered by $\alpha(\text{HP}, x)$ and $\Lambda_u(\mathsf{tag}, x)$ if $\mathsf{tag} \neq \widehat{\mathsf{tag}}$.
- (PROJECTIVE TAG INDISTINGUISHABILITY.) For any tag $\mathsf{tag} \in \text{TAG}$, it is hard to determine whether the tag tag is a projective tag $\widehat{\mathsf{tag}}$ or not ($\mathsf{tag} \neq \widehat{\mathsf{tag}}$).
- (EXTRACTOR PSEUDORANDOMNESS INDISTINGUISHABILITY.) For any function extractor $\mathsf{Ext}(\mathcal{X}, \mathcal{R}) : \mathcal{X} \times \mathcal{R} \rightarrow \mathcal{P}$, it is hard to distinguish the $\mathsf{Ext}(\cdot, \cdot)$ value from a randomly chosen element σ of $\mathcal{P}$, i.e., $(\mathsf{Ext}(\mathcal{X}, \mathcal{R}), \mathcal{R}) \approx_c (\sigma, \mathcal{R})$.

In addition, we formalize the *subset indistinguishability*, *full trapdoor indistinguishability* and *partial trapdoor indistinguishability* to support the introduced projective tag indistinguishability and the extractor pseudorandomness indistinguishability in the leakage setting, which are described in Lemma 1 and Lemma 2.

In particular, our UDPH considers the continuous leakage model of invisible key updates, where an adversary can ask unbounded leakage and cannot issue any leakage query during trapdoor updating [10]. Technically, we introduce a new algorithm $\mathsf{Update}(\mathsf{td}, \mathsf{utd})$ to use an updatable trapdoor utd to update an initial trapdoor td invisibly for generating an updated trapdoor td^*, which leaks no any knowledge to the adversary. Furthermore, since an updatable trapdoor utd is sampled via an algorithm $\mathsf{SampUtd}(\text{HP})$ with the kernel, the original trapdoor td and its new updated trapdoor td^* will be equivalent on every YES instance sampled by an algorithm $\mathsf{SampYes}(\text{HP})$ from the set Π_Y and extractor value $\mathsf{Ext}(\mathcal{X}, \text{HP})$. Thus, an adversary can break the underlying subset membership assumption of (ABO) DPH and the pseudorandomness of reconstructive extractor by checking whether the two trapdoors are equivalent on the challenge instance and the challenge extractor value respectively. Therefore, we put forth the subset indistinguishability and the extractor pseudorandomness indistinguishability to guarantee that the adversary cannot distinguish a challenge instance or a challenge extractor value $\mathsf{Ext}(\mathcal{X}, \text{HP})$ even by launching a continuous leakage attack on td.

Leakage-Resilient All-But-One Lossy Trapdoor Functions. The leakage-resilient (ABO) LTDFs [12,13] is a variant of (ABO) LTDFs [14] to deal with bounded leakage or continuous leakage. For a collection of leakage-resilient ABO LTDFs, the inputs are a branch b and a function index pp, where there exits at least one branch to be a lossy branch for defining a lossy trapdoor function $\mathsf{Eval}(\cdot, \cdot)$ and the fraction of all lossy branches is negligible. The function $\mathsf{Eval}(b, \cdot)$ is injective when $b \neq \widehat{b}$, whose pre-image can be recovered with a regularly updated trapdoor td^*. While the function $\mathsf{Eval}(\widehat{b}, \cdot)$ is lossy when $b = \widehat{b}$, in which the size of an image is much smaller than the size of its pre-image. However, it is hard to determine whether the b is lossy or injective even given continuous leakage information of updated trapdoors $\mathcal{L}(\tau^*)$.

More formally, for any trapdoor function defined as $\mathsf{Eval} = \alpha(\text{HP}, x)|| \Lambda_u(\mathsf{tag}, x)$ under a collection of leakage-resilient ABO LTDFs, an instance u generated by the $\mathsf{KeyGen}(\mathsf{mtd}, \widehat{\mathsf{tag}})$ algorithm acts as a function index pp of Eval and a tag acts as a branch of LTDFs, hence the function $\mathsf{Eval}(\mathsf{tag}, x)$ is injective when $\mathsf{tag} \neq \widehat{\mathsf{tag}}$; otherwise, the function $\mathsf{Eval}(\mathsf{tag}, x)$ is lossy when $\mathsf{tag} = \widehat{\mathsf{tag}}$. Therefore, the injective property guarantees that the hash key x can be recovered from the injective function value $\Lambda_u(\mathsf{tag}, x)$. When the function $\Lambda_u(\mathsf{tag}, x) = \Lambda_u(\widehat{\mathsf{tag}}, x)$ is lossy, it is completely determined by $\alpha(\text{HP}, x)$ and the witness w of the instance u, while the information of x is lost about at most $log\ |\alpha(x)|$ bits. Moreover, the trapdoor $\tau^* = \mathsf{td}^*$ of the inversion function $\mathsf{Inv}(\mathsf{tag}, \tau^*, y)$ is regularly updated with a trapdoor updating algorithm $\mathsf{U}(\mathsf{pp}, \tau)$ via calling the updatable algorithm Update of UDPH in essence. Hence, the indistinguishability between *injective* case and *lossy* case of the function $\mathsf{Eval}(\mathsf{tag}, x)$ is implied by the *projective tag indistinguishability* of the UDPH (c.f. Sect. 4).

Continuous Leakage-Resilient Deterministic PKE. Different from continuous leakage-resilient deterministic PKE schemes from specific leakage-resilient ABO LTDFs [12], we give a modular construction framework under the introduced *continuous-leakage-resilient strong privacy indistinguishability-based* security model of invisible key update (CLR-PRIV-sIND, c.f. Sect. 5), which derives

Table 1. Comparison with leakage-resilient deterministic PKE Instantiations

Schemes	Assumption	leakage rate	$\|m\|$-bits[a]	Group	Pairing	Model[b]
[12]	MDDH	1/2	1	Prime order	YES	CML
	SXDH	$1-O(1)$	1	Prime order	YES	CML
Our work	k-LIN	$1/k$	n	Prime order	NO	CML*
	DCR	$1-O(1)$	n	Composite order	NO	CML*
	QR	$1-O(1)$	n	Composite order	NO	CML*
	LWE	$\log p/O(n\log q)$	$O(n\log q)$	Lattice-based	NO	CML*

[a]The $|m|$-bits denotes the length of the encrypted message.
[b]The CML* model implies the CML model of "invisible key updates".

from the UDPH in Sect. 3. To consider continuous leakage resilience and find a tag for deterministic encryption, the tags in UDPH are required to be determinately sampled with private information, since an adversary cannot check whether the tag is projective or not. In addition, the projective map $\alpha(\text{HP}, x)$ in underlying UDPH is a reconstructive extractor Ext such that the proposed deterministic PKE is secure with respect to hard-to invert auxiliary input. Note that the pseudorandomness indistinguishability of reconstructive extractor Ext in the floppy model is guaranteed by the extractor pseudorandomness indistinguishability of UDPH.

Instantiations. We give a variety of instantiations of UDPH from some widely-accepted assumptions (c.f. Sect. 6), such as *DDH*-based assumptions like k-LIN, *number-theoretic* assumptions like QR and DCR and *lattice-based* assumptions like LWE. Inspired by the work [1,3,12], we employ the $\alpha(\text{HP}, x)$ instantiated with random linear functions to be a strong and reconstructive extractor Ext, and use a concept of matrix kernel $\mathsf{Ker}(\Pi_Y) = \{\mathsf{utd}|\forall u \in \Pi_Y, \mathsf{utd} = \mathsf{kernel}(u)\}$ to get an updatable trapdoor utd from the set Π_Y, where the UDPH is described in a vector or a matrix form. In addition, some leakage-resilient ABO LTDFs and leakage-resilient deterministic PKEs are provided. Table 1 shows a comparison about leakage-resilient deterministic PKEs, where efficient instantiations and acceptable leakage rate and message length are achieved in our work.

Related Work. There has been important follow up work on extending deterministic PKEs and LTDFs. Mironov et al. [15] modelled the incrementality of deterministic PKEs to avoid efficiency constraints. Huang et al. [16] gave a generic framework of CCA-secure deterministic PKEs. A couple of leakage-resilient LTDFs [13,17] and their all-but-one variants [12,18] were also proposed. Particularly, Yang et al. [6] introduced the updatable hash proof system concept to construct leakage-resilient CCA secure PKE schemes.

2 Preliminaries

Notations. We denote $\log x$ as the discrete logarithm of x in base 2 and $s \xleftarrow{\$} S$ as the process of uniformly and randomly picking an element s from a set S.

For a column vector $\mathbf{s} = (s_1, s_2, \ldots, s_n) \in \mathbb{Z}_q^n$, we define $g^{\mathbf{s}} = (g^{s_1}, g^{s_2}, \ldots, g^{s_n}) \in \mathbb{G}^n$ as a vector of group elements where g is a generator of a group $\mathbb{G}$ whose prime order is q, as well as defining a matrix $\mathbf{A}$ and $g^{\mathbf{A}}$. Moreover, we use $\mathsf{kernel}(\mathbf{A})$ to denote by the vectors $\mathbf{x}$ that satisfy $\mathbf{Ax} = \mathbf{0}$, and use $\mathsf{span}(\mathbf{s})$ to denote the linear space spanned by the vector $\mathbf{s}$. Throughout, we denote λ as the security parameter, and use $\cdot$ to denote the group operation or component-wise multiplication and use $\mathrm{negl}(\cdot)$ to denote a negligible function. PPT stands for "probabilistic polynomial-time".

Hard-to-Invert Auxiliary Input [19]. Given an auxiliary function $f(x)$, it is difficult to recover x, which is derived from the computational and information-theoretic hardness. An efficiently computable function $\mathcal{F} = \{f_\lambda\}$ is assumed to be *δ-hard-to-invert* over an efficient sampling distribution $\mathcal{D}$, if for any PPT algorithm $\mathcal{A}$, it holds $\Pr[\mathcal{A}(1^n, f_\lambda(x)) = x] \leq \delta$, where the probability is taken over $\mathcal{D}$ and the internal tosses of $\mathcal{A}$, and δ is a negligible function.

Definition 1 (Reconstructive Extractor [20]**).** *An (ϵ, δ) reconstructive extractor is a pair of functions* $(\mathsf{Ext}, \mathsf{Rec})$*, where* Ext *is an extractor that maps elements from $\{0,1\}^{n_1} \times \{0,1\}^{n_2}$ to Ω, and* Rec *is an oracle machine that on input $(1^{n_1}, 1/\epsilon)$ with poly$(n_1, 1/\epsilon, log|\Omega|)$ running time complexity. For any $x \in \{0,1\}^{n_1}$ and any distinguishable function* Dis *such that* $|\Pr[\mathsf{Dis}(r, \mathsf{Ext}(x, r)) = 1 | r \xleftarrow{\$} \{0,1\}^{n_2}] - \Pr[\mathsf{Dis}(r, \omega) = 1 | r \xleftarrow{\$} \{0,1\}^{n_2}, \omega \xleftarrow{\$} \Omega]| \geq \epsilon$*, we always have* $\Pr[\mathsf{Rec}^{\mathsf{Dis}}(1^{n_1}, 1/\epsilon) = x] \geq \delta$ *where the probability is over the coin tosses of* Rec*. Note that the output of (ϵ, δ) reconstructive extractor is pseudorandom for $\delta \cdot \mathrm{negl}(\cdot)$-hard-to-invert auxiliary inputs.*

Definition 2 (All-But-One Dual Projective Hashing (ABO-DPH) [3]**).** *Let $\lambda \in \mathbb{N}$ be the security parameter, an ABO dual projective hashing consists of the following* PPT *algorithms:* $\mathsf{Setup}, \mathsf{KeyGen}, \mathsf{Pub}, \mathsf{Priv}, \mathsf{Tdinv}$.

- $\mathsf{Setup}(\lambda)$*: Inputs a security parameter λ and generates a tuple of instances* $\mathsf{para} = (\text{HP}, \mathsf{mtd}, \text{TAG}, \mathcal{H}, \mathcal{X}, \mathcal{Y}, \mathcal{P}, \mathcal{U} = \Pi_Y \cup \Pi_N, \mathcal{W}, \mathcal{T}, \alpha)$*, where the random master trapdoor* mtd *is used to generate global public parameters* HP*, $\mathcal{H} = \{\Lambda_u : \text{TAG} \times \mathcal{X} \to \mathcal{Y}\}_{u \in \mathcal{U}}$ is a family of hash functions indexed by $u \in \mathcal{U}$ and $\alpha : \mathcal{X} \to \mathcal{P}$ is a projective map. In addition, $\mathcal{U}$ is divided to a pair of disjoint sets Π_Y and Π_N corresponding to YES instances sampled by* $\mathsf{SampYes}(\text{HP})$ *and NO instances sampled by* $\mathsf{SampNo}(\text{HP})$ *respectively.*
- $\mathsf{KeyGen}(\mathsf{mtd}, \widehat{\mathsf{tag}})$*: Inputs* mtd *and a projective tag* $\widehat{\mathsf{tag}} \in \text{TAG}$*, and outputs a public parameter $u \in \mathcal{U}$, a witness $w \in \mathcal{W}$, and an inversion trapdoor* $\mathsf{td} \in \mathcal{T}$.
- $\mathsf{Priv}(\mathsf{tag}, u, x)$*: Inputs* $\mathsf{tag} \in \text{TAG}$*, $u \in \mathcal{U}$ and $x \in \mathcal{X}$, the deterministic private evaluation algorithm outputs $y \in \mathcal{Y}$.*
- $\mathsf{Pub}(\mathsf{tag}, u, \alpha(x), w)$*: Inputs* $\mathsf{tag} \in \text{TAG}, \alpha(x) \in \mathcal{P}, u \in \mathcal{U}$ *with its witness w, the public evaluation algorithm outputs $y \in \mathcal{Y}$ if* $\mathsf{tag} = \widehat{\mathsf{tag}}$.
- $\mathsf{Tdinv}(\mathsf{tag}, \mathsf{td}, \alpha(x), \Lambda_u(\mathsf{tag}, x))$*: Inputs a trapdoor* $\mathsf{td} \in \mathcal{T}, \mathsf{tag} \in \text{TAG}, \alpha(x) \in \mathcal{P}$*, for any $x \in \mathcal{X}$, and a hash value* $\Lambda_u(\mathsf{tag}, x) \in \mathcal{Y}$*, outputs $x' \in \mathcal{X}$ if* $\mathsf{tag} \neq \widehat{\mathsf{tag}}$.

Moreover, an ABO DPH has the following requirements [3]:

Correctness. For all $\lambda \in \mathbb{N}$, all $\mathsf{para} \leftarrow \mathsf{Setup}(\lambda)$, all $\widehat{\mathsf{tag}} \in \text{TAG}$, all $x \in \mathcal{X}$, and all $(u, w, \mathsf{td}) \leftarrow \mathsf{KeyGen}(\mathsf{mtd}, \widehat{\mathsf{tag}})$, we have $\mathsf{Priv}(\mathsf{tag}, u, x) = \Lambda_u(\mathsf{tag}, x)$.

Projectiveness. For all $\lambda \in \mathbb{N}$, all $\mathsf{para} \leftarrow \mathsf{Setup}(\lambda)$, all $\widehat{\mathsf{tag}} \in \text{TAG}$, all $x \in \mathcal{X}$, and all $(u, w, \mathsf{td}) \leftarrow \mathsf{KeyGen}(\mathsf{mtd}, \widehat{\mathsf{tag}})$, we have $\mathsf{Pub}(\widehat{\mathsf{tag}}, u, \alpha(x), w) = \Lambda_u(\widehat{\mathsf{tag}}, x)$.

Invertibility. For all $\lambda \in \mathbb{N}$, all $\mathsf{para} \leftarrow \mathsf{Setup}(\lambda)$, all $\mathsf{tag}, \widehat{\mathsf{tag}} \in \text{TAG}$, all $x \in \mathcal{X}$, and all $(u, w, \mathsf{td}) \leftarrow \mathsf{KeyGen}(\mathsf{mtd}, \widehat{\mathsf{tag}})$, we have $\mathsf{Tdinv}(\mathsf{tag}, \mathsf{td}, \alpha(x), \Lambda_u(\mathsf{tag}, x)) = x$ if $\mathsf{tag} \neq \widehat{\mathsf{tag}}$.

Hidden Projective Tag. For all $\lambda \in \mathbb{N}$, all $\mathsf{para} \leftarrow \mathsf{Setup}(\lambda)$, for any PPT adversary $\mathcal{A} = (\mathcal{A}_1, \mathcal{A}_2)$, the following advantage function is negligible in λ.

$$\mathsf{Adv} = \Pr\left[b' = b \,\middle|\, \begin{array}{c} ((\mathsf{tag}_0, \mathsf{tag}_1), \mathit{state}) \xleftarrow{\$} \mathcal{A}_1(\text{HP}), b \xleftarrow{\$} \{0,1\}, \\ (u, w, \mathsf{td}) \xleftarrow{\$} \mathsf{KeyGen}(\mathsf{mtd}, \mathsf{tag}_b), b' \xleftarrow{\$} \mathcal{A}_2(\text{HP}, u, \mathit{state}) \end{array} \right] - \frac{1}{2}$$

3 Updatable All-But-One Dual Projective Hashing

This section introduces the updatable ABO DPH (UDPH) primitive, which considers ABO DPH with continuous leakage resilience of invisible key update.

Definition 3. *Let ρ be a polynomial of the security parameter λ, which represents the leakage tolerance of the challenge information. An updatable ρ-ABO dual projective hashing Σ_{UDPH} consists of the following* PPT *algorithms.*

$\mathsf{Setup}(\lambda)$: *Inputs a security parameter λ and generates a tuple of instances $\mathsf{para} = (\text{HP}, \mathsf{mtd}, \text{TAG}, \mathcal{H}, \mathcal{X}, \mathcal{Y}, \mathcal{P}, \mathcal{U} = \Pi_Y \cup \Pi_N, \mathcal{W}, \mathcal{T}, \alpha)$, where the random master trapdoor* mtd *is used to generate global public parameters* HP, *and $\mathcal{H} = \{\Lambda_u : \text{TAG} \times \mathcal{X} \to \mathcal{Y}\}_{u \in \mathcal{U}}$ is a family of hash function indexed by $u \in \mathcal{U}$ and $\alpha : \mathcal{X} \to \mathcal{P}$ is a projective map. In particular, there exists a sampling algorithm* $\mathsf{SampUtd}(\text{HP})$, *which outputs the updatable trapdoor* $\mathsf{utd} \leftarrow \mathsf{Ker}(\Pi_Y)$ *with the kernel of a matrix.*

$\mathsf{KeyGen}(\mathsf{mtd}, \widehat{\mathsf{tag}})$: *Inputs* mtd *and a projective tag $\widehat{\mathsf{tag}} \in \text{TAG}$, outputs a public parameter $u \in \mathcal{U}$, a witness $w \in \mathcal{W}$, and an initial trapdoor $\mathsf{td} \in \mathcal{T}$.*

$\mathsf{Priv}(\mathsf{tag}, u, x)$: *Inputs $u \in \mathcal{U}$, a tag $\mathsf{tag} \in \text{TAG}$ and $x \in \mathcal{X}$, then the deterministic private evaluation algorithm outputs $y \in \mathcal{Y}$.*

$\mathsf{Pub}(\mathsf{tag}, u, \alpha(\text{HP}, x), w)$: *Inputs $u \in \mathcal{U}, \mathsf{tag} \in \text{TAG}, \alpha(\text{HP}, x) \in \mathcal{P}$ with its witness w, then the public evaluation algorithm outputs $y \in \mathcal{Y}$ if $\mathsf{tag} = \widehat{\mathsf{tag}}$.*

$\mathsf{Tdinv}(\mathsf{tag}, \mathsf{td}, \alpha(\text{HP}, x), \Lambda_u(\mathsf{tag}, x))$: *Inputs $\mathsf{td} \in \mathcal{T}, \mathsf{tag} \in \text{TAG}, \alpha(\text{HP}, x) \in \mathcal{P}$, for any $x \in \mathcal{X}$ and a hash value $\Lambda_u(\mathsf{tag}, x) \in \mathcal{Y}$, then outputs $x' \in \mathcal{X}$ if $\mathsf{tag} \neq \widehat{\mathsf{tag}}$.*

$\mathsf{Update}(\mathsf{utd}, \mathsf{td})$: *Inputs an updatable trapdoor* utd *and the initial trapdoor $\mathsf{td} \in \mathcal{T}$, then outputs an updated trapdoor td^* such that $|\mathsf{td}^*| = |\mathsf{td}|$.*

Note that, the set Π_Y and the updatable trapdoor $\mathsf{utd} \leftarrow \mathsf{Ker}(\Pi_Y)$ are closely related with mtd, since Π_Y is sampled by $\mathsf{SampYes}(\text{HP})$ and HP is generated by mtd. Then the Update algorithm is required to randomize utd as $\mathsf{utd}^* \leftarrow \mathsf{span}(\mathsf{utd})$ and the Pub algorithm is required to have additive homomorphism, i.e., $\mathsf{Pub}(\mathsf{tag}, u, \alpha(\text{HP}, x), w_1 + w_2) = \mathsf{Pub}(\mathsf{tag}, u, \alpha(\text{HP}, x), w_1) + \mathsf{Pub}(\mathsf{tag}, u, \alpha(\text{HP}, x), w_2)$. That is, our UDPH has the following requirements:

1. **Correctness.** For all $\lambda \in \mathbb{N}$, all $\mathsf{para} \leftarrow \mathsf{Setup}(\lambda)$, all $\widehat{\mathsf{tag}} \in \text{TAG}$, all $x \in \mathcal{X}$, and all $(u, w, \mathsf{td}) \leftarrow \mathsf{KeyGen}(\mathsf{mtd}, \widehat{\mathsf{tag}})$, we have $\mathsf{Priv}(\mathsf{tag}, u, x) = \Lambda_u(\mathsf{tag}, x)$.
2. **Projectiveness.** For all $\lambda \in \mathbb{N}$, all $\mathsf{para} \leftarrow \mathsf{Setup}(\lambda)$, all $x \in \mathcal{X}$, and all $(u, w, \mathsf{td}) \leftarrow \mathsf{KeyGen}(\mathsf{mtd}, \widehat{\mathsf{tag}})$, we have $\mathsf{Pub}(\widehat{\mathsf{tag}}, u, \alpha(x), w) = \Lambda_u(\widehat{\mathsf{tag}}, x)$.
3. **Invertibility.** For all $\lambda \in \mathbb{N}$, all $\mathsf{para} \leftarrow \mathsf{Setup}(\lambda)$, all $x \in \mathcal{X}$, all $\mathsf{tag}, \widehat{\mathsf{tag}} \in \text{TAG}$, and all $(u, w, \mathsf{td}) \leftarrow \mathsf{KeyGen}(\mathsf{mtd}, \widehat{\mathsf{tag}})$, if $\mathsf{tag} \neq \widehat{\mathsf{tag}}$ we always have $\mathsf{Tdinv}(\mathsf{tag}, \mathsf{td}, \alpha(x), \Lambda_u(\mathsf{tag}, x)) = x$.
4. **Projective Tag Indistinguishability.** For any PPT adversary $\mathcal{A}$, it is hard to distinguish a projective tag $\widehat{\mathsf{tag}}$ from a tag tag with ρ bits leakage information at each time interval, that is, for any leakage function $\mathcal{L}_i$ and $i = 0, 1, \cdots, t = poly(\lambda)$, the advantage function

$$\mathsf{Adv}_{\mathcal{A}}^{\mathsf{ProT}}(\lambda) = \Pr\left[b' = b \,\middle|\, \begin{array}{c} \mathsf{tag}, \widehat{\mathsf{tag}} \xleftarrow{\$} \text{TAG}, (u, \mathsf{td}_0) \leftarrow \mathsf{KeyGen}(\mathsf{mtd}, \widehat{\mathsf{tag}}), \\ \{state_i \leftarrow \mathcal{A}^{\mathcal{L}_i(\mathsf{td}_i)}(\text{HP}), \mathsf{td}_{i+1} \leftarrow \mathsf{Update}(\mathsf{utd}, \mathsf{td}_i)\}_{i=0}^t \\ b \xleftarrow{\$} \{0,1\}, b' \leftarrow \mathcal{A}(\text{HP}, \{state_i\}_{i=0}^t, u) \end{array} \right] - \frac{1}{2}$$

is negligible in λ, where the challenger sends tag to $\mathcal{A}$ when $b = 0$, otherwise sends the projective tag $\widehat{\mathsf{tag}}$ to $\mathcal{A}$.
5. **Extractor Pseudorandomness Indistinguishability.** For any PPT adversary $\mathcal{A}$, it is hard to distinguish a function extractor $\mathsf{Ext}(\mathcal{X}, \mathcal{R}) : \mathcal{X} \times \mathcal{R} \to \mathcal{P}$ from a random element $\sigma \in \mathcal{P}$, that is, for arbitrary positive integer n, the advantage function

$$\mathsf{Adv}_{\mathcal{A}}^{\mathsf{Ext}}(\lambda) = \Pr\left[\mathcal{A}(\mathsf{para}, \mathsf{Ext}(\mathcal{X}, \mathcal{R}), \mathcal{R}, \{\mathsf{utd}_i\}_{i=1}^n) = 1 \,\middle|\, \begin{array}{c} \mathsf{para} \xleftarrow{\$} \mathsf{Setup}(\lambda), \\ \{\mathsf{utd}_i\}_{i=1}^n \xleftarrow{\$} \mathsf{Ker}(\Pi_Y) \end{array} \right]$$
$$- \Pr\left[\mathcal{A}(\mathsf{para}, \sigma, \mathcal{R}, \{\mathsf{utd}'_i\}_{i=1}^n) = 1 \,\middle|\, \begin{array}{c} u \xleftarrow{\$} \Pi_N, \mathsf{para} \xleftarrow{\$} \mathsf{Setup}(\lambda), \sigma \xleftarrow{\$} \mathcal{P}, \\ \{\mathsf{utd}'_i\}_{i=1}^n \xleftarrow{\$} \mathsf{Ker}(\Pi_Y \cup \{u\}) \end{array} \right]$$

is negligible in λ.
6. **Subset Indistinguishability.** For any PPT adversary $\mathcal{A}$, it is hard to distinguish a random YES instance $u_Y \xleftarrow{\$} \Pi_Y$ and a random NO instance $u_N \xleftarrow{\$} \Pi_N$, that is, for arbitrary positive integer n, the advantage function

$$\mathsf{Adv}_{\mathcal{A}}^{\mathsf{Subet}}(\lambda) = \Pr\left[\mathcal{A}(u_Y, \{\mathsf{utd}_i\}_{i=1}^n) = 1 \,\middle|\, u_Y \xleftarrow{\$} \Pi_Y, \{\mathsf{utd}_i\}_{i=1}^n \xleftarrow{\$} \mathsf{Ker}(\Pi_Y) \right]$$
$$- \Pr\left[\mathcal{A}(u_N, \{\mathsf{utd}'_i\}_{i=1}^n) = 1 \,\middle|\, u_N \xleftarrow{\$} \Pi_N, \{\mathsf{utd}'_i\}_{i=1}^n \xleftarrow{\$} \mathsf{Ker}(\Pi_Y \cup \{u_N\}) \right]$$

is negligible in λ. Note that, an adversary can break the hidden projective tag of ABO DPH and pseudorandomness of reconstructive extractor (Definition 1) by checking whether they are equivalent on the challenge instance and extractor value respectively, the two properties above have considered the regularly updated trapdoors utd in the advantage functions.
7. **Full Trapdoor Indistinguishability.** For any PPT adversary $\mathcal{A} = (\mathcal{A}_1, \mathcal{A}_2)$, it is hard to distinguish the linear dependency between two updatable trapdoors, that is, the advantage function

$$\mathsf{Adv}_{\mathcal{A}}^{\mathsf{FullTd}}(\lambda) = \Pr\left[b' = b \,\middle|\, \begin{array}{c} \mathsf{mtd}' \xleftarrow{\$} \mathcal{A}_1(\lambda, \mathsf{mtd}), \mathsf{utd}_0, \mathsf{utd}_1 \xleftarrow{\$} \mathsf{Ker}(\Pi_Y), \\ b \xleftarrow{\$} \{0,1\}, \mathsf{utd}_b^* \xleftarrow{\$} \mathsf{span}(\mathsf{utd}_b), \\ b' \leftarrow \mathcal{A}_2(\mathsf{utd}_0, \mathsf{utd}_1, \mathsf{utd}_b^*) \end{array} \right] - \frac{1}{2}$$

is negligible in λ. Note that, Π_Y and utd are closely related with mtd, mtd is outputted by $\mathcal{A}_1$ so that mtd is kept outside the view of the adversary $\mathcal{A}_2$ who wants to break the full trapdoor indistinguishability actually.

8. **Partial Trapdoor Indistinguishability.** For any PPT adversary $\mathcal{A}$, it is hard to determine the legitimacy of utd only given partial information from a leakage function $\mathcal{L}$ with range $\{0,1\}^\rho$, that is, the advantage function

$$\mathsf{Adv}_{\mathcal{A}}^{\mathsf{PartTd}}(\lambda) = \Pr\left[\mathcal{A}\begin{pmatrix} \mathsf{para}, u, \mathsf{utd}_1, \\ \mathcal{L}(\mathsf{utd}_1, \mathsf{utd}_2) \end{pmatrix} = 1 \,\middle|\, \begin{array}{c} \mathsf{para} \leftarrow \mathsf{Setup}(\lambda), u \xleftarrow{\$} \Pi_N, \\ \mathsf{utd}_1, \mathsf{utd}_2 \xleftarrow{\$} \mathsf{Ker}(\Pi_Y \cup \{u\}) \end{array} \right]$$
$$- \Pr\left[\mathcal{A}\begin{pmatrix} \mathsf{para}, u, \mathsf{utd}_1, \\ \mathcal{L}(\mathsf{utd}_1, \mathsf{utd}_2') \end{pmatrix} = 1 \,\middle|\, \begin{array}{c} \mathsf{para} \leftarrow \mathsf{Setup}(\lambda), u \xleftarrow{\$} \Pi_N, \\ \mathsf{utd}_1 \xleftarrow{\$} \mathsf{Ker}(\Pi_Y \cup \{u\}), \\ \mathsf{utd}_2' \xleftarrow{\$} \mathsf{Ker}(\Pi_Y) \end{array} \right]$$

is negligible in λ.

In the following, we give Lemma 1 for projective tag indistinguishability and Lemma 2 for extractor pseudorandomness indistinguishability that are used for our security proof, which can be concluded from the subset indistinguishability, full trapdoor indistinguishability and partial trapdoor indistinguishability.

Lemma 1. *Suppose that the adversary $\mathcal{A}$ makes at most $\mathcal{Q}(\lambda)$ leakage queries, we have* $\mathsf{Adv}_{\mathcal{A}}^{\mathsf{ProT}} \leq \mathsf{Adv}_{\mathcal{A}}^{\mathsf{Subet}} \leq \mathcal{Q}(\lambda) \cdot \mathsf{Adv}_{\mathcal{A}}^{\mathsf{FullTd}} + \mathcal{Q}(\lambda) \cdot \mathsf{Adv}_{\mathcal{A}}^{\mathsf{PartTd}}$.

Sketch of Proof. If an adversary breaks the *projective tag indistinguishability*, this implies that it distinguishes tag and $\widehat{\mathsf{tag}}$ and certainly determines u_Y and u_N, but this seems impossible since the *subset indistinguishability* holds in essence. If an adversary breaks the *subset indistinguishability*, this implies that it distinguishes u_Y and u_N and certainly determines $\mathsf{utd}_i \xleftarrow{\$} \mathsf{Ker}(\Pi_Y)$ and $\mathsf{utd}_i' \xleftarrow{\$} \mathsf{Ker}(\Pi_Y \cup u_N)$. However, the indistinguishability between utd and utd′ is guaranteed by the *full trapdoor indistinguishability* and the *partial trapdoor indistinguishability.* Therefore, we can sample u_Y with a linear combination of master trapdoor mtd and its witness w to deal with continuous leakage in the floppy model.

Lemma 2. *Suppose that the adversary $\mathcal{A}$ makes at most $\mathcal{Q}(\lambda)$ leakage queries, we have* $\mathsf{Adv}_{\mathcal{A}}^{\mathsf{Ext}} \leq \mathcal{Q}(\lambda) \cdot \mathsf{Adv}_{\mathcal{A}}^{\mathsf{FullTd}} + \mathcal{Q}(\lambda) \cdot \mathsf{Adv}_{\mathcal{A}}^{\mathsf{PartTd}}$.

Sketch of Proof. If an adversary breaks the *extractor pseudorandomness indistinguishability*, this implies that it distinguishes the challenge extractor Ext^* and a random element from $\mathcal{P}$ and certainly determines utd_i and utd_i'. However, the indistinguishability between utd and utd′ is guaranteed by the *full trapdoor indistinguishability* and the *partial trapdoor indistinguishability*. Therefore, we can employ Ext to be a projective map $\alpha(\text{HP}, x)$ of $\mathsf{Pub}(\mathsf{tag}, \alpha(\text{HP}, x), \mathsf{td})$ under continuous leakage in the floppy model.

4 Updatable All-But-One Lossy Trapdoor Functions

In this section, we construct a family of updatable ABO LTDFs from the presented UDPH in Sect. 3.

Definition 4 ([12,13]). *A collection of updatable ABO (ℓ, j, ρ)-lossy trapdoor functions consists of the following* PPT *algorithms* $(\mathsf{S_{abo}}, \mathsf{Eval}, \mathsf{U}, \mathsf{Inv})$, *where j is called the lossiness, $\ell(\lambda) = poly(\lambda)$ represents the input length of* Eval *and ρ indicates the leakage tolerance of the challenge information.*

$\mathsf{S_{abo}}(\lambda, \widehat{b})$: *Inputs the security parameter λ and the lossy branch $\widehat{b}$, and outputs the function index* pp *and the initial trapdoor τ.*

$\mathsf{Eval}(\mathsf{pp}, b, x)$: *Inputs the function index* pp, *a branch b and a pre-image x, the evaluation algorithm outputs an image y.*

$\mathsf{U}(\tau, \mathsf{pp})$: *Inputs an initial trapdoor τ and a function index* pp, *the update algorithm outputs an updated trapdoor τ^* such that $|\tau^*| = |\tau|$.*

$\mathsf{Inv}(b, \tau^*, y)$: *Inputs b, τ^* and an image y, the inversion algorithm outputs x'. Particularly, τ^* is the initial τ or an updated $\tau^* \leftarrow \mathsf{U}(\cdot, \mathsf{pp})$.*

Our Construction. Given an updatable ABO dual projective hashing $\Sigma_{\mathsf{UDPH}} =$ (Setup, KeyGen, Priv, Pub, Tdinv, Update), a family of updatable ABO LTDFs can be generally constructed in a modular way.

$\mathsf{S}_{abo}(\lambda, \widehat{\mathsf{tag}})$: The algorithm runs to obtain $(\text{HP}, \mathsf{utd}) \leftarrow \Sigma_{\mathsf{UDPH}}.\mathsf{Setup}(\lambda)$, gets $(u, w, \mathsf{td}) \leftarrow \Sigma_{\mathsf{UDPH}}.\mathsf{KeyGen}(\mathsf{mtd}, \widehat{\mathsf{tag}})$, and sets $\mathsf{pp} = u||\text{HP}$ and $\tau = \mathsf{td}$.

$\mathsf{Eval}(\mathsf{pp}, \mathsf{tag}, x)$: On input $(\mathsf{pp}, \mathsf{tag})$ and x, the evaluation algorithm outputs an image $y = y_0||y_1 = \alpha(\text{HP}, x)||\Lambda_u(\mathsf{tag}, x)$.

$\mathsf{U}(\tau, \mathsf{pp})$: The algorithm runs to obtain $\tau^* \leftarrow \Sigma_{\mathsf{UDPH}}.\mathsf{Update}(\tau, \mathsf{utd})$, and outputs an updated trapdoor τ^* such that $|\tau^*| = |\tau|$.

$\mathsf{Inv}(\mathsf{tag}, \tau^*, y)$: On input τ^*, tag and an image $y = y_0||y_1$, the algorithm outputs $x' = \Sigma_{\mathsf{UDPH}}.\mathsf{Tdinv}(\mathsf{tag}, \tau^*, y_0||y_1)$.

Theorem 1. *Suppose that Σ_{UDPH} is an updatable ABO dual projective hashing as defined in Sect. 3, then the above construction yields a collection of $(x, x - \log|\mathsf{Image}(\alpha)|, \rho)$-updatable ABO LTDFs in the floppy model.*

Proof. The correctness for injective function Eval follows from the invertibility property of UDPH, and the lossiness for lossy branch follows from the projective property of UDPH. Since $\Lambda_u(\mathsf{tag}, x)$ is determined by $\alpha(\text{HP}, x)$ and u when $\mathsf{tag} = \widehat{\mathsf{tag}}$, hence the size of the image set $\mathsf{Image}(\Lambda_u(\widehat{\mathsf{tag}}, x))$ is at most $\mathsf{Image}(\alpha(\text{HP}, x))$. Based on the projective tag indistinguishability and extractor pseudorandomness indistinguishability of UDPH, the security of the updatable ABO LTDFs holds.

5 Continuous Leakage-Resilient Deterministic PKE from Updatable All-But-One Dual Projective Hashing

This section introduces the security notion for deterministic PKE under continuous leakage of invisible key update, i.e., *continuous-leakage-resilient strong privacy indistinguishability-based* (CLR-PRIV-sIND), and gives a modular framework for constructing CLR-PRIV-sIND secure deterministic PKEs from the UDPH.

5.1 Deterministic Encryption

A continuous leakage-resilient deterministic PKE consists of the following algorithms (Gen, Enc, KeyUpdate, Dec) where Gen, KeyUpdate are probabilistic algorithms and Enc, Dec are deterministic algorithms. Generally, the key generation algorithm Gen inputs the security parameter λ and outputs a public/secret key pair (PK, SK). The encryption algorithm Enc inputs PK and a plaintext m and produces a ciphertext CT. And the decryption algorithm Dec inputs SK, CT and returns a message m. Note that the KeyUpdate(PK, SK) algorithm inputs PK, SK and outputs an updated secret key SK* such that $|\text{SK}^*| = |\text{SK}|$, where SK is either an initial secret key or a secret key updated by KeyUpdate.

Followed by the PRIV-sIND security definition [1,19], we formally define the CLR-PRIV-sIND security model, where the adversary can issue polynomial-times leakage queries before receiving the challenge ciphertext.

CLR-PRIV-SIND SECURITY WITH AUXILIARY INPUT. A deterministic PKE is *continuous leakage-resilient strong privacy indistinguishablitiy-based* (CLR-PRIV-sIND) secure with leakage parameter ρ in the floppy model, if for any PPT adversary $\mathcal{A}$ and auxiliary input functions aux $= \{\mathcal{F}_\lambda\}$, the advantage function $\mathsf{Adv}^{\mathsf{CLR\text{-}PRIV\text{-}sIND}}_{\Sigma_{\mathsf{D\text{-}PKE}},\mathcal{A},\mathsf{aux}}(\lambda) = |\Pr[\mathsf{Exp}^{\mathsf{CLR\text{-}PRIV\text{-}sIND}}_{\Sigma_{\mathsf{D\text{-}PKE}},\mathcal{A},\mathsf{aux}}(\lambda,0) = 1] - \Pr[\mathsf{Exp}^{\mathsf{CLR\text{-}PRIV\text{-}sIND}}_{\Sigma_{\mathsf{D\text{-}PKE}},\mathcal{A},\mathsf{aux}}(\lambda,1) = 1]|$ is negligible in λ, where $\mathsf{Exp}^{\mathsf{CLR\text{-}PRIV\text{-}sIND}}_{\Sigma_{\mathsf{D\text{-}PKE}},\mathcal{A},\mathsf{aux}}(\lambda,b)$ is an experiment played by a challenger and an adversary $\mathcal{A} = (\mathcal{A}_1, \mathcal{A}_2)$ that is formally defined below:

Initialization: The challenger runs Gen(λ) to generate (PK, SK) and sends PK to $\mathcal{A}_2$, and $\mathcal{A}_1(\lambda)$ samples two messages (m_0, m_1).

Leakage Queries: For the i-th leakage query issued by $\mathcal{A}_2$, the challenger directly sets $\text{SK}_1 = \text{SK}$ when $i = 1$; otherwise it responds $\mathcal{L}_i(\text{SK}_i)$ to $\mathcal{A}_2$ under a received computable leakage function $\mathcal{L}_i$ (whose outputs are at most ρ bits), and runs KeyUpdate(PK, SK_{i-1}) to get SK_i with $i = i+1$.

Challenge: The challenger randomly picks $b \xleftarrow{\$} \{0,1\}$ and computes a challenge ciphertext $\text{CT}^* \leftarrow \mathsf{Enc}(\text{PK}, m_b)$, and finally sends the CT^* to $\mathcal{A}_2$.

Guess: The adversary outputs $b' \leftarrow \mathcal{A}_2(state, \text{CT}^*, \mathcal{F}(m_0), \mathcal{F}(m_1))$, and finally returns 1 if $b' = b$ else returns 0.

Note that the existence of $\mathcal{A}_1$ who has to sample two messages is to ensure that the sampled messages are kept completely outside the view of the adversary $\mathcal{A}_2$. At period i, $\mathcal{A}_2$ learns at most ρ bits leakage information of SK_i via $\mathcal{L}_i(\text{SK}_i)$; then the SK_i for the leakage function $\mathcal{L}_i$ will be updated via KeyUpdate(PK, SK_{i-1}).

5.2 Our Construction

Given the UDPH $\Sigma_{\mathsf{UDPH}} = (\mathsf{Setup}, \mathsf{KeyGen}, \mathsf{Priv}, \mathsf{Pub}, \mathsf{Tdinv}, \mathsf{Update})$ in Sect. 3, let $\mathsf{h} : \mathcal{M} \to \text{TAG}$ be a universal hash function and set $\mathsf{tag} = \mathsf{h}(m)$, and we give a modular framework for a leakage-resilient deterministic PKE $\Sigma_{\mathsf{D\text{-}PKE}}$:

$\mathsf{Gen}(\lambda)$: The algorithm samples a projective tag $\widehat{\mathsf{tag}} \xleftarrow{\$} \text{TAG}$, and runs to obtain $(\text{HP}, \mathsf{utd}, \mathsf{mtd}) \leftarrow \Sigma_{\mathsf{UDPH}}.\mathsf{Setup}(\lambda)$ and $(u, w, \mathsf{td}) \leftarrow \Sigma_{\mathsf{UDPH}}.\mathsf{KeyGen}(\mathsf{mtd}, \widehat{\mathsf{tag}})$. It sets public key $\text{PK} = (\text{HP}, u, \mathsf{h})$ and initial secret key $\text{SK} = \mathsf{td}$.

$\mathsf{Enc}(\text{PK}, m)$: On input PK and a message m, the encryption algorithm computes $C_2 = \mathsf{tag} = \mathsf{h}(m)$ and outputs a ciphertext $\text{CT} = C_0||C_1||C_2 = \alpha(\text{HP}, m)||\Lambda_u(\mathsf{h}(m), m)||\mathsf{h}(m)$.

$\mathsf{KeyUpdate}(\text{PK}, \text{SK})$: The algorithm runs to obtain $\mathsf{td}^* \leftarrow \Sigma_{\mathsf{UDPH}}.\mathsf{Update}(\text{SK}, \mathsf{utd})$, and outputs an updated secret key $\text{SK}^* = \mathsf{td}^*$.

$\mathsf{Dec}(\text{PK}, \text{SK}^*, \text{CT})$: On input SK^* and a ciphertext $\text{CT} = C_0||C_1||C_2$, the decryption algorithm outputs $m' = \Sigma_{\mathsf{UDPH}}.\mathsf{Tdinv}(\text{SK}^*, C_0||C_1||C_2)$.

Correctness. The correctness directly follows the correctness of the UDPH in Sect. 3, where the $\mathsf{KeyUpdate}$ algorithm is repeated by i times to update SK_i. For any honestly generated ciphertext $\text{CT} = \alpha(\text{HP}, m)||\Lambda_u(\mathsf{h}(m), m)||\mathsf{h}(m)$, we always have $\Sigma_{\mathsf{UDPH}}.\mathsf{Tdinv}(\text{SK}_i, \alpha(\text{HP}, m)||\Lambda_u(\mathsf{h}(m), m)||\mathsf{h}(m)) = m$.

Theorem 2. *Assume an updatable ABO DPH Σ_{UDPH} with projective tag indistinguishability and extractor pseudorandomness indistinguishability exists (where $\alpha(\text{HP}, x)$ is a (ϵ, δ)-reconstructive extractor), the deterministic PKE is* CLR-PRIV-sIND *secure with hard-to-invert auxiliary inputs in the floppy model.*

Proof. We define and use the following games to prove the Theorem 2.

Game 0: This is the real $\mathsf{Exp}^{\mathsf{CLR\text{-}PRIV\text{-}sIND}}_{\Sigma_{\mathsf{D\text{-}PKE}},\mathcal{A},\mathsf{aux}}(\lambda, b)$ game. The challenger generates $(\text{PK}, \text{SK}) \leftarrow \mathsf{Gen}(\lambda)$ and sends PK to $\mathcal{A}_2$, and responses $\mathcal{L}_i(\text{SK}_i)$ to $\mathcal{A}_2$ for each leakage query $\mathcal{L}_i$. Based on two equal-length messages m_0, m_1 from $\mathcal{A}_1$, the challenger randomly picks $b \xleftarrow{\$} \{0, 1\}$ and sends the challenge ciphertext $\text{CT}^* = \mathsf{Enc}(\text{PK}, m_b) = \alpha(\text{HP}, m_b)||\Lambda_u^*(\mathsf{tag}, m_b)||\mathsf{h}(m_b)$ along with the auxiliary function $\mathsf{aux} = (\mathcal{F}(m_0), \mathcal{F}(m_1))$ to $\mathcal{A}_2$. Finally, $\mathcal{A}_2$ outputs a guess b' of b. Hence, we have $\mathsf{Exp}^{\mathsf{CLR\text{-}PRIV\text{-}sIND}}_{\Sigma_{\mathsf{D\text{-}PKE}},\mathcal{A},\mathsf{aux}}(\lambda, b) = |\Pr[\mathcal{A} \text{ wins in } \textbf{Game 0}] - 1/2|$.

Game 1: This game is like **Game 0** except for the tag generation in the **Challenge** phase, where the challenger sets $\mathsf{tag} = \widehat{\mathsf{tag}}$ instead of $\mathsf{tag} = \mathsf{h}(m_b)$. By the projective tag indistinguishability of UDPH and Lemma 1, we have $|\Pr[\mathcal{A} \text{ wins in } \textbf{Game 1}] - \Pr[\mathcal{A} \text{ wins in } \textbf{Game 0}]| \le \mathsf{Adv}^{\mathsf{ProT}}_{\mathcal{A}} \le \mathcal{Q}(\lambda) \cdot (\mathsf{Adv}^{\mathsf{FullTd}}_{\mathcal{A}} + \mathsf{Adv}^{\mathsf{PartTd}}_{\mathcal{A}})$ after $\mathcal{A}_2$ makes at most $\mathcal{Q}(\lambda)$ leakage queries.

Game 2: This game is like **Game 1** except that $\Lambda_u^*(\widehat{\mathsf{tag}}, m_b)$ is computed by $\Sigma_{\mathsf{UDPH}}.\mathsf{Pub}(\widehat{\mathsf{tag}}, \text{PK}, \alpha(\text{HP}, m_b), w)$ instead of $\Sigma_{\mathsf{UDPH}}.\mathsf{Priv}(\widehat{\mathsf{tag}}, \text{PK}, m_b)$ in the **Challenge** phase. Based on the projective property of UDPH, we thus have $\Pr[\mathcal{A} \text{ wins in } \textbf{Game 2}] = \Pr[\mathcal{A} \text{ wins in } \textbf{Game 1}]$.

Game 3: This game is like **Game 2** except that $\alpha(\text{HP}, m_b)$ in the challenge ciphertext CT^* is replaced by a random element σ from $\mathcal{P}$, that is $\alpha(\text{HP}, m_b)||\Sigma_{\mathsf{UDPH}}.\mathsf{Pub}(\widehat{\mathsf{tag}}, \text{PK}, \alpha(\text{HP}, m_b), w) \Rightarrow \sigma||\Sigma_{\mathsf{UDPH}}.\mathsf{Pub}(\widehat{\mathsf{tag}}, \text{PK}, \sigma, w)$. By the Lemma 2 and the extractor pseudorandomness indistinguishability of UDPH, we have $|\Pr[\mathcal{A} \text{ wins in } \textbf{Game 3}] - \Pr[\mathcal{A} \text{ wins in } \textbf{Game 2}]| \leq 2\mathsf{Adv}_{\mathcal{A}}^{\mathsf{Ext}} \leq 2\mathcal{Q}(\lambda) \cdot (\mathsf{Adv}_{\mathcal{A}}^{\mathsf{FullTd}} + \mathsf{Adv}_{\mathcal{A}}^{\mathsf{PartTd}})$ after $\mathcal{A}_2$ makes at most $\mathcal{Q}(\lambda)$ leakage queries.

As claimed in the Definition 1, the auxiliary function $\mathcal{F}$ gives no advantage for $\mathcal{A}$ to win the **Game 3**, since the message m_b is completely hidden from $\mathcal{F}(m_b)$ in CT^* (inverts the auxiliary function $\mathcal{F}$). As a result, the challenge ciphertext CT^* in **Game 3** is statistically independent of the random bit b picked by the challenger. Hence, we have $\Pr[\mathcal{A} \text{ wins in } \textbf{Game 3}] = 1/2$.

Finally, we conclude that

$$\mathsf{Exp}_{\Sigma_{\mathsf{D\text{-}PKE}},\mathcal{A},\mathsf{aux}}^{\mathsf{CLR\text{-}PRIV\text{-}sIND}}(\lambda, b) \leq 3\mathcal{Q}(\lambda) \cdot \mathsf{Adv}_{\mathcal{A}}^{\mathsf{FullTd}} + 3\mathcal{Q}(\lambda) \cdot \mathsf{Adv}_{\mathcal{A}}^{\mathsf{PartTd}}.$$

6 Instantiations

In this section, we instantiate the *updatable all-but-one dual projective hashing* (c.f. Sect. 3) with some categories of cryptographic assumptions, such as *DDH*-based assumptions like k-LIN, *number-theoretic* assumptions like QR and DCR, and *lattice-based* assumptions like LWE.

6.1 Instantiations from k-LIN

Let $\mathbb{G}$ be a group of prime order q and g be a generator of $\mathbb{G}$. The k-LIN assumption implies that given $g_1, g_2, \cdots, g_{k+1}, g_1^{r_1}, \cdots, g_k^{r_k}$, it is hard to distinguish $g_{k+1}^{r_1+r_2+\cdots+r_k}$ from a random element from $\mathbb{G}$. Note that 1-LIN (i.e., $k = 1$) refers to the *Decisional Diffie-Hellman* (DDH) assumption.

$\mathsf{Setup}(\lambda)$: Inputs a security parameter λ and samples $\mathbf{P} \xleftarrow{\$} \mathbb{Z}_q^{k \times n}$ and $\mathsf{tag}, \widehat{\mathsf{tag}} \xleftarrow{\$} \mathbb{Z}_q$, and sets the master trapdoor $\mathsf{mtd} = \mathbf{P}$ and the updatable trapdoor $\mathsf{utd} = \mathbf{V} \xleftarrow{\$} \mathsf{kernel}(\mathbf{P})^k$.

$\mathsf{KeyGen}(\mathsf{mtd}, \widehat{\mathsf{tag}})$: Inputs mtd and $\widehat{\mathsf{tag}}$, samples the witness $\mathbf{W} \xleftarrow{\$} \mathbb{Z}_q^{n \times k}$, and sets $u = g^{\mathbf{WP} - \widehat{\mathsf{tag}}\mathbf{I}_n}$ and the initial trapdoor $\mathsf{td} = \mathbf{W}$.

$\mathsf{Priv}(\mathsf{tag}, u, \mathbf{x})$: Inputs a hash key $\mathbf{x} \xleftarrow{\$} \{0,1\}^n$ and the tag tag, then computes $y = \Lambda_u(\mathsf{tag}, \mathbf{x}) = (u \cdot g^{\mathsf{tag}})^{\mathbf{x}}$.

$\mathsf{Pub}(\mathsf{tag}, u, \alpha(\text{HP}, \mathbf{x}), \mathbf{W})$: Inputs u with its witness $\mathbf{W}$ and a projective map $\alpha(\text{HP}, \mathbf{x}) = g^{\mathbf{Px}}$, then computes $y = g^{\mathbf{W}(\mathbf{Px})}$.

$\mathsf{Tdinv}(\mathsf{tag}, \mathsf{td}, \alpha(\text{HP}, \mathbf{x}), \Lambda_u(\mathsf{tag}, \mathbf{x}))$: Inputs a trapdoor $\mathsf{td} = \mathbf{W}$, and $\alpha(\text{HP}, \mathbf{x})$ and a hash value $y = (u \cdot g^{\mathsf{tag}})^{\mathbf{x}} = g^{\mathbf{WPx} + (\mathsf{tag} - \widehat{\mathsf{tag}})\mathbf{x}}$ and a tag tag, then computes $g^{(\mathsf{tag} - \widehat{\mathsf{tag}})\mathbf{x}}$ and thus $\mathbf{x}$.

$\mathsf{Update}(\mathsf{utd}, \mathsf{td})$: Inputs an updatable trapdoor utd and the initial trapdoor td, randomly picks $\mathsf{utd}^* = \mathbf{V}^* \xleftarrow{\$} \mathsf{span}(\mathsf{utd})$, then outputs an updated trapdoor $\mathsf{td}^* = \mathsf{td} + \mathsf{utd}^* = \mathbf{W} + \mathbf{V}^*$.

6.2 Instantiations from QR

Let a Blum integer $N = PQ$, where P and Q are strong primes such that $P, Q \equiv 3(mod\ 4)$ and $|N| = \lambda$. The *Quadratic Residuosity* (QR) assumption implies it is hard to distinguish random elements in the subgroup of $\mathbb{Z}_N^*$ with Jacobi symbol +1 from random elements in the cyclic subgroup of squares of $\mathbb{Z}_N^*$ (i.e., $\mathbb{QR}_N$).

$\mathsf{Setup}(\lambda)$: Inputs a security parameter λ and chooses an RSA modulus $N = PQ$. Samples $\mathbf{p} \xleftarrow{\$} \mathbb{Z}_{N/2}^n, g \xleftarrow{\$} \mathbb{QR}_N, \mathsf{tag}, \widehat{\mathsf{tag}} \xleftarrow{\$} \{0, \cdots, 2^{\lambda/2-1}\}$, and sets the master trapdoor $\mathsf{mtd} = \mathbf{p}$ and the updatable trapdoor $\mathsf{utd} = \mathbf{v} \xleftarrow{\$} \mathsf{kernel}(\mathbf{p})$.

$\mathsf{KeyGen}(\mathsf{mtd}, \widehat{\mathsf{tag}})$: Inputs mtd and $\widehat{\mathsf{tag}}$, samples the witness $\mathbf{w} \xleftarrow{\$} \mathbb{Z}_{N/2}^n$, and sets $u = (-1)^{-\widehat{\mathsf{tag}}\mathbf{I}_n} g^{\mathbf{w}\mathbf{p}^\top}$ and the initial trapdoor $\mathsf{td} = \mathbf{w}$.

$\mathsf{Priv}(\mathsf{tag}, u, \mathbf{x})$: Inputs a hash key $\mathbf{x} \xleftarrow{\$} \{0,1\}^n$, the tag tag and the instance u, then computes $y = \Lambda_u(\mathsf{tag}, \mathbf{x}) = ((-1)^{\mathsf{tag}\mathbf{I}_n} \cdot u)^{\mathbf{x}}$.

$\mathsf{Pub}(\mathsf{tag}, u, \alpha(\text{HP}, \mathbf{x}), \mathbf{w})$: Inputs an instance u with its witness $\mathbf{w}$, a tag tag and a projective map $\alpha(\text{HP}, x) = \alpha(g^{\mathbf{p}}, \mathbf{x}) = g^{\mathbf{p}^\top \mathbf{x}}$, then computes $y = (g^{\mathbf{p}^\top \mathbf{x}})^{\mathbf{w}}$.

$\mathsf{Tdinv}(\mathsf{tag}, \mathsf{td}, \alpha(\text{HP}, x), \Lambda_u(\mathsf{tag}, \mathbf{x}))$: Inputs a trapdoor td, and $\alpha(x)$ and a hash value $y = ((-1)^{\mathsf{tag}\mathbf{I}_n} \cdot u)^{\mathbf{x}} = (-1)^{(\mathsf{tag}-\widehat{\mathsf{tag}})\mathbf{x}} \cdot g^{\mathbf{w}\mathbf{p}^\top \mathbf{x}}$, then computes $(-1)^{(\mathsf{tag}-\widehat{\mathsf{tag}})\mathbf{x}}$ and thus $\mathbf{x}$.

$\mathsf{Update}(\mathsf{utd}, \mathsf{td})$: Inputs an updatable trapdoor utd and the initial trapdoor td, randomly picks $\mathsf{utd}^* = \mathbf{v}^* \xleftarrow{\$} \mathsf{span}(\mathsf{utd})$ then outputs an updated trapdoor $\mathsf{td}^* = \mathsf{td} + \mathsf{utd}^* = \mathbf{w} + \mathbf{v}^*$.

6.3 Instantiations from DCR

Let a Blum integer $N = PQ$, where P and Q are strong primes such that $P, Q \equiv 3(mod\ 4)$ and $|N| = \lambda$, and let the multiplicative group $\mathbb{Z}_{N^{s+1}}^*$ be isomorphic to $\mathbb{Z}_{N^s} \times \mathbb{Z}_N^*$ where s is a positive integer. The *Decision Composite Residuosity* (DCR) assumption implies that it is hard to distinguish random elements in $\mathbb{Z}_{N^{s+1}}^*$ from random elements in N^sth power in $\mathbb{Z}_{N^{s+1}}^*$.

$\mathsf{Setup}(\lambda)$: Inputs a security parameter λ and chooses an RSA modulus $N = PQ$. Samples $\mathbf{p} \xleftarrow{\$} \mathbb{Z}_N^k, g \xleftarrow{\$} \mathbb{Z}_{N^{s+1}}^*, \mathsf{tag}, \widehat{\mathsf{tag}} \xleftarrow{\$} \{0, \cdots, 2^{\lambda/2-1}\}$ and sets the master trapdoor $\mathsf{mtd} = \mathbf{p}$ and $g_1 = g^{N^s}$, and the updatable trapdoor $\mathsf{utd} = \mathbf{v} \xleftarrow{\$} \mathsf{kernel}(\mathbf{p})$.

$\mathsf{KeyGen}(\mathsf{mtd}, \widehat{\mathsf{tag}})$: Inputs mtd and $\widehat{\mathsf{tag}}$, samples the witness $\mathbf{w} \xleftarrow{\$} \mathbb{Z}_{N^{s+1}}^n$, and sets $u = (1+N)^{-\widehat{\mathsf{tag}}\mathbf{I}_n} g_1^{\mathbf{w}\mathbf{p}^\top}$ and the initial trapdoor $\mathsf{td} = \mathbf{w}$.

$\mathsf{Priv}(\mathsf{tag}, u, x)$: Inputs a hash key $\mathbf{x} \xleftarrow{\$} \{0,1\}^n$, the tag tag and the instance u, then computes $y = \Lambda_u(\mathsf{tag}, \mathbf{x}) = ((1+N)^{\mathsf{tag}\mathbf{I}_n} \cdot u)^{\mathbf{x}}$.

$\mathsf{Pub}(\mathsf{tag}, u, \alpha(\text{HP}, x), \mathbf{w})$: Inputs the instance u with its witness $\mathbf{w}$ and a projective map $\alpha(\text{HP}, x) = \alpha(g_1^{\mathbf{p}}, \mathbf{x}) = g_1^{\mathbf{p}^\top \mathbf{x}}$, then computes $y = (g_1^{\mathbf{p}^\top \mathbf{x}})^{\mathbf{w}}$.

$\mathsf{Tdinv}(\mathsf{tag}, \mathsf{td}, \alpha(\text{HP}, x), \Lambda_u(\mathsf{tag}, \mathbf{x}))$: Inputs a trapdoor td, $\alpha(\text{HP}, x)$ and a hash value $y = ((1+N)^{\mathsf{tag}\mathbf{I}_n} \cdot u)^{\mathbf{x}} = (1+N)^{(\mathsf{tag}-\widehat{\mathsf{tag}})\mathbf{x}} \cdot g_1^{\mathbf{wp}^\top \mathbf{x}}$, then computes $(1+N)^{(\mathsf{tag}-\widehat{\mathsf{tag}})\mathbf{x}}$ and thus $\mathbf{x}$.

$\mathsf{Update}(\mathsf{utd}, \mathsf{td})$: Inputs utd and td, randomly picks $\mathsf{utd}^* = \mathbf{v}^* \xleftarrow{\$} \mathsf{span}(\mathsf{utd})$, and outputs an updated trapdoor $\mathsf{td}^* = \mathsf{td} + \mathsf{utd}^* = \mathbf{w} + \mathbf{v}^*$.

6.4 Instantiations from LWE

We give a LWE-based updatable ABO DPH based on [14]'s lossy trapdoor functions. Let $r : \{0,1\} \to \mathbb{Z}_q^{k \times n_1}$ be a function mapping a tag value into the distribution $\mathcal{U}$, and let Ψ_β be the distribution over $\mathbb{R}/\mathbb{Z}$ of a normal variable with means 0 and standard deviation $\beta/\sqrt{2\pi}$ then reduced modulo 1, and $\overline{\Psi}_\beta$ be the discrete distribution over $\mathbb{Z}_q$ of the random variable $\lfloor q\mathsf{X} \rfloor \bmod q$, in which the random variable X has a distribution Ψ_β. The parameters of *learning with errors* (LWE) are $k = O(n \log q), \beta = \Theta(1/q), n_1 = k/\log p$, and $p \le q/4n$. In particular, let γ be a constant, we thus have $q = \Theta(n^{(1+1/\gamma)})$ and $p = \Theta(n^{1/\gamma})$.

$\mathsf{Setup}(\lambda)$: Inputs a security parameter λ and samples $\mathbf{A} \xleftarrow{\$} \mathbb{Z}_q^{n \times k}, \mathbf{tag}, \widehat{\mathbf{tag}} \xleftarrow{\$} \{0,1\}^{n_1}$ and sets the master trapdoor $\mathsf{mtd} = \mathbf{A}$ and the updatable trapdoor $\mathsf{utd} = \mathbf{V} \xleftarrow{\$} \mathsf{kernel}(\mathbf{A})^{n_1}$.

$\mathsf{KeyGen}(\mathsf{mtd}, \widehat{\mathsf{tag}})$: Inputs mtd and $\widehat{\mathbf{tag}}$, samples the witness $\mathbf{W} = \mathbf{S} \xleftarrow{\$} \mathbb{Z}_q^{n \times n_1}$, and sets $u = \mathbf{A}^\top \mathbf{S} + \mathbf{E} - r(\widehat{\mathbf{tag}})$ and the initial trapdoor $\mathsf{td} = \mathbf{S}$.

$\mathsf{Priv}(\mathbf{tag}, u, \mathbf{x})$: Inputs a hash key $\mathbf{x} \xleftarrow{\$} \{0,1\}^k$ and a tag $\mathbf{tag}$ and the instance u, then computes $y = \Lambda_u(\mathbf{tag}, \mathbf{x}) = \mathbf{x}^\top(u + r(\mathbf{tag}))$.

$\mathsf{Pub}(\mathbf{tag}, u, \alpha(\text{HP}, \mathbf{x}), \mathbf{W})$: Inputs an instance u with its witness $\mathbf{W}$ and a projective map $\alpha(\text{HP}, \mathbf{x}) = \alpha(\mathbf{A}, \mathbf{x}) = \mathbf{A}\mathbf{x}$, then computes $y = (\mathbf{A}\mathbf{x})^\top \mathbf{W}$.

$\mathsf{Tdinv}(\mathbf{tag}, \mathsf{td}, \alpha(\text{HP}, \mathbf{x}), \Lambda_u(\mathbf{tag}, \mathbf{x}))$: Inputs a trapdoor td, $\alpha(\text{HP}, \mathbf{x})$ and a hash value $y = \mathbf{x}^\top(u + r(\mathbf{tag})) = \mathbf{x}^\top(\mathbf{A}^\top \mathbf{S}) + \mathbf{x}^\top(\mathbf{E} + r(\mathbf{tag} - \widehat{\mathbf{tag}}))$, then recovers $\mathbf{x}^\top r(\mathbf{tag} - \widehat{\mathbf{tag}})$ from $\mathbf{x}^\top(\mathbf{E} + r(\mathbf{tag} - \widehat{\mathbf{tag}}))$ based on the bounded-error decoding and thus $\mathbf{x}$. Note that the quantity $\mathbf{x}^\top \mathbf{E}$ has small norm.

$\mathsf{Update}(\mathsf{utd}, \mathsf{td})$: Inputs an updatable trapdoor utd and the initial trapdoor td, randomly picks $\mathsf{utd}^* = \mathbf{V}^* \xleftarrow{\$} \mathsf{span}(\mathsf{utd})$, then outputs an updated trapdoor $\mathsf{td}^* = \mathsf{td} + \mathsf{utd}^* = \mathbf{S} + \mathbf{V}^*$.

7 Conclusions

In this work, we introduce the updatable ABO DPH (UDPH) that extends the ABO DPH into the leakage-resilient setting. Based on the newly introduced UDPH, we present a simple modular framework for constructing leakage-resilient ABO LTDFs and deterministic PKE schemes in the floppy model from various well-known assumptions including k-LIN, DCR, QR and LWE.

Acknowledgments. We would like to thank Rupeng Yang for invaluable feedback and anonymous reviewers for insightful comments. This work was partially supported by National Natural Science Foundation of China (61802248, U1936213, 62002120), the "Chenguang Program" supported by Shanghai Municipal Education Commission (No.18CG62), NSFC-ISF Joint Scientific Research Program (61961146004) and Innovation Program of Shanghai Municipal Education Commission (2021-01-07-00-08-E00101).

References

1. Wee, H.: Dual projective hashing and its applications — lossy trapdoor functions and more. In: Pointcheval, D., Johansson, T. (eds.) EUROCRYPT 2012. LNCS, vol. 7237, pp. 246–262. Springer, Heidelberg (2012). https://doi.org/10.1007/978-3-642-29011-4_16
2. Cramer, R., Shoup, V.: Universal hash proofs and a paradigm for adaptive chosen ciphertext secure public-key encryption. In: Knudsen, L.R. (ed.) EUROCRYPT 2002. LNCS, vol. 2332, pp. 45–64. Springer, Heidelberg (2002). https://doi.org/10.1007/3-540-46035-7_4
3. Zhang, Z., Chen, Yu., Chow, S.S.M., Hanaoka, G., Cao, Z., Zhao, Y.: All-but-one dual projective hashing and its applications. In: Boureanu, I., Owesarski, P., Vaudenay, S. (eds.) ACNS 2014. LNCS, vol. 8479, pp. 181–198. Springer, Cham (2014). https://doi.org/10.1007/978-3-319-07536-5_12
4. Ma, S., Huang, Q.: A new framework of IND-CCA secure public key encryption with keyword search. Comput. J. **63**(12), 1849–1858 (2020)
5. Li, Z., Yang, Z., Szalachowski, P., Zhou, J.: Building low-interactivity multifactor authenticated key exchange for industrial internet of things. IEEE Internet Things J. **8**(2), 844–859 (2020)
6. Yang, R., Xu, Q., Zhou, Y., Zhang, R., Hu, C., Yu, Z.: Updatable hash proof system and its applications. In: Pernul, G., Ryan, P.Y.A., Weippl, E. (eds.) ESORICS 2015. LNCS, vol. 9326, pp. 266–285. Springer, Cham (2015). https://doi.org/10.1007/978-3-319-24174-6_14
7. Bellare, M., Boldyreva, A., O'Neill, A.: Deterministic and efficiently searchable encryption. In: Menezes, A. (ed.) CRYPTO 2007. LNCS, vol. 4622, pp. 535–552. Springer, Heidelberg (2007). https://doi.org/10.1007/978-3-540-74143-5_30
8. Brakerski, Z., Kalai, Y.T., Katz, J., Vaikuntanathan, V.: Overcoming the hole in the bucket: Public-key cryptography resilient to continual memory leakage. In: 2010 IEEE 51st Annual Symposium on Foundations of Computer Science, pp. 501–510. IEEE (2010)
9. Dodis, Y., Haralambiev, K., López-Alt, A., Wichs, D.: Cryptography against continuous memory attacks. In: 2010 IEEE 51st Annual Symposium on Foundations of Computer Science, pp. 511–520. IEEE (2010)
10. Agrawal, S., Dodis, Y., Vaikuntanathan, V., Wichs, D.: On continual leakage of discrete log representations. In: Sako, K., Sarkar, P. (eds.) ASIACRYPT 2013. LNCS, vol. 8270, pp. 401–420. Springer, Heidelberg (2013). https://doi.org/10.1007/978-3-642-42045-0_21
11. Akavia, A., Goldwasser, S., Vaikuntanathan, V.: Simultaneous hardcore bits and cryptography against memory attacks. In: Reingold, O. (ed.) TCC 2009. LNCS, vol. 5444, pp. 474–495. Springer, Heidelberg (2009). https://doi.org/10.1007/978-3-642-00457-5_28

12. Koppula, V., Pandey, O., Rouselakis, Y., Waters, B.: Deterministic public-key encryption under continual leakage. In: Manulis, M., Sadeghi, A.-R., Schneider, S. (eds.) ACNS 2016. LNCS, vol. 9696, pp. 304–323. Springer, Cham (2016). https://doi.org/10.1007/978-3-319-39555-5_17
13. Huang, M., Yang, B., Zhang, M., Zhang, L., Hou, H.: Updatable lossy trapdoor functions under consecutive leakage. Comput. J. (4), 4 (2019)
14. Peikert, C., Waters, B.: Lossy trapdoor functions and their applications. SIAM J. Comput. **40**(6), 1803–1844 (2011)
15. Mironov, I., Pandey, O., Reingold, O., Segev, G.: Incremental deterministic public-key encryption. J. Cryptol. **31**(1), 134–161 (2018)
16. Huang, M., Yang, B., Zhao, Y., Wang, X., Zhou, Y., Xia, Z.: A generic construction of CCA-secure deterministic encryption. Inf. Process. Lett. **154**, 105865 (2020)
17. Li, S., Mu, Y., Zhang, M., Zhang, F.: Updatable lossy trapdoor functions and its application in continuous leakage. In: Chen, L., Han, J. (eds.) ProvSec 2016. LNCS, vol. 10005, pp. 309–319. Springer, Cham (2016). https://doi.org/10.1007/978-3-319-47422-9_18
18. Zhao, Y., Yong, Yu., Yang, B.: Leakage resilient CCA security in stronger model: Branch hidden abo-LTFS and their applications. Comput. J. **62**(4), 631–640 (2019)
19. Brakerski, Z., Segev, G.: Better security for deterministic public-key encryption: the auxiliary-input setting. In: Rogaway, P. (ed.) CRYPTO 2011. LNCS, vol. 6841, pp. 543–560. Springer, Heidelberg (2011). https://doi.org/10.1007/978-3-642-22792-9_31
20. Paterson, K.G., Schuldt, J.C.N., Sibborn, D.L., Wee, H.: Security against related randomness attacks via reconstructive extractors. In: Groth, J. (ed.) IMACC 2015. LNCS, vol. 9496, pp. 23–40. Springer, Cham (2015). https://doi.org/10.1007/978-3-319-27239-9_2

On Tightly-Secure (Linkable) Ring Signatures

Guofeng Tang[1,2(✉)]

[1] TCA Lab of State Key Laboratory of Computer Science, Institute of Software, Chinese Academy of Sciences, Beijing, China
guofeng2016@iscas.ac.cn

[2] University of Chinese Academy of Sciences, Beijing, China

Abstract. Tight security is increasingly gaining importance in real-world cryptography, as it allows to deploy the cryptosystem without compensating the security loss of a reduction with larger parameters. In this paper, we point out the difficulties of creating tightly-secure ring signatures (RS) and linkable ring signatures (LRS), then present solutions to overcome them. As a result, we construct a tightly-secure RS scheme that is more efficient than the previous construction (ESORICS'18), and the first tightly-secure LRS scheme. The security is based on the Computational and Decisional Diffie-Hellman assumptions in the random oracle model.

Keywords: Tight security · Ring signature · Linkable ring signature · Logarithmic size

1 Introduction

1.1 Background

In modern cryptography it is standard to propose a new cryptographic construction along with a proof of security. The security proof usually describes a reduction which turns an efficient adversary $\mathcal{A}$ breaking the proposed cryptosystem into an efficient adversary $\mathcal{B}$ breaking the underlying complexity assumption. If $\mathcal{B}$'s success probability $\epsilon_{\mathcal{B}}$ and running time $t_{\mathcal{B}}$ are the same as $\epsilon_{\mathcal{A}}, t_{\mathcal{A}}$ of $\mathcal{A}$ (up to a constant factor) respectively, then the reduction is said to be *tight*. However in many proofs, we are only able to show that $\mathcal{B}$ has running time $t_{\mathcal{B}} \approx t_{\mathcal{A}}$, but success probability $\epsilon_{\mathcal{B}} \geq \epsilon_{\mathcal{A}}/L$, where L is the security loss. When we choose the cryptographic parameters in a theoretically-sound way, a larger loss L must be compensated by larger parameters which in turn has a direct impact on efficiency. Thus in order to be able to deploy the cryptosystem with "optimal" parameters, we need a tight security proof.

The notion of ring signatures (RS) was first proposed by Rivest *et al.* [24], which allows a signer to sign a message on behalf of a self-formed group called a *ring*, while hiding his identity. Unlike group signatures [8], RS does not require

D. Gao et al. (Eds.): ICICS 2021, LNCS 12919, pp. 375–393, 2021.
https://doi.org/10.1007/978-3-030-88052-1_22

any centralized group manager or coordination among the various ring members, neither does it involve a tracing authority to de-anonymize signatures. This makes RS has a variety of applications which have been suggested already in previous works [10,21]. The main motivation was to allow secrets to be leaked anonymously, by concealing the identity of a source (*e.g.*, a whistleblower in a political scandal) while simultaneously providing reliability.

As an extension of RS, Liu *et al.* [19] first proposed the concept of linkable ring signatures (LRS). Besides anonymity, LRS requires linkability which guarantees a public procedure can link two signatures signed by the same signer, and nonslanderaility which guarantees a signer should not be entrapped that he has signed twice. It can be applied in the e-voting system [9,29] to ensure that the voters can vote anonymously and will not vote twice. Moreover, LRS has received much attention in cryptocurrencies, such as Monero [28,31], in order to defeat the double-spending attack.

Wang *et al.* [30] proposed a generic construction that adds linkability to any RS scheme with one-time signature scheme. The linkability of LRS is reduced to the unforgeability of RS. However the proof has a security loss $Q_{\mathcal{H}}$ that is the number of random oracle queries. Thus, a tightly-secure LRS cannot be constructed directly from a tightly-secure RS scheme using transformation in [30].

So far, the only known tightly-secure RS construction was due to Libert *et al.* [18] in ESORICS 2018. It applies the idea of lossy identification paradigm [1] where security proofs proceed by replacing a well-formed public key by a lossy key, with respect to which forging an RS becomes statistically impossible. It resorts to a lossy encryption scheme [4], in order to be compatible with lossy modes. The first drawback is that using lossy encryption is *not* efficient enough, with more group elements and exponentiations than ElGamal encryption. The second drawback is the lossy identification paradigm cannot be extended into an LRS scheme. Concretely if we add a linkability tag to their RS construction, the lossiness property will not be satisfied any more. Thus their solution can *not* be extended into an LRS scheme preserving tight security.

In this paper, we aim to create a more efficient RS scheme and add linkability to it preserving tight security, obtaining the first tightly-secure LRS.

1.2 Our Results

In this paper, we first construct a tightly-secure RS scheme. Since we apply ElGamal encryption which has better performance than lossy encryption used in [18], our RS are more efficient with shorter signature size, lower computational cost as shown in Table 1. More importantly, our techniques of avoiding reduction loss for an RS scheme can be extended to an LRS scheme, that is the first LRS construction with tight security.

Difficulties of Constructing Tightly-Secure RS and LRS. For an RS scheme, the main challenge is to prove tight unforgeability. In the unforgeability game, the adversary $\mathcal{A}$ can query the key generation queries at most Q_V times, and receives as input a list $\{PK_i\}_{i\in[Q_V]}$ of public keys. We denote the corresponding secret

Table 1. A comparison of performance between our tightly-secure (linkable) RS constructions versus the prior one [18]. (Let N be the ring size. Let e_N denote one multi-exponentiation in $\mathbb{G}$ of size N. Using multi-exponentiation techniques [20], computing e_{2N} is much more efficient than computing two e_N operations.)

RS	Signature size		Signing (# $\mathbb{G}$ exponentiation)	Verifying (# $\mathbb{G}$ exponentiation)
	$\mathbb{G}$	$\mathbb{Z}_q$		
[18]	$10\log N+2$	$5\log N+4$	$2\log N\cdot e_N+27\log N+6$	$2e_N+17\log N+12$
Our RS	$9\log N+2$	$3\log N+2$	$\log N\cdot e_{2N}+15\log N+3$	$e_{2N}+12\log N+6$
Our LRS	$8\log N+1$	$3\log N+1$	$\log N\cdot e_{2N}+12\log N+1$	$e_{2N}+11\log N+3$

keys with $\{SK_i\}_{i\in[Q_V]}$. In the proof, there exist two relevant dimensions for tightness: (i) the number Q_V of key generation queries, and (ii) the number $Q_{\mathcal{H}}$ of random oracle queries.

i A straightforward reduction guesses the index π of $\mathcal{A}$'s targeted public key PK_π and embeds the underlying hard problem into PK_π, which incurs a security loss that is linear in Q_V. In order to avoid the need to guess $\mathcal{A}$'s target, $\mathcal{B}$ must know all secret keys $SK_1,\cdots,SK_{Q_V}$ in order to be able to answer corruption queries. However if $\mathcal{B}$ knows all secret keys, then it seems $\mathcal{B}$ can generate $\mathcal{A}$'s forgery. That is to say that $\mathcal{B}$ is able to solve the underlying hard problem by itself, which is not meaningful.

ii A common approach to construct RS in the random oracle model (ROM) [5] is to use Fiat-Shamir methodology [12], in combination with Schnorr-type [25] or Stern-type [27] proof of knowledge, such as logarithmic-size constructions [11,16,17]. The only known reduction applies the Forking Lemma [23]. It needs to rewind the adversary $\mathcal{A}$ with the same random tape which incurs a security loss that is polynomial in $Q_{\mathcal{H}}/\epsilon_{\mathcal{A}}$. Thus a Fiat-Shamir-like proof of knowledge is difficult to prove tightly secure due to known impossibility results [13,22,26].

For instance, the first known logarithmic-size RS construction was due to Groth and Kohlweiss [16], which is a Fiat-Shamir-like proof of knowledge proving that one of N commitments opens to 0. To prove unforgeability, the reduction rewinds the forger $\log N$ times where N is the ring cardinality, leading to $\epsilon_{\mathcal{B}}\approx\frac{\epsilon_{\mathcal{A}}^{\log N}}{Q_V\cdot Q_{\mathcal{H}}}$. This means we need to multiply the security parameter by a factor $\log N$ to compensate for the reduction loss, even without taking into account the factors Q_V and $Q_{\mathcal{H}}$.

For an LRS scheme, the main challenge is to prove tight linkability. In the linkability game, the adversary $\mathcal{A}$ is allowed to ask corruption queries to obtain all secret keys, which means the reduction $\mathcal{B}$ must know all secret keys. Thus, it requires a security proof such that $\mathcal{B}$ cannot solve the underlying hard problem without $\mathcal{A}$'s help, even though $\mathcal{B}$ knows all secret keys. Furthermore, we can not use rewinding technique. Therefore, constructing tightly-secure LRS is faced with similar technical challenges with constructing tightly-secure RS.

Our Solutions. In order to avoid a loss Q_V in i, we construct an RS scheme in which each user's public key PK consists of two group elements $PK = (X^{(0)}, X^{(1)})$, the associated secret key consists of a random bit $b \xleftarrow{\$} \{0,1\}$ and the discrete logarithm x of $X^{(b)} = g^x$. The basic idea is inspired by previously known signatures with tight multi-user security [3,14]. The reduction $\mathcal{B}$ basically knows each user's secret key (b, x) and thus is able to respond all corruption queries of $\mathcal{A}$, but it hopes that $\mathcal{A}$ produces a forgery under $X^{(1-b)}$. If the adversary $\mathcal{A}$ cannot learn information about (b, x) from signing queries, then it outputs a forgery under $X^{(1-b)}$ with the probability $\frac{1}{2}$. In this way, $\mathcal{B}$ can embed a computationally-hard problem into each user's $X^{(1-b)}$ and can only solve it with $\mathcal{A}$'s help, since $\mathcal{B}$ does not know the secret key of $X^{(1-b)}$.

In order to avoid a loss $Q_{\mathcal{H}}/\epsilon_{\mathcal{A}}$ in ii, the adversary $\mathcal{A}$ must be run only once by the reduction $\mathcal{B}$. At a high level, we invoke the idea from [15], which gives a tightly-secure signature. It sets the key pair (x, g^x), the signature includes h^x and a proof that (g^x, h, h^x) is DDH tuple. The reduction embeds a CDH problem in (g^x, h), then it solves the problem after receiving $\mathcal{A}$'s forgery. However the RS cannot output h^x since it will break anonymity under full key exposure (that is the adversary knows secret key of all users). Thus, our RS involves a commitment of h^x to hide h^x, but we need to make sure $\mathcal{B}$ can extract h^x from the commitment in $\mathcal{A}$'s forgery. For this reason, we use ElGamal encryption as a commitment scheme which allows $\mathcal{B}$ to decrypt. Then the heart of an RS construction is an one-out-of-many proof. In this paper, our one-out-of-many proof builds on the Groth-Kohlweiss proof system [16].

Since our solutions of avoiding losses $Q_V, Q_{\mathcal{H}}$ can be extended into an LRS scheme, our RS can be added linkability preserving tight security. The difference is LRS requires a linkability tag to link signatures signed by the same signer. In our construction, we use h^x as the linkability tag, then tweak our RS construction to generate a proof that one of $\{X_i, h, h^x\}_{i\in[2N]}$ is a DDH tuple with $\{X_i\}_{i\in[2N]} = \{X_\xi^{(0)}, X_\xi^{(1)}\}_{\xi\in[N]}$.

2 Preliminary

2.1 Notations and Hardness Assumptions

We use $\mathbb{Z}$ to denote the set of integers. For $N \in \mathbb{Z}$ we define $[N]$ as shorthand for the set $\{0, 1, \cdots, N-1\}$. If S is a set then $s \xleftarrow{\$} S$ denotes the operation of uniformly sampling an element s from S at random. We use the same notation to denote sampling an element s from a distribution S. The function log denotes the logarithm with the base 2. Let $\mathbb{G}$ denote a cyclic group of prime order q and let g be a generator. We use $|\mathbb{G}|$ to denote the length of a element in $\mathbb{G}$, similarly for $|\mathbb{Z}_q|$. Let $\mathcal{DDH}$ be the set of DDH tuples $\{(g^a, g^b, g^{ab})|a, b \in \mathbb{Z}_q\}$.

Definition 1. *Let $\mathcal{A}$ be an algorithm that takes two group elements as input and outputs a group element. The success probability of $\mathcal{A}$ against the Computational Diffie-Hellman (CDH) problem is*

$$\mathsf{Adv}_{\mathsf{CDH}}(\mathcal{A}) = \Pr[\mathcal{A}(X, Y) = Z | (X, Y, Z) \in \mathcal{DDH}].$$

Definition 2. *Let $\mathcal{A}$ be an algorithm that takes three group elements as input and outputs 0 or 1. The advantage of $\mathcal{A}$ against the Decisional Diffie-Hellman (DDH) problem [7] is*

$$\mathsf{Adv}_{\mathsf{DDH}}(\mathcal{A}) = |\Pr[\mathcal{A}(X,Y,Z)=0|(X,Y,Z) \xleftarrow{\$} \mathcal{DDH}] - \Pr[\mathcal{A}(X,Y,Z)=0|(X,Y,Z) \xleftarrow{\$} \mathbb{G}^3]|.$$

2.2 Ring Signature and Linkable Ring Signature

An RS scheme consists of four algorithms (**Setup**, **KeyGen**, **Sign**, **Verify**):

Setup(1^λ)**:** On input the security parameter 1^λ, outputs public parameter pp.
KeyGen(pp)**:** On input pp, outputs secret key SK and public key PK.
Sign$(pp, SK_\pi, \mathcal{R}, M)$**:** On input pp, the signer's secret key SK_π for some $\pi \in [N]$, a ring $\mathcal{R} = \{PK_\xi\}_{\xi\in[N]}$ and a message M, outputs a signature σ.
Verify$(pp, M, \mathcal{R}, \sigma)$**:** On input pp, a signing message M, a ring $\mathcal{R}$, and a signature σ, outputs 0 or 1.

Correctness. For any $\{PK_\xi, SK_\xi\}_{\xi\in[N]}$ output by **KeyGen**(pp), any $\pi \in [N]$, and any message M, we have **Verify**$(pp, M, \mathcal{R}, $ **Sign**$(pp, SK_\pi, \mathcal{R}, M)) = 1$ with $\mathcal{R} = \{PK_\xi\}_{\xi\in[N]}$.

Security. Before introducing the security definitions of RS [6], we first assume there are three oracles as following:

- Key generation oracle KGO: At each query, it generates $(PK, SK) \leftarrow$ **KeyGen**(pp) and returns only PK.
- Corruption oracle $\mathsf{CO}(PK)$: On input a public key PK, returns the associated secret key SK.
- Signing oracle $\mathsf{SO}(M, \mathcal{R}, \pi)$: On input a message M, a ring $\mathcal{R}$ and an index π, it returns $\sigma \leftarrow$ **Sign**$(pp, SK_\pi, \mathcal{R}, M)$.

Definition 3. *An RS scheme is said to be* ***anonymous*** *under* ***full key exposure*** *if for any probabilistic polynomial time (PPT) adversary $\mathcal{A}$, $\mathsf{Adv}_{\mathsf{anon}}(\mathcal{A})$ is negligible in λ where*

$$\mathsf{Adv}_{\mathsf{anon}}(\mathcal{A}) = |\Pr[pp \leftarrow \textbf{\textit{Setup}}(1^\lambda); (M, \mathcal{R}, \pi_0, \pi_1) \leftarrow \mathcal{A}^{\mathsf{KGO},\mathsf{CO},\mathsf{SO}}(pp); b \xleftarrow{\$} \{0,1\}; \sigma \leftarrow \textbf{\textit{Sign}}(pp, SK_{\pi_b}, \mathcal{R}, M) : \mathcal{A}(\sigma) = b] - 1/2|$$

such that $PK_{\pi_0}, PK_{\pi_1} \in \mathcal{R}$, all public keys in $\mathcal{R}$ are produced by KGO and $\mathcal{A}$ is allowed to corrupt all secret keys.

Definition 4. *An RS scheme is said to be* ***unforgeable*** *if for any PPT adversary $\mathcal{A}$, $\mathsf{Adv}_{\mathsf{forge}}(\mathcal{A})$ is negligible in λ where*

$$\mathsf{Adv}_{\mathsf{forge}}(\mathcal{A}) = \Pr[pp \leftarrow \textbf{\textit{Setup}}(1^\lambda); (M^*, \sigma^*, \mathcal{R}^*) \leftarrow \mathcal{A}^{\mathsf{KGO},\mathsf{SO},\mathsf{CO}}(pp) : \textbf{\textit{Verify}}(pp, M^*, \mathcal{R}^*, \sigma^*) = 1]$$

such that each public key in $\mathcal{R}^*$ is produced by KGO and has never been queried to CO, and no query of the form $(M^*, \mathcal{R}^*, \cdot)$ has been made to SO.

An LRS consists of five algorithms (**Setup**, **KeyGen**, **Sign**, **Verify**, **Link**). The definitions of **Setup**, **KeyGen**, **Sign**, **Verify** are the same with an RS scheme.

Link$(pp, (M, \mathcal{R}, \sigma), (M', \mathcal{R}', \sigma'))$**:** On input two message-ring-signature triples, outputs linked or unlinked description

Correctness. For any $\{PK_\xi, SK_\xi\}_{\xi\in[N]}$, $\{PK'_\xi, SK'_\xi\}_{\xi\in[N']}$ output by **KeyGen**(pp), any $\pi \in [N], \pi' \in [N']$, and any message M, M', we have

$$\mathbf{Verify}(pp, M, \mathcal{R}, \mathbf{Sign}(pp, SK_\pi, \mathcal{R}, M)) = 1 \text{ and}$$

$$\mathbf{Link}(pp, (M, \mathcal{R}, \mathbf{Sign}(pp, SK_\pi, \mathcal{R}, M)), (M', \mathcal{R}', \mathbf{Sign}(pp, SK'_{\pi'}, \mathcal{R}', M'))) = \mathsf{linked}$$

with $PK_\pi \in \mathcal{R}$, $PK'_{\pi'} \in \mathcal{R}'$, $PK_\pi = PK'_{\pi'}$ and $SK_\pi = SK'_{\pi'}$.

Security. A secure LRS scheme requires three properties: anonymity, linkability and nonslanderability. The unforgeability of LRS can be implied by the linkability and nonslanderability according to [2]. Unlike RS, an LRS scheme cannot provide anonymity against full key exposure.

Definition 5. *An LRS scheme is* ***anonymous*** *if for any PPT adversary $\mathcal{A}$, $\mathsf{Adv}_{\mathsf{anon}}(\mathcal{A})$ is negligible in λ where*

$$\mathsf{Adv}_{\mathsf{anon}}(\mathcal{A}) = |\Pr[pp \leftarrow \textbf{Setup}(1^\lambda); (M,\mathcal{R},\pi_0,\pi_1) \leftarrow \mathcal{A}^{\mathsf{KGO,CO,SO}}(pp); b \xleftarrow{\$} \{0,1\}; \\ \sigma \leftarrow \textbf{Sign}(pp, SK_{\pi_b}, \mathcal{R}, M) : \mathcal{A}(\sigma) = b] - 1/2|$$

such that all public keys in $\mathcal{R}$ are produced by KGO, $PK_{\pi_0}, PK_{\pi_1} \in \mathcal{R}$ have never been queried to CO and as a ring member to SO.

Definition 6. *An LRS scheme is* ***linkable*** *w.r.t.* ***insider corruption*** *if for any PPT adversary $\mathcal{A}$, $\mathsf{Adv}_{\mathsf{link}}(\mathcal{A})$ is negligible in λ where*

$$\mathsf{Adv}_{\mathsf{link}}(\mathcal{A}) = \Pr[pp \leftarrow \textbf{Setup}(1^\lambda); \{M_k, \sigma_k, \mathcal{R}^*\}_{k\in[N+1]} \leftarrow \mathcal{A}^{\mathsf{KGO,CO,SO}}(pp) : \\ \textbf{Verify}(pp, M_k, \mathcal{R}^*, \sigma_k) = 1 \text{ for each } k \in [N+1]; \\ \textbf{Link}(pp, (M_{k_1}, \mathcal{R}^*, \sigma_{k_1}), (M_{k_2}, \mathcal{R}^*, \sigma_{k_2})) = \mathsf{unlinked} \text{ for any } k_1 \neq k_2]$$

such that $\mathcal{R}^*$ contains N public keys, all of them are produced by KGO and $\mathcal{A}$ is allowed to corrupt all secret keys.

Definition 7. *An LRS scheme is* ***nonslanderable*** *if for any PPT adversary $\mathcal{A}$, $\mathsf{Adv}_{\mathsf{slander}}(\mathcal{A})$ is negligible in λ where*

$$\mathsf{Adv}_{\mathsf{anon}}(\mathcal{A}) = \Pr[pp \leftarrow \textbf{Setup}(1^\lambda); (M, \mathcal{R}, \pi) \leftarrow \mathcal{A}^{\mathsf{KGO,CO,SO}}(pp); \\ \sigma \leftarrow \textbf{Sign}(pp, SK_\pi, \mathcal{R}, M); (M^*, \mathcal{R}^*, \sigma^*) \leftarrow \mathcal{A}(\sigma) : \\ \textbf{Verify}(pp, M^*, \mathcal{R}^*, \sigma^*) = 1; \textbf{Link}(pp, (M, \mathcal{R}, \sigma), (M^*, \mathcal{R}^*, \sigma^*)) = \mathsf{linked}]$$

such that $PK_\pi \in \mathcal{R}$ has never been queried to CO and as a ring member to SO, all public keys in $\mathcal{R}$ and $\mathcal{R}^*$ are produced by KGO.

3 A Tightly-Secure Ring Signature

3.1 Rationale

In our RS construction, each user's public key consists of two group elements $PK = (X^{(0)}, X^{(1)})$, the associated secret key consists of a random bit $b \xleftarrow{\$} \{0,1\}$ and the discrete logarithm of $X^{(b)}$. To sign a message M on behalf of a ring $\mathcal{R} = \{X_\xi^{(0)}, X_\xi^{(1)}\}_{\xi \in [N]} = \{X_i\}_{i \in [2N]}$, the signer is one of N users with the knowledge of secret key SK_π. Note that $SK_\pi = (b, x)$ is the secret key of $PK_\pi = (X_\pi^{(0)}, X_\pi^{(1)})$ such that $X_\pi^{(b)} = g^x$. In signing algorithm, the signer computes solution h^x of the CDH input (g^x, h) and then computes an ElGamal encryption $(g^r, H^r \cdot h^x)$ of h^x. The key point is to construct an one-out-of-many proof for relation $R = \{(Z_1, Z_2, \{X_i\}_{i \in [2N]}); (l, r, x) | Z_1 = g^r \wedge Z_2 = H^r \cdot h^x \wedge X_l = g^x\}$ to prove (Z_1, Z_2) is an encryption of h^x and one of $\{X_i, h, h^x\}_{i \in [2N]}$ is a DDH tuple.

With the knowledge of l, write $l = l_1 \cdots l_n$ in binary with $n = \lceil \log 2N \rceil$. For each $j \in [1, n]$, compute an ElGamal ciphertext $\mathbf{C}_{l_j}$ of message g^{l_j} which can be seen as a perfectly binding, computationally hiding commitment on l_j. In order to prove that each $\mathbf{C}_{l_j}$ opens to 0 or 1, we will utilize the Σ-protocol in [16]. The response $f_j = l_j \cdot c + a_j$ is viewed as a degree-one polynomial in challenge $c \in \mathbb{Z}_q$ and used to define polynomials

$$P_i[C] = \prod_{j=1}^{n} F_{j,i_j}[C] = \delta_{i,j} \cdot C^n + \sum_{k=0}^{n-1} p_{i,k} \cdot C^k \in \mathbb{Z}_q[C] \quad \forall i \in [2N] \qquad (1)$$

where $F_{j,1}[C] = l_j \cdot C + a_j$ and $F_{j,0}[C] = C - F_{j,1}[C]$, which have degree n ($\delta_{i,j} = 1$) if $i = l$ and degree $n-1$ ($\delta_{i,j} = 0$) otherwise. We have the product $\prod_{i \in [2N]} X_i^{P_i(c)} = X_l^{c^n} \cdot \prod_{i \in [2N]} X_i^{\sum_{k=0}^{n-1} p_{i,k} \cdot c^k}$. If $X_l = g^x$, we have $\prod_{i \in [2N]} X_i^{P_i(c)} = g^{x \cdot c^n} \cdot \prod_{k=0}^{n-1} \prod_{i \in [2N]} X_i^{p_{i,k} \cdot c^k}$. In order to prove that one of $\{X_i\}_{i \in [2N]}$ has logarithm x without revealing which one, we compute $B_k = \prod_{i \in [2N]} X_i^{p_{i,k}} \cdot g^{\rho_k}$ for $k \in [0, n-1]$ and output them in the commitment phase. In order to cancel out the terms of degree 0 to $n-1$ in the exponent and add new randomness, we multiply $\prod_{i \in [2N]} X_i^{P_i(c)}$ with $\prod_{k=0}^{n-1} B_k^{-c^k}$, which should be equal to $g^{x \cdot c^n - \sum_{k=0}^{n-1} \rho_k \cdot c^k}$. The response contains $z_d = x \cdot c^n - \sum_{k=0}^{n-1} \rho_k \cdot c^k$. The soundness of the proof relies on the Schwartz-Zippel lemma, which ensures that $\prod_{i \in [2N]} X_i^{P_i(c)} \cdot \prod_{k=0}^{n-1} B_k^{-c^k}$ is unlikely to be g^{z_d} if $X_l \neq g^x$. We finally use the Fiat-Shamir heuristic to transform this one-out-of-many proof into a ring signature scheme.

3.2 Construction

In this section, we present our RS scheme $\mathsf{RS} = (\mathbf{Setup}, \mathbf{KeyGen}, \mathbf{Sign}, \mathbf{Verify})$.

Setup(1^λ): Given a security parameter λ, choose a cyclic group $\mathbb{G}$ of prime order q with the generators $g, h \xleftarrow{\$} \mathbb{G}$. Choose hash functions $\mathcal{H} : \{0,1\}^* \to \mathbb{G}$ and $\mathcal{H}_{\mathsf{FS}} : \{0,1\}^* \to \mathbb{Z}_q$ which will be modeled as random oracles. Output the common public parameter $pp = (\lambda, \mathbb{G}, g, h)$.

KeyGen(pp): Given pp, pick $b \xleftarrow{\$} \{0,1\}$, $x \xleftarrow{\$} \mathbb{Z}_q$ and $X^{(1-b)} \xleftarrow{\$} \mathbb{G}$, compute $X^{(b)} = g^x$. The secret key is $SK = (b, x)$ and the public key is $PK = (X^{(0)}, X^{(1)})$.

Sign($pp, SK_\pi, \mathcal{R}, M$): To sign a message $M \in \{0,1\}^*$ on behalf of $\mathcal{R} = \{PK_\xi\}_{\xi\in[N]}$, the signer uses SK_π to produce a ring signature as follows. We remark that $SK_\pi = (b, x)$ is the secret key of the π-th member in $\mathcal{R}$. For convenience, we rewrite $\mathcal{R} = \{X_\xi^{(0)}, X_\xi^{(1)}\}_{\xi\in[N]} = \{X_i\}_{i\in[2N]}$ where $X_\xi^{(0)} = X_{2\xi}$ and $X_\xi^{(1)} = X_{2\xi+1}$ for each $\xi \in [N]$. For $l = 2\pi + b$, we have $X_l = g^x \in \mathcal{R}$. Let $n = \lceil \log 2N \rceil$ and write $l = l_1 \cdots l_n$ in binary.

1. Choose $r_j \xleftarrow{\$} \mathbb{Z}_q$ for each $j \in [1, n]$, compute $H = \mathcal{H}(\mathcal{R}, M, \{g^{r_j}\}_{j\in[1,n]}) \in \mathbb{G}$. Choose $r \xleftarrow{\$} \mathbb{Z}_q$, compute $\mathbf{Z} = (Z_1, Z_2) = (g^r, H^r \cdot h^x)$. The next step is to prove knowledge of witness (r, x) such that $\mathbf{Z} = (Z_1, Z_2) = (g^r, H^r \cdot h^x)$ and $X_l = g^x$ for some $l \in [2N]$.
2. For each $j \in [1, n]$, choose $a_j, s_j, t_j, \rho_{j-1}, \tau_{j-1} \xleftarrow{\$} \mathbb{Z}_q$, compute

$$\begin{aligned} \mathbf{C}_{l_j} &= (g^{r_j}, H^{r_j} \cdot g^{l_j}) \\ \mathbf{C}_{a_j} &= (g^{s_j}, H^{s_j} \cdot g^{a_j}) \\ \mathbf{C}_{b_j} &= (g^{t_j}, H^{t_j} \cdot g^{l_j a_j}) \end{aligned} \qquad \begin{aligned} B_{j-1} &= \prod_{i\in[2N]} X_i^{p_{i,j-1}} \cdot g^{\rho_{j-1}} \\ D_{j-1} &= Z_1^{\sum_{i\in[2N]} p_{i,j-1}} \cdot g^{\tau_{j-1}} \\ E_{j-1} &= Z_2^{\sum_{i\in[2N]} p_{i,j-1}} \cdot H^{\tau_{j-1}} \cdot h^{\rho_{j-1}} \end{aligned}$$

   For each $i \in [2N]$, write $i = i_1 \cdots i_n \in \{0,1\}^n$ in binary, $p_{i,0}, \cdots, p_{i,n-1} \in \mathbb{Z}_q$ are the coefficients of the polynomial defined in Eq. (1).
3. Compute $c = \mathcal{H}_{\mathsf{FS}}(M, \mathcal{R}, \{\mathbf{C}_{l_j}, \mathbf{C}_{a_j}, \mathbf{C}_{b_j}, B_{j-1}, D_{j-1}, E_{j-1}\}_{j\in[1,n]}) \in \mathbb{Z}_q$.
4. For each $j \in [1, n]$, compute

$$\begin{aligned} f_j &= l_j \cdot c + a_j \\ z_{a_j} &= r_j \cdot c + s_j \end{aligned} \qquad z_{b_j} = r_j(c - f_j) + t_j$$

   and compute

$$z_d = x \cdot c^n - \sum_{k=0}^{n-1} \rho_k \cdot c^k$$

$$z_r = r \cdot c^n - \sum_{k=0}^{n-1} \tau_k \cdot c^k$$

   Output the ring signature

$$\sigma = (\mathbf{Z}, \{\mathbf{\Sigma}_j\}_{j\in[1,n]}, z_d, z_r) \tag{2}$$

   with $\mathbf{\Sigma}_j = (\mathbf{C}_{l_j}, \mathbf{C}_{a_j}, \mathbf{C}_{b_j}, B_{j-1}, D_{j-1}, E_{j-1}, f_j, z_{a_j}, z_{b_j})$.

Verify$(pp, M, \mathcal{R}, \sigma)$: Given a ring $\mathcal{R} = \{X_\xi^{(0)}, X_\xi^{(1)}\}_{\xi\in[N]} = \{X_i\}_{i\in[2N]}$ and a pair (M, σ), parse σ as Eq. (2) and define $f_{j,1} = f_j$ and $f_{j,0} = c - f_j$ for each $j \in [1, n]$.

1. Denote $\mathbf{C}_{l_j} = (R_{j,1}, R_{j,2})$ for each $j \in [1, n]$. Compute $H = \mathcal{H}(\mathcal{R}, M, \{R_{j,1}\}_{j\in[1,n]}) \in \mathbb{G}$ and
$$c = \mathcal{H}_{\mathsf{FS}}(M, \mathcal{R}, \{\mathbf{C}_{l_j}, \mathbf{C}_{a_j}, \mathbf{C}_{b_j}, B_{j-1}, D_{j-1}, E_{j-1}\}_{j\in[1,n]}) \in \mathbb{Z}_q.$$
2. For each $i \in [2N]$, write $i = i_1 \cdots i_n \in \{0,1\}^n$ in binary and compute $p_i = P_i[c] = \prod_{j=1}^n f_{j,i_j}$. Return 1 if and only if for each $j \in [1, n]$,
$$(g^{z_{a_j}}, H^{z_{a_j}} \cdot g^{f_j}) = \mathbf{C}_{l_j}^c \cdot \mathbf{C}_{a_j} \tag{3}$$
$$(g^{z_{b_j}}, H^{z_{b_j}}) = \mathbf{C}_{l_j}^{c-f_j} \cdot \mathbf{C}_{b_j} \quad \text{and} \tag{4}$$
$$g^{z_d} = \prod_{i\in[2N]} X_i^{p_i} \cdot \prod_{k=0}^{n-1} B_k^{-c^k} \tag{5}$$
$$g^{z_r} = Z_1^{\sum_{i\in[2N]} p_i} \cdot \prod_{k=0}^{n-1} D_k^{-c^k} \tag{6}$$
$$H^{z_r} \cdot h^{z_d} = Z_2^{\sum_{i\in[2N]} p_i} \cdot \prod_{k=0}^{n-1} E_k^{-c^k}. \tag{7}$$

Otherwise, output 0.

Correctness. In Sect. 3.1, we have shown the correctness of Eq. (5). For Eqs. (6) and (7), we have

$$Z_1^{\sum_{i\in[2N]} p_i} \cdot \prod_{k=0}^{n-1} D_k^{-c^k} = Z_1^{c^n + \sum_{k=0}^{n-1} \sum_{i\in[2N]} p_{i,k} \cdot c^k} \cdot \prod_{k=0}^{n-1} D_k^{-c^k}$$
$$= Z_1^{c^n} \cdot \prod_{k=0}^{n-1} g^{-\tau_k \cdot c^k} = g^{r \cdot c^n - \sum_{k=0}^{n-1} \tau_k \cdot c^k}$$

$$Z_2^{\sum_{i\in[2N]} p_i} \cdot \prod_{k=0}^{n-1} E_k^{-c^k} = Z_2^{c^n + \sum_{k=0}^{n-1} \sum_{i\in[2N]} p_{i,k} \cdot c^k} \cdot \prod_{k=0}^{n-1} E_k^{-c^k}$$
$$= Z_2^{c^n} \cdot \prod_{k=0}^{n-1} H^{-\tau_k \cdot c^k} \cdot \prod_{k=0}^{n-1} h^{-\rho_k \cdot c^k}$$
$$= H^{r \cdot c^n - \sum_{k=0}^{n-1} \tau_k \cdot c^k} \cdot h^{x \cdot c^n - \sum_{k=0}^{n-1} \rho_k \cdot c^k}$$

3.3 Security

Theorem 1. *Let $\mathcal{A}$ be a PPT adversary against **unforgeability** in the ROM, making at most Q_V queries to the key generation oracle* KGO*, Q_S signing queries* *to SO as well as $Q_{\mathcal{H}}$ and $Q_{\mathcal{H}_{FS}}$ queries to the random oracle $\mathcal{H}$ and $\mathcal{H}_{FS}$, respectively. Then there exists adversaries $\mathcal{B}$ and $\mathcal{C}$ against DDH and CDH, respectively, such that*

$$\mathsf{Adv}_{\mathsf{forge}}(\mathcal{A}) \leq 2\mathsf{Adv}_{\mathsf{CDH}}(\mathcal{C}) + \mathsf{Adv}_{\mathsf{DDH}}(\mathcal{B}) + \frac{Q_S \cdot (2Q_S + Q_{\mathcal{H}} + Q_{\mathcal{H}_{FS}} + 1)}{q^2} + \frac{Q_{\mathcal{H}_{FS}} \cdot (\log(Q_V) + 2) + 2}{q}.$$

Proof. We use a sequence of games between the adversary $\mathcal{A}$ and the challenger $\mathcal{CH}$. For each i, W_i stands for the event that $\mathcal{A}$ wins in Game i.

Game 0. This is the original game in Definition 4. $\mathsf{Adv}_{\mathsf{forge}}(\mathcal{A}) = \Pr[W_0]$.

Game 1. We modify the random oracle $\mathcal{H}$. It may be queried directly, or triggered by a signing query. At each direct $\mathcal{H}$ query $(\mathcal{R}, M, \{R_{j,1}\}_{j\in[1,n]})$, the challenger $\mathcal{CH}$ returns the previously defined value if it exists. Otherwise, it picks $\gamma \xleftarrow{\$} \mathbb{Z}_q$ and defines the hash value as $\mathcal{H}(\mathcal{R}, M, \{R_{j,1}\}_{j\in[1,n]}) = g^\gamma$. $\mathcal{CH}$ remembers $(\mathcal{R}, M, \{R_{j,1}\}_{j\in[1,n]}, \gamma)$. Since γ is sampled uniformly from $\mathbb{Z}_q$, the hash value $\mathcal{H}(M, \mathcal{R}, \{R_{j,1}\}_{j\in[1,n]})$ is distributed uniformly over $\mathbb{G}$, like in **Game 0**. Each signing query triggers a random oracle query $\mathcal{H}(\cdot)$, if this was already defined, $\mathcal{B}$ aborts. Since each $R_{j,1}$ is chosen uniformly the probability to abort is at most $\frac{Q_S\cdot(Q_S+Q_{\mathcal{H}})}{q^2}$. Thus we have $|\Pr[W_1] - \Pr[W_0]| < \frac{Q_S\cdot(Q_S+Q_{\mathcal{H}})}{q^2}$.

Game 2. We introduce failure events which cause $\mathcal{CH}$ fails. When $\mathcal{A}$ outputs a forgery $(M^*, \sigma^*, \mathcal{R}^*)$, it first parses σ^* as in Eq. (2) and computes $H = \mathcal{H}(\mathcal{R}^*, M^*, \{R_{j,1}\}_{j\in[1,n]})$. If $\mathcal{H}(\mathcal{R}^*, M^*, \{R_{j,1}\}_{j\in[1,n]})$ was defined in response to a signing query or has never been queried, the challenger aborts. Here the probability to abort is at most $\frac{Q_S}{q^2} + \frac{1}{q}$. Recall the hash value was defined such that $H = g^\gamma$. Then $\mathcal{CH}$ uses γ to decrypt the ciphertexts $\{\mathbf{C}_{l_j}\}_{j\in[1,n]}$. The challenger $\mathcal{CH}$ fails if one of these ciphertexts turns out not to encrypt a bit $l_j \in \{0,1\}$. Lemma 1 shows that the probability is at most $\frac{Q_{\mathcal{H}_{FS}}+1}{q}$. We have $|\Pr[W_2] - \Pr[W_1]| \leq \frac{Q_{\mathcal{H}_{FS}}+2}{q} + \frac{Q_S}{q^2}$.

Game 3. We now modify the key generation algorithm used by $\mathcal{CH}$ so that instead of sampling $X^{(1-b)} \xleftarrow{\$} \mathbb{G}$, it samples $x' \xleftarrow{\$} \mathbb{Z}_q$ and computes $X^{(1-b)} = g^{x'}$. $\mathcal{CH}$ stores x' along with the original secret key as (b, x, x'), but it still returns (b, x) when $\mathcal{A}$ asks for a signing key.
Since x' is sampled from the uniform distribution on $\mathbb{Z}_q$, $X^{(1-b)}$ will also be sampled from the same distribution, just like in **Game 2**. $\Pr[W_3] = \Pr[W_2]$.

Game 4. When $\mathcal{A}$ outputs a forgery $(M^*, \sigma^*, \mathcal{R}^*)$, $\mathcal{C}$ parses σ^* as in Eq. (2). It first decrypts $\{\mathbf{C}_{l_j}\}_{j\in[1,n]}$ to produce an n-bit string $l_1 \cdots l_n \in \{0,1\}^n$ as the bit representation of $l \in [2N]$. Then it decrypts $\mathbf{Z} = (Z_1, Z_2)$ by computing $Z = Z_2/Z_1^\gamma$. At this point, $\mathcal{CH}$ rewrites $\mathcal{R}^* = \{X_i\}_{i\in[2N]}$ and recalls the l-th element $X_l = g^{x_l}$ of $\mathcal{R}^*$. In this game, we determine $\mathcal{A}$ fails if $\log_h Z \neq x_l$. Lemma 2 shows that $|\Pr[W_4] - \Pr[W_3]| \leq \frac{Q_{\mathcal{H}_{FS}}\cdot(\log(Q_V)+1)}{q}$.

Game 5. We now modify the signing algorithm used by the challenger $\mathcal{CH}$. On each signing query $(M, \mathcal{R} = \{PK_\xi\}_{\xi\in[N]}, \pi)$, $\mathcal{CH}$ computes $\mathbf{Z}$ and $\{\mathbf{C}_{l_j}\}_{j\in[1,n]}$ as in real signing algorithm. Then it chooses $f_j, z_{a_j}, z_{b_j} \xleftarrow{\$} \mathbb{Z}_q$ for each j and $c, z_d, z_r \xleftarrow{\$} \mathbb{Z}_q$, and computes $\mathbf{C}_{a_j} = (g^{z_{a_j}} \cdot R_{j,1}^{-c}, H^{z_{a_j}} \cdot g^{f_j} \cdot R_{j,2}^{-c})$ and $\mathbf{C}_{b_j} = (g^{z_{b_j}} \cdot R_{j,1}^{f_j-c}, H^{z_{b_j}} \cdot R_{j,2}^{f_j-c})$. For each $k \in [1, n-1]$, it computes B_k, D_k, E_k as in real signing algorithm, but it computes $B_0 = g^{-z_d} \cdot \prod_{i\in[2N]} X_i^{p_i} \cdot \prod_{k=1}^{n-1} B_k^{-c^k}$, $D_0 = g^{-z_r} \cdot Z_1^{\sum_{i\in[2N]} p_i} \cdot \prod_{k=1}^{n-1} D_k^{-c^k}$ and $E_0 = H^{-z_r} \cdot h^{-z_d} \cdot Z_2^{\sum_{i\in[2N]} p_i} \cdot \prod_{k=1}^{n-1} E_k^{-c^k}$ where $p_i = \prod_{j=1}^{n} f_{j,i_j}$ and $f_{j,1} = f_j$, $f_{j,0} = c - f_j$. Finally, $\mathcal{CH}$ programs

$$c = \mathcal{H}_{\mathsf{FS}}(M, \mathcal{R}, \{\mathbf{C}_{l_j}, \mathbf{C}_{a_j}, \mathbf{C}_{b_j}, B_{j-1}, D_{j-1}, E_{j-1}\}_{j\in[1,n]})$$

where $c \xleftarrow{\$} \mathbb{Z}_q$.
Although we change the way of generating $\{\mathbf{C}_{a_j}, \mathbf{C}_{b_j}, f_j, z_{a_j}, z_{b_j}\}_{j\in[1,n]}$ and B_0, D_0, E_0, z_d, z_r, they are distributed identically to those in the real signatures. Therefore, as long as no collision occurs in the simulation of random oracle $\mathcal{H}_{\mathsf{FS}}$, $\mathcal{A}$'s view is the same as that in **Game 4**. The probability that reprogramming attempts of $\mathcal{H}_{\mathsf{FS}}$ fail is at most $Q_S \cdot (Q_{\mathcal{H}_{\mathsf{FS}}+Q_S})/q^2$. Thus, $|\Pr[W_5] - \Pr[W_4]| \le \frac{Q_S\cdot(Q_{\mathcal{H}_{\mathsf{FS}}}+Q_S)}{q^2}$.

Game 6. We continue to modify the signing algorithm used by the challenger. On each signing query $(M, \mathcal{R} = \{PK_\xi\}_{\xi\in[N]}, \pi)$, $\mathcal{CH}$ chooses $Z_1, Z_2 \xleftarrow{\$} \mathbb{G}$ and sets $\mathbf{Z} = (Z_1, Z_2)$. For each $j \in [1, n]$, it chooses $R_{j,1}, R_{j,2} \xleftarrow{\$} \mathbb{G}$, sets $\mathbf{C}_{l_j} = (R_{j,1}, R_{j,2})$. For each $k \in [1, n-1]$, it chooses $B_k, D_k, E_k \xleftarrow{\$} \mathbb{G}$, other operations are the same with **Game 5**.
The challenger takes $\{\bar{A}, \bar{B}, \bar{C}\} \in \mathbb{G}^3$ as input. On the i-th signing query with input $(M, \mathcal{R}, \pi)$ for each $i \in [Q_S]$, $\mathcal{CH}$ first choose a random value $\chi_i, \eta_i \xleftarrow{\$} \mathbb{Z}_q$, computes $(Z_1, Z_2) = (\bar{A}^{\chi_i}, \bar{C}^{\eta_i\cdot\chi_i} \cdot h^x)$. For each $j \in [1, n]$, $\mathcal{B}$ chooses $\theta_j \xleftarrow{\$} \mathbb{Z}_q$, sets $\mathbf{C}_{l_j} = (\bar{A}^{\chi_i\cdot\theta_j}, \bar{C}^{\eta_i\cdot\chi_i\cdot\theta_j} \cdot g^{l_j})$ and reprograms the hash oracle so that $\mathcal{H}(M, \mathcal{R}, \{\bar{A}^{\chi_i\cdot\theta_j}\}_{j\in[1,n]}) = \bar{B}^{\eta_i}$. For each $k \in [1, n-1]$, it picks $\rho_k, \bar{\theta}_k \xleftarrow{\$} \mathbb{Z}_q$, and computes $B_k = \prod_{i\in[2N]} X_i^{p_{i,k}} \cdot g^{\rho_k}$, $D_k = Z_1^{\sum_{i\in[2N]} p_{i,k}} \cdot \bar{A}^{\chi_i\cdot\bar{\theta}_k}$ and $E_k = Z_2^{\sum_{i\in[2N]} p_{i,k}} \cdot h^{\rho_k} \cdot \bar{C}^{\eta_i\cdot\chi_i\cdot\bar{\theta}_k}$.
If $(\bar{A}, \bar{B}, \bar{C}) \in \mathcal{DDH}$, then $\{\bar{A}^{\chi_i\cdot\theta_j}, \bar{B}^{\eta_i}, \bar{C}^{\eta_i\cdot\chi_i\cdot\theta_j}\}_{i\in[1,Q_S],j\in[1,n]}$ are DDH tuples and $\{\bar{A}^{\chi_i\cdot\bar{\theta}_k}, \bar{B}^{\eta_i}, \bar{C}^{\eta_i\cdot\chi_i\cdot\bar{\theta}_k}\}_{i\in[1,Q_S],k\in[1,n-1]}$ are DDH tuples. In this case, $\mathcal{B}$ successfully simulates **Game 5** as long as no collision occurs in simulating oracle $\mathcal{H}$. Since $\mathcal{CH}$ aborts if $\mathcal{H}(M, \mathcal{R}, \{\bar{A}^{\chi_i\cdot\theta_j}\}_{j\in[1,n]})$ has already defined from **Game 1**, no collision occurs. Else if $(\bar{A}, \bar{B}, \bar{C})$ are random elements on $\mathbb{G}^3$, $\mathbf{Z}, \{\mathbf{C}_{l_j}\}_{j\in[1,n]}$ are uniformly distributed over $\mathbb{G}^2$ due to the presence of $\chi_i, \eta_i, \theta_j \xleftarrow{\$} \mathbb{Z}_q$, and similarly $\{B_k, D_k, E_k\}_{k\in[1,n-1]}$ are uniformly distributed over $\mathbb{G}^3$, just like in **Game 6**. Thus we have that $|\Pr[W_6] - \Pr[W_5]| \le \mathsf{Adv}_{\mathsf{DDH}}$.

Consider a CDH solver $\mathcal{C}$ who takes $(\bar{X}, \bar{Y})$ as input and aims to compute $\bar{Z}$ such that $\log_g \bar{X} = \log_{\bar{Y}} \bar{Z}$. It proceeds to run **Game 6** with $\mathcal{A}$ with the following modifications:

1. $\mathcal{C}$ sets $h = \bar{Y}$ instead of picking $h \xleftarrow{\$} \mathbb{G}$, sends the public parameter $pp = (\lambda, \mathbb{G}, g, h)$ to $\mathcal{A}$.
2. On each key generation query, $\mathcal{C}$ picks $\alpha \xleftarrow{\$} \mathbb{Z}_q$ and sets $X^{(1-b)} = \bar{X}^{\alpha}$. The algorithm adds $(X^{(1-b)}, \alpha)$ in table $\mathcal{L}$.

When the forger $\mathcal{A}$ outputs a valid forgery $(M^*, \sigma^*, \mathcal{R}^* = \{X_\xi^{(0)}, X_\xi^{(1)}\}_{\xi \in [N]})$, $\mathcal{C}$ parses σ^* as in Eq. (2) and does as follows.

1. Denote $\mathbf{C}_{l_j} = (R_{j,1}, R_{j,2})$. Compute $H = \mathcal{H}(\mathcal{R}^*, M^*, \{R_{j,1}\}_{j \in [1,n]})$, recall the previously defined exponent $\gamma \in \mathbb{Z}_q$ such that $H = g^\gamma$. Denote $\mathbf{C}_{l_j} = (R_{j,1}, R_{j,2})$, compute $g^{l_j} = R_{j,2}/R_{j,1}^\gamma$, determine $l_j \in \{0,1\}$ for each $j \in [1,n]$.
2. Having obtained the n-bit string $l_1 \cdots l_n \in \{0,1\}^n$ as the bit representation of l, compute $\pi = \lfloor l/2 \rfloor \in [N]$ and $b' = l - 2\pi \in \{0,1\}$. Recall the secret key $SK_\pi = (b_\pi, x_\pi)$ of the π-th member of the ring $\mathcal{R}^*$.
3. If $b' = 1 - b_\pi$, recall $(X_\pi^{(b')}, \alpha_\pi) \in \mathcal{L}$. Compute $Z = Z_2/{Z_1}^\gamma$. Output $\bar{Z} = Z^{\frac{1}{\alpha_\pi}}$. Otherwise, output $\perp$.

It is clear that $\mathcal{C}$ perfectly simulates **Game 6**. In this game, $\mathcal{A}$ wins meaning that $\log_h Z = \log_g X_l$ for the n-bit string $l_1 \cdots l_n$ decoded from $\{\mathbf{C}_{l_j}\}_{j \in [1,n]}$ and $l = \sum_{j \in [1,n]} l_j \cdot 2^{j-1}$. Since the forger $\mathcal{A}$ has no information about b_π in **Game 6**, it follows that $\mathcal{A}$'s forgery is about $b' = 1 - b_\pi$ at least half the time, that is $(X_\pi^{(b')}, h, Z) = (\bar{X}^{\alpha_\pi}, \bar{Y}, Z)$ is a DDH tuple. Finally, $\mathcal{C}$ solves the CDH problem by outputting $\bar{Z} = Z^{\frac{1}{\alpha_\pi}}$. We have $\Pr[W_6] \leq 2\mathsf{Adv}_{\mathsf{CDH}}(\mathcal{C})$. Finally, we obtain

$$\mathsf{Adv}_{\mathsf{forge}}(\mathcal{A}) \leq 2\mathsf{Adv}_{\mathsf{CDH}}(\mathcal{C}) + \mathsf{Adv}_{\mathsf{DDH}}(\mathcal{B}) + \frac{Q_S \cdot (2Q_S + Q_{\mathcal{H}} + Q_{\mathcal{H}_{\mathsf{FS}}} + 1)}{q^2} + \frac{Q_{\mathcal{H}_{\mathsf{FS}}} \cdot (\log(Q_V) + 2) + 2}{q}.$$

Lemma 1. *For any PPT adversary $\mathcal{A}$, if it outputs a valid forgery σ^* parsed as in Eq. (2), then the probability that one of $\mathbf{C}_{l_j}$ turns out not to decrypt a bit is upper bounded by $\frac{Q_{\mathcal{H}_{FS}}+1}{q}$.*

Following Lemma 2 of [18], the proof is trivial.

Lemma 2. *For any PPT adversary $\mathcal{A}$, it outputs a valid forgery $(M^*, \sigma^*, \mathcal{R}^* = \{X_i\}_{i \in [2N]})$, σ^* is parsed as in Eq. (2). Having decoded the n-bit string $l_1 \cdots l_n$ as the bit representation of $l \in [2N]$ from $\{\mathbf{C}_{l_j}\}_{j \in [1,n]}$ and decrypted Z from $\mathbf{Z}$, the probability that $\log_g X_l \neq \log_h Z$ is upper bounded by $\frac{Q_{\mathcal{H}_{FS}} \cdot (\log(Q_V)+1)}{q}$.*

Proof. We assume that $Z_1 = g^r$, $Z_2 = H^r \cdot h^{\bar{x}}$, $X_i = g^{x_i}$ for each $i \in [2N]$, $B_k = g^{b_k}$, $D_k = g^{d_k}$ and $E_k = H^{d_k} h^{e_k}$ with $b_k, d_k, e_k \in \mathbb{Z}_q$ for each $k \in [n-1]$.

Note that Eq. (3) implies that $f_j = a_j + l_j \cdot c$ for each $j \in [1, n]$ where a_j is encrypted by $\mathbf{C}_{a_j}$. Defining $f_{j,1} = f_j$ and $f_{j,0} = c - f_j$,

$$p_i = \prod_{j=1}^{n} f_{j,i_j} = \delta_{i,l} \cdot c^n + \sum_{k=0}^{n-1} p_{i,k} c^k \qquad \forall i \in [2N].$$

And Eq. (5) implies that

$$z_d = x_l \cdot c^n + \sum_{i=0}^{2N-1} \sum_{k=0}^{n-1} x_i \cdot p_{i,k} \cdot c^k - \sum_{k=0}^{n-1} b^k \cdot c^k \tag{8}$$

Since H and h are independent of each other from $\mathcal{A}$'s view, Eqs. (6) and (7) imply that

$$z_d = \bar{x} \cdot c^n + \sum_{i=0}^{2N-1} \sum_{k=0}^{n-1} \bar{x} \cdot p_{i,k} \cdot c^k - \sum_{k=0}^{n-1} e_k \cdot c^k \tag{9}$$

Combine Eqs. (8) and (9), we obtain

$$(\bar{x} - x_l) \cdot c^n + \sum_{k=0}^{n-1} (\sum_{i=0}^{2N-1} \bar{x} \cdot p_{i,k} - \sum_{i=0}^{2N-1} x_i \cdot p_{i,k} - e_k + b_k) \cdot c^k = 0 \tag{10}$$

If $\bar{x} \neq x_l$, Eq. (10) implies that c is a root of a non-zero polynomial of degree n. However, c is uniformly distributed over $\mathbb{Z}_q$ and the Schwartz-Zippel Lemma implies that Eq. (10) can only be hold with probability $\frac{n}{q} < \frac{\log(Q_V)+1}{q}$. Taking a union bound over all hash queries of $\mathcal{H}_{\mathsf{FS}}$, we obtain the probability of $\log_g X_l \neq \log_h Z$ for a valid signature is upper bounded by $\frac{Q_{\mathcal{H}_{\mathsf{FS}}} \cdot (\log(Q_V)+1)}{q}$.

Theorem 2. *Let $\mathcal{A}$ be a PPT adversary against* ***anonymity*** *against* ***full key exposure*** *in the ROM, making at most $Q_{\mathcal{H}_{\mathsf{FS}}}$ and $Q_{\mathcal{H}}$ queries to the random oracle $\mathcal{H}$ and $\mathcal{H}_{\mathsf{FS}}$. Then there exists a DDH distinguisher $\mathcal{B}$ such that $\mathsf{Adv}_{\mathsf{anon}}(\mathcal{A}) \leq \mathsf{Adv}_{\mathsf{DDH}}(\mathcal{B}) + \frac{Q_{\mathcal{H}} + Q_{\mathcal{H}_{\mathsf{FS}}}}{q^2}$.*

4 A Tightly-Secure Linkable Ring Signature

In our LRS construction, each user has public key with two group elements, same with RS construction in Sect. 3. In signing algorithm, the signer computes solution h^x of the CDH input (g^x, h), and then outputs h^x as signer's linkability tag. Finally, the signer outputs an one-out-of-many proof for relation $R' = \{(Z, \{X_i\}_{i \in [2N]}); (l, x) | Z = g^x \wedge X_l = g^x\}$ to prove one of $\{X_i, h, Z\}_{i \in [2N]}$ is a DDH tuple. This proof is obtained by tweaking the one-out-of-many proof for relation R in Sect. 3.

4.1 Construction

In this section, we present our LRS scheme LRS = (**Setup**, **KeyGen**, **Sign**, **Verify**, **Link**) with LRS.**Setup** = RS.**Setup** and LRS.**KeyGen** = RS.**KeyGen**.

Sign($pp, SK_\pi, \mathcal{R}, M$): To sign a message $M \in \{0,1\}^*$ on behalf of $\mathcal{R}$, the signer uses SK_π to produce a ring signature as follows. We remark that $SK_\pi = (b, x)$, $\mathcal{R} = \{X_\xi^{(0)}, X_\xi^{(1)}\}_{\xi\in[N]} = \{X_i\}_{i\in[2N]}$. We have $X_l = g^x \in \mathcal{R}$ where $l = 2\pi + b$. Let $n = \lceil \log 2N \rceil$ and write $l = l_1 \cdots l_n$ in binary.

1. Compute $Z = h^x$ and the next step is to prove that one of $\{X_i, h, Z\}_{i\in[2N]}$ is a DDH tuple such that $\log_g X_l = \log_h Z$ for some $l \in [2N]$.
2. For each $j \in [1, n]$, choose $r_j, a_j, s_j, t_j, \rho_{j-1} \xleftarrow{\$} \mathbb{Z}_q$, compute $H = \mathcal{H}(\mathcal{R}, M, \{g^{r_j}\}_{j\in[1,n]}) \in \mathbb{G}$ and

$$\begin{aligned} \mathbf{C}_{l_j} &= (g^{r_j}, H^{r_j} \cdot g^{l_j}) & B_{j-1} &= \prod_{i\in[2N]} X_i^{p_{i,j-1}} \cdot g^{\rho_{j-1}} \\ \mathbf{C}_{a_j} &= (g^{s_j}, H^{s_j} \cdot g^{a_j}) & & \\ \mathbf{C}_{b_j} &= (g^{t_j}, H^{t_j} \cdot g^{l_j a_j}) & D_{j-1} &= Z^{\sum_{i\in[2N]} p_{i,j-1}} \cdot h^{\rho_{j-1}} \end{aligned}$$

   For each $i \in [2N]$, $p_{i,0}, \cdots, p_{i,n-1}$ are coefficients of the polynomial defined in Eq. (1).
3. Compute $c = \mathcal{H}_{\mathsf{FS}}(M, \mathcal{R}, \{\mathbf{C}_{l_j}, \mathbf{C}_{a_j}, \mathbf{C}_{b_j}, B_{j-1}, D_{j-1}\}_{j\in[1,n]}) \in \mathbb{Z}_q$.
4. For each $j \in [1, n]$, compute

$$\begin{aligned} f_j &= l_j \cdot c + a_j & z_{b_j} &= r_j(c - f_j) + t_j \\ z_{a_j} &= r_j \cdot c + s_j \end{aligned}$$

   and compute $z_d = x \cdot c^n - \sum_{k=0}^{n-1} \rho_k \cdot c^k$. Output the ring signature

$$\begin{aligned} \sigma = (\mathbf{\Pi}, Z) \quad &\text{with } \mathbf{\Pi} = (\{\mathbf{\Sigma}_j\}_{j\in[1,n]}, z_d) \\ \text{and } \mathbf{\Sigma}_j &= (\mathbf{C}_{l_j}, \mathbf{C}_{a_j}, \mathbf{C}_{b_j}, B_{j-1}, D_{j-1}, f_j, z_{a_j}, z_{b_j}) \end{aligned} \tag{11}$$

Verify($pp, M, \mathcal{R}, \sigma$): Given a ring $\mathcal{R} = \{X_\xi^{(0)}, X_\xi^{(1)}\}_{\xi\in[N]} = \{X_i\}_{i\in[2N]}$ and a pair (M, σ), parse σ as in Eq. (11) and define $f_{j,1} = f_j$ and $f_{j,0} = c - f_j$ for each $j \in [1, n]$.

1. Denote $\mathbf{C}_{l_j} = (R_{j,1}, R_{j,2})$ for each $j \in [1, n]$. Compute $H = \mathcal{H}(\mathcal{R}, M, \{R_{j,1}\}_{j\in[1,n]}) \in \mathbb{G}$ and

$$c = \mathcal{H}_{\mathsf{FS}}(M, \mathcal{R}, \{\mathbf{C}_{l_j}, \mathbf{C}_{a_j}, \mathbf{C}_{b_j}, B_{j-1}, D_{j-1}\}_{j\in[1,n]}) \in \mathbb{Z}_q.$$

2. For each $i \in [2N]$, write it as $i = i_1 \cdots i_n \in \{0,1\}^n$ and compute $p_i = \prod_{j=1}^n f_{j,i_j}$. Return 1 if and only if for each $j \in [1, n]$,

$$(g^{z_{a_j}}, H^{z_{a_j}} \cdot g^{f_j}) = \mathbf{C}_{l_j}^c \cdot \mathbf{C}_{a_j}, \quad (g^{z_{b_j}}, H^{z_{b_j}}) = \mathbf{C}_{l_j}^{c-f_j} \cdot \mathbf{C}_{b_j}$$

   and

$$g^{z_d} = \prod_{i\in[2N]} X_i^{p_i} \cdot \prod_{k=0}^{n-1} B_k^{-c^k}, \quad h^{z_d} = Z^{\sum_{i\in[2N]} p_i} \cdot \prod_{k=0}^{n-1} D_k^{-c^k}.$$

   Otherwise, output 0.

Link$(pp, (M, \mathcal{R}, \sigma), (M', \mathcal{R}', \sigma'))$: Given two message-ring-signature triples, run **Verify** $(pp, M, \mathcal{R}, \sigma)$ and **Verify**$(pp, M', \mathcal{R}', \sigma')$, parse σ, σ' as

$$\sigma = (\{\boldsymbol{\Sigma}_j\}_{j\in[1,n]}, z_d, Z), \qquad \sigma' = (\{\boldsymbol{\Sigma}'_j\}_{j\in[1,n]}, z'_d, Z')$$

Return linked if and only if **Verify**$(pp, M, \mathcal{R}, \sigma) = 1$, **Verify**$(pp, M', \mathcal{R}', \sigma') = 1$ and $Z = Z'$. Otherwise, return unlinked.

4.2 Security

Theorem 3. *Let $\mathcal{A}$ be a PPT adversary against* **linkability** *of our LRS scheme in the ROM, making at most Q_V queries to the key generation oracle KGO, Q_S signing queries to SO as well as $Q_{\mathcal{H}}$ and $Q_{\mathcal{H}_{FS}}$ queries to the random oracle $\mathcal{H}$ and $\mathcal{H}_{FS}$, respectively, then there exists a CDH solver $\mathcal{C}$ such that*

$$\mathsf{Adv}_{\mathsf{forge}}(\mathcal{A}) \le \mathsf{Adv}_{\mathsf{CDH}}(\mathcal{C}) + \frac{Q_S \cdot (Q_S + Q_{\mathcal{H}} + N + 1)}{q^2} + \frac{(N+1)\cdot(Q_{\mathcal{H}_{FS}} \cdot \log(Q_V) + 2Q_{\mathcal{H}_{FS}} + 2)}{q}.$$

Proof. We proceed via a sequence of games between the adversary $\mathcal{A}$ and the challenger $\mathcal{CH}$, let W_i be the event that $\mathcal{A}$ wins in Game i.

Game 0. This is the original linkability game in Definition 6. $\Pr[W_0] = \mathsf{Adv}_{\mathsf{link}}(\mathcal{A})$.

Game 1. We modify the random oracle $\mathcal{H}$. It is the same with **Game 1** in proof of Theorem 1. $|\Pr[W_1] - \Pr[W_0]| < \frac{Q_S\cdot(Q_S+Q_{\mathcal{H}})}{q^2}$.

Game 2. We introduce failure events which cause $\mathcal{CH}$ fails. It is the same with **Game 2** in proof of Theorem 1. Since we consider $N+1$ forgeries in this case, $|\Pr[W_2] - \Pr[W_1]| \le \frac{(N+1)\cdot(Q_{\mathcal{H}_{FS}}+2)}{q} + \frac{(N+1)\cdot Q_S}{q^2}$.

Game 3. We now modify the key generation algorithm used by $\mathcal{CH}$. It is the same with **Game 3** in proof of Theorem 1. We have $\Pr[W_3] = \Pr[W_2]$.

Game 4. The adversary $\mathcal{A}$ outputs $N+1$ valid forgeries $\{M_k, \sigma_k, \mathcal{R}^* = \{X_i\}_{i\in[2N]}\}_{k\in[N+1]}$. For each signature $\sigma_k = (\boldsymbol{\Pi}_k, Z_k)$ parsed as in Eq. (11), $\mathcal{CH}$ first decrypts $\{\mathbf{C}_{l_j}\}_{j\in[1,n]}$ to obtain $l_1 \cdots l_n$. Then it computes $l = \sum_{j\in[1,n]} l_j \cdot 2^{j-1} \in [2N]$. From Lemma 3, we have $\log_g X_l = \log_h Z_k$ except with the probability $\frac{Q_{\mathcal{H}_{FS}}\cdot(\log(Q_V)+1)}{q}$. Thus we have $|\Pr[W_4] - \Pr[W_3]| \le \frac{Q_{\mathcal{H}_{FS}}\cdot(N+1)\cdot(\log(Q_V)+1)}{q}$

If $\mathcal{A}$ wins in **Game 4**, we construct a CDH solver $\mathcal{C}$ who takes $(\bar{X}, \bar{Y})$ as input, successfully outputs $\bar{Z}$ such that $\log_g \bar{X} = \log_{\bar{Y}} \bar{Z}$. At the end of this game, the forger $\mathcal{A}$ outputs $\{M_k, \sigma_k, \mathcal{R}^* = \{X_\xi^{(0)}, X_\xi^{(1)}\}_{\xi\in[N]}\}_{k\in[N+1]}$, $\mathcal{C}$ parses each signature σ_k as $\sigma_k = (\boldsymbol{\Pi}_k, Z_k)$ and recalls each secret key $SK_\xi = (b_\xi, x_\xi)$ with $X_\xi^{(b_\xi)} = g^{x_\xi}$. Since $\{M_k, \sigma_k, \mathcal{R}^*\}_{k\in[N+1]}$ are $N+1$ unlinked signatures on N public keys, so there exists at least one of $\{Z_k\}_{k\in[N+1]}$ which does not belong to $\{h^{x_\xi}\}_{\xi\in[N]}$. We assume it is Z_t in $\sigma_t = (\boldsymbol{\Pi}_t, Z_t)$ for some $t \in [N+1]$. The solver $\mathcal{C}$ proceeds to run **Game 4** with $\mathcal{A}$ with the following modifications:

1. $\mathcal{C}$ sets $h = \bar{Y}$ instead of picking $h \xleftarrow{\$} \mathbb{G}$, sends the common public parameter $pp = (\lambda, \mathbb{G}, g, h)$ to $\mathcal{A}$.
2. On each key generation query, $\mathcal{C}$ picks $\alpha \xleftarrow{\$} \mathbb{Z}_q$ and sets $X^{(1-b)} = \bar{X}^{\alpha}$. The algorithm adds $(X^{(1-b)}, \alpha)$ in table $\mathcal{L}$.

Upon receiving $\{M_k, \sigma_k, \mathcal{R}^*\}_{k \in [N+1]}$, $\mathcal{C}$ finds one signature $\sigma_t = (\mathbf{\Pi}_t, Z_t)$ parsed as in Eq. (11) such that Z_t does not belong to $\{h^{x_\xi}\}_{\xi \in [N]}$ for some $t \in [N+1]$. Then it does as follows.

1. Denote $\mathbf{C}_{l_j} = (R_{j,1}, R_{j,2})$. Compute $H = \mathcal{H}(\mathcal{R}^*, M_t, \{R_{j,1}\}_{j \in [1,n]})$, recall the previously defined exponent $\gamma \in \mathbb{Z}_q$ such that $H = g^{\gamma}$. Compute $g^{l_j} = R_{j,2}/R_{j,1}^{\gamma}$, determine $l_j \in \{0,1\}$ for each $j \in [1,n]$.
2. Having obtained the n-bit string $l_1 \cdots l_n \in \{0,1\}^n$ as the bit representation of l, compute $\pi = \lfloor l/2 \rfloor \in [N]$ and recall $(X_{\pi}^{(1-b_\pi)}, \alpha_\pi) \in \mathcal{L}$. Output $\bar{Z} = Z_t^{\frac{1}{\alpha_\pi}}$.

It is clear that $\mathcal{C}$ perfectly simulates **Game 4** for the adversary $\mathcal{A}$. In this game, the winning of $\mathcal{A}$ requires that each forgery $\sigma_k = (\mathbf{\Pi}_k, Z_k)$ satisfies that $\log_h Z_k = \log_g X_l$ where l is decoded from $\{\mathbf{C}_{l_j}\}_{j \in [1,n]}$ in $\mathbf{\Pi}_k$. Thus, for the signature $\sigma_t = (\mathbf{\Pi}_t, Z_t)$ such that $Z_t \neq h^{x_\pi}$, we have the fact that $\log_h Z_t = \log_g X_{\pi}^{(1-b_\pi)}$. That is $\log_{\bar{Y}} Z_t = \log_g \bar{X}^{\alpha_\pi}$, which implies $\log_{\bar{Y}} Z_t^{\frac{1}{\alpha_\pi}} = \log_g \bar{X}$. $\Pr[W_3] = \mathsf{Adv}_{\mathsf{CDH}}(\mathcal{C})$.

In conclusion, we have that

$$\mathsf{Adv}_{\mathsf{forge}}(\mathcal{A}) \leq \mathsf{Adv}_{\mathsf{CDH}}(\mathcal{C}) + \frac{Q_S \cdot (Q_S + Q_{\mathcal{H}} + N + 1)}{q^2} + \frac{(N+1) \cdot (Q_{\mathcal{H}_{\mathsf{FS}}} \cdot \log(Q_V) + 2Q_{\mathcal{H}_{\mathsf{FS}}} + 2)}{q}.$$

Lemma 3. *For any PPT adversary $\mathcal{A}$, it outputs a valid forgery $(M^*, \sigma^*, \mathcal{R}^* = \{X_i\}_{i \in [2N]})$ such that **Verify**$(pp, M^*, \mathcal{R}^*, \sigma^*) = 1$, $\sigma^* = (\mathbf{\Pi}, Z)$ is parsed as in Eq. (11). Having decoded the n-bit string $l_1 \cdots l_n$ as the bit representation of $l \in [2N]$ from $\{\mathbf{C}_{l_j}\}_{j \in [1,n]}$, the probability of $\log_g X_l \neq \log_h Z$ is upper bounded by $\frac{Q_{\mathcal{H}_{FS}} \cdot (\log(Q_V)+1)}{q}$. (The proof of this lemma is similar to the proof of Lemma 2.)*

Theorem 4. *Let $\mathcal{A}$ be a PPT adversary against **anonymity** of our LRS scheme in the ROM, making at most $Q_{\mathcal{H}}$ and $Q_{\mathcal{H}_{FS}}$ queries to the random oracle $\mathcal{H}$ and $\mathcal{H}_{FS}$ respectively, then there exists a DDH distinguisher $\mathcal{B}$ such that $\mathsf{Adv}_{\mathsf{anon}}(\mathcal{A}) \leq \mathsf{Adv}_{\mathsf{DDH}}(\mathcal{B}) + \frac{Q_{\mathcal{H}} + Q_{\mathcal{H}_{FS}}}{q^2}$.*

Theorem 5. *Let $\mathcal{A}$ be a PPT adversary against **nonslanderability** of our LRS scheme in the ROM, making at most Q_V queries to the key generation oracle, $Q_{\mathcal{H}}$ and $Q_{\mathcal{H}_{FS}}$ queries to the random oracle $\mathcal{H}$ and $\mathcal{H}_{FS}$ respectively, then there exists a DDH distinguisher $\mathcal{B}$ such that $\mathsf{Adv}_{\mathsf{slander}} \leq \mathsf{Adv}_{\mathsf{DDH}}(\mathcal{B}) + \frac{Q_{\mathcal{H}_{FS}} \cdot \log(Q_V) + 2Q_{\mathcal{H}_{FS}} + 2}{q} + \frac{Q_{\mathcal{H}} + Q_{\mathcal{H}_{FS}}}{q^2}$.*

Acknowledgments. The work is supported by the National Key Research and Development Program of China (No. 2020YFA0309705), and the National Natural Science Foundation of China (No. 61802376).

References

1. Abdalla, M., Fouque, P.-A., Lyubashevsky, V., Tibouchi, M.: Tightly-secure signatures from lossy identification schemes. In: Pointcheval, D., Johansson, T. (eds.) EUROCRYPT 2012. LNCS, vol. 7237, pp. 572–590. Springer, Heidelberg (2012). https://doi.org/10.1007/978-3-642-29011-4_34
2. Au, M.H., Susilo, W., Yiu, S.-M.: Event-oriented k-times revocable-iff-linked group signatures. In: Batten, L.M., Safavi-Naini, R. (eds.) ACISP 2006. LNCS, vol. 4058, pp. 223–234. Springer, Heidelberg (2006). https://doi.org/10.1007/11780656_19
3. Bader, C.: Efficient signatures with tight real world security in the random-oracle model. In: Gritzalis, D., Kiayias, A., Askoxylakis, I. (eds.) CANS 2014. LNCS, vol. 8813, pp. 370–383. Springer, Cham (2014). https://doi.org/10.1007/978-3-319-12280-9_24
4. Bellare, M., Hofheinz, D., Yilek, S.: Possibility and impossibility results for encryption and commitment secure under selective opening. In: Joux, A. (ed.) EUROCRYPT 2009. LNCS, vol. 5479, pp. 1–35. Springer, Heidelberg (2009). https://doi.org/10.1007/978-3-642-01001-9_1
5. Bellare, M., Rogaway, P.: Random oracles are practical: a paradigm for designing efficient protocols. In: CCS, pp. 62–73. ACM (1993)
6. Bender, A., Katz, J., Morselli, R.: Ring signatures: stronger definitions, and constructions without random oracles. In: Halevi, S., Rabin, T. (eds.) TCC 2006. LNCS, vol. 3876, pp. 60–79. Springer, Heidelberg (2006). https://doi.org/10.1007/11681878_4
7. Boneh, D.: The decision Diffie-Hellman problem. In: Buhler, J.P. (ed.) ANTS 1998. LNCS, vol. 1423, pp. 48–63. Springer, Heidelberg (1998). https://doi.org/10.1007/BFb0054851
8. Chaum, D., van Heyst, E.: Group signatures. In: Davies, D.W. (ed.) EUROCRYPT 1991. LNCS, vol. 547, pp. 257–265. Springer, Heidelberg (1991). https://doi.org/10.1007/3-540-46416-6_22
9. Chow, S.S.M., Liu, J.K., Wong, D.S.: Robust receipt-free election system with ballot secrecy and verifiability. In: NDSS. The Internet Society (2008)
10. Dodis, Y., Kiayias, A., Nicolosi, A., Shoup, V.: Anonymous identification in *Ad Hoc* groups. In: Cachin, C., Camenisch, J.L. (eds.) EUROCRYPT 2004. LNCS, vol. 3027, pp. 609–626. Springer, Heidelberg (2004). https://doi.org/10.1007/978-3-540-24676-3_36
11. Esgin, M.F., Steinfeld, R., Sakzad, A., Liu, J.K., Liu, D.: Short lattice-based one-out-of-many proofs and applications to ring signatures. In: Deng, R.H., Gauthier-Umaña, V., Ochoa, M., Yung, M. (eds.) ACNS 2019. LNCS, vol. 11464, pp. 67–88. Springer, Cham (2019). https://doi.org/10.1007/978-3-030-21568-2_4
12. Fiat, A., Shamir, A.: How to prove yourself: practical solutions to identification and signature problems. In: Odlyzko, A.M. (ed.) CRYPTO 1986. LNCS, vol. 263, pp. 186–194. Springer, Heidelberg (1987). https://doi.org/10.1007/3-540-47721-7_12
13. Garg, S., Bhaskar, R., Lokam, S.V.: Improved bounds on security reductions for discrete log based signatures. In: Wagner, D. (ed.) CRYPTO 2008. LNCS, vol. 5157, pp. 93–107. Springer, Heidelberg (2008). https://doi.org/10.1007/978-3-540-85174-5_6

14. Gjøsteen, K., Jager, T.: Practical and tightly-secure digital signatures and authenticated key exchange. In: Shacham, H., Boldyreva, A. (eds.) CRYPTO 2018. LNCS, vol. 10992, pp. 95–125. Springer, Cham (2018). https://doi.org/10.1007/978-3-319-96881-0_4
15. Goh, E.-J., Jarecki, S.: A signature scheme as secure as the Diffie-Hellman problem. In: Biham, E. (ed.) EUROCRYPT 2003. LNCS, vol. 2656, pp. 401–415. Springer, Heidelberg (2003). https://doi.org/10.1007/3-540-39200-9_25
16. Groth, J., Kohlweiss, M.: One-out-of-many proofs: or how to leak a secret and spend a coin. In: Oswald, E., Fischlin, M. (eds.) EUROCRYPT 2015. LNCS, vol. 9057, pp. 253–280. Springer, Heidelberg (2015). https://doi.org/10.1007/978-3-662-46803-6_9
17. Libert, B., Ling, S., Nguyen, K., Wang, H.: Zero-knowledge arguments for lattice-based accumulators: logarithmic-size ring signatures and group signatures without trapdoors. In: Fischlin, M., Coron, J.-S. (eds.) EUROCRYPT 2016. LNCS, vol. 9666, pp. 1–31. Springer, Heidelberg (2016). https://doi.org/10.1007/978-3-662-49896-5_1
18. Libert, B., Peters, T., Qian, C.: Logarithmic-size ring signatures with tight security from the DDH assumption. In: Lopez, J., Zhou, J., Soriano, M. (eds.) ESORICS 2018. LNCS, vol. 11099, pp. 288–308. Springer, Cham (2018). https://doi.org/10.1007/978-3-319-98989-1_15
19. Liu, J.K., Wei, V.K., Wong, D.S.: Linkable spontaneous anonymous group signature for ad hoc groups. In: Wang, H., Pieprzyk, J., Varadharajan, V. (eds.) ACISP 2004. LNCS, vol. 3108, pp. 325–335. Springer, Heidelberg (2004). https://doi.org/10.1007/978-3-540-27800-9_28
20. Möller, B., Rupp, A.: Faster multi-exponentiation through caching: accelerating (EC)DSA signature verification. In: Ostrovsky, R., De Prisco, R., Visconti, I. (eds.) SCN 2008. LNCS, vol. 5229, pp. 39–56. Springer, Heidelberg (2008). https://doi.org/10.1007/978-3-540-85855-3_4
21. Naor, M.: Deniable ring authentication. In: Yung, M. (ed.) CRYPTO 2002. LNCS, vol. 2442, pp. 481–498. Springer, Heidelberg (2002). https://doi.org/10.1007/3-540-45708-9_31
22. Paillier, P., Vergnaud, D.: Discrete-log-based signatures may not be equivalent to discrete log. In: Roy, B. (ed.) ASIACRYPT 2005. LNCS, vol. 3788, pp. 1–20. Springer, Heidelberg (2005). https://doi.org/10.1007/11593447_1
23. Pointcheval, D., Stern, J.: Security proofs for signature schemes. In: Maurer, U. (ed.) EUROCRYPT 1996. LNCS, vol. 1070, pp. 387–398. Springer, Heidelberg (1996). https://doi.org/10.1007/3-540-68339-9_33
24. Rivest, R.L., Shamir, A., Tauman, Y.: How to leak a secret. In: Boyd, C. (ed.) ASIACRYPT 2001. LNCS, vol. 2248, pp. 552–565. Springer, Heidelberg (2001). https://doi.org/10.1007/3-540-45682-1_32
25. Schnorr, C.P.: Efficient identification and signatures for smart cards. In: Brassard, G. (ed.) CRYPTO 1989. LNCS, vol. 435, pp. 239–252. Springer, New York (1990). https://doi.org/10.1007/0-387-34805-0_22
26. Seurin, Y.: On the exact security of Schnorr-type signatures in the random oracle model. In: Pointcheval, D., Johansson, T. (eds.) EUROCRYPT 2012. LNCS, vol. 7237, pp. 554–571. Springer, Heidelberg (2012). https://doi.org/10.1007/978-3-642-29011-4_33
27. Stern, J.: A new paradigm for public key identification. IEEE Trans. Inf. Theory **42**(6), 1757–1768 (1996)

28. Sun, S.-F., Au, M.H., Liu, J.K., Yuen, T.H.: RingCT 2.0: a compact accumulator-based (linkable ring signature) protocol for blockchain cryptocurrency Monero. In: Foley, S.N., Gollmann, D., Snekkenes, E. (eds.) ESORICS 2017. LNCS, vol. 10493, pp. 456–474. Springer, Cham (2017). https://doi.org/10.1007/978-3-319-66399-9_25
29. Tsang, P.P., Wei, V.K.: Short linkable ring signatures for E-voting, E-cash and attestation. In: Deng, R.H., Bao, F., Pang, H.H., Zhou, J. (eds.) ISPEC 2005. LNCS, vol. 3439, pp. 48–60. Springer, Heidelberg (2005). https://doi.org/10.1007/978-3-540-31979-5_5
30. Wang, X., Chen, Y., Ma, X.: Adding linkability to ring signatures with one-time signatures. In: Lin, Z., Papamanthou, C., Polychronakis, M. (eds.) ISC 2019. LNCS, vol. 11723, pp. 445–464. Springer, Cham (2019). https://doi.org/10.1007/978-3-030-30215-3_22
31. Yuen, T.H., et al.: RingCT 3.0 for blockchain confidential transaction: shorter size and stronger security. In: Bonneau, J., Heninger, N. (eds.) FC 2020. LNCS, vol. 12059, pp. 464–483. Springer, Cham (2020). https://doi.org/10.1007/978-3-030-51280-4_25

More Efficient Construction of Anonymous Signatures

Yunfeng Ji[1,2], Yang Tao[1(✉)], and Rui Zhang[1,2(✉)]

[1] State Key Laboratory of Information Security, Institute of Information Engineering, Chinese Academy of Sciences, Beijing 100093, China
{jiyunfeng,taoyang,r-zhang}@iie.ac.cn

[2] School of Cyber Security, University of Chinese Academy of Sciences, Beijing 100049, China

Abstract. Anonymous signature is a cryptographic tool where the signature of a message can hide its identity of the signer as long as part of the signature is hidden from the verifier. It gives a handy protection of signer identity and is useful in key exchange, auctions and voting.

In this paper, we present a new generic construction of anonymous signatures, which is more practical and efficient than all the previous known constructions. For more practicability, we rewrite anonymous signature as two phases, namely signature-commit phase and identity-open phase, and manage to reduce operations in the signature-commit phase where all the participants should proceed, and generate a verification token using the secret key in the identity-open phase which is only required for minority. Moreover, our construction can utilize the structure of the underlying signature, hence it achieves a better efficiency than all the previous ones.

As an independent interest, we investigate whether the signatures from the third round finalists of NIST's PQC standardization are anonymous. Note that they were not designed to be anonymous. Though most of them are not anonymous, interestingly, using the above method we can transform them into anonymous signatures with almost no costs.

Keywords: Anonymous signature · Post-quantum security · Lattice-based signature

1 Introduction

The Concept. In an anonymous paper review system, an author Alice wants to reveal her identity if her paper is accepted, but to remain anonymous, otherwise. A cryptographic tool called anonymous signature [3,9,17–19] allows her to achieve the goal as follows. When Alice submits her paper, instead of a normal digital signature, she appends an anonymous signature to the paper, called signature-commit, which cannot be verified under Alice's verification key. Therewith, reviewers can not decide the authors of the papers, which has a protection against collusion between authors and reviewers. Later, when the paper is

D. Gao et al. (Eds.): ICICS 2021, LNCS 12919, pp. 394–411, 2021.
https://doi.org/10.1007/978-3-030-88052-1_23

accepted, Alice and only Alice can provide a verification token, called identity-open. Together with the anonymous signature, Alice's identity can be verified under her public key.

Anonymous signature was first formalized by Yang et al. [18]. Unlike group signature [4,7] and ring signature [5,16] with more advanced functionalities and complicated operations, anonymous signature offers a handy way to obtain anonymity in certain situations, for instance, key exchange protocols, auction systems, and anonymous paper reviewing.

There are three security requirements for anonymous signatures, i.e. unforgeability, anonymity, and unpretendability. Unforgeability not only means adversaries cannot forge a signature pair (i.e. anonymous signature and verification token) on a new message, but also requires they cannot forge a valid verification token even though given an anonymous signature on a message. Anonymity means that the signature-creator's identity cannot be determined from the message and anonymous signature without a verification token. Only the full signature pair can be verified under the public key. Unpretendability guarantees that even though given the message and anonymous signature, adversaries are unable to create a legal verification token under a freshly public key and pretend the ownership of the anonymous signature.

In the earliest work [18], Yang et al. presented three anonymous signatures with unforgeability and anonymity from Schnorr, RSA signature, and RSA-PSS respectively. Subsequently, Fischlin [9] proposed a generic construction of anonymous signatures without random oracles. Zhang and Imai [19] pointed out a limitation of the model of [9,18], and introduced a stronger model as well as a generic construction. Later, unpretendability was added to the model independently by Saraswat and Yun [17] and Bellare and Duan [3], also with generic constructions. Their frameworks essentially follow the same idea: The anonymous signature runs the underlying signature scheme at first, then generates a commitment of the public key and signature of the underlying scheme. In the signature-commit phase, the commitment is presented as the anonymous signature, and in the identity-open phase, a verification token (the decommitment and the signature of the underlying scheme) is presented, so signer's identity can be verified.

Motivation of This Work. Our key observation stems from the unbalanced computations in the above scenarios and generic constructions [3,17], where most of expensive computations (i.e. generating a signature and a commitment) are required in the signature-commit phase while few signatures are proceeded to open an identity. However, when revisiting the application of anonymous signature in the real-life, such as an anonymous paper reviewing system, we find that each author should proceed the signature-commit phase, while only few authors whose papers are accepted need to open their identities. That means, such most of the expensive computations in the signature-commit phase will be in vain since only minority should be opened.

Besides, with the rapid development of quantum computers, the security of the classical public-key cryptography has been threatened. In order to achieve a long-term security, it seems necessary to instantiate the generic construction using a post-quantum secure commitment and signature. But considering the bad efficiency and bandwidth of the known post-quantum commitments and signatures, "handy" anonymous signature seems difficult for a post-quantum era. On the other hand, since the signature-commit and identity-open phases together forms a normal signature, it is easy to see that the minimum computation cost is at least that of a normal signature. Hence, it is natural to ask:

Can we construct (post-quantum) secure anonymous signatures which are more efficient and practical in the real-life?

Our Treatments. In this paper, we study the above problem and give an affirmative answer. An anonymous signature contains two parts which can be used in two phases, namely signature-commit phase (Phase 1) and identity-open phase (Phase 2). The output of Phase 1 (i.e. anonymous signature σ) satisfies anonymity, and the output of the two phases (i.e. σ and verification token τ) should satisfy unforgeability and unpretendability. Notice all participators in the anonymous paper reviewing system should proceed Phase 1 and a minority of them take part in Phase 2, our strategy is making an adjustment between the two phases to reduce operations in Phase 1.

Note that [3,17] used a sign-then-commit strategy where in Phase 1, a signer presents a commitment of the public key and signature of the ordinary unforgeable signature. However, we find it suffices to make the anonymous signature σ a commitment of the message and public key for anonymity and unpretendability. Suppose $(\sigma, r) \leftarrow \mathsf{Com}(m, pk)$ with the commit algorithm Com, message m, signer's public key pk, and the decommitment r. In the signature-commit phase, only σ needs to be presented. Later, in the identity-open phase, to open the anonymity, a verification token $\tau \leftarrow (\sigma^*, r)$ is generated by $\sigma^* \leftarrow \mathsf{Sig}(sk, \sigma)$, where Sig is a signing algorithm with the secret key sk. Then given τ, the signature pair (m, σ, τ) can be publicly verified using pk.

Our construction is secure, and it enjoys fewer operations in Phase 1 than [3,17]. Roughly speaking, anonymity requires that given m, the output of Phase 1 should reveal no information of pk. That can be satisfied since Com can hide the information of the input. Unforgeability requires that adversaries cannot forge a full signature pair even if given σ, which can be satisfied if the underlying signature is unforgeable. And unpretendability requires that given σ, it is hard to find pk' and τ', s.t. $pk \neq pk'$ and (σ, τ') can be verified. Due to σ is binding on pk and m, it is difficult to find an appropriate pair of pk' and τ'. So unpretendability is satisfied.

In practice, one always uses hash-then-sign approach. Therefore, in the standard model, when a hash function is instantiated with a collision-resistant exposure resilient function (CR-ERF) [19] which can be viewed as a commitment, we can sign the commitment directly in the identity-open phase rather than hashing the commitment then signing. When considering instantiations in the random oracle model, we can use a hash function (treated as a random oracle) as a commitment in Phase 1 and then sign its output directly in Phase 2.

The above treatments bring almost no additional computation cost, and much less computation in Phase 1 than [3,17]. In particular, in the above mentioned scenarios, most anonymous signatures will not be opened, hence our construction is more desirable. In addition, an "instant open" is possible in Phase 2, if one does the computations till that required by the identity-open phase offline.

Our Results. Our contributions are two-fold. First, we present an efficient and practical generic framework for anonymous signatures. Second, we investigate whether NIST's third round signature candidates are anonymous signatures.

In comparison with the previous generic constructions [3,17][1], our method is more practical and efficient. As shown in Table 1, our construction is "commit-then-sign", while the existing constructions in [3,17] are "sign-then-commit". Thus, we can reduce lots of operations in Phase 1. Besides, the commitment in our work can take place of the random oracle or hash function of Sig, which allows our construction to make full use of the underlying signature, so the signing algorithm Sig in our construction has better performance in total computation than [3,17].

As an independent interest, we also analyze whether the signature candidates in NIST's third round, i.e. Dilithium [11], Falcon [15] and Rainbow [8], are anonymous signatures. Interestingly, Dilithium is a secure anonymous signature (with proper treatments), while Falcon and Rainbow are not. However, using our

Table 1. Comparisons on the known constructions of anonymous signature

Constructions	[17]	[3]	This work
Phase 1	$\sigma^* \leftarrow \mathsf{Sig}(sk, m)$ $(\sigma, r) \leftarrow \mathsf{Com}(\sigma^*\|\|pk)$ output σ	$\tau \leftarrow \mathsf{Sig}(sk, m)$ $\sigma \leftarrow \mathsf{H}(\tau\|\|pk)$ output σ	$(\sigma, r) \leftarrow \mathsf{Com}(m, pk)$ output σ
Phase 2	$\tau \leftarrow r\|\|\sigma^*$ output τ	output τ	$\sigma^* \leftarrow \mathsf{Sig}(sk, \sigma)$ $\tau \leftarrow (\sigma^*, r)$ output τ

‡ We denote Sig a signing algorithm, Com a commitment algorithm and H a random oracle.

Table 2. Comparisons on the efficiency of post-quantum anonymous signatures

Constructions		Falcon	Dilithium	Rainbow
Ordinary schemes		291.886 μs	1167.127 μs	1329.718 μs
This work	**Phase 1**	**17.745** μs	**13.597** μs	**16.532** μs
	Phase 2	275.369 μs	1167.186 μs	1328.657 μs
	Total	293.114 μs	1180.783 μs	1345.189 μs
[3,17]	**Phase 1**	**312.496** μs	**1181.263** μs	**1348.172** μs
	Phase 2	0.816 μs	0.742 μs	0.953 μs
	Total	313.312 μs	1182.005 μs	1349.125 μs

[1] Since the construction in [19] did not consider unpretendability, we just compare our work with [17] and [3].

framework, we can transform all of them into practical anonymous signatures with almost no additional cost. For more accurate discussions, we implement the anonymous signatures under the above generic constructions based on these three schemes. The commitments are instantiated with random oracles for efficiency. As shown in Table 2, our construction brings a marginal increase in the cost of time compared with the ordinary schemes, and it has better performance in terms of time complexity than [3,17] in Phase 1, which is only 1.2% of [3,17] for Dilithium and Rainbow and 5.6% of [3,17] for Falcon.

Organization of the Rest of the Paper. In Sect. 2, we review some useful notations, definitions and facts. In Sect. 3, we present a generic construction of anonymous signatures and give two instantiations of anonymous signatures in the random oracle model. Then we analyze whether NIST's third round finalist signature schemes are anonymous in Sect. 4. Finally, we give the conclusion in Sect. 5.

2 Preliminary

In this section, we review some useful notations, definitions and facts.

Notations. Throughout the paper, we denote the real number by $\mathbb{R}$, natural number by $\mathbb{N}$, integers by $\mathbb{Z}$, and finite field by $\mathbb{F}$. We assume that q is a prime number and identify $\mathbb{Z}_q$ with the interval $[-\frac{q}{2}, \frac{q}{2}) \cap \mathbb{Z}$. Vectors are assumed to be in column form. We denote column vectors over $\mathbb{R}$ and $\mathbb{Z}$ with boldface small letters (e.g. $\mathbf{x}$), and matrices by boldface capital letters (e.g. $\mathbf{A}$). We denote the matrix $\mathbf{A_1}||\mathbf{A_2}$ as the matrix concatenating matrices $\mathbf{A_1}$ and $\mathbf{A_2}$. The l_p-norm of a vector $\mathbf{a}$ is denoted by $\|\mathbf{a}\|_p = (\sum_i |a_i|^p)^{\frac{1}{p}}$. If S is a set, denote the uniform distribution over S as $U(S)$ and choosing s uniformly from S as $s \leftarrow S$. We write $s||t$ as the string concatenation of s and t. If $k \in \mathbb{N}$, a function $f(k)$ is negligible if $\exists k_0 \in \mathbb{N}, \forall k > k_0, f(k) < 1/k^c$, where $c > 0$ is a constant.

2.1 Lattices and Gaussian

Below we review some facts regarding lattices and Gaussian.

Lattices. An n-dimension (full-rank) lattice $\Lambda \subseteq \mathbb{R}^n$ is a set of all integer linear combinations of some set of independent basis vectors $\mathbf{B} = \{\mathbf{b}_1, \ldots, \mathbf{b}_n\} \subseteq \mathbb{R}^n$, $\Lambda = \mathcal{L}(\mathbf{B}) = \{\sum_{i=1}^n z_i \mathbf{b}_i | z_i \in \mathbb{Z}\}$. The dual lattice of $\Lambda \subseteq \mathbb{R}^n$ is defined as $\Lambda^* = \{\mathbf{x} \in \mathbb{R}^n | \langle \Lambda, \mathbf{x} \rangle \subseteq \mathbb{Z}\}$. Define the determinant of Λ to be $\det(\Lambda) = \sqrt{\det(\mathbf{B}^\mathsf{T}\mathbf{B})}$. We have $\det(\Lambda) = \dfrac{1}{\det(\Lambda^*)}$. For integers $n \geq 1$, modulus $q \geq 2$ and $\mathbf{A} \in \mathbb{Z}_q^{n \times \bar{m}}$, an $\bar{m}$-dimensional lattice is defined as $\Lambda^\perp(\mathbf{A}) = \{\mathbf{x} \in \mathbb{Z}^{\bar{m}} | \mathbf{A}\mathbf{x} = \mathbf{0} \in \mathbb{Z}_q^n\} \subseteq \mathbb{Z}^{\bar{m}}$. For any $\mathbf{y}$ in the subgroup of $\mathbb{Z}_q^n$, we also define the coset $\Lambda_\mathbf{y}^\perp(\mathbf{A}) = \{\mathbf{x} \in \mathbb{Z}^{\bar{m}} | \mathbf{A}\mathbf{x} = \mathbf{y} \bmod q\} = \Lambda^\perp(\mathbf{A}) + \bar{\mathbf{x}}$, where $\bar{\mathbf{x}} \in \mathbb{Z}^{\bar{m}}$ is an arbitrary solution to $\mathbf{A}\bar{\mathbf{x}} = \mathbf{y}$.

Gaussian. For any $\mathbf{c} \in \mathbb{R}^n$ and $\sigma > 0$, the n-dimensional Gaussian function $\rho_{\sigma,\mathbf{c}} : \mathbb{R}^n \to (0, 1]$ is defined as $\rho_{\sigma,\mathbf{c}}(\mathbf{x}) := (\frac{1}{\sqrt{2\pi}\sigma})^n \exp(-\|\mathbf{x} - \mathbf{c}\|_2^2/2\sigma^2)$.[2] Let Λ be a lattice in $\mathbb{Z}^n$, the discrete Gaussian distribution over Λ with parameter σ and center $\mathbf{c}$ (abbreviated as $D_{\Lambda,\sigma,\mathbf{c}}$) is defined as $\forall \mathbf{y} \in \Lambda, D_{\Lambda,\sigma,\mathbf{c}}(\mathbf{y}) := \frac{\rho_{\sigma,\mathbf{c}}(\mathbf{y})}{\rho_{\sigma,\mathbf{c}}(\Lambda)}$, where $\rho_{\sigma,\mathbf{c}}(\Lambda) = \sum_{\mathbf{y}\in\Lambda} \rho_{\sigma,\mathbf{c}}(\mathbf{y})$. When $\mathbf{c} = \mathbf{0}$, we write ρ_σ and $D_{\Lambda,\sigma}$ for short.

Lemma 1 ([14]). *For any n-dimensional lattice Λ, center $\mathbf{c} \in \mathbb{R}^n$, positive $\epsilon > 0$, and $s \geq 2\eta_\epsilon(\Lambda)$, and for every $\mathbf{x} \in \Lambda$, we have*

$$D_{\Lambda,s,\mathbf{c}}(\mathbf{x}) \geq \frac{1+\epsilon}{1-\epsilon} \cdot 2^{-n}.$$

In particular, for $\epsilon < \frac{1}{3}$, the min-entropy of $D_{\Lambda,s,\mathbf{c}}$ is at least $n - 1$.

2.2 Lattice-Based Signatures in the Random Oracle Model

We now review two types of lattice-based signature schemes in the random oracle model.

Full-Domain Hash Signature. At STOC 2008, Gentry, Peikert and Vaikuntanathan [10] presented a framework for obtaining secure full-domain hash lattice-based signature schemes in the random oracle model. The framework can be described as follows.

- Key Generation $(sk, pk) \leftarrow \mathsf{KeyGen}(1^\lambda)$: Given a security parameter λ, the algorithm generates a random matrix $\mathbf{A} \in \mathbb{Z}_q^{n\times\bar{m}}$ as the public key pk, and a short basis $\mathbf{B} \in \mathbb{Z}_q^{\bar{m}\times\bar{m}}$ of the orthogonal lattice $\Lambda^\perp(\mathbf{A})$ as the secret key sk.
- Signing $(r, \mathbf{s}) \leftarrow \mathsf{Sig}(sk, m)$: Given a message m, the algorithm samples $r \leftarrow \{0, 1\}^l$, then computes $\mathbf{c} \leftarrow H(m, r)$ and an arbitrary "specific solution" $\mathbf{y} \in \mathbb{Z}_q^{\bar{m}}$ satisfying $\mathbf{Ay} = \mathbf{c}$, where $H : \{0, 1\}^* \to \mathbb{Z}_q^n$ is a random oracle. Then using $\mathbf{B}$, the algorithm samples $\mathbf{x} \leftarrow D_{\Lambda^\perp(\mathbf{A}),\sigma,-\mathbf{y}}$, and computes $\mathbf{s} \leftarrow \mathbf{y} + \mathbf{x}$. The signature of m is $(r, \mathbf{s})$.
- Verification $\beta \leftarrow \mathsf{Ver}(pk, m, (r, \mathbf{s}))$: Given the message m and signature $(r, \mathbf{s})$, the algorithm outputs a symbol $\beta \in \{0, 1\}$. $\beta = 1$ (accept the signature) if and only if $\|\mathbf{s}\|_2$ is indeed short and $\mathbf{As} = H(m, r)$.

Fiat-Shamir with Aborts Signature. The lattice-based Fiat-Shamir signature schemes use a 3-round public-coin identification scheme and a hash function as a random oracle, which can be described as follows[3].

[2] In [1,10,12,13], Gaussian function can also be denoted as $\rho_{r,\mathbf{c}}(\mathbf{x}) := \exp(-\pi\|\mathbf{x} - \mathbf{c}\|_2^2/r^2)/r$. The two descriptions of Gaussian functions are equivalent when $r = \sqrt{2\pi}\sigma$.

[3] For simplicity, we just consider the algorithms defined in the plain lattices, which can be trivially extended to algebraic lattices.

- Key Generation $(sk, pk) \leftarrow \mathsf{KeyGen}(1^\lambda)$: Given a security parameter λ, the algorithm generates an uniform matrix $\mathbf{S} \in \{-d, \cdots, 0, \cdots, d\}^{\bar{m} \times k}$ as the secret key sk, and matrices $(\mathbf{A}, \mathbf{T})$ as the public key pk, where $\mathbf{A} \leftarrow \mathbb{Z}_q^{n \times \bar{m}}$ and $\mathbf{T} = \mathbf{AS} \mod q$.
- Signing $(\mathbf{c}, \mathbf{z}) \leftarrow \mathsf{Sig}(sk, m)$: Given a message m, the algorithm samples a randomness $\mathbf{y} \leftarrow D_\sigma^{\bar{m}}$, and computes $\mathbf{c} \leftarrow H(\mathbf{Ay}, m)$, where $H : \{0,1\}^* \to \mathbb{B}_\kappa$ acts as a random oracle with $\mathbb{B}_\kappa = \{\mathbf{v} : \mathbf{v} \in \{-1, 0, 1\}^k, \|\mathbf{v}\|_1 \leq \kappa\}$. Then using secret key $\mathbf{S}$, the algorithm computes $\mathbf{z} \leftarrow \mathbf{Sc} + \mathbf{y}$ and outputs the signature $(\mathbf{c}, \mathbf{z})$ of the message m with probability $\min\{\frac{D_\sigma^{\bar{m}}(\mathbf{z})}{M D_{\mathbf{Sc},\sigma}^{\bar{m}}(\mathbf{z})}, 1\}$, where M is a constant. Otherwise, repeat the whole signing algorithm from the beginning.
- Verification $\beta \leftarrow \mathsf{Ver}(pk, m, (\mathbf{c}, \mathbf{z}))$: Given the message m and signature $(\mathbf{c}, \mathbf{z})$, the algorithm outputs a symbol $\beta \in \{0, 1\}$. $\beta = 1$ (accept the signature) if and only if $\|\mathbf{z}\|_2$ is indeed short and $\mathbf{c} = H(\mathbf{Az} - \mathbf{Tc}, m)$.

2.3 Anonymous Signature

An anonymous signature scheme $\mathrm{A}\Sigma = (\mathsf{AKeyGen}, \mathsf{ASig}, \mathsf{AVer})$ consists of 3 probabilistic polynomial time (PPT) algorithms.

- Key Generation $(sk, pk) \leftarrow \mathsf{AKeyGen}(1^\lambda)$: The randomized key generation algorithm $\mathsf{AKeyGen}$ takes a security parameter λ as input, and generates a pair of secret key sk and public key pk.
- Signing $(\sigma, \tau) \leftarrow \mathsf{ASig}(sk, pk, m)$: The possibly randomized signing algorithm ASig takes the secret key sk, public key pk and $m \in \mathcal{M}$ as input, where m is a message and $\mathcal{M}$ is the message space.
  - In the signature-commit phase (Phase 1), the algorithm outputs an anonymous signature σ.
  - In the identity-open phase (Phase 2), the algorithm outputs a verification token τ.

  Output the signature (σ, τ) of message m.
- Verification $\beta \leftarrow \mathsf{AVer}(pk, m, (\sigma, \tau))$: The deterministic verification algorithm AVer takes public key pk, message m, and signature pair (σ, τ) as input, then outputs a symbol $\beta \in \{0, 1\}$. $\beta = 1$ if and only if accepting the signature pair, otherwise $\beta = 0$.

We require that for any key pair $(sk, pk) \leftarrow \mathsf{AKeyGen}(1^\lambda)$ and any message $m \in \mathcal{M}$, $\mathsf{AVer}(pk, m, \mathsf{ASig}(sk, m)) = 1$. For a secure anonymous signature, there are three security requirements, i.e. unforgeability, anonymity [19] and unpretendability [3,17].

Unforgeability. Besides an adversary cannot forge a signature pair (i.e. anonymous signature and verification token) on a new message, unforgeability also need an adversary cannot forge a valid verification token, even given an anonymous signature on a message. Let λ be a security parameter, $\mathrm{A}\Sigma = (\mathsf{AKeyGen}, \mathsf{ASig}, \mathsf{AVer})$ be an anonymous signature scheme, and $\mathcal{A}$ be a PPT adversary. Denote $\mathcal{L}_1$ as the transcript containing all the interactions between $\mathcal{A}$ and $\mathcal{SO}_1$, where $\mathcal{SO}_1$ is a signing oracle that for the input message m, returns a corresponding full signature pair $(\sigma, \tau) \leftarrow \mathsf{ASig}(sk, m)$. Denote $\mathcal{L}_2$ as the interactions between $\mathcal{A}$ and $\mathcal{SO}_2$. The difference of $\mathcal{SO}_2$ from $\mathcal{SO}_1$ is that it only returns an anonymous signature σ.

Definition 1 (Unforgeability). *We say* $\mathrm{A}\Sigma$ *is unforgeable if the advantage of any PPT adversary* $\mathcal{A}$ *is negligible in the following experiment.*

$$Adv^{\mathsf{UF}}_{\mathrm{A}\Sigma,\mathcal{A}}(1^\lambda) = \Pr[(sk, pk) \leftarrow \mathsf{AKeyGen}(1^\lambda); (m^*, \sigma^*, \tau^*) \leftarrow \mathcal{A}^{\mathcal{SO}_1, \mathcal{SO}_2}(pk) : \mathsf{AVer}(pk, m^*, (\sigma^*, \tau^*)) = 1 \wedge m^* \notin \mathcal{L}_1].$$

Anonymity. Let λ be a security parameter, $\mathrm{A}\Sigma = (\mathsf{AKeyGen}, \mathsf{ASig}, \mathsf{AVer})$ be an anonymous signature scheme, and $\mathcal{A}$ be a PPT adversary. Denote $\mathcal{SO}$ as a signing oracle that returns the corresponding full signature pair (σ, τ) on a signing query m, and st be the state information for $\mathcal{A}$. Intuitively, anonymity means given the challenge anonymous signature part σ^* (without its verification token τ^*), the adversary cannot distinguish its public key.

Definition 2 (Anonymity). *We say* $\mathrm{A}\Sigma$ *is anonymous if the advantage of any PPT adversary* $\mathcal{A}$ *is negligible in the following experiment.*

$$\begin{aligned} Adv^{\mathsf{Anon}}_{\mathrm{A}\Sigma,\mathcal{A}}(1^\lambda) = |\Pr[&(sk_0, pk_0) \leftarrow \mathsf{AKeyGen}(1^\lambda); \\ &(sk_1, pk_1) \leftarrow \mathsf{AKeyGen}(1^\lambda); (m, st) \leftarrow \mathcal{A}^{\mathcal{SO}}(pk_0, pk_1); b \leftarrow \{0,1\}; \\ &(\sigma^*, \tau^*) \leftarrow \mathsf{ASig}(sk_b, pk_b, m); b' \leftarrow \mathcal{A}^{\mathcal{SO}}(\sigma^*, st) : b' = b] - 1/2|. \end{aligned}$$

Unpretendability. Unpretendability means an adversary pretends the ownership of an anonymous signature with a verification token under its chosen fresh public key is infeasible. Let λ be a security parameter, $\mathcal{A}$ be a PPT adversary, and $\mathrm{A}\Sigma = (\mathsf{AKeyGen}, \mathsf{ASig}, \mathsf{AVer})$ be an anonymous signature scheme. Denote $\mathcal{SO}$ as a signing oracle that returns the corresponding full signature pair (σ, τ) on a signing query m, and st be the state information for $\mathcal{A}$.

Definition 3 (Unpretendability). *We say* $\mathrm{A}\Sigma$ *is unpretendable if the advantage of any PPT adversary* $\mathcal{A}$ *is negligible in the following experiment.*

$$\begin{aligned} Adv^{\mathsf{UP}}_{\mathrm{A}\Sigma,\mathcal{A}}(1^\lambda) = \Pr[&(sk^*, pk^*) \leftarrow \mathsf{AKeyGen}(1^\lambda); (m^*, st) \leftarrow \mathcal{A}^{\mathcal{SO}}(pk^*); \\ &(\sigma^*, \tau^*) \leftarrow \mathsf{ASig}(sk^*, pk^*, m^*); (\tau, pk) \leftarrow \mathcal{A}^{\mathcal{SO}}(\sigma^*, \tau^*, st) : \\ &\mathsf{AVer}(pk, m^*, (\sigma^*, \tau)) = 1 \wedge (pk \neq pk^*)]. \end{aligned}$$

If $\mathrm{A}\Sigma = (\mathsf{AKeyGen}, \mathsf{ASig}, \mathsf{AVer})$ is unforgeable, anonymous and unpretendable, we say it is a secure anonymous signature scheme.

2.4 Commitment Schemes

A commitment scheme allows a party to commit to a message m by publishing a commitment *com*, which can be opened with a decommitment *dec* at a later point in time, and the receiver will be convinced that the sender did not change his mind. A commitment scheme $\Gamma = (\mathsf{Com}, \mathsf{CVer})$ consists of a pair of algorithms satisfying the following.

- Commitment $(com, dec) \leftarrow \mathsf{Com}(m)$: The commitment algorithm Com takes a message m from a message space $\mathcal{M}$ as input, and generates a pair of commitment *com* and decommitment *dec*.
- Commitment Verification $\beta \leftarrow \mathsf{CVer}(m, (com, dec))$: The commitment verification algorithm CVer takes a message m, a pair of commitment *com* and decommitment *dec* as input, then outputs a symbol $\beta \in \{0,1\}$. $\beta = 1$ if and only if accepting the commitment, otherwise $\beta = 0$.

We require that for any message $m \in \mathcal{M}$, $\mathsf{CVer}(m, \mathsf{Com}(m)) = 1$. Besides, a secure commitment scheme should satisfies the following security properties:

Hiding. Hiding means that the receiver cannot learn anything about the committed message m from the commitment *com*. Let λ be a security parameter, and $\Gamma = (\mathsf{Com}, \mathsf{CVer})$ be a commitment scheme. Denote $\mathcal{A}$ as a PPT adversary, and *st* as the state information for $\mathcal{A}$.

Definition 4 (Hiding). *We say Γ satisfies hiding if the advantage of any PPT adversary $\mathcal{A}$ is negligible in the following experiment.*

$$Adv^{\mathsf{Hide}}_{\Gamma,\mathcal{A}}(1^\lambda) = |\Pr[(m_0, m_1, st) \leftarrow \mathcal{A}(1^\lambda); b \leftarrow \{0,1\}; (com, dec) \leftarrow \mathsf{Com}(m_b); \\ b' \leftarrow \mathcal{A}(com, st) : b' = b] - 1/2|.$$

We require the adversary $\mathcal{A}$ to output m_0, m_1 of the same length.

Binding. The binding property means that the sender cannot open a commitment *com* to two different messages m and m'. Let λ be a security parameter, and $\Gamma = (\mathsf{Com}, \mathsf{CVer})$ be a commitment scheme. Denote $\mathcal{A}$ as a PPT adversary, and *st* as the state information for $\mathcal{A}$.

Definition 5 (Binding). *We say Γ satisfies binding if the advantage of any PPT adversary $\mathcal{A}$ is negligible in the following experiment.*

$$Adv^{\mathsf{Bind}}_{\Gamma,\mathcal{A}}(1^\lambda) = \Pr[(com, dec, m, dec', m') \leftarrow \mathcal{A}(1^\lambda); \beta \leftarrow \mathsf{CVer}(m, (com, dec)); \\ \beta' \leftarrow \mathsf{CVer}(m', (com, dec')) : \beta \wedge \beta' \wedge (m \neq m')].$$

An efficient construction of commitment using a random oracle can be described as follows.

- Commitment $(c, r) \leftarrow \mathsf{Com}(m)$: The commitment algorithm samples $r \leftarrow \{0,1\}^l$, then computes $c \leftarrow H(m, r)$, where $H : \{0,1\}^* \rightarrow \{0,1\}^k$ is a random oracle. c is a commitment and r is the decommitment.
- Commitment Verification $\beta \leftarrow \mathsf{CVer}(m, (c, r))$: Given a message m, a pair of commitment c and decommitment r, the algorithm outputs a symbol $\beta \in \{0,1\}$. $\beta = 1$ (accepting the commitment) if and only if $c = H(m, r)$.

3 A Generic Construction of Anonymous Signatures

In this section, we propose a generic construction of anonymous signatures, which consists of two phases, namely signature-commit phase (Phase 1) and identity-open phase (Phase 2). Phase 1 of the construction needs a commitment scheme, while Phase 2 needs an unforgeable signature scheme. Moreover, we give some instantiations in the random oracle model, interestingly, our construction can make full use of the structure of the underlying signature schemes and achieve anonymous signatures with marginal cost.

3.1 Construction of Anonymous Signatures

Supposed $\Sigma = (\mathsf{KeyGen}, \mathsf{Sig}, \mathsf{Ver})$ is a signature scheme, and $\Gamma = (\mathsf{Com}, \mathsf{CVer})$ is a commitment scheme, our construction $\mathrm{A}\Sigma = (\mathsf{AKeyGen}, \mathsf{ASig}, \mathsf{AVer})$ can be described as follows.

- Key Generation $(sk, pk) \leftarrow \mathsf{AKeyGen}(1^\lambda)$: Given a security parameter λ, the algorithm calls $\mathsf{KeyGen}(1^\lambda)$ to generate a pair of secret key sk and public key pk.
- Signing $(\sigma, \tau) \leftarrow \mathsf{ASig}(sk, pk, m)$: The signing algorithm is divided into two phases by invoking the algorithm Sig and Com.
  - In the signature-commit phase (Phase 1), the algorithm calls Com with the input $m||pk$ and gets the output $(\sigma, r) \leftarrow \mathsf{Com}(m||pk)$. Then, it returns σ as the anonymous signature.
  - In the identity-open phase (Phase 2), given the output σ of Phase 1 and the decommitment r, the algorithm calls Sig with the secret key sk and σ to get the output $\sigma^* \leftarrow \mathsf{Sig}(sk, \sigma)$, then it returns $\tau \leftarrow (\sigma^*, r)$ as the verification token.
- Verification $\beta \leftarrow \mathsf{AVer}(pk, m, (\sigma, \tau))$: Given the public key pk, message m and signature pair (σ, τ) as input, the algorithm parses τ as (τ_1, τ_2) and outputs a symbol $\beta \in \{0, 1\}$. $\beta = 1$ (accept the signature pair) if and only if $\mathsf{Ver}(pk, \sigma, \tau_1) = 1$ and $\mathsf{CVer}(m||pk, \sigma, \tau_2) = 1$.

Theorem 1. *If the underlying signature scheme Σ is unforgeable, then $\mathrm{A}\Sigma$ is a secure anonymous signature.*

Proof. We show that $\mathrm{A}\Sigma$ satisfies the unforgeability, anonymity and unpretendability.

Unforgeability. Let $\mathcal{A}_{\mathrm{A}\Sigma}$ be a PPT adversary attacking the unforgeability of the signature scheme $\mathrm{A}\Sigma$, we can construct an efficient adversary $\mathcal{A}_\Sigma$ that attacks the unforgeability of Σ using $\mathcal{A}_{\mathrm{A}\Sigma}$ as a subroutine.

For setup, $\mathcal{A}_\Sigma$ runs $\mathsf{AKeyGen}(1^\lambda)$ to generate a pair of key (sk, pk), then gives pk to $\mathcal{A}_{\mathrm{A}\Sigma}$. When $\mathcal{A}_{\mathrm{A}\Sigma}$ makes its signing query to $\mathcal{SO}_1$ on m_1, $\mathcal{A}_\Sigma$ computes $(\sigma_{m_1}, r_{m_1}) \leftarrow \mathsf{Com}(m_1||pk)$, then makes a query on σ_{m_1} to its own signing oracle. After getting an answer $\sigma^*_{m_1}$, it sets $\tau_{m_1} \leftarrow (\sigma^*_{m_1}, r_{m_1})$ and returns $(\sigma_{m_1}, \tau_{m_1})$

to $\mathcal{A}_{\mathrm{A}\Sigma}$. When $\mathcal{A}_{\mathrm{A}\Sigma}$ makes its signing query to $\mathcal{SO}_2$ on m_2, $\mathcal{A}_\Sigma$ just computes $(\sigma_{m_2}, r_{m_2}) \leftarrow \mathsf{Com}(m_2||pk)$ and returns σ_{m_2} to $\mathcal{A}_{\mathrm{A}\Sigma}$.

Denote $\mathcal{L}_1(\mathcal{L}_2)$ as the interactions between $\mathcal{A}_{\mathrm{A}\Sigma}$ and $\mathcal{SO}_1(\mathcal{SO}_2)$. If $\mathcal{A}_{\mathrm{A}\Sigma}$ outputs a forged signature pair (σ', τ') on a message $m' \notin \mathcal{L}_1$ for $\mathrm{A}\Sigma$, $\mathcal{A}_\Sigma$ can parse τ' as (τ'_1, τ'_2) and get a valid forgery (σ', τ'_1), since σ' is a new message which is never queried to $\mathcal{A}_\Sigma$'s signing oracle. We insist that m' should be allowed in $\mathcal{L}_2$, which means $\mathcal{A}_{\mathrm{A}\Sigma}$ is allowed to made its signing query to $\mathcal{SO}_2$ on m' before giving a forgery, since $\mathcal{A}_\Sigma$ did not query to its signing oracle on σ'. Therefore, $\mathcal{A}_\Sigma$'s success probability is exactly that of $\mathcal{A}_{\mathrm{A}\Sigma}$.

Anonymity. Suppose that $\mathcal{A}_{\mathrm{A}\Sigma}$ is a PPT adversary attacking the anonymity of $\mathrm{A}\Sigma$, then using $\mathcal{A}_{\mathrm{A}\Sigma}$, we can construct an adversary $\mathcal{A}_\Gamma$ attacking the hiding property of Γ.

For setup, $\mathcal{A}_\Gamma$ generates two key pairs (sk_0, pk_0) and (sk_1, pk_1), and gives pk_0, pk_1 to $\mathcal{A}_{\mathrm{A}\Sigma}$. When $\mathcal{A}_{\mathrm{A}\Sigma}$ chooses a message m and hands it to $\mathcal{A}_\Gamma$, $\mathcal{A}_\Gamma$ gives $m||pk_0$ and $m||pk_1$ to the challenger, the challenger chooses $b \leftarrow \{0,1\}$ and computes $(\sigma_b, r_b) \leftarrow \mathsf{Com}(m||pk_b)$, then returns σ_b to $\mathcal{A}_\Gamma$. $\mathcal{A}_\Gamma$ gives σ_b to $\mathcal{A}_{\mathrm{A}\Sigma}$ and obtains an output b', then outputs b' to the challenger. Thus, $\mathcal{A}_\Gamma$'s success probability is exactly that of $\mathcal{A}_{\mathrm{A}\Sigma}$.

Unpretendability. Let $\mathcal{A}_{\mathrm{A}\Sigma}$ be a PPT adversary attacking the unpretendability of $\mathrm{A}\Sigma$ which succeeds with non-negligible probability, then using $\mathcal{A}_{\mathrm{A}\Sigma}$, we can construct an adversary $\mathcal{A}_\Gamma$ attacking the binding of Γ.

For setup, $\mathcal{A}_\Gamma$ runs $\mathsf{AKeyGen}(1^\lambda)$ to generate a pair of keys (sk, pk), then gives pk to $\mathcal{A}_{\mathrm{A}\Sigma}$. When $\mathcal{A}_{\mathrm{A}\Sigma}$ makes its signing query on m and hands it to $\mathcal{A}_\Gamma$, $\mathcal{A}_\Gamma$ runs $(\sigma_m, r_m) \leftarrow \mathsf{Com}(m||pk')$ and $\sigma^*_m \leftarrow \mathsf{Sig}(sk, pk, \sigma_m)$, then sets $\tau_m \leftarrow (\sigma^*_m, r_m)$ and returns the signature pair (σ_m, τ_m) to $\mathcal{A}_{\mathrm{A}\Sigma}$. When $\mathcal{A}_{\mathrm{A}\Sigma}$ chooses a message m' and sends it to $\mathcal{A}_\Gamma$, $\mathcal{A}_\Gamma$ will generate the signature pair $(\sigma_{m'}, \tau_{m'} = (\tau_1, \tau_2))$ as a reply, which satisfies $\mathsf{Ver}(pk, \sigma_{m'}, \tau_1) = 1$ and $\mathsf{CVer}(m'||pk, (\sigma_{m'}, \tau_2)) = 1$. After making several signing queries, $\mathcal{A}_{\mathrm{A}\Sigma}$ finally outputs a new verification token $\tau' = (\tau'_1, \tau'_2)$ and a fresh public key pk' satisfying $pk' \neq pk$, $\mathsf{Ver}(pk', \sigma_{m'}, \tau'_1) = 1$ and $\mathsf{CVer}(m'||pk', (\sigma_{m'}, \tau'_2)) = 1$ with non-negligible probability. Since $pk' \neq pk$, $\mathcal{A}_\Gamma$ finds a commitment $\sigma_{m'}$ that can be opened in two different ways, which breaks the binding of Γ.

Summarizing the above discussions, we conclude that $\mathrm{A}\Sigma$ is a secure anonymous signature. □

3.2 Instantiations in the Random Oracle Model

In practice, a hash function is usually applied to compress a message of arbitrary length into a fixed-length string before signing. Based on this observation, we can use a compressed commitment (e.g. CR-ERF) instead of the hash function to compress messages when constructing an anonymous signature, and the scheme just signs the commitment in the identity-open phase rather than hashing then signing. Moreover, random oracles can be regarded as commitments already, so when it comes to the anonymous signature based on our construction in the random oracle model, the scheme needs a random oracle as the commitment in the signature-commit phase, and it also runs a random oracle in the identity-open phase when invoking the signing algorithm of the underlying scheme. It seems fairly natural to consider whether the two random oracle can be reduced to one. We give the discussion based on two types of lattice-based signature schemes, which are the most promising candidate for post-quantum cryptography.

There are two paradigms for lattice-based signature schemes in the random oracle model, i.e. full-domain hash and Fiat-Shamir signature. We now discuss the instantiations of anonymous signatures from these two types of schemes.

Full-Domain Hash. For a lattice-based signature following the full-domain hash paradigm (also named hash-and-sign) described in Sect. 2.2, its hash phase is a random oracle whose output is $\mathbf{c}$, and its sign phase is signing $\mathbf{c}$ then outputting $(r, \mathbf{s})$. Since a random oracle can act as a commitment, which is needed in our construction (Sect. 3.1), we can regarded $\mathbf{c}$ as the output of Phase 1 and $(r, \mathbf{s})$ as the output of Phase 2 in the corresponding anonymous signature via our construction. In other words, the scheme runs a random oracle in the underlying scheme as the commitment in Phase 1, and just signs $\mathbf{c}$ without a random oracle in Phase 2. So the anonymous signature $\mathrm{A}\Sigma^{\mathsf{FDH}} = (\mathsf{AKeyGen}^{\mathsf{FDH}}, \mathsf{ASig}^{\mathsf{FDH}}, \mathsf{AVer}^{\mathsf{FDH}})$ can be described as follows.

- Key Generation $(sk, pk) \leftarrow \mathsf{AKeyGen}^{\mathsf{FDH}}(1^\lambda)$: Given a security parameter λ, generate a random matrix $\mathbf{A} \in \mathbb{Z}_q^{n\times\bar{m}}$ as the public key pk, and a short basis $\mathbf{B} \in \mathbb{Z}_q^{\bar{m}\times\bar{m}}$ of the lattice $\Lambda^\perp(\mathbf{A})$ as the secret key sk.
- Signing $(\sigma, \tau) \leftarrow \mathsf{ASig}^{\mathsf{FDH}}(sk, pk, m)$:
  - In the signature-commit phase, given a message m and the public key pk, the algorithm samples a random number $r \leftarrow \{0,1\}^l$ and computes $\mathbf{c} \leftarrow H(m||r||pk)$, where $H : \{0,1\}^* \to \mathbb{Z}_q^n$ is a random oracle. It returns $\sigma \leftarrow \mathbf{c}$ as an anonymous signature.
  - In the identity-open phase, given the output $\mathbf{c}$ of H, secret key sk, and the random number r, the algorithm computes an arbitrary "specific solution" $\mathbf{y} \in \mathbb{Z}_q^{\bar{m}}$ satisfying $\mathbf{Ay} = \mathbf{c}$. Using the secret key $\mathbf{B}$, it samples $\mathbf{x} \leftarrow D_{\Lambda^\perp(\mathbf{A}),\sigma,-\mathbf{y}}$, and compute $\mathbf{s} \leftarrow \mathbf{y} + \mathbf{x}$. It returns $\tau \leftarrow (\mathbf{s}, r)$ as a verification token.

  The signature pair of the message m is (σ, τ).
- Verification $\beta \leftarrow \mathsf{AVer}^{\mathsf{FDH}}(pk, m, (\sigma, \tau))$: Given the message m and signature pair (σ, τ), the algorithm parses τ as $(\mathbf{s}, r)$ and σ as $\mathbf{c}$, and outputs a symbol $\beta \in \{0,1\}$. Accept the signature ($\beta = 1$) if and only if $||\mathbf{s}||_2$ is indeed short, $\mathbf{As} = H(m||r||pk)$ and $\mathbf{c} = H(m||r||pk)$.

Remark 1. As shown in the proof in Sect. 3.1, our construction makes use of the binding and hiding properties of commitment. Since quantum random oracles have this two security properties against quantum adversaries and full-domain hash signatures are secure in the quantum random oracle model [6], we have $\mathrm{A}\Sigma^{\mathsf{FDH}}$ is also secure in the quantum random oracle model.

Fiat-Shamir with Aborts. As we can see from Sect. 2.2, the signature of a lattice-based Fiat-Shamir with aborts signature scheme contains $\mathbf{c}$ and $\mathbf{z}$. Among them, $\mathbf{c}$ is the output of a random oracle and reveals no information of the public key, which can be regarded as the output of the signature-commit phase like full-domain hash signatures. And $\mathbf{z}$ can be viewed as a verification token. It seems that lattice-based Fiat-Shamir with aborts signature schemes are secure anonymous signatures with this treatment. However, it is possible that the output $\mathbf{c}$ of H is rejected in the signing algorithm due to the rejection sampling. We need to compute all the steps including $\mathbf{z}$ and then check whether rejection sampling succeeds, and only after a successful rejection sampling check, we could output a valid $\mathbf{c}$. So we cannot just generate $\mathbf{c}$ in the signature-commit phase of the corresponding anonymous signature since computation of $\mathbf{c}$ alone does not guarantee $\mathbf{z}$ will be valid.

Therefore, when we transform the schemes into efficient anonymous signatures using our construction in Sect. 3.1, it needs to generate a commitment in Phase 1 and complete a full signing algorithm in Phase 2 rather than omitting the random oracle like $\mathsf{A}\Sigma^{\mathsf{FDH}}$, even if the random oracle can be considered as a commitment. As for their quantum random oracle security, similar as $\mathsf{A}\Sigma^{\mathsf{FDH}}$, anonymous signatures transformed from lattice-based Fiat-Shamir with aborts schemes using our construction are secure in the quantum random oracle model.

To sum up, when generating anonymous signatures via our construction in the random oracle model, we can consider to make use of the structure of underlying scheme and reduce the random oracle in Phase 2. But with few exceptions, like the schemes use rejection sampling, the two random oracles are irreplaceable.

4 Analysis of NIST's Round Three Finalists

In this section, we investigate whether the NIST's third round finalist signatures, namely Dilithium, Falcon and Rainbow, are anonymous signatures. Interestingly, we found that Dilithium is a secure anonymous signature scheme while Falcon and Rainbow are not. Then via our generic construction, we can transform them into efficient anonymous signatures with almost no additional cost.

4.1 Falcon

Falcon is one of two lattice-based signature in the third round, and it utilizes the full-domain hash paradigm. However, we found that lattice-based schemes following the full-domain hash paradigm (Sect. 2.2) is not anonymous, and here are the details.

The signature of the schemes consists of r and $\mathbf{s}$. Therefore, there are two possible cases acting as the output of the signature-commit phase (Phase 1) and the identity-open phase (Phase 2) to achieve an anonymous signature by itself.

Case 1: We regard r as the output of Phase 1 and $\mathbf{s}$ as the verification token. Then, the scheme does not satisfy the unpretendability, thus not a secure anonymous signature. Concretely, the adversary attacking the unpretendability proceeds as follows. When we choose a random string r as the output of

Phase 1, the adversary can generate his own (fresh) public/secret key pair and easily forge a legal verification token $\mathbf{s}'$ with his own secret key, which can be verified on his own fresh public key, thus breaking the unpretendability.
Case 2: We regard $\mathbf{s}$ as the output of Phase 1 and r as the verification token. Then, the scheme may not satisfy the anonymity. On an intuitive level, $\mathbf{s}$ belongs to the orthogonal lattice $\Lambda^{\perp}(\mathbf{A})$, where $\mathbf{A}$ is the public key, and different orthogonal lattices almost have no intersection. Thus, an adversary may distinguish the public key of $\mathbf{s}$ through such "domain separation" and break the anonymity. For simplicity, signature $\mathbf{s}$ is written as the form of $\Lambda^{\perp}(\mathbf{A}) + \mathbf{c}$, where $\mathbf{c}$ is sampled from $U(\mathbb{Z}_q^n)$. We demonstrate the above intuition in Theorem 2.

Theorem 2. *Let $\mathbf{A}_1, \mathbf{A}_2 \in \mathbb{Z}_q^{n\times m}$, $\mathbf{c}_1$ and $\mathbf{c}_2$ are uniform vectors from $\mathbb{Z}_q^n$, the probability of sampling $\mathbf{s}$ from $D_{\Lambda^{\perp}(\mathbf{A}_1)+\mathbf{c}_1,\sigma}$ which is also in $\Lambda^{\perp}(\mathbf{A}_2) + \mathbf{c}_2$ is approximately $\frac{1}{q^n}$.*

Proof. If $\mathbf{s} \in (\Lambda^{\perp}(\mathbf{A}_1)+\mathbf{c}_1) \wedge (\Lambda^{\perp}(\mathbf{A}_2)+\mathbf{c}_2)$, then it satisfies $(\mathbf{A}_2-\mathbf{A}_1)\mathbf{s} = \mathbf{A}_2\mathbf{c}_2 - \mathbf{A}_1\mathbf{c}_1$. Thus, it suffices to compute the probability $\Pr[\mathbf{s} \leftarrow D_{\Lambda^{\perp}(\mathbf{A}_1)+\mathbf{c}_1,\sigma} | (\mathbf{A}_2 - \mathbf{A}_1)\mathbf{s} = \mathbf{A}_2\mathbf{c}_2 - \mathbf{A}_1\mathbf{c}_1]$, when $\mathbf{c}_1$ and $\mathbf{c}_2$ are uniform vectors. There are two cases according to $\mathbf{c}_1 = \mathbf{c}_2$ and $\mathbf{c}_1 \neq \mathbf{c}_2$ respectively. For $\mathbf{c}_1 = \mathbf{c}_2$,

$$\begin{aligned}
&\Pr[\mathbf{s} \leftarrow D_{\Lambda^{\perp}(\mathbf{A}_1)+\mathbf{c}_1,\sigma} | (\mathbf{A}_2 - \mathbf{A}_1)\mathbf{s} = (\mathbf{A}_2 - \mathbf{A}_1)\mathbf{c}_1] \\
=& \Pr[\mathbf{s} \leftarrow D_{\Lambda^{\perp}(\mathbf{A}_1)+\mathbf{c}_1,\sigma} | \mathbf{s} \in \Lambda^{\perp}(\mathbf{A}_2 - \mathbf{A}_1) + \mathbf{c}_1] \\
=& \Pr[\mathbf{t} \leftarrow D_{\Lambda^{\perp}(\mathbf{A}_1),\sigma} | \mathbf{s} = \mathbf{t} + \mathbf{c}_1, \mathbf{A} = \begin{pmatrix}\mathbf{A}_1\\ \mathbf{A}_2\end{pmatrix}, \mathbf{A}\mathbf{t} = \mathbf{0}] \\
=& \frac{\rho_\sigma(\Lambda^{\perp}(\mathbf{A}))}{\rho_\sigma(\Lambda^{\perp}(\mathbf{A}_1))} \approx \frac{\det((\Lambda^{\perp}(\mathbf{A}))^*)}{\det((\Lambda^{\perp}(\mathbf{A}_1))^*)} \\
=& \frac{1}{q^n}.
\end{aligned}$$

For $\mathbf{c}_1 \neq \mathbf{c}_2$,

$$\begin{aligned}
&\Pr[\mathbf{s} \leftarrow D_{\Lambda^{\perp}(\mathbf{A}_1)+\mathbf{c}_1,\sigma} | (\mathbf{A}_2 - \mathbf{A}_1)\mathbf{s} = \mathbf{A}_2\mathbf{c}_2 - \mathbf{A}_1\mathbf{c}_1] \\
=& \Pr[\mathbf{t} \leftarrow D_{\Lambda^{\perp}(\mathbf{A}_1),\sigma} | \mathbf{s} = \mathbf{t} + \mathbf{c}_1, \mathbf{A} = \begin{pmatrix}\mathbf{A}_1\\ \mathbf{A}_2\end{pmatrix}, \mathbf{A}\mathbf{t} = \begin{pmatrix}\mathbf{0}\\ \mathbf{A}_2\mathbf{c}_2 - \mathbf{A}_2\mathbf{c}_1\end{pmatrix}] \\
=& \frac{\rho_{\mathbf{y}_0,\sigma}(\Lambda^{\perp}(\mathbf{A}))}{\rho_\sigma(\Lambda^{\perp}(\mathbf{A}_1))} \approx \frac{\det((\Lambda^{\perp}(\mathbf{A}))^*)}{\det((\Lambda^{\perp}(\mathbf{A}_1))^*)} \\
=& \frac{1}{q^n}.
\end{aligned}$$

Therefore, the probability of sampling $\mathbf{s}$ from $D_{\Lambda^{\perp}(\mathbf{A}_1)+\mathbf{c}_1,\sigma}$ which is also in $\Lambda^{\perp}(\mathbf{A}_2) + \mathbf{c}_2$ is approximately $\frac{1}{q^n}$. □

Summarizing the above discussions, we conclude that Falcon is not anonymous. However, we can transform it into an anonymous signature similar as $\mathrm{A}\Sigma^{\mathsf{FDH}}$ using our generic construction (Sect. 3) almost for free.

4.2 Dilithium

Dilithium is the other lattice-based signatures in the third round. It follows the Fiat-Shamir with aborts technique, and it has a strong and balanced performance in terms of sizes and speed. As we can see from Sect. 3.2, even though Dilithium is an anonymous signature with proper treatment, we can make it more efficient using our generic construction.

4.3 Rainbow

Rainbow is a multivariate signature scheme with a layered construction based on the Unbalanced Oil-Vinegar (UOV) signature scheme. It enjoys fast speed and has a very short signature but suffers from a very large public key. For completeness, we review the scheme in Fig. 1.

$\mathsf{KeyGen}(q, v_1, o_1, o_2)$

$\bar{m} \leftarrow o_1 + o_2, n \leftarrow \bar{m} + v_1$
$\mathbf{M}_S \leftarrow \mathsf{Matrix}(q, \bar{m}, \bar{m})$
$c_S \leftarrow \mathbb{F}^{\bar{m}}$
$\mathcal{S} \leftarrow \mathsf{Aff}(\mathbf{M}_S, c_S)$
$InvS \leftarrow \mathbf{M}_S^{-1}$
$\mathbf{M}_T \leftarrow \mathsf{Matrix}(q, n, n)$
$c_T \leftarrow \mathbb{F}^{\bar{m}}$
$\mathcal{T} \leftarrow \mathsf{Aff}(\mathbf{M}_T, c_T)$
$InvT \leftarrow \mathbf{M}_T^{-1}$
$\mathcal{F} \leftarrow \mathsf{Rainbowmap}(q, v_1, o_1, o_2)$
$\mathcal{P} \leftarrow \mathcal{S} \circ \mathcal{F} \circ \mathcal{T}$
return $pk = \mathcal{P}, sk = (InvS, c_S, \mathcal{F}, InvT, c_T)$

$\mathsf{Sign}(sk, m)$

$\mathbf{h} \leftarrow H(m)$
$\mathbf{x} \leftarrow InvS \cdot (\mathbf{h} - c_S)$
$\mathbf{y} \leftarrow \mathsf{InvF}(\mathcal{F}, \mathbf{x})$
$\mathbf{z} \leftarrow InvT \cdot (\mathbf{y} - c_T)$
return $\sigma = \mathbf{z}$

$\mathsf{Ver}(pk, m, \sigma)$

$\mathbf{h} \leftarrow H(m)$
$\mathbf{h}' \leftarrow \mathcal{P}(\mathbf{z})$
if $\mathbf{h}' = \mathbf{h}$ **then**
  accept
else
  reject

Fig. 1. Rainbow

The signature of Rainbow is $\mathbf{z}$. If we output $\mathbf{z}$ in the signature-commit phase, an adversary can distinguish pk easily by using the verification algorithm, thus breaking the anonymity. However, if we set an empty string as the output of Phase 1 and regard $\mathbf{z}$ as the verification token, then the adversary can generate a fresh public/secret key pair and forge another legal verification token $\mathbf{z}'$ with its own secret key, which can be verified under his fresh public key and breaks the unpretendability. Therefore, Rainbow is not an anonymous signature.

Moreover, there does not exist a formal security proof of Rainbow, so we will not go into details about the UOV signature scheme. And if Rainbow is unforgeable, we can obtain an anonymous signature using our generic construction with almost no efficiency loss.

4.4 The Efficiency of Post-quantum Anonymous Signatures

In order to have a comparison of the efficiency and the extra cost to transform the schemes (i.e. Falcon, Dilithium and Rainbow) into post-quantum anonymous signatures, we give comparisons on the performance of the ordinary schemes and anonymous signatures from the constructions in this work and in [3,17] by implementing these schemes in C. To minimize changes to the implementations of the schemes, we use the random oracles of the ordinary schemes to instantiate the commitment in Falcon and Dilithium. Besides, there are not formal security proofs of Rainbow, we also instantiate the commitment with a random oracle in Rainbow, which is more efficient than the most efficient commitment in the standard model [2]. The implementations were achieved on an Intel Core i5-8257U CPU(1.40 GHz).

As shown in Table 2, compared with the ordinary schemes, the total time of the anonymous signatures is in a limited increase. Moreover, in the real-life applications, most participants do the operations in Phase 1 is enough, while only a few participants need to advance to Phase 2. Our construction is much more efficient than [3,17] in Phase 1, which running time is only 1% of [3,17] for Dilithium and Rainbow and 5.6% of [3,17] for Falcon. Therefore, our construction of anonymous signatures is more practical than [3,17].

5 Conclusion

In this paper, we propose a new generic construction of anonymous signatures, which has better performance and more practical to the real-life applications than previous work. Different from the existing strategy "sign-then-commit", our constructions utilize "commit-then-sign" to reduce operations in the signature-commit phase. In addition, we divide anonymous signatures into two phases, make full use of the underlying signatures and achieve anonymous signatures with marginal cost. Furthermore, we also investigate the NIST's third round signature candidates and transform them into anonymous signatures almost for free.

Acknowledgments. This work was supported in part by National Natural Science Foundation of China (Nos. 61772520, 61802392, 61972094).

References

1. Bai, S., Langlois, A., Lepoint, T., Stehlé, D., Steinfeld, R.: Improved security proofs in lattice-based cryptography: using the Rényi divergence rather than the statistical distance. In: Iwata, T., Cheon, J.H. (eds.) ASIACRYPT 2015. LNCS, vol. 9452, pp. 3–24. Springer, Heidelberg (2015). https://doi.org/10.1007/978-3-662-48797-6_1
2. Baum, C., Damgård, I., Lyubashevsky, V., Oechsner, S., Peikert, C.: More efficient commitments from structured lattice assumptions. In: Catalano, D., De Prisco, R. (eds.) SCN 2018. LNCS, vol. 11035, pp. 368–385. Springer, Cham (2018). https://doi.org/10.1007/978-3-319-98113-0_20

3. Bellare, M., Duan, S.: Partial signatures and their applications. Cryptology ePrint Archive, Report 2009/336 (2009). https://eprint.iacr.org/2009/336
4. Bellare, M., Micciancio, D., Warinschi, B.: Foundations of group signatures: formal definitions, simplified requirements, and a construction based on general assumptions. In: Biham, E. (ed.) EUROCRYPT 2003. LNCS, vol. 2656, pp. 614–629. Springer, Heidelberg (2003). https://doi.org/10.1007/3-540-39200-9_38
5. Bender, A., Katz, J., Morselli, R.: Ring signatures: stronger definitions, and constructions without random oracles. In: Halevi, S., Rabin, T. (eds.) TCC 2006. LNCS, vol. 3876, pp. 60–79. Springer, Heidelberg (2006). https://doi.org/10.1007/11681878_4
6. Boneh, D., Dagdelen, Ö., Fischlin, M., Lehmann, A., Schaffner, C., Zhandry, M.: Random oracles in a quantum world. In: Lee, D.H., Wang, X. (eds.) ASIACRYPT 2011. LNCS, vol. 7073, pp. 41–69. Springer, Heidelberg (2011). https://doi.org/10.1007/978-3-642-25385-0_3
7. Chaum, D., van Heyst, E.: Group signatures. In: Davies, D.W. (ed.) EUROCRYPT 1991. LNCS, vol. 547, pp. 257–265. Springer, Heidelberg (1991). https://doi.org/10.1007/3-540-46416-6_22
8. Ding, J., et al.: Rainbow: algorithm specification and documentation the 3rd round proposal. In: NIST Post-Quantum Cryptography Standardization Round 3 Submission (2020). https://csrc.nist.gov/Projects/post-quantum-cryptography/round-3-submissions
9. Fischlin, M.: Anonymous signatures made easy. In: Okamoto, T., Wang, X. (eds.) PKC 2007. LNCS, vol. 4450, pp. 31–42. Springer, Heidelberg (2007). https://doi.org/10.1007/978-3-540-71677-8_3
10. Gentry, C., Peikert, C., Vaikuntanathan, V.: Trapdoors for hard lattices and new cryptographic constructions. In: STOC 2008, pp. 197–206. ACM, New York (2008). https://doi.org/10.1145/1374376.1374407
11. Lyubashevsky, V., et al.: CRYSTALS-Dilithium: algorithm specifications and supporting documentation. In: NIST Post-Quantum Cryptography Standardization Round 3 Submission (2020). https://pq-crystals.org/dilithium/index.shtml
12. Micciancio, D., Peikert, C.: Trapdoors for lattices: simpler, tighter, faster, smaller. In: Pointcheval, D., Johansson, T. (eds.) EUROCRYPT 2012. LNCS, vol. 7237, pp. 700–718. Springer, Heidelberg (2012). https://doi.org/10.1007/978-3-642-29011-4_41
13. Micciancio, D., Regev, O.: Worst-case to average-case reductions based on gaussian measures. In: FOCS 2004, pp. 372–381. IEEE (2004). https://doi.org/10.1109/FOCS.2004.72
14. Peikert, C., Rosen, A.: Efficient collision-resistant hashing from worst-case assumptions on cyclic lattices. In: Halevi, S., Rabin, T. (eds.) TCC 2006. LNCS, vol. 3876, pp. 145–166. Springer, Heidelberg (2006). https://doi.org/10.1007/11681878_8
15. Prest, T., et al.: Falcon: Fast-Fourier lattice-based compact signatures over NTRU specifications v1.2. In: NIST Post-Quantum Cryptography Standardization Round 3 Submission (2020). https://csrc.nist.gov/Projects/post-quantum-cryptography/round-3-submissions
16. Rivest, R.L., Shamir, A., Tauman, Y.: How to leak a secret. In: Boyd, C. (ed.) ASIACRYPT 2001. LNCS, vol. 2248, pp. 552–565. Springer, Heidelberg (2001). https://doi.org/10.1007/3-540-45682-1_32
17. Saraswat, V., Yun, A.: Anonymous signatures revisited. In: Pieprzyk, J., Zhang, F. (eds.) ProvSec 2009. LNCS, vol. 5848, pp. 140–153. Springer, Heidelberg (2009). https://doi.org/10.1007/978-3-642-04642-1_13

18. Yang, G., Wong, D.S., Deng, X., Wang, H.: Anonymous signature schemes. In: Yung, M., Dodis, Y., Kiayias, A., Malkin, T. (eds.) PKC 2006. LNCS, vol. 3958, pp. 347–363. Springer, Heidelberg (2006). https://doi.org/10.1007/11745853_23
19. Zhang, R., Imai, H.: Strong anonymous signatures. In: Yung, M., Liu, P., Lin, D. (eds.) Inscrypt 2008. LNCS, vol. 5487, pp. 60–71. Springer, Heidelberg (2009). https://doi.org/10.1007/978-3-642-01440-6_7

Author Index

Printed in the United States
by Baker & Taylor Publisher Services